Excursions in Literature
for Christian Schools

Donna L. Hess

Bob Jones University Press
Textbook Division, Greenville, South Carolina 29614

Advisory Committee

Julaine K. Appling, B.A., B.S., M.A.
Educational Advisor.
Dr. Kenneth Frederick, B.A., M.A., Ph.D.
Chairman of the Division of Practical Studies, Bob Jones University.
William L. Yost, B.S., M.A., Ph.D.
Chairman of the Division of Secondary Education, Bob Jones University.

EXCURSIONS IN LITERATURE for Christian Schools®
Donna L. Hess

Produced in cooperation with the Bob Jones University Division of English Language and Literature of the College of Arts and Science, the School of Religion, and Bob Jones Junior High School.

ISBN 0-89084-274-4

© 1985 Bob Jones University Press.
Greenville, South Carolina 29614

Acknowledgments

Bob Jones University Press, Inc.: *Wine of Morning* by Bob Jones. Reprinted by permission of the author.

Bobbs-Merrill and Company, Inc.: "Knights of the Silver Shield" by Raymond McDonald Alden from WHY THE CHIMES RANG, Bobbs-Merrill Company, 1906, 1908.

Charles Coombs: "Rock Hounds" by Charles Coombs. Copyright 1965. Reprinted by permission of the author.

Curtis Publishing Company: "Wolves of Fear" by Richard Savage. Reprinted from THE SATURDAY EVENING POST. Copyright 1941. The Curtis Publishing company.

Doubleday & Company, Inc: "After Twenty Years," from THE FOUR MILLION by O. Henry. Copyright 1904 by Press Publishing Co. Reprinted by permission of Doubleday & Company, Inc.

"One Minute Longer," from BUFF, A COLLIE, AND OTHER DOG STORIES by Albert Payson Terhune. Copyright 1921 by George H. Doran Company. Reprinted by permission of Doubleday and Company, Inc.

Harcourt Brace Jovanovich, Inc.: "Mama and the Graduation Present" from MAMA'S BANK ACCOUNT, copyright 1943 by Kathryn Forbes; renewed 1971 by Richard E. McLean and Robert McLean. Reprinted by permission of Harcourt Brace Jovanovich, Inc.

Harold Matson Company, Inc.: "Weep No More My Lady" by James Street. Copyright 1941 by James Street. Copyright renewed 1969 by Lucy Nash Street. Reprinted by permission of the Harold Matson Company, Inc.

Harold Ober Associates, Inc.: "A Most Important Person" by Margaret Weymouth Jackson. Reprinted by permission of Harold Ober Associates Incorporated. Copyright 1937 by Curtis Publishing Company. Copyright renewed 1965 by Margaret Weymouth Jackson.

"You've Got to Learn," by Robert Murphy. Reprinted by permission of Harold Ober Associates, Incorporated. Copyright renewed 1945 by Robert Murphy.

Houghton Mifflin Company: "The Art of Seeing Things" from LEAF AND TENDRIL by John Burroughs. Copyright 1907 and copyright renewed 1935 by Julian Burroughs. Houghton Mifflin Company.

Irving Shepard: "The Banks of the Sacramento," from *Dutch Courage and Other Stories* by Jack London.

Plays, Inc.: "The Necklace" by Walter Hackett. Reprinted by permission from *Radio Plays for Young People*, by Walter hackett. Copyright 1950 by Plays, Inc. This play is for reading purposes only; for permission to broadcast, write to Plays, Inc., 8 Arlington St., Boston, MA, 02116.

A careful effort has been made to trace the ownership of selections included in this anthology in order to secure permission to reprint copyright material and to make full acknowledgment of their use. If any error of omission has occurred, it is purely inadvertent and will be corrected in subsequent editions, provided written notification is made to the publisher.

Contents

ADVENTURERS

DISCOVERIES

HEROES AND VILLAINS

Preface

As I walked through the wilderness of this world, I lighted on a certain place, where was a den; and I laid me down in that place to sleep: and as I slept I dreamed a dream, and behold I saw a man clothed in rags, standing in a certain place, with a book in his hand and a great burden upon his back. I looked, and saw him open the book, and read therein; and not being able longer to contain, he brake out with a lamentable cry; saying, What shall I do?

The description above is taken from the opening of *The Pilgrim's Progress*, which was written by John Bunyan in the seventeenth century. In this story, Bunyan portrays the world as a dangerous wilderness. Christian, the hero of the story, must hazard this vast terrain in order to reach the Celestial City. Although his adventures are often perilous, there is also much along the way to delight and instruct him. Bunyan intended that Christian's journey be a reflection of the journey each of us must travel in life. Consequently, in the story Christian faces many of the same dangers you will face; and he enjoys many of the same delights you will enjoy.

The unit introductions in this book are designed to help you understand these dangers and delights, and the stories were chosen to illustrate the principles in the introductions. But before you begin reading, let's examine some of Christian's significant experiences.

When the story begins, we find Christian wandering on the outskirts of the City of Destruction. Here he meets Evangelist who opens God's Word to him, explains how he can rid himself of his burden, and shows him the path that leads to the Celestial City. After hearing Evangelist's words, Christian makes the **choice** to flee the City of Destruction to seek the heavenly kingdom.

From the outset of his journey, he experiences many dangers. One of these dangers is the Valley of the Shadow of Death, a valley full of snares, traps, nets, pits, and deep holes. At the end of this valley, Christian falls and cannot rise until a fellow pilgrim named Faithful comes to help him. Through Faithful's companionship, Christian begins to understand the value of true **friends**. The two pilgrims joyfully continue their journey together until they reach Vanity Fair, where they are scorned for refusing the Fair's tempting merchandise. Eventually the Fair's inhabitants become so enraged that they martyr Faithful. Christian escapes, and his grief over Faithful's death is lessened somewhat when he is joined by another pilgrim, Hopeful.

At this point in the journey, Christian shifts his focus from the Celestial City to By-path meadow, and persuades Hopeful to leave the King's highway to travel through this pleasant pasture. Christian assures Hopeful that the forbidden ground is but a harmless detour. Once they have entered the meadow, however, they quickly realize that from this **viewpoint** they totally lose sight of the Celestial City. Before they can find their way back to the King's highway they are captured by Giant Despair, taken to Doubting Castle, and cast into a dungeon to await execution. As the time of execution nears, Christian remembers a key called promise that he received early in his travels. He tries the key in the lock, the door swings open, and the pilgrims flee. Once they are safely back on the right path, Christian erects a milestone to signify their deliverance and to warn others against turning aside.

Having overcome all "hardships, terrors, and amazements," our **adventurer** nears the end of his journey. He enters the River of Death and, passing over to the other side, at last **discovers** the Celestial City. The gates of the city open, and the weary pilgrim beholds the eternal beauties of the heavenly kingdom.

As you read through your units on **Choices, Friends, Viewpoints, Adventurers,** and **Discoveries**, remember that Christian's journey illustrates your travels through the "wilderness of this world." Thus, if you seek to understand and apply the principles presented in each unit, you will be better prepared to make your own pilgrimage. When you have completed your studies, we hope that you can say with Christian:

Here have I seen things rare and profitable;
Things pleasant, dreadful, things to make me stable
In what I have begun to take in hand:
Then let me think on them, and understand.

Choices

"Certain things are right and certain things are wrong," Uncle Jesse told Skeeter. "And nothing ain't gonna ever change that. When you learn that your fit'n to be a man."

In the story "Weep No More, My Lady," Skeeter has an important decision to make. As he sits down to think about this choice, Uncle Jesse's words come to his mind. Skeeter's decision is difficult, but the difficulty of his choice makes you appreciate and enjoy the story. Making any decision causes one either to move forward or backward; so when a character like Skeeter decides, he moves. He may take only one step, but he is one step closer to eventual success or failure. There is a simple rule in fiction: intriguing characters in intriguing stories never stand still. And neither do people in real life.

Consider yourself. You, like Skeeter, face choices every day. Of course, some of your choices are more important than others. But the ones that determine whether you will eventually become "fit'n" or "unfit," as Uncle Jesse said, are choices between right and wrong. Yet how are you to determine right from wrong? You must first establish a fixed standard. You cannot, however, rely on men's laws and values for this standard, for men's ideas of right and wrong change constantly. As an old Puritan preacher once observed, "Men make laws like tailors make garments—to fit the crooked bodies they serve." The only unfailing, absolute authority you have for determining what is right is the Bible, and it is essential that you examine God's Word whenever you are faced with an important choice.

Making *one* right choice is a good beginning, but it is by no means the end of the decision-making process. Sir Roland, a young knight in the story "Knights of the Silver Shield," comes to realize this truth. His desire to "show what knightly stuff he is made of" is thwarted when the lord of the castle commands him to stay behind and guard the palace gate. Despite his disappointment, Roland chooses to obey his lord. Once he is alone, however, this initial choice is tested, and through this testing Roland discovers the "domino theory." What is the "domino theory"? Well, take a set of dominos and set them up one behind the other. Then push the first one into the second one. What happens? Not just two, but the whole set topples. After Roland made his initial decision, he found that there were several more choices lined up behind this first one and that his initial decision greatly influenced which direction the succeeding choices "toppled."

Happily for Sir Roland, his initial choice was right. But the domino theory also applies when one makes an initial wrong decision. One wrong choice is often followed by a whole series of costly wrong choices.

EVANGELIST: Wherefore dost thou cry?

CHRISTIAN: Sir, I perceive, by the book in my hand, that I am condemned to die, and after that to come to judgment.

EVANGELIST: If this be thy condition, why standest thou here? Fly from the wrath to come.

This idea of cost exemplifies the sowing and reaping principle in decision-making. Your choices bring consequences. A striking example of this truth is portrayed in the novel *Ben-Hur*. The story centers on the conflict between a Jew named Judah Ben-Hur and a Roman named Messala. These two young men were once close childhood friends, but their opposing choices in youth destroy their friendship and create an enduring hostility between them. Following them through their turbulent experiences vividly illustrates the outworking of God's principle of sowing and reaping.

Ben-Hur also powerfully illustrates the most important choice in life, the choice of whether to accept or to reject Christ. This choice is presented in the climax of the novel, and all preceding events lead up to this key point. As the story progresses, it becomes increasingly clear that the value of Ben-Hur's early decisions is that they lead him closer to Christ and to understanding why He has come to earth. On the other hand, Messala's early choices lead him away from the knowledge of God toward ultimate calamity.

As you read the following stories, carefully consider the choices presented. Remember also that the rule for fiction is equally true in life: people never stand still. Your daily choices may move you only one step, but like the characters in the stories, you are moving one step closer to eventual success or failure. Your success or failure, however, is far more important than the success or failure of a fictional character. In life you cannot simply "turn the page" when your choices become difficult, nor can you "close the book" when the consequences of those choices face you. You are going to live forever, and as God appealed to the children of Israel hundreds of years ago, so He appeals to you today: "I have set before you [spiritual] life and death, blessing and cursing: therefore *choose* life, that thou and thy seed may live" (Deuteronomy 30:19b).

The strange, haunting laugh drew Skeeter and his Uncle Jesse out of their cabin and into the swamp. Slowly they crept forward until they could see a small unfamiliar animal crouching on a nearby slope. Skeeter strained to see through the night shadows. "It's a dog all right," he said. From the moment of this discovery, Skeeter and My Lady become inseparable friends. But another discovery soon threatens their bond and creates a tug-of-war for Skeeter, forcing him to choose between his conscience and his desires.

Weep No More, My Lady

James Street

The moonlight symphony of swamp creatures hushed abruptly, and the dismal bog was as peaceful as unborn time and seemed to brood in its silence. The gaunt man glanced back at the boy and motioned for him to be quiet, but it was too late. Their presence was discovered. A jumbo frog rumbled a warning, and the swamp squirmed into life as its denizens [inhabitants] scuttled to safety.

Foxfire was glowing to the west and the bayou was slapping the cypress trees when suddenly a haunting laugh echoed through the wilderness, a strange chuckling yodel ending in a weird "gro-o-o."

The boy's eyes were wide and staring. "That's it, Uncle Jesse. Come on! Let's catch it!"

"Uh, oh." The man gripped his shotgun. "That ain't no animal. That's a thing."

They hurried noiselessly in the direction of the sound that Skeeter had been hearing for several nights. Swamp born and reared, they feared nothing they could shoot or outwit, so they slipped out of the morass and to the side of a ridge. Suddenly, Jesse put out his hand and stopped the child; then he pointed up the slope. The animal, clearly visible in the moonlight, was sitting on its haunches, its head cocked sideways as it chuckled. It was a merry and rather melodious little chuckle.

Skeeter grinned in spite of his surprise, then said, "Sh-h-h. It'll smell us."

Jesse said, "Can't nothing smell that far. Wonder what the thing is?" He peered up the ridge, studying the creature. He had no intention of shooting unless attacked, for Jesse Tolliver and his nephew never killed wantonly.

The animal, however, did smell them and whipped her nose into the wind, crouched and braced. She was about sixteen inches high and weighed about twenty-two pounds. Her coat was red and silky, and there was a blaze of white down her throat. Her face was wrinkled and sad, like a wise old man's.

Jesse shook his head. "Looks som'n like a mixture of bloodhound and terrier from here," he whispered. "It beats me—"

"It's a dog, all right," Skeeter said.

"Can't no dog laugh."

"That dog can." The boy began walking toward the animal, his right hand outstretched. "Heah, heah. I ain't gonna hurt you."

The dog, for she was a dog, cocked her head from one side to the other and watched Skeeter. She was trembling, but she didn't run. And when Skeeter knelt by her, she stopped trembling, for the ways of a boy with a dog are mysterious. He stroked her, and the trim little creature looked up at him and blinked her big hazel eyes. Then she turned over, and Skeeter scratched her. She closed her eyes, stretched, and chuckled, a happy mixture of chortle and yodel. Jesse ambled up, and the dog leaped to her feet and sprang between the boy and the man.

Skeeter calmed her. "That's just Uncle Jesse."

Jesse, still bewildered, shook his head again. "I still say that ain't no dog. She don't smell and she don't bark. Ain't natural. And look at her! Licking herself like a cat."

"Well, I'll be catty wampus," Skeeter said. "Never saw a dog do that before." However, he was quick to defend any mannerism of his friend and said, "She likes to keep herself clean. She's a lady, and I'm gonna name her that, and she's mine 'cause I found her."

"Lady, huh?"

"No, sir. My Lady. If I name her Lady, how folks gonna know she's mine?" He began stroking his dog again. "Uncle Jesse, I ain't never had nothing like this before."

"It still don't make sense to me," Jesse said. But he didn't care, for he was happy because the child was happy.

Like most mysteries, there was no mystery at all about My Lady. She was a lady, all right, an aristocratic basenji, one of those strange barkless dogs of Africa. Her ancestors were pets of the Pharaohs, and her line was well established. A bundle of nerves and muscles, she would fight anything and could scent game up to eighty yards. She had the gait of an antelope and was odorless, washing herself before and after meals. However, the only noises she could make were a piercing cry that sounded almost human and that chuckling little chortle. She could chuckle only when happy, and she had been happy in the woods. Now she was happy again.

As most men judge values, she was worth more than all the possessions of Jesse and his nephew. Several of the dogs had been shipped to New Orleans to avoid the dangerous upper route, thence by motor to a northern kennel. While crossing Mississippi, My Lady had escaped from a station wagon. Her keeper had advertised in several papers, but Jesse and Skeeter never saw papers.

Skeeter said, "Come on, M'Lady. Let's go home."

The dog didn't hesitate, but walked proudly at the boy's side to a cabin on the bank of the bayou. Skeeter crumbled corn bread, wet it with potlikker [a juice produced by cooking greens and meat together] and put it before her. She sniffed the food disdainfully at first, eating it only when she saw the boy fix a bowl for his uncle. She licked herself clean and explored the cabin, sniffing the brush brooms, the piles of wild pecans and hickory nuts, and then the cots. Satisfied at last, she jumped on Skeeter's bed, tucked her nose under her paws, and went to sleep.

"Acts like she owns the place," Jesse said.

"Where you reckon she came from?" The boy slipped his overall straps from his shoulders, flexed his stringy muscles, and yawned.

"Circus maybe." He looked at M'Lady quickly. "Say, maybe she's freak and run off from some show. Bet they'd give us two dollars for her."

Skeeter's face got long. "You don't aim to get rid of her?"

The old man put his shotgun over the mantel and lit his pipe. "Skeets, if you want that thing, I wouldn't get shed of her for a piece of bottom land a mile long. Already plowed and planted."

"I reckoned you wouldn't, 'cause you like me so much. And I know how you like dogs, 'cause I saw you cry when yours got killed. But you can have part of mine."

Jesse sat down and leaned back, blowing smoke into the air to drive away mosquitos. The boy got a brick and hammer and began cracking nuts, pounding the meat to pulp so his uncle could chew it. Skeeter's yellow hair hadn't been cut for months and was tangled. He had freckles, too. And his real name was Jonathan. His mother was Jesse's only sister and died when the child was born. No one thereabouts ever knew what happened to his father. Jesse, a leathery, toothless old man with faded blue eyes, took him to bring up and called him Skeeter because he was so little.

In the village, where Jesse seldom visited, folks wondered if he were fit'n to rear a little boy. They considered him shiftless and no-count. Jesse had lived all his sixty years in the swamp. He earned a few dollars selling jumbo frogs and pelts, but mostly he just paddled around the swamp, watching things and teaching Skeeter about life.

The villagers might have tried to send Skeeter to an orphanage, but for Joe (Cash) Watson, the storekeeper. Cash was a hard man, but fair. He often hunted with Jesse, and the old man trained Cash's bird dogs. When there was talk of sending Skeeter away, Cash said, "You ain't gonna do it. You just don't take young'uns away from their folks." And that's all there was to it.

Jesse yearned for only two things— a twenty-gauge shotgun for Skeeter and a set of Roebuckers for himself, as he called store-bought teeth. Cash had promised him the gun and the best false teeth in the catalog for forty-six dollars. Jesse had saved nine dollars and thirty-seven cents.

"Someday I'm gonna get them Roebuckers," he often told Skeeter. "Then I'm gonna eat me enough roastin' ears to kill a goat. Maybe I can get a

set with a couple of gold teeth in 'em. I seen a man once with six gold teeth."

The boy cracked as many nuts as his uncle wanted, then put the hammer away. He was undressing when he glanced over at his dog. "Uncle Jesse, I'm scared somebody'll come get her."

"I ain't heard of nobody losing no things around here. If'n they had, they'd been to me fo' now, beings I know all about dogs and the swamp."

"That's so," Skeeter said. "But you don't reckon she belonged to another fellow like me, do you? I know how I'd feel if I had a dog like her and she got lost."

Jesse said, "She don't belong to another fellow like you. If'n she had, she wouldn't be so happy here."

Skeeter fed M'Lady biscuits and molasses for breakfast, and although the basenji ate it, she still was hungry when she went into the swamp with the boy. He was hoping he could find a bee tree or signs of wild hogs. They were at the edge of a clearing when M'Lady's chokebore [tapered] nose suddenly tilted and she froze to a flash point, pausing only long enough to get set. Then she darted to the bayou, at least sixty yards away, dived into a clump of reeds, and snatched a water rat. She was eating it when Skeeter ran up.

"Don't do that," he scolded. "Ain't you got no more sense than to run into the water after things? A snake or a 'gator might snatch you."

The basenji dropped the rat and tucked her head. She knew the boy was displeased, and when she looked up at him, her eyes were filled, and a woebegone expression was on her face.

Skeeter tried to explain. "I didn't mean to hurt your feelings. Don't cry." He stepped back quickly and stared at her, at the tears in her eyes. "She is crying!" Skeeter called her and ran toward the cabin, where Uncle Jesse was cutting splinters.

"Uncle Jesse! Guess what else my dog can do!"

"Whistle," the old man laughed.

"She can cry! I declare! Not out loud, but she can cry just the same."

Jesse knew that most dogs will get watery-eyed on occasion, but, not wanting to ridicule M'Lady's accomplishments, asked, "What made her cry?"

"Well, sir, we were walking along an all of a sudden she got scent and flash-pointed and then . . ." Skeeter remembered something.

"Then what?"

Skeeter sat on the steps. "Uncle Jesse," he said slowly, "we must have been fifty or sixty yards from that rat when she smelled it."

"What rat? What's eating you?"

The child told him the story, and Jesse couldn't believe it. For a dog to pick up the scent of a water rat at sixty yards simply isn't credible. Jesse reckoned Skeeter's love for M'Lady had led him to exaggerate.

Skeeter knew Jesse didn't believe the story, so he said, "Come on. I'll show you." He whistled for M'Lady.

The dog came up. "Hey," Jesse said. "That thing knows what a whistle means. Shows she's been around folks." He caught the dog's eye and commanded, "Heel!"

But M'Lady cocked her head quizzically. Then she turned to the boy and chuckled softly. She'd never heard the order before. That was obvious. Her nose came up into the breeze and she wheeled.

Her curved tail suddenly was still and her head was poised.

"Flash pointing," Jesse said. "Well, I'll be a monkey's uncle!"

M'Lady held the strange point only for a second, though, then dashed toward a corn patch about eighty yards from the cabin.

Halfway to the patch, she broke her gait and began creeping. A whir of feathered lightning sounded in the corn, and a covey [small group] of quail exploded almost under her nose. She sprang and snatched a bird.

"Partridges!" Jesse's jaw dropped.

The child was motionless as stone, his face white and his eyes wide in amazement. Finally he found his voice, "She was right here when she smelled them birds. A good eighty yards."

"I know she ain't no dog now," Jesse said. "Can't no dog do that."

"She's fast as greased lightning and ain't scared of nothing." Skeeter still was under the spell of the adventure. "She's a hunting dog from way back."

"She ain't no dog a-tall, I'm telling you. It ain't human." Jesse walked toward M'Lady and told her to fetch the bird, but the dog didn't understand. Instead, she pawed it. "Well," Jesse said. "One thing's certain. She ain't no bird hunter."

"She can do anything," Skeeter said. "Even hunt birds. Maybe I can make a bird dog out'n her. Wouldn't that be som'n?"

"You're batty. Maybe a coon dog, but not a bird dog. I know 'bout dogs."

"Me too," said Skeeter. And he did. He'd seen Jesse train many dogs, even pointers, and had helped him train Big Boy, Cash Watson's prize gun dog.

Jesse eyed Skeeter and read his mind.

"It can't be done, Skeets."

"Maybe not, but I aim to try. Ain't no sin in trying, is it?"

"Naw," Jesse said slowly. "But she'll flush [frighten from cover] birds."

"I'll learn her not to."

"She won't hold no point. Any dog'll flash point. And she'll hunt rats."

"I'm gonna learn her just to hunt birds," Skeeter said.

"Wanta bet?" Jesse issued the challenge in an effort to keep Skeeter's enthusiasm and determination at the high-water mark.

"Yes, sir. If I don't train my dog, then I'll cut all the splinters for a year. If I do, you cut 'em."

"It's a go," Jesse said.

Skeeter ran to the bayou and recovered the rat M'Lady had killed. He tied it round his dog's neck. The basenji was indignant and tried to claw off the hateful burden. Failing, she ran into the house and under the bed, but Skeeter made her come out. M'lady filled up then, and her face assumed that don't-nobody-love-me look. The boy steeled himself, tapped M'Lady's nose with the rat, and left it around her neck.

"You done whittled out a job for yourself," Jesse said. "If'n you get her trained, you'll lose her in the brush. She's too fast and too little to keep up with."

"I'll bell her," Skeeter said. "I'm gonna learn her ever'thing. I got us a gun dog, Uncle Jesse."

The old man sat on the porch and propped against the wall. "Bud, I don't know what that thing is. But you're a thoroughbred. John dog my hide!"

If Skeeter had loved M'Lady one bit less, his patience would have exploded during the ordeal of training the basenji. It takes judgment and infinite patience to train a bird dog properly, but to train a basenji, that'll hunt anything, to concentrate only on quail took something more than discipline and patience. It never could have been done except for that strange affinity between a boy and a dog, and the blind faith of a child.

M'Lady's devotion to Skeeter was so complete that she was anxious to do anything to earn a pat. It wasn't difficult to teach her to heel and follow at Skeeter's feet regardless of the urge to dash away and chase rabbits. The boy used a clothesline as a guide rope and made M'Lady follow him. The first time the dog tried to chase an animal, Skeeter pinched the rope around her neck just a bit and commanded "Heel!" And when she obeyed, Skeeter released the noose. It took M'Lady only a few hours to associate disobedience with disfavor.

The dog learned that when she chased and killed a rat or rabbit, the thing would be tied around her neck. The only things she could hunt without being disciplined were quail. Of course, she often mistook the scent of game chickens for quail and hunted them, but Skeeter punished her by scolding. He never switched his dog, but to M'Lady a harsh word from the boy hurt more than a hickory limb.

Jesse watched the dog's progress and pretended not to be impressed. He never volunteered suggestions. M'Lady learned quickly, but the task of teaching her to point birds seemed hopeless. Skeeter knew she'd never point as pointers do, so he worked out his own system. He taught her to stand motionless when he shouted "Hup!" One day she got a scent of birds, paused and pointed for a moment as most animals will, and was ready to spring away when Skeeter said "Hup!"

M'Lady was confused. Every instinct urged her to chase the birds, but her master had said stand still. She broke, however, and Skeeter scolded her. She pouted at first, then filled up, but the boy ignored her until she obeyed the next command, then he patted her and she chuckled.

The lessons continued for days and weeks, and slowly and surely M'Lady learned her chores. She learned that the second she smelled birds she must stop and stand still until Skeeter flushed them; that she must not quiver when he shot.

Teaching her to fetch was easy, but teaching her to retrieve dead birds without damaging them was another matter. M'Lady had a hard mouth— that is, she sank her teeth into the birds. Skeeter used one of the oldest hunting tricks of the backwoods to break her.

He got a stick and wrapped it with wire and taught his dog to fetch it. Only once did M'Lady bite hard on the stick, and then the wire hurt her sensitive mouth. Soon she developed a habit of carrying the stick on her tongue and supporting it lightly with her teeth. Skeeter tied quail feathers on the stick, and soon M'Lady's education was complete.

Skeeter led Jesse into a field one day and turned his dog loose. She flashed to a point almost immediately. It was a funny point, and Jesse almost laughed. The dog's curved tail poked up over her back, she straddled her front legs and sort of squatted, her nose pointing the birds, more than forty yards away. She remained rigid until the boy flushed and shot, then she leaped away; seeking and fetching dead birds.

Jesse was mighty proud. "Well, Skeets, looks like you got yourself a bird hunter."

"Yes, sir," Skeeter said. "And you got yourself a job." He pointed toward the kindling pile.

The swamp was dressing for winter when Cash Watson drove down that day to give his Big Boy a workout in the wild brush.

He locked his fine pointer in the corncrib for the night and was warming himself in the cabin when he noticed M'Lady for the first time. She was sleeping in front of the fire.

"What's that?" he asked.

"My dog," said Skeeter. "Ain't she a beaut?"

"She sure is," Cash grinned at Jesse. Skeeter went out to the well, and Cash asked his old friend, "What kind of mutt is that?"

"Search me," said Jesse. "Skeets found her in the swamp. I reckon she's got a trace of bloodhound in her and some terrier and a heap of just plain dog."

M'Lady cocked one ear and got up and stretched; then, apparently not liking the company, she turned her tail toward Cash and strutted out, looking for Skeeter.

The men laughed. "Som'n wrong with her throat," Jesse said. "She can't bark. When she tries, she makes a funny sound, sort of a cackling, chuckling yodel. Sounds like she's laughing."

"Well," Cash said, "trust a young'un to love the orner'st dog he can find."

"Wait a minute," Jesse said. "She ain't no-count. She's a bird-hunting fool."

Just then Skeeter entered and Cash jestingly said, "Hear you got yourself a bird dog, son."

The boy clasped his hands behind him and rocked on the balls of his feet as he had seen men do. "Well, now, I'll tell you, Mr. Cash. M'Lady does ever'thing except tote the gun."

"She must be fair to middling. Why not take her out with Big Boy tomorrow? Do my dog good to hunt in a brace."

"Me and my dog don't want to show Big Boy up. He's a pretty good ol' dog."

"Whoa!" Cash was every inch a bird-dog man and nobody could challenge him without a showdown. Besides, Skeeter was shooting up and should be learning a few things about life. "Any old boiler can pop off steam." Cash winked at Jesse.

"Well, sir, if you're itching for a run, I'll run your dog against mine."

Cash admired the boy's confidence. "All right, son. What are the stakes?"

Skeeter started to mention the twenty-gauge gun he wanted, but changed his mind quickly. He reached down and patted M'Lady, then looked up. "If my dog beats yours, then you get them Roebuckers for Uncle Jesse."

Jesse's chest suddenly was tight. Cash glanced from the boy to the man, and he, too, was proud of Skeeter. "I

wasn't aiming to go that high. But all right. What do I get if I win?"

"I'll cut ten cords of stove wood."

"And a stack of splinters?"

"Yes, sir."

Cash offered his hand, and Skeeter took it. "It's a race," Cash said. "Jesse will be the judge."

The wind was rustling the sage and there was a nip in the early-morning air when they took the dogs to a clearing and set them down. Skeeter snapped a belt around M'Lady's neck, and, at a word from Jesse, the dogs were released.

Big Boy bounded away and began circling, ranging into the brush. M'Lady tilted her nose into the wind and ripped away toward the sage, her bell tinkling.

Cash said, "She sure covers ground." Skeeter made no effort to keep up with her, but waited until he couldn't hear the bell, then ran for a clearing where he had last heard it. And there was M'Lady on a point.

Cash laughed out loud. "That ain't no point, son. That's a squat."

"She's got birds."

"Where?"

Jesse leaned against a tree and watched the fun.

Skeeter pointed toward a clump of sage. "She's pointing birds in that sage."

Cash couldn't restrain his mirth. "Boy, now that's what I call some pointing. Why, Skeeter, it's sixty or seventy yards to that sage."

Just then Big Boy flashed by M'Lady, his head high. He raced to the edge of the sage, caught the wind, then whipped around, freezing to a point. Cash called Jesse's attention to the point.

"That's M'Lady's point," Skeeter said. "She's got the same birds Big Boy has."

Jesse sauntered up. "The boy's right, Cash. I aimed to keep my mouth out'n this race, but M'Lady's pointing them birds. She can catch scents up to eighty yards."

Cash said, "Aw, go on. You're crazy." He walked over and flushed the birds.

Skeeter picked one off and ordered M'Lady to fetch it. When she returned with the bird, the boy patted her, and she began chuckling.

Cash really studied her then for the first time. "Hey!" he said suddenly. "A basenji! That's a basenji!"

"A what?" Jesse asked.

"I should have known." Cash was very excited. "That's the dog that was lost by them rich Yankees. I saw about it in the paper." He happened to look at Skeeter then and wished he had cut out his tongue.

The boy's lips were compressed and his face drawn and white. Jesse had closed his eyes and was rubbing his forehead.

Cash, trying to dismiss the subject, said, "Just 'cause it was in the paper don't make it so. I don't believe that's the same dog, come to think of it."

"I know she's the same dog," Skeeter said. "On account of I just know it. But she's mine now." His voice rose and trembled. "And ain't nobody gonna take her away from me." He ran into the swamp. M'Lady was at his heels.

Cash said, "I'm sorry, Jesse. If I'd kept my mouth shut he'd never known the difference."

"It can't be helped, now," Jesse said.

"'Course she beat Big Boy. Them's the best hunting dogs in the world. And she's worth a mint of money."

They didn't feel like hunting and returned to the cabin and sat on the porch. Neither had much to say, but kept glancing toward the swamp where Skeeter and M'Lady were walking along the bayou.

"Don't you worry," Skeeter said tenderly, "ain't nobody gonna bother you." He sat on a stump and M'Lady put her head on his knee. She wasn't worrying. Nothing could have been more contented than she was.

"I don't care if the sheriff comes down." Skeeter pulled her onto his lap and held her. "I don't give a whoop if the governor comes down. Even the President of the United States! The whole shebang can come, but ain't nobody gonna mess with you."

His words gave him courage, and he felt better, but only for a minute. Then the tug-of-war between him and his conscience started.

"Once I found a Barlow knife and kept it, and it was all right," he mumbled.

"But this is different."

"Finders, keepers; losers, weepers."

"No, Skeeter."

"Well, I don't care. She's mine."

"Remember what your Uncle Jess said."

"He said a heap of things."

"Yes, but you remember one thing more than the rest. He said, 'Certain things are right and certain things are wrong. And nothing ain't gonna ever change that. When you learn that, then you're fit'n to be a man.' Remember, Skeeter?"

A feeling of despair and loneliness almost overwhelmed him. He fought off the tears as long as he could, but finally he gave in, and his sobs caused M'Lady to peer into his face and wonder why he was acting that way when she was so happy. He put his arms around her neck and pulled her to him. "My li'l old puppy dog. Poor li'l old puppy dog. But I got to do it."

He sniffed back his tears and got up and walked to the cabin. M'Lady curled up by the fire, and the boy sat down, watching the logs splutter for several minutes. Then he said, almost in a whisper, "Uncle Jesse, if you keep som'n that ain't yours, it's the same as stealing, ain't it?"

Jesse puffed his pipe slowly. "Son, that's som'n you got to settle with yourself."

Skeeter stood and turned his back to the flames warming his hands. "Mr. Cash," he said slowly, "when you get back to your store, please let them folks know their dog is here."

"If that's how it is—"

"That's how it is," Skeeter said.

The firelight dancing on Jesse's face revealed the old man's dejection, and Skeeter, seeing it, said quickly, "It's best for M'Lady. She's too good for the swamp. They'll give her a good home."

Jesse flinched, and Cash, catching the hurt in his friend's eyes, said, "Your dog outhunted mine, Skeets. You win them Roebuckers for your uncle."

"I don't want 'em," Jesse said, rather childishly. "I don't care if'n I never eat no roastin' ears." He got up quickly and hurried outside. Cash reckoned he'd better be going and left Skeeter by the fire, rubbing his dog.

Jesse came back in directly and pulled up a chair. Skeeter started to speak, but Jesse spoke first. "I been doing a heap of thinking lately. You're sprouting up. The swamp ain't no place for you."

Skeeter forgot about his dog and faced his uncle, bewildered.

"I reckon you're too good for the swamp too," Jesse said. "I'm aiming to send you into town for a spell. I can make enough to keep you in fit'n clothes and all." He dared not look at the boy.

"Uncle Jesse!" Skeeter said reproachfully. "You don't mean that. You're just saying that on account of what I said about M'Lady. I said it just to keep you from feeling so bad about our dog going away. I ain't ever gonna leave you." He buried his face in his uncle's shoulder. M'Lady put her head on Jesse's knee, and he patted the boy and rubbed the dog.

"Reckon I'll take them Roebuckers," he said at last. "I been wanting some for a long, long time."

Several days later Cash drove down and told them the man from the kennels was at his store. Skeeter didn't say a

word, but called M'Lady and they got in Cash's car. All the way to town, the boy was silent. He held his dog's head in his lap.

The keeper took just one look at M'Lady and said, "That's she, all right. Miss Congo III." He turned to speak to Skeeter, but the boy was walking away. He got a glance at Skeeter's face, however. "I wish you fellows hadn't told me," he muttered. "I hate to take a dog away from a kid."

"Mister"—Jesse closed his left eye and struck his swapping pose—" I'd like to swap you out'n that hound. Now, course she ain't much 'count . . ."

The keeper smiled in spite of himself. "If she was mine, I'd give her to the kid. But she's not for sale. The owner wants to breed her and establish her line in this country. And if she was for sale, she'd cost more money than any of us will ever see." He called Skeeter and offered his hand. Skeeter shook it.

"You're a good kid. There's a reward for this dog."

"I don't want no reward." The boy's words tumbled out. "I don't want nothing, except to be left alone. You've got your dog, mister. Take her and go on. Please." He walked away again, fearing he would cry.

Cash said, "I'll take the reward and keep it for him. Some day he'll want it."

Jesse went out to the store porch to be with Skeeter. The keeper handed Cash the money. "It's tough, but the kid'll get over it. The dog never will."

"Is that a fact?"

"Yep. I know the breed. They never forget. That dog'll never laugh again. They never laugh unless they're happy."

He walked to the post where Skeeter had tied M'Lady. He untied the leash and started toward his station wagon. M'lady braced her front feet and looked around for the boy. Seeing him on the porch, she jerked away from the keeper and ran to her master.

She rubbed against his legs. Skeeter tried to ignore her. The keeper reached for the leash again, and M'lady crouched, baring her fangs. The keeper shrugged, a helpless gesture.

"Wild elephants couldn't pull that dog away from that boy," he said.

"That's all right, mister." Skeeter unsnapped the leash and tossed it to the keeper. Then he walked to the station wagon, opened the door of a cage, and called, "Heah, M'Lady!" She bounded to him. "Up!" he commanded. She didn't hesitate, but leaped into the cage. The keeper locked the door.

M'Lady, having obeyed a command poked her nose between the bars, expecting a pat. The boy rubbed her head. She tried to move closer to him, but the bars held her. She looked quizzically at the bars, then tried to nudge them aside. Then she clawed them. A look of fear suddenly came to her eyes, and she fastened them on Skeeter, wistfully at first, then pleadingly. She couldn't make a sound, for her unhappiness had sealed her throat. Slowly her eyes filled up.

"Don't cry no more, M'Lady. Ever'thing's gonna be all right." He reached out to pat her, but the station wagon moved off, leaving him standing there in the dust.

Back on the porch, Jesse lit his pipe and said to his friend, "Cash, the boy has lost his dog, and I've lost a boy."

"Aw, Jesse, Skeeter wouldn't leave you."

"That ain't what I mean. He growed up that day in the swamp."

Skeeter walked into the store and Cash followed him. "I've got that reward money for you, Jonathan."

It was the first time anyone ever had called him that, and it sounded like man talk.

"And that twenty-gauge is waiting for you," Cash said. "I'm gonna give it to you."

"Thank you, Mr. Cash." The boy bit his lower lip. "But I don't aim to do no more hunting. I don't never want no more dogs."

"Know how you feel. But if you change you mind, the gun's here for you."

Skeeter looked back toward the porch where Jesse was waiting, and said, "Tell you what, though. When you get them Roebuckers, get some with a couple of gold teeth in 'em. Take it out of the reward money."

"Sure, Jonathan."

Jesse joined them and Skeeter said, "We better be getting back toward the house."

"I'll drive you down," Cash said. "But first I aim to treat you to some lemon pop and sardines."

"That's mighty nice of you," Jesse said, "but we better be gettin' on."

"What's your hurry?" Cash opened the pop.

"It's my time to cut splinters," Jesse said. "That's what I get for betting with a good man."

Reading Check

1. What are some characteristics that make M'Lady unusual?
2. What are some specific actions in the story that illustrate the close bond between Skeeter and M'Lady?
3. How does Skeeter choose to spend his reward money?
4. Why does Cash call Skeeter *Jonathan* at the end of the story?
5. How does Skeeter's choice to return M'Lady to her owner indicate that he is as Uncle Jesse says, "fit'n to be a man"?

Young Sir Roland believes that adventure awaits him only on the battlefield. But the choices he faces while guarding the lonely castle teach him that danger is not limited to the battleground and that the enemy does not always carry a sword.

Knights of the Silver Shield

Raymond Macdonald Alden

There was once a splendid castle in a forest, with great stone walls and a high gateway, and turrets that rose away above the tallest trees. The forest was dark and dangerous, and many cruel giants lived in it; but in the castle was

a company of knights, who were kept there by the king of the country, to help travelers who might be in the forest and to fight with the giants whenever they could.

Each of these knights wore a beautiful suit of armor and carried a long spear, while over his helmet there floated a great red plume that could be seen a long way off by any one in distress.

But the most wonderful thing about the knights' armor was their shields. They were not like those of other knights but had been made by a great magician who had lived in the castle many years before. They were made of silver and sometimes shone in the sunlight with dazzling brightness; but at other times the surface of the shields would be clouded as though by a mist, and one could not see his face reflected there as he could when they shown brightly.

Now, when each young knight received his spurs and his armor, a new shield was also given him from among those that the magician had made; and when the shield was new its surface was always cloudy and dull. But as the knight began to do service against the giants, or went on expeditions to help poor travelers in the forest, his shield grew brighter and brighter, so that he could see his face clearly reflected in it. But if he proved to be a lazy or cowardly knight, and let the giants get the better of him, or did not care what became of the travelers, then the shield grew more and more cloudy, until the knight became ashamed to carry it.

But this was not all. When any one of the knights fought a particularly hard battle and won the victory, or when he went on some hard errand for the lord

of the castle and was successful, not only did his silver shield grow brighter, but when one looked into the center of it he could see something like a golden star shining in its very heart. This was the greatest honor that a knight could achieve, and the other knights always spoke of such a one as having "won his star." It was usually not till he was pretty old and tried as a soldier that he could win it. At the time when this story begins, the lord of the castle himself was the only one of the knights whose shield bore the golden star.

There came a time when the worst of the giants in the forest gathered themselves together to have a battle against the knights. They made a camp in a dark hollow not far from the castle, and gathered all their best warriors together, and all the knights made ready to fight them. The windows of the castle were closed and barred; the air was full of the noise of armor being made ready for use; and the knights were so excited that they could scarcely rest or eat.

Now there was a young knight in the castle named Sir Roland, who was among those most eager for the battle. He was a splendid warrior, with eyes that shone like stars whenever there was anything to do in the way of knightly deeds. And although he was still quite young, his shield had begun to shine enough to show plainly that he had done bravely in some of his errands through the forest. This battle, he thought, would be the great opportunity of his life. And on the morning of the day when they were to go forth to it, and all the knights assembled in the great hall of the castle to receive the commands of their leaders, Sir Roland hoped that he would be put in the most dangerous place of all, so that he could show what knightly stuff he was made of.

But when the lord of the castle came to him, as he went about in full armor giving his commands, he said: "One brave knight must stay behind and guard the gateway of the castle, and it is you, Sir Roland, being one of the youngest, whom I have chosen for this."

At these words Sir Roland was so disappointed that he bit his lip and closed his helmet over his face so that the other knights might not see it. For a moment he felt as if he must reply angrily to the commander and tell him that it was not right to leave so sturdy a knight behind when he was eager to fight. But he struggled against this feeling and went quietly to look after his duties at the gate. The gateway was high and narrow and was reached from outside by a high, narrow bridge that crossed the moat, which surrounded the castle on every side. When an enemy approached, the knight on guard rang a bell just inside the gate, and the bridge was drawn up against the castle wall so that no one could come across the moat. So the giants had long ago given up trying to attack the castle itself.

Today the battle was to be in the dark hollow in the forest, and it was not likely that there would be anything to do at the castle gate except to watch it like a common doorkeeper. It was not strange that Sir Roland thought someone else might have done this.

Presently all the other knights marched out in their flashing armor, their red plumes waving over their heads, and their spears in their hands. The lord of the castle stopped only to

tell Sir Roland to keep guard over the gate until they had all returned, and to let no one enter. Then they went into the shadows of the forest and were soon lost to sight.

Sir Roland stood looking after them long after they had gone, thinking how happy he would be if he were on the way to battle like them. But after a little he put this out of his mind and tried to think of pleasanter things. It was a long time before anything happened, or any word came from the battle.

At last Sir Roland saw one of the knights come limping down the path to the castle, and he went out on the bridge to meet him. Now this knight was not a brave one, and he had been frightened away as soon as he was wounded.

"I have been hurt," he said, "so that I cannot fight any more. But I could watch the gate for you if you would like to go back in my place."

At first Sir Roland's heart leaped with joy at this, but then he remembered what the commander had told him on going away, and he said, "I should like to go, but a knight belongs where his commander has put him. My place is here at the gate, and I cannot open it even for you. Your place is at the battle."

The knight was ashamed when he heard this, and he presently turned about and went into the forest again.

So Sir Roland kept guard silently for another hour. Then there came an old beggar woman down the path to the castle, and asked Sir Roland if she might come in and have some food. He told her that no one could enter the castle that day, but that he would send a servant out to her with food, and that she might sit and rest as long as she would.

"I have been past the hollow in the forest where the battle is going on," said the old woman while she was waiting for her food.

"And how do you think it is going?" asked Sir Roland.

"Badly for the knights, I am afraid," said the old woman. "The giants are fighting as they have never fought before. I should think you had better go and help your friends."

"I should like to, indeed," said Sir Roland. "But I am set to guard the gateway of the castle, and cannot leave."

"One fresh knight would make a great difference when they are all weary with fighting," said the old woman. "I should think that, while there are no enemies about, you would be much more useful there."

"You may well think so," said Sir Roland, "and so may I; but it is neither you nor I that is commander here."

"I suppose," said the old woman then, "that you are one of the kind of knights who like to keep out of fighting. You are lucky to have so good an excuse for staying at home." And she laughed a thin and taunting [mocking] laugh.

Then Sir Roland was very angry, and thought that if it were only a man instead of a woman, he would show him whether he liked fighting or no. But as it was a woman, he shut his lips and set his teeth hard together, and as the servant came just then with the food he had sent for, he gave it to the old woman quickly, and shut the gate that she might not talk to him any more.

It was not very long before he heard someone calling outside. Sir Roland opened the gate and saw standing at the other end of the drawbridge a little old man in a long black cloak. "Why are you knocking here?" he said. "The castle is closed today."

"Are you Sir Roland?" said the little old man.

"Yes," said Sir Roland.

"Then you ought not to be staying here when your commander and his knights are having so hard a struggle with the giants, and when you have the chance to make of yourself the greatest knight in this kingdom. Listen to me! I have brought you a magic sword!"

As he said this, the old man drew from under his coat a wonderful sword that flashed in the sunlight as if it were covered with diamonds. "This is the sword of all swords," he said, "and it is for you, if you will leave your idling here by the castle gate and carry it to the battle. Nothing can stand before it. When you lift it the giants will fall back, your master will be saved, and you will be crowned the victorious knight—the one who will soon take his commander's place as lord of the castle."

Now Sir Roland believed that it was a magician who was speaking to him, for it certainly appeared to be a magic sword. It seemed so wonderful that the sword should be brought to him that he reached out his hand as though he would take it, and the little old man came forward as though he would cross the drawbridge into the castle. But as he did so, it came to Sir Roland's mind again that the bridge and the gateway had been entrusted to him, and he called out "No!" to the old man, so that he stopped where he was standing. But he waved the shining sword in the air again and said, "It is for you! Take it and win the victory!"

Sir Roland was really afraid that if he looked any longer at the sword, or listened to any more words of the old man, he would not be able to hold himself within the castle. For this reason he struck the great bell at the gateway, which was the signal for the servants inside to pull in the chains of the drawbridge, and instantly they began to pull, and the drawbridge came up, so that the old man could not cross it to enter the castle, nor Sir Roland to go out.

Then, as he looked across the moat, Sir Roland saw a wonderful thing. The little old man threw off his black cloak, and as he did so he began to grow bigger and bigger, until in a minute more he was a giant as tall as any in the forest. At first Sir Roland could scarcely believe his eyes. Then he realized that this must be one of their giant enemies, who had changed himself to a little old man through some magic power, that he might make his way into the castle while all the knights were away. Sir Roland shuddered to think what might have happened if he had taken the sword and left the gate unguarded. The giant shook his fist across the moat that lay between them, and then, knowing that he could do nothing more, he went angrily back into the forest.

Sir Roland now resolved not to open the gate again, and to pay no attention to any other visitor. But it was not long before he heard a sound that made him spring forward in joy. It was the bugle of the lord of the castle, and there came sounding after it the bugles of many of the knights that were with him, pealing so joyfully that Sir Roland was sure they were safe and happy. As they came nearer, he could hear their shouts of victory. So he gave the signal to let down the drawbridge again and went out to meet them. They were dusty and blood-stained and weary, but they had won the battle with the giants; and it had never been a happier home-coming.

Sir Roland greeted them all as they passed in over the bridge, and then, when he had closed the gate and fastened it, he followed them into the great hall of the castle. The lord of the castle took his place on the highest seat, with the other knights about him, and Sir Roland came forward with the key of the gate to give his account of what he had done in the place to which the commander had appointed him. The lord of the castle bowed to him as a sign for him to begin, but just as he opened his mouth to speak, one of the knights cried out, "The shield! The shield! Sir Roland's shield!"

Everyone turned and looked at the shield which Sir Roland carried on his left arm. He himself could see only the top of it and did not know what they could mean. But what they saw was the golden star of knighthood, shining brightly from the center of Sir Roland's shield. There had never been such amazement in the castle before.

Sir Roland knelt before the lord of the castle to receive his commands. He still did not know why everyone was looking at him so excitedly, and wondered if he had in some way done wrong.

"Speak, Sir Knight," said the commander, as soon as he could find his voice after his surprise, "and tell us all

that has happened today at the castle. Have you been attacked? Have any giants come hither? Did you fight them alone?"

"No, my Lord," said Sir Roland. "Only one giant has been here, and he went away silently when he found he could not enter."

Then he told all that had happened through the day.

When he had finished, the knights all looked at one another, but no one spoke a word. Then they looked again at Sir Roland's shield to make sure that their eyes had not deceived them, and there the golden star was still shining.

After a little silence the lord of the castle spoke.

"Men make mistakes," he said, "but our silver shields are never mistaken. Sir Roland has fought and won the hardest battle of all today."

Then the others all rose and saluted Sir Roland, who was the youngest knight that ever carried the golden star.

Reading Check

1. Why is the knight's shield the most important piece of his armor?
2. What is Sir Roland's first response to his lord's command?
3. While guarding the castle gate, Sir Roland encounters three visitors. How does he choose to deal with each of the three?
4. What does Sir Roland discover about the third visitor?
5. What is the result of Sir Roland's choice to obey his lord's command in spite of temptations to do otherwise?

Before 600 B.C. Rome was a small insignificant Latin settlement. By 509 B.C., however, this small settlement had grown into a powerful city-state. This city-state was to become the center of one of the world's greatest empires, an empire that dominated the Mediterranean world for more than four hundred years.

Our story takes place at the peak of Rome's power at the time of Christ. Judea had been a Roman province for more than eighty years. A Roman guard kept the gates of the palace, a Roman judge dispensed justice both civil and criminal, and a Roman system of taxation crushed both city and country. Daily, hourly, and in a thousand ways, the Jews were taught the difference between a life of independence and a life of subjection.

Let us look now into one of the palace gardens on Mount Zion. The time is noonday in the middle of July when the heat of the summer is at its highest. Unmindful of the sun shining full upon them, two friends, one nineteen and the other seventeen, sit engaged in earnest conversation.

Both boys are handsome and, at first glance, might be pronounced brothers, for both have dark hair and eyes, and their faces are deeply browned. The elder, Messala, wears a tunic of soft, gray-tinted wool. His costume certifies him as a Roman.

Messala's friend, Judah Ben-Hur, is slighter in form, and his distinctive features as well as his white linen garments confirm that he is of Jewish descent.

Ben-Hur

(an adaptation)

Lew Wallace

Part I   The Betrayal of Ben Hur

"You say the new procurator [Roman administrator] of Judea is to arrive tomorrow?" inquired Ben-Hur.

"Yes, tomorrow," Messala answered.

"Who told you?"

"I heard Ishmael, the new governor, tell my father so last night." Messala dismissed the subject as insignificant and turned his mind to other thoughts. "Our farewell took place in this garden. Your last words to me were, 'The peace of the Lord go with you.' 'The gods keep you,' I replied. Do you remember?"

"Yes. I watched you start for Rome, and wept. Five years are gone, and you have come back educated and princely—and yet—I wish you were the same Messala who went away."

"Tell me, friend, in what way have I changed?"

Ben-Hur reddened under Messala's scornful gaze, but he replied firmly, "You talk with the ease of a master, but your speech carries a sting. The old Messala had no poison in his nature. Not for the world would he have hurt the feelings of a friend."

Messala smiled as if complimented. "Be plain, Judah, wherein have I hurt you?"

Ben-Hur drew a long breath and said, "In these five years, I too have learned, though my masters at the temple are not as those you heard in Rome. Their learning goes not out into forbidden paths. Those who sit at their feet arise enriched simply with the knowledge of God, the law, and Israel; and the effect is love and reverence for everything that pertains to them."

Messala raised his head a toss higher. "All things, even heaven and earth, change; but a Jew never! To him there is no backward, no forward; he is what his ancestors were in the beginning. Watch, Judah. In this sand I draw you a circle—there! Now tell me what more a Jew's life is? Round and round, Abraham here, Isaac and Jacob yonder, God in the middle!"

Ben-Hur arose, his face flushed.

"No, no; keep your place, Judah, keep your place," Messala cried, extending his hand.

"You mock me!"

"Listen a little further," urged Messala. "I am mindful of your goodness in walking from your father's house to welcome me back and to renew the love of our childhood. But if we are to remain friends you must see the world as it truly is. Judah, my teacher, in his last lecture said to us, 'Go, and to make your lives great, remember Mars [Roman god of war] reigns and Eros [Roman god of love] has found his eyes.' He meant that love is nothing, war everything. It is so in Rome, and Rome is now the world. Remember our childhood dreams? We were to be great warriors together."

Ben-Hur turned and moved closer to the garden pool. Messala's drawl deepened and a flush of pride kindled on his haughty Roman face. "The world is not all conquered. Look to the glories that await us."

Ben-Hur looked hard at Messala, hesitated, then turned to go.

"Do not leave," said Messala.

"We had better part," Judah answered. "I wish I had not come. I sought a friend and find a—"

"Roman?" said Messala quickly. "Judah, renounce the follies of Moses and the traditions of Israel. They are past. Give yourself and your father's wealth to Rome. Together we will rule the future."

Ben-Hur's hands clenched tightly, and he started for the gate. Messala followed. When he reached Ben-Hur's side, he put his hand on his young friend's shoulder. "This is the way—my hand thus—we used to walk when we were children. Let us keep it as far as the gate." Judah permitted the familiarity, but when they reached the garden's entrance he stopped.

"I understand you because you are a Roman," he said taking Messala's hand gently from his shoulder. "But you cannot understand me, for I am an Israelite and will remain so. You have given me great suffering today by convincing me that we can never be the friends we once were—never. As we said our first farewell in this garden, so we shall say our last. The peace of the God of my fathers abide with you."

Messala offered him his hand, but Ben-Hur walked on through the gateway. When he was gone, Messala was silent a moment, then he too passed through the gate, saying to himself with a toss of the head, "Be it so. Eros is dead, Mars reigns!"

* * *

Ben-Hur was soon before the western gate of his house. He entered hastily, passed to the stairway, and ascended to the terrace. Making his way to a doorway on the north side, he entered his apartment.

About nightfall a woman servant came to the door. Ben-Hur was lying motionless on his divan. "Supper is long over. Are you not hungry?" she asked.

"No," he replied.

"Are you sick?"

"I am indifferent, Amrah. Life does not seem as pleasant now as it did this morning."

"Your mother has asked for you."

"Where is she?"

"In the summer-house on the roof."

He stirred himself and sat up. "Very well. Bring me something to eat; then I shall go to her."

"What do you want?"

"What you please, Amrah."

After a while she returned, bearing on a wooden platter a bowl of milk, some thin cakes, a delicate paste of brayed wheat, a bird broiled, and honey and salt. Amrah was an Egyptian slave to whom not even the sacred fiftieth year could have brought freedom; she would not have accepted it, for the boy she was attending was her life.

"You remember, Amrah," he said as she placed the meal before him, "Messala who used to visit me here for days at a time?"

"I remember him."

"He went to Rome some years ago and is now back. I called upon him today." Ben-Hur shuddered in disgust.

"I knew something had happened," said Amrah, deeply interested. "I never liked Messala. Tell me all."

But Ben-Hur fell into musing and to her repeated inquiries only said, "He is much changed, and I shall have nothing more to do with him."

When Amrah took the platter away, Ben-Hur went out from his apartment and up to the roof. Through one of the openings, he saw his mother reclining against a cushion on the divan. At the sound of his steps upon the floor, the fan in her hand stopped, and he saw it glisten where the starlight struck the jewels with which it was sprinkled. She sat up and called his name.

"Judah, my son?"

"Yes, mother," he answered, quickening his approach. His mother resumed her easy position against the cushion, while Ben-Hur took his place on the divan. The city was still. Only the winds stirred.

"Amrah tells me something has happened," she said. Ben-Hur remained silent. "When you were a child, I allowed small things to trouble you, but now you are a man and you must face your doubts and find a way to banish them."

The words appeared to set him thinking anew. "Today, mother, I have been made to think of many things that never had place in my mind before. Tell me, what am I to be?"

Her voice became very soft. "One day you are to be my hero."

"I will be your hero," he continued, "but you must put me in the way. You know the law—every son of Israel must have some occupation. Today I visited Messala." A certain change in his voice attracted his mother's attention. "He is very much changed."

"You mean he has come back a Roman?"

"Yes. I suppose all great people are proud," he went on, "but the pride of this people is unlike all others."

The young Israelite then rehearsed his conversation with Messala, dwelling on the Roman's speeches in contempt of the Jews and their customs.

His mother listened, discerning the matter plainly. Her voice became firm. "Your friend—or former friend—charged, if I understand you rightly, that we have had no great men. A just consideration of this charge requires a definition. A great man, my son, is one whose life proves him to be recognized, if not called, by God. In light of this definition, set our great men before you. You find patriarchs, legislators, warriors, singers, and prophets. Compare them to the best of Rome. Place Caesar against King David; Rome's consuls [highest official of the Roman Republic] against our judges; Augustus against Solomon. But do not stop here. Go on to the prophets—greatest of the great. Think of Elijah sitting on the hilltop outside Samaria amid the smoking bodies of captains and their fifties warning the son of Ahab of the wrath of our God. Finally, Judah, if such speech be reverent, place Jehovah against Jupiter. Comparison ends here. You may judge our God by what His servants have done in His name. Rome and her gods are but the passing folly of vain men's imaginings.

"And as for what you shall do—" She spoke these last words slowly, "you, my son, shall serve the Lord, the Lord God of Israel, not Rome. For a child of Abraham there is no glory except in the Lord's ways, and in them there is much glory."

"But can I be both a soldier and a servant of God?" inquired Judah.

There was a long silence in the summer chamber. "Your father, Judah, was a great merchant. But though all Rome recognized him as a wealthy man, they knew him first as a prince of Israel. You have my permission to pursue whatever occupation you desire if you will be as your father in this one point: remember that you serve the Lord, not Caesar."

* * *

When Judah awoke, the sun was up over the mountains, and the pigeons were abroad in flocks, filling the air with the gleams of their white wings. On the edge of the divan sat Tirzah his sister, scarcely fifteen. She was singing.

"Very pretty, Tirzah, very pretty!" he said with animation.

"The song?" she asked.

"Yes—and the singer, too. I am proud of you. Have you another song as good as the first?"

"Many. But let them go now. Amrah sent me to tell you that she will bring your breakfast and that you need not come down. She should be here by this time. She thinks you are sick and that a dreadful accident happened yesterday. What is it? Tell me and I will help Amrah doctor you. She knows the cures of the Egyptians who were always a stupid set; but I have a great many recipes of the Arabs who—"

"Are even more stupid than the Egyptians," he said, shaking his head.

"Do you think so? Very well, then," she replied, "we will have nothing to do with any of them."

"Tirzah," he continued cautiously, "I am going away."

"Going away? When? Where? For what?"

He laughed. "Three questions all in one breath! But the next instant he became serious. "I am going to Rome."

"I will go with you."

"You must stay with Mother. If both of us leave her, she will die."

The brightness faded from her face. "But—must you go? Here in Jerusalem you can learn all that is needed to be a merchant as Father was."

"The law does not require a son to be what his father was."

"What else can you be?"

"A soldier," he replied, with a certain pride in his voice.

Tears came into her eyes. "You will be killed."

"If God wills, be it so. But, Tirzah, the soldiers are not all killed. War is a trade," he continued soberly. "To learn it thoroughly, one must go to school, and there is no school like a Roman Camp."

"You would fight for Rome?" she asked.

"Yes, I will fight for her, if, in return, she will teach me how one day to fight against her."

"When will you go?"

Amrah's steps were then heard.

"Hush!" he said. "Do not let her know what I am thinking."

The faithful slave came in with breakfast and placed it on the stool before them. Then she remained to serve them. They dipped their fingers into a bowl of water and were rinsing them when a noise arrested their attention.

"Soldiers from the Praetorium, I must see them," Judah cried, springing from the divan and running out.

In a moment he was leaning over the parapet [protective railing] of tiles which guarded the roof, so absorbed that he did not immediately notice Tirzah, who was now at his side resting one hand on his shoulder.

Ben-Hur knew of the custom by which chief commanders, to indicate their rank, appeared in public with a laurel vine upon their heads. By that sign he knew the officer—Valerius Gratus, the new procurator of Judea!

Judah leaned yet farther over the parapet to see him go by and in the act rested his hand on a tile which had long been cracked. The pressure was strong enough to displace the outer piece which started to fall. A thrill of horror shot through him. He reached out to catch the tile, and when he did so, it looked exactly as if he were pitching something from him. His effort failed. He shouted with all his might. The soldiers of the guard looked up; so did Valerius Gratus, and at that moment the tile struck him. He fell from his seat as dead. The cohort [a division of the Roman legion] halted; the guards leaped from their horses and hastened to cover their chief with their shields.

Judah arose from the parapet his face pale.

"Judah, what has happened?" Tirzah asked in sudden alarm.

"I have killed the Roman governor. The tile fell upon him. I did not do it purposely, Tirzah—it was an accident!"

"What will they do?" she asked.

To evade an answer, he peered over the parapet again and saw that the guards were assisting the Roman to remount his horse. "He lives, he lives, Tirzah! Blessed be the Lord God of our fathers! Do not be afraid. I will explain how it happened, and they will remember our father and his services and not hurt us."

He was leading her to the summerhouse when the roof jarred under their feet. A cry of surprise and agony arose from the courtyard below. He stopped.

The cry was repeated and followed by a rush of many feet and voices lifted in rage blending with voices lifted in fear. Then came the screams of women in mortal terror. He began to realize that the servants were being butchered.

The terrace at the foot of the steps was crowded with soldiers. Many other officers with drawn swords were running in and out of the chambers. At one place several women on their knees clung to each other and prayed for mercy. Apart from them, his mother, with torn garments, was struggling to tear loose from a man. Her cries were shrillest of all. Cutting through the clamor, they had arisen distinguishably to the roof. Judah sprang to her; his steps were long and swift, almost a winged flight. "Mother! Mother!" he shouted. She stretched her hand towards him; but when almost touching her, he was seized and forced aside. Then he heard someone cry aloud, "That is he!" Judah looked and saw—Messala. "That is his mother; yonder his sister. You now have the whole family."

Judah's love for his family made him forget his earlier quarrel with the young Roman. "Help them, Messala! Remember our childhood and help them. I—Judah—pray you!"

Messala pretended not to hear, and turning to the officer said, "I cannot be of further use to you. There is richer entertainment in the street. Down Eros, up Mars!" With these words he disappeared.

Judah understood; and in the bitterness of his soul, he prayed to heaven, "In the hour of Thy vengeance, Oh Lord, be mine the hand to put it upon Messala!"

Reading Check

1. Ben-Hur and his childhood friend Messala have been separated for five years. Where has Messala been?

2. At the reunion in the garden, Ben-Hur describes Messala as having "poison in his nature." What does he mean by this statement?

3. As a result of the changes in Messala, what choice does Ben-Hur make concerning their friendship?

4. Before Ben-Hur's tragic accident what choice does he make concerning his life occupation and why does he make this choice?

5. At the time of Ben-Hur's tragedy, how does Messala manifest the poison in his nature?

Part II *The Captivity of Ben-Hur*

The next day a detachment of legionaries [soldiers of the Roman Army] went to the desolated place of the Hurs and, closing the gates permanently, nailed at each entrance the following notice:

"This is the property of the Emperor."

Several days later, a decurion [Roman cavalry officer] with his command of ten horsemen approached Nazareth from Jerusalem. His prisoner, Ben-Hur, was forced to make the long journey on foot. Upon reaching the well of Nazareth, the young Jew was in the last stage of exhaustion. The villagers would have helped him, but the hard look of the decurion as he dismounted, stopped them. Ben-Hur sank down in the dust of the road unattended.

While the pitchers of water were passed among the soldiers, a man came down the road. At the sight of him one of the village women whispered, "Look!

Yonder comes the carpenter. Now we will hear something." The man stopped close to the well to survey the crowd. "Good Rabbi Joseph," said the woman approaching him, "there is a Jewish prisoner here. Come ask the Roman soldiers about him that we may know who he is, what he has done, and what they are going to do with him."

The rabbi glanced at Ben-Hur, then went to the officer. "The peace of the Lord be with you," he said.

"And the gods with you," the decurion replied.

"Are you from Jerusalem?"

"Yes."

"Your prisoner is young."

"In years, yes."

"May I ask what he has done?"

"He is an assassin."

"Is he a son of Israel?"

"He is a Jew," said the Roman dryly. "I know nothing of your tribes, but I can speak of his family. You may have heard of the prince of Jerusalem named Hur—Ben-Hur they called him. He lived in Herod's day."

"I have seen him," Joseph said.

"Well, this is his son."

Exclamations became general, and the decurion hastened to stop them. "In the streets of Jerusalem, day before yesterday, he nearly killed the noble Gratus by flinging a tile upon his head."

There was a pause in the conversation, and the Nazarenes gazed at young Ben-Hur as at a wild beast.

"Did he kill him?" asked the rabbi at length.

"No."

"Is he under sentence?"

"Yes—the galleys for life."

"The Lord help him!" said Joseph.

At this time, a youth who had come up with Joseph laid down the axe he had been carrying. Going to the great stone standing by the well, he took a pitcher and filled it with water. The action was so quiet that before the guards could interfere he was stooping over Ben-Hur and offering him a drink. He laid his hand gently on Ben-Hur's shoulder. Judah revived; and, looking up, he saw a face he never forgot—the face of a boy about his own age. Ben-Hur's spirit, hardened though it was by suffering, melted under the stranger's look and became as a child's. He put his lips to the pitcher and drank long and deep. Not a word was said.

When the draught [drink] was finished, the hand that had been resting on Judah's shoulder was placed on his head to say a blessing. Then the stranger returned the pitcher to its place on the stone and taking his axe again, went back to Rabbi Joseph. All eyes went with

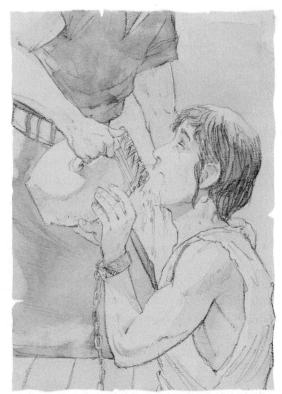

him, the decurion's as well as those of the villagers. And so, for the first time, Judah and the son of Mary met and parted.

* * *

For three years Ben-Hur had labored as a galley slave. No one knew his story nor even his name. There was no need of keeping the proper names of slaves brought to the galleys as to their graves. They were identified by the numerals painted on the benches to which they were assigned. Thus, Ben-Hur was known only as number sixty on the ship *Astroea.*

Having been appointed the new master of the ship, the tribune, Quintus Arrius, came to examine his slaves. His sharp eyes moved from seat to seat and came at last to number sixty. There they rested. Arrius observed Ben-Hur's youth. He also observed that he seemed of good height and that his limbs were a mass of muscle, which swelled and knotted like kinking cords as he rowed. Altogether there was in Ben-Hur's action a certain harmony which provoked Arrius's curiosity, and soon the tribune found himself waiting to catch a glimpse of Ben-Hur's face in full. Directly he caught the view he wished, for the young rower turned and looked at him.

"A Jew and a boy!" he said to himself. "What could have brought a young Jew to this place reserved for barbarian convicts? I will know more of him." Arrius moved to the horator [man in charge of rowers]. "Do you know the man at number sixty?" he asked.

The chief looked sharply at the rower then going forward. "No," he replied.

"He is a Jew," Arrius remarked thoughtfully.

"The noble Quintus is shrewd," said the other.

"He is very young," Arrius continued.

"But our best rower."

"What is his disposition?"

"He is obedient. Otherwise I know nothing of him."

"Nothing of his history?"

"Not a word."

The tribune reflected awhile then turned to go. "If I should be on deck when his rowing time is up," he paused to say, "send him to me. Let him come alone."

About two hours later Arrius saw Ben-Hur approaching. "The chief said

it was your will that I should seek you here. I am come."

Arrius spoke as an older man to a younger, not as a master to a slave. "The horator tells me you are his best rower."

"The horator is very kind," Ben-Hur answered.

"Have you seen much service?"

"About three years."

"At the oars?"

"I cannot recall a day of rest from them."

"From your speech you are a Jew," said Arrius pointedly.

"My ancestors, further back than the first Roman, were Hebrews," answered Ben-Hur.

"The stubborn pride of your race is not lost in you," said Arrius, observing a flush on Ben-Hur's face.

"Pride is never so loud as when in chains."

"But what cause have you for pride?"

"That I am a Jew."

Arrius smiled. "I have not been to Jerusalem," he said. "But I have heard of its princes. I knew one of them. He was a merchant and sailed the seas. He was fit to have been a king. Of what degree [station] are you?"

"My father was a prince of Jerusalem; and as a merchant, he sailed the seas. He was known and honored in the guest chamber of the great Augustus."

"His name?"

"Ithamar, of the house of Hur."

The tribune raised his hand in astonishment. "A son of Hur—you? What brought you here?" he said more sternly.

Judah lowered his head, and when his feelings were sufficiently mastered, he looked again at the tribune and answered, "I was accused of attempting to assassinate Valerius Gratus, the procurator."

"You?" cried Arrius, yet more amazed. "All Rome rang with the story!" His manner became more severe. "Do you admit your guilt?"

The change that came over Ben-Hur was wonderful to see; it was so instant and extreme. His voice sharpened, every fiber thrilled, and his eyes flamed. "You have heard of the God of my fathers," he said, "of the infinite Jehovah. By His truth and almightiness, I am innocent!"

The tribune was moved. "Did you have no trial?" he asked.

"No!"

The Roman raised his head surprised. "No trial—no witnesses? Who passed judgment on you?"

"They bound me with chords and dragged me to a vault in the tower of Antonia. I saw no one, and no one spoke to me. After what seemed several days of this torturous solitude, soliders came, took me to the seaside, and placed me aboard this ship. I have been at the gallies ever since."

"Who was with you when the blow was struck?"

"Tirzah, my sister, was with me. Together we leaned over the parapet to see the legion pass. A tile gave way under my hand and fell upon Gratus. I thought I had killed him. Ah, what horror I felt!"

"Where was your mother?"

"In the chamber below."

"What became of her?"

Ben-Hur drew a breath like a gasp. "I do not know. I saw them drag her away—that is all. I, too, ask for her. Oh, for one word. She at least was innocent!"

Arrius listened intently. A whole family blotted out to atone an accident! The thought shocked him. For once Arrius was uncertain. His power was ample, and Ben-Hur had won his faith. Yet, he said to himself, there is no haste. The best rower cannot be spared. I will wait and learn more. I will at least be sure that this is the prince Ben-Hur and that he is of the right disposition. Ordinarily slaves are liars. "It is enough," he said aloud. "Go back to your place."

Ben-Hur bowed, looked once more into his master's face, but saw nothing for hope. As he turned away, he said, "If you think of me again, tribune, let it not be lost in your mind that I prayed you only for a word of my people— mother and sister." Ben-Hur moved on.

"Stay," said Arrius. Ben-Hur stopped; the tribune went to him. "If you were free, what would you do?"

"The noble Arrius mocks me," said Judah bitterly.

"No. No."

"Then I will answer. I would know no rest until my mother and Tirzah were restored to home. I would give every day and hour to their happiness. I would wait on them, never a slave more faithful. They have lost much; but, by the God of my fathers, I would find them more!"

The answer was unexpected by the Roman, and he momentarily lost his purpose. "I spoke of your ambition," he said, recovering. "If your mother and sister were dead, or not to be found, what would you do?"

"Tribune, I will tell you truthfully. Only the night before the dreadful day of which I have spoken, I obtained

permission to be a soldier. I am of the same mind yet."

A short while after, Ben-Hur was at his bench again. That he had been called by a great man and asked his story was the bread on which he fed his hungry spirit. Surely something good would come of it. The light about his bench was clear and bright with promises, and he prayed, "Oh God, I am a true son of Israel whom thou hast loved! Help me, I pray Thee!"

When the sun, going down, withdrew its last ray from the cabin, the galley still held northward. About nightfall, the smell of incense floated down the gangways from the deck. Ben-Hur noted this. The tribune is at the altar, he thought to himself. Could it be that we are going into battle? He became more observant.

Since becoming a galley slave, Ben-Hur had been in many battles though he had never seen one. He only heard them above and about him, and he was familiar with all the notes, almost as a singer with a song. He waited anxiously, and it was not long before he heard Arrius addressing the commander of the marines. "The pirates are close by. Up and ready!"

Everyone aboard, even the ship, awoke now. Officers went to their quarters. The marines took arms and were led out. Sheaves of arrows and armfuls of javelins were carried on deck. The rowers assembled under guard in front of the chief while overhead could be heard the muffled noises of final preparations.

Presently, quiet settled about the galley again—quiet full of vague dread and expectation. No sound from without, none from within, yet each man in the cabin instinctively poised himself for a shock. The very ship seemed to catch the sense, hold its breath, and go crouched, tiger-like.

At last there was the sound of trumpets—full, clear, long blown. The chief beat the sounding board until it

rang. The rowers reached forward, full length and deepening the dip of their oars, pulled suddenly with all their united force. The galley, quivering in every timber, answered with a leap. Forward rushed the *Astroea*; and as it went, sailors ran down into the cabin and plunging large cotton swabs into oil tanks, tossed them dripping to comrades at the head of the stairs. From this action Ben-Hur concluded that fire was to be added to the horrors of the combat. But he did not dwell long on this thought, for suddenly the *Astroea* stopped. The oars were dashed from the hands of the rowers, and the rowers from their benches. In the midst of this panic a body was plunged headlong down the hatchway falling at the feet of Ben-Hur. He beheld the face—a barbarian from the white-skinned nations of the North. Had an iron hand snatched him from the pirate's deck? Then the thought struck him—the *Astroea* had been boarded! The Romans were now fighting on their own deck!

A chill of horror smote the young Jew. Arrius was hard pressed. All Ben-Hur's hope of freedom rested in the noble tribune. What if Arrius were killed in battle? The tumult thundered above him; he looked around; in the cabin all was confusion. Only the chief kept his chair, unchanged, calm as ever—weaponless. A short space lay between Ben-Hur and the hatchway aft. He gave the chief a last look, then broke away—not in flight but to seek the tribune. With a single leap he was halfway up the steps—up far enough to catch a glimpse of the sky, blood-red with fire. The floor when he reached it seemed to be lifting itself and breaking into pieces; then, the whole after-part of the hull broke asunder. The sea, hissing and foaming, leaped in, and all became darkness and surging water to Ben-Hur.

The time he was under water seemed an age longer than it really was; at last he gained the top. With a great gasp he filled his lungs afresh and tossing the water from his hair and eyes, climbed higher on a plank he'd managed to grasp. He looked about him. Death had pursued him closely under the waves, and he found it waiting for him still when he reached the surface. The battle was yet on, nor could he say who was victor. But he had nothing to do with their struggles. They were all his enemies. There was not one of them who would not kill him for the plank on which he floated. He made haste to get away.

He struck out, pushing the plank, which was broad and unmanageable. Seconds were precious; half a second might save or lose him. He struggled with all his might, and in the crisis of this effort, up from the sea, within an arms reach, a helmet shot like a gleam of gold. Then appeared two hands with fingers extended; they were large, strong hands. Ben-Hur swerved from them appalled. Then up came two arms which began to beat the water violently. The head turned back and gave the face to the light. Ben-Hur had never seen a more ghastly sight. The mouth was gaping wide, the eyes were open but sightless, and the face had a bloodless pallor. As the drowning man was going under again, Ben-Hur caught the chain of the man's helmet and drew him to the plank. The man was Arrius, the tribune.

The water beat violently about them, taxing all Ben-Hur's strength to hold to the plank and at the same time keep the Roman's head above the surface. A short distance from them were several others adrift. He turned toward them just as several galleys were heading toward them. The ships drove right through the floating men. In wild alarm Ben-Hur swerved, and he and the tribune barely escaped the stroke of the oars.

The battle moved on. Resistance had turned to flight. But who were the victors? Ben-Hur pushed the plank more securely under Arrius, then took care to keep him there.

*   *   *

The dawn came slowly, and Ben-Hur watched it coming with hope and fear, for he realized that both his freedom and the life of the tribune were dependent on the previous day's battle. At last the morning broke in full, the air without a breath. Ben-Hur looked about him. The sea was blackened by charred and sometimes smoking fragments, and in the distance could be seen a battered galley floating motionless, the oars all idle. Further on he noticed some moving specks, but he could not discern if they were ships or white birds a wing.

As the hours passed, his anxiety increased. If relief came not speedily, Arrius would die. Sometimes he seemed already dead, he lay so still. Ben-Hur took the Roman's helmet off, and then, with greater difficulty, the cuirass [Roman soldier breastplate]; he found the heart fluttering. He took hope at the sign and held on. There was nothing to do but wait, and, after the manner of his people, pray.

* * *

The throes of recovering from drowning are more painful than the drowning. These Arrius passed through and at length, to Ben-Hur's delight, reached the point of speech. "Our rescue, I see, depends on the result of that fight. I see also what you have done for me. To speak fairly, you have saved my life at the risk of your own. I make the acknowledgment broadly; and whatever comes you have my thanks.

More than that, if fortune serves me kindly and we escape this peril, I will do you such a favor as becomes a Roman who has power and opportunity to prove his gratitude." Arrius rested again. "Are you indeed a son of Hur, the Jew?" he next asked.

"It is as I have said," Ben-Hur replied.

"I knew your father—" Judah drew himself nearer and listened eagerly; at last he thought to hear of home. "I knew him and loved him," Arrius continued. There was another pause, during which something diverted the speaker's thought. "Before I speak of my acquaintance with your father, let us discuss a more urgent matter. It is the custom of gentlemen in Rome to wear a ring. There

is one on my hand. Take it now and put it on your own." Judah did as he was told. "This trinket has its uses. I have property and money, and am accounted rich even in Rome. I have no family, however, no heir to pass these fortunes on to. If you are rescued, show that ring to my freedman; he has control in my absence. You will find him in a villa near Misenum. Tell him how it came to you and ask anything or all he may have. He will refuse you nothing. If we both are rescued by the Romans, I will do better by you." The tribune drew a deep breath to regain strength, then said, "Now, I desire a pledge from you."

"Tell me first your wish."

"Will you promise then?"

"That were to give the pledge, and— blessed be the God of my fathers! Yonder comes a ship!"

"In what direction?" asked Arrius.

"From the north."

"Can you tell her nationality by outward signs?"

"No. My service has been at the oars," said Ben-Hur.

"Has she a flag?"

"I cannot see one."

Arrius remained quiet some time, apparently in deep reflection. "Does the ship hold this way?" he said at length.

"Still this way," said Ben-Hur.

"Look for the flag now."

"She has none."

"Nor any other sign?"

"She has a sail set, is of three banks, and comes swiftly—that is all I can say of her."

"A Roman in triumph would have out many flags. She must be an enemy. Hear now," said Arrius, becoming grave

again, "hear, while I may yet speak. If the galley be a pirate, your life is safe. They may not give you freedom. They may put you to the oar again, but they will not kill you. On the other hand, I—" The tribune faltered, "I am too old to submit to dishonor. In Rome let them tell how Quintus Arrius, as became a Roman tribune, went down with his ship in the midst of the foe. I want you to pledge me that if the galley prove a pirate, you will push me from the plank and drown me. Swear you will do it."

"I will not swear," said Ben-Hur firmly. "I will not do the deed. The Jewish law, which is to me most binding, tribune, would make me answerable for your life. Take back your ring." Ben-Hur took the seal from his finger. "Take it back, and all your promises of favor in the event of delivery from this peril. The judgment which sent me to the oar for life made me a slave, yet I am not a slave; and no more am I your freedman. I am a son of Israel and this moment, at least, my own master. Take back the ring." Arrius remained passive. "You will not?" Judah continued. "Not in anger then, nor in any despite, but to free myself from a hateful obligation, I will give your gift to the sea." He tossed the ring away. Arrius heard the splash where it struck and sank, though he did not look. "In the three years of my servitude, you are the first to treat me kindly—no, there was one other." His voice dropped, and he saw plainly, as if it were then before him, the face of the boy who helped him by the well in Nazareth. He pushed the thought aside and continued. "Tribune, I pray you to believe me. I would rather die with you than be your slayer. My mind is as firmly set as yours. Though you were to offer me all Rome, I would not kill you."

For a time they waited silently, Ben-Hur often looking at the coming ship and Arrius resting with his eyes closed, indifferent. "Are you sure she is an enemy?" Ben-Hur asked at length.

"I think so," was the reply.

"She is stopping to put a boat over the side."

Arrius became alert. "Do you see her flag?"

"Is there no other sign by which we may know if she is Roman?"

"If Roman, she will have a helmet over the mast's top."

"Then be of cheer. I see the helmet."

Arrius threw off his calm. "Thank your God," he said to Ben-Hur after straining to see the galley. "Thank your God, as I do my many gods." Judah raised himself on the plank, waved his hand, called with all his might, and at last drew the attention of the sailors.

* * *

Upon his return to Rome, Arrius had a warm welcome, and the young man attending him attracted the attention of his friends. To their questions about who he was, Arrius proceeded in a most affectionate manner to tell the story of his rescue and introduce Ben-Hur. He carefully omitted, however, any information that pertained to the young Jew's previous history. At the end of the narrative, the tribune called Ben-Hur to his side. "Good friends," he said, "this is now my son and heir, who, as he is to take my property, shall be known to you by my name. I pray you all to love him as you love me." As speedily as the opportunity permitted, the adoption was formally perfected, and Ben-Hur became the son of Arrius.

Reading Check

1. Why is Ben-Hur taken to Nazareth by the decurion and his soldiers?
2. Whom does Ben-Hur meet at the well of Nazareth?
3. Why does Ben-Hur decide to escape from the cabin to the deck during the battle?
4. What request does Arrius make of Ben-Hur and why does Ben-Hur choose to deny the tribune's request?
5. How does Arrius repay Ben-Hur for saving his life?

Part III   The Discovery

Arrius died soon after adopting Ben-Hur, but not before he had given the young Jew introduction into the Imperial world. Five years had passed since Ben-Hur had been taken from Jerusalem, and in that time he had learned to be cautious. For safety he desired to be known only as the son of Arrius, and he moved and carried out his business under that protective title. He had completed his training as a soldier in Rome and set out to travel the world and to enjoy the privileges reserved for wealthy Roman citizens. Presently, he was on board a ship bound for Antioch. For an hour or more he had occupied a seat in the shade of the sail. In that time several passengers of his own nationality had tried to engage him in conversation but without avail. His replies to their questions were brief, though gravely courteous, and in the Latin tongue.

It happened, however, that the galley stopped at a port in Cyprus and picked up a Hebrew of most respectable appearance: quiet, reserved, paternal. Ben-Hur could not refrain from speaking to the man. He ventured to ask him some questions, and the man's replies so won Ben-Hur's confidence that an extended conversation resulted.

During this conversation, the galley entered the receiving bay of the Orontes and two other vessels, which had been sighted out in sea, passed the river at the same time. As they did so, each threw out a flag of brightest yellow. There was much speculation as to the meaning of this signal, and at length one passenger interrupted Ben-Hur and addressed himself to the respectable Hebrew. "Do you know the meaning of those flags?" he inquired.

"Yes," replied the Hebrew. "They are simply marks of ownership."

"Do you know the owner?" asked another passenger.

"I have dealt with him," the Hebrew said.

All of the passengers, including Ben-Hur, looked at the speaker as if requesting him to go on.

"He lives in Antioch," the speaker continued in his quiet way. "He is vastly rich, and the talk about him is not always kind. You see, there used to be in Jerusalem a prince of an ancient family named Hur." Judah's heart beat quicker, but he managed to remain composed. "The prince was a merchant with a genius for business. He set on foot many enterprises, some reaching far east, others west. In the great cities he had branch houses. The one in Antioch was in the charge of a Greek in name, yet an Israelite. The master drowned at sea. His business, however, went on and was scarcely less prosperous. After a while misfortune overtook the family. The prince's only son, nearly grown, tried to kill the procurator Gratus in one of Jerusalem's streets. He failed by a narrow chance and has not been heard of since. In fact, Gratus's rage took in the whole house—not one of the name was left alive. Their palace was sealed up and is now a rookery for pigeons. The estate was confiscated as was everything that could be traced to the Hur's.

"To go on, Simonides, once the Prince Hur's agent, now opened his own trade and in an incredibly brief time became the master merchant of the city. They say nothing goes amiss with him. His camels do not die, except of old age; his ships never founder; if he throws a chip into the river, it will come back to him gold."

"How long has he been going on thus?"

"Not ten years."

"He must have had a good start."

"Yes, they say the procurator took only the prince's property ready at hand—his horses, cattle, houses, land, vessels, and goods. The money could not

be found, though there must have been vast sums of it. What became of it has been an unsolved mystery—a mystery that haunts the procurator still."

"It is no mystery to me," said a passenger with a scorn.

"I understand you," the Hebrew answered. "Others have had your idea—that it furnished old Simonides his start is a common belief. The procurator is of that opinion, or has been, for twice in five years he has caught the merchant and put him to torture."

Judah gripped the rope he was holding with crushing force. "It is said," the narrator continued, "that there is not a sound bone in the man's body. The last time I saw him he sat in a chair, a shapeless cripple, propped against cushions."

"So tortured?" exclaimed several listeners in one breath.

"Disease could not have produced such deformity. Still, the suffering made no impression on him. All he had was his lawfully, and he was making lawful use of it—that was the most they wrung from him. Now, however, he is past

persecution. He has a license to trade signed by Tiberius himself!"

"He paid roundly for it, I warrant," said a sympathetic listener.

The story ended just as the city of Antioch came into full view. All the passengers now crowded on deck, eager that nothing of the scene might escape them, for the shores of this city were unsurpassed in beauty. But Judah scarcely noticed, and as the ship turned and made her way slowly to the wharf, he turned once again to the Hebrew. "Before saying farewell, let me trouble you for one moment more. Your story of the merchant has made me curious to see him. You called him Simonides."

"Yes, he is a Jew with a Greek name."

"Where is he to be found?"

The man considered an instant. Then approving of Ben-Hur, he gave the information requested. "One would think," he replied, "that the richest merchant in Antioch would have a house for business corresponding to his wealth. But if you would find him, you must follow the river to the bridge, then to a building that looks like the buttress of a wall. Before the door there is an immense landing always covered with cargoes. The fleet that lies moored [anchored] there is his. You will find him in that building."

"I give you thanks," said Ben-Hur.

"The peace of our fathers go with you," said the Hebrew.

"And with you," replied Ben-Hur courteously.

Early the next day, Ben-Hur sought out Simonides. Now, at last, he thought to hear of his mother and sister. But if indeed Simonides had been his father's slave, would the man acknowledge the

relation? To do so meant that he must give up his riches. This thought caused Ben-Hur to hesitate a moment, but he derived strength for the interview from faith in his rights and the hope in his heart. If the story which the Hebrew told of Simonides was true, then by right Simonides, as well as his riches, belonged to Ben-Hur. For the wealth he cared nothing. He only wished to hear of his family. When he started to the door, it was with this promise to himself; "Let him tell me of mother and Tirzah, and I will give him his freedom without account."

As he entered, a man approached and spoke to him. "What would you have?"

"I would see Simonides, the merchant." He was led to the end of a darkened passage.

"A stranger to see the master," the man called out through a half parted curtain.

"Let him enter," a clear voice replied. Ben-Hur entered. In the middle of the room were two people. One was sitting in an ornate divan. This Ben-Hur assumed was Simonides. At the merchant's left, leaning against the back of the divan, was a girl well forward into womanhood.

"If you are Simonides, the merchant, and a Jew, then the peace of the God of our father Abraham on you and yours," said Ben-Hur.

"I am Simonides," the man answered in a voice singularly clear, "and a Jew. I return your salutation, with a prayer to know who calls on me."

"I am Judah, son of Ithamar, the late head of the House of Hur and a prince of Jerusalem."

Simonides right hand lay outside the robe—a long, thin hand. It closed tightly. Otherwise, there was not the slightest expression of feeling on the merchant's part; nothing to warrant surprise or interest; nothing but his calm answer. "The princes of Jerusalem, of the pure blood, are always welcome in my house. You are welcome. Give the young man a seat, Esther." The girl took an ottoman and carried it to Ben-Hur.

He courteously refused the offered seat; his business was too urgent.

"I pray good master Simonides," began Ben-Hur cautiously, "that you will not hold me an intruder. But coming up the river yesterday, I heard you knew my father."

"I knew the prince Hur. We were associated in some business enterprises."

Ben-Hur threw off his cautious manner. "Simonides, my father, at his death, had a trusted servant and I am told that you are that man!"

There was a sudden start of the wrenched limbs under the robe, but Simonides quickly regained himself and answered coldly, "Show me proofs of who you are."

Ben-Hur was stunned by the demand. He stammered then turned away at a loss. Simonides pressed him. "The proofs, the proofs, I say! Set them before me! Lay them in my hands!"

Ben-Hur had not anticipated such a requirement. Now that it had been made, the awful fact came to him that the three years in the galley had carried away all proofs of his identity. With his mother and sister gone, he did not live in the knowledge of any human being. Many were acquainted with him as the son of Arrius, but that was all. "Master Simonides," he said at length, "all my Roman connection with the noble Quintus Arrius I can prove. I have only to call the consul, at present the guest of the governor of this city, but I cannot prove your demand on me. I cannot prove I am my father's son. Those who would serve me in that, alas, are dead or lost! Since I have no proof, I will go and trouble you no further. Only let me say I did not seek your return to servitude nor account of your fortune. I have no need of any part thereof. When the good Quintus, my adopted father, died, he left me as his heir princely rich. If, therefore, you think of me again, let it be remembered that the chief purpose of my coming here was to know what you could tell me of my mother and sister. Can you tell me anything of them—even one word?"

Though Ben-Hur's earnestness brought Esther to tears, Simonides remained willful. In a clear voice he replied, "I have said I knew the Prince Ben-Hur. I also remember hearing of the misfortune which overtook his family, and I received the news with bitterness. Gratus and his officers, who wrought such misery on the widow of my friend, are the same who have since mercilessly tortured me. I will go further and say to you that I have made diligent search concerning the family, but—I have nothing to tell you of them. They are lost."

"Then the last hope is broken," he said, struggling with his feelings. "I am used to disappointments. I pray you to pardon my intrusion. If I have annoyed you, forgive it because of my sorrow. Farewell. I have nothing now to live for but vengeance on all that is Roman." With these words he departed.

Scarcely had Ben-Hur gone when Simonides seemed to wake as from sleep. His countenance flushed. The sullen light of his eyes changed to brightness, and he said with animation, "Esther, ring—quickly!" She rang a bell and behind them a door swung open and a man entered, passed round to the front of the merchant's divan and saluted him.

"Malluch, here—closer, closer to the divan," the master said excitedly. "I have a mission which shall not fail though the sun should. Listen! A young man is now descending to the storeroom—tall, comely, and in the garb of Israel. Follow him, his shadow not more faithful, and every night send me report of where he is, what he does, and the company he keeps. Do you understand? If he leaves the city, go after him—and mark my words, Malluch, be a friend to him." The man bowed and was gone.

When Ben-Hur exited the great warehouse, depression curtained him about with a sense of utter loneliness. He passed out of the city gate wandering aimlessly and eventually found himself one of a large procession. He had not enough interest to ask where they were going, yet he had a vague impression that they were in movement to the temples, the central attraction of Antioch's famous Grove of Daphne.

As the procession neared the grove, a breeze brought a wave of sweet smells toward them. Ben-Hur stopped as did the others and looked to see where the fragrance came from. "It is coming from a garden over there," Ben-Hur said to a man at his elbow.

"It looks like some priestly ceremony in performance—something to Diana or Pan or a deity of the woods," said the man. His answer was in Ben-Hur's mother tongue.

"A Hebrew?" questioned Ben-Hur, turning toward the speaker.

The man replied with a smile, "I was born within a stone's throw of the market place in Jerusalem."

"Are you going my way?" asked Judah.

"I am going to the stadium, if that is your way."

"The stadium! Good, friend," said Ben-Hur frankly, "I admit my ignorance of the grove. I did not know such a place had a stadium. If you will let me be your follower, I would be grateful."

"I would be delighted. Listen! I hear the wheels of the chariots now. They are taking the track."

Ben-Hur listened a moment, then completed the introduction by laying his hand on the man's arm and saying, "I am the son of Arrius, and you?"

"I am Malluch, a merchant of Antioch." With the introductions completed, they moved on.

They came to a field with a track laid out on it. The course was of soft earth, rolled and sprinkled. There were also several stands shaded by awnings which provided seats for the scattered spectators. In one of these stands the two newcomers found places.

The chariots were already moving along the track. Ben-Hur counted them as they passed—nine in all. Eight of the fours [teams of four horses] passed in front of them, some walking, others trotting, and all unexceptionally handled. Then the ninth one came on at a gallop. Ben-Hur burst into exclamation. "I have been in the stables of the emperor, Malluch; but by our father Abraham, I have never seen horses like these!" But before Ben-Hur stopped speaking, the horses fell into confusion. Someone in the stand uttered a sharp cry. Ben-Hur turned as he saw an old man half risen from an upper seat, his hands clenched, his eyes fiercely bright, and his long beard quivering in anger. The driver was exerting himself without

avail to quiet the four. "Accursed Roman!" shouted the old man shaking his fist at the driver. "Did he not swear he could drive them—swear by all his Latin gods?" His servants tried to calm him. "Nay, hands off me—off, I say! Oh, fool, fool, that I was to put trust in a Roman!" Ben-Hur sympathized with him, while the others in the stand began to laugh.

"They should at least respect his age," said Ben-Hur. "Who is he?"

"Sheik Ilderim, a mighty man from the desert, somewhere beyond Moab," replied Malluch. "He owns those horses. They say that they are racers descended from the time of the first Pharaoh."

Suddenly a new contestant came into view. His progress was signalized by clapping and cheering. All eyes turned from the sheik and his driver to this new spectacle. The new driver's beautiful horses and resplendent chariot drew Ben-Hur's attention as well. While looking at the driver, Ben-Hur was struck with a vague sense of familiarity. "Who is that man?" Ben-Hur asked himself. He could not see the man's face

or even his full figure yet. But the air and manner of the man pricked him keenly with a reminder of a period long gone.

From the shouting and the turnout, it was thought he might be some official favorite or a famous prince. Ben-Hur arose and forced a passage down nearly to the railing. His face was earnest, his manner eager. Directly the whole person of the driver was in view. Ben-Hur stood transfixed. His instinct and memory had served him faithfully—the driver was Messala!

Ben-Hur was yet staring at Messala, when an Arab arose and cried out, "Men of the east and west—listen! The good Sheik Ilderim needs a mighty man to drive his magnificent horses. Whoever will take them to his satisfaction, to him is promised enrichment forever. So says my master, Sheik Ilderim the Generous."

The proclamation awakened a great buzz among the people. Ben-Hur quickly turned his attention from Messala to the sheik. He then addressed Malluch who was by now at his side.

"Good Malluch, may a man forget his mother?" The question was abrupt and without direction.

Malluch looked into Ben-Hur's face for some hint of meaning, but saw none. Thus, he answered mechanically, "No, never," he said. Then recovering himself he added with fervor, "If he is an Israelite, never!"

"Your words bring back my childhood," said Ben-Hur, "and, Malluch, they prove you a genuine Jew. I believe I can trust you. My father bore a good name and was not without honor in Jerusalem, where he dwelt. My mother at his death was in the prime of womanhood; and it is not enough to say of her she was good and beautiful. In her tongue was the law of kindness, and her words were the praise of all in the gates. I also had a little sister; she and I were the family, and we were a happy family. But one day an accident happened to a Roman authority as he

was riding past our palace. The legionaries burst the gate and rushed in to seize us. I have not seen my mother or sister since. I cannot say if they are dead or living. But, Malluch, the man in the chariot yonder was present at that separation. He gave us over to the captors, and despite my mother's prayer for her children, he laughed as they dragged her away. It is hard for me to say which lives deepest in my memory of that day, love or hate." Ben-Hur caught the listener's arm. "Malluch, that man knows and takes with him now the secret I would give my life for. He knows if my mother and sister live, where they are, and their condition. If they are dead, he could at least tell me where they died and where their bones await my finding."

"And he will not?"

"No."

"Why?"

"Because I am a Jew and he a Roman."

"But Romans have tongues; and Jews, though despised by Romans, have methods to beguile [deceive] them."

"Not for such as he," said Ben-Hur bitterly. "Besides the secret is one of state."

Malluch nodded his head slowly, admitting the argument. Then he asked, "Would he recognize you?"

"He could not. I was sent to the galleys to die and have long been accounted as dead."

"I am amazed you did not rush at him and strike him," said Malluch yielding to a touch of passion.

"That would have been to put him past serving me forever. I would have had to kill him, and death keeps secrets even better than a guilty Roman." After a brief pause Ben-Hur resumed speaking. "I would not take his life, good Malluch, against that extreme the knowledge he possesses of my family's whereabouts is his safeguard. Yet I may punish him; and if you will help me, I will try."

"He is a Roman," said Malluch without hesitation, "and I am of the tribe of Judah. I will help you. If you choose, put me under oath—under the most solemn oath."

"Give me your hand; that will suffice." As their hands fell apart Ben-Hur said with lightened feeling, "What I would charge you with is not difficult, good friend; neither is it dreadful to the conscience. Do you know Ilderim the sheik?"

"Yes. His Orchard of Palms lies beyond the village two hours by horse and one by swift camel."

"These games in which the chariots will race, have they been widely published?"

"Oh, yes."

"When will the games be?"

"They are scheduled for the sixth day from this."

"Then time is short, Malluch, but it is enough." The last words were spoken decisively. "One thing more now, Malluch. Can I be assured that Messala will drive?"

"He is committed to the race in many ways," said Malluch. "He has published it in the streets, in the palace, and in the soldiers barracks. Moreover, his name is on the tablets of every spend-thrift in Antioch. He could not withdraw from the race now even if he desired to do so."

"Then I am satisfied. Now guide me to the Orchard of Palms and give me introduction to Sheik Ilderim the Generous."

"Now?"

"Now. I want to engage his horses, and by tomorrow someone else may have received the commission."

"You like them then?"

"They are of the blood which is the glory of the deserts. If all that is said of them be true and I can bring their spirit under control of mine, then I can—"

"Win the sesterii!" said Malluch with enthusiasm.

"No," said Ben-Hur quickly. "I will do much better than that, my friend. I will humble my enemy in a most public place, and as you and I know a Roman can bear anything but humiliation!"

Reading Check

1. Why is the Hebrew's story about the merchant Simonides of such interest and importance to Ben-Hur?
2. Why does Ben-Hur choose to be known as the son of Arrius rather than Ben-Hur?
3. What does Simonides tell Ben-Hur of his family?
4. How and where does Ben-Hur discover Messala?
5. As a result of this discovery what decision does Ben-Hur make and why does he make this choice?

Simonides sat on the terrace looking down over the river. "Malluch is a laggard tonight," he said, showing where his thoughts were.

"Do you believe he will come?" Esther asked.

"Unless he has taken to the sea or the desert and is yet following the young man, he will come." Simonides said with quiet confidence. Just then a footstep was heard on the terrace—"Ha! Did I not tell you he would come, Esther? We will now have tidings."

Malluch approached. "Peace be to you, good master," he said "and to you, Esther, most excellent of daughters."

Simonides, as was his habit in business, after answering the salutation went straight to the subject. "What of the young man, Malluch?"

Malluch recounted the events of the day in the simplest words; and until he was through, there was no interruption.

"You have done well—no one could have done better," said Simonides heartily. "Now, what say you of the young man's nationality?"

"He is an Israelite, good master, and of the tribe of Judah."

"You are positive?"

"Very positive."

"He appears to have told you only bits and pieces of his life."

"He has learned to be prudent. I might call him distrustful, but I can answer with much assurance nonetheless. He is devoted to finding his mother and sister—that first. Then he has a grievance against Rome. Messala whom I mentioned has something to do with

that wrong, and the present object of the young Jew is to humiliate this Roman."

"Messala is influential," said Simonides thoughtfully.

"Yes, but the meeting will be at the games."

"Well—what then?"

"The son of Arrius will win."

"How do you know?"

Malluch smiled. "I am judging by what he says."

"Is that all?"

"No, there is a much better sign—his spirit."

"Enough, Malluch. Go eat and make ready to return to the Orchard of Palms. You must help the young man in his coming trial. I will send a letter to Ilderim and tell him our secret. But make certain Ben-Hur remains ignorant of our acquaintance. He must not know I have sent you—at least not yet." Then in an undertone, as if to himself, he added, "I may attend the games myself this year."

*   *   *

Ben-Hur, having immediately answered Sheik Ilderim's publication, received the commission. The young Jew's skill with horses proved astounding, and Ilderim's enthusiasm knew no bounds. There was only one week for training, but when the time for the race arrived Ilderim, Malluch, and Ben-Hur were all confident—the fours and their driver were ready.

The afternoon before the games Ilderim's racing property was transported to the city and put in quarters adjoining the circus. As the shiek and Ben-Hur made their way into the city,

Malluch approached them. He exchanged salutations, as usual, then produced a paper for the sheik saying, "I have here the notice of the editor of the games. It was just issued. In it you will find your horses published for the race. You will also find in it the order of the other exercises. And may I say even now, good sheik, that I congratulate you on your victory." He gave the paper to Ilderim and turned to Ben-Hur. "To you also, son of Arrius, my congratulations. There is nothing now to prevent your meeting Messala. Every condition preliminary to the race is complied with. I have assurance from the creditor himself, and may I add that I am certain you shall win."

"Thank you, Malluch," said Ben-Hur.

"Your color is white," Malluch continued, "and Messala's mixed scarlet and gold. The good effects are visible already. Boys are now hawking [peddling] white ribbons along the streets. Tomorrow I assure you every Arab and Jew in the city will wear them. In the circus you will see the white fairly divide the galleries with the red."

"Malluch, would you serve me perfectly?" said Ben-Hur.

"I would," replied Malluch.

"Then help me fix all the public eye on our race—Messala's and mine. Draw their attention away from all other contestants. Can that be done?"

"It can!"

"Then do it," said Ben-Hur.

At that moment the conversation was interrupted by a cry from Ilderim. "Ha! What is this!" He drew near Ben-Hur with a finger pointing on the face of the notice. "Read here!"

Ben-Hur took the paper. The names of the competitors were given, with their several nationalities and schools of training, the trials in which they had been engaged, the prizes they had won, and the prizes now offered. Over these parts of the program, Ben-Hur sped with rapid glance. At last he came to the announcement of the chariot race. He read it slowly. One thousand sesteria and a crown of laurel were the prizes. Then followed the particulars.

"I. A four of Lysippus the Corinthian—two grays, a bay, and a black; entered at Alexandria last year, and again at Corinth, where they were winners. Lysippus, driver. Color, yellow.

"II. A four of Messala of Rome—two white, two black; victors of the Circensian as exhibited in the Circus Maximus last year. Messala, driver. Colors, scarlet and gold.

"III. A four of Cleanthes the Athenian—three gray, one bay; winners at the Isthmian last year. Cleanthes, driver. Color, green.

"IV. A four of Dicaeus the Byzantine—two black, one gray, one bay; winners, this year at Byzantium. Dicaeus, driver. Color, black.

"V. A four Admetus the Sidonian—all grays. Thrice entered at Casarea, and thrice victors. Admetus, driver. Color, blue.

"VI. A four of Ilderim, sheik of the Desert. All bays; first race. Ben-Hur, a Jew, driver. Color, white."

Ben-Hur, a Jew, driver!

Why that name instead of Arrius?

Ben-Hur raised his eyes to Ilderim. He had found the cause of the Arab's outcry. Both rushed to the same conclusion.

The hand was the hand of Messala! He knew Ben-Hur!

* * *

In the purest sense the games were a gift to the public; consequently, everyone was free to attend. At midnight the day before the games were to start, the entrances were thrown open, and the rabble [common people] came surging into every quarter. Nothing less than an earthquake or an army with spears could have dislodged them from their benches. They dozed the night away and breakfasted there, and in the morning they were found waiting, patient and sight-hungry.

As the charioteers moved into the circus, the excitement increased. The people in the galleries filled the air with screams.

"Messala! Messala!"

"Ben-Hur! Ben-Hur!

On hearing the crowd Ben-Hur knew his prayers had been answered. Malluch had done his work well. The eyes of the East were on his contest with Messala. In the midst of this excitement, four stout servants entered carrying the merchant Simonides up the aisle. Curiosity was much excited. Presently someone called out, "Simonides, that's Simonides; he's come to the games!" Those about caught it and passed it along the benches. There was a hurried climbing on seats to get sight of the man about whom common report had coined a romance so mixed of good and bad fortune that everyone was interested. Ilderim, who entered with Simonides and Esther, also brought attention. The merchant and his party were only just seated when the trumpet sounded short and sharp. The starters, one for each chariot, leaped down from behind the pillars of the goal, ready to give assistance if any of the four proved unmanageable. Again the trumpet sounded and simultaneously the gate-keepers threw open the stalls. The race was on and the souls of the racers were in it.

Ben-Hur was on the extreme left of the six racers. For a moment, like the others, he was half-blinded by the lights in the arena; yet he managed to catch sight of his antagonists and divine their purpose. At Messala, he gave one searching look. As he did so, he saw the soul of the man—cruel, cunning, desperate—not so much excited as determined, a soul in a tension of watchfulness and fierce resolve. In a time no longer than was required to turn his eyes back to his horses, Ben-Hur felt his own resolution harden to like temper. At whatever cost, at all hazards, he determined to humble this enemy!

At the outset of the race, Ben-Hur swept around and took the course neck and neck with Messala, though on the outside. The marvelous skill shown in making the change from the extreme left across to the right without losing ground, did not fail the sharp eyes of the spectators. The circus rocked with prolonged applause.

Now, racing together side by side, the two opponents neared the goal. Making this first turn was in all respects considered the telling test of a chariot-eer. A hush fell over all the circus so that, for the first time in the race, the rattle and clang of the cars plunging after the tugging steeds was distinctly heard.

Messala observed Ben-Hur. As they rounded the perilous curve, he turned to Ben-Hur and cried out, "Down Eros, Up Mars!" and with this shout he whirled his whip to lash Ben-Hur's steeds. The whip caught the horses a cut the like of which they had never known. The four Arabs sprang forward affrighted! The blow was seen in every

quarter of the galleries, and the spectator's amazement was universal. The silence deepened until up on the benches behind the consul the boldest held his breath, waiting for the outcome. The strength obtained from years of rowing helped Ben-Hur now. He called to the four in a soothing voice and with both might and skill he gripped the reins to guide the horses safely around the dangerous turn. The people cheered Ben-Hur then turned their attention to Messala. Down from the balcony, as thunder falls, burst their indignant cry. Their feeling was so vigorous in its manifestation that Messala felt it unsafe to trifle further. Before the people's fever abated, Ben-Hur had totally regained the mastery of his horses, and on approaching the first goal, he was again side by side with Messala, bearing with him the sympathy and admiration of all in the crowd who were not Roman.

As the cars whirled around the goal, Esther caught sight of Ben-Hur's face. He was pale, but otherwise calm. There were yet five rounds to go. After three rounds Messala still held the inside position, but Ben-Hur moved closely at his side.

Messala had now attained his utmost speed, and slowly but certainly he was beginning to forge ahead. His horses were running with their heads low; from the balcony their bodies appeared to skim the earth; their nostrils showed blood-red in expansion; their eyes seemed straining in their sockets.

When the last round began, Ben-Hur turned in behind the Roman's car, and the joy of the Messala faction reached its bound. They screamed and howled and tossed the red and yellow colors. Malluch in the lower gallery found it hard to keep his cheer. Ben-Hur was barely holding a place at the tail of his enemy's car. Over in the east end, Simonides' party was silent. The merchant's head was bent low. Ilderim tugged at his beard and dropped his eyebrows till there was nothing to be seen of his eyes but an occasional sparkle of light. Esther scarcely breathed.

Messala, fearful of losing his place, hugged the stony wall with a perilous clasp. As they whirled by Esther saw Ben-Hur's face again; it was whiter than before. Simonides, shrewder than Esther, said to Ilderim, "I am no judge, good sheik, if Ben-Hur be not about to execute some design. His face has that look."

All factions except the Romans joined hope in Ben-Hur and openly indulged their feeling.

"Ben-Hur! Ben-Hur!" they shouted.

From the benches above him as he passed, he heard the favor descend in fierce injunctions, "Speed thee, Jew!" some cried. "Take the wall now! On, loose the Arabs! Give them rein and scourge! Do not let the Roman have the turn on you again!" others cried.

Either Ben-Hur refused to listen or could not do better, for halfway round the course in the last round, he was still following. Now, to make the last turn, Messala began to draw in his left-hand steeds, an act which necessarily slackened their speed. His spirit was high, and confident, for they were only six-hundred feet from the finish.

At that moment Malluch saw Ben-Hur lean forward over his Arabs and give them the reins. Out flew the many-

folded lash in his hand. Over the backs of the startled steeds it writhed and hissed and writhed again and again. Though it did not fall, there was both sting and menace in its quick report. Instantly, not one, but the four as one, answered with a leap that landed them alongside the Roman's car. Messala heard, but dared not look. At that moment the iron shod point of Ben-Hur's axle caught Messala's wheel and crushed it. A crash loud enough to send a thrill throughout the circus was heard. Quicker than thought, out over the course a spray of shining red and yellow fragments flew. Down on its right side toppled the bed of Messala's chariot! There was a rebound as the axle hit the

hard earth; then another. The car dashed against the wall and went to pieces. Messala, entangled in the reigns, pitched forward headlong! To increase the horror of the sight, the Sidonian, who was behind Ben-Hur, could not stop or turn out. He drove into the wreck full speed, over Messala and into his horses all mad with fear. Presently, out of the turmoil, the fighting horses, the resound of blows, and the murky clouds of dust, crawled Messala. The race had been delayed only an instant.

The people arose, leaped on the benches, shouted and screamed. Their enthusiasm was beyond all restraint. Those who looked toward the wreckage caught glimpses of Messala, now under the trampling fours, now under the abandoned car. He was still; they thought him dead. But a far greater number never even looked that way. Instead they followed Ben-Hur. When the Byzantine and Corinthian were halfway down the course, Ben-Hur made the last turn. The race was won.

* * *

The chariot race proved only the beginning of Messala's humiliation. He had escaped death, but his legs were crushed and forever useless. This proud Roman, who had encouraged Gratus to torture Simonides in an effort to find the Hur's fortune, was now compelled to suffer the same affliction. His misery, however, was far greater than the noble merchant's. For all Messala's wealth was lost with the race, and the friends that had doted on him in prosperous times now deserted him. Only his pride remained as a bitter companion to mock him and daily remind him of lost dreams and the tragic life he was destined to endure.

Reading Check

1. Why does Shiek Ilderim cry out when he reads the program for the games?
2. As the racers stand waiting in the arena, Ben-Hur looks toward his enemy and sees "the soul of the man." What does this look reveal about Messala?
3. List some of Messala's specific actions during the race that prove the accuracy of this revelation.
4. As a result of this revelation what resolve does Ben-Hur make?
5. In Galatians Paul tells us, "Be not deceived; God is not mocked: for whatsoever a man soweth, that shall he also reap" (Gal. 6:7). How does this verse apply to Messala?

Part V   The Tower of Antonia

Ben-Hur moved toward the house of Simonides with the excitement of the race still in his mind. After the race, Simonides had revealed his acquaintance with Ilderim, and now the whole party waited for Ben-Hur at the merchant's house. Malluch greeted him at the door and showed him into the main room. It was exactly as it had been at Ben-Hur's first interview.

"Son of Hur," said Simonides, repeating the address slowly, "son of Hur take thou the peace of the Lord God of our fathers—take it from me and mine." The salutation could not be misunderstood. Simonides' address confirmed that he now recognized Ben-Hur as master.

Unable to find the appropriate words to convey his emotion, Ben-Hur remained silent while Simonides continued, "I have here a statement covering your property first, and then our relation. Will it please you to read it now."

"Later, Simonides," he managed to say. "Later I will read the papers carefully. For the present I would prefer you to summarize their contents."

From the separate sheets, Simonides read the following:

Credit

By ships	*60 talents*
By goods in store	*110 talents*
By cargoes in transit	*75 talents*
By camels, horses, etc.	*20 talents*
By warehouses	*10 talents*
By bills due	*54 talents*
By money on hand and subject draft	*224 talents*
Total	*553 talents*

"To these five hundred and fifty-three talents gained, add the original capital I had from your father and you have six hundred and seventy-three talents! You are now, son of Hur, the richest Roman subject in the world!" Ben-Hur gazed at the speaker. Despite the broken limbs and the bloodless face, Simonides had a masterful air and a royal manner. His black eyes looked out under the white brows steadily, but not sternly. The pride perceptible in the faithful servant's manner was not offensive, for it was from a sense of duty well done. Simonides rolled the papyri and offered them to Ben-Hur, who took them gently from the old man's hand. "Now, concerning our relation," said Simonides, dropping his voice but not his eyes, "What is your desire?"

The moment was one of absorbing interest to all present, for a man is never so on trial as in the moment of excessive good fortune. Simonides folded his hands and waited. Esther scarcely breathed, and Ilderim fingered his beard anxiously.

Ben-Hur arose. He was yet struggling with emotion, but he mastered himself and began. "All this is to me as a light from heaven sent to drive away a night which has been so long I feared it would not end, so dark I had lost hope of seeing. I give thanks to the Lord, Who has not abandoned me, and next, to you, good Simonides. Your faithfulness outweighs the cruelty of others, and my father would have richly rewarded you. I desire to be like him. You have said there is nothing I cannot do; be it so. The goods recorded here—the ships, houses, camels, horses, money, and of course your freedom, I give back to you. It is all yours with one exception and on one condition. That exception is that the hundred and twenty talents which were my father's be returned to me; and that condition is that you shall join me in the search for my mother and sister, holding all your wealth, as I shall mine, subject to the expense of their discovery." It was heartily agreed on, and before nightfall Ben-Hur was on his way to Jerusalem, with the promise that Simonides and Esther would soon follow.

* * *

A great change had come to pass in Jerusalem. Valerius Gratus had been succeeded by Pontius Pilate. As his first administrative command, Pilate ordered an inspection of all the prisons in Judea and a return of the names of persons in custody with a statement of the crimes they had committed.

This order was received and promptly executed at the Tower of Antonia in Jerusalem. The next morning an officer from the tower appeared at Pilate's palace.

"Ah, Gesius! Come in," Pilate said.

The newcomer entered. Everyone present looked at him, and observing a certain expression of alarm on his face, became silent that they might hear what he had to say. "Tribune," he began, bending low, "I fear to tell you the news I bring."

"Another mistake—ah, Gesius?"

"If I could persuade myself it was but a mistake, I would not be afraid."

"A crime then, or worse, a breach of duty. You may laugh at Caesar and live; but if you have offended the eagles [emblem of Rome]—ah, Gesius you know your fate. Go on."

"It has been about eight years now since Valerius Gratus selected me to be keeper of the Tower Antonia," said the man deliberately. "I remember the morning I entered upon the duties of my office. There had been a riot the day before. We slew many Jews and suffered on our side as well. The affair came, it was said, from an attempt to assassinate Gratus. I found him sitting where you now sit, his head wrapped in bandages. He told me of my selection and gave me these keys. They are numbered to correspond with the number of each cell in the Tower. He told me they were the badges of my office and not to be parted with. He also laid a roll of parchment on the table, and calling me over to him, he opened the roll. 'Here are the maps of the cells,' he said. There were three maps. He pointed to one. 'This one,' he said, 'shows the arrangement of the lower floor.' He then took care to spread the map out on the table. 'Notice this cell—cell number V.' He laid his finger on the picture of the cell. 'There are three men confined in that cell,' he continued, 'desperate characters, who by some means got hold of a state secret and suffer for their curiosity. They are blind and tongueless and are placed in this cell for life. They are to have nothing but food and drink, and that is to be given them through a hole which you will find in the wall. Do you understand, Gesius?' I nodded assent. 'It is well that you do.' He looked at me threateningly. 'One thing more, the door of their cell—cell number V—shall never be opened for any purpose, neither to let anyone in or out, not even yourself.'

"But if they die," I asked.

"'If they die,' he said, 'the cell shall be their tomb. They were put there to die. The cell is leprous. They cannot last long.' With that he gave me the parchments and let me go."

Gesius stopped and from the breast of his tunic drew three parchments, all much yellowed by time and use. Selecting one of them, he laid it before the tribune. "This is the lower floor as the map of Gratus gave me shows." The

whole company looked at the map. "But," Gesius continued, "this is not a true map," said the keeper. It shows but five cells on that floor and there are six."

"Six, you say?"

"I will show you the floor as it is, or as I believe it to be." On the page of his tablet, Gesius drew another diagram and gave it to the tribune.

"You have done well," said Pilate, examining the drawing and thinking the narrative at an end. "I will have the map corrected; or, better, I will have a new one made and given to you. Come for it in the morning." Pilate then rose to go.

"But hear me further, tribune. The prisoners of state—those blind and without tongues—that was not a true story either."

"No?" said the tribune with returning interest.

"Hear and judge for yourself. As required, I visited all cells. Gratus's order that cell number V should not be opened had been respected all these years. Food and drink only had been passed through the wall for the three men; that was all. I went to the door yesterday, curious to see the wretches who, against all expectation, had lived so long. The locks refused the key. We pulled a little and the door fell down, rusted from its hinges. Going in, I found but one man—old, blind, and tongueless. His hair dropped in stiffened mats below his waist. His skin was like the parchment there, and as he held out his hands, his fingernails curled and twisted like the claws of a bird. I asked him where his companions were. He shook his head in denial. Thinking to find the others, we searched the cell. The floor was dry; so were the walls. If three men had been shut up in the cell and two of them had died, at least their bones would have endured."

"What are you saying?"

"I believe that there has been but one prisoner there in the eight years."

The tribune regarded the keeper sharply and said, "Are you saying that Gratus lied?"

Gesius bowed, "I am saying he might have been mistaken."

"No, he must have been correct," the tribune said. "By your own admission he was right. For did you not say that for eight years food and drink were furnished for three men?"

"There is an explanation," Gesius continued. "Today the prisoner came back. He was brought to me. By signs and tears he at last made me understand that he wished to return to his cell, and I so ordered. As they were leading him off, he broke away and kissed my feet and by piteous dumb imploration [pleading] insisted that I should go also. I went. When we were in the cell again, the prisoner caught my hand eagerly and led me to the back wall of his cell. There I found a hole exactly like the one through which we passed the prisoner's food and drink. He pushed me aside and put his face to the hole and gave a beast-like cry. A sound came faintly back. I was astonished and drew him away. I called out, 'Ho, here!' At first there was no answer. I called again and received a reply. 'Be Thou praised, O Lord,' a faint voiced cried. What was more astonishing was that the voice was a woman's voice. 'Who are you?' I called. The reply came, 'A woman of Israel, entombed with her daughter. Help us quickly, or we die.' I told them to be of cheer and hurried here to know your will in the matter."

The tribune arose hastily. "You were right, Gesius," he said. "I see now. The map was a lie, and so was the tale of the three men. There have been better Romans than Valerius Gratus."

"I gleaned from the prisoner that he had regularly given the women of the food and drink that he received," continued Gesius excitedly.

"It is accounted for," replied the tribune. "Come let us rescue the women."

"We will have to pierce the wall," the keeper warned. "I found where a door had been, but it was filled solidly with stones and mortar."

"Send workman after me with tools," the tribune said to a clerk.

In a short time Ben-Hur's mother and his sister were released from their living tomb. As they emerged from their long confinement, however, the light revealed for them a fate worse than death—they were leprous.

* * *

About the same hour that Gesius was visiting the tribune, Ben-Hur was climbing the eastern face of Mount Olivet. He had left Simonides' house thirty days before and was now just arriving in Judea. The road was rough and dusty, for it was the dry season. He proceeded slowly, approaching his home town as one approaches an old acquaintance after a long separation, as if he were saying, "I'm glad to be with you again; let me see how you have changed."

His search for his mother and sister as yet had no definite plan. From

Simonides he learned that Amrah, the Egyptian servant, was still living. On the morning the calamity overtook the Hurs, the faithful creature broke from the guard and ran back into the palace. She was sealed up there. Simonides, while searching for the family, had discovered Amrah and secretly began supplying her with enough money to live comfortably. The Roman authorities assumed she had starved to death.

Gratus had tried diligently to sell the palace but could not. Its reputation was that of a haunted house. This idea was probably derived from the infrequent glimpses of poor old Amrah by passersby. Sometimes she would be seen on the roof, other times through a latticed window. Never was a palace so shunned or fitted for ghostly habitation after that tragic day.

Ben-Hur decided first to go to the old house and find Amrah. He would make further plans then. As he stopped at the gate on the north side, he saw plainly that the wax used in sealing the corners was still intact. No one had gone in or out of the gate since that fateful day. Should he knock as in old times? It was useless, he knew. Still, he could not resist the temptation. Amrah might hear and look out one of the windows on that side. He mounted the broad stone step and tapped three times. A dull echo replied. He tried again, louder than before, pausing each time to listen. The silence was mocking, and he finally gave up and passed from the north side to the west.

There were four windows on this side and he watched them long and anxiously, hoping Amrah would appear. But when she made no sign, he stole round to the south. There, too, the gate was sealed and inscribed with the hated words: *This is the property of the Emperor.* The mellow splendor of the August moon brought the lettering boldly out. As he read the inscription Ben-Hur was filled with rage. He wrenched the board from its nailing and hurled it into the ditch. Then he sat down on the step and prayed until his blood cooled. After sitting a while, however, he began to feel the weariness caused by his long journey in the summer heat. He sank down lower and at last slept.

About this time two women approached the palace from the direction of the Tower of Antonia. They advanced with timid steps, pausing to make certain no one was about. They neared the house. "This is it, Tirzah," the widow said. Tirzah, after a look, caught her mother's hand and leaned heavily on her, quietly weeping.

"We must go on now, my child," the mother said. She hesitated and then added, "If they find us within the city in the morning, they will stone us. We must be out of the gates and to the lepers' tombs by then." At these words Tirzah sank almost to the stones. Her mother, however, supported her and encouraged her to move on. As she did so, she gave one last glance back toward the house and stopped. "Wait," she said. "I think I see someone lying on the steps—a man."

Looking carefully about her, the mother stepped cautiously into the street leading Tirzah closer to the house. As they emerged from the darkness, the bright moonlight revealed the extent of their affliction. Their faces and hands were dry and cracked. Their eyes were bleary. Their hair was long, stiff, loathsome, and ghastly white. Nor was it possible to tell the daughter from the mother, for they both seemed witch-like old. They crossed to the opposite side of the street quickly and moved on till they were before the gate. They were careful to keep close to the wall in the shadows.

"He is asleep, Tirzah! Stay here and I will get a closer look. She moved close to the gate. Looking down, she gasped, looked again, then ran back to Tirzah. "As the Lord lives, the man is my son—your brother!" she said in a frenzied whisper.

"Judah?" said Tirzah, unbelieving.

Her mother caught her hand eagerly. "Come!" she said, in the same enforced whisper. "Let us look at him together—once more—only once!" They moved close hand in hand ghostly-quickly, ghostly-still. When their shadows fell upon him, they stopped. One of his hands was draped across a step. Tirzah fell on her knees and would have kissed it, but her mother drew her back. "No! We are unclean!" Tirzah shrank from him, as if he were the leper. He stirred at that moment. They moved back. He muttered in his restless dreaming, "Mother! Amrah, where is—" He moved fitfully and then fell off into a deep sleep once again.

Tirzah stared wistfully. Her mother covered her face, struggling to suppress a sob so deep and strong it seemed her heart would burst. Almost she wished he would awaken. But he had asked for her, and she knew she was not forgotten. This had to be enough. She beckoned Tirzah and they arose, taking one more look, as if to imprint his image on their minds. They then turned and crossed the street again. When safely on the other side, they hovered in the shadows waiting—waiting for some revelation, they knew not what.

By and by another woman appeared at the corner of the palace. Tirzah and her mother saw her plainly in the light, a small figure, much bent, dark-skinned, gray-haired, and dressed neatly in servant's garb. She was carrying a basket full of vegetables. At the sight of Ben-Hur on the steps, the newcomer stopped. Then as if deciding to walk on, very lightly she drew the wicket gate latch easily to one side and put her hand in the opening. One of the boards swung ajar without noise. She put her basket through and was about to follow, when, yielding to her curiosity, she lingered to have one look at the stranger. The spectators across the street heard her low exclamation and saw the woman rub her eyes as if to renew their power. She then leaned closer, gazed wildly about, and awoke the sleeper.

"Amrah! Oh, Amrah!" exclaimed Ben-Hur when he had regained his sense. "Is it really you?"

Amrah made no answer in words; she simply fell upon his neck, crying for joy. He gently kissed her. His tears of joy were only a little less than hers. Tirzah and her mother straining to listen from their hiding place heard him say, "Mother and Tirzah, tell me of them, Amrah. Speak, Speak I pray you." Amrah only cried the more. "Have you seen them, Amrah? Tell me are they at home?"

Tirzah moved forward as if to run to her brother, but her mother caught her firmly by the arm and whispered urgently, "You cannot go—not for life!" Her mother's love was in a tyrannical mood. Even though both of them desired more than anything to see him, the greater fear of making him leprous overruled.

In another moment Amrah and Ben-Hur disappeared into the house, leaving the two outsiders staring blankly at the gate—the gate which they might never enter more. Nestling together in the dust, they gave way to their despair.

The next morning they were found and driven from the city with stones,

the sentence of their doom ringing in their ears as they went forth. "Begone! You are of the dead! Go to the dead."

* * *

Amrah had been accustomed to going to the market after nightfall. Stealing out unobserved, she would quickly make her purchases of meat and vegtables and return to shut herself within the palace. She had been on this errand the night she found Ben-Hur.

The pleasure she derived from his return was even more than she imagined it would be. Her only regret was that she could tell him nothing of his mother and sister. She desired that he move into the palace and take his own room again but the danger of discovery would be too great and he refused. He came to see her as often as possible, however. She was satisfied and at once set about contriving ways of making him happy.

Several nights after his arrival she stole out with her basket to the Fish Gate market. Ben-Hur was coming to visit and she was in search of the best honey. Wandering about, she chanced to hear a man telling a story, and immediately her attention went to the storyteller. She could scarcely believe her ears for he was relating the particulars of the rescue of the widow and Tirzah. Quickly she made her purchases and returned home as if in a dream, thinking only of the joy she would have in telling Ben-Hur the news.

As she entered the gate, however, another thought struck her. They were lepers. She had heard the man say so, and yet she had not let that idea sink

into her mind until now, and it struck with crushing force. Such knowledge she knew would kill Ben-Hur. He would relentlessly wander through the tombs where the lepers lived until he found them, and eventually their fate would be his. Wringing her hands in despair, she sat down to think what she should do.

Like many others before her, she derived wisdom from her affliction and came to a profitable conclusion. The lepers, she knew, were accustomed to come down from their grave-like abodes every morning to get water from the well. Bringing their jars, they would set them on the ground and move far from the well, waiting for some merciful soul to take up the jars and fill them. The mistress and Tirzah must surely come to the well with the others, for a rich leper was no better than a poor one. Thus, Amrah decided not to speak to Ben-Hur of her discovery until she had gone to the well in the morning.

Shortly after sunrise the lepers began to appear, moving slowly from their tombs. Amrah kept watch on the ghostly group, moving slowly. At first, distance softened the misery of the outcasts, but as they neared their true condition became clear. Some leaned on the shoulders of others. A few—the utterly helpless—lay, like heaps of rags, on litters [stretchers]. She had never seen such a ghastly spectacle. But she was determined. Those she sought must come down and she would wait.

At length Amrah beheld two women. They remained at the back of the crowd awhile. Then slowly, painfully they moved forward toward the well. They were fearful and obviously unaware that they could not come themselves to fill the jars. Several voices were raised to stop them from approaching. Someone even picked up some pebbles and made ready to drive them back. The company of lepers behind them shouted shrilly, "Unclean! Unclean!"

"Surely," thought Amrah, "surely they are strangers to the usage of lepers and have only recently come to the tombs." She arose and went to meet them, taking a jar of water. The alarm at the well immediately subsided and was replaced by mocking and laughter.

"What a fool," said one observer, "what a fool to serve water to the dead."

"And to think of her going so far," said another as she watched Amrah proceed without hesitation.

The further Amrah went, however, the more she doubted. What if she should be mistaken? Her heart rose to her throat. Four or five yards from where they stood she stopped. That woman could not be the mistress she loved, not the woman of matronly loveliness that Amrah treasured faithfully in her memory. Nor could the other leper be Tirzah whom she had nursed through babyhood, whose pains she had soothed and whose sports she had shared. Amrah's soul sickened at the sight of them. "These women are old," she said to herself. "I never saw them before. I will go back." She turned away.

"Amrah," one of the lepers called to her. The Eygptian nurse dropped the jar she was holding, spilling the water it

contained. She looked back trembling.

"Who called me?" she asked.

"Amrah."

The servant's wondering eyes settled on the speaker's face. "Who are you?" she cried.

"We are those you are seeking," said the woman softly. Amrah fell on her knees. "Oh my mistress, my mistress! As I have made your God my God, be He praised that He has led me to you!" The poor, overwhelmed creature moved forward to embrace them.

"Stay, Amrah! Don't come near." The words sufficed to stop her approach, but she was so overcome with her helplessness that she fell on her face and began to sob loudly. The people at the well heard her and wondered.

"Please, Amrah, rise, and bring us water."

The habit of the servant renewed itself. Immediately Amrah rose and taking up the jar she went to the well and refilled it. The people under whose eyes all this had passed made way for her and even helped her, for her countenance was so grief stricken, they could not help showing mercy.

"Who are they?" one woman asked.

Amrah answered meekly, "They used to be good to me." Raising the jar on her shoulder, she hurried back. She would have served them both, but the mistress restrained her, "No, Amrah. They may stone you and refuse us drink. Leave the jar, and we will carry it to the tomb with us. You have rendered us all the service that is lawful."

Amrah obeyed, and placing the jar on the ground, she stepped back a little way. "Is there nothing else I can do for you?" she asked.

"Yes," she said firmly. "I know that Judah has come home. I saw him at the gate asleep the same night you found him. I watched you awaken him."

"Mistress, you saw it and did not come?"

"That would have been to kill him. I can never take him in my arms again, never kiss him more," she paused to gain strength. "Oh, Amrah, I know you love him."

"I would die for him," said the servant earnestly.

"Then prove what you say."

"What do you want me to do?"

"Do not tell him where we are or that you have seen us—only that, Amrah."

"But he has come so far to find you."

"He must not! You shall tell us of him, but never, never, say anything of us. Do you hear?"

"It will be hard to hear him speak of you and see him constantly searching for you and say nothing—not so much as that you are alive."

"Can you tell him we are well, Amrah?"

"No," said the servant, grieved.

"Then be silent altogether. Go now and come again when you have news. Until then, farewell."

Reading Check

1. How does Ben-Hur decide to use his newly acquired fortune?
2. How does he choose to deal with the faithful Simonides?
3. Who has succeeded Valerius Gratus as procurator of Rome?
4. What discovery was made by the officer of the Tower of Antonia?
5. Why did Ben-Hur's mother and sister refuse to inform him that they were still alive?

Part VI   The Beloved are Restored

Throughout the passing months, Amrah remained obedient to her mistress's command. Though daily she carried news of Ben-Hur to the leper's tomb, she returned to the palace bearing only the guarded silence of her hidden sorrow. She gave Ben-Hur no cause to hope, and eventually his hope died and was replaced by bitterness against all that was Rome.

Jerusalem's political situation was ripe for harvesting a bitterness like Ben-Hur's. The Nazarene had recently gained many followers, and rumors flourished that He would soon overthrow Rome and set up a kingdom of

His own. By the time Simonides and Esther arrived in Jerusalem, Ben-Hur had formed a faithful band of Galileans who followed the son of Mary expectantly. Simonides joined their ranks, and though he could not join them in roaming the Judean countryside, he gave of his wealth to further their cause.

One evening as Ben-Hur was recounting the day's events to Simonides, Amrah chanced to overhear the conversation. As she listened to him, she became increasingly excited, for Judah spoke of the Nazarene's cleansing of ten lepers. By the time Simonides and Ben-Hur departed Amrah had determined to bear the news to the widow and Tirzah.

As the first traces of dawn colored the sky, she hurried out of the city, hastened to the eastern valley, and made her way past the well of En-rogel to the lepers' refuge. Early as it was, her unhappy mistress was up sitting outside with Tirzah.

"Mistress, mistress," called Amrah excitedly, "I have news!"

"Of Judah?" asked the widow.

"There is a wonderful man," Amrah continued, "who has the power to cure you. He speaks a word and the sick are made well. Even the dead come to life! Come, we must go to Him."

"Poor Amrah," said Tirzah thinking the servant had gone mad.

"No!" cried Amrah, detecting Tirzah's thoughts. "As the Lord lives, I speak the truth. Come with me; let us lose no time. This morning He will pass this way on His way to the city. Come. Come," she urged.

The mother listened eagerly. She had heard of this man but not heard of this wonderful story. "Who told you about this?" she asked.

"Judah."

The widow was silent awhile then asked, "Did my son send you to tell us this?"

"No, I have kept my word. He still believes you dead."

"How does he know this man?"

"He has been traveling with him these past months. He believes as many others that the Nazarene will use his powers to conquer Rome. Judah has formed a band of soldiers, Galileans, who travel with the Master and await the time when He shall need them."

"Does the Nazarene know of his band of soldiers?"

"No—they say nothing; they only follow and wait. That is how Judah saw the miracle of healing.

The widow sat musing awhile, then at length said, "There was a time when Jerusalem was filled with the story that the Messiah had been born. This must be He." She did not speak coldly like one reasoning away doubt, but rather as a woman of Israel familiar with God's promises to her race. "We will go with you," she said turning to Amrah.

The journey, though short, was difficult. The good servant toiled faithfully to lighten the way as they descended the hillside, but Tirzah moaned at every step. When they reached the roadside, she fell down exhausted. "Go on with Amrah, Mother. Leave me. I cannot go further."

"No, Tirzah. What would be the gain to me if I were healed and you were not? And when Judah asks for you, as he will, what would I say to him?"

"Tell him simply that I love him."

At that moment the widow noticed a stranger approaching "Courage, Tirzah," she said. "Here comes one who may tell us of the Nazarene."

Amrah helped the girl sit up and supported her. "In your goodness, Mother, you forget what we are. The stranger will go round us. His best gift to us will be a curse, if not a stone."

"We will see," said the widow, though she knew that her daughter's fears were well-founded. The road was little more than a path or trail, and if the stranger kept his direction he must meet them face to face. He did so. When he was near enough to hear the cry, the widow called out shrilly, "Unclean, unclean!"

To her surprise the man came steadily on, and stopping not four yards off, he asked, "What can I do for you?"

"You see our condition; be cautious."

"Woman," the man said, "I am the messenger of Him who speaks but once to people as you are and they are healed. I am not afraid."

"Do you speak of the Nazarene?"

"I speak of the Messiah."

"Is it true that He is coming to the city today?"

"He is now at Bethphage."

"On what road, Master?"

"This one, but for whom do you take Him?"

"The Son of God," she replied firmly.

"Then stay here but remain by the rock yonder, for there is a multitude with him. When he goes by, do not fail to call to Him. Call and fear not." With these words the stranger moved on.

"Did you hear, Tirzah? Did you hear? Let us go to the rock. It is but a step."

The road became gradually more and more frequented until by the fourth hour a great crowd appeared. Many carried freshly cut palm branches. "He is coming," said the widow to Tirzah. Then turning to Amrah she asked, "When Judah spoke of the healing of the ten, what words did he say the lepers used to call to the Nazarene?"

"Some said, 'Lord, have mercy on us,' and others simply said, 'Master, have mercy.'"

"Only that?"

"No more that I heard."

By now the foremost of the crowd was in sight, but the gaze of the lepers fixed on the man riding in the midst of the company, the wonderful Nazarene.

"Come, my child," the widow urged moving to the front of the rock. Directly her daughter and servant were by her side. As the procession drew near, she arose, staggered forward, and called out. The people turned, saw her hideous face,

and stopped awestruck. Tirzah drew back frightened.

"Lepers!" someone cried.

"Stone them!"

"The accursed of God! Kill them!"

Despite these cries the widow continued to move forward. Those familiar with the nature of the One to whom she appealed remained silent. Jesus rode up and stopped in front of her. "Master, you see our need. Have mercy on us—make us clean."

"Believest thou that I am able to do this?"

"Thou art He of whom the prophets spake—thou art Messiah!"

His eyes grew radiant, his manner confident. "Woman," he said, "great is thy faith; be it unto thee even as thou wilt." He lingered an instant after, unconscious of the throng—an instant—then He rode away.

Ben-Hur, was in the midst of the multitude and glancing past the lepers he saw Amrah. He hurried to her,

passing his mother and sister without recognizing them. "Amrah, what are you doing here?"

"Oh master, master," she cried weeping for joy, "thy God and mine, how good He is!" Amrah knew the transformation the lepers were undergoing, knew it and shared all their feeling to the full. Her expression, her words, her whole manner betrayed her thoughts. With swift perception, Ben-Hur knew that her mission was in some way connected with the women he had just passed. He turned quickly, just as the widow and Tirzah were rising to their feet.

His heart stood still. He would have run to them, but he was rooted in his tracks. Could he be mistaken? "Amrah, Amrah—my mother! Tirzah! Tell me if I see rightly!"

"Go. Speak to them, master!"

He waited no longer but ran with outstretched arms and embraced them.

The first ecstasy over, his mother said, "In this happiness, my children, let us not be ungrateful. Let us begin life anew by acknowledging Him to whom we are all so indebted." They knelt together and the mother's prayer was outspoken in a psalm. Tirzah repeated it word for word; so did Ben-Hur, but not with the same clear mind and unquestionable faith. He was waiting, waiting until the Nazarene proved Himself by setting up His kingdom—until He had overcome Rome.

*   *   *

Tirzah and her mother had to remain outside the city nine days. They could then enter the temple, be purified, and once again be accepted into the community. Ben-Hur went to the palace to await their return. Five of these days had passed when two of the Galileans rode full speed to the palace and, dismounting, urged Amrah to summon Ben-Hur.

"Peace be to you," he said as he entered the chamber where the men were waiting for him. "Be seated."

"No," said the older of the two Galileans, "to be at ease would be to let the Nazarene die! Rise, Judah, and go with us. Judgment has been given and the tree of the cross is already at Golgotha."

Ben-Hur stared at them in disbelief. How could this king whom the people had praised with hosannas be condemned to the cross? He quickly made preparations to depart. He sent the men ahead to give Simonides instructions to meet them at Golgotha.

When the party—Ben-Hur, Simonides, Esther, and the two Galileans—reached the place of crucifixion, Ben-Hur was leading them. When he caught sight of Jesus he stopped spellbound. Gazing at the figure on the hill, he became conscious of a change. The force of his bitterness began to fade. He heard again the saying of the Nazarene, *I am the Resurrection and the life.* The words repeated themselves over and over in his mind. He tried to grasp the meaning. Who is the resurrection? He pondered. Who is the life? *I AM* the figure seemed to say—and say it for him. Judah was sensible of a peace such as he had never known, a peace which is the end of all doubt and mystery and the beginning of faith, love, and clear understanding.

From this dreamy state Ben-Hur was aroused by the sound of hammering. On the summit of the hill he observed then what had escaped him before, the soldiers and workmen preparing the crosses.

"The crosses are ready," said the centurion to the pontiff.

The high priest received the report and with the wave of his hand said, "Let the blasphemer go first. We shall see if the Son of God is able to save Himself."

The people, who to this time had assailed [verbally attacked] the hill with continual cries of impatience, permitted a lull which directly became a universal hush, for the part of the infliction, the most shocking part, was at hand. As the soldiers laid their hands on Jesus, a shudder passed through the crowd.

"How very still it is!" Esther said, as she put her arm about her father's neck.

Remembering the torture he himself had suffered in times past, he drew her face down on his breast and said trembling, "Avoid it, Esther, avoid it. I do not know but that all who stand and see this, the innocent as well as the guilty, may be cursed from this hour." Growing increasingly anxious, Simonides added, "Son of Hur, if Jehovah does not stretch forth His hand and quickly, Israel is lost. We are lost."

Ben-Hur answered calmly, "I have been as in a dream, Simonides, and heard in it why all this should be, and why it should go on. It is the will of the Nazarene; it is God's will. It is not for us to try to rescue him. Let us hold our peace and pray."

The Nazarene's back was yet bloody from the morning's scourging when he was laid down on the wooden cross. The careless soldiers stretched his arms across the transverse [crosswise] beams and roughly drove the first sharp spike through His tender palms. Then drawing His knees up until the soles of His feet rested flat against the wood, they placed one foot on the other and thrust in the final spike. Yet the spectators heard only the dull sound of hammering; there was no cry, nor word of rebuke from the sufferer.

The workmen carried the cross to its place of planting and dropped it into the hole prepared. The body of the Nazarene hung heavily by bleeding hands. A cry was then heard—not of pain but of pity. "Father, forgive them, for they know not what they do." To this selfless proclamation the people answered with curses and jeers. Again and again their mocking salutation, "Hail, King of the Jews!" echoed across the darkening hillside. The dimness that filled the sky and covered the earth at first appeared only as the fading of day. But the blackness deepened. Only then did the noise of laughter and shouting

subside, for men, doubting their senses, paused to gaze at one another curiously.

"It is only a mist or a passing cloud," said Simonides to comfort Esther. "It will brighten presently."

"It is not a mist or cloud," Ben-Hur said. "The spirits who live in the air—the prophets and the saints—are at work in mercy to themselves and nature. I say to you, Simonides, truly as God lives, He who hangs on that cross is the Son of God."

But even the darkness did not long silence the reckless jeering. "If you are the king of the Jews, save yourself," one soldier shouted.

"Yes," said a priest, "if He will come down to us now, we will believe Him."

"He called himself the Son of God; let us see if God will save Him," others called.

"Let's go home," Esther pleaded. "This darkness is the frown of God, Father. What other dreadful things may happen we cannot tell?"

But Simonides would not be moved. Though he said little, it was plain that he was under great agitation.

The second hour passed like the first one. For the Nazarene they were hours of insult, provocation, and slow dying. He spoke but once in that time. Some women came and knelt at the foot of His cross. Among them he recognized His mother with the beloved disciple. "Woman," He said raising His voice, "behold thy son!" And to the disciple, "Behold thy mother!"

The third hour came, and still people surged round the hill, held to it by some strange attraction. When the hour was about half gone, some men of the rudest class came and stopped in front of the center cross. "This is He, King of the Jews," said one of them.

The others cried out with laughter, "Hail, all hail, King!" Receiving no reply, they went closer.

"If you are the Son of God, come down," said one man boldly.

At this, one of the thieves quit groaning and called to the Nazarene, "Yes, if you are the Christ, save yourself and us!"

The people laughed and applauded; then, while they were listening for a reply, the other felon spoke, "Do you have no fear of God? We received due reward for our deeds, but this man has done nothing wrong." The bystanders were astonished. In the midst of the hush, the second felon spoke again, "Lord," he said, "remember me when you come into your kingdom."

Simonides gave a start. "When you come into your kingdom!" This was the very point of doubt in his mind.

"Did you hear?" said Ben-Hur. "The kingdom cannot be of this world. The felon declares that He is but going to His kingdom."

"Hush!" said Simonides to Judah. "Hush, the Nazarene may answer."

And as he spoke the Nazarene did answer, in a clear voice, full of confidence: "Verily, I say unto thee, today shalt thou be with me in paradise!"

Simonides folded his hands and said, "The darkness is gone, Lord. I see with the eyes of perfect faith." At last he understood. New life was now shown him, a life beyond this one, and its name was paradise. There he would find the kingdom which he and Ben-Hur had longed for. There his broken body would be restored and all the memories of undeserved suffering blotted out.

The breathing of the Nazarene grew harder, and his sighs became great gasps. Then there went out through the gloom, over the heads of those gathered on the hill, a cry of despair, "My God! My God! Why hast Thou forsaken me?" The voice startled all who heard it. But it touched Ben-Hur more than any; for there came to his memory a time long ago when he had despaired by the well of Nazareth. Quickly he moved toward the soldiers. They had brought with them a vessel of wine and water. Catching up a sponge on the end of a stick, he dipped it into the vessel and pushed his way through the crowd toward the cross.

"Let Him be!" the people in the way shouted angrily. But Ben-Hur pressed on, remembering the drink he had received at the well so long ago.

Reaching the Nazarene, Judah gazed up at the loving face now bruised and black with blood and dust, and at that moment the eyes opened wide and fixed on someone in the far heavens. In relief, even triumph, He gave a shout, "It is finished! It is finished!"

Ben-Hur quickly put the sponge to the Nazarene's lips, but the light in the eyes had dimmed and the head was slowly sinking on the laboring breast. "I am too late," he thought. But the fainting soul recollected itself and in a low voice said, "Father, into thy hands I commend my spirit." A tremor shook the tortured body. There was a scream of fiercest anguish, and the mission and earthly life were over. The heart, with all its love, broke and He died.

There was a murmur, at first a little more than a whisper, which spread from the hill in every direction. "He is dead! He is dead!" The people had their wish. Yet on hearing the news they drew back, as if for the first time they realized that His blood was upon them! While they stood staring, the ground began to tremble, and each man took hold of his neighbor to support himself. The crosses were reeling drunken-like on the hill, and Ben-Hur could scarcely make his way back to his company.

Every man among them who had jeered at the Nazarene, everyone who

had struck Him; everyone who had voted to crucify Him; everyone whose heart had wished Him dead, felt at that moment that he was being individually singled out for judgment. They started to run and ran with all their might to get away. Some mounted horses, others camels, and others tried escaping on foot. But the earthquake pursued them, tossed them about, flung them down, and terrified them yet more by the horrible noise of the great rocks grinding and rending beneath them. They shrieked in fear. If they called on the Lord, the outraged earth answered for Him in fury and dealt with them all alike. The high priest was no better than his guilty brethren. Overtaking him, the rumbling earth tripped him, smirched the fringing of his robe, and filled his mouth with dust. They were all to blame. The blood of the Nazarene was on them all!

* * *

When the sunlight finally broke upon the crucifixion, the hill had nearly cleared. Only the mother of Jesus, the beloved disciple, the faithful women of Galilee, the centurion and his soldiers, and Ben-Hur's party remained. They had not observed the flight of the multitude, for they were too engaged in caring for their own safety. Realizing they need no longer fear, Ben-Hur turned to Esther and said, "Cover your eyes, and do not look up, simply trust in God and the spirit of that just man so foully slain."

"No," said Simonides reverently, "call Him not a man. Let us henceforth speak of Him only as the Christ."

"Be it so," said Ben-Hur as he lifted Simonides in his strong arms to bear him home.

From that day forward, all who entered the palace of Ben-Hur were to hear not only of the crucifixion and resurrection but also of the coming kingdom of *GOD THE FATHER AND CHRIST THE SON*.

Reading Check

1. How does Amrah learn of Jesus' healing the ten lepers and to whom does she repeat this story?
2. Why is Ben-Hur among the crowd traveling with Jesus?
3. What does the widow Hur say that reveals her belief in Christ as the Son of God?
4. How does Ben-Hur's attitude differ from his mother's and sister's when they kneel to give thanks for Christ's miracle?
5. What specific portions of the novel reveal Ben-Hur's ultimate choice to believe in Christ as Messiah?

Christian Beholds the Cross

from *The Pilgrim's Progress*

John Bunyan

Thus far did I come loaden with my sin,
Nor could aught ease the grief that I was in,
Till I came hither. What a place is this!
Must here be the beginning of my bliss?
Must here the burden fall from off my back?
Must here the strings that bound it to me, crack?
Blessed Cross! Blessed Sepulchre! Blessed rather be
The man that there was put to shame for me.

Beneath the Cross of Jesus

Elizabeth C. Clephane

Christ Crucified by Flemish or Dutch Artist
Active in Italy in the XVII Century from
The Bob Jones University Collection of Sacred Art

Beneath the cross of Jesus
I fain would take my stand,
The shadow of a mighty rock
Within a weary land;
A home within the wilderness,
A rest upon the way,
From the burning of the noontide heat,
And the burden of the day.

Upon that cross of Jesus,
Mine eye at times can see
The very dying form of One
Who suffered there for me;
And from my smitten heart with tears
Two wonders I confess,—
The wonders of His glorious love
And my unworthiness.

I take, O Cross, thy shadow
For my abiding place;
I ask no other sunshine than
The sunshine of His face;
Content to let the world go by,
To know no gain nor loss,
My sinful self my only shame,
My glory all the cross.

THE PRODIGAL

And he said, A certain man had two sons:

And the younger of them said to his father, Father, give me the portion of goods that falleth to me. And he divided unto them his living.

And not many days after the younger son gathered all together, and took his journey into a far country, and there wasted his substance with riotous living.

And when he had spent all, there arose a mighty famine in that land; and he began to be in want.

And he went and joined himself to a citizen of that country; and he sent him into his fields to feed swine.

And he would fain have filled his belly with the husks that the swine did eat: and no man gave unto him.

And when he came to himself, he said, How many hired servants of my father's have bread enough and to spare, and I perish with hunger!

I will arise and go to my father, and will say unto him, Father, I have sinned against heaven, and before thee,

And am no more worthy to be called thy son: make me as one of thy hired servants.

And he arose, and came to his father. But when he was yet a great way off, his father saw him, and had compassion, and ran, and fell on his neck, and kissed him.

And the son said unto him, Father, I have sinned against heaven, and in thy sight, and am no more worthy to be called thy son.

But the father said to his servants, Bring forth the best robe, and put it on him; and put a ring on his hand, and shoes on his feet:

And bring hither the fatted calf, and kill it; and let us eat, and be merry:

For this my son was dead, and is alive again; he was lost, and is found. And they began to be merry.   (Luke 15:11-24)

FRIENDS

Friends

Now as Christian went on his way he saw Faithful before him on his journey. Then said Christian aloud,"Ho, stay and I will be your companion." At that Faithful turned and looked behind him. Then Christian, not taking heed to his feet, stumbled and fell, and could not rise again until Faithful came to help him up. Then I saw in my dream that they went lovingly on together and had sweet discourse of all things that happened to them on their pilgrimage.

Rising slowly, Franz moved from his easel to the open window. Every limb ached, for he and Albrecht had sketched all night. Now it was dawn. He sighed deeply as he listened to the faint ringing of the cathedral bells. They echoed softly over the silent city like a mother's whisper awakening her sleeping child. Turning to Albrecht, Franz toyed with the idea of speaking, but seeing his friend still absorbed in sketching, he paused.

He so admired Albrecht's driving discipline. The melancholy which grew out of financial strain and repeated disappointments at times wearied Franz—never Albrecht. Indeed these obstacles seemed only to harden his determination to succeed. Albrecht's mind knew only one purpose, the creation of images, and his heart only one love, a finished work of art.

Franz studied the lean, intense figure silhouetted in the waning candlelight. "The candle," he suddenly thought. "It's the last one." He caught himself. There it was again. There was that dogged fretfulness crowding in upon the lovely morning. Still . . . there were pressing needs and someone had to care for them. "Put the candle out," he said aloud to Albrecht. "The sun has risen." Albrecht obeyed without glancing up.

Franz knew Albrecht must be hungry, for they had not eaten since the previous afternoon. He cut a slice of bread, and with this meager offering he approached Albrecht like a penitent approaching a confessor. He was reluctant, but his sense of duty drew him to unburden his mind. Albrecht took the bread and continued working. "You know," Franz began, "we cannot feed ourselves solely on artistic dreams, and the fires of imagination will do little to warm us when the winter comes."

Albrecht made no reply. He simply got up and wandered from the easel. Franz understood his thoughts. The comment had been an intrusion, and wandering was Albrecht's means of putting distance between himself and the problem at hand. Desperately Franz sought for something encouraging to say, but found nothing. He understood their failure no better than Albrecht did. Why had their talent and persistence brought them nothing? Oh, there had been vague promises, promises from wealthy landowners who desired lavish portraits. But Franz had come to realize that the promises of the rich are often poor hopes for the needy.

He turned his thoughts to Albrecht's sketch. The picture was of an old German peasant. The intricate facial lines created through Albrecht's delicate technique portrayed the weathered skin of the aging woman so perfectly that his hand unwittingly reached out to touch her face. Then he paused. "The world must one day recognize such genius—yes, they must—must recognize it one day." The words seemed to echo through his mind and each time he rehearsed them his conviction grew. He knew what he must do. For a moment, a brief moment, his own ambition rose up before him. But the beautiful painting drew his thoughts back to the needs of his friend, and he found the courage to deny himself. Turning to Albrecht he said, "I have an idea. It is senseless for both of us to abandon our studies to earn bread. You shall continue to paint. I will go out and earn enough for both of us."

The suggestion stirred Albrecht from his moody silence. "That's unfair."

"It will be fair in time," continued Franz. "When you've obtained a commission, you can support us. Then I can go back to my studies with an easy mind. We shall both succeed. Time is all that is needed—time and bread."

"No I—"

"It is settled," Franz flatly stated.

Several winters passed before Albrecht was able to obtain a solid commission, but at last the long awaited day arrived. As Franz, weary from his long day's labor, entered the cottage, Albrecht rushed to greet him. "I have sold a painting—here—here is the money; and more important I have a commission, so there is sure promise of more!" The jubilant friends agreed that Franz would immediately return to his art studies.

When Franz and Albrecht rose, the darkness before the dawn still cloaked the city. Franz lit a candle, for there were several now, no need to worry. Albrecht's tools were already waiting, and he began work immediately. But Franz, who had not painted for months, had much to do.

While preparing his paints he listened to the sounds of the morning. A cock crowed loudly as he placed his easel before the window. Sitting down he noticed that a gray mist had wrapped itself about the houses and the trees along the river. He paused to watch the misty shroud unwrap itself as he knew it would. Soon a myriad of bright colors splashed across the grayed horizon. Franz eagerly lifted his brush to capture the sunrise but. . . .

Albrecht turned to see his friend struggling. Vainly Franz tried to manipulate his brush, but the knotted muscles would not obey the artistic command. He tried and tried until he was weary with trying. At last he rested. Albrecht gazed in dumb silence at his friend's stiffened gnarled hands. For the first time he realized the sacrifice Franz had made. The years of rustic labor had deformed the sensitive hands. Greatly distressed he went to his friend and kneeling beside him, clasped his hands within his own. Franz nodded and gave Albrecht a reassuring but solemn smile then gently said, "Put the candle out. The sun has risen."

* * *

As Franz predicted, the world did recognize Albrecht's genius. His art is now housed in museums throughout the world. One work, however, is more familiar and beloved than the rest. The expressive, intricate lines which captured Franz's attention in Albrecht's early sketch are refined in this piece. The work is entitled *Hands of the Apostle* but is more widely known as *The Praying Hands*. The drawing has become a universal symbol for humble devotion, and according to legend, Franz was the model Durer used for this masterpiece. Five hundred years later, those who admire this drawing of Albrecht's can also be touched by the humble devotion of Franz.

The need and value of true friendship is evident in the story of these two friends. But how does one build such a friendship? There must first be a solid base, and that base is biblical love. You must realize, however, that biblical love is not sentimental. A sentimental love will change as feelings change. But biblical love is an act of your will, your choice to place another's needs above your own. Consequently, this love is as stable and enduring as God's love for us.

Now that you understand the basis for true friendship, what type of person do you think would be a good friend? Through studying the Scripture we find that Christ is our best example of true friendship (John 15:13). Thus, it is logical to assume that a good friend would be striving to have the mind of Christ. In Philippians we are told, "Let this mind be in you which was also in Christ Jesus: Who being in the form of God, thought it not robbery to be equal with God: But made himself of no reputation, and took upon him the form of a servant, and was made in the likeness of men: And being found in fashion as a man, he humbled himself, and became obedient unto death, even the death of the cross" (Philippians 2:5-8). Christ was humble and self-sacrificing, and a person who is to be a good friend must possess these same qualities.

This Christ-likeness will manifest itself in a person's behavior. He will act in a certain way. He will be loyal, patient, gracious, generous, honest, and forgiving (I Corinthians 13).

Having established the basis, attitudes, and actions of a good friendship, how would you evaluate Franz as a friend? Was he humble and self-sacrificing? Was he sympathetic toward the problems that Albrecht faced? In his dealings with Albrecht was he patient, gracious, generous, honest, loyal, and forgiving? The answers to these questions are clear when you examine the story.

Considering what you have learned about friendship, you can also evaluate the stories you are going to read in this unit. For example, in the selection "Being Neighborly" you will see Jo's determination to help Laurie overcome shyness, and the creative plan she initiates to do so. The attitude of self-sacrifice is clearly evidenced in the story "Half a Gift," and in each of the succeeding stories you will be able to see this attitude worked out through the characters' actions. You will see the value of loyalty in the story "One Minute Longer," patience in the story "Rock Hounds," generosity and graciousness in "A Most Important Person," and honesty in "After Twenty Years."

Most important, however, what you have learned can help you evaluate your own friendships. Think for a moment. What is the basis of your friendships? Are you a friend like Franz? Do those whom you have chosen as friends exemplify the qualities you've read about? If you can answer "yes" to those questions, then you are privileged to enjoy and understand true friendship. But if you had to answer "no," then you must realize that the "friendships" you have formed are not friendships at all. At best they are a convenience; at worst they are a destructive influence. If you find yourself involved in such destructive relationships, it may be profitable for you to consider seriously the truth expressed in the following ancient Jewish proverb: *A man who insists on lying down with the dogs will rise up with fleas.*

Though Jo, Amy, Beth, and Meg were sisters, they were as different in appearance and personality as the brightly colored leaves on an autumn tree. Beth was like the soft golden color; Meg, the deep crimson; Amy, the fresh yellow-green, and Jo? Well, Jo was the fiery red. She was bold—at times brash. Nonetheless, her sincere concern for others made her a delightful friend. And as you read this episode from Little Women, *you will find, as Theodore Laurence found, that her spirit and freshness made even the dreariest afternoon an adventure.*

Being Neighborly

from Little Women

Louisa May Alcott

"What in the world are you going to do now, Jo?" asked Meg one snowy afternoon as her sister came tramping through the hall in rubber boots, old sack [loose coat] and hood, with a broom in one hand and a shovel in the other.

"Going out for exercise," answered Jo.

"I should think two long walks this morning would have been enough! It's cold and dull out, and I advise you to stay warm and dry by the fire, as I do," said Meg with a shiver.

"Never take advice! Can't keep still all day, and not being a pussycat, I don't like to doze by the fire. I like adventures, and I'm going to find some."

Meg went back to toast her feet and read *Ivanhoe,* and Jo began to dig paths with great energy. The snow was light, and with her broom she soon swept a path all round the garden. Now the garden separated the Marches' house from that of Mr. Laurence. Both stood in a suburb of the city, which was still countrylike, with groves and lawns, large gardens, and quiet streets. A low hedge parted the two estates. On one side was an old brown house, looking rather bare and shabby robbed of the vines that in summer covered its walls and the flowers which then surrounded it. On the other side was a stately stone mansion, plainly betokening every sort of comfort and luxury, from the big coach house and well-kept grounds to the conservatory. Yet it seemed a lonely, lifeless sort of house; for no children frolicked on the lawn, no motherly face ever smiled at the windows, and few people went in and out except the old gentleman and his grandson.

To Jo's lively fancy, this fine house seemed a kind of enchanted palace full of splendors and delights which no one enjoyed. She had long wanted to behold these hidden glories, and to know the "Laurence boy," who looked as if he would like to be known if he only knew how to begin. Since the party, she had been more eager than ever and had planned many ways of making friends with him; but he had not been seen lately, and Jo began to think he had gone away when she one day spied a brown face at the upper window, looking wishfully down into their garden, where Beth and Amy were snowballing one another.

"That boy is suffering for society and fun," she said to herself. "His grandpa does not know what's good for him and keeps him shut up all alone. He needs a party of jolly boys to play with, or somebody young and lively. I've a great mind to go over and tell the old gentleman so!"

The idea amused Jo, who liked to do daring things and was always scandalizing Meg by her odd performances. The plan of "going over" was not forgotten, and when the snowy afternoon came, Jo resolved to try what could be done. She saw Mr. Laurence drive off, and then sallied out to dig her way down to the hedge, where she paused and took a survey. All quiet— curtains down at the lower windows, servants out of sight, and nothing human visible but a curly black head leaning on a thin hand at the upper window.

"There he is," thought Jo, "poor boy! All alone and sick this dismal day. It's a shame! I'll toss up a snowball and make him look out, and then say a kind word to him."

Up went a handful of soft snow, and the head turned at once, showing a face which lost its listless look in a minute.

Jo nodded and laughed, and flourished her broom as she called out: "How do you do? Are you sick?" Laurie* opened the window, and croaked out as hoarsely as a raven:

"Better, thank you. I've had a bad cold and been shut up a week."

"I'm sorry. What do you amuse yourself with?"

"Nothing. It's as dull as tombs up here."

"Don't you read?"

"Not much. They won't let me."

"Can't somebody read to you?"

---

*Laurie: Nickname for Theodore Laurence

"Grandpa does, sometimes; but my books don't interest him, and I hate to ask Brooke* all the time."

"Have someone come and see you, then."

"There isn't anyone I'd like to see. Boys make such a row, and my head is weak."

"Isn't there some nice girl who'd read and amuse you? Girls are quiet, and like to play nurse."

"Don't know any."

"You know us," began Jo, then laughed, and stopped.

*Brooke: Laurie's private teacher

"So I do! Will you come, please?" cried Laurie.

"I'm not quiet and nice, but I'll come if Mother will let me. I'll go ask her. Shut that window, like a good boy, and wait till I come."

With that, Jo shouldered her broom and marched into the house, wondering what they would all say to her. Laurie was in a flutter of excitement at the idea of having company and flew about to get ready. Presently there came a loud ring, then a decided voice asking for "Mr. Laurie," and a surprised-looking servant came running up to announce a young lady.

"All right, show her up. It's Miss Jo," said Laurie, going to the door of his little parlor to meet Jo, who appeared with a covered dish in one hand and Beth's three kittens in the other.

"Here I am, bag and baggage," she said briskly. "Mother sent her love, and was glad if I could do anything for you. Meg wanted me to bring some of her blancmange [a cornstarch pudding]— she makes it very nicely—and Beth thought her cats would be comforting. I knew you'd laugh at them, but I couldn't refuse, she was so anxious to do something."

It so happened that Beth's funny loan was just the thing, for in laughing over the kits Laurie forgot his bashfulness, and grew sociable at once.

"That looks too pretty to eat," he said, smiling with pleasure as Jo uncovered the dish and showed the blancmange, surrounded by a garland of green leaves and the scarlet flowers of Amy's pet geranium.

"It isn't anything, only they all felt kindly, and wanted to show it. Tell the girl to put it away for your tea. It's so simple you can eat it, and it will slip down without hurting your sore throat. What a cozy room this is!"

"It might be if it was kept nice."

"I'll right it up in two minutes; for it only needs to have the hearth brushed, so—and the things made straight on the mantelpiece, so—and the books put here, and the bottles there, and your sofa turned from the light, and the pillows plumped up a bit. Now then, you're fixed."

And so he was, for as she laughed and talked Jo had whisked things into place and given quite a different air to the room. Laurie watched her in respectful silence and when she beckoned him to his sofa, he sat down with a sigh of satisfaction, saying gratefully: "How kind you are! Yes, that's what it wanted. Now please take the big chair, and let me do something to amuse my company."

"No—I came to amuse you. Shall I read aloud?" And Jo looked affectionately toward some inviting books near by.

"Thank you, I've read all those, and if you don't mind, I'd rather talk," answered Laurie.

"Not a bit. I'll talk all day if you'll only set me going. Beth says I never know when to stop."

"Is Beth the rosy one who stays at home a good deal, and sometimes goes out with a little basket?" asked Laurie.

"Yes, that's Beth. She's my girl, and a regular good one she is, too."

"The pretty one is Meg, and the curly-haired one is Amy, I believe?"

"How did you find that out?"

Laurie colored up, but answered frankly: "Why, you see I often hear you calling to one another, and when I'm alone up here, I can't help looking over at your house, you always seem to be having such good times. I beg your pardon for being so rude, but sometimes you forget to put down the curtain at the window where the flowers are; and when the lamps are lighted, it's like looking at a picture to see the fire, and you all round the table with your mother. I can't help watching it. I haven't got any mother, you know."

The solitary, hungry look in his eyes went straight to Jo's warm heart. She had been so simply taught that there was no nonsense in her head, and at fifteen she was as innocent and frank as any child. Laurie was sick and lonely, and feeling how rich she was in home, love and happiness, she gladly tried to share it with him. Her face was very friendly and her sharp voice unusually gentle as she said:

"We'll never draw that curtain any more, and I give you leave to look as much as you like. I just wish, though, instead of peeping, you'd come over and see us. Mother is so splendid she'd do you heaps of good, and Beth would sing to you if I begged her to, and Amy would dance, Meg and I would make you laugh over our funny stage properties, and we'd have jolly times. Wouldn't your grandpa let you?"

"I think he would, if your mother asked him. He's very kind, though he does not look so; and he lets me do what I like, pretty much, only he's afraid I might be a bother to strangers," began Laurie, brightening more and more.

"We are not strangers, we are neighbors, and you needn't think you'd be a bother. We *want* to know you, and I've been trying to do it this ever so long. We haven't been here a great while, you know, but we have got acquainted with all our neighbors but you."

"You see Grandpa lives among his books, and doesn't mind much what happens outside. Mr. Brooke, my tutor, doesn't stay here, you know, and I have no one to go about with me, so I just stop at home and get on as I can."

"That's bad. You ought to make an effort, and go visiting everywhere you are asked. Then you'll have plenty of friends and pleasant places to go to.

Never mind being bashful; it won't last long if you keep going."

Laurie turned red again, but wasn't offended at being accused of bashfulness, for there was so much goodwill in Jo it was impossible not to take her blunt speeches as kindly as they were meant.

"Do you like your school?" asked the boy, changing the subject.

"Don't go to school. I'm a businessman—girl, I mean. I go to wait on my great-aunt, and a dear, cross old soul she is, too," answered Jo.

Laurie opened his mouth to ask another question, but remembering just in time that it wasn't good manners to make too many inquiries into people's affairs, he shut it again, and looked uncomfortable. Jo liked his good breeding, and didn't mind having a laugh at Aunt March, so she gave him a lively description of the fidgety old lady, her fat poodle, the parrot, and the library where she reveled. Laurie enjoyed that immensely.

"Oh, that does me no end of good! Tell on, please."

Much elated with her success, Jo did "tell on," all about their plays and plans, their hopes and fears for father,* and the most interesting events of the little world in which the sisters lived. Then they got to talking about books, and to Jo's delight, she found that Laurie loved them as well as she did, and had read even more than herself.

"If you like them so much, come down and see ours. Grandpa is out, so you needn't be afraid," said Laurie.

---

*"hopes and fears for father": Mr. March was a chaplain in the Civil War; thus, his family was much concerned for his safety.

"I'm not afraid," returned Jo, with a toss of the head.

"I don't believe you are!" exclaimed the boy, looking at her with much admiration, though he privately thought she would have good reason to be a trifle afraid of the old gentleman if she met him in some of his moods.

The atmosphere of the whole house being summerlike, Laurie led the way from room to room, letting Jo stop to examine whatever struck her fancy; and so at last they came to the library, where she clapped her hands and pranced, as she always did when especially delighted. It was lined with books, and there were pictures and statues, and distracting little cabinets full of coins and curiosities, and sleepy-hollow chairs, and odd tables, and bronzes; and best of all a great open fireplace, with quaint tiles all round it.

"What richness!" sighed Jo, sinking into the depth of a velvet chair and gazing about her with an air of intense satisfaction. "Theodore Laurence, you ought to be the happiest boy in the world," she added impressively.

"A fellow can't live on books," said Laurie, shaking his head.

Before he could say more, a bell rang, and Jo flew up, exclaiming with alarm: "Mercy me! It's your grandpa!"

"Well, what if it is? You aren't afraid of anything, you know," returned the boy, looking wicked.

"I think I am a little bit afraid of him, but I don't know why I should be. Marmee said I might come, and I don't think you're any the worse for it," said Jo, composing herself.

"I'm a great deal better for it, and ever so much obliged. I'm only afraid you are very tired talking to me. It was so pleasant I couldn't bear to stop," said Laurie gratefully.

"The doctor to see you, sir," and the maid beckoned as she spoke.

"Would you mind if I left you for a minute? I suppose I must see him," said Laurie.

"Don't mind me. I'm as happy as a cricket here."

Laurie went away, and his guest amused herself in her own way. She was standing before a fine portrait of the old gentleman when the door opened again, and, without turning, she said decidedly: "I'm sure now that I shouldn't be afraid of him, for he's got kind eyes, though his mouth is grim and he looks as if he had a tremendous will of his own. He isn't as handsome as my grandfather, but I like him."

"Thank you, ma'am," said a gruff voice behind her, and there, to her great dismay, stood old Mr. Laurence.

Poor Jo blushed till she couldn't blush any redder, and her heart began to beat uncomfortably fast as she thought what she had said. For a minute a wild desire to run away possessed her; but that was cowardly, and the girls would laugh at her, so she resolved to stay and get out of the scrape as she could. A second look showed her that the living eyes under the bushy gray eyebrows were kinder even than the painted ones, and there was a sly twinkle in them which lessened her fear a good deal. The gruff voice was gruffer than ever as the old gentleman said abruptly, "So you're not afraid of me, hey?"

"Not much, sir."

"And you don't think me as handsome as your grandfather?"

"Not quite, sir."

"And I've got a tremendous will, have I?"

"I only said I thought so."

"But you like me, in spite of it?"

"Yes, I do, sir."

That answer pleased the old gentleman. He gave a short laugh, shook hands with her, and putting his finger under her chin, turned up her face, examined it gravely, and let it go, saying with a nod:

"You've got your grandfather's spirit, if you haven't his face. He was a fine man, my dear, but what is better, he was a brave and an honest one, and I was proud to be his friend."

"Thank you, sir."

"What have you been doing to this boy of mine, hey?" was the next question, sharply put.

"Only trying to be neighborly, sir." And Jo told how her visit came about.

"You think he needs cheering up a bit, do you?"

"Yes, sir. He seems a little lonely, and young folks would do him good perhaps. We are only girls, but we should be glad to help if we could, for we don't forget the splendid Christmas present you sent us," said Jo eagerly.

"I shall come and see your mother some fine day. Tell her so. There's the tea bell; we have it early, on the boy's account. Come down, and go on being neighborly."

"If you'd like to have me, sir."

"Shouldn't ask you if I didn't." And Mr. Laurence offered her his arm with old-fashioned courtesy.

"What would Meg say to this?" thought Jo as she was marched away.

"Hey! Why, what the dickens has come to the fellow?" said the old gentleman as Laurie came running downstairs and brought up with a start of surprise at the astonishing sight of Jo arm-in-arm with his redoubtable grandfather.

"I didn't know you'd come, sir."

"That's evident by the way you racket downstairs. Come to your tea, sir, and behave like a gentleman." And having pulled the boy's hair by way of a caress, Mr. Laurence walked on, while

Laurie went through a series of comic evolutions behind their backs which nearly produced an explosion of laughter from Jo.

The old gentleman did not say much as he drank his four cups of tea, but he watched the young people, who soon chatted away like old friends, and the change in his grandson did not escape him. There was color, light, and life in the boy's face now, vivacity [liveliness] in his manner, and genuine merriment in his laugh.

"She's right, the lad is lonely. I'll see what these little girls can do for him," thought Mr. Laurence. He liked Jo, for her odd, blunt ways suited him, and she seemed to understand the boy almost as well as if she had been one herself.

If the Laurences had been what Jo called "prim and poky," she would not have got on at all, for such people always made her shy and awkward; but finding them free and easy, she was so herself, and made a good impression. When they rose she proposed to go, but Laurie said he had something more to show her and took her away to the conservatory. It seemed quite fairylike to Jo as she went up and down the walks enjoying the blooming walls on either side, the soft light, the damp sweet air, and the wonderful vines and trees that hung above her. Her new friend cut the finest flowers till his hands were full; then he tied them up, saying, with the happy look Jo liked to see: "Please give these to your mother, and tell her I like the medicine she sent me very much."

Reading Check

1. Why does Jo choose to befriend Laurie?
2. Why doesn't she feel free to simply go over and visit the Laurence home?
3. How does Jo arrange to meet Laurie?
4. When Jo finally meets old Mr. Laurence he tells her: "You've got your grandfather's spirit. . . . He was a fine man, . . . a brave and honest one and I was proud to be his friend." List some of Jo's specific actions that show us that Mr. Laurence's opinion of Jo was correct.

A nineteenth century Bible scholar once wrote, "God designs us to learn many lessons from His creatures in the natural world, for there is in each creature some excellency testifying against our deficiencies." This truth is well illustrated in the following story. The example of self-sacrifice and loyalty, which are instinctive characteristics of the collie Wolf, can provide for us an excellent lesson on the attitudes portrayed in a true friendship.

One Minute Longer

Albert Payson Terhune

Wolf was a collie, red-gold and white of coat, with a shape more like his long-ago wolf ancestors' than like a domesticated dog's. It was from this ancestral throw back that he was named Wolf.

He looked not at all like his great sire, Sunnybank Lad, nor like his dainty, thoroughbred mother, Lady. Nor was he like them in any other way, except that he inherited old Lad's stanchly gallant spirit and loyalty, and uncanny brain. No, in traits as well as in looks, he was more wolf than dog. He almost never barked, his snarl supplying all vocal needs.

The Mistress, or the Master, or the Boy—any of these three could romp with him, roll him over, tickle him, or subject him to all sorts of playful indignities. And Wolf entered gleefully into the fun of the romp. But let any human, besides these three, lay a hand on his slender body, and a snarling plunge for the offender's throat was Wolf's invariable reply to the caress.

It had been so since his puppyhood. He did not fly at accredited [authorized] guests, nor, indeed, pay any heed to their presence, so long as they kept their hands off him. But to all of these the Boy was forced to say at the very outset of the visit:

"Pat Lad and Bruce all you want to, but please leave Wolf alone. He doesn't care for people. We've taught him to stand for a pat on the head from guests—but don't touch his body."

Then, to prove his own immunity [exemption], the Boy would proceed to tumble Wolf about, to the delight of them both.

In romping with humans whom they love, most dogs will bite, more or less gently—or pretend to bite—as a part of the game. Wolf never did this. In his wildest and roughest romps with the Boy or with the Boy's parents, Wolf did not so much as open his mighty jaws. Perhaps because he dared not trust himself to bite gently. Perhaps because he realized that a bite is not a joke, but an effort to kill.

There had been only one exception to Wolf's hatred for mauling at strangers' hands. A man came to The Place on a business call, bringing along a chubby two-year-old daughter. The Master warned the baby that she must not go near Wolf, although she might pet any of the other collies. Then he became so much interested in the business talk that he and his guest forgot all about the child.

Ten minutes later the Master chanced to shift his gaze to the far end of the room. And he broke off, with a gasp, in the very middle of a sentence.

The baby was seated astride Wolf's back, her tiny heels digging into the dog's sensitive ribs, and each of her chubby fists gripping one of his ears. Wolf was lying there, with an idiotically happy grin on his face and wagging his tail in ecstasy.

No one knew why he had submitted to the baby's tugging hands, except because she was a baby, and because the gallant heart of the dog had gone out to her helplessness.

Wolf was the official watchdog of The Place; and his name carried dread to the loafers and tramps of the region. Also, he was the Boy's own special dog. He had been born on the Boy's tenth birthday, five years before this story of ours begins; and ever since then the two had been inseparable chums.

One sloppy afternoon in late winter, Wolf and the Boy were sprawled, side by side, on the fur rug in front of the library fire. The Mistress and the Master had gone to town for the day. The house was lonely, and the two chums were left to entertain each other.

The Boy was reading a magazine. The dog beside him was blinking in drowsy comfort at the fire. Presently, finishing the story he had been reading, the Boy looked across at the sleepy dog.

"Wolf," he said, "here's a story about a dog. I think he must have been something like you. Maybe he was your great-great-great-great-grandfather. He lived an awfully long time ago—in Pompeii. Ever hear of Pompeii?"

Now, the Boy was fifteen years old, and he had too much sense to imagine that Wolf could possibly understand the story he was about to tell him. But, long since, he had fallen into a way of talking to his dog, sometimes, as if to another human. It was fun for him to note the almost pathetic eagerness wherewith Wolf listened and tried to grasp the meaning of what he was saying. Again and again, at sound of some familiar word or voice inflection, the collie would prick up his ears or wag his tail, as if in the joyous hope that he had at last found a clew to his owner's meaning.

"You see," went on the Boy, "this dog lived in Pompeii, as I told you. You've never been there, Wolf."

Wolf was looking up at the Boy in wistful excitement, seeking vainly to guess what was expected of him.

"And," continued the Boy, "the kid who owned him seems to have had a regular knack for getting into trouble all the time. And his dog was always on hand to get him out of it. It's a true story, the magazine says. The kid's father was so grateful to the dog that he bought him a solid silver collar. Solid silver! Get that, Wolfie?"

Wolf did not "get it." But he wagged his tail hopefully, his eyes alight with bewildered interest.

"And," said the Boy, "what do you suppose was engraved on the collar? Well, I'll tell you: 'This dog has thrice saved his little master from death. Once

by fire, once by flood, and once at the hands of robbers!' How's that for a record, Wolf? For one dog, too!"

At the words "Wolf" and "dog," the collie's tail smote the floor in glad comprehension. Then he edged closer to the Boy as the narrator's voice presently took on a sadder note.

"But at last," resumed the Boy, "there came a time when the dog couldn't save the kid. Mount Vesuvius erupted. All the sky was pitch-dark, as black as midnight, and Pompeii was buried under lava and ashes. The dog could easily have got away by himself— dogs can see in the dark, can't they, Wolf?—but he couldn't get the kid away.

And he wouldn't go without him. You wouldn't have gone without me, either, would you, Wolf? Pretty nearly two thousand years later, some people dug through the lava that covered Pompeii. What do you suppose they found? Of course they found a whole lot of things. One of them was that dog—silver collar and inscription and all. He was lying at the feet of a child. The child he couldn't save. He was one grand dog— hey, Wolf?"

The continued strain of trying to understand began to get on the collie's high-strung nerves. He rose to his feet, quivering, and sought to lick the Boy's face, thrusting one upraised white forepaw at him in appeal for a hand-shake. The Boy slammed shut the magazine.

"It's slow in the house, here, with nothing to do," he said to his chum. "I'm going up the lake with my gun to see if any wild ducks have landed in the marshes yet. It's almost time for them. Want to come along?"

The last sentence Wolf understood perfectly. On the instant he was dancing with excitement at the prospect of a walk. Being a collie, he was of no earthly help in a hunting trip; but, on such tramps, as everywhere else, he was the Boy's inseparable companion.

Out over the slushy snow the two started, the Boy with his light single-barreled shotgun slung over one shoulder, the dog trotting close at his heels. The March thaw was changing to a sharp freeze. The deep and soggy snow was crusted over, just thick enough to make walking a genuine difficulty for both dog and Boy.

The Place was a promontory that ran out into the lake, on the opposite bank from the mile-distant village. Behind, across the high-road, lay the winter-choked forest. At the lake's northerly end, two miles beyond The Place, were the reedy marshes where, a month hence, wild duck would congregate. Thither, with Wolf, the Boy plowed his way though the biting cold.

The going was heavy and heavier. A quarter mile below the marshes, the Boy struck out across the upper corner of the lake. Here the ice was rotten at the top, where the thaw had nibbled at it, but beneath it was still a full eight inches thick; easily strong enough to bear the Boy's weight.

Along the gray ice field the two plodded. The skim of water, which the thaw had spread an inch thick over the ice, had frozen in the day's cold spell. It crackled like broken glass as the chums walked over it. The Boy had on big hunting boots. So, apart from the extra effort, the glasslike ice did not bother him. To Wolf it gave acute pain. The sharp particles were forever getting between the callous black pads of his feet, pricking and cutting him acutely.

Little smears of blood began to mark the dog's course; but it never occurred to Wolf to turn back, or to betray by any sign that he was suffering. It was all a part of the day's work—a cheap price to pay for the joy of tramping with his adored young master.

Then, forty yards or so on the hither side of the marshes, Wolf beheld a right amazing phenomenon [occurrence]. The Boy had been walking directly in front of him, gun over shoulder. With no warning at all the youthful hunter fell, feet foremost, out of sight, through the ice.

The light shell of new-frozen water that covered the lake's thicker ice also masked an air hole nearly three feet wide. Into this, as he strode carelessly along, the Boy had stepped. Straight down he had gone, with all the force of his hundred-and-twenty pounds and with all the impetus of his forward stride.

Instinctively, he threw out his hands to restore his balance. The only effect of this was to send the gun flying ten feet away.

Down went the Boy through less than three feet of water (for the bottom of the lake at this point had started to slope upward toward the marshes) and through nearly two feet more of sticky marsh mud that underlay the lake bed.

His outflung hands struck against the ice on the edges of the air hole, and clung there.

Sputtering and gurgling, the Boy brought his head above the surface and tried to raise himself by his hands, high enough to wriggle out upon the surface of the ice. Ordinarily, this would have been simple enough for so strong a lad. But the gluelike mud had imprisoned his feet and the lower part of his legs; and held them powerless.

Try as he would, the Boy could not wrench himself free of the slough. The water, as he stood upright, was on a level with his mouth. The air hole was too wide for him, at such a depth, to get a good purchase [grip] on its edges and lift himself bodily to safety.

Gaining such a fingerhold as he could, he heaved with all his might, throwing every muscle of his body into the struggle. One leg was pulled almost free of the mud, but the other was driven deeper into it. And, as the Boy's fingers slipped from the smoothly wet ice edge, the attempt to restore his balance drove the free leg back, knee-deep into the mire.

Ten minutes of this hopeless fighting left the Boy panting and tired out. The icy water was numbing his nerves and chilling his blood into torpidity [dormancy]. His hands were without sense of feeling, as far up as the wrists. Even if he could have shaken free his legs from the mud now, he had not strength enough left to crawl out of the hole.

He ceased his uselessly frantic battle and stood dazed. Then he came sharply to himself. For, as he stood, the water crept upward from his lips to his nostrils. He knew why the water seemed to be rising. It was not rising. It was he who was sinking. As soon as he stopped moving, the mud began, very slowly, but very steadily, to suck him downward.

This was not a quicksand, but it was a deep mud bed. And only by constant motion could he avoid sinking farther and farther down into it. He had less than two inches to spare, at best, before the water should fill his nostrils; less than two inches of life, even if he could keep the water down to the level of his lips.

There was a moment of utter panic. Then the Boy's brain cleared. His only hope was to keep on fighting—to rest when he must, for a moment or so, and then to renew his numbed grip on the ice edge and try to pull his feet a few inches higher out of the mud. He must do this as long as his chilled body could be scourged into obeying his will.

He struggled again, but with virtually no result in raising himself. A second struggle, however, brought him chin-high above the water. He remembered confusedly that some of these earlier struggles had scarce budged him, while others had gained him two or three inches. Vaguely, he wondered why. Then turning his head, he realized.

Wolf, as he turned, was just loosing his hold on the wide collar of the Boy's mackinaw [jacket]. His cut forepaws were still braced against a flaw of ragged ice on the air hole's edge, and all his tawny body was tense.

His body was dripping wet, too. The Boy noted that; and he realized that the repeated effort to draw his master to safety must have resulted, at least once, in pulling the dog down into the water with the floundering Boy.

"Once more, Wolfie! Once more!" chattered the Boy through teeth that clicked together like castanets.

The dog darted forward, caught his grip afresh on the edge of the Boy's collar, and tugged with all his fierce strength; growling and whining ferociously the while.

The Boy seconded the collie's tuggings by a supreme struggle that lifted him higher than before. He was able to get one arm and shoulder clear. His numb fingers closed about an upthrust tree limb which had been washed downstream in the autumn freshets [overflow of stream caused by heavy rain] and had been frozen into the lake ice.

With this new purchase, and aided by the dog, the boy tried to drag himself out of the hole. But the chill of the water had done its work. He had not the strength to move farther. The mud still sucked at his calves and ankles. The big hunting boots were full of water that seemed to weigh a ton.

He lay there, gasping and chattering. Then, through the gathering twilight, his eyes fell on the gun, lying ten feet away.

"Wolf!" he ordered, nodding toward the weapon. "Get it! Get it!"

Not in vain had the Boy talked to Wolf, for years, as if the dog were human. At the words and the nod, the collie trotted over to the gun, lifted it by the stock, and hauled it awkwardly along over the bumpy ice to his master, where he laid it down at the edge of the air hole.

The dog's eyes were cloudy with trouble, and he shivered and whined as with ague [a fever much like malaria]. The water on his thick coat was freezing to a mass of ice. But it was from anxiety that he shivered, and not from cold.

Still keeping his numb grasp on the tree branch, the boy balanced himself as best he could, and thrust two fingers of his free hand into his mouth to warm them into sensation again.

When this was done, he reached out to where the gun lay, and pulled its trigger. The shot boomed deafeningly through the twilight winter silences. The recoil sent the weapon sliding sharply back along the ice, spraining the Boy's trigger finger and cutting it to the bone.

"That's all I can do," said the Boy to himself. "If anyone hears it, well and good. I can't get at another cartridge. I couldn't put it into the breech if I had it. My hands are too numb."

For several minutes he clung there, listening. But this was a desolate part of the lake, far from any road; and the season was too early for other hunters to be abroad. The bitter cold, in any case, tended to make sane folk hug the fireside rather than to venture so far into the open. Nor was the single report of a gun uncommon enough to call for investigation in such weather.

All this the Boy told himself, as the minutes dragged by. Then he looked again at Wolf. The dog, head on one side, still stood protectingly above him. The dog was cold and in pain. But, being only a dog, it did not occur to him to trot off home to the comfort of the library fire and leave his master to fend for himself.

Presently, with a little sigh, Wolf lay down on the ice, his nose across the Boy's arm. Even if he lacked strength to save his beloved master, he could stay and share the Boy's sufferings.

But the Boy himself thought otherwise. He was not at all minded to freeze to death, nor was he willing to let Wolf imitate the dog of Pompeii by dying helplessly at his master's side. Controlling for an instant the chattering of his teeth, he called:

"Wolf!"

The dog was on his feet again at the word; alert, eager.

"Wolf!" repeated the Boy. "Go! Hear me? Go!"

He pointed homeward.

Wolf started at him, hesitant. Again the Boy called in vehement command, "Go!"

The collie lifted his head to the twilight sky with a wolf howl hideous in its grief and appeal—a howl as wild and discordant as that of any of his savage ancestors. Then, stooping first to lick the numb hand that clung to the branch, Wolf turned and fled.

Across the cruelly sharp rim of ice he tore, at top speed, head down; whirling through the deeping dusk like a flash of tawny light.

Wolf understood what was wanted of him. Wolf always understood. The pain in his feet was nothing. The stiffness of his numbed body was forgotten in the urgency for speed.

The Boy looked drearily after the swift-vanishing figure which the dusk was swallowing. He knew the dog would try to bring help; as has many another and lesser dog in times of need. Whether or not that help could arrive in time, or at all, was a point on which the Boy would not let himself dwell. Into his benumbed brain crept the memory of an old Norse proverb he had read in school:

"Heroism consists of hanging on, one minute longer."

Unconsciously he tightened his feeble hold on the tree branch and braced himself.

From the marshes to The Place was a full two miles. Despite the deep and sticky snow, Wolf covered the distance in less than nine minutes. He paused in front of the gate lodge, at the highway entrance to the drive. But the superintendent and his wife had gone to Paterson, shopping, that afternoon.

Down the drive to the house he dashed. The maids had taken advantage of their employers' day in New York, to walk across the lake to the village, to a motion picture show.

Wise men claim that dogs have not the power to think or to reason things out in a logical way. So perhaps it was mere chance that next sent Wolf's flying feet across the lake to the village. Perhaps it was chance, and not the knowledge that where there is a village there are people.

Again and again, in the car, he had sat upon the front seat alongside the Mistress when she drove to the station to meet guests. There were always people at the station. And to the station Wolf now raced.

The usual group of platform idlers had been dispersed by the cold. A solitary baggageman was hauling a trunk and some boxes out of the express coop on to the platform; to be put aboard the five o'clock train from New York.

As the baggageman passed under the clump of station lights, he came to a sudden halt. For out of the darkness dashed a dog. Full tilt, the animal rushed up to him and seized him by the skirt of the overcoat.

The man cried out in scared surprise. He dropped the box he was carrying and struck at the dog, to ward off the seemingly murderous attack. He recognized Wolf, and he knew the collie's repute.

But Wolf was not attacking. Holding tight to the coat skirt, he backed away, trying to draw the man with him, and all the while whimpering aloud like a nervous puppy.

A kick from the heavy-shod boot broke the dog's hold on the coat skirt, even as a second yell from the man brought four or five other people running out from the station waiting room.

One of these, the telegraph operator, took in the scene at a single glance. With great presence of mind he bawled loudly: "Mad Dog!"

This, as Wolf, reeling from the kick, sought to gain another grip on the coat skirt. A second kick sent him rolling over and over on the tracks, while other voices took up the panic cry of "Mad dog!"

Now, a mad dog is supposed to be a dog afflicted by rabies. Once in ten thousand times, at the very most, a mad-dog hue and cry is justified. Certainly not oftener. A harmless and friendly dog loses his master on the street. He runs about, confused and frightened, looking for the owner he has lost. A boy throws a stone at him. Other boys chase him. His tongue hangs out, and his eyes glaze with terror. Then some fool bellows: "Mad dog!"

And the cruel chase is on—a chase that ends in the pitiful victim's death. Yes, in every crowd there is a voice ready to raise that murderously cruel shout.

So it was with the men who witnessed Wolf's frenzied effort to take aid to the imperiled Boy.

Voice after voice repeated the cry. Men groped along the platform edge for stones to throw. The village policeman ran puffingly upon the scene, drawing his revolver.

Finding it useless to make a further attempt to drag the baggageman to the rescue, Wolf leaped back, facing the ever larger group. Back went his head again in that hideous wolf howl. Then he galloped away a few yards, trotted back, howled once more, and again galloped lakeward.

All of which only confirmed the panicky crowd in the belief that they were threatened by a mad dog. A shower of stones hurled about Wolf as he came back a third time to lure these dull humans into following him.

One pointed rock smote the collie's shoulder, glancingly, cutting it to the bone. A shot from the policeman's revolver fanned the fur of his ruff, as it whizzed past.

Knowing that he faced death, he nevertheless stood his ground, not troubling to dodge the fusilade [rapid discharge] of stones, but continuing to run lakeward and then trot back, whining with excitement.

A second pistol shot flew wide. A third grazed the dog's hip. From all directions people were running toward the station. A man darted into a house next door, and emerged carrying a shotgun. This he steadied on the veranda rail not forty feet away from the leaping dog, and made ready to fire.

It was then the train from New York came in. and, momentarily, the sport of "mad-dog" killing was abandoned, while the crowd scattered to each side of the track.

From a front car of the train the Mistress and the Master emerged into a bedlam of noise and confusion.

"Best hide in the station, Ma'am!" shouted the telegraph operator, at sight of the Mistress. "There is a mad dog loose out here! He's chasing folks around, and—"

"Mad dog!" repeated the Mistress in high contempt. "If you knew anything about dogs, you'd know mad ones never 'chase folks around,' anymore than diphtheria patients do. Then—"

A flash of tawny light beneath the station lamp, a scurrying of frightened idlers, a final wasted shot from the policeman's pistol as Wolf dived headlong through the frightened crowd toward the voice he heard and recognized.

Up to the Mistress and the Master galloped Wolf. He was bleeding, his eyes were bloodshot, his fur was rumpled. He seized the astounded Master's gloved hand lightly between his teeth and sought to pull him across the tracks and toward the lake.

The Master knew dogs. Especially he knew Wolf. And without a word he suffered himself to be led. The Mistress and one or two inquisitive men followed.

Presently, Wolf loosed his hold on the Master's hand and ran on ahead, darting back every few moments to make certain he was followed.

"Heroism—consists—in—hanging—on—one—minute—longer," the Boy was whispering deliriously to himself for the hundredth time, as Wolf pattered up to him in triumph, across the ice, with the human rescuers a scant ten yards behind.

Reading Check

1. How was Wolf more like a wolf than a dog?
2. What specific actions characterize Wolf's loyalty toward his Master?
3. What specific actions characterize Wolf's self-sacrifice for his Master?
4. Why do the townspeople initially attack Wolf?
5. Why does the old Norse Proverb, "Heroism consists in hanging on one minute longer," prove valuable to the boy?

Nick and Joe understood that "it is better to give than to receive," and they thoroughly enjoyed secretly planning the purchase of a special Mother's Day gift. But their secret plan was also to teach them another principle, the principle that "at times, true love will withhold rather than give."

Half a Gift

Robert Zacks

I was ten years old then, and my brother, Nick, was fourteen. For both of us, this purchase of a gift for our mother on Mother's Day was an occasion of excitement and great importance.

It was our first gift to her. We were very poor. It was just after the first World War and we lived in a time of trouble. Our father worked now and then as a waiter. Birthday and Christmas gifts were taken care of by him as well as he could, but such a thing as a Mother's Day gift was an out-of-the-ordinary luxury. But we had been fortunate, Nick and myself. A second-hand furniture store had opened on the block, and deliveries were made by means of loading the furniture on a wobbly pushcart which we carefully pushed through traffic to the customer's home. We had a nickel each and, perhaps, a tip.

I remember how Nick's thin, dark face blazed with the joy of the present. He had been given the thought in school; and the anticipation of surprise and giving grew in him, and myself, until we were almost frantic.

When we secretly told our father, he was very pleased. He stroked our heads proudly.

"It's a fine idea," he said. "It will make your mother very happy."

From his wistful tone, we knew what he was thinking. He had given our mother little enough in their life together. She worked all day, cooking and buying and tending to us in illness and stoking the stove in the kitchen with wood and coal to keep us warm in winter. She did her own washing of the family clothes in the bathtub. And she did all these things silently. She did not laugh much, but when she smiled at us it was a beautiful thing—well worth waiting for.

"What are you going to give her?" asked father, thoughtfully. "How much money have you?"

"We're going to give separate presents," I announced importantly.

"Pick carefully," my father counseled.

"You tell Mother," said Nick, looking at me for approval, "so she can enjoy thinking about it."

I nodded. My father said, "That is a big thought to come from so small a head. And wise."

Nick flushed with joy. Then he put a hand on my shoulder and said quickly, "Joe thought of it, too."

"No," I said, "I didn't." I wanted no credit for what was not mine. "But my present will make up for it."

"The thought belongs to everybody," said Father smiling. "Everybody. Nick, too, got the thought elsewhere."

For the next few days we enjoyed the game of secrecy with my mother. A shining look came into her face as

his and scooted around like a fly in summertime.

"We might get the same thing," I wailed.

"No, we won't," said Nick. "I have more money than you."

I did not like this remark, though it was fair enough, since I had spent some of my earnings for candy, while Nick had determined to spend everything on the gift.

After careful deliberation I bought for my mother a comb decorated with little shiny stones that could even be mistaken for diamonds. Nick came back from the store with a pleased look. He liked my gift very much and wouldn't tell about his.

"We will give the gifts at a certain moment I have picked," he said.

"What moment?" I asked mystified.

"I can't tell, because it has something to do with my gift. And don't ask me again what it is."

The next morning Nick kept me close and when my mother got ready to wash the floor he nodded to me and we ran to get our gifts. When I came back, Mother was, as usual, on her knees, wearily scrubbing the floor with scouring powder and scrubbing brush, and mopping up the dirty water with old rags made of discarded underwear. It was the job she hated most in the world.

Then Nick returned with his present, and Mother sat back on her heels staring unbelievingly at the gift. Her face went pale with disappointment as she looked at the new scrubbing pail with the wringer and the fresh mop in it.

"A scrubbing pail?" she said. Her voice almost broke.

she worked near us, pretending not to know, and she smiled often. The air was full of love.

Nick and I discussed what to buy. We became involved in competition of taste.

"Let's not tell each other what we're getting," said Nick, exasperated with me, for my mind was not as settled as

Tears sprang to Nick's eyes. Without a word he picked up the scrubbing pail and mop. "I will take it back," he sobbed.

"No," said Father, taking the pail. He soaked the puddle of dirty water up with the mop and using the foot wringer on the bucket, neatly squeezed it dry.

"You did not let Nick finish," he said to Mother. "Part of his gift is that he is going to wash the floor from now on." He looked at Nick. "Isn't that so, Nick?"

With a flush of shame Nick understood the lesson. "Yes, oh, yes," he said in a low, eager tone.

Quickly, repentantly, Mother said, "It is too heavy work for a fourteen-year-old boy."

It was then I realized how smart Father was. "Ah," he said cunningly, "not with this wonderful wringer and scrub pail. It's much easier. Your hands stay clean, and your knees don't hurt." Again Father demonstrated quickly.

Mother said, looking sadly at Nick, "Ah, a woman can become so stupid." She kissed Nick and he felt better. Then they turned to me.

"What is your gift?" asked Father. Nick looked at me and paled. I felt the comb in my pocket. It would make the scrubbing pail, again, just a scrubbing pail. After all, a comb with shining stones just like diamonds.

"Half the scrubbing pail," I said mournfully, and Nick looked at me with love in his eyes.

Reading Check

1. Why is the purchase of a Mother's Day gift so special in Nick and Joe's family?
2. What does each boy buy?
3. What makes Joe realize how "smart" his father is?
4. In I Corinthians 13 Paul lists several characteristics of true love. One of these characteristics is that "Charity seeketh not her own." How does Paul's statement apply to Nick?
5. How does Paul's statement apply to Joe?

Though the boys of the Redwood Mineralogical Club took great pains to avoid Arden Sawyer, they found that Arden was "unavoidable." Yet before the afternoon was over, Arden's patient determination proved to the boys that he was more than unavoidable. He was invaluable.

Rock Hounds

Charles Coombs

"Careful as we pass this line of trees," cautioned Cal Martin. "If Arden Sawyer sees us, he'll be out here determined to go along." Cal was president of our "rock-hunting" club; and since he owned all our equipment, his word was law.

Cal, Brick, Jerry, and I made up the Redwood Mineralogical Club; and gathering different kinds of rock to add to collections was our hobby. Every weekend when the weather permitted, we rock hounds would be out combing

the hillsides and river banks for specimens. This October Saturday was a special occasion, for we had heard that autunite could be found in an old mine on the Sawyer farm.

We were very eager to get some autunite, not because it is such a valuable mineral, but because it's so much in demand by other rock hounds. Half the fun of being a rock hound is the contacts that you have with members of other clubs. You're always getting letters from other hounds who want to exchange their surplus specimens with you. You see, not all kinds of rocks are found in all parts of our country.

It's easy to spot autunite in a cave or mine if you use a portable mineral light. The ultraviolet rays from the mineral light make the autunite glow with a brilliant green color. I was carrying the light, and Jerry was panting under the weight of the battery that would produce the electric current for the light. Brick had brought a coil of rope, needed to lower us into the mine. And each of us had a flashlight and a pick for digging purposes.

Normally, when we want to scout around on a person's land, we go directly to the owner and ask permission. But this farm belonged to Arden Sawyer's father. And if we went up to the house, Arden would be sure to want to go along. The Sawyers were new people in the community, and—well, Arden was such a funny-looking little guy.

Now you know why we were quietly sneaking along the line of trees that served as a windbreak for the Sawyers' house. The old mine lay just over the next hill. Ten more minutes and we'd be there.

"I see it!" cried Jerry, who was in the lead. We dashed up to him. At the bottom of the hill a sort of boxlike structure protruded from the undergrowth. It was the old shaft that used to serve as the entrance to the mine.

"That's it, all right," confirmed Cal. "Let's rest a bit and catch our breath."

We sat down, gazing at the mine shaft with mixed feelings of anticipation and foreboding. Somehow, now that we were almost there, the idea of going down into that deep hole didn't seem as attractive as it once had.

Suddenly there was a rustling in the bushes nearby. We jumped up, nearly frightened out of our skins.

"Hi, fellows!" cried a cheerful voice. It was Arden. In spite of our attempts to avoid him, he had seen us. And now he insisted on knowing our plans.

When he heard them, he stated flatly that he was going along. There was nothing for us to do except to say that he could—but only as a spectator. And, to keep him from getting any ideas about joining the club, we loaded upon him the battery, the mineral light, and the big coil of rope. If he hadn't been such a dope, he would have left us right then and there. But he grimly shouldered his burden and started off for the bottom of the hill.

As we lifted the cover of weather-beaten planks from the top of the shaft and gazed down into the pitch-black pit, we were plenty excited. Then the musty odor of rotting wood and stagnant water smacked us in the face.

"Don't mind that," Cal assured us in the tone of an expert. "Any damp pit would have that odor. Here, give me a rock, someone."

It was Arden who handed him a good-sized piece of granite. Cal dropped it straight down the shaft. After a wait of a couple of seconds, we heard a shallow splash.

"Must be about twenty feet down to the bottom," said Arden. "and not much water." We glared at him.

"Give me a flashlight, somebody," ordered Cal, ignoring him. Arden grabbed mine and put it in Cal's hands before you could have said Jack Robinson.

The beam of the light showed an old rusted winch [hoisting machine] straddling the hole. Though its rope had long since disappeared, the winch was still in working order. And at one side, there was a small wooden platform that could be fastened to the rope and used as a sort of elevator for making the descent.

It was only a matter of minutes until we had uncoiled our rope and tied one end of it securely to the platform. Then the rope was placed correctly in the winch and wound around its shaft. We were ready to make the descent.

Flashlights in hand, we stood there trembling. None of us had the slightest idea of what we would find at the bottom of that deep dark hole. We began to wonder whether we really wanted to go down. If it hadn't been for Arden, we might have given the whole thing up.

Cal went first. Everyone but Brick, who was working the winch, watched the beam of Cal's flashlight as it cut downward through the blackness.

"Easy now." Cal's voice echoed hollowly up to the surface. "I'm about down. Got to see how deep the water is. . . . Just a couple of inches. Come on, fellows."

Jerry went down. And Brick. Then Arden and I stood looking at each other. Someone had to stay on top to work the winch. Arden had such a pleading look on his face I said I'd stay. At least I told myself that that was the reason why I made my magnanimous [generous] offer.

The rope went slack as Arden touched bottom. "Everything down there O.K.?" I shouted.

"Sure," Cal's muffled voice replied. "Come on down."

"How? Fly?"

"It's easy," said Cal impatiently. "Drop the loose end of the rope down here. It's a good long rope. We'll lower you from down here. Then we'll fasten the rope; and when we get ready to go back up, the first guy up can be raised from down here. See? It's simple."

Well, it sounded logical enough, although I could hear someone protesting that, for safety's sake, I should stay on top. It sounded like Arden's voice and, of course, that made me suddenly determined to go down.

When we were all together at the bottom of the shaft, Cal put a big rock over the loose end of the rope to anchor it. Then we busied ourselves hooking up the mineral light to the battery.

A tunnel angled off to the right, and soon our flashlight beams were stabbing into its blackness. The rhythmical drip-drip-drip of water from the roof of the tunnel became louder the farther we went. Soon it seemed to be pounding in our ears. As we plodded onward, the chill damp air kept hitting us in the face like a cold wet blanket.

"You shouldn't all have your lights on," observed Arden. "You're wasting them." We didn't deign to answer him, but one by one everybody but Cal turned his off.

At last the tunnel opened into a large room where water dripped from the ceiling. Cal played his flashlight over the walls.

"This must have been the main part of the mine," he said with awe in his voice. "Boy, it must have taken some digging."

"I never dreamed all this was under our farm!" gasped Arden.

But Jerry was thinking about our purpose in coming. "Let's get busy and find some autunite."

Cal turned on the mineral light, and we all clustered around as he moved the almost invisible ray along the wall. Every once in a while something would catch the light and sparkle back. Perhaps it would sparkle blue, like a chunk of aurichalcite. Perhaps it would sparkle a pinkish red, like cinnabar. Whatever it was, if it glittered in the ultraviolet light, we dug it out with our picks and stuffed it into our pockets. Later, we would consult our mineral charts in Cal's garage and find out what each new specimen was.

Then there was a gleam of green. Autunite! Soon everyone was busy digging out bits of it for himself. We forgot to talk.

Gradually my teeth began to chatter with the cold. When I could bear no more, I said, "L-let's get out of here. W-we can c-come back sometime when we've g-got sweaters and raincoats."

"I s-second the motion," Jerry chattered.

"O.K.," Cal agreed. "Who'd ever guess it'd be so cold down here!"

With Cal at the front and Arden at the rear, we worked our way back toward the shaft. The tunnel seemed endless, and we were so eager to get there that we soon found ourselves almost running.

A few yards from the shaft, Cal stumbled on some loose shale and fell. I sailed headfirst over him, and sprawled on the rocky floor.

At that moment I heard the squeak of the winch overhead. "Hey!" I yelled. "The rope's going up. We knocked it loose!"

I made a desperate leap for the loose end as it went past, but I missed. The rumble of the winch increased, and we watched horrified as the winch continued to roll, pulling the rope upward. Then the loose end passed over the winch, and the rope came snaking down to lie at our feet. We were stranded at the bottom of the shaft!

"Oh-h!" groaned Brick. "What are we going to do! We'll all freeze to death if we stay down here much longer, and—"

The hopelessness of our situation sank upon us. We gazed upward. The rough, perpendicular walls that rose like the inside of a giant chimney seemed to leer back at us. We began to feel panicky.

We shouted and shouted until we were hoarse. But who was there to hear? And when would anyone come to look for us? Our folks knew that we were out on a rock hunting excursion, but none of us had thought to say where we were going.

I had an idea. Turning to Arden, I cried, "Maybe your dad will come hunting for you!"

He shook his head. "Dad doesn't know. He and Mom had gone over to Georgetown before you fellows even came on the farm. They went to see my sick aunt, and they're not coming back again until tomorrow night. I stayed home to care for the livestock."

Cal made a strange sound and turned away. Was he struggling with tears? We sat down limply. The sound of our breathing and the dripping of the water were all we could hear. Time seemed to be standing still.

After a year or two, Arden said, "If-if you fellows would form a base so as to raise me up in the shaft, I think I

could brace myself across it. By digging in with my heels and then working my shoulders upward, I think I could inch my way toward the top."

"You couldn't!" cried Brick. "And anyway, the rope would be down here."

"I've thought of that," said Arden quietly. "I'll tie one end of it to my belt and pull it up with me."

"You'd never make it, Arden," Jerry interrupted. "It's more than twenty feet up that shaft. Even if you did get part way up, you'd probably slip—and then!"

We shuddered at the thought.

"I'm going to try it," said Arden firmly, "and that's that. Jerry, Brick, Tom—you fellows stand up, close together, and lock your arms around each other's shoulders." His tone was so crisp that we hurried to obey him. Even Cal came over to help boost Arden up.

It hurt plenty as Arden dug his heels in to get started. But pretty soon his weight lessened. He had begun his climb.

Inch by inch he struggled upward. First with his feet, then with his shoulders. Stones the size of hens' eggs were dislodged and came raining down. I could just imagine what those stones were doing to his back as he forced his shoulders upward over that rough surface.

It seemed a year before he reached the top, and each of us ached all over from doing the climb with him.

Then came a shout of victory!

We laughed and cried and cheered, slapping each other on the shoulders and dashing the tears from our eyes.

Suddenly the winch began to turn. Arden had fastened the rope in it and was pulling up the slack.

One by one we took our place on the platform and were hauled up. First Brick—then Jerry—and I. Cal insisted on being last. Sunshine and the sight of brown hills had never seemed so beautiful to me as they did when I was brought up from that hole.

We all looked at Arden. He was trying hard to force a grin, but you could see it was a tremendous effort. We turned him around. His shirt hung in shreds, and his back was a mass of cuts and bruises. We looked at each other and none of us said a word.

Arden protested like anything but we made him go with us to see Dr. Bowman. And then we took him home and made him lie down while we cared for the livestock. Our folks gave us permission to stay out at the farm until Mr. and Mrs. Sawyer got back the next night. After all, we didn't want anything more to happen to the newest and most valuable member of the Redwood Mineralogical Club.

And next spring, when it's time to choose our president— Well, you just wait and see!

Reading Check

1. What does Cal say and do that indicates that he is selfish and proud?
2. How does the group show Arden that they do not want him along?
3. How does Arden react to their disapproval?
4. What happens at the mine to prove that Arden is actually a better friend and leader than Cal?
5. After reading the last sentence in the story, what do you think will happen next year when the club elects a new president?

Miss Lucy Quinn was a gracious, refined, wealthy lady. Chester was an energetic, mischievous young boy. But in spite of these differences, Miss Lucy firmly believed that her new friend Chester was "the most important person" she had ever known.

A Most Important Person

Margaret Weymouth Jackson

The old-fashioned high-bodied automobile drew up at the curbing at Fourth Street and the Boulevard, and the liveried [uniformed] chauffeur descended and opened the car door as grandly as though it were some new imported model carrying a queen. Miss Lucy Quinn hesitated with one gloved hand on the open car door and one small foot on the pavement. She looked as though she did not want to get out of the car, and the elderly chauffeur said quickly, kindly:

"Maybe you'd better not walk today, Miss Quinn. The wind is cold and it might snow again."

"Yes, Arthur, I must walk, thank you," Miss Quinn said firmly and stepped down onto the pavement.

It was her custom always to stop at this corner and walk the six blocks down the Boulevard and around the corner to her house on Maple Drive. She walked off now, her narrow back erect, the little hat bobbing on her smooth gray hair, and the chauffeur looked after her.

"It's the Christmas trimmings," he told himself. "She's that lonely."

It was true. It was Christmas and Miss Lucy Quinn was lonely. There was no one for whom she could make a Christmas. The rest of the year she endured her loneliness with composure, but at Christmas it came upon her like an illness.

"It's the way we were brought up," Miss Quinn told herself; and then, hastily: "Yet we had a happy childhood. Our parents were always good and kind to us."

But Miss Lucy and her sister Agatha had been brought up on the fixed idea that there was only a small group of people in the city with whom they might associate. The idea once planted, the years had done the rest. Miss Lucy's parents, loving though they were, had had to die. Miss Lucy's sister Agatha and her husband had died. All the friends of Miss Lucy's youth had either died or moved away or lost touch with her, until now there was no one left—no one at all near Miss Lucy. The society of the town moved briskly on without her, bristling with strange names.

There had been three delightful years when Miss Lucy's grandnephew, Agatha's only grandson, George, had lived in her house and studied at the university. He had been a quiet, studious young man, a true Quinn and a scholar, not much given to gaiety, but Miss Lucy had enjoyed him tremendously. Now he was studying in England; and in the casual manner of young males, he occasionally wrote to her.

There must be many interesting things one could do in a great city, Miss Lucy knew, but she did not know how to do them. The aloof manner imposed on her in her youth imprisoned her now like a suit of armor.

She was reflecting rather vaguely on these and wishing—almost—for a catastrophe that might hurl her out of her rut, when suddenly, it seemed right out of the pavement beneath her feet, a violent fight sprang up. Miss Lucy stopped and trembled. She did not like fighting at all, and this was nothing more than a brawl. Three small boys, two larger than the other, were fighting in deadly earnest, with the sounds like a dogfight which arise from small boys in battle. Miss Lucy looked at them horrified. The two big boys were beating and pounding the small one, and though he fought like a young wildcat, he was being overcome.

Miss Lucy looked all around. No one was near. No policeman was in sight. The horrible idea occurred to her that the little boy might be killed, right before her eyes. Briskly she raised her umbrella and brought it down smartly on first one pair of young shoulders and then the other. The bigger boys howled and departed as abruptly and inexplicably [incapable of being explained] as they had come, and the small boy stood, still braced for battle, still snorting through his nose, and looked at Miss Lucy.

Miss Lucy was very upset. She had never struck another human being in her life. She was completely demoralized [disheartened] and astonished, and she also felt a strange glow. She pulled herself together and resumed her walk. The small boy reached up and put his hand inside of hers and walked beside her. His hand was shaking a little and he was still breathing very hard. Miss Lucy looked down at him but went on

walking, and the small boy measured his step to hers and walked with her. They proceeded so to the very corner and the small boy drew a deep quivering breath and said:

"You saved me!"

Miss Lucy did not know what to say. She walked on across the street, holding the little hand firmly now, because of the traffic. In the next block her young friend, who had quite recovered, said to her again:

"You saved me! I have never been saved before."

Miss Lucy felt required to make some answer. "I'm glad," she told him, "glad I was there." And she found that she was very glad. He was such a dear little boy!

"I know how you feel," he answered eagerly. "I know just how you feel. I saved a cat once. I was awf'ly fond of it afterwards. "It wasn't much of a cat," he explained. "Its ears were chewed and it had fleas, but then—it liked me."

"Yes, indeed," said Miss Lucy. The little hand was now warm and safe and friendly in her own.

"I think you are a very good fighter for your size," Miss Lucy said, a little shyly.

"Yes," he agreed complacently, "I'm a good fighter. And I like to fight. But not two at once, and both so big."

"Little boys should not fight on the street," said Miss Lucy, but she did not say it severely, and he answered at once:

"I know. It is better to get in an alley, or somewheres where the cops or teachers won't stop you."

They had come unaccountably to her very door. Miss Lucy was amazed. The walk had never seemed so short. She stopped and explained, "I live here. This is my house."

The little boy looked at the house.

"I think that I'll come in and visit you awhile," he offered then. "I don't have to be home until dark, and I like to go visiting. I like to visit my friends."

"I always have tea when I come in from my walk," said Miss Lucy, who was ashamed that he had needed to invite himself. "Wouldn't you like to come in and have tea with me?"

"I don't care," he said, and they went up the steps and Mitzie, the grizzled parlormaid, opened the door for Miss Lucy.

Miss Lucy walked in proudly with her guest. "There will be two of us for tea, Mitzie," she said, and Mitzie said, "Yes, Ma'am," and helped Miss Lucy out of her coat and took the small boy's jacket and cap. Miss Lucy led him into the little parlor where she always sat. A coal fire was burning on the hearth. The brass coal scuttle [pail] and the brass fender [screen] were shining. He stood and looked all around. Miss Lucy felt suddenly proud of her parlor. It seemed to her it had never looked so nice. But the small boy said:

"Where is your Christmas tree?"

"Why," said Miss Lucy, "I haven't got it up yet."

"Oh," he said, and his face broke into a vivid smile, "I know! You are keeping it back for a surprise for someone. Will you have it up tomorrow? May I come to see it?"

"Yes," said Miss Lucy, "I will have the tree up tomorrow. I'll be glad if you will come to see it."

"I'll come early," he assured her. "I love Christmas trees. I'll bet I've seen every tree on our whole street and I'll bet that you will have the biggest tree and the best tree of all!"

Mitzie appeared with the tea tray and placed it on the low table before Miss Lucy. Cook had put a chocolate pot beside the silver teapot, and there was a plate with three great sugary buns on the usually Spartan tray. But they had made a mistake. A large kitchen cup and saucer stood on the tray. Miss Lucy picked them up and handed them to Mitzie with a stern glance.

"Bring me the delft-blue cup," she said. "The big one that my father used."

Mitzie turned red and took the cup without a word and brought back Miss Lucy's great treasure, her father's cup which held almost a pint. Miss Lucy filled it with chocolate and gave it to her guest, who placed it carefully on the edge of a small table. She gave him a

fringed napkin and passed the buns. He began at once to eat in a businesslike manner and with much pleasure.

"My mother says the lankest part of the day is between school's out and supper," he remarked.

Miss Lucy felt a vague disappointment. She didn't know why. "Oh, you have a mother?" she said.

The small boy looked astonished. *Whoever heard of anyone without a mother?* his look said. "Sure," he told her. "I have a mother and father and two brothers and two sisters, besides the baby."

"And the baby?" Miss Lucy asked.

"The baby is a girl," he said. "Her name is Marie. She's got blue eyes and she's bowlegged."

"Oh, I'm sorry," said Miss Lucy.

"It's on account of her temper'ment," the boy explained. "She has such a for'd [forward] temper'ment."

Miss Lucy put her cup down and looked at him. "I don't understand," she said.

"She does everything before she should," he answered. "She's that way. She wanted to sit up too soon, and now she is walking before she should and that makes her bowlegged. My mother says she doesn't know how she is going to cope with her, her being always so for'd."

"Oh," said Miss Lucy.

"Our baby is quite a care," he admitted.

"Now she is causing a lot of trouble because she is determined to eat things off the Christmas tree; and when she is determined, she is determined, and there's nothing anyone can do about it. She's a nice baby. You mustn't think we don't like her. I'm just telling you about her."

"I understand," Miss Lucy assured him. "She sounds like an interesting baby. But I shouldn't think Christmas-tree ornaments would be very good for her."

"They're not! But what does she care? They are pretty and she wants to eat them—that's the way she is."

"Wouldn't you like another bun?" said Miss Lucy.

He would. He said, eating it, "If you would like to see our baby—since you're so interested in her and everything—I could bring her over to see you. Not in the morning when I come to see the tree, but after lunch, I could bring her. I take her out every day. That's what the fight was about," he added, "because those guys think it is sissy to take the baby out. But my mother says family responsibility is not sissy."

Miss Lucy almost said she always took a nap after lunch, but she caught herself back in time. Her young guest was offering her a great favor, in showing her the baby. "I will be looking for you," she said. She rang the bell and Mitzie came and took the tray away and Miss Lucy said: "It is getting almost dark. You mustn't worry your mother. You haven't told me yet what your name is, or where you live."

"My name is Chester," he said, embarrassed, "Chester Chilton. My mother is smart but she admits herself that my name was a mistake, and my father thinks so too. However, what can they do about it now? But everyone calls me Chuck, so it isn't important, I guess. I live on Basalt-1028. On the third floor. It isn't far from here."

Miss Lucy went to the door with him. She knew where Basalt Street was. A crowded street, three blocks long, a half mile or so to the west of the Boulevard. "I have enjoyed your visit," she said, "and you must come again."

"I'm coming in the morning," he reminded her, "to see your Christmas tree. School's out so I can come early."

Miss Lucy closed the door gently after him and looked out through the glass and saw him hop down the stairs and light out for Basalt Street on the run. She returned to her fire. She rang the bell again.

"Please send Arthur to me," she said and in a moment the chauffeur stood in the door. "I want to go out again," Miss Lucy told him. "Are the shops still open? I want to buy a Christmas tree."

"I can get it for you, Miss Quinn," said Arthur.

But Miss Lucy thought to herself that one thing that made her so lonely was that she never did anything for herself, or for anyone else. She simply said, "Mitzie, do this," or "Cook, I want so and so—" She smiled, thinking what the child had said about family responsibilities. He would expect something pretty wonderful of her, in the way of a tree. She wanted to choose it herself!

It was very crowded and busy at the market. After some searching they found a tree that suited Miss Lucy. It filled up the back of the car and stuck out of the window and Miss Lucy had to ride with Arthur.

"We will have to go downtown for ornaments," she said. "There is a box of things in the attic, but I am sure there are not enough."

So they went to the dime store and Arthur went in with Miss Lucy. She was

almost crushed to death. White people and black ones jammed the aisles, and babies in their mothers' arms wailed or slept or gazed around at the great world. They bought boxes and boxes of ornaments.

"I need a gift for him too," Miss Lucy shouted at Arthur. Her hat was on one side of her head and she said in a firm, annoyed tone, "Please take your elbow out of my ribs," to a tall, thin man who tried to oblige her. "What do you buy," she shouted again, "for a seven-year-old who lives on Basalt and likes to fight, and for a girl baby who eats Christmas-tree ornaments?"

Arthur blinked a little. "I'd buy him boxing gloves," said Arthur, solemn as an owl. "And I'd buy her some of these candy canes."

So they left the car where it was and found a sporting goods store, and a candy store. When they got back to the car, they found that the tires were marked with chalk, and they had been given a ticket! Arthur took it out from under the windshield wiper. He was quite disconcerted.

"I've not had a ticket for years, Miss Quinn," he said.

"Never mind," said Miss Lucy, "We'll just pay the fine."

"They're getting very strict about traffic violations," explained Arthur, stowing packages away under the tree. "But if you'll call Mr. Henderson, ma'am."

"No," said Miss Lucy firmly, "I will pay the fine."

When they got home again, Mitzie ran out to help Arthur with all the packages, and Cook came to see what they had bought.

Miss Lucy was very excited. "We'll have dinner," she announced, "and then you will all have to help me with the tree. There are some boxes in the attic. But I am very hungry now."

"If you will tell me what you want, Miss Quinn," Mitzie said, when she served Miss Lucy, "I will get it from the attic."

"No," said Miss Lucy, "I want to get it. I know where the things are. The last time we had a tree in this house was when George was twelve years old, the year before my father died. I put the things away then."

When Miss Lucy went up to the attic, Arthur and Cook and Mitzie all followed her. The attic was in perfect order. Miss Lucy found the box just where she had expected to find it and Mitzie helped Arthur carry it down.

Cook looked around. "My, wouldn't a lively young one have a time up here," said Cook, "dressing up in these old clothes and parading around?"

"Yes," said Miss Lucy. "I'm sure I don't know why I have saved all this junk. It is no good to anyone."

Cook followed Miss Lucy down, talking a blue streak. They discussed the position of the tree, and had some trouble making it stand up straight. Arthur had to take his coat off and go down to the basement and hammer and pound until he contrived a sturdy base. At last the tree was in place and Cook brought the ladder they used for window washing, and they began to trim the tree.

Miss Lucy wanted the same old angel on the top of the tree they had had when she was a child.

"It is faded," she said, "but it is like Chester's cat—it is mine," and she told them about the cat. "You mustn't put anything near the bottom that the baby might eat," said Miss Lucy and she told them about the baby who was determined to eat Christmas-tree things, and when she was determined, she was determined!

Cook knew a child that had done the same thing and Arthur said, "I had a cat when I was a lad that simply went wild over a Christmas tree—simply wild. Once he got so excited he sprang right into the middle of the tree—just lost all reason!"

Mitzie got the giggles at this, and Miss Lucy laughed aloud. They worked very hard and by nine o'clock there the tree stood, covered with gorgeous bright balls and silver icicles, and strung with lights, with candy canes on the lower branches for the baby.

Miss Lucy had to sit down and admire it, and she could not hear enough praise from the others. She was so tired she was no sooner in bed than asleep and she slept so soundly that Mitzie had to waken her.

"The young gentleman is here," Mitzie explained. "I thought you would want to see him."

Miss Lucy got downstairs in a hurry. Chester was standing in the middle of the parlor staring at the tree with round excited eyes.

"I knew it!" he said, when he saw her. "I told my mother you would have the best tree of anyone. I told her, 'That's the way she is!'"

Miss Lucy glowed with pride. "I haven't had my breakfast," she said. "Wouldn't you like to eat with me?" That was one thing she remembered—George could always eat, when he was little.

Chester said politely, "I will be glad to keep you company," and Mitzie put a plate on the dining-room table for him.

But before they had finished with breakfast Mitzie summoned her mistress to the door, and Chester followed her. There was a policeman with a summons. Miss Lucy had to appear in the police court at ten o'clock.

"Have you been arrested?" Chester asked with eager interest.

"Yes," said Miss Lucy, bragging about it, and she explained: "We got a ticket, Arthur and I, for parking too long on Front Street."

The last fine touch of glamor had been added to Miss Lucy. Her young friend looked at her with shining eyes. "Will you have to go to jail?" he said hopefully. "I will come and visit you if you do."

"No," said Miss Lucy, "I am afraid they will not imprison me. I will be home before you get here with the baby."

Chester offered to ride down to the courthouse with them, but Miss Lucy dropped him off at his own door. The police court was crowded. Arthur stood very stiff and severe beside Miss Lucy. They had to wait their turn. The judge was cross. He was scolding and fining everyone. A young man at a table near the judge's bench nudged another young man and they watched Miss Lucy when she came forward to answer the complaint.

"Miss Lucy Quinn," said the judge. "Parking on Front Street for forty-five minutes, between five and six." He looked over his glasses. "You are certainly the last person I expected to see in this court, Miss Lucy."

"Yes, Your Honor—yes, Judge Hennesy."

The judge turned to Arthur. "You are Miss Quinn's chauffeur?" he demanded.

"Yes sir."

"Don't you know the traffic rules?"

"Yes sir."

"It was my fault," said Miss Quinn. "I was buying a Christmas tree and boxing gloves and candy—you see, the child thinks things on the tree are to eat. The dime store was crowded, and it took us a long time. I will pay my fine."

"Seven dollars and costs," said the judge. "And I want to speak to you in my chambers."

Miss Lucy paid her fine to the clerk, and went into the judge's little room. When the door closed he shook hands with her, his blue eyes twinkling.

"So you have a Christmas tree, Miss Lucy?" he said. "My wife and I were speaking about you the other day. We haven't seen you for years."

"Why don't you come to call on me, and see my tree?" said Miss Lucy Quinn. "I will leave it up until the New Year."

"We'll do it. We will come to see you some time next week, Miss Lucy."

When they reached home Miss Lucy got out of the car and looked at their front door. "We ought to have a wreath on our door, Arthur—a big one, with a great red bow of ribbon on it. Everyone has a wreath on the front door." So she got back into the car and they went and bought a wreath for the door.

Inside, Miss Lucy was surprised to see that there were packages tucked under the tree, and she went up to her room and got the gifts she had purchased for Mitzie and Cook and Arthur and put them under the tree. She was a little late for luncheon, but it seemed the servants did not mind anything today.

Chester arrived with the baby tied securely into a small cart, and he untied her and carried her up the stairs, staggering a little. Mitzie ran to help him and Miss Lucy stood in the door. When Mitzie had unwrapped the baby from her blankets and taken off her bonnet and coat, there she stood, no bigger than a minute, with bright red cheeks and bright blue eyes and silky-soft fair hair.

The baby put her arms up to Miss Lucy. "Up!" she said, and Miss Lucy lifted her uncertainly. They went into the parlor and Miss Lucy sat down with the baby in her lap. But the baby gave a great lunge at sight of the tree and almost leaped out of Miss Lucy's arms. Miss Lucy gave a cry and clutched the infant firmly.

"She wants down," explained Chester, and Miss Lucy put the baby on the floor. She went on her active small legs, which were undeniably a little bowed, straight for the tree and grabbed one of the candy canes and stuffed it in her mouth and looked around with a defiant "come-and-get-it" air. Cook and Arthur hovered in the doorway, smiling and murmuring.

Chester's visit was a great success. Marie was an altogether delightful small person, noisy and gay and not afraid of anyone or anything in the world. She got into the desk and into the bookcase, and the magazine stand and the bric-a-brac. She was quick as a flash and curious as a monkey. It took both Cook and Mitzie to regulate her. But a delicate sense of loyalty prevented Miss Lucy from becoming too enamored of the baby. She made Chester her special guest and responsibility. She told him

about the police court, and about Judge Hennesy, who had been the policeman on this very beat when they were both young. He had married their upstairs girl, as pretty a girl as ever came from the country to work in town. Then he had studied law and he had become a lawyer and a politician and now he was a judge!

"And a very fine judge too," Miss Lucy said, who knew nothing at all of what kind of judge he was.

"I am going to be a pilot," Chester told her and they talked about that.

Finally the baby began to rub her eyes and cry, and Arthur took Marie and Chester home in the car with the little cart strapped onto the trunk! Miss Lucy toiled upstairs to her nap. She was as sleepy as Marie. When she came downstairs again, the evening paper was lying on the table near her chair by the fireplace and the tree was blazing with lights. Miss Lucy felt very happy.

She opened the paper and there on the first page was a candid-camera picture of Miss Lucy and Judge Hennesy! "Society Leader in Traffic Court" the legend ran. Miss Lucy blushed bright red, and then looked at the picture critically. It was really quite good. She was looking very pert, and Judge Hennesy was leaning down with his mouth open, and Arthur looked like an undertaker!

Miss Lucy read the story through twice. It was most absurd. It told a great deal about her family, about her position as "titular [nominal] head of local Society," and went on about how simple everything would be when people stepped up and paid their fines instead of using their influence to get stickers "fixed." While Miss Lucy was reading the story the third time the telephone rang for her. It was old Mr. Henderson, for many years the family lawyer. He said, quite excited, that Miss Lucy should have called him and he would have taken care of the ticket for her, or at least taken care of the fine without her appearing in court. She must always let him know—

"It was no trouble at all," said Miss Lucy.

She asked after Mr. Henderson's health, and his wife's health.

"We are quite well," said Mr. Henderson.

Before she knew it she had agreed to go to Hendersons' to dinner the following Tuesday.

Before she had finished her dinner, she was called again. It was her sister Agatha's husband's niece, Mrs. Morrison.

"We wondered, Miss Lucy, if you would not like to go to the community Christmas tree, at the Settlement House. We will call for you and take you home again, if you would go, as a favor to the committee."

Miss Lucy almost refused, and then she remembered that Chester had seen every tree on his block, and that Agatha's husband's family had given a great deal of money to the Settlement House. Miss Lucy was far too excited to eat any more dinner. But she was ready when Mrs. Morrison came for her.

There was an enormous tree at the Settlement House, and there were swarms of children from the ghetto. Miss Lucy was quite confused; but after she had recovered herself sufficiently to watch the games being played on the floor, she decided it was the lights in the great dark room which confused her.

"Something should be done about these lights," she told Mrs. Morrison. "And the room shouldn't be brown— it is such a dreary, sad color. Couldn't the room be painted cream—or even pink? And couldn't the lights be softer?"

Mrs. Morrison explained that this was the gymnasium and it got very dirty, and there was never enough money for decorating and lighting the place—there were so many needs.

"If you could come to a committee meeting," she suggested, "if you feel strong enough—you would see what our problems are."

"I am perfectly well," Miss Lucy told her tartly. "There isn't a thing the matter with me. And I will come to your committee meeting. There," she said, pointing down at a shy child, smitten with stage fright, trying to hide behind an older brother, "there is your real problem—people shouldn't be allowed to grow up to be shy."

Mrs. Morrison agreed, but Miss Lucy did not listen to what they were saying about child psychology. It had come to Miss Lucy that the problems were always the same; people had the same things to overcome, wherever they lived! And she grew suddenly warmly interested in what they were trying to do for all these children. If she worked on this committee, they would have to listen to her.

When she reached home, Arthur and Cook and Mitzie were all waiting up, to see that their mistress got home safely and safely to bed. Miss Lucy was quite touched.

"I am going to be going out a good deal," she scolded them, "and you must not begin waiting up for me."

In the morning they gathered around the tree, Arthur and Cook and Mitzie and Miss Lucy, and opened their gifts. Miss Lucy was exceedingly gratified at the little things her old servants had given her. And she was even more gratified at the things she had given them, and their pleasure in them! And there, under the tree, was a grimy little package, labeled, "To Miss Quinn from her friend Chuck." Miss Lucy opened it with brimming eyes. It was a string of glass beads with a huge brass clasp.

When she went out for her drive that afternoon, Arthur took her to Basalt Street, and delivered the boxing gloves for Chester, and a bright ball for Marie. Chester came down to the car to see Miss Lucy and they took him for a short ride. He chattered all the way, and Miss Lucy was very much surprised to find

that she had invited him and his brothers and sisters and a few friends, if he liked, to come to her house to an attic party the next week.

Chester was vivid with excitement, and he asked her, in a whisper, to park in the street for a minute, so that all the "kids" could see her.

Miss Lucy sat parked while Chester went and got some of his friends. They were clean, rosy children. The street, though crowded, was not a slum, and the other children, like Chester, looked healthy and well cared for. And Miss Lucy did not know that the ancient high-bodied car was a great curiosity to the children.

But she felt dissatisfied to go home and eat the small turkey Cook had prepared for Christmas dinner, all by herself. For two years George had had a young friend of his in for Christmas dinner, a young professor who had no family.

"But he wouldn't want to eat with an old woman like me," Miss Lucy thought. And then she remembered how Chester had invited himself visiting, remembered the baby who could not wait until time to taste of life, and she was ashamed. She spoke to Arthur. "Do you know where Professor Tilden lives?" She asked him. "The young man George had for dinner last Christmas."

"Yes, Miss Quinn," said Arthur. "He lives near the university."

So they drove there, and Arthur went into Professor Tilden's boarding house and found him sitting alone over his book. He came down to the car. He would be delighted to have dinner with Miss Quinn.

"How kind you are to remember me," he said.

He was a very shy young man. And all through the formal dinner he and Miss Quinn talked about poetry. And later by the fire he said to her:

"I wonder if you would be kind enough to come to visit the Shelley Club? We have some gifted young people, trying to write verse. You are so gracious and kind—you might be a great help to them, and I think you would enjoy it."

Miss Lucy said she had got out of touch with the university since her father died.

"But he was a regent [board member] for years," Professor Tilden objected. "You ought to know what we are doing out there."

When Professor Tilden had gone home, Miss Lucy sat by the fire looking at the Christmas tree and thinking about Chester.

"What a dear little boy he is," she thought, and then she stared, amazed at all that had happened to her in the last two days. Since she had lifted her umbrella to Chester's adversaries all her life had changed. She decided soberly, "I am seventy years old, and he is the most important person I ever knew—and Christmas the most important time."

Reading Check

1. Why is Miss Lucy lonely?
2. How does she meet Chester?
3. List some things Chester likes about Miss Lucy.
4. List some things Miss Lucy likes about Chester.
5. Why does Miss Lucy call Chester "the most important person" she has ever known?

"I desire to so conduct my affairs that if, in the end, I have lost every other friend, I shall at least have one friend left—that friend shall be down inside me" (Abraham Lincoln).

After Twenty Years

O. Henry

The policeman on the beat moved up the avenue impressively. The impressiveness was habitual and not for show, for spectators were few. The time was barely ten o'clock at night, but chilly gusts of wind with a taste of rain in them had well nigh depeopled the streets.

Trying doors as he went, twirling his club with many intricate and artful movements, turning now and then to cast his watchful eye adown the pacific thoroughfare, the officer, with his stalwart [robust] form and slight swagger, made a fine picture of a guardian of the peace. The vicinity was one that kept early hours. Now and then you might see the lights of a cigar store or of an all-night lunch counter; but the majority of the doors belonged to business places that had long since been closed.

When about midway of a certain block the policeman suddenly slowed his walk. In the doorway of a darkened hardware store a man leaned, with an unlighted cigar in his mouth. As the policeman walked up to him, the man spoke up quickly.

"It's all right, officer," he said, reassuringly. "I'm just waiting for a friend. It's an appointment made twenty years ago. Sounds a little funny to you, doesn't it? Well, I'll explain if you'd like to make certain it's all straight. About that long ago there used to be a restaurant where this store stands—'Big Joe' Brady's restaurant."

"Until five years ago," said the policeman. "It was torn down then."

The man in the doorway struck a match and lit his cigar. The light showed a pale, square-jawed face with keen eyes, and a little white scar near his right eyebrow. His scarfpin was a large diamond, oddly set.

"Twenty years ago tonight," said the man, "I dined here at 'Big Joe' Brady's with Jimmy Wells, my best chum, and the finest chap in the world. He and I were raised here in New York, just like two brothers, together. I was eighteen and Jimmy was twenty. The next morning I was to start for the West to make my fortune. You couldn't have dragged Jimmy out of New York; he thought it was the only place on earth. Well, we agreed that night that we would meet here again in exactly twenty years from that date and time, no matter what our conditions might be or from what distance we might have to come. We figured that in twenty years each of us

You see, the West is a pretty big proposition, and I kept hustling around over it pretty lively. But I know Jimmy will meet me here if he's alive, for he always was the truest, staunchest old chap in the world. He'll never forget. I came a thousand miles to stand in this door tonight, and it's worth it if my old partner turns up."

The waiting man pulled out a handsome watch, the lids of it set with small diamonds.

"Three minutes to ten," he announced. "It was exactly ten o'clock when we parted here at the restaurant door."

"Did pretty well out West, didn't you?" asked the policeman.

"You bet! I hope Jimmy has done half as well. He was a kind of plodder, though, good fellow as he was. I've had to compete with some of the sharpest wits going to get my pile. A man gets in a groove in New York. It takes the West to put a razor-edge on him."

The policeman twirled his club and took a step or two. "I'll be on my way. Hope your friend comes around all right. Going to call time on him sharp?"

"I should say not!" said the other. "I'll give him half an hour at least. If Jimmy is alive on earth, he'll be here by that time. So long, officer."

"Good night, sir," said the policeman, passing on along his beat, trying doors as he went.

There was now a fine, cold drizzle falling, and the wind had risen from its uncertain puffs into a steady blow. The few foot passengers astir in that quarter hurried dismally and silently along with coat collars turned high and pocketed hands. And in the door of the hardware

ought to have our destiny worked out and our fortunes made, whatever they were going to be."

"It sounds pretty interesting," said the policeman. "Rather a long time between meets, though, it seems to me. Haven't you heard from your friend since you left?"

"Well, yes, for a time we corresponded," said the other. "But after a year or two we lost track of each other.

store the man who had come a thousand miles to fill an appointment, uncertain almost to absurdity, with the friend of his youth, smoked his cigar and waited.

About twenty minutes he waited, and then a tall man in a long overcoat, with collar turned up to his ears, hurried across from the opposite side of the street. He went directly to the waiting man.

"Is that you, Bob?" he asked, doubtfully.

"Is that you, Jimmy Wells?" cried the man in the door.

"Bless my heart!" exclaimed the new arrival, grasping both the other's hands with his own. "It's Bob, sure as fate. I was certain I'd find you here if you were still in existence. Well, well, well! Twenty years is a long time. The old restaurant's gone, Bob; I wish it had lasted, so we could have had another dinner there. How has the West treated you, old man?"

"Bully; it has given me everything I asked it for. You've changed lots, Jimmy. I never thought you were so tall by two or three inches."

"Oh, I grew a bit after I was twenty."

"Doing well in New York, Jimmy?"

"Moderately. I have a position in one of the city departments. Come on, Bob; we'll go around to a place I know of, and have a good long talk about old times."

The two men started up the street, arm in arm. The man from the West, his egotism enlarged by success, was beginning to outline the history of his career. The other, submerged in his overcoat, listened with interest.

At the corner stood a drugstore, brilliant with electric lights. When they came into this glare, each of them turned simultaneously to gaze upon the other's face.

The man from the West stopped suddenly and released his arm.

"You're not Jimmy Wells," he snapped. "Twenty years is a long time, but not long enough to change a man's nose from a Roman to a pug."

"It sometimes changes a good man into a bad one," said the tall man. "You've been under arrest for ten minutes, 'silky' Bob. Chicago thinks you may have dropped over our way and wires us she wants to have a chat with you. Going quietly, are you? That's sensible. Now, before we go to the station, here's a note I was asked to hand to you. You may read it here at the window. It's from Patrolman Wells."

The man from the West unfolded the little piece of paper handed him. His hand was steady when he began to read, but it trembled a little by the time he had finished. The note was rather short.

Bob: I was at the appointed place on time. When you struck the match to light your cigar, I saw it was the face of the man wanted in Chicago. Somehow I couldn't do it myself, so I went around and got a plainclothesman to do the job. JIMMY

Reading Check

1. How does the author describe Bob?
2. What does this description reveal about Bob's character?
3. How does Bob describe his friend, Jimmy?
4. Does Jimmy meet Bob?
5. How does the opening quotation by Abraham Lincoln apply to the story?

*Greater love hath no man
than this, that he lay down
his life for his friends.*

(John 15:13)

Isaiah 53

Who hath believed our report? and to whom is the arm of the Lord revealed?

For he shall grow up before him as a tender plant, and as a root out of a dry ground: he hath no form nor comeliness; and when we shall see him, there is no beauty that we should desire him.

He is despised and rejected of men; a man of sorrows, and acquainted with grief: and we hid as it were our faces from him; he was despised, and we esteemed him not.

Surely he hath borne our griefs, and carried our sorrows: yet we did esteem him stricken, smitten of God, and afflicted.

But he was wounded for our transgressions, he was bruised for our iniquities: the chastisement of our peace was upon him; and with his stripes we are healed.

All we like sheep have gone astray; we have turned every one to his own way; and the Lord hath laid on him the iniquity of us all.

He was oppressed, and he was afflicted, yet he opened not his mouth: he is brought as a lamb to the slaughter, and as a sheep before her shearers is dumb, so he openeth not his mouth.

He was taken from prison and from judgment: and who shall declare his generation? for he was cut off out of the land of the living: for the transgression of my people was he stricken.

And he made his grave with the wicked, and with the rich in his death; because he had done no violence, neither was any deceit in his mouth.

Yet it pleased the Lord to bruise him; he hath put him to grief: when thou shalt make his soul an offering for sin, he shall see his seed, he shall prolong his days, and the pleasure of the Lord shall prosper in his hand.

He shall see of the travail of his soul, and shall be satisfied: by his knowledge shall my righteous servant justify many; for he shall bear their iniquities.

Therefore will I divide him a portion with the great, and he shall divide the spoil with the strong; because he hath poured out his soul unto death: and he was numbered with the transgressors; and he bare the sin of many, and made intercession for the transgressors.

What a Friend We Have in Jesus

Joseph Scriven

What a Friend we have in Jesus,
All our sins and griefs to bear!
What a privilege to carry
Everything to God in prayer!
O what peace we often forfeit,
O what needless pain we bear,
All because we do not carry
Everything to God in prayer!

Have we trials and temptations?
Is there trouble anywhere?
We should never be discouraged,
Take it to the Lord in prayer.

Can we find a friend so faithful
Who will all our sorrows share?
Jesus knows our every weakness,
Take it to the Lord in prayer.

Are we weak and heavy laden,
Cumbered with a load of care?
Precious Savior, still our refuge
Take it to the Lord in prayer.
Do thy friends despise, forsake thee?
Take it to the Lord in prayer;
In His arms He'll take and shield thee,
Thou wilt find a solace there.

DAVID AND JONATHAN

And as David returned from the slaughter of the Philistine [Goliath], Abner took him, and brought him before Saul with the head of the Philistine in his hand.

And Saul said to him, Whose son art thou, thou young man? And David answered, I am the son of thy servant Jesse the Bethlehemite.

And it came to pass, when he had made an end of speaking unto Saul, that the soul of Jonathan was knit with the soul of David, and Jonathan loved him as his own soul.

And Saul took him that day, and would let him go no more home to his father's house.

Then Jonathan and David made a covenant, because he loved him as his own soul.

And David went out withersoever Saul sent him, and behaved himself wisely: and Saul set him over the men of war, and he was accepted in the sight of all the people, and also in the sight of Saul's servants.

Wherefore when Saul saw that he behaved himself very wisely, he was afraid of him.

But all Israel and Judah loved David, because he went out and came in before them.

(I Samuel 17:57, 58; 18:1-3, 5, 15-16)

And Saul spake to Jonathan his son, and to all his servants, that they should kill David.

But Jonathan Saul's son delighted much in David: and Jonathan told David saying, Saul my father seeketh to kill thee: now therefore, I pray thee, take heed to thyself until the morning, and abide in a secret place, and hide thyself:

And I will go out and stand beside my father in the field where thou art, and I will commune with my father of thee; and what I see, that I will tell thee.

And Jonathan spake good of David unto Saul his father, and said unto him, Let not the king sin against his servant, against David; because he hath not sinned against thee, and because his works have been to thee-ward very good.

For he did put his life in his hand, and slew the Philistine, and the Lord wrought a great salvation for all Israel: thou sawest it, and didst rejoice: wherefore then wilt thou sin against innocent blood, to slay David without a cause.

And Saul hearkened unto the voice of Jonathan: and Saul sware, As the Lord liveth, he shall not be slain.

And Jonathan called David, and Jonathan shewed him all those things. And Jonathan brought David to Saul, and he was in his presence, as in times past.

And there was war again: and David went out, and fought with the Philistines, and slew them with a great slaughter; and they fled from him.

And the evil spirit from the Lord was upon Saul, as he sat in his house with his javelin in his hand: and David played with his hand [on the harp].

And Saul sought to smite David even to the wall with the javelin; but he slipped away out of Saul's presence, and he smote the javelin into the wall: and David fled, and escaped that night.

(I Samuel 19:1-10)

And Jonathan Saul's son arose, and went to David into the wood, and strengthened his hand in God.

And he said unto him, Fear not: for the hand of Saul my father shall not find thee; and thou shalt be king over Israel, and I shall be next unto thee; and that also Saul my father knoweth.

And they two made a covenant before the Lord: and David abode in the wood, and Jonathan went to his house.

(I Samuel 23:16-18)

Now the Philistines fought against Israel: and the men of Israel fled from before the Philistines, and fell down slain in mount Gilboa.

And the Philistines followed hard upon Saul and upon his sons; and the Philistines slew Jonathan, and Abinadab, and Melchishua, Saul's sons.

And the battle went sore against Saul, and the archers hit him; and he was sore wounded of the archers.

Then said Saul unto his armourbearer, Draw thy sword, and thrust me through therewith; lest these uncircumcised come and thrust me through, and abuse me. But his armourbearer would not; for he was sore afraid. Therefore Saul took a sword, and fell upon it.

And when his armourbearer saw that Saul was dead, he fell likewise upon his sword, and died with him.

So Saul died, and his three sons, and his armourbearer, and all his men, that same day together.

(I Samuel 31:1-6)

And David lamented with this lamentation over Saul and over Jonathan his son:
The beauty of Israel is slain upon thy high places: how are the mighty fallen!
Saul and Jonathan were lovely and pleasant in their lives, and in their death they were not divided: they were swifter than eagles, they were stronger than lions.
How are the mighty fallen in the midst of the battle! O Jonathan, thou wast slain in thine high places.

(II Samuel 1:17, 19, 23, 25)

And David said, Is there yet any that is left of the house of Saul, that I may show him kindness for Jonathan's sake?
And there was of the house of Saul a servant whose name was Ziba. And when they had called him unto David, the king said unto him, Art thou Ziba? And he said, Thy servant is he.
And the king said, Is there not yet any of the house of Saul, that I may shew the kindness of God unto him? And Ziba said unto the king, Jonathan hath yet a son, which is lame on his feet.
And the king said unto him, Where is he? And Ziba said unto the king, Behold he is in the house of Machir, the son of Ammiel, in Lodebar.
Then king David sent, and fetched him out of the house of Machir, the son of Ammiel, from Lodebar.
Now when Mephibosheth, the son of Jonathan, the son of Saul, was come unto David, he fell on his face, and did reverence. And David said, Mephibosheth. And he answered, Behold thy servant!
And David said unto him, Fear not: for I will surely shew thee kindness for Jonathan thy father's sake, and will restore thee all the land of Saul thy father [grandfather]; and thou shalt eat bread at my table continually.
So Mephibosheth dwelt in Jerusalem: for he did eat continually at the king's table; and he was lame on both his feet.

(II Samuel 9:1-7, 13)

Viewpoints

Now Peter sat without in the palace: and a damsel came unto him, saying, Thou also wast with Jesus of Galilee. But he denied before them all, saying, I know not what thou sayest. And when he was gone out into the porch, another maid saw him, and said unto them that were there, This fellow was also with Jesus of Nazareth. And again he denied with an oath, I do not know the man. And after a while came unto him they that stood by, and said to Peter, Surely thou also art one of them; for thy speech bewrayeth thee. Then began he to curse and to swear, saying, I know not the man. And immediately the cock crew. And Peter remembered the word of Jesus, which said unto him, Before the cock crow, thou shalt deny me thrice. And he went out, and wept bitterly.
(Matthew 26:69-75)

Only a few short hours before, Peter had been with the Lord at the Passover feast, boldly and sincerely declaring, "Though all men shall be offended because of thee, yet will I never be offended" (Matthew 26:31). Why did Peter, the first disciple to proclaim "Thou art the Christ," deny the Saviour? Peter's statement at the Passover gives us a clue that his viewpoint was not what it should have been. Peter was focusing on self rather than on Christ.

Unfortunately Peter's sad experience is not unique. An improper viewpoint has caused many of Christ's followers to wander from the right path "to tread upon forbidden ground." And as Peter, they have always found the consequences of such wanderings painful.

Yet, this painful experience proved to be a milestone in Peter's life; for, following this denial, he confessed his sin and became the courageous, immovable servant he imagined himself to be before his fall. The book of Acts is a testimony to Peter's change in viewpoint. Failure had taught him his total dependence on Jesus Christ, not just for salvation, but also for the grace needed to walk the right path.

You need not, however, suffer this same kind of defeat if you learn by such examples to keep your focus right. But how can you determine if you are viewing things correctly? Carefully examine yourself. If your viewpoint is not as it should be, your behavior will betray an overemphasis on self, others, or things.

To help you better understand this principle, let's look briefly at this unit's stories. In the characters of Katrin and Paul, you will see clearly the results of an overemphasis on self. In the first unit story "Mama and the Graduation Present," Katrin views her world from a totally selfish perspective. She is absorbed with her own importance and the importance of the events that affect her personally. This pride blinds her to the needs and desires of others.

In the second story "Wolves of Fear," you will see the problem of self take on a different form. Paul, the central character, is consumed with feelings of inadequacy, and he views every situation from this vantage point. It is fear, rather than pride, that paralyzes him. In both stories, however, it is this overemphasis on "I" that renders the characters powerless to see or meet the needs of others.

This concern with self also produces a second problem: the problem of an overemphasis on others' opinions. In both Paul's and Katrin's stories, this problem is a logical outgrowth of pride and fear, for both of these viewpoints eventually drive a person to desire too much the approval of others.

A striking example of this truth is recorded for us in I Samuel. Throughout Saul's life he wavered between fear and pride, and a study of his life will show you the consequences of such instability. But let's look at one specific example. In I Samuel 15, Saul was commanded by the prophet Samuel to destroy utterly the Amalekites. Saul did destroy *most* of the Amalekite people, but he spared King Agag and preserved the best livestock of the enemy. Hearing of Saul's disobedience, Samuel rose early, went to Saul, and boldly accused him of rejecting God's command. Initially Saul lied. But when he could no longer conceal his sin, he excused himself by saying, "I have transgressed the commandment of the Lord, and thy words: *because I feared the people, and obeyed their voice*" (I Samuel 15:24). Samuel, however, would accept no such excuse. He declared, "The Lord hath rent the kingdom of Israel from thee this day, and hath given it to a neighbor of thine, that is better than thou" (I Samuel 15:28). Saul's disobedience, which was an outgrowth of fear and of a desire to gain approval from others, cost him God's continued blessing.

Besides an overemphasis on self and others, an overemphasis on things will also render your influence ineffective. The story of the crotchety old Scrooge is an excellent illustration of this truth. In *A Christmas Carol* Scrooge views the world as a shrine for his idol of gold. This perspective blinds him to what is truly valuable. Only after his unnerving experience with the three Christmas spirits does Scrooge consent to relinquish his idol.

Though few of us are of the same disposition as Scrooge, many of us are as reluctant to change our viewpoints. Stop and consider for a moment. What does your behavior reveal about you to others?

Do your actions show others that you view the world as a shrine for your idols of self, others, or things? If so, turn your focus to Christ that He may restore you to the right path. "Seek ye first the kingdom of God and his righteousness" (Matthew 6:33a), that as the penitent Peter you may become a truly courageous, immovable servant of God.

Out of the way we went, and then we found
What 'twas to tread upon forbidden ground;
And let them that come after have a care,
Lest heedlessness makes them as we to fare,
Lest they for trespassing his prisoners are,
Whose castle's Doubting, whose name's Despair.

The past months had proven very difficult financially. But now that Papa was home from the hospital, and the new boarders were happily settled, finances were bound to improve. Everyone in the family was feeling genuinely grateful—everyone except Katrin.

Mama and the Graduation Present

Kathryn Forbes

During the last week that Papa was in the hospital, we rented the big downstairs bedroom to two brothers, Mr. Sam and Mr. George Stanton.

The Stantons worked in the office of the Gas and Electric Company, and they paid a whole month's rent in advance, which was a very good thing

for us. They were nice young men, and after dinner every night they would come out to the kitchen to tell Mama how much they enjoyed her cooking.

After they got better acquainted with Miss Durant, they teased her about her "rabbit food" and made bets with each other as to which of them would be the

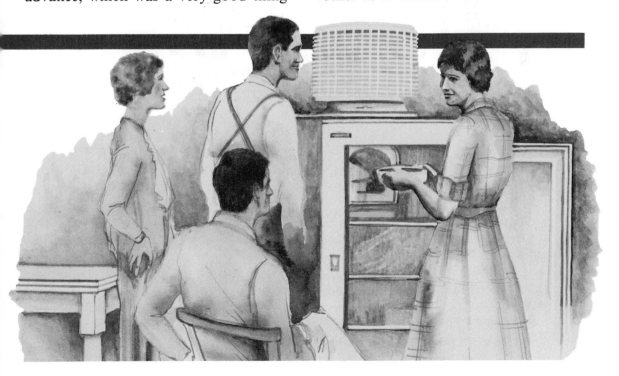

first to coax her to eat a big, thick steak—medium rare.

Mama was very proud of her three boarders; she listened to their chattering and laughter and said it was going to be fine when we had the hospital bills paid up and the money back to the Aunts. Then we would get more furniture and more boarders. Enough to fill all the chairs in the dining room. The Stanton brothers said they knew two more men from their place who would like to board with us.

On the day that Papa came home from the hospital, it was like a big party. We all stayed home from school, and Mama let Dagmar decorate the table real fancy.

Everything seemed all right again when Papa walked carefully into the kitchen and sat down in the rocking chair. His face was white, and he looked thinner, but his smile was just the same.

He had a bandage on his head, and he made little jokes about how they shaved off his hair when he wasn't looking.

It was strange, having Papa about the house during the day, but it was nice, too. He would be there in the kitchen when I came home from school, and I would tell him all that had happened.

Winford School had become the most important thing in life to me. I was friendly with the girls, and Carmelita and I were invited to all their parties. Every other Wednesday they came to my house, and we would sit up in my attic, drink chocolate, eat cookies, and make plans about our graduation.

We discussed "High" [high school] and vowed that we would stay together all through the next four years. We were the only ones in our class going on to Lowell. Lowell, we told each other loftily, was "academic."

We were enthralled with our superiority. We were going to be the first class at Winford to have evening graduation exercises; we were having a graduation play; and we were making our own graduation dresses in sewing class.

And when I was given the second lead in the play—the part of the Grecian boy—I found my own great importance hard to bear. I alone, of all the girls, had to go downtown to the costumer's to rent a wig. A coarse black wig that smelled of disinfectant, but made me feel like Geraldine Farrar. At every opportunity, I would put it on and have Papa listen to my part of the play.

Then the girls started talking about their graduation presents.

Madeline said she was getting an onyx ring with a small diamond. Hester was getting a real honest-to-goodness wrist watch, and Thyra's family was going to add seven pearls to the necklace they had started for her when she was a baby. Even Carmelita was getting something special; her sister Rose was putting a dollar every payday into an ivory manicure set.

I was intrigued, and wondered what great surprise my family had in store for me. I talked about it endlessly, hoping for some clue. It would be terrible if my present weren't as nice as the rest.

"It is the custom, then," Mama asked, "the giving of gifts when one graduates?"

"My goodness, Mama," I said, "it's practically the most important time there is in a girl's life—when she graduates."

I had seen a beautiful pink celluloid dresser set at Mr. Schiller's drugstore, and I set my heart upon it. I dropped hint after hint, until Nels took me aside and reminded me that we did not have money for that sort of thing. Had I forgotten that the Aunts and the hospital must be paid up? That just as soon as Papa was well enough, he must do the Beauchamp job for no pay?

"I don't care," I cried recklessly, "I must have a graduation present. Why, Nels, think how I will feel if I don't get any. When the girls ask me—"

Nels got impatient and said he thought I was turning into a spoiled brat. And I retorted that since he was a boy, he naturally couldn't be expected to understand.

When Mama and I were alone one day, she asked me how I would like her silver brooch for a graduation present. Mama thought a lot of that brooch— it had been her mother's.

"Mama," I said reasonably, "what in the world would I want an old brooch for?"

"It would be like an—an heirloom, Katrin. It was your grandmother's."

"No, thank you, Mama."

"I could polish it up, Katrin."

I shook my head. "Look, Mama, a graduation present is something like— well, it's like that beautiful dresser set in Mr. Schiller's window."

There, now, I had told. Surely, with such a hint—

Mama looked worried, but she didn't say anything. Just pinned the silver brooch back on her dress

I was so sure that Mama would find some way to get me the dresser set, I bragged to the girls as if it were a sure thing. I even took them by Schiller's window to admire it. They agreed with me that it was wonderful. There was a comb, a clothesbrush, and even something called a "hair receiver."

Graduation night was a flurry of excitement.

I didn't forget a single word of my part in the play. Flushed and triumphant, I heard Miss Scanlon say that I was every bit as good as Hester, who had taken elocution [art of speaking which emphasizes gesture, manner, and delivery] lessons for years. And when I went up to the platform for my diploma, the applause for me was long and loud. Of course, the Aunts and Uncles were all there, and Uncle Ole and Uncle Peter could clap very loud, but I pretended that it was because I was so popular.

And when I got home—there was the pink celluloid dresser set!

Mama and Papa beamed at my delight, but Nels and Christine, I noticed, didn't say anything. I decided that they were jealous, and felt sorry that they would not join me in my joy.

I carried the box up to my attic and placed the comb and brush carefully on my dresser. It took me a long while to arrange everything to my satisfaction. The mirror, so. The pinchushion, here. The hair receiver, there.

Mama let me sleep late the next morning. When I got down for breakfast, she had already gone downtown

to do her shopping. Nels was reading the want-ad section of the paper. Since it was vacation, he was going to try to get a job. He read the jobs aloud to Papa, and they discussed each one.

After my breakfast, Christine and I went upstairs to make the beds. I made her wait while I ran up to my attic to look again at my wonderful present. Dagmar came with me, and when she touched the mirror, I scolded her so hard she started to cry.

Christine came up then and wiped Dagmar's tears and sent her down to Papa. She looked at me for a long time.

"Why do you look at me like that, Christine?"

"What do you care? You got what you wanted, didn't you?" And she pointed to the dresser set. "Trash," she said, "cheap trash."

"Don't you dare talk about my lovely present like that! You're jealous, that's what. I'll tell Mama on you."

"And while you're telling her," Christine said, "ask her what she did with her silver brooch. The one her very own dear mother gave her. Ask her that."

I looked at Christine with horror. "What? You mean—did Mama—?"

Christine walked away.

I grabbed up the dresser set and ran down the stairs to the kitchen. Papa was drinking his second cup of coffee, and Dagmar was playing with her doll in front of the stove. Nels had left. "Papa, oh, Papa!" I cried. "Did Mama— Christine says—" I started to cry then, and Papa had me sit on his lap.

"There now," he said, and patted my shoulder. "There now."

And he dipped a cube of sugar into his coffee and fed it to me. We were not allowed to drink coffee—even with lots of milk in it—until we were considered grown-up, but all of us children loved that occasional lump of sugar dipped in a cup of coffee.

After my hiccuping and sobbing had stopped, Papa talked to me very seriously. It was like this, he said. I had wanted the graduation present. Mama had wanted my happiness more than she had wanted the silver brooch. So she had traded it to Mr. Schiller for the dresser set.

"But I never wanted her to do that, Papa. If I had known—I would never have let her—"

"It was what Mama wanted to do, Katrin."

"But she loved it so. It was all she had of Grandmother's."

"She always meant it to be for you, Katrin."

I stood up slowly, I knew what I must do.

And all the way up to Mr. Schiller's drugstore, the graduation present in my arms, I thought of how hard it must have been for Mama to ask Mr. Schiller to take the brooch as payment. It was never easy for Mama to talk to strangers.

Mr. Schiller examined the dresser set with care. He didn't know, he said, about taking it back. After all, a bargain was a bargain, and he had been thinking of giving the brooch to his wife for her birthday next month.

Recklessly, I mortgaged my vacation.

If he would take back the dresser set, if he would give me back my brooch, I would come in and work for him every single day, even Saturdays. "I'll shine the showcases," I begged. "I'll sweep the floor for you."

Mr. Schiller said that would not be necessary. Since I wanted the brooch back so badly, he would call the deal off. But if I was serious about working during vacation, he might be able to use me.

So I walked out of Mr. Schiller's drugstore not only with Mama's brooch, but with a job that started the next morning. I felt very proud. The dresser set suddenly seemed a childish and silly thing.

I put the brooch on the table in front of Papa.

He looked at me proudly. "Was it so hard to do, Daughter?"

"Not so hard as I thought." I pinned the brooch to my dress. "I'll wear it always," I said. "I'll keep it forever."

"Mama will be glad, Katrin."

Papa dipped a lump of sugar and held it out to me. I shook my head. "Somehow," I said, "I just don't feel like it, Papa."

"So?" Papa said. "So?"

And he stood up and poured out a cup of coffee and handed it to me.

"For me?" I asked wonderingly.

Papa smiled and nodded. "For my grown-up daughter," he said.

I sat up straight in my chair. And felt very proud as I drank my first cup of coffee.

Reading Check

1. What is the financial situation of Katrin's family at the time of this story?
2. List several of Katrin's actions that reveal to us that she is focusing on herself.
3. When Katrin receives the graduation present she has wanted, how do her brother and sister react?
4. At what specific point in the story does Katrin realize her selfishness?
5. What action shows us that her viewpoint has changed?

Wolves of Fear

Richard Savage

It was late at night in early December, and the veteran trapper's eighteen-year-old companion stirred sleeplessly in the rough, hand-hewn bunk, rustling the hay and marsh grass beneath him. The iron stove in the center of the cabin still threw off some heat, although he and the trapper, who snored softly on the other side of the room, had gone to bed several hours earlier. Why he had awakened suddenly, Paul didn't know at first—he had been tired enough after a day of sawing logs and making practice runs out from the cabin on snowshoes. He turned his head so he could gaze at one of the two small

windows high off the floor. The thick, wavy glass was so frosted he could not see through, but the moon was out and the window pane shone a luminous [shining] white against dark logs.

Then suddenly the youth shivered, and he knew what must have awakened him. A long, quavering howl rose from the far shore of the lake, then another and another. Breaking the profound quiet of the snow-covered wilderness, the sound seemed to fill the woods around them and the cabin itself. He tried to fight back his fear, keenly aware of how disappointed and scornful his father would be if he gave in to it and proved a failure on his trapping expedition.

When his father had arranged for him to spend these six months in the wilderness with an old trapper friend with whom he had gone through high school in Duluth years ago, he had talked of what a wonderful experience it would be for Paul before he started college. But Paul knew all too well why his father had urged him to go on this trip. He could almost remember when it all started.

When Paul was ten years old, his father had bought him a small tent one summer and helped him to pitch it at the edge of the wooded lot behind their home on the outskirts of Minneapolis. Then he had suggested that Paul try sleeping in it alone. Paul had been frightened at the idea to begin with, but he had been game to try, and even joined his father in overcoming his mother's protests.

Lying wide-eyed and sleepless in the tent, Paul had listened to the rustling noises in the little patch of woods behind the tent and had shivered when an owl hooted. Then the howling of a dog nearby had jerked him upright into a sitting position, stiff with fear. As he stared out the opening of the tent, he began to see fearful shapes of animals prowling about the edge of the wooded lot. It was all he could do to keep from crying out in terror. But he was too frightened even to move, and he sat there clutching with icy hands at the ground cloth beneath his father's sleeping bag.

At last from several blocks away, he heard a car door slam and voices calling good night. This comforting sound had given him just enough momentary reassurance. He scrambled out of the sleeping bag, grabbed his flashlight, and raced barefoot in his pajamas across the lawn to the back door. He opened it quickly but silently and tiptoed up to his room, praying that no one would hear him. He could tell his father that he came into the house to go to the bathroom in the early morning and then decided to stay in his room till breakfast.

But as he slipped his feet under the covers, the bedroom door opened, and there was his father, outlined by the hall light, standing large and forbidding in the doorway. "So you couldn't stick it out?" asked his father, trying to control the scorn in his voice.

The boy swallowed and turned his head away, unable to meet his father's gaze. "No," he whispered. "There were—I saw . . ." His voice trailed off in fear and humiliation.

There was a moment of silence, while his father shook his head and gazed at his son. "I hoped you wouldn't give in

so easily," he said at last. "There was nothing out there that could harm you. Why were you afraid?"

"I—I don't know. I couldn't help it."

"Look, Paul," said his father, walking over to his bed, "maybe a person can't help being afraid, but they can keep from running away. Every time you run away you lose a little bit of yourself. You lose some respect for yourself. Remember the story I used to read to you about the gingerbread boy who ran away? And in the version we read he gets smaller and smaller as he runs? That's what happens when we let our fears make us run away. We get smaller."

As Paul lay there remembering all this, he suddenly realized the howling of the wolves had stopped. A deep silence settled again on the white solitude, broken only by the occasional sharp cracking of the frost in the trees. Struggling to push back the slow, dark waves of uneasiness, of fear, he tried to relax and drift back to sleep.

All at once the quavering chorus of wolves began again, moving along the shore of the lake, and so close now that the youth sat upright in bed, a cold tingling at the nape of his neck and a coldness at his heart. This time the trapper heard it too, and Paul could see him in the dim light sitting up and shaking his head, running a muscular hand through the thick iron-gray hair. Then Mac was out of bed and pulling on his heavy pants and boots.

"Come on, boy! Let's see what those wolves are up to. They'll not do the trapping any good. Come on, maybe we can bag a couple!"

Paul jumped out of bed and dressed hurriedly. He grabbed his old Remington rolling block rifle just as the trapper started out the door. With his long legs the youth made better time through the deep snow and caught up with the stocky trapper. They headed for the lake about a hundred yards beyond the cabin. The howling had stopped now, and in its place they heard a muted frenzy of vicious snarls. A three-quarter moon lighted the white world around them, and when they reached the lake, they could see what was happening on the ice a little way up the shore toward the outlet of the river.

Four wolves were attacking a moose they had driven into the open, their ghostly gray and brown forms whipping in and out like pursuing demons. The great moose was fighting a courageous but losing battle. Already the huge creature was down, almost in a sitting position, tossing its great antlers in a dying frenzy.

Mac stepped back from the shore

into a thicket of balsam and spruce. "Come on," he said. "Keep to the trees. They might be too hungry to frighten away, but we won't take chances." Crouching low, he began to move through the trees up the shore, and Paul followed, clutching his rifle so tightly his hands grew numb. About fifty yards away from the scene, the trapper stopped and then crept to the edge of the trees. The moose was completely down now, and the timber wolves were tearing at the flesh.

"Now!" whispered Mac, taking aim from a kneeling position. Several shots rang out. One wolf dropped instantly

to the side and lay still. Another wolf, apparently wounded, gave a little leap into the air then, in snarling confusion headed almost directly toward the two men. The animal had covered nearly half the distance before Mac brought it down with one shot. The two remaining wolves sniffed the air for just an instant and then started toward the heavy timber, moving like gray ghosts in the dim light of the moon. Then they disappeared amidst several more shots.

"So!" exclaimed Mac, standing up. "There's two wolves that won't rob traps or scare game. But what happened to you, boy? Didn't you—" He stopped suddenly as he realized his young companion was no longer with him. "Hey, boy!" He gazed around, perplexed and a little annoyed. Then he spotted tracks that led back to the cabin.

When the trapper stepped inside, stamping snow from his boots, he saw the youth sitting on the edge of the bunk, his head in his hands and staring at the floor. Paul didn't look up. Mac hung up his rifle and lighted one of the deer-tallow candles they had made. Then he put several logs into the stove and began stripping down to his woolen underwear. It wasn't until he had taken off his boots that the trapper spoke. "What's the matter, boy? You get sick or something?"

Slowly Paul raised his head, his large, soft-gray eyes gazing almost blankly into the semidarkness. "No," he said, his voice nearly a whisper.

"No, I—I—"

The trapper's jaw tightened underneath his beard, and the dark, piercing eyes smoldered with angry impatience.

"Look here, boy," he began, and his voice had a threatening rumble to it. Then he stopped. Perhaps it was something that he had glimpsed in the boy's open and sensitive face, or a sudden remembrance that he was the son of a friend.

He shrugged at last, and his voice softened a little. "Guess a pack of wolves can be frightening the first time. But they're not ever likely to attack a man. That wounded critter didn't know where he was headed—just wanted to hit the timber."

Paul shifted on the edge of the bunk and shook his head. "I'm sorry, Mac." Drawing a deep breath, Paul tried to speak more forcefully. "I'll snap out of it, Mac. I'm not going to be a handicap to you."

After a few minutes he lay down on his bunk. "Mac," he said at last, trying to keep his voice casual, "if—if something did happen, like—like the cabin burning down and we had to go back before the ice broke, where would we head for?"

"Why, I suppose we'd head for that settlement that's about two days due south of here. If my old Indian-trapper friend is up here this winter, maybe we could head for his cabin if we needed. That's only a day's haul from here. Now, let's get some sleep, boy!"

Then all was still, except for the occasional loud snapping of the frost in the trees. A silence so deep that the earth itself seemed to have dropped away, leaving them in a cold, white void. Paul closed his eyes and eventually slipped off into a fitful sleep. But the wolves of fear ran through his dreams.

At breakfast the next morning nothing was said about the incident of the night before. Paul, however, could not bring himself to look the old trapper in the face—he was ashamed and afraid of what he might see there. While Paul cleaned up the breakfast utensils, Mac went out to see what could be salvaged from the moose. It appeared that no wolves had returned, wary perhaps of the two dead ones lying nearby, but the flesh was badly torn in places from the initial attack. He quickly set about to dress the animal. Paul came out as he was finishing, and they lugged the hindquarters back to the meat shelter.

The sky had become overcast, and the temperature had risen, becoming unexpectedly mild, though far from the point of melting. The trapper got together his equipment for a day's run and then knelt outside the cabin door to bind on his snowshoes. Paul stood by, gazing out over the lake toward the south.

"In a few more days, boy," said Mac. "I'll be able to take you along on some of the shorter runs. Right now I want to move around fairly fast and get the trap lines out in good shape. Maybe you can spend some time making that extra shelf we thought we could use—and taking an excursion [short journey] on your snowshoes. By this time you ought to be getting good enough so you won't slow me down. And see what you can think up for supper, eh?"

The youth nodded, mumbled goodbye, and watched the trapper set out on a line northeast of the cabin. He had really been looking forward to accompanying Mac as he made the rounds of the trap lines, but now he could only gaze miserably after the departing trapper.

All at once, his face strangely set, Paul hurried inside. He began to make up a bedroll and gather together food supplies and a few clothes. When his packsack was filled and ready to shoulder, he paused for a moment. Then he quickly began to search on his shelf for a pencil and a piece of paper. Having found them, he sat down at the table and scrawled a note.

Mac: Please don't try to follow me. I've headed for the settlement, and I'll make it O.K. It's better that I leave. Thanks for all you've done. Dad will understand.

Paul

He shouldered his packsack, picked up his rifle, and went outside. He bound on his snowshoes and then, without looking back, headed directly across the lake, past the mouth of the river up which they had traveled in canoes during the beautiful days of mid-October. How long ago that seemed now! Driven by shame and by his haunting fear of the violent primitive forces of this wilderness, Paul felt there was nothing else to do but try to escape. Once at the settlement he could find a way to reach a train—but not to his home. He couldn't go back now to face his father. He would have to get a job somewhere and give up college, at least for a while.

As he plunged into the tamarack swamp on the other side of the lake, he saw out of the corner of his eye the tracks of the wolves in the snow. He shuddered and hurried on. He traveled through dense stands of pines, across open meadows, over wooded hills, and across small lakes. He looked frequently at his compass and was satisfied that he was heading due south. Around noon he stopped. But so desperately did he want to continue on that he didn't bother to light a fire. Instead he cleared a place for himself in the protected hollow of a great hemlock and collapsed wearily onto the ground, where he munched on some pemmican [dried beef product] and cold biscuits from the morning's breakfast. The sky was still partly overcast, and the mild temperature continued.

When Paul started on again, he was suddenly aware of a pain in both ankles—a pain that seemed to increase with almost every step. He was suffering from snowshoe lameness, which had actually been coming on for some time; but he had been concentrating so fiercely on covering as much ground as possible that he hadn't noticed it at first. Nonetheless, he kept on, even though the pain finally became so intense that his teeth were clenched and the tears came constantly to his eyes.

At last, when the pain in his ankles became so intense that he realized he could not go much farther, he began searching for a place to spend the night. It was while he was looking about him that one of his snowshoes caught under a fallen bough which arched a fraction above the snow. Because of the pain and weariness he had become careless, and now he was flung onto the snow in a crumpled heap. The breath went out of him, and he gave a groan as he felt his right leg twist beneath him. When he

tried to get to his feet, he cried out in pain, realizing with a sickening shock that he had wrenched the leg so badly he could not stand on it.

He struggled out of the packsack and then lay there in the snow, so exhausted, so stricken with pain from the twisted leg and the lameness in his ankles that he sank into a daze. Lying there with his eyes closed, listening to the deep soughing of the wind in the tops of the pines and hemlocks, he felt the exhaustion and the pain recede at last. In their place a wave of drowsy contentment crept over him, drugging him. No longer was there any thought of moving, even to try to build a fire. He wanted only to lie there and rest, forgetting everything—forgetting his plight and all the torment and humiliation his fears had brought him.

Yet as he drifted closer toward complete unconsciousness and snuggled with drowsy comfort in his snow cocoon, he was still aware of a warning signal far back in his mind—a persistent, urgent nudging to move, to move, to move. . . . Then it seemed as if the warning took strangely the form of the barking of a dog—a barking that became as irritating and disturbing as the buzzing of a mosquito which won't let one make the final descent into sleep.

The barking continued and even seemed to become louder. Was he awake or dreaming? Finally with a grimace Paul half raised himself on one elbow. Gradually he became once more aware of his surroundings and at last realized bewilderedly, that he was not dreaming, that it was the barking of a dog.

Groaning slightly with the pain and the effort, he struggled onto his knees and crawled through the snow to where his rifle had landed. Then raising his head to determine where the barking was coming from, he began to crawl with painful slowness to the top of a little ridge a few yards ahead of him. There was still enough light to see the outlines of things, but the darkness was coming fast. Paul reached the top of the ridge and stared in disbelief into the hollow just a little below him.

No more than fifty yards away were a large bear, a gray dog, and an Indian

boy. With the dog barking and snapping at its rear quarters, the bear, looming frighteningly large in the dim light, was lumbering in a dazed and awkward manner toward the boy, who was armed with only a bow and arrow. Legs apart, with the arrow notched and the bow bent, the boy courageously stood his ground. For a moment the bear paused to swat clumsily at the dog. The Indian released the arrow and then retreated a few paces and notched another. There was a low, hoarse growl from the bear, and it swung forward again and continued to advance, two arrows sticking from its shoulder and chest like banderillas [darts stuck in a bull during a bullfight] in a bull.

In a moment Paul had shaken himself free of his dazed condition. He grasped at least partially what had happened. The boy had been hunting rabbits or other small game, and the dog had routed the bear out of its winter den. This accounted for the slow, stupefied approach of the animal as it weaved toward the young hunter.

Lying on his stomach, Paul took off his mittens and raised the rifle. He hesitated. If I miss, he thought. If I only wounded the bear and draw his attention toward me? Then in his fear and indecision he heard himself gasping to the boy, "Run, you little fool! Run quick before it's too late." He had meant to shout, but it came out no more than a whisper.

Even as Paul wavered indecisively, the undaunted Indian boy drew back the arrow for another shot—and there was in that movement, in that stance, a timeless element which seemed to have in it all that men knew of resolution and courage. Sensing this, Paul clenched the rifle. Something within him clicked with the clean, sharp finality of a released trigger. In that instant he saw himself standing again before the oncoming wolf, as the boy stood before the bear, only this time he did not run— and knew now that he could not run again.

Taking a deep breath, Paul squeezed the trigger. At the sharp report the feisty dog gave a loud yelp and ran to its master. The bear stopped suddenly and sat down in the snow, snarling and tossing its head. With numbed fingers Paul reloaded and fired again, and the great creature crumpled onto the snow. The gray dog raced over to the body, sniffing and growling.

The boy dropped his bow, gazed at the bear for a moment, and then began jumping up and down, clapping his hands. "Good!" Good!" he cried with boyish delight, as if he'd been in no danger at all. "Fine shot!" Then he stopped and peered about him.

At last he spied Paul in the near darkness and without any hesitation walked directly up the ridge toward him. He stood in front of Paul, grinning down at him in the friendliest kind of manner. "You shot just in time, mister. A little while, maybe, and there would not be much of me." He continued to smile as if the thought did not disturb him.

Paul saw that he was no more than fourteen or fifteen and noted with surprise that although he was dressed in Indian fashion, almost entirely in buckskin, his skin was very light and his features only slightly resembled the characteristic Indian face. Paul couldn't help smiling too. "And if you hadn't come along with your dog, a little while, maybe, and I'd have been a frozen corpse."

The boy looked puzzled.

"My leg is twisted," said Paul. "I can't walk on it."

The Indian lad gave him a quizzical glance and then said, "Oh. You wait here. I'll bring back hunting sled."

In what seemed a relatively short time the Indian boy returned, dragging after him what looked like a narrow toboggan—two hand-hewn boards about six feet long and held in place by cross pieces with rawhide lashings and curved slightly in front. Paul got on with difficulty. He was numb with cold from lying so long in the snow.

Then the boy lugged the packsack to the sled. Paul motioned with his hand. "Leave it. You'll have a hard enough time as it is. We can get it later."

The boy hesitated a moment and then nodded. "Yes. I'll get it later. I'll come back to skin the bear." He hesitated again. "You'll let me have some bear meat?" he added, a look of real concern on his face. "My mother and I—"

"It's yours," said Paul with a smile, wondering curiously what the circumstances were of the boy and his mother living here in the midst of this wilderness. Why were they here? What had driven the boy to—

Suddenly the sled began to move with such vigor that Paul was nearly jerked into the snow. It was totally dark now, but the boy seemed to know exactly where he was going. After about a half mile they came to a clearing, and Paul, lying on his stomach with his rifle at his side, could see the dim outline of a small cabin and beyond that a broad expanse of frozen lake.

With great difficulty he rolled himself off the sled and crawled through the doorway that the boy held open for him. Inside it was lighted dimly by a single deer-tallow candle. In the center of the single room stood a Chippewa squaw. She motioned him toward a deerskin rug that had been placed near the stove.

"There," she said. "Lie down."

Paul took off his fur-lined jacket, the bearskin cap that had been his father's, his mittens, and his boots. But instead of lying down, he sat holding his hands and feet toward the warmth of the stove.

The boy squatted beside him. "My name is John—John Burton. This is my mother." The woman nodded, smiled a little, and then set about preparing something to eat.

Paul introduced himself and then said. "Your son came along just in time, Mrs. Burton. He saved me from freezing to death in the snow."

Again the squaw smiled a slow, hesitant smile. "He says you saved him," she said softly.

"Oh, I could not run," broke in the boy quickly. "Not while I had arrows to kill the bear. If I turn and run before then, I am nothing."

Paul stared at him in wonderment, remembering suddenly his father's whimsical words years ago about the gingerbread boy who ran away.

Then John held up a forefinger in front of Paul. "But you could not have run if the bear had come after you when you shot," he said softly. There was a pause. "We saved each other!" laughed John suddenly, clapping his hands in that childlike gesture so incongruous with the amazingly calm and courageous manner he had faced the bear.

Paul nodded and smiled, noticing then how strongly built the boy was, with his black hair and attractive, though somewhat dirty, features. He noticed also that he was too thin; so too was his mother, who was a strikingly attractive squaw—probably in her middle thirties, Paul decided, though it was hard to tell.

In a short time they began eating their meal, which consisted of nothing more than rice, bread, and tea, and Paul wished then that he had his packsack with him. So well did he and John strike it off that before long he had their confidence and was hearing, bit by bit from the woman and her son, their story. The woman's English was limited and hesitant, and the boy did most of the talking.

His mother was a full-blooded Chippewa and had married a white man, who had worked in a trading post in the settlement to the south. When he died a year ago—they didn't say how—several persons began to try to have the boy taken away from her. She had fled with her son to this cabin her husband had built some years ago when he was trapping. They had planned late last October to travel back to the settlement

by canoe for more supplies. They had Indian friends there whom they could stay with and who would get for them the things they needed without betraying their presence. But the mother had become very ill, and before she was well enough to travel, the lake and river had frozen. Then the journey was impossible. Paul could see that she was still weak and had probably been giving most of what little food they had to her son.

Now they were almost without supplies of any kind, and the old rifle they had been so dependent upon had broken down two months before. They were subsisting almost entirely on what small game John could shoot with his bow and arrow. The mother planned to travel farther south when summer came,

where she would not be known, and there she and John would sell woven baskets and moccasins to the tourists. Paul could see in the corner some of the beaded moccasins and baskets she had been working on.

When their story was finished, there was a brief silence. Then Paul put down his tin cup of tea. "I'll help you," he said quietly. "Somehow."

At eleven o'clock the next morning Mac came barging into the cabin, having set out around six and traveling in five hours the distance it had taken Paul eight or nine hours to cover. He had known of the existence of the cabin, though he had not realized it was occupied now. Paul was not really surprised to see him. Deep in his subconscious he had known Mac would follow him. But in keeping with the inexplicable folly of his whole attempted escape, he had pretended it was not so.

Mac stood over the youth and began to roar angrily, ignoring the squaw who shrank into a corner of the cabin. "What kind of foolishness is this! Did you think I could let you go like that and ever face your dad again? If it weren't for your dad being my friend, I sure would have let you go—let you go so you could get lost and freeze to death or starve, or—"

Suddenly he was startled to feel small hands pushing and pounding against his shoulders and chest. "No, no!" cried the squaw. "He saved my son. He killed meat for us. It's not right to talk so!"

Mac stopped, backing away and staring at the woman, half in irritation, half in amusement. He shrugged and fell silent; presently he heard the story, not from her or from Paul, but from John, who had been standing wide-eyed just inside the door, having just returned from dressing the bear.

"So you stuck it out this time, eh?" muttered Mac, and then was sorry for having said it. Paul looked away—and then with an effort went about the formality of introducing him to the woman and her son. Then he fell silent, not knowing what to say to the trapper.

Mac removed some of his outer clothing and knelt beside Paul to examine his leg. The woman withdrew to a corner to weave a basket, and John went outside to finish dressing the bear. "It will be all right in another day or two," said Mac, his voice quieter and showing some regret at his outburst. "Look, boy," he began after an awkward pause, "yesterday I met my Indian trapper friend while I was out on the trail. If you're really set on getting back to the city, he'll take care of my trap lines, and I'll take you out of here. Maybe that's what we'd better do, eh?"

Paul clenched his fists hard against his knees. "I want to stay, Mac," he said with quiet intensity. "I'm sure sorry for the trouble I've caused, and you have every right to be angry and want me to go. But, please—now I have to stay. I must stay! I must stay," he repeated in a fierce whisper.

The trapper seemed to understand the urgency in the voice and all that was left unspoken. He nodded and in a gruffly embarrassed gesture patted the youth's knee.

Then in a low voice Paul told him briefly the story of the Indian woman and her son. When he had finished, Mac nodded and said, "We'll give them some help. We'll see them through the winter." He glanced speculatively toward the Chippewa squaw. "I'll do more than that. I'll give some help when she leaves here and see that she doesn't lose her son."

There was a long pause. Then the veteran trapper spoke again, looking directly at the youth. "I think things will go all right for us this winter, Paul. You'll make out in good shape. And it'll make your dad proud to hear it."

Paul lay back, stretching his slim body on the deerskin rug, his hands behind his head and a broad smile on his lips. He was pleased with Mac's words. Pleased mostly that the trapper had addressed him for the first time by his name. It was as if a hand of partnership had been extended to him.

When the trapper left his side a moment later, Paul closed his eyes, still smiling. "The gingerbread boy won't get any smaller," he murmured.

Reading Check

1. Why is Paul staying with Mac?
2. What are some specific things Paul fears?
3. How does the opening quotation in the head note apply to this story?
4. How does Paul's decision to return to Mac reveal his change in focus?
5. What is Paul really saying by his last statement: "The gingerbread boy won't get any smaller"?

As Scrooge sat and stared at Marley's ghost, his bony fingers clutched the overstuffed chair with a strength he had not known since youth. He sat still as a statue, not because he wanted to stay with Marley, but because he was too frightened to budge. Scrooge did manage, however, to collect a remnant of his wit and in a frightened whisper say, "You are fettered. Tell me why."

"I wear the chain I forged in life," Old Marley said. "I made it link by link. . . ." With this introduction, Marley began his lesson—a lesson that would bring the "squeezing, grasping, clutching, covetous old Scrooge" to some frightening discoveries.

A Christmas Carol

Charles Dickens

Part I   Marley's Ghost

Marley was dead: to begin with. There is no doubt whatever about that. Old Marley was as dead as a door-nail.

Scrooge knew he was dead? Of course he did. How could it be otherwise? Scrooge and he were partners for I don't know how many years.

Scrooge never painted out Old Marley's name. There it stood, years afterwards, above the warehouse door: Scrooge and Marley. Sometimes people new to the business called Scrooge Scrooge, and sometimes Marley, but he answered to both names: it was all the same to him.

Oh! But he was a tight-fisted hand at the grindstone, Scrooge! a squeezing, wrenching, grasping, scraping, clutching, covetous, old sinner. Hard and sharp as flint, from which no steel had ever struck out generous fire; secret, and self-contained, and solitary as an oyster. The cold within him froze his old features, nipped his pointed nose, shrivelled his cheek, stiffened his gait; made his eyes red, his thin lips blue; and spoke out shrewdly in his grating voice.

Nobody ever stopped him in the street to say, "My dear Scrooge, how are you? When will you come to see me?" No beggars implored him to bestow a trifle, no children asked him what it was o'clock, no man or woman ever once in all his life inquired the way to such and such a place, of Scrooge. Even the blind men's dogs appeared to know him; and when they saw him coming on, would tug their owners into doorways and up courts; and then would wag their tails as though they said, "No eye at all is better than an evil eye, dark master!"

But what did Scrooge care? It was the very thing he liked.

Once upon a time—of all the good days in the year, on Christmas Eve—old Scrooge sat busy in his counting-house. It was cold, bleak, biting weather, and he could hear the people in the court outside go wheezing up and down, beating their hands upon their breasts, and stamping their feet upon the pavement-stones to warm them. The City clocks had only just gone three, but it was quite dark already: it had not been light all day: and candles were flaring in the windows of the neighbouring offices, like ruddy smears upon the palpable [capable of being touched] brown air.

The door of Scrooge's counting-house was open that he might keep his eye upon his clerk [Bob Cratchit], who in a dismal little cell beyond was copying letters. Scrooge had a very small fire, but the clerk's fire was so very much smaller that it looked like one coal. But he couldn't replenish it, for Scrooge kept the coal-box in his own room; and so surely as the clerk came in with the shovel, the master predicted it would be necessary for them to part. Wherefore the clerk put on his white comforter, and tried to warm himself at the candle.

"A Merry Christmas, uncle! God save you!" cried a cheerful voice. It was the voice of Scrooge's nephew, who came upon him so quickly that this was the first intimation he had of his approach.

"Bah!" said Scrooge. "Humbug*!"

He had so heated himself with rapid walking in the fog and frost, this nephew of Scrooge's, that he was all in a glow; his face was ruddy and handsome; his eyes sparkled, and his breath smoked again.

"Christmas a humbug, uncle!" said Scrooge's nephew. "You don't mean that, I am sure."

"I do," said Scrooge. "Merry Christmas! What right have you to be merry? What reason have you to be merry? You're poor enough."

"Come, then" returned the nephew, gayly. "What right have you to be dismal [depressing]? What reason have you to be morose [gloomy]? You're rich enough."

Scrooge having no better answer ready on the spur of the moment, said, "Bah!" again; and followed it up with "Humbug."

"Don't be cross, uncle," said the nephew.

"What else can I be," returned the uncle, "when I live in such a world of fools as this? Merry Christmas! Out upon merry Christmas! What's Christmas time to you but a time for paying bills without money; a time for finding yourself a year older, but not an hour richer? If I could work my will," said

---

*Humbug: a term meaning "all is deceit or fraud."

Scrooge, indignantly, "every idiot who goes about with 'Merry Christmas,' on his lips should be boiled with his own pudding, and buried with a stake of holly through his heart. He should!"

"Uncle!" pleaded the nephew.

"Nephew!" returned the uncle, sternly, "keep Christmas in your own way, and let me keep it in mine."

"Keep it!" repeated Scrooge's nephew. "But you don't keep it."

"Let me leave it alone, then," said Scrooge. "Much good may it do you! Much good it has ever done you!"

"There are many things from which I might have derived good, but which I have not profited, I dare say," returned the nephew: "Christmas among the rest. But I am sure I have always thought of Christmas time, when it has come round—apart from the veneration [reverence] due to its sacred name and origin, if anything belonging to it can be apart from that—as a good time: a kind, forgiving, charitable, pleasant time: the only time I know of, in the long calendar of the year, when men and women seem by one consent to open their shut-up hearts freely, and to think of people below them as if they really were fellow-passengers to the grave, and not another race of creatures bound on other journeys. And therefore, uncle, though it has never put a scrap of gold or silver in my pocket, I believe it has done me good, and will do me good; and I say, God bless it!"

The clerk involuntarily applauded.

"Let me hear another sound from *you*," said Scrooge, "and you'll keep your Christmas by losing your situation [job]. You're quite a powerful speaker,

Sir," he added, turning to his nephew. "I wonder you don't go into Parliament."

"Don't be angry, uncle. Come! Dine with us tomorrow."

Scrooge said that he would not.

"But why?" cried Scrooge's nephew. "Why?"

"Why did you get married?" said Scrooge.

"Because I fell in love."

"Because you fell in love!" growled Scrooge, as if that were the only one thing in the world more ridiculous than a merry Christmas. "Good afternoon!"

"Nay, uncle, but you never came to see me before that happened. Why give it as a reason for not coming now?"

"Good afternoon," said Scrooge.

"I am sorry, with all my heart, to find you so resolute. We have never had

any quarrel, to which I have been a party. But I have made the trial in a homage to Christmas, and I'll keep my Christmas humour to the last. So a Merry Christmas, uncle!"

"Good afternoon!" said Scrooge.

"And a Happy New Year!"

His nephew left the room without an angry word, notwithstanding. He stopped at the outer door to bestow the greetings of the season on the clerk, who cold as he was, was warmer than Scrooge; for he returned them cordially.

"There's another fellow," muttered Scrooge; who overheard him: "my clerk, with fifteen shilling a-week, and a wife and family, talking about a merry Christmas."

Scrooge's nephew had let two other people in. They were portly gentlemen, pleasant to behold, and now stood, with their hats off, in Scrooge's office. They had books and papers in their hands, and bowed to him.

"Scrooge and Marley's, I believe," said one of the gentlemen, referring to his list. "Have I the pleasure of addressing Mr. Scrooge, or Mr. Marley?"

"Mr. Marley has been dead seven years," Scrooge replied. "He died seven years ago, this very night."

"We have no doubt his liberality [generosity] is well represented by his surviving partner," said the gentleman, presenting his credentials.

It certainly was; for they had been two kindred spirits. At the ominous [threatening] word "liberality," Scrooge frowned, and shook his head, and handed the credentials back.

"At this festive season of the year, Mr. Scrooge," said the gentleman, taking up a pen, "it is more than usually desirable that we should make some slight provision for the poor and destitute, who suffer greatly at the present time. Many thousands are in want of common necessaries; hundreds of thousands are in want of common comforts, Sir."

"Are there no prisons?" asked Scrooge.

"Plenty of prisons," said the gentleman, laying down the pen again.

"And the Union workhouses?" demanded Scrooge. "Are they still in operation?"

"They are." returned the gentleman.

"Oh! I was afraid, from what you said at first, that something had occurred to stop them in their useful course," said Scrooge. "I'm very glad to hear it."

"Under the impression that they scarcely furnish Christian cheer of mind or body to the multitude," returned the gentleman, "a few of us are endeavouring to raise a fund to buy the Poor some meat and drink, and means of warmth. We choose this time, because it is a time, of all others, when Want is keenly felt, and Abundance rejoices. What shall I put you down for?"

"Nothing!" Scrooge replied.

"You wish to be anonymous?"

"I wish to be left alone," said Scrooge. "Since you ask me what I wish, gentlemen, that is my answer. I don't make merry myself at Christmas, and I can't afford to make idle people merry. I help to support the establishments I have mentioned: they cost enough: and those who are badly off must go there."

"Many can't go there; and many would rather die."

"If they would rather die," said Scrooge, "they had better do it, and decrease the surplus [excess] population."

Seeing clearly that it would be useless to pursue their point, the gentlemen withdrew.

Meanwhile a scant young singer gnawed by hungry cold as bones are gnawed by dogs, stooped down at Scrooge's keyhole to regale [entertain] him with a Christmas carol: but at the first sound of

"God bless you, merry gentleman!
May nothing you dismay!"

Scrooge seized a ruler with such energy of action, that the singer fled in terror.

At length the hour of shutting up the counting-house arrived. With an ill-will Scrooge dismounted from his stool,

and tacitly [without words] admitted the fact to the expectant clerk, who instantly snuffed his candle out, and put on his hat.

"You'll want all day tomorrow, I suppose?" said Scrooge.

"If quite convenient, Sir."

"It's not convenient," said Scrooge, "and it's not fair. If I was to stop half-a-crown for it, you'd think yourself ill-used, though you don't think *me* ill-used, when I pay a day's wages for no work. But I suppose you must have the whole day. Be here all the earlier next morning."

The clerk promised that he would; and Scrooge walked out with a growl.

Scrooge took his melancholy dinner in his usual melancholy tavern; and having read all the newspapers, and beguiled the rest of the evening with his banker's-book, went home.

He lived in chambers which had once belonged to his deceased partner [Marley]. Now, it is a fact, that there was nothing at all particular about the knocker on the door, except that it was very large. It is also a fact, that Scrooge had seen it, night and morning, during his whole residence in that place; also that Scrooge had as little of what is called fancy about him as any man in the City of London. Let it also be borne in mind that Scrooge had not bestowed one thought on Marley since his last mention of his seven-years' dead partner that afternoon. And then let any man explain to me, if he can, how it happened that Scrooge, having his key in the lock of the door, saw in the knocker, not a knocker, but Marley's face.

Marley's face. It was not in shadow as the other objects in the yard were, but had a dismal light about it like a bad lobster in a dark cellar. It was not angry or ferocious, but looked at Scrooge as Marley used to look: with ghostly spectacles turned up on its ghostly forehead. The hair was curiously stirred, as if by breath or hot air; and though the eyes were wide open, they were perfectly motionless. That, and its livid color, made it horrible.

As Scrooge looked fixedly at this phenomenon, it was a knocker again.

To say that he was not startled, or that his blood was not conscious of a terrible sensation to which it had been a stranger from infancy, would be untrue. But he put his hand upon the key he had relinquished, turned it sturdily, walked in, and lighted his candle.

He *did* pause before he shut the door; and he *did* look cautiously behind it first, as if he half-expected to be terrified with the sight of Marley's pigtail sticking out into the hall. But there was nothing on the back of the door, except the screws and nuts that held the knocker on; so he said "Pooh, pooh!" and closed it with a bang. The sound resounded through the house like thunder. He fastened the door, and walked across the hall, and up the stairs: slowly too: trimming his candle as he went.

Half-a-dozen gas-lamps out of the street wouldn't have lighted the entry too well, so you may suppose that it was pretty dark.

Up Scrooge went, not caring a button for that: darkness is cheap, and Scrooge liked it. He walked through his rooms to see that all was right. He had just enough recollection of the face to desire to do that.

Sitting-room, bedroom. All as they should be. Quite satisfied, he closed his door, and locked himself in; double-locked himself in, which was not his custom. Thus secured against surprise, he took off his cravat [neck scarf]; put on his dressing-gown and slippers, and his nightcap; and sat down before the fire to take his gruel.

It was a very low fire indeed; nothing on such a bitter night. He was obliged to sit close to it, and brood over it, before he could extract the least sensation of warmth from such a handful of fuel.

His glance happened to rest upon a bell, a disused bell, that hung in the room, and communicated for some purpose now forgotten with a chamber in the highest story of the building. It was with great astonishment, and with a strange, inexplicable dread, that as he looked he saw this bell begin to swing. It swung so softly in the outset that it scarcely made a sound; but soon it rang out loudly, and so did every bell in the house.

This might have lasted half a minute, or a minute, but it seemed an hour. The bells ceased as they had begun, together. They were succeeded by a clanking noise, deep down below; as if some person were dragging a heavy chain over the casks in the wine-merchant's cellar. Scrooge then remembered to have heard that ghosts in haunted houses were described as dragging chains.

The cellar-door flew open with a booming sound, and then he heard the noise much louder, on the floors below; then coming up the stairs; then coming straight towards his door.

"It's humbug!" said Scrooge. "I won't believe it."

His color changed though, when, without a pause, it came on through the heavy door, and passed into the room before his eyes. Upon its coming in, the dying flame leaped up, as though it cried "I know him! Marley's Ghost!" and fell again.

The same face: the very same. Marley in his pigtail, usual waistcoat, tights and boots. The chain he drew was clasped about his middle. It was long, and wound about him like a tail; and it was made (for Scrooge observed it closely) of cashboxes, keys, padlocks, ledgers, deeds, and heavy purses wrought in steel. His body was transparent; so that Scrooge, observing him, and looking through his waistcoat, could see the two buttons on his coat behind.

He looked the phantom through and through, and saw it standing before him; though he felt the chilling influence of its death-cold eyes; and marked the very texture of the folded kerchief bound about its head and chin, which wrapper he had not observed before: he was still incredulous [unbelieving] and fought against his senses.

"How now!" said Scrooge, caustic [bitter] and cold as ever. "What do you want with me?"

"Much!"—Marley's voice, no doubt about it.

"Who are you?"

"Ask me who I *was*."

"Who *were* you then?" said Scrooge, raising his voice.

"In life I was your partner, Jacob Marley."

"Can you—can you sit down?" asked Scrooge, looking doubtfully at him.

"I can."

"Do it then."

The Ghost sat down on the opposite side of the fireplace.

"You don't believe in me," observed the Ghost.

"I don't," said Scrooge.

"What evidence would you have of my reality beyond that of your senses?"

"I don't know," said Scrooge.

"Why do you doubt your senses?"

"Because," said Scrooge, "a little thing affects them. A slight disorder of the stomach makes them cheats. You may be an undigested bit of beef, a blot of mustard, a crumb of cheese, a fragment of an underdone potato. There's more of gravy than of grave about you, whatever you are!"

Scrooge was not much in the habit of cracking jokes, nor did he feel, in his heart, by any means waggish [humorous] then. The truth is, that he tried to be smart, as a means of distracting his own attention, and keeping down his terror; for the spectre's voice disturbed the very marrow in his bones.

"You see this toothpick?" said Scrooge, wishing to divert the vision's stony gaze from himself.

"I do," replied the Ghost.

"You are not looking at it," said Scrooge.

"But I see it," said the Ghost, "notwithstanding."

"Well!" returned Scrooge. "I have but to swallow this, and be for the rest of my days persecuted by a legion of goblins, all of my own creation. Humbug, I tell you—humbug!"

At this the spirit raised a frightful cry, and shook its chain with such a dismal and appalling noise, that Scrooge held on tight to his chair, to save himself from falling in a swoon. But how much greater was his horror, when the phantom taking off the bandage round its head, as if it were too warm to wear indoors, its lower jaw dropped down upon its breast!

Scrooge fell upon his knees, and clasped his hands before his face.

"Mercy!" he said. "Dreadful apparition, why do you trouble me?"

"Man of the worldly mind!" replied the Ghost, "do you believe in me or not?"

"I do," said Scrooge. "I must. But why do spirits walk the earth, and why do they come to me?"

"It is required of every man," the Ghost returned, "that the spirit within him should walk abroad among his fellowmen, and travel far and wide; and if that spirit goes not forth in life, it is condemned to do so after death. It is doomed to wander through the world—oh, woe is me!—and witness what it cannot share, but might have shared on earth, and turned to happiness!" Again the spectre raised a cry, and shook its chain, and wrung its shadowy hands.

"You are fettered," said Scrooge, trembling. "Tell me why?"

"I wear the chain I forged in life," replied the Ghost.

"I made it link by link, and yard by yard; I girded it on of my own free will, and of my own free will I wore it. Is its pattern strange to *you*?"

Scrooge trembled more and more.

"Or would you know," pursued the Ghost, "the weight and length of the strong coil you bear yourself? It was full as heavy and as long as this, seven Christmas Eves ago. You have laboured on it since. It is a ponderous chain."

Scrooge glanced about him on the floor, in the expectation of finding himself surrounded by some fifty or sixty fathoms of iron cable: but he could see nothing.

"Jacob," he said imploringly. "Old Jacob Marley, tell me more. Speak comfort to me, Jacob."

"I have none to give," the Ghost replied. "It comes from other regions, Ebenezer Scrooge, and is conveyed by other ministers, to other kinds of men. Nor can I tell you what I would. A very little more, is all permitted to me. I cannot rest, I cannot stay, I cannot linger anywhere. My spirit never walked beyond our counting-house—mark me!—in life my spirit never roved beyond the narrow limits of our money-changing hole; and weary journeys lie before me!"

It was a habit with Scrooge, whenever he became thoughtful, to put his hands in his breeches pockets. Pondering on what the Ghost had said, he did so now, but without lifting up his eyes, or getting off his knees.

"You must have been very slow about it, Jacob," Scrooge observed, in a business-like manner, though with humility and deference.

"Slow!" the Ghost repeated.

"Seven years dead," mused Scrooge. "And travelling all the time!"

"The whole time," said the Ghost. "No rest, no peace. Incessant [continuous] torture of remorse."

"You travel fast?" said Scrooge.

"On the wings of the wind," replied the Ghost.

"You might have got over a great quantity of ground in seven years," said Scrooge.

The Ghost, on hearing this, set up another cry, and clanked its chain hideously in the dead silence of the night.

"Oh! captive, bound, and double-ironed," cried the phantom, "not to

know, that ages of incessant labour, by immortal creatures, for this earth must pass into eternity before the good of which it is susceptible is all developed. Not to know that any Christian spirit working kindly in its little sphere, whatever it may be, will find its mortal life too short for its vast means of usefulness. Not to know that no space of regret can make amends for one life's opportunity misused! Yet such was I! Oh! such was I!"

"But you were always a good man of business, Jacob," faltered Scrooge, who began to apply this to himself.

"Business!" cried the Ghost, wringing its hands again. "Mankind was my business. The common welfare was my business; charity, mercy, forbearance, and benevolence were all my business. The dealings of my trade were but a drop of water in the comprehensive ocean of my business!"

It held up its chain at arm's length, as if that were the cause of all its unavailing grief, and flung it heavily upon the ground again.

Scrooge was very much dismayed to hear the spectre going on at this rate, and began to quake exceedingly.

"Hear me!" cried the Ghost. "My time is nearly gone."

"I will," said Scrooge. "But don't be hard upon me! Don't be flowery, Jacob! Pray!" [expression of pleading]

"How it is that I appear before you in a shape that you can see, I may not tell. I have sat invisible beside you many and many a day."

It was not an agreeable idea. Scrooge shivered, and wiped the perspiration from his brow.

"That is no light part of my penance," pursued the Ghost. "I am here to-night to warn you, that you have yet a chance and hope of escaping my fate. You will be haunted by Three Spirits."

Scrooge's countenance fell almost as low as the Ghost's had done.

"I—I think I'd rather not," said Scrooge.

"Without their visits," said the Ghost, "you cannot hope to shun the path I tread. Expect the first tomorrow, when the bell tolls one."

"Couldn't I take 'em all at once, and have it over, Jacob?" hinted Scrooge.

"Expect the second one the next night at the same hour. The third upon the next night when the last stroke of twelve has ceased to vibrate. Look to see me no more; and look that, for your own sake, you remember what has passed between us!"

When it had said these words, the spectre took its wrapper from the table, and bound it round its head, as before. Scrooge knew this, by the smart sounds its teeth made, when the jaws were brought together by the bandage.

The apparition walked backward from him; and at every step it took, the window raised itself a little, so that when the spectre reached it, it was wide open. It beckoned Scrooge to approach, which he did. When they were within two paces of each other, Marley's Ghost held up its hand, warning him to come no nearer. Scrooge stopped.

Not so much in obedience, as in surprise and fear: for on the raising of the hand, he became sensible of confused noises in the air; incoherent sounds of lamentation and regret; wailings inexpressibly sorrowful and self-accusatory. The spectre, after listening for a moment, joined in the mournful dirge; and floated out upon the bleak, dark night.

Whether these creatures faded into mist, or mist enshrouded them, he could not tell. But they and their spirit voices faded together; and the night became as it had been when he walked home.

Scrooge closed the window, and examined the door by which the Ghost had entered. It was double-locked, as he had locked it with his own hands, and the bolts were undisturbed. He tried to say "Humbug!" but stopped at the first syllable. And being much in need of repose, went straight to bed, without undressing, and fell asleep upon the instant.

Reading Check

1. What do we learn about Scrooge's attitudes from the author's description?
2. How do Scrooge's actions reveal his viewpoint?
3. How does Scrooge's house reflect his viewpoint?
4. Why has Marley come to pay old Scrooge a visit?

Part II   The First of the Three Spirits

When Scrooge awoke, it was so dark, that looking out of bed, he could scarcely distinguish the transparent window from the walls of his chamber. He was endeavouring to pierce the darkness with his ferret [weasel-like] eyes, when the chimes of a neighboring church struck the four quarters. So he listened for the hour.

To his great astonishment the heavy bell went on from six to seven, and from seven to eight, and regularly up to twelve; then stopped. Twelve! It was past two when he went to bed. The clock was wrong. An icicle must have got into the works. Twelve!

"Why, it isn't possible," said Scrooge, "that I can have slept through a whole day and far into another night. It isn't possible that anything has happened to the sun, and this is twelve at noon!"

The idea being an alarming one, he scrambled out of bed, and groped his way to the window. All he could make out was, that it was still very foggy and extremely cold, and that there was no noise of people running to and fro, and making a great stir, as there unquestionably would have been if night had beaten off bright day, and taken possession of the world. This was a great relief.

Scrooge went to bed again, and thought, and thought, and thought it over and over and over, and could make nothing of it. Marley's Ghost bothered him exceedingly. "Was it a dream or not?"

As Scrooge lay in this state he remembered, on a sudden, that the Ghost had warned him of a visitation when the bell tolled one. He resolved to lie awake until the hour was passed; and, considering that he could no more go to sleep than go to Heaven, this was perhaps the wisest resolution in his power.

The quarter was so long, that he was more than once convinced he must have sunk into a doze unconsciously, and missed the clock. At length it broke upon his listening ear.

"Ding, dong!"

"A quarter past," said Scrooge, counting.

"Ding, dong!"

"Half-past!" said Scrooge.

"Ding, dong!"

"A quarter to it," said Scrooge.

"Ding, dong!"

"The hour itself," said Scrooge, triumphantly, "and nothing else!"

He spoke before the hour bell sounded, which it now did with a deep, dull, hollow, melancholy *One*. Light flashed up in the room upon the instant, and the curtains of his bed were drawn.

The curtains of his bed were drawn aside, I tell you, by a hand, and Scrooge, starting up into a half-recumbent [reclining] attitude, found himself face to face with the unearthly visitor who drew them.

It was a strange figure—like a child: yet not so like a child as like an old man, viewed through some supernatural medium, which gave him the appearance of having receded from the view, and being diminished to a child's proportions. Its hair, which hung about its neck and down its back, was white as if with age; and yet the face had not a wrinkle in it, and the tenderest bloom was on the skin. The arms were very long and muscular; the hands the same, as if its hold were of uncommon strength. Its legs and feet, most delicately formed, were, like those upper members, bare. It wore a tunic of the purest white; and round its waist was bound a lustrous belt, the sheen of which was beautiful. It held a branch of fresh green holly in its hand; and, in singular contradiction of that wintry emblem, had its dress trimmed with summer flowers. But the strangest thing about it was, that from the crown of its head there sprang a bright clear jet of light, by which all this was visible; and which was doubtless the occasion of its using, in its duller moments, a great extinguisher for a cap, which it now held under its arm.

Even this, though, when Scrooge looked at it with increasing steadiness, was not its strangest quality. For as its belt sparkled and glittered now in one part and now in another, and what was light one instant, at another time was dark, so the figure itself fluctuated in

its distinctness: being now a thing with one arm, now with one leg, now with twenty legs, now a pair of legs without a head, now a head without a body.

"Are you the Spirit, Sir, whose coming was foretold to me?" asked Scrooge.

"I am!"

The voice was soft and gentle.

"Who, and what are you?" Scrooge demanded.

"I am the Ghost of Christmas Past."

"Long past?" inquired Scrooge: observant of its dwarfish stature.

"No. Your past."

Perhaps, Scrooge could not have told anybody why, if anybody could have asked him: but he had a special desire to see the Spirit in his cap; and begged him to be covered.

"What!" exclaimed the Ghost, "would you so soon put out, with worldly hands, the light I give? Is it not enough that you are one of those whose passions make this cap, and force me through whole trains of years to wear it low upon my brow!"

Scrooge reverently disclaimed all intention to offend, or any knowledge of having wilfully "bonneted" the Spirit at any period of his life. He then made bold to inquire what business brought him there.

"Your welfare!" said the Ghost.

It put out its strong hand and clasped him gently by the arm.

"Rise! and walk with me!"

It would have been in vain for Scrooge to plead that the weather and the hour were not adapted to pedestrian purposes; that bed was warm, and the thermometer a long way below freezing; that he was clad but lightly in his slippers, dressing-gown, and nightcap; and that he had a cold upon him at that time. The grasp, though gentle as a woman's hand, was not to be resisted. He rose: but finding that the Spirit made towards the window, clasped its robe in supplication.

"I am a mortal," Scrooge remonstrated, "and liable to fall."

"Bear but a touch of my hand there," said the Spirit, laying it upon his heart, "and you shall be upheld in more than this!"

As the words were spoken, they passed through the wall and stood upon an open country road, with fields on either hand. It was a clear, cold, winter day, with snow upon the ground.

"Good Heaven!" said Scrooge, clasping his hands together, as he looked about him. "I was bred in this place. I was a boy here!"

He was conscious of a thousand odours floating in the air, each one connected with a thousand thoughts, and hopes, and joys, and cares long, long forgotten!

"You recollect the way?" inquired the Spirit.

"Remember it!" cried Scrooge with fervour—"I could walk it blindfold."

They walked along the road; Scrooge recognizing every gate, and post, and tree; until a little market-town appeared in the distance, with its bridge, its church, and winding river. Some shaggy ponies now were seen trotting towards them with boys upon their backs, who called to other boys in country gigs and carts, driven by farmers. All these boys were in great spirits, and shouted to each other, until the broad fields were so full of merry music, that the crisp air laughed to hear it.

"These are but shadows of the things that have been," said the Ghost. "They have no consciousness of us."

The jocund [merry] travellers came on; and as they came, Scrooge knew and named them every one. Why was he rejoiced beyond all bounds to see them! Why did his cold eye glister, and his heart leap up as they went past! Why was he filled with gladness when he heard them give each other Merry Christmas, as they parted at cross-roads and by-ways, for their several homes!

What was merry Christmas to Scrooge? Out upon merry Christmas! What good had it ever done to him?

"The school is not quite deserted," said the Ghost. "A solitary child, neglected by his friends, is left there still."

Scrooge said he knew it. And he sobbed.

They left the high-road, by a well-remembered lane, and soon approached a mansion of dull red brick. It was a large house, but one of broken fortunes; for the spacious offices were little used, their walls were damp and mossy, their windows broken, and their gates decayed. Entering the dreary hall, and glancing through the open doors of many rooms, they found them poorly furnished, cold and vast.

They went, the Ghost and Scrooge, across the hall, to a door at the back of the house. It opened before them, and disclosed a long, bare, melancholy room, made barer still by lines of plain deal forms and desks. At one of these a lonely boy was reading near a feeble fire; and Scrooge sat down upon a form, and wept to see his poor forgotten self as he had used to be.

The Spirit touched him on the arm, and pointed to his younger self, intent upon his reading. Suddenly a man, in foreign garments: wonderfully real and distinct to look at: stood outside the window, with an axe stuck in his belt, and leading an ass laden with wood by the bridle.

"Why, it's Ali Baba!" Scrooge exclaimed in ecstasy. "It's dear old honest Ali Baba! One Christmas time, when yonder solitary child was left here all alone, he *did* come, for the first time, just like that. And Valentine," said Scrooge, "and his wild brother, Orson; there they go! And what's his name, who was put down in his drawers, asleep at the Gate of Damascus; don't you see him! And the Sultan's Groom turned upside down by the Genii; there he is upon his head! Serve him right. I'm glad of it. What business had *he* to be married to the Princess!"

To hear Scrooge expending all the earnestness of his nature on such subjects, would have been a surprise to his business friends in the City, indeed.

Then, with a rapidity of transition very foreign to his usual character, he said, in pity for his former self, "Poor boy!" and cried.

"I wish," Scrooge muttered, putting his hand in his pocket, and looking about him, after drying his eyes with his cuff: "but it's too late now."

"What is the matter?" asked the Spirit.

"Nothing," said Scrooge. "Nothing. There was a boy singing a Christmas Carol at my door last night. I should like to have given him something: that's all."

The Ghost smiled thoughtfully, and waved his hand: saying as it did so, "Let us see another Christmas!"

Scrooge's former self grew larger at the words, and the room became a little darker and more dirty. The panels shrank, the windows cracked; fragments of plaster fell out of the ceiling, and the naked laths were shown instead; but how all this was brought about, Scrooge knew no more than you do. He only knew that it was quite correct; that

everything had happened so; that there he was, alone again, when all the other boys had gone home for the jolly holidays. He was not reading now, but walking up and down despairingly. Scrooge looked at the Ghost, and with a mournful shaking of his head, glanced anxiously towards the door.

It opened; and a little girl, much younger than the boy, came darting in, and putting her arms about his neck, and often kissing him, addressed him as her "Dear, dear brother."

"I have come to bring you home, dear brother!" said the child.

"Home, little Fan?" returned the boy.

"Yes!" said the child, brimful of glee. "Home, for good and all. Home, for ever and ever. Father is so much kinder than he used to be, that home's like Heaven! He spoke so gently to me one dear night when I was going to bed, that I was not afraid to ask him once more if you might come home; and he said Yes, you should; and sent me in a coach to bring you. And you're to be a man!" said the child, opening her eyes, "and are never to come back here; but first, we're to be together all the Christmas long, and have the merriest time in all the world."

She clapped her hands and laughed, and tried to touch his head; but being too little, laughed again, and stood on tiptoe to embrace him. Then she began to drag him, in her childish eagerness, towards the door; and he, nothing loath to go, accompanied her.

"Always a delicate creature, whom a breath might have withered," said the Ghost. "But she had a large heart!"

"So she had," cried Scrooge. "You're right. I'll not gainsay [deny] it, Spirit. God forbid!"

"She died a woman," said the Ghost, "and had, as I think, children."

"One child," Scrooge returned.

"True," said the Ghost. "Your nephew!"

Scrooge seemed uneasy in his mind; and answered briefly, "Yes."

They had left the school behind them, and they were now in the busy thoroughfares of a city, where shadowy passengers passed and repassed; where shadowy carts and coaches battled for the way. It was made plain enough, by the dressing of the shops, that here too it was Christmas time again; but it was evening, and the streets were lighted up.

The Ghost stopped at a certain warehouse door, and asked Scrooge if he knew it.

"Know it!" said Scrooge. "I was apprenticed [trained] here."

They went in. At sight of an old gentleman in a Welsh wig, sitting behind a high desk, Scrooge cried in great excitement:—

"Why, it's old Fezziwig!"

Old Fezziwig laid down his pen, and looked up at the clock, which pointed to the hour of seven. He rubbed his hands; adjusted his capacious [roomy] waistcoat; laughed all over himself, and called out in a comfortable, oily, rich, fat, jovial voice:—

"Yo ho, there! Ebenezer! Dick!"

Scrooge's former self, now grown a young man, came briskly in, accompanied by his fellow-'prentice.

"Dick Wilkins, to be sure!" said Scrooge to the Ghost. "Bless me, yes. There he is. He was very much attached to me, was Dick. Poor Dick! Dear, dear!"

"Yo ho, my boys!" said Fezziwig. "No more work tonight. Christmas Eve, Dick. Christmas, Ebenezer! Let's have the shutters up," cried old Fezziwig, with a sharp clap of his hands.

You wouldn't believe how those two fellows went at it! They charged into the street with the shutters—one, two, three—had 'em up in their places—four, five, six—barred 'em and pinned 'em—seven, eight, nine—and came back before you could have got to twelve, panting like race-horses.

"Hilli-ho!" cried old Fezziwig, skipping down from the high desk, with wonderful agility. "Clear away, my lads, and let's have lots of room here!"

Clear away! There was nothing they wouldn't have cleared away, or couldn't have cleared away, with old Fezziwig looking on. It was done in a minute.

Every movable was packed off, as if it were dismissed from public life for evermore; the floor was swept, the lamps were trimmed, fuel was heaped upon the fire; and the warehouse was as snug, and warm, and dry, and bright a ball-room, as you would desire to see upon a winter's night.

In came a fiddler with a music-book, and went up to the lofty desk, and made an orchestra of it, and tuned like fifty stomach-aches. In came Mrs. Fezziwig, one vast substantial smile. In came the three Miss Fezziwigs, beaming and lovable. In came the six young followers whose hearts they broke. In came all the young men and women employed in the business. In came the housemaid, with her cousin, the baker. In came the cook, with her brother's particular friend, the milkman. In they all came, one after another.

There were dances, and there were forfeits, and more dances, and there was cake, and there was negus [sweet, spicy, hot beverage], and there was a great piece of Cold Roast, and there was a great piece of Cold Boiled, and there were mince-pies. But the great effect of the evening came after the Roast and Boiled, when the fiddler (an artful dog, mind! The sort of man who knew his business better than you or I could have told it him!) struck up "Sir Roger de Coverley." Then old Fezziwig stood out to dance with Mrs. Fezziwig. Top couple, too; with a good stiff piece of work cut out for them; three or four and twenty pair of partners; people who were not to be trifled with; people who *would* dance, and had no notion of walking.

But if they had been twice as many: ah, four times: old Fezziwig would have been a match for them, and so would Mrs. Fezziwig.

When the clock struck eleven, this domestic ball broke up. Mr. and Mrs. Fezziwig took their stations, one on either side the door, and shaking hands with every person individually as he or she went out, wished him or her a Merry Christmas. When everybody had retired but the two 'prentices, they did the same to them; and thus the cheerful voices died away, and the lads were left to their beds; which were under a counter in the back-shop.

During the whole of this time, Scrooge had acted like a man out of his wits. His heart and soul were in the scene, and with his former self. He enjoyed everything and underwent the strangest agitation.

"A small matter," said the Ghost, "to make these silly folks so full of gratitude."

The Spirit signed to him to listen to the two apprentices, who were pouring out their hearts in praise of Fezziwig: and when he had done so, said,

"Why! He has spent but a few pounds of your mortal money: three or four, perhaps. Is that so much that he deserves this praise?"

"It isn't that," said Scrooge, heated by the remark, and speaking unconsciously like his former, not his latter, self. "It isn't that, Spirit. He has the power to render us happy or unhappy; to make our service light or burdensome; a pleasure or a toil. Say that his power lies in words and looks; in things so slight and insignificant that it is impossible to add and count 'em up: what then? The happiness he gives is quite as great as if it cost a fortune." He felt the Spirit's glance, and stopped.

"What is the matter?" asked the Ghost.

"Nothing particular," said Scrooge.

"Something, I think?" the Ghost insisted.

"No," said Scrooge. "No. I should like to be able to say a word or two to my clerk just now! That's all."

His former self turned down the lamps as he gave utterance to the wish; and Scrooge and the Ghost again stood side by side in the open air.

"My time grows short," observed the Spirit. "Quick."

This was not addressed to Scrooge, or to anyone whom he could see, but it produced an immediate effect. For again Scrooge saw himself. He was older now; a man in the prime of life. His face had not the harsh and rigid lines of later years; but it had begun to wear the signs of care and avarice [greed].

He was not alone, but sat by the side of a fair young girl in a mourning-dress:

"It matters little," she said, softly. "To you, very little. Another idol has displaced me; and if it can cheer and comfort you in time to come, as I would have tried to do, I have no just cause to grieve."

"What idol has displaced you?" he rejoined.

"A golden one."

"This is the even-handed dealing of the world!" he said. "There is nothing on which it is so hard as poverty; and there is nothing it professes to condemn with such severity as the pursuit of wealth!"

"You fear the world too much," she answered, gently. "All your other hopes have merged into the hope of being beyond the chance of its sordid [base] reproach. I have seen your nobler aspirations [ambitions] fall off one by one, until the master-passion, Gain, engrosses you. Have I not?"

"What then?" he retorted. "Even if I have grown so much wiser, what then? I am not changed towards you."

"Our contract is an old one. It was made when we were both poor and

content to be so, until, in good season, we could improve our worldly fortune by our patient industry. You are changed. When it was made, you were another man."

"I was a boy," he said impatiently.

"Your own feeling tells you that you were not what you are," she returned. "I am. That which promised happiness when we were one in heart, is fraught with misery now that we are two. How often and how keenly I have thought of this, I will not say. It is enough that I have thought of it, and can release you."

"Have I ever sought release?"

"In words? No. Never."

"In what, then?"

"In a changed nature; in an altered spirit; in another atmosphere of life; another Hope as its great end. In everything that made my love of any worth or value in your sight. If this had never been between us," said the girl, looking mildly, but with steadiness, upon him; "tell me, would you seek me out and try to win me now? Ah, no!"

He seemed to yield to the justice of this supposition in spite of himself. But he said with a struggle, "You think not."

"I would gladly think otherwise if I could," she answered, "Heaven knows! When I have learned a Truth like this, I know how strong and irresistible it must be. But if you were free to-day, to-morrow, yesterday, can even I believe that you would choose a dowerless [without a dowery; poor] girl—you who, in your very confidence with her, weigh everything by Gain: or, choosing her, if for a moment you were false enough to your one guiding principle to do so, do I not know that your repentance and regret would surely follow? I do; and I release you. With a full heart, for the love of him you once were."

She left him, and they parted.

"Spirit!" said Scrooge, "show me no more! Conduct me home. Why do you delight to torture me?"

"One shadow more!" exclaimed the Ghost.

"No more!" cried Scrooge. "No more. I don't wish to see it. Show me no more!"

But the relentless Ghost pinioned [held by force] him in both his arms, and forced him to observe what happened next.

They were in another scene and place; a room, not very large or handsome, but full of comfort. Near to the winter fire sat a beautiful young girl, so like the last that Scrooge believed it was the same, until he saw her, now a comely matron, sitting opposite her daughter. The noise in this room was perfectly tumultuous, for there were more children there, than Scrooge in his agitated state of mind could count.

Now the father came home attended by a man laden with Christmas toys and presents. The shouts of wonder and delight with which the development of every package was received!

The joy, and gratitude, and ecstasy! They are all indescribable alike. By degrees the children and their emotions got out of the parlour and by one stair at a time, up to the top of the house; where they went to bed, and so subsided.

And now Scrooge looked on more attentively than ever, when the master of the house, having his daughter leaning fondly on him, sat down with her and her mother at his own fireside.

"Belle," said the husband, turning to his wife with a smile, "I saw an old friend of yours this afternoon."

"Who was it?"

"Mr. Scrooge. I passed his office window; and as it was not shut up, and he had a candle inside, I could scarcely help seeing him. His partner lies upon the point of death, I hear; and there he sat alone. Quite alone in the world, I do believe."

"Spirit!" said Scrooge in a broken voice, "remove me from this place."

"I told you these were shadows of the things that have been," said the Ghost. "That they are what they are, do not blame me!"

"Remove me!" Scrooge exclaimed, "I cannot bear it!"

He turned upon the Ghost, and seeing that it looked upon him with a face, in which in some strange way there were fragments of all the faces it had shown him, wrestled with it.

"Leave me! Take me back. Haunt me no longer!"

In the struggle, if that can be called a struggle in which the Ghost with no visible resistance on its own part was undisturbed by any effort of its adversary, Scrooge observed that its light was burning high and bright; and dimly

connected that with its influence over him, he seized the extinguisher-cap, and by a sudden action pressed it down upon his head.

The Spirit dropped beneath it, so that the extinguisher covered its whole form; but though Scrooge pressed it down with all his force, he could not hide the light, which streamed from under it, in an unbroken flood upon the ground.

He was conscious of being exhausted, and overcome by an irresistible drowsiness; and, further, of being in his own bedroom. He gave the cap a parting squeeze, in which his hand relaxed; and had barely time to reel to bed, before he sank into a heavy slumber.

Reading Check

1. Describe the first of the three spirits sent to visit Scrooge.
2. Who is little Fan, and why is Scrooge uneasy when the spirit speaks of her child?
3. Who is old Fezziwig?
4. List some differences between the viewpoints of the older Scrooge and the younger Scrooge.
5. By the time Scrooge reaches young manhood, what idol has he chosen to replace all other loves in his life?

Part III   The Second of the Three Spirits

Awaking in the middle of a prodigiously tough snore, and sitting up in bed to get his thoughts together, Scrooge had no occasion to be told that the bell was again upon the stroke of One. He felt that he was restored to consciousness in the right nick of time, for the especial purpose of holding a conference with the second messenger despatched to him through Jacob Marley's intervention.

He was ready for a good broad field of strange appearance, and nothing between a baby and a rhinoceros would have astonished him very much.

Now, being prepared for almost anything, he was not by any means prepared for nothing; and, consequently, when the Bell struck One, and no shape appeared, he was taken with a violent fit of trembling. Five minutes, ten minutes, a quarter of an hour went by, yet nothing came. All this time, he lay upon his bed, the very core and centre of a blaze of ruddy light, which streamed upon it when the clock

proclaimed the hour; and which, being only light, was more alarming than a dozen ghosts, as he was powerless to make out what it meant. At last, however, he began to think—that the source and secret of this ghostly light might be in the adjoining room, from whence, on further tracing it, it seemed to shine. This idea taking full possession of his mind, he got up softly and shuffled in his slippers to the door.

The moment Scrooge's hand was on the lock, a strange voice called him by his name, and bade him enter. He obeyed.

It was his own room. There was no doubt about that. But it had undergone a surprising transformation. The walls and ceiling were hung with living green. The crisp leaves of holly, mistletoe, and ivy reflected back the light, as if so many little mirrors had been scattered there; and a mighty blaze went roaring up the chimney. Heaped up on the floor, to form a kind of throne, were turkeys, geese, game, poultry, brawn, great joints of meat, sucking-pigs, long wreaths of

sausages, mince pies, plum-puddings, barrels of oysters, red-hot chestnuts, cherry-cheeked apples, juicy oranges, luscious pears, immense twelfth-cakes, and seething bowls of punch, that made the chamber dim with their delicious steam. In easy state upon this couch, there sat a jolly Giant, glorious to see; who bore a glowing torch, in shape not unlike Plenty's horn, and held it up, high up, to shed its light on Scrooge, as he came peeping round the door.

"Come in!" exclaimed the Ghost. "Come in! and know me better, man!"

Scrooge entered timidly, and hung his head before this Spirit. He was not the dogged Scrooge he had been; and though the Spirit's eyes were clear and kind, he did not like to meet them.

"I am the Ghost of Christmas Present," said the Spirit. "Look upon me!"

Scrooge reverently did so. It was clothed in one simple deep green robe, or mantle, bordered with white fur. This garment hung loosely on the figure. Its feet, observable beneath the ample folds of the garment, were bare; and on its head it wore no other covering than a holly wreath set here and there with shining icicles. Its dark brown curls were long and free; free as its genial face, its sparkling eyes, its open hand, its cheery voice, its unconstrained demeanour, and its joyful air. Girded round its middle was an antique scabbard; but no sword was in it, and the ancient sheath was eaten up with rust.

"Spirit," said Scrooge, submissively, "conduct me where you will. I went forth last night on compulsion [under constraint], and I learnt a lesson which is working now. To-night, if you have aught to teach me, let me profit by it."

"Touch my robe!"

Scrooge did as he was told, and held it fast.

Holly, mistletoe, ivy, turkeys, geese, game, poultry, brawn, meat, pigs, sausages, oysters, pies, puddings, fruit, and punch, all vanished instantly. So did the room, the fire, the ruddy glow,

the hour of night, and they stood in the city streets on Christmas morning, where (for the weather was severe) the people made a rough, but brisk and not unpleasant kind of music, in scraping the snow from the pavement in front of their dwellings.

The poulterers' shops were still half open, and the fruiterers' were radiant in their glory. There were great, round, potbellied baskets of chestnuts, shaped like the waistcoats of jolly old gentlemen, lolling at the doors, and tumbling out into the street. There were pears and apples, clustered high in blooming pyramids; there were oranges and lemons, urgently entreating and beseeching to be carried home in paper bags and eaten after dinner.

Soon the steeples called good people all, to church and chapel, and away they came, flocking through the streets in their best clothes, and with their gayest faces. And at the same time there emerged from scores of by-streets, lanes,

and nameless turnings, innumerable people, carrying their dinners to the bakers' shops. The sight of these poor revellers appeared to interest the Spirit very much, for he stood with Scrooge beside him in a baker's doorway, and taking off the covers as their bearers passed, sprinkled incense on their dinners from his torch. And it was a very uncommon kind of torch, for once or twice when there were angry words between some dinner-carriers who had jostled with each other, he shed a few drops of water on them from it, and their good humour was restored directly. For they said, it was a shame to quarrel upon Christmas Day. And so it was! God love it, so it was.

They went on, invisible, as they had been before, into the suburbs of the town—straight to Scrooge's clerk's; and on the threshold of the door the Spirit smiled, and stopped to bless Bob Cratchit's dwelling with the sprinklings of his torch. Think of that! Bob had but fifteen "Bob" [English shillings] a-week himself; and yet the Ghost of Christmas Present blessed his four-roomed house!

Then up rose Mrs. Cratchit, dressed out but poorly in a twice-turned gown, but brave in ribbons, which are cheap and make a goodly show for sixpence; and she laid the cloth, assisted by Belinda Cratchit, second of her daughters, also brave in ribbons; while Master Peter Cratchit plunged a fork into the saucepan of potatoes. And now two smaller Cratchits, boy and girl, came tearing in, screaming that outside the baker's they had smelt the goose, and known it for their own; and basking in luxurious thoughts of sage and onion, these young Cratchits danced about the table.

"What has ever got your precious father?" said Mrs. Cratchit. "And your brother, Tiny Tim! And Martha warn't as late last Christmas Day by half-an-hour!"

"Here's Martha, mother!" said a girl, appearing as she spoke.

"Why, bless your heart alive, my dear, how late you are!" said Mrs. Cratchit, kissing her a dozen times, and taking off her shawl and bonnet for her with officious [unnecessary] zeal.

"We'd a deal of work to finish up last night," replied the girl, "and had to clear away this morning, mother!"

"Well! Never mind so long as you are come," said Mrs. Cratchit. "Sit ye down before the fire, my dear, and have a warm, Lord bless ye!"

"There's father coming," cried the two young Cratchits, who were everywhere at once.

In came Bob, the father, and Tiny Tim upon his shoulder. Alas for Tiny Tim, he bore a little crutch, and had his limbs supported by an iron frame!

The two young Cratchits hustled Tiny Tim, and bore him off into the wash-house, that he might hear the pudding singing in the copper.

"And how did little Tim behave?" asked Mrs. Cratchit.

"As good as gold," said Bob, "and better. Somehow he gets thoughtful, sitting by himself so much, and thinks the strangest things you ever heard. He told me, coming home, that he hoped the people saw him in the church, because he was a cripple, and it might be pleasant to them to remember upon Christmas Day, who made lame beggars walk and blind men see."

The active little crutch was heard upon the floor, and back came Tiny Tim before another word was spoken, escorted by his brother and sister to his stool before the fire; and while Bob compounded some hot mixture in a jug and stirred it round and round and put it on the hob to simmer; Master Peter, and the two young Cratchits went to fetch the goose, with which they soon returned in high procession.

Such a bustle ensued that you might have thought a goose the rarest of all birds; and in truth it was something very like it in that house. At last the dishes were set on, and grace was said. It was succeeded by a breathless pause, as Mrs. Cratchit, looking slowly all along the carving-knife, prepared to plunge it in the goose; but when she did, and when the long expected gush of stuffing issued forth, one murmur of delight arose all around the board, and even Tiny Tim, excited by the two young Cratchits, beat on the table with the handle of his knife, and feebly cried Hurrah!

There never was such a goose. Its tenderness and flavour, size and cheapness, were the themes of universal admiration. It was a sufficient dinner for the whole family; indeed, as Mrs. Cratchit said with great delight (surveying one small atom of a bone upon the dish), they hadn't eaten it all at last! Yet everyone had had enough. But now, the plates being changed by Miss Belinda, Mrs. Cratchit left the room alone—too nervous to bear witnesses— to take the pudding up and bring it in.

Suppose it should not be done enough! Suppose it should break in turning out! Suppose somebody should have got over the wall of the back-yard, and stolen it, while they were merry with the goose—a supposition at which the two young Cratchits became livid [pale]! All sorts of horrors were supposed.

In half a minute Mrs. Cratchit entered—flushed, but smiling proudly— with the pudding, like a speckled cannon-ball, and bedight with Christmas holly stuck into the top.

At last the dinner was all done, the cloth was cleared, the hearth swept, and the fire made up. The compound in the jug being tasted, and considered perfect, apples and oranges were put upon the table, and a shovelful of chestnuts on

the fire. Then all the Cratchit family drew around the hearth, in what Bob Cratchit called a circle, meaning half a one; and at Bob Cratchit's elbow stood the family display of glass. Two tumblers and a custard-cup without a handle.

These held the hot stuff from the jug, however, as well as golden goblets would have done; and Bob served it out with beaming looks, while the chestnuts on the fire sputtered and cracked noisily. Then Bob proposed:—

"A Merry Christmas to us all, my dears. God bless us!"

Which all the family re-echoed.

"God bless us every one!" said Tiny Tim, the last of all.

He sat very close to his father's side upon his little stool. Bob held his withered little hand in his, as if he loved the child, and wished to keep him by his side, and dreaded that he might be taken from him.

"Spirit," said Scrooge, with an interest he had never felt before, "tell me if Tiny Tim will live."

"I see a vacant seat," replied the Ghost, "in the poor chimney-corner, and a crutch without an owner, carefully preserved. If these shadows remain unaltered by the Future, the child will die."

"No, no," said Scrooge. "Oh, no, kind Spirit! say he will be spared."

"If these shadows remain unaltered by the Future, none other of my race," returned the Ghost, "will find him here. What then? If he be like to die, he had better do it, and decrease the surplus population."

Scrooge hung his head to hear his own words quoted by the Spirit and,

trembling, cast his eyes upon the ground. But he raised them speedily, on hearing his own name.

"Mr. Scrooge!" said Bob, "I'll give you Mr. Scrooge, the Founder of the Feast!"

"The Founder of the Feast indeed!" cried Mrs. Cratchit, reddening. "I wish I had him here. I'd give him a piece of my mind to feast upon, and I hope he'd have a good appetite for it."

"My dear," said Bob, "the children! Christmas Day."

"It should be Christmas Day, I am sure, on which one drinks the health of such a stingy, hard, unfeeling man as Mr. Scrooge," said Mrs. Cratchit. "I'll drink his health for your sake and the Day's, not for his."

The children drank the toast after her. It was the first of their proceedings which had no heartiness in it. Tiny Tim drank it last of all, but he didn't care twopence for it. Scrooge was the Ogre [cruel man] of the family. The mention of his name cast a dark shadow on the party, which was not dispelled [driven away] for full five minutes. But after it passed away, they were then merrier than before.

They were not a handsome family; they were not well-dressed; their clothes were scanty. But, they were happy, grateful, pleased with one another, and contented with the time; and when they faded, and looked happier yet in the bright sprinklings of the Spirit's torch at parting, Scrooge had his eye upon them, and especially on Tiny Tim, until the last.

By this time it was getting dark, and snowing pretty heavily; and as Scrooge and the Spirit went along the streets, the brightness of the roaring fires in kitchens, parlours, and all sorts of rooms, was wonderful. But the Spirit did not tarry here, but bade Scrooge hold his robe, and sped on, above the black and heaving sea—on, on—until, being far away, as he told Scrooge, from any shore, they lighted on a ship. They stood beside the helmsman at the wheel, the look-out in the bow, the officers who had the watch; dark, ghostly figures in their several stations; but every man among them hummed a Christmas tune, or had a Christmas thought, or spoke below his breath to his companion of some by-gone Christmas Day, with homeward hopes belonging to it. And every man on board, walking or sleeping, good or bad, had had a kinder word for another on that day than on any day in the year; and had shared to some extent in its festivities; and had remembered those he cared for at a distance, and had known that they delighted to remember him.

It was a great surprise to Scrooge, while listening to the moaning of the wind, and thinking what a solemn thing it was to move on through the lonely darkness over an unknown abyss [bottomless gulf] whose depths were secrets as profound as Death: it was a great surprise to Scrooge, while thus engaged, to hear a hearty laugh. It was a much greater surprise to Scrooge to recognize it as his own nephew's and to find himself in a bright, dry, gleaming room, with the Spirit standing smiling by his side, and looking at that same nephew with approving affability [kindliness].

"Ha, ha!" laughed Scrooge's nephew. "Ha, ha, ha!"

Scrooge's nephew laughed: holding his sides, rolling his head, and twisting his face into the most extravagant contortions. Scrooge's niece, by marriage, laughed as heartily as he. And their assembled friends being not a bit behindhand, roared out, lustily.

"Ha, ha! Ha, ha, ha, ha!"

"He said that Christmas was a humbug, as I live!" cried Scrooge's nephew. "He believed it too!"

"More shame for him, Fred!" said Scrooge's niece, indignantly.

She was very pretty: exceedingly pretty. With a dimpled, surprised-looking, capital face; a ripe little mouth, that seemed made to be kissed—as no doubt it was; all kinds of good little dots about her chin, that melted into one another when she laughed; and the sunniest pair of eyes you ever saw in any little creature's head.

"He's a comical old fellow," said Scrooge's nephew, "that's the truth; and not so pleasant as he might be. However, his offences carry their own punishment, and I have nothing to say against him."

"I'm sure he is very rich, Fred," hinted Scrooge's niece. "At least you always tell *me* so."

"What of that, my dear!" said Scrooge's nephew. "His wealth is of no use to him. He doesn't do any good with it. He don't make himself comfortable with it."

"I have no patience with him," observed Scrooge's niece. Scrooge's niece's sisters, and all the other ladies, expressed the same opinion.

"Oh, I have!" said Scrooge's nephew. "I am sorry for him; I couldn't be angry with him if I tried. Who suffers by his ill whims? Himself, always. Here, he takes it into his head to dislike us, and he won't come and dine with us. What's the consequence? He doesn't lose much of a dinner."

"Indeed, I think he loses a very good dinner," interrupted Scrooge's niece. Everybody else said the same, and they must be allowed to have been competent judges, because they had just had dinner; and, with the dessert upon the table, were clustered around the fire, by lamplight.

"Well! I'm very glad to hear it," said Scrooge's nephew, "because I haven't any great faith in these young housekeepers. What do *you* say, Topper?"

Topper had clearly got his eyes upon one of Scrooge's niece's sisters, for he answered that a bachelor was a wretched outcast, who had no right to express an opinion on the subject. Whereat Scrooge's niece's sister—the plump one with the lace tucker: not the one with the roses—blushed.

"Do go on, Fred," said Scrooge's niece, clapping her hands. "He never finishes what he begins to say! He is such a ridiculous fellow!"

"I was only going to say," said Scrooge's nephew, "that the consequence of his taking a dislike to us, and not making merry with us, is, as I think, that he loses some pleasant moments, which could do him no harm. I am sure he loses pleasanter companions than he can find in his own thoughts, either in his mouldy old office, or his dusty chambers. I mean to give him the same chance every year, whether he likes it or not, for I pity him. He may rail at Christmas till he dies, but he can't help thinking better of it—I defy him—if he finds me going there, in good temper, year after year, and saying 'Uncle Scrooge, how are you?' If it only put him in the vein to leave his poor clerk fifty pounds, that's something; and I think I shook him yesterday."

After tea, they had some music. When the music sounded, all the things the Ghost had shown him, came upon his mind; he softened more and more; and thought that if he could have listened to it often, years ago, he might have cultivated the kindnesses of life.

The Ghost was greatly pleased to find him in this mood, and looked upon him with such favour, that he begged like a boy to be allowed to stay until the guests departed. But this the Spirit said could not be done.

And he and the Spirit were again upon their travels.

Much they saw, and far they went, and many homes they visited, but always with a happy end. The Spirit stood beside sick beds and they were cheerful; on foreign lands, and they were close at home; by struggling men, and they were patient in their greater hope; by poverty, and it was rich. In almshouse, hospital, and jail, in misery's every refuge, where vain man in his little brief authority had not made fast the door, and barred the Spirit out, he left his blessing, and taught Scrooge his precepts.

It was a long night, if it were only a night; but Scrooge had his doubts of this, because the Christmas Holidays appeared to be condensed into the space of time they passed together. It was strange, too, that while Scrooge remained unaltered in his outward form, the Ghost grew older, clearly older. Scrooge had observed this change, but never spoke of it, until they left a children's Twelfth Night party, when, looking at the Spirit as they stood together in an open place, he noticed that its hair was gray.

"Are spirits' lives so short?" asked Scrooge.

"My life upon this globe, is very brief," replied the Ghost. "It ends to-night."

"To-night!" cried Scrooge.

"To-night! at midnight. Hark! The time is drawing near."

The chimes were ringing the three quarters past eleven at that moment.

"Forgive me if I am not justified in that I ask," said Scrooge, looking intently at the Spirit's robe, "but I see something strange, and not belonging to yourself, protruding from your skirts. Is it a foot or a claw?"

"It might be a claw, for the flesh there is upon it," was the Spirit's sorrowful reply. "Look here."

From the foldings of its robe, it brought two children; wretched, frightful, hideous, miserable. They knelt down at its feet, and clung upon the outside of its garment.

"Oh, Man! look here. Look, look, down here!" exclaimed the Ghost.

There were a boy and girl. Yellow, meagre, ragged, scowling, wolfish; but prostrate, too, in their humility. Where graceful youth should have filled their features out, and touched them with its freshest tints, a stale and shrivelled hand, like that of age, had pinched, and twisted them, and pulled them into shreds. Where angels might have sat enthroned, devils lurked, and glared out menacing. No change, no degradation, no perversion of humanity, in any grade, through all the mysteries of wonderful creation, has monsters half so horrible and dread.

Scrooge started back, appalled. Having them shown to him in this way, he tried to say they were fine children, but the words choked themselves, rather than be parties to a lie of such enormous magnitude.

"Spirit! are they yours?" Scrooge could say no more.

"They are Man's," said the Spirit, looking down upon them. "And they cling to me, appealing from their fathers. This boy is Ignorance. This girl is Want. Beware them both, and all their degree, but most of all beware this boy, for on his brow I see that written which is Doom, unless the writing be erased. Deny it!" cried the Spirit, stretching out his hand toward the city. "Slander those who tell it ye! Admit it for your factious [divisive] purposes, and make it worse! And bide the end!"

"Have they no refuge or resource?" cried Scrooge.

"Are there no prisons?" said the Spirit, turning on him for the last time with his own words. "Are there no workhouses?"

The bell struck twelve.

Scrooge looked about him for the Ghost, and saw it not. As the last stroke ceased to vibrate, he remembered the prediction of old Jacob Marley, and lifting up his eyes, beheld a solemn Phantom, draped and hooded, coming, like a mist along the ground, towards him.

Reading Check

1. Who is the second Spirit to visit Scrooge, and how does he differ from the first?
2. Has Scrooge's viewpoint changed since the previous Spirit's visit?
3. Where does this Spirit take Scrooge, and what do they see?
4. How does Scrooge's nephew's view of wealth differ from that of Scrooge?
5. Who are the two children that cling to the Spirit's robes, and why does the Spirit show them to Scrooge?

Part IV The Last of the Spirits

The Phantom slowly, gravely, silently approached. When it came near him, Scrooge bent down upon his knees; for in the very air through which this Spirit moved it seemed to scatter gloom and mystery.

It was shrouded in a deep black garment, which concealed its head, its face, its form, and left nothing of it visible save one outstretched hand. But for this it would have been difficult to detach its figure from the night, and separate it from the darkness by which it was surrounded.

"I am in the presence of the Ghost of Christmas Yet To Come?" said Scrooge.

The Spirit answered not, but pointed downward with its hand.

Although well used to ghostly company by this time, Scrooge feared the silent shape so much that his legs trembled beneath him, and he found that he could hardly stand when he prepared to follow it. The Spirit paused a moment, as observing his condition, and giving him time to recover.

"Ghost of the Future!" he exclaimed, "I fear you more than any Spectre I have seen. But, as I know your purpose is to do me good, and as I hope to live to be another man from what I was, I am prepared to bear you company, and do it with a thankful heart. Will you not speak to me?"

It gave him no reply. The hand was pointed straight before them.

"Lead on!" said Scrooge. "Lead on! The night is waning fast, and it is precious time to me, I know. Lead on, Spirit!"

The Phantom moved away as it had come towards him. Scrooge followed in

the shadow of its dress, which bore him up, he thought, and carried him along.

The Spirit stopped beside one little knot of business men. Observing that the hand was pointed to them, Scrooge advanced to listen to their talk.

"No," said a great fat man with a monstrous chin, "I don't know much about it, either way. I only know he's dead."

"When did he die?" inquired another.

"Last night, I believe."

"Why, what was the matter with him?" asked a third, taking a vast quantity of snuff out of a very large snuff-box. "I thought he'd never die."

"God knows," said the first, with a yawn.

"What has he done with his money?" asked a red-faced gentleman.

"I haven't heard," said the man with the large chin, yawning again. "Left it to his Company, perhaps. He hasn't left it to *me*. That's all I know."

This pleasantry was received with a general laugh.

"It's likely to be a very cheap funeral," said the same speaker; "for upon my life I don't know of anybody to go to it. Suppose we make up a party and volunteer?"

"I don't mind going if a lunch is provided," observed the red-faced gentleman. "But I must be fed, if I make one."

Another laugh.

Speakers and listeners strolled away, and mixed with other groups.

Scrooge was at first inclined to be surprised that the Spirit should attach importance to conversations apparently so trivial; but feeling assured that they must have some hidden purpose, he set himself to consider what it was likely to be. For he had an expectation that the conduct of his future self would give him the clew he missed, and would render the solution of these riddles easy.

He looked about in that very place for his own image; but another man stood in his accustomed corner, and though the clock pointed to his usual time of day for being there, he saw no likeness of himself among the multitudes that poured in through the Porch. It gave him little surprise, however; for he had been revolving in his mind a change of life, and thought and hoped he saw his new-born resolutions carried out in this.

They left the busy scene, and went into an obscure part of the town, where Scrooge had never penetrated before, although he recognized its situation, and its bad repute [reputation]. The ways were foul and narrow; the shops and houses wretched; and people half-naked, drunken, slipshod, ugly. Alleys and archways, like so many cesspools, disgorged [emptied] their offences of smell, and dirt, and life, upon the straggling streets; and the whole quarter reeked with crime, with filth, and misery.

Far in this den of infamous resort, there was a low-browed, beetling [machine used for finishing cloth] shop, below a pent-house roof, where iron, old rags, bottles, bones, and greasy offal [garbage] were brought. Upon the floor within, were piled up heaps of rusty keys, nails, chains, hinges, files, scales, weights, and refuse iron of all kinds.

Secrets that few would like to scrutinize were bred and hidden in mountains of unseemly rags, masses of corrupt fat, and sepulchres of bones. Sitting in among the wares he dealt in, by a charcoal-stove, made of old bricks, was a gray-haired rascal, nearly seventy years of age; who had screened himself from the cold air without, by a frowzy [dirty, untidy] curtaining of miscellaneous tatters, hung upon the line, and smoked his pipe in all the luxury of calm retirement.

Scrooge and the Phantom came into the presence of this man, just as a woman with a heavy bundle slunk into the shop. But she had scarcely entered, when another woman, similarly laden, came in too; and she was closely followed by a man in faded black, who was no less startled by the sight of them, than they had been upon the recognition of each other. After a short period of blank astonishment, in which the old man with the pipe had joined them, they all three burst into a laugh.

"Let the charwoman alone to be the first!" cried she who had entered first. "Let the laundress alone to be the second, and let the undertaker's man alone to be the third. Look here, old Joe, here's a chance! If we haven't all three met here without meaning it!"

"You couldn't have met in a better place," said old Joe, removing his pipe from his mouth. "Come into the parlour.

The parlour was the space behind the screen of rags. The old man raked the fire together with an old stair-rod, and having trimmed his smoky lamp (for it was night) with the stem of his pipe, put it in his mouth again.

While he did this, the woman who had already spoken threw her bundle on the floor, and sat down in a flaunting [impudent] manner on a stool; crossing her elbows on her knees, and looking with a bold defiance at the other two.

"What odds then! What odds, Mrs. Dilber?" said the woman. "Every person has a right to take care of themselves. *He* always did!"

"That's true, indeed!" said the laundress. "No man more so."

"Very well, then!" cried the woman. "That's enough. Who's the worse for the loss of a few things like these? Not a dead man, I suppose."

"No, indeed," said Mrs. Dilber, laughing.

"If he wanted to keep 'em after he was dead," pursued the woman, "why wasn't he natural in his lifetime? If he had been, he'd have had somebody to look after him when he was struck with Death, instead of lying gasping out his last there, alone by himself."

"It's the truest word that ever was spoke," said Mrs. Dilber. "It's a judgment on him."

"I wish it was a little heavier one," replied the woman; "and it would have been, you may depend upon it, if I could have laid my hands on anything else. Open that bundle, old Joe, and let me know the value of it. Speak out plain. I'm not afraid to be the first, nor afraid for them to see it. We knew pretty well that we were helping ourselves, before we met here, I believe. It's no sin. Open the bundle, Joe."

But the gallantry of her friends would not allow of this; and the man in faded black, mounting the breach first, produced *his* plunder. It was not extensive. A seal or two, a pencil-case, a pair of sleeve-buttons, and a brooch of no great value, were all. They were severally examined and appraised by old Joe, who chalked the sums he was disposed to give for each, upon the wall, and added them up into a total when he found there was nothing more to come.

"That's your account," said Joe, "and I wouldn't give another sixpence, if I was to be boiled for not doing it. Who's next?"

Mrs. Dilber was next. Sheets and towels, a little wearing apparel, two old-fashioned silver teaspoons, a pair of sugar-tongs, and a few boots. Her account was stated on the wall in the same manner.

"And now undo my bundle, Joe," said the first woman.

"What do you call this?" said Joe. "Bed-curtains!"

"Ah!" returned the woman, laughing and leaning forward on her crossed arms. "Bed-curtains!"

"You don't mean to say you took 'em down, rings and all, with him lying there?" said Joe.

"Yes I do," replied the woman. "Why not?"

"His blankets?" asked Joe.

"Whose else's do you think?" replied the woman. "He isn't likely to take cold without 'em, I dare say."

"I hope he didn't die of anything catching? Eh?" said old Joe, stopping in his work, and looking up.

"Don't you be afraid of that," returned the woman. "I ain't so fond of his company that I'd loiter about him for such things, if he did. Ah! you may look through that shirt till your eyes ache; but you won't find a hole in it, nor a threadbare place. It's the best he had, and a fine one too. They'd have wasted it, if it hadn't been for me."

"What do you call wasting of it?" asked old Joe.

"Putting it on him to be buried in, to be sure," replied the woman with a laugh. "Somebody was fool enough to do it, but I took it off again. If calico ain't good enough for such a purpose, it isn't good enough for anything. It's quite as becoming to the body. He can't look uglier than he did in that one."

Scrooge listened to this dialogue in horror. As they sat grouped about their spoil, in the scanty light afforded by the old man's lamp, he viewed them with a detestation and disgust, which could hardly have been greater, though they had been obscene demons, marketing the corpse itself.

"Ha, ha!" laughed the same woman, when old Joe, producing a flannel bag with money in it, told out their several gains upon the ground. "This is the end of it, you see! He frightened everyone away from him when he was alive, to profit us when he was dead! Ha, ha, ha!"

"Spirit!" said Scrooge, shuddering from head to foot, "I see, I see. The case of this unhappy man might be my own. My life tends that way, now. Merciful Heaven, what is this!"

He recoiled in terror, for the scene had changed, and now he almost touched a bed: a bare, uncurtained bed: on which, beneath a ragged sheet, there lay a something covered up, which, though it was dumb, announced itself in awful language.

Scrooge glanced towards the Phantom. Its steady hand was pointed to the head. The cover was so carelessly adjusted that the slightest raising of it, the motion of a finger upon Scrooge's part, would have disclosed the face. He thought of it, felt how easy it would be to do, and longed to do it; but had no more power to withdraw the veil than to dismiss the spectre at his side.

Oh cold, cold, rigid, dreadful Death, set up thine altar here, and dress it with such terrors as thou hast at thy command: for this is thy dominion! But of the loved, revered, and honoured head, thou canst not turn one hair to thy dread purposes, or make one feature odious.

No voice pronounced these words in Scrooge's ears, and yet he heard them when he looked upon the bed. He thought, if this man could be raised up now, what would be his foremost thoughts? Avarice, hard dealing, griping cares? They have brought him to a rich end, truly!

He lay, in the dark empty house, with not a man, a woman, or a child, to say that he was kind to me in this or that, and for the memory of one kind word I will be kind to him. A cat was tearing at the door, and there was a sound of gnawing rats beneath the hearth-stone. What *they* wanted in the room of death, and why they were so restless and disturbed, Scrooge did not dare to think.

"Spirit!" he said, "this is a fearful place. In leaving it, I shall not leave its lesson, trust me. Let us go!"

Still the Ghost pointed with an unmoved finger to the head.

"I understand you," Scrooge returned, "and I would do it, if I could. But I have not the power, Spirit. I have not the power."

The Ghost conducted him through several streets familiar to his feet; and as they went along, Scrooge looked here and there to find himself, but nowhere was he to be seen. They entered poor Bob Cratchit's house; the dwelling he had visited before; and found the mother and the children seated round the fire.

Quiet. Very quiet. The noisy little Cratchits were as still as statues in one corner, and sat looking up at Peter, who had a book before him. The mother and her daughters were engaged in sewing. But surely they were very quiet!

The mother laid her work upon the table, and put her hand up to her face.

"The colour hurts my eyes," she said.

The colour? Ah, poor Tiny Tim!

"They're better now again," said Cratchit's wife. "It makes them weak by candlelight; and I wouldn't show weak eyes to your father when he comes home, for the world. It must be near his time."

"Past it rather," Peter answered, shutting up his book. "But I think he's walked a little slower than he used, these few last evenings, mother."

They were very quiet again. At last she said, and in a steady cheerful voice, that only faltered once:—

"I have known him walk with—I have known him walk with Tiny Tim upon his shoulder, very fast indeed."

"But he was very light to carry," she resumed, intent upon her work, "and his father loved him so, that it was no trouble—no trouble. And there is your father at the door!"

Bob was very cheerful with them, and spoke pleasantly to all the family.

He looked at the work upon the table, and praised the industry and speed of Mrs. Cratchit and the girls. They would be done long before Sunday he said.

"Sunday! You went today, then, Robert?" said his wife.

"Yes, my dear," returned Bob. "I wish you could have gone. It would have done you good to see how green a place it is. But you'll see it often. I promised him that I would walk there on a Sunday. My little, little child!" cried Bob. "My little child!"

He broke down all at once. He couldn't help it. If he could have helped it, he and his child would have been farther apart perhaps than they were.

He left the room, and went upstairs into the room above, which was lighted cheerfully, and hung with Christmas.

There was a chair set close beside the child, and there were signs of someone having been there, lately. Poor Bob sat down in it, and when he had thought a little and composed himself, he kissed the little face. He was reconciled to what had happened, and went down again quite happy.

"Spectre," said Scrooge, "something informs me that our parting moment is at hand. I know it, but I know not how. Tell me what man that was whom we saw lying dead?"

The Ghost of Christmas Yet To Come conveyed him, as before—though at a different time, he thought: indeed, there seemed no order in these latter visions, save that they were in the Future—into the resorts of business men, but showed him not himself.

Indeed, the Spirit did not stay for anything, but went straight on, as to the end just now desired, until besought by Scrooge to tarry for a moment.

"This court," said Scrooge, "through which we hurry now, is where my place of occupation is, and has been for a length of time. I see the house. Let me behold what I shall be in days to come!"

The Spirit stopped; the hand was pointed elsewhere. "The house is yonder," Scrooge exclaimed. "Why do you point away?"

The inexorable [unrelenting] finger underwent no change.

Scrooge hastened to the window of his office, and looked in. It was an office still, but not his. The furniture was not the same, and the figure in the chair was not himself. The Phantom pointed as before.

He joined it once again, and wondering why and whither he had gone, accompanied it until they reached an iron gate. He paused to look round before entering.

A churchyard. Here, then, the wretched man whose name he had now to learn, lay underneath the ground. It was a worthy place. Walled in by houses; overrun by grass and weeds, the growth of vegetation's death, not life; choked up with too much burying; fat with repleted appetite. A worthy place!

The Spirit stood among the graves, and pointed down to One. He advanced towards it trembling. The Phantom was exactly as it had been, but he dreaded that he saw new meaning in its solemn shape.

"Before I draw nearer to that stone to which you point," said Scrooge, "answer me one question. Are these the shadows of the things that Will be, or are they shadows of things that May be, only?"

Still the Ghost pointed downward to the grave by which it stood.

"Men's courses will foreshadow certain ends, to which, if persevered in, they must lead," said Scrooge. "But if the courses be departed from, the ends will change. Say it is thus with what you show me!"

The Spirit was immovable as ever.

Scrooge crept towards it, trembling as he went; and following the finger, read upon the stone of the neglected grave his own name, EBENEZER SCROOGE.

"Am I that man who lay upon the bed?" he cried, upon his knees.

The finger pointed from the grave to him, and back again.

"No, Spirit! Oh no, no!"

The finger still was there.

"Spirit!" he cried, tight clutching at its robe, "hear me! I am not the man I was. Why show me this, if I am past all hope!"

For the first time the hand appeared to shake.

"Good Spirit," he pursued, as down upon the ground he fell before it: "Your nature intercedes for me, and pities me. Assure me that I yet may change these shadows you have shown me, by an altered life!"

The kind hand trembled.

"I will honour Christmas in my heart, and try to keep it all the year. I will live in the Past, the Present, and the Future. The Spirits of all Three shall strive within me. I will not shut out the lessons that they teach. Oh, tell me I may sponge away the writing on this stone!"

In his agony, he caught the spectral hand. It sought to free itself, but he was strong in his entreaty, and detained it. The Spirit, stronger yet, repulsed him.

Holding up his hands in one last prayer to have his fate reversed, he saw an alteration in the Phantom's hood and dress. It shrank, collapsed, and dwindled down into a bedpost.

Reading Check

1. Who is the last of the three spirits, and what is he like?
2. Why do you think this third Spirit is the most frightening to Scrooge?
3. Where does this third Spirit take Scrooge, and what do they see?
4. How are the vagrants like Scrooge at the opening of the story?
5. What is the difference between the mourners view of Tiny Tim and their view of Scrooge?

Part V   The End of It

Yes! and the bedpost was his own. The bed was his own, the room was his own. Best and happiest of all, the Time before him was his own, to make amends in!

"I will live in the Past, the Present, and the Future!" Scrooge repeated, as he scrambled out of bed. "The Spirits of all Three shall strive within me. Oh Jacob Marley! Heaven, and the Christmas Time be praised for this! I say it on my knees, old Jacob, on my knees!"

He was so fluttered and so glowing with his good intentions, that his broken voice would scarcely answer to his call. He had been sobbing violently in his conflict with the Spirit, and his face was wet with tears.

"They are not torn down," cried Scrooge, folding one of his bed-curtains in his arms, "they are not torn down, rings and all. They are here: I am here: the shadows of the things that would have been, may be dispelled. They will be. I know they will!"

His hands were busy with his garments all this time: turning them inside out, putting them on upside down, tearing them, misleading them, making them parties to every kind of extravagance.

"I don't know what to do!" cried Scrooge, laughing and crying in the same breath; and making a perfect Laocoön of himself with his stockings. "I am as light as a feather, I am as happy

as an angel, I am as merry as a schoolboy. I am as giddy as a drunken man. A Merry Christmas to everybody! A Happy New Year to all the world. Hallo here! Whoop! Hallo!"

He had frisked into the sitting-room, and was now standing there: perfectly winded.

"There's the saucepan that the gruel was in!" cried Scrooge, starting off again, and frisking round the fireplace. "There's the door, by which the Ghost of Jacob Marley entered! There's the corner where the Ghost of Christmas Present sat! There's the window where I saw the wandering Spirits! It's all right, it's all true, it all happened. Ha, ha, ha!"

Really, for a man who had been out of practice for so many years, it was a splendid laugh, a most illustrious laugh. The father of a long, long line of brilliant laughs!

"I don't know what day of the month it is!" said Scrooge. "I don't know how long I've been among the Spirits. I don't know anything. I'm quite a baby. Never mind. I don't care. I'd rather be a baby. Hallo! Whoop! Hallo here!" He was checked in his transports by the churches ringing out the lustiest peals he had ever heard. Clash, clang, hammer, ding, dong, bell. Bell, dong, ding, hammer, clang, clash! Oh, glorious, glorious!

Running to the window, he opened it, and put out his head. No fog, no mist; clear, bright, jovial, stirring, cold; cold, piping for the blood to dance to; golden sunlight; heavenly sky; sweet fresh air; merry bells. Oh, glorious. Glorious!

"What's today?" cried Scrooge, calling downward to a boy in Sunday clothes, who perhaps had loitered in to look about him.

"EH?" returned the boy, with all his might of wonder.

"What's today, my fine fellow?" said Scrooge.

"Today!" replied the boy. "Why, CHRISTMAS DAY."

"It's Christmas Day!" said Scrooge to himself. "I haven't missed it. The Spirits have done it all in one night. They can do anything they like. Of course they can. Of course they can. Hallo, my fine fellow?"

"Hallo!" returned the boy.

"Do you know the Poulterer's, in the next street the one, at the corner?" Scrooge inquired.

"I should hope I did," replied the lad.

"An intelligent boy!" said Scrooge. "A remarkable boy! Do you know whether they've sold the prize Turkey that was hanging up there? Not the little prize Turkey: the big one?"

"What, the one as big as me?" returned the boy.

"What a delightful boy!" said Scrooge. "It's a pleasure to talk to him. Yes, my buck!"

"It's hanging there now," replied the boy.

"Is it?" said Scrooge. "Go and buy it."

"Walk-ER!" exclaimed the boy.

"No, no," said Scrooge, "I am in earnest. Go and buy it, and tell 'em to bring it here, that I may give them the direction where to take it. Come back with the man, and I'll give you a shilling. Come back with him in less than five minutes, and I'll give you half-a-crown!"

The boy was off like a shot. He must have had a steady hand at a trigger who could have got a shot off half so fast.

"I'll send it to Bob Cratchit's!" whispered Scrooge, rubbing his hands, and splitting with a laugh. "He shan't know who sends it. It's twice the size of Tiny Tim. Joe Miller never made such a joke as sending it to Bob's will be!"

The hand in which he wrote the address was not a steady one, but write it he did, somehow, and went down stairs to open the street door, ready for the coming of the poulterer's man. As he stood there, waiting his arrival, the knocker caught his eye.

"I shall love it, as long as I live!" cried Scrooge, patting it with his hand.

"I scarcely ever looked at it before. What an honest expression it has in its face! It's a wonderful knocker!—Here's the Turkey. Hallo! Whoop! How are you! Merry Christmas!"

It *was* a Turkey! He could never have stood upon his legs, that bird. He would have snapped 'em short off in a minute, like sticks of sealing-wax.

"Why, it's impossible to carry that to Camden Town," said Scrooge. "You must have a cab."

The chuckle with which he said this, and the chuckle with which he paid for the turkey, and the chuckle with which he paid for the cab, and the chuckle with which he recompensed the boy, were only to be exceeded by the chuckle with which he sat down breathless in his chair again, and chuckled till he cried.

Shaving was not an easy task, for his hand continued to shake very much; and shaving requires attention, even when you don't dance while you are at it. But if he had cut the end of his nose off, he would have put a piece of sticking-plaster over it, and been quite satisfied.

He dressed himself "all in his best," and at last got out into the streets. The people were by this time pouring forth, as he had seen them with the Ghost of Christmas Present; and walking with his hands behind him, Scrooge regarded everyone with a delighted smile. He looked so irresistibly pleasant, in a word, that three or four good-humoured fellows said, "Good morning, Sir! A Merry Christmas to you!" And Scrooge said often afterwards, that of all the blithe sounds he had ever heard, those were the blithest in his ears.

He had not gone far, when coming on towards him he beheld the portly gentleman, who had walked into his counting-house the day before and said, "Scrooge and Marley's, I believe?" It sent a pang across his heart to think how this old gentleman would look upon him when they met; but he knew what path lay straight before him, and he took it.

"My dear Sir," said Scrooge, quickening his pace, and taking the old gentleman by both his hands. "How do you do? I hope you succeeded yesterday. It was very kind of you. A Merry Christmas to you, Sir!"

"Mr. Scrooge?"

"Yes," said Scrooge. "That is my name, and I fear it may not be pleasant to you. Allow me to ask your pardon. And will you have the goodness"—here Scrooge whispered in his ear.

"Lord bless me!" cried the gentleman, as if his breath were gone. "My dear Mr. Scrooge, are you serious?"

"If you please," said Scrooge. "Not a farthing less. A great many back-payments are included in it, I assure you. Will you do me that favour?"

"My dear Sir," said the other, shaking hands with him. "I don't know what to say to such munifi—"

"Don't say anything, please," retorted Scrooge. "Come and see me. Will you come and see me?"

"I will!" cried the old gentleman. And it was clear he meant to do it.

"Thank'ee," said Scrooge. "I am much obliged to you. I thank you fifty times. Bless you!"

He went to church, and walked about the streets, and watched the

people hurrying to and fro, and patted children on the head, and questioned beggars, and looked down into the kitchens of houses, and up to the windows; and found that everything could yield him pleasure. He had never dreamed that any walk—that anything—could give him so much happiness. In the afternoon, he turned his steps towards his nephew's house.

He passed the door a dozen times, before he had the courage to go up and knock. But he made a dash, and did it:—

"Is your master at home, my dear?" said Scrooge to the girl.

"Yes, Sir."

"Where is he, my love?" said Scrooge.

"He's in the dining-room, Sir, along with mistress. I'll show you upstairs, if you please."

"Thank'ee. He knows me," said Scrooge, with his hand already on the

dining-room lock. "I'll go in here, my dear."

He turned it gently, and sidled his face in, round the door. They were looking at the table (which was spread out in great array [display]) for these young housekeepers are always nervous on such points, and like to see that everything is right.

"Fred!" said Scrooge.

Dear heart alive, how his niece by marriage started! Scrooge had forgotten, for the moment, about her sitting in the corner with the footstool, or he wouldn't have done it, on any account.

"Why, bless my soul!" cried Fred, "who's that?"

"It's I. Your uncle Scrooge. I have come to dinner. Will you let me in, Fred?"

Let him in! It is a mercy he didn't shake his arm off. He was at home in five minutes. Nothing could be done heartier. His niece looked just the same.

So did Topper when *he* came. So did the plump sister, when *she* came. So did everyone when *they* came. Wonderful party, wonderful games, wonderful unanimity [complete agreement], wonder-ful happiness!

But he was early at the office next morning. Oh, he was early there. If he could only be there first, and catch Bob Cratchit coming late! That was the thing he had set his heart upon.

And he did it; yes he did! The clock struck nine. No Bob. A quarter past. No Bob. He was full eighteen minutes and a half behind his time. Scrooge sat with his door wide open, that he might see him come in.

His hat was off, before he opened the door; his comforter too. He was on his stool in a jiffy; driving away with his pen, as if he were trying to overtake nine o'clock.

"Hallo!" growled Scrooge, in his accustomed voice as near as he could

feign it. "What do you mean by coming here at this time of day?"

"I am very sorry, Sir," said Bob. "I *am* behind my time."

"You are?" repeated Scrooge. "Yes. I think you are. Step this way, Sir, if you please."

"It's only once a year, Sir," pleaded Bob. "It shall not be repeated. I was making rather merry yesterday, Sir."

"Now, I'll tell you what, my friend," said Scrooge, "I am not going to stand this sort of thing any longer. And therefore," he continued, leaping from his stool, and giving Bob such a dig in the waistcoat that he staggered back again: "and therefore I am about to raise your salary!"

Bob trembled, and got a little nearer to the ruler. He had a momentary idea of knocking Scrooge down with it; holding him; and calling to the people in the court for help and a strait-waistcoat.

"A Merry Christmas, Bob!" said Scrooge, with an earnestness that could not be mistaken, as he clapped him on the back. "A merrier Christmas, Bob, my good fellow, than I have given you for many a year! I'll raise your salary, and endeavour to assist your struggling family, and we will discuss your affairs this very afternoon, over a Christmas bowl of smoking bishop, Bob! Make up the fires, and buy another coal-scuttle before you dot another *i,* Bob Cratchit!"

Scrooge was better than his word. He did it all, and infinitely more; and to Tiny Tim, who did NOT die, he was a second father. He became as good a friend, as good a master, and as good a man, as the good old city knew, or any other good old city, town, or borough, in the good old world. Some people laughed to see the alteration in him, but he let them laugh, and little heeded them; for he was wise enough to know that nothing ever happened on this globe, for good, at which some people did not have their fill of laughter in the outset; and knowing that such as these would be blind anyway, he thought it quite as well that they should wrinkle up their eyes in grins, as have the malady in less attractive forms. His own heart laughed: and that was quite enough for him.

He had no further intercourse with Spirits, but lived upon the Total Abstinence Principle, ever afterwards; and it was always said of him, that he knew how to keep Christmas well, if any man alive possessed the knowledge. May that be truly said of us, and all of us! And so, as Tiny Tim observed, God Bless Us, Every One!

Reading Check

1. What is Scrooge's reaction to awakening in his own bed?
2. List some incidents that reveal the fact that the three spirits' visits have helped change Scrooge's viewpoint.
3. List at least one specific action that shows us that Scrooge has relinquished his idol of money.
4. How do others view Scrooge after his change?

If we confess our sins, he is faithful and just to forgive us our sins, and to cleanse us from all unrighteousness.

(I John 1:9)

The Meaning of the Look

Elizabeth Barrett Browning

I think that look of Christ might seem to say—
"Thou Peter! art thou then a common stone
Which I at last must break my heart upon,
For all God's charge to his high angels may
Guard my foot better? Did I yesterday
Wash thy feet, my beloved, that they should run
Quick to deny me 'neath the morning sun?
And do thy kisses, like the rest, betray?
The cock crows coldly.—Go, and manifest
A late contrition, but no bootless fear!
For when thy final need is dreariest,
Thou shalt not be denied, as I am here;
My voice to God and angels shall attest,
Because I KNOW this man, let him be clear."

Peter Denying Christ by Christoph Paudiss from
The Bob Jones University Collection of Sacred Art

Spirit of God, Descend Upon My Heart

George Croly

Spirit of God, descend upon my heart;
Wean it from earth, through all its pulses move;
Stoop to my weakness, mighty as Thou art,
And make me love Thee as I ought to love.

Hast Thou not bid us love Thee, God and King?
All, all Thine own, soul, heart and strength and mind;
I see Thy cross—there teach my heart to cling:
O let me seek Thee, and O let me find.

Teach me to feel that Thou art always nigh;
Teach me the struggles of the soul to bear.
To check the rising doubt, the rebel sigh;
Teach me the patience of unanswered prayer.

Teach me to love Thee as Thine angels love.
One holy passion filling all my frame;
The baptism of the heav'n-descended Dove,
My heart an altar; and Thy love the flame.

And it came to pass after these things, that God did tempt Abraham, and said unto him, Abraham: and he said, Behold, here I am.

And he said, Take now thy son, thine only son Isaac, whom thou lovest, and get thee into the land of Moriah; and offer him there for a burnt offering upon one of the mountains which I will tell thee of.

And Abraham rose up early in the morning, and saddled his ass, and took two of his young men with him, and Isaac his son, and clave the wood for the burnt offering, and rose up, and went unto the place of which God had told him.

Then on the third day Abraham lifted up his eyes, and saw the place afar off.

And Abraham said unto his young men, Abide ye here with the ass; and I and the lad will go yonder and worship, and come again to you.

And Abraham took the wood of the burnt offering, and laid it upon Isaac his son; and he took the fire in his hand, and a knife; and they went both of them together.

And Isaac spake unto Abraham his father, and said, My father: and he said, Here am I, my son. And he said, Behold the fire and the wood: but where is the lamb for a burnt offering?

And Abraham said, My son, God will provide himself a lamb for a burnt offering: so they went both of them together.

And they came to the place which God had told him of; and Abraham built an altar there, and laid the wood in order, and bound Isaac his son, and laid him on the altar upon the wood.

And Abraham stretched forth his hand, and took the knife to slay his son.

And the angel of the Lord called unto him out of heaven, and said, Abraham, Abraham: and he said, Here am I.

And he said, Lay not thine hand upon the lad, neither do thou anything unto him: for now I know that thou fearest God, seeing thou hast not withheld thy son, thine only son from me.

And Abraham lifted up his eyes, and looked, and behold behind him a ram caught in a thicket by his horns: and Abraham went and took the ram, and offered him up for a burnt offering in the stead of his son.

And Abraham called the name of that place Jehovah-jireh: as it is said to this day, In the mount of the Lord it shall be seen.

And the angel of the Lord called unto Abraham out of heaven the second time,

And said, By myself have I sworn, saith the Lord, for because thou hast done this thing, and hast not withheld thy son, thine only son:

That in blessing I will bless thee, and in multiplying I will multiply thy seed as the stars of the heaven, and as the sand which is upon the sea shore; and thy seed shall possess the gate of his enemies;

And in thy seed shall all the nations of the earth be blessed; because thou hast obeyed my voice.

(Genesis 22:1-18)

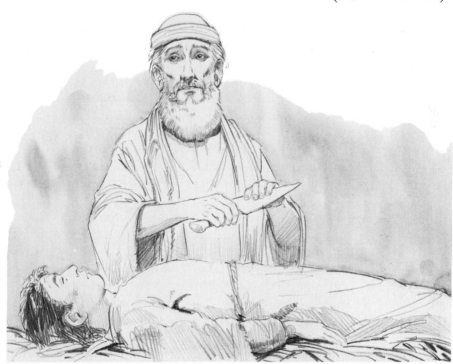

Adventurers

When they reached the haunted house there was something so weird and grisly about the dead silence that reigned there under the baking sun, and something so depressing about the loneliness and desolation of the place, that they were afraid for a moment to venture in. Then they crept to the door and took a trembling peep.

In a little while familiarity modified their fears and they gave the place a critical and interested examination. Next they wanted to look upstairs. Up there were the same signs of decay. They were about to go and begin work when—

"Sh!" said Tom.

"What is it?" whispered Huck.

"Sh! . . . There! . . . Hear it?"

"Yes! . . . Oh, my! Let's run!"

"Keep still! Don't budge! They're coming right toward the door."   The boys stretched themselves upon the floor with their eyes to knot-holes in the planking, and lay waiting, in a misery of fear.

Do you find yourself wanting to know what happened to Tom and Huck? The fact that you are curious is not surprising, for the excitement, hazard, and suspense that characterize their adventure keep you interested and make you want to know more.

Like Tom and Huck all the adventurers you will read about in this unit confront danger. Unlike the boys, however, the succeeding adventurers are unselfish and brave. They are characters who act courageously in hazardous settings despite the sacrifice required of them. To aid in our discussion of these noble adventurers, let's divide them into two groups: the "responders" and the "contenders."

Jerry in "The Banks of the Sacramento" and the missionary family in "The Swiss Family Robinson" are responders. These characters are unexpectedly confronted with life-and-death adventures. But even though they are caught off guard they respond courageously, and the courage each manifests is admirable.

A scriptural example of such bravery is found in the book of Daniel. Nebuchadnezzar, the Babylonian king, had set up a golden image and demanded that all in his kingdom bow down and worship his idol. Those who refused were to be cast into a burning fiery furnace. The Jews, at this time captives in Babylon, were also required to obey the king's decree. But three young Israelites named Shadrach, Meshach, and Aded-nego refused. And when they were brought before Nebuchadnezzar and given one final chance to obey, they replied without hesitation, "We are not careful to answer thee in this matter. If it be so, our God whom we serve is able to deliver us from the burning fiery furnace, and he will deliver us out of thine hand, O king. But if not, be it known unto thee . . . that we will not serve thy gods, nor worship the golden image which thou hast set up" (Daniel 3:16b-18). These three young men did not expect to face this perilous adventure, but once confronted with the danger they responded bravely.

When therefore we hear that robberies are done on the king's highway, two things become us to do. We need first to be sure to take a shield with us for He hath said, "Above all take the shield of faith, wherewith ye shall be able to quench all the fiery darts of the wicked." 'Tis good also that we desire that the King himself go with us. For if He will but go along, what need have we to be afraid though ten thousand shall set themselves against us.

Our second group of adventurers is called "contenders." These adventurers do not simply respond to unexpected perils; they willingly accept hazardous challenges. Though each character could have avoided personal risk, each one chose to contend with danger to protect others. The major characters in "Incident of the French Camp," "Emily Geiger," and "The Princess and Curdie" are contenders who prove to be wise and determined as well as courageous.

The patriarch Abraham was such a contender. In Genesis 14 Lot, Abraham's nephew, separates from him and settles in Sodom. Soon after, Sodom comes under the attack of several neighboring kings. During these skirmishes Lot is taken captive and his goods are confiscated. When Abraham hears of his nephew's dilemma, he immediately devises a plan to rescue Lot. This plan is so successful that Abraham is able not only to save Lot and retrieve his goods but also to rescue the entire city from the enemy.

Such scriptural examples teach us that adventures demanding courage, wisdom, and determination are not limited to storybooks. Nor should you be deceived into thinking that such adventurers are only found among the Old Testament heroes. God challenges each Christian to be a noble adventurer, and He promises success to those who accept the challenge. "Be thou strong therefore, . . . And keep the charge of the Lord thy God, to walk in his ways, to keep his statutes, and his commandments, and his judgments, and his testimonies, . . . that thou mayest prosper in all that thou doest, and whithersoever thou turnest thyself" (I Kings 2:2b-3).

Tom Sawyer was a clever, mischievous boy who often chafed under the strict supervision of his well-intentioned Aunt Polly. Huck Finn, on the other hand, was a homeless orphan who was not as clever as Tom nor as inclined to seek out trouble. But despite these differences, the boys shared a common love—the love for adventure.

The Adventures of Tom Sawyer

Mark Twain

There comes a time in every rightly constructed boy's life when he has a raging desire to go somewhere and dig for hidden treasure. This desire suddenly came upon Tom one day. Presently he stumbled upon Huck Finn and taking him to a private place, opened the matter to him confidentially. Huck was willing to take the enterprise into hand.

"Where'll we dig?" he said.

Tom considered awhile, and then said:

"The ha'nted house. That's it!"

"Blame it, I don't like ha'nted houses, Tom. Why, they're worse'n dead people. Dead people might talk, maybe, but they don't come sliding around in a shroud, when you ain't noticing, and peep over your shoulder all of a sudden and grit their teeth, the way a ghost does. I couldn't stand such a thing as that, Tom—nobody could."

"Yes, but, Huck, ghosts don't travel around only at night. They won't hinder us from digging there in the daytime."

"Well, that's so. But you know mighty well people don't go about that ha'nted house in the day nor the night."

"Well, that's mostly because they don't like to go where a man's been murdered, anyway—but nothing's ever been seen around that house except in the night—just some blue lights slipping by the windows—no regular ghosts."

"Well, where you see one of them blue lights flickering around, Tom, you can bet there's a ghost mighty close behind it. It stands to reason. Becuz *you* know that they don't anybody but ghosts use 'em."

"Yes, that's so. But anyway they don't come around in the daytime, so what's the use of our being afeard?"

"Well, all right. We'll tackle the ha'nted house if you say so—but I reckon it's taking chances."

So they got a crippled pick and shovel and started down the hill.

When they reached the haunted house there was something so weird and grisly about the dead silence that reigned there under the baking sun, and something so depressing about the loneliness and desolation of the place, that they were afraid, for a moment, to venture in. Then they crept to the door and took a trembling peep. They saw a weed-grown, floorless room, unplastered, an ancient fireplace, vacant windows, a ruinous [decayed] staircase; and here, there, and everywhere hung ragged and abandoned cobwebs. They presently entered, softly, with quickened pulses, talking in whispers, ears alert to catch the slightest sound, and muscles tense and ready for instant retreat.

In a little while familiarity modified their fears and they gave the place a critical and interested examination, rather admiring their own boldness, and wondering at it, too. Next they wanted to look upstairs. This was something like cutting off retreat, but they got to daring each other, and of course there could be but one result—they threw their tools into a corner and made the ascent. Up there were the same signs of decay. In one corner they found a closet that promised mystery, but the promise was a fraud—there was nothing in it. Their courage was up now and well in hand. They were about to go down and begin work when—

" 'Sh!" said Tom.

"What is it?" whispered Huck, blanching [turning pale] with fright.

" 'Sh! . . . There! . . . Hear it?"

"Yes! . . . Oh, my! Let's run!"

"Keep still! Don't you budge! They're coming right toward the door."

The boys stretched themselves upon the floor with their eyes to knot-holes in the planking, and lay waiting, in a misery of fear.

"They've stopped. . . . No—coming. . . . Here they are. Don't whisper another word, Huck. My goodness, I wish I was out of this!"

Two men entered. Each boy said to himself: "There's the old deaf and dumb Spaniard* that's been about town once or twice lately—never saw t'other man before."

"T'other" was a ragged, unkempt creature, with nothing very pleasant in his face. The Spaniard was wrapped in a *serape* [wool cloak]; he had bushy white whiskers; long white hair flowed from under his sombrero, and he wore green goggles. When they came in, "t'other" was talking in a low voice; they sat down on the ground, facing the door, with their backs to the wall.

"No," said he, "I've thought it all over, and I don't like it. It's dangerous."

"Dangerous!" grunted the "deaf and dumb" Spaniard—to the vast surprise of the boys.

This voice made the boys gasp and quake. It was Injun Joe's!

The two men got out some food and made a luncheon. After a long and thoughtful silence, Injun Joe said:

"Look here, lad—you go back up the river where you belong. Wait there till you hear from me. I'll take the chances on dropping into this town just once more, for a look. We'll do that 'dangerous' job after I've spied around a little and think things look well for it. Then for Texas! We'll leg it together!"

This was satisfactory. Both men presently fell to yawning, and Injun Joe said:

"I'm dead for sleep! It's your turn to watch."

He curled down in the weeds and soon began to snore. His comrade stirred him once or twice and he became quiet. Presently the watcher began to nod; his head drooped lower and lower, both men began to snore now.

The boys drew a long, grateful breath. Tom whispered:

"Now's our chance—come!"

Huck said:

"I can't—I'd die if they was to wake."

Tom urged—Huck held back. At last Tom rose slowly and softly, and started alone. But the first step he made wrung such a hideous creak from the crazy floor that he sank down almost dead with fright. He never made a second attempt. The boys lay there counting the dragging moments till it seemed to them that time must be done and eternity growing gray; and then they were grateful to note that at last the sun was setting.

---

*"old deaf and dumb Spaniard": Injun Joe, a noted criminal, has disguised himself as a deaf and dumb Spaniard. He has done so that he might go into town unrecognized. Tom, who recently testified against this outlaw, is terrified that he will return to take revenge.

Now one snore ceased. Injun Joe sat up, stared around—smiled grimly upon his comrade, whose head was drooping upon his knees—stirred him up with his foot and said:

"Here! *You're* a watchman, ain't you! All right, though—nothing's happened."

"My! have I been asleep?"

"Oh, partly, partly. Nearly time for us to be moving, pard. What'll we do with that little swag [stolen money] we've got left?"

"I don't know—leave it here as we've always done, I reckon. No use to take it away till we start south. Six hundred and fifty in silver's something to carry."

"Well—all right—it won't matter to come here once more."

"No—but I'd say come in the night as we used to do—it's better."

"Yes: but look here; it may be a good while before I get the right chance at that job; accidents might happen; 'tain't in such a very good place; we'll just regularly bury it—and bury it deep."

"Good idea," said the comrade, who walked across the room, knelt down, raised one of the hearthstones and took out a bag that jingled pleasantly. He subtracted from it twenty or thirty dollars for himself and as much for Injun Joe and passed the bag to the latter, who was on his knees in the corner, now, digging with his bowie-knife.

The boys forgot all their fears, all their miseries in an instant. With gloating eyes they watched every movement. Six hundred dollars was money enough to make half a dozen boys rich! Here was treasure-hunting under the happiest auspices—there would not be any bothersome uncertainty as to where to dig. They nudged each other every moment—eloquent nudges and easily understood, for they simply meant—"Oh, but ain't you glad *now* we're here!"

Joe's knife struck upon something.

"Hello!" said he.

"What is it?" said his comrade.

"Half-rotten plank—no, it's a box, I believe. Here—bear a hand and we'll see what it's here for. Never mind I've broke a hole."

He reached his hand in and drew it out—

"Man, it's money!"

The two men examined the handful of coins. They were gold. The boys above were as excited as themselves, and as delighted.

Joe's comrade said:

"We'll make quick work of this. There's an old rusty pick over amongst the weeds in the corner the other side of the fireplace—I saw it a minute ago."

He ran and brought the boys' pick and shovel. Injun Joe took the pick, looked it over critically, shook his head, muttered something to himself, and then began to use it. The box was soon unearthed. It was not very large; it was ironbound and had been very strong before the slow years had injured it. The men contemplated the treasure awhile in blissful silence.

"Pard, there's thousands of dollars here," said Injun Joe.

"'Twas always said that Murrel's gang used to be around here one summer," the stranger observed.

"I know it," said Injun Joe; "and this looks like it, I should say."

"*Now* you won't need to do that job."

The half-breed frowned. Said he:

"You don't know me. Least you don't know all about that thing. 'Tain't robbery altogether—it's *revenge*!" and a wicked light flamed in his eyes. "I'll need your help in it. When it's finished—then Texas. Go home to your Nance and your kids, and stand by till you hear from me."

"Well—if you say so. What'll we do with this—bury it again?"

"Yes. (Ravishing delight overhead.) No! No! (Profound distress overhead.) I'd nearly forgot. That pick had fresh earth on it! (The boys were sick with terror in a moment.) What business has a pick and a shovel here? What business with fresh earth on them? Who brought them here—and where are they gone? Have you heard anybody—seen anybody? What! Bury it again and leave them to come and see the ground disturbed? Not exactly—not exactly. We'll take it to my den."

"Why, of course! Might have thought of that before. You mean Number One?"

"No—Number Two—under the cross. The other place is bad—too common."

"All right. It's nearly dark enough to start."

Injun Joe got up and went about from window to window cautiously peeping out. Presently he said:

"Who could have brought those tools here? Do you reckon they can be upstairs?"

The boys' breath forsook them. Injun Joe put his hand on his knife, halted a moment, undecided, and then turned toward the stairway. The boys thought of the closet, but their strength was gone. The steps came creaking up the stairs—the intolerable distress of the situation woke the stricken resolution of the lads—they were about to spring for the closet, when there was a crash of rotten timbers and Injun Joe landed on the ground amid the debris of the ruined stairway. He gathered himself up, and his comrade said:

"Now what's the use of all that? If it's anybody, and they're up there, let them stay there—who cares? If they want to jump down, now, and get into trouble, who objects? It will be dark in fifteen minutes—and then let them follow us if they want to. I'm willing."

Joe grumbled awhile; then he agreed with his friend that what daylight was left ought to be economized in getting things ready for leaving. Shortly afterward they slipped out of the house in the deepening twilight, and moved toward the river with their precious box.

Tom and Huck rose up, weak but vastly relieved, and stared after them through the chinks between logs of the house. Follow? Not they. They were content to reach ground again without broken necks, and take the townward track over the hill. They did not talk much. They were too absorbed in hating themselves—hating the ill luck that made them take the spade and the pick there. But for that, Injun Joe never would have suspected. He would have hidden the silver with the gold to wait there till his "revenge" was satisfied, and then he would have had the misfortune to find that money turn up missing. Bitter, bitter luck that the tools were ever brought there!

They resolved to keep a lookout for that Spaniard when he should come to town spying out for chances to do his revengeful job, and follow him to "Number Two," wherever that might be.

Reading Check

1. Do you think Tom really believes that he is going to find buried treasure? Why or why not?
2. Do you believe Huck actually thinks that they are going to find treasure? Why or why not?
3. List some of the incidents in the story that make it exciting.
4. At what point in the story does the boys' search for buried treasure become hazardous?
5. In the headnote Tom is described as "clever" and "mischievous." List some specific actions that confirm this description.

Trembling on the Trail

The adventure of the day mightily tormented Tom's dreams that night. Sleep forsook him. As he lay in the early morning recalling the incidents of his great adventure, he noticed that they seemed curiously subdued and far away. It occurred to him that the great adventure itself must be a dream! There was one strong argument in favor of this idea—namely, that the quantity of coin he had seen was too vast to be real.

But the incidents of his adventure grew sensibly sharper and clearer after thinking them over, and so he presently found himself leaning to the impression that the thing might not have been a dream, after all. This uncertainty must be swept away. He would snatch a hurried breakfast and go and find Huck.

Huck was sitting on the gunwale of a flatboat, listlessly dangling his feet in the water and looking very melancholy. Tom concluded to let Huck lead up to the subject. If he did not do it, then the adventure would be proven to have been only a dream.

"Hello, Huck!"

"Hello, yourself."

Silence for a minute.

"Tom, if we'd 'a' left the tools at the dead tree, we'd 'a' got the money. Oh, ain't it awful!"

"'Tain't a dream, then, 'tain't a dream! Somehow I most wish it was. Dog'd if I don't, Huck."

"What ain't a dream?"

"Oh, that thing yesterday. I been half thinking it was."

"Dream! If them stairs hadn't broke down you'd 'a' seen how much dream it was! I've had dreams enough all night—with that patch-eyed Spanish devil going for me all through 'em—rot him!"

"No, not rot him. *Find* him! Track the money!"

"Tom, we'll never find him. A feller don't have only one chance for such a pile—and that one's lost. I'd feel mighty shaky if I was to see him, anyway."

"Well, so'd I; but I'd like to see him, anyway—track him out—to his Number Two."

"Number Two—yes, that's it. I be thinking 'bout that. But I can't make nothing out of it. What do you reckon it is?"

"I dunno. It's too deep. Say, Huck—maybe it's the number of a house!"

"Goody! . . . No, Tom, that ain't it. If it is, it ain't in this one-horse town. They ain't no numbers here."

"Well, that's so. Lemme think a minute. Here—it's the number of a room—in a tavern, you know!"

"Oh, that's the trick! They ain't only two taverns. We can find out quick."

"You stay here, Huck, till I come."

Tom was off at once. He did not care to have Huck's company in public places. He was gone half an hour. He found that in the best tavern, No. 2 had long been occupied by a young lawyer, and was still so occupied. In the less ostentatious house No. 2 was a mystery.

"Now what you going to do?" asked Huck on hearing the news.

Tom thought a long time. Then he said:

"I'll tell you. The back door of that No. 2 is the door that comes out into that little close alley between the tavern and the old rattletrap of a brick store. Now you get hold of all the door keys you can find, and I'll nip all of auntie's, and the first dark night we'll go there and try 'em. And mind you, keep a lookout for Injun Joe, because he said he was going to drop into town and spy around once more for a chance to get his revenge. If you see him, you just follow him; and if he don't go to that No. 2, that ain't the place."

In the Lair of Injun Joe

That night Tom and Huck were ready for their adventure. They hung about the neighborhood of the tavern until after nine, one watching the alley at a distance and the other the tavern door. Nobody entered the alley or left it; nobody resembling the Spaniard entered or left the tavern door. The night promised to be a fair one; so Tom went home with the understanding that if a considerable degree of darkness came on, Huck was to come and "meow," whereupon he would slip out and try the keys. But the night remained clear, and Huck closed his watch and retired to bed in an empty sugar hogshead about twelve.

Tuesday the boys had the same ill luck. Also Wednesday. But Thursday night promised better. Tom slipped out in good season with his aunt's old tin lantern, and a large towel to blindfold it with. He hid the lantern in Huck's sugar hogshead and the watch began. An hour before midnight the tavern closed up and its lights (the only ones thereabouts) were put out. No Spaniard had been seen. Nobody had entered or left the alley.

Tom got his lantern, lit it in the hogshead, wrapped it closely in the towel, and the two adventurers crept in the gloom toward the tavern. Huck stood sentry and Tom felt his way into the alley. Then there was a season of waiting that weighed upon Huck's spirits like a mountain. He began to wish he could see a flash from the lantern— it would frighten him, but it would at least tell him that Tom was alive yet. It seemed hours since Tom had disappeared. Surely he must have fainted; maybe he was dead; maybe his heart had burst under terror and excitement. In his uneasiness Huck found himself drawing closer and closer to the alley; fearing all sorts of dreadful things, and

momentarily expecting some catastrophe to happen that would take his breath away, for he seemed only able to inhale it by thimblefuls, and his heart would soon wear itself out, the way it was beating. Suddenly there was a flash of light and Tom came tearing by him:

"Run!" said he; "run for your life!"

He needn't have repeated it; once was enough; Huck was making thirty or forty miles an hour before the repetition was uttered. The boys never stopped till they reached the shed of a deserted slaughter-house at the lower end of the village. Just as they got within its shelter the storm burst and the rain

poured down. As soon as Tom got his breath he said:

"Huck, it was awful! I tried two of the keys, just as soft as I could; but they seemed to make such a power of racket that I couldn't hardly get my breath I was so scared. They wouldn't turn in the lock, either. Well, without noticing what I was doing, I took hold of the knob, and open comes the door! It warn't locked! I hopped in, and shook off the towel, and, *great Caesar's ghost*!"

"What—what'd you see, Tom?"

"Huck, I most stepped onto Injun Joe's hand!"

"No!"

"Yes! He was laying there, sound asleep on the floor, with his old patch on his eye and his arms out."

"What did you do? Did he wake up?"

"No, never budged. I just grabbed the towel and started!"

There was a long time for reflection, and then Tom said:

"Lookyhere, Huck, le's not try that thing any more till we know Injun Joe's not in there. It's too scary. Now, if we watch every night, we'll be dead sure to see him go out, some time or other, and then we'll snatch that box quicker'n lightning."

"Well, I'm agreed. I'll watch the whole night long, and I'll do it every night, too, if you'll do the other part of the job."

"All right, I will. All you got to do is trot up Hooper Street a block and meow—and if I'm asleep, you throw some gravel at the window and that'll fetch me."

"Agreed, and good as wheat!"

"Now, Huck, the storm's over, and I'll go home. It'll begin to be daylight in a couple of hours. You go back and watch that long, will you?"

"I said I would, Tom, and I will. I'll ha'nt that tavern every night for a year! I'll sleep all day and I'll stand watch all night."

"That's all right. Now, where you going to sleep?"

"In Ben Rogers's hayloft. He let's me."

"Well, if I don't want you in the daytime, I'll let you sleep. I won't come bothering around. Any time you see something's up, in the night, just skip right around and meow."

Huck Saves the Widow

The first thing Tom heard on Friday morning was a glad piece of news— Judge Thatcher and his family had come back to town the night before. Both Injun Joe and the treasure sank into secondary importance for a moment, and Becky took the chief place in the boy's interest. He saw her, and they had an exhausting good time playing "hi-spy" and "gully-keeper" with a crowd of their schoolmates. The day was completed and crowned in a peculiarly satisfactory way: Becky teased her mother to appoint the next day for the long-promised picnic, and she consented. The child's delight was boundless; and Tom's not more moderate. The invitations were sent out before sunset, and straightway the young folks of the village were thrown into a fever of preparation and pleasurable anticipation.

Morning came, eventually, and by ten or eleven o'clock a giddy and rollicking company were gathered at Judge Thatcher's, and everything was ready for a start.

Three miles below town the ferryboat stopped at the mouth of woody hollow and tied up. The crowd swarmed ashore and soon the forest distances and craggy heights echoed far and near with shoutings and laughter. By and by somebody shouted:

"Who's ready for the cave?"

Everybody was. Bundles of candles were procured, and straightway there was a general scamper up the hill. The mouth of the cave was up the hillside—an opening shaped like a letter A. It's massive oaken door stood unbarred. Within was a small chamber, chilly as an icehouse, and walled by nature with a solid limestone that was dewy with a cold sweat. It was romantic and mysterious in the deep gloom. The procession moved along together for awhile, and then groups and couples began to slip aside into branch avenues and dismal corridors. By and by, one group after another came straggling back to the mouth of the cave, panting, hilarious, smeared from head to foot with tallow drippings, daubed with clay, and entirely delighted with the success of the day. When the ferryboat with her wild freight pushed into stream, nobody cared sixpence for the wasted time but the captain of the craft.

Huck was already upon his watch when the ferryboat's lights went glinting past the wharf. He heard no noise on board, for the young people were as subdued and still as people usually are who are nearly tired to death. He wondered what boat it was, and why she did not stop at the wharf—and then

he dropped her out of his mind and put his attention upon his business.

A noise fell upon his ear. He was all attention in an instant. The alley door closed softly. He sprang to the corner of the brick store. The next moment two men brushed by him, and one seemed to have something under his arm. It must be that box! So they were going to remove the treasure. Why call Tom now? It would be absurd—the men would get away with the box and never be found again. No, he would stick to their wake and follow them.

They moved up the river street three blocks then turned to the left up a cross-street. They went straight ahead, then, until they came to the path that led up Cardiff Hill to the Widow Douglas's. They passed the servants' quarters where the old Welshman lived, without hesitating, and still climbed upward. Good,

Huck thought; they will bury it in the old quarry. But they never stopped at the quarry. They passed on, up the summit. They plunged into the narrow path between the tall sumac bushes, and were at once hidden in the gloom. Huck closed up and shortened his distance, now, for they would never be able to see him. He trotted along awhile; then slackened his pace, fearing he was gaining too fast; moved on a piece, then stopped altogether; listened; no sound; none, save that he seemed to hear the beating of his own heart. The hooting of an owl came from over the hill—ominous sound! But no footsteps. He was about to spring with winged feet, when a man cleared his throat not four feet from him! Huck's heart shot into his throat, but he swallowed it again; and then he stood there shaking as if a dozen agues had taken charge of him

at once, and so weak that he thought he must surely fall to the ground. He knew where he was. He knew he was within five steps of the stile leading to the Widow Douglas's grounds. Very well, he thought, let them bury it here; it won't be hard to find.

Now there was a voice—a very low voice—Injun Joe's:

"There's lights, late as it is."

"I can't see any."

This was that stranger's voice—the stranger of the haunted house. A deadly chill went to Huck's heart—this, then, was the "revenge" job! His thought was, to fly. Then he remembered that the Widow Douglas had been kind to him more than once, and maybe these men were going to murder her. He wished he dared venture to warn her; but he knew he didn't dare—they might come and catch him. He thought all this and more in the moment that elapsed between the stranger's remark and Injun Joe's next—which was—

"Because the bush is in your way. Now—this way—now you see, don't you?"

"Yes. Well, there *is* company there, I reckon. Better give it up."

"Give it up, and I just leaving this country forever! Give it up and maybe never have another chance. I tell you again, as I've told you before, I don't care for her swag—you may have it. But her husband was rough on me—many times he was rough on me—and mainly he was the justice of the peace that judged me for a vagrant. And that ain't all. It ain't a millionth part of it! He had me *horsewhipped*—horsewhipped in front of the jail!—with all the town looking on! HORSEWHIPPED!—do you understand? He took advantage of me and died. But I'll take it out on *her*. My friend, you'll help in this thing—for *my* sake—that's why you're here—I mightn't be able alone. If you flinch, I'll kill you. Do you understand that?"

"Well, if it's to be done, let's get at it. The quicker the better—I'm all in a shiver."

"Do it *now*? And company there? Look here—I'll get suspicious of you, first thing you know. No—we'll wait till the lights are out—there's no hurry."

Huck felt that a silence was going to ensue—a thing more awful than any amount of murderous talk; so he held his breath and stepped gingerly back; planted his foot carefully and firmly, after balancing, one-legged, in a precarious way and almost toppling over, first on one side and then on the other. He took another step back, with the same elaboration and the same risks; then another and another, and—a twig snapped under his foot! His breath stopped and he listened. There was no sound—the stillness was perfect. His gratitude was measureless. Now he turned in his tracks, between the walls of sumac bushes—turned himself as carefully as if he were a ship—and then stepped quickly but cautiously along. When he emerged at the quarry he felt secure, and so he picked up his nimble heels and flew. Down, down he sped, till he reached the Welshman's. He

banged at the door, and presently the heads of the old man and his two stalwart sons were thrust from windows.

"What's the row there? Who's banging? What do you want?"

"Let me in—quick! I'll tell everything."

"Why, who are you?"

"Huckleberry Finn—quick, let me in!"

"Huckleberry Finn, indeed! It ain't a name to open many doors, I judge! But let him in, lads, and let's see what's the trouble."

"Please don't ever tell I told you," were Huck's first words when he got in. "Please don't—I'd be killed, sure—but the widow's been good friends to me sometimes, and I want to tell—I *will* tell if you'll promise you won't ever say it was me."

"By George, he *has* got something to tell, or he wouldn't act so!" exclaimed the old man; "out with it an' nobody here'll ever tell, lad."

Three minutes later the old man and his sons, well-armed, were up the hill, and just entering the sumac path on tiptoe, their weapons in their hands. Huck accompanied them no further. He hid behind a great boulder and fell to listening. There was a lagging, anxious silence, and then all of a sudden there was an explosion of firearms and a cry.

Huck waited for no particulars. He sprang away and sped down the hill as fast as his legs could carry him.

As the earliest suspicion of dawn appeared on Sunday morning, Huck came groping up the hill and rapped gently at the old Welshman's door. The inmates were asleep, but it was a sleep that was set on a hair-trigger, on account of the exciting episode of the night. A call came from the window:

"Who's there!"

Huck's scared voice answered in a low tone:

"Please let me in! It's only Huck Finn!"

"It's a name that can open this door night or day, lad!—and welcome! I and the boys hoped you'd turn up and stop here last night."

"I was awful scared," said Huck, "and I run. I took out when the pistols went off, and I didn't stop for three mile. I've come now becuz I wanted to know about it, you know; and I come before daylight becuz I didn't want to run acrost them devils, even if they was dead."

"Well, poor chap, you do look as if you'd had a hard night of it—but there's a bed here for you when you've had your breakfast. No, they ain't dead, lad—we are sorry enough for that. You see we knew right where to put our hands on them, by your description; so we crept along on tiptoe till we got within fifteen feet of them—dark as a cellar that sumac path was—and just then I found I was going to sneeze. It was the meanest kind of luck! I tried to keep it back, but no use—'twas bound to come, and it did come! I was in the lead with my pistol raised, and when the sneeze started those scoundrels a-rustling to get out of the path, I sung out, 'Fire, boys!' and blazed away at the place where the rustling was. So did the boys. But they were off in a jiffy, those villains, and we after them, down through the woods. I judge we never touched them. They fired a shot apiece as they started, but their bullets whizzed by and didn't do us any harm. As soon as we lost the sound of their feet we quit chasing, and went down and stirred up the constables. They got a posse together, and went off to guard the river-bank, and as soon as it is light the sheriff and a gang are going to beat up the woods. I wish we had some sort of description of those rascals—'twould help a good deal. But you couldn't see what they were like, in the dark, lad, I suppose?

"Oh, yes, I saw them down-town and follered them,"

"Splendid! Describe them—describe them, my boy!"

"One's the deaf old Spaniard that's been around here once or twice, and t'other's a mean-looking, ragged—"

"That's enough, lad, we know them! Happened on them in the woods back of the widow's one day, and they slunk away. Off with you, boys, and tell the sheriff—get your breakfast tomorrow morning!"

The Welshman's sons departed at once. As they were leaving the room Huck sprang up and exclaimed:

"Oh, please don't tell *any*body it was me that blowed on them! Oh, please!"

"All right if you say it, Huck, but you ought to have the credit of what you did."

"Oh, no, no! Please don't tell!"

When the young men were gone, the old Welshman said:

"They won't tell—and I won't."

There was no Sabbath-school during day-school vacation, but everybody was early at church. The stirring event at the widow's was well rehearsed. Not a sign of the two villains had been yet discovered. As the sermon finished, Judge Thatcher's wife came up to Mrs. Harper and said:

"Is my Becky going to sleep all day? I just expected she would be tired to death."

"Your Becky?"

"Yes," said Mrs. Thatcher with a startled look—"didn't she stay with you last night?"

"Why, no."

Mrs. Thatcher turned pale, and sank into a pew, just as Aunt Polly, talking briskly with a friend, passed by and said:

"Good morning, Mrs. Thatcher. Good morning, Mrs. Harper. I've got a boy that's turned up missing. I reckon my Tom stayed at your house last night—one of you. And now he's afraid to come to church. I've got to settle with him."

Mrs. Thatcher shook her head feebly and turned paler than ever.

"He didn't stay with us," said Mrs. Harper, beginning to look uneasy. A marked anxiety came into Aunt Polly's face.

"Joe Harper, have you seen my Tom this morning?"

"No'm."

"When did you see him last?"

Joe tried to remember, but was not sure he could say.

The alarm swept from lip to lip, from group to group, from street to street, and within five minutes the bells were wildly clanging and the whole town was up! The Cardiff Hill episode sank into instant insignificance, the burglars were forgotten, horses were saddled, skiffs were manned, the ferryboat ordered out, and before the horror was half an hour old two hundred men were pouring down highroad and river toward the cave.

All the long afternoon the village seemed empty and dead. Many women visited Aunt Polly and Mrs. Thatcher and tried to comfort them.

The old Welshman came home toward daylight, spattered with candle-grease, smeared with clay, and almost worn out. He found Huck still in the bed that had been provided for him, and delirious with fever. The physicians were all at the cave, so the Widow Douglas came and took charge of the patient. She said she would do her best by him, because, whether he was good, bad, or indifferent, he was the Lord's, and nothing that was the Lord's was a thing to be neglected.

Three dreadful days and nights dragged their tedious hours along, and the village sank into a hopeless stupor. No one had heart for anything.

Reading Check

1. Why do you think Tom's statement, "'Tain't a dream, then, 'tain't a dream [finding the treasure]! Somehow I most wish it was!" is not really how he feels?
2. How do the boys decide to track down Injun Joe?
3. Why does Tom come dashing down the alley crying, "Run! run for your life!"?
4. What adventure does Huck have while he and Tom are separated?
5. What adventure does Tom have while he and Huck are separated?

Tom and Becky in the Cave

Tom and Becky wandered along, hand in hand and hopeless. They tried to estimate how long they had been in the cave, but all they knew was that it seemed days and weeks, and yet it was plain that this could not be, for their candles were not gone yet. A long time after this—they could not tell how long—Tom said they must go softly and listen for dripping water—they must find a spring. They found one presently, and Tom said it was time to rest again. Both were cruelly tired, yet Becky said she thought she could go a little farther.

She was surprised to hear Tom dissent. She could not understand it. They sat down, and Tom fastened his candle to the wall in front of them with some clay. Thought was soon busy; nothing was said for some time.

By and by Becky suggested that they move on again. Tom was silent a moment. Then he said:

"Becky, can you bear it if I tell you something?"

Becky's face paled, but she thought she could.

"Well, then, Becky, we must stay here, where there's water to drink. That little piece is our last candle!"

Becky gave loose to tears and wailings. Tom did what he could to comfort her, but with little effect. At length Becky said:

"When would they miss us, Tom?"

"When they get back to the boat, I reckon."

"Tom, it might be dark then—would they notice we hadn't come?"

"I don't know. But anyway, your mother would miss you as soon as they got home."

They fastened their eyes upon their bit of candle and watched it melt slowly and pitilessly away; saw the half-inch of wick stand alone at last; saw the feeble flame rise and fall, climb the thin column of smoke, linger at its top a moment, and then—the horror of utter darkness reigned!

By and by Tom said:

" 'Sh! Did you hear that?"

Both held their breath and listened. There was a sound like the faintest, far-off shout. Instantly, Tom answered it, and, leading Becky by the hand, started groping down the corridor in its direction. Presently, he listened again; again the sound was heard, and apparently a little nearer.

"It's them!" said Tom; "they're coming! Come along, Becky—we're all right now!"

The joy of the prisoners was almost overwhelming. Their speed was slow, however, because pitfalls were somewhat common, and had to be guarded against. They shortly came to one and had to stop. It might be three feet deep, it might be a hundred—there was no passing it, at any rate. Tom got down on his breast and reached as far down as he could. No bottom. They must stay

there and wait until the searchers came. They listened; evidently the distant shoutings were growing more distant! a moment or two longer and they had gone altogether. The heart-sinking misery of it! Tom whooped until he was hoarse, but it was of no use. He talked hopefully to Becky; but an age of anxious waiting passed and no sounds came again.

The children groped their way back to the spring. The weary time dragged on; they slept again, and awoke famished and woe-stricken. Tom believed it must be Tuesday by this time.

Now an idea struck him. There were some side passages near at hand. It would be better to explore some of these than bear the weight of the heavy time in idleness. He took a kite-line from his pocket, tied it to a projection, and he and Becky started, Tom in the lead, unwinding the line as he groped along. At the end of twenty steps the corridor ended in a "jumping-off place." Tom got down on his hands and knees and felt below, and then as far around the corner as he could reach with his hands conveniently; he made an effort to

stretch yet a little farther to the right, and at that moment, not twenty yards away, a human hand, holding a candle, appeared from behind a rock! Tom lifted up a glorious shout, and instantly that hand was followed by the body it belonged to—Injun Joe's! Tom was paralyzed; he could not move. He was vastly gratified the next moment to see the "Spaniard" take to his heels and get himself out of sight. Tom wondered that Joe had not recognized his voice and come over and killed him for testifying in court. But the echoes must have disguised the voice. Without doubt, that was it, he reasoned. Tom's fright weakened every muscle in his body. He said to himself that if he had strength enough to get back to the spring he would stay there, and nothing should tempt him to run the risk of meeting Injun Joe again. He was careful to keep from Becky what it was he had seen. He told her he had only shouted "for luck."

Another tedious wait at the spring and another long sleep brought changes. The children awoke tortured with raging hunger. Tom believed that it must be Wednesday or Thursday or even Friday or Saturday, now, and that the search had been given over. He proposed to explore another passage. He felt willing to risk Injun Joe and all other terrors. But Becky was very weak. She had sunk into a dreary apathy and would not be roused. She said she would wait, now, where she was, and die—it would not be long. She told Tom to go with the kite-line and explore if he chose; but she implored him to come back every little while and speak to her; and she made him promise that when the awful time came, he would stay by her and hold her hand until it was all over.

Tom made a show of being confident of finding the searchers or an escape from the cave; then he took the kite-line in his hand and went groping down one of the passages on his hands and knees, distressed with hunger and sick with bodings of coming doom.

"Turn Out! They're Found!"

Tuesday afternoon came, and waned to the twilight. The village of St. Petersburg still mourned. The lost children had not been found.

The village went to its rest on Tuesday night, sad and forlorn, but away in the middle of the night a wild peal burst from the village bells. In a moment the streets were swarming with frantic half-clad people, who shouted, "Turn out! Turn out! They're found! They're found!" Tin pans and horns were added to the din, the population massed itself and moved toward the river, met the children coming in an open carriage drawn by shouting citizens, thronged around it, joined its homeward march, and swept magnificently up the main street roaring hurrah after hurrah!

Three days and nights of toil and hunger in the cave were not to be shaken off at once, as Tom and Becky soon discovered. They were bedridden all of Wednesday and Thursday, and seemed to grow more and more tired and worn all the time. Tom got about a little on Thursday, was down-town on Friday, and nearly as whole as ever Saturday; but Becky did not leave her room until Sunday, and then she looked as if she had passed through a wasting illness.

Tom learned of Huck's sickness and went to see him on Friday, but could not be admitted to the bedroom; neither could he on Saturday or Sunday. He was admitted daily after that, but warned to keep still about his adventure and introduce no exciting topic. The Widow Douglas stayed close by to see that he obeyed. At home Tom learned of the Cardiff Hill event; also that the "ragged man's" body had eventually been found in the river near the ferry landing; he had been drowned while trying to escape, perhaps.

About a fortnight after Tom's rescue from the cave, he started off to visit Huck, who had grown plenty strong enough, now, to hear exciting talk, and Tom had some that would interest him, he thought. Judge Thatcher's house was on Tom's way, and he stopped to see Becky. The judge and some friends set Tom to talking, and some one asked him ironically if he wouldn't like to go to the cave again. Tom said he thought he wouldn't mind it. The judge said:

"Well, there are others just like you, Tom, I've not the least doubt. But we have taken care of that. Nobody will ever get lost in that cave anymore."

"Why?"

"Because I had its big door sheathed with boiler iron two weeks ago, and triple-locked—and I've got the keys."

Tom turned as white as a sheet.

"What's the matter, boy! Here, run, somebody! Fetch a glass of water!"

The water was brought and thrown into Tom's face.

"Ah, now you're all right. What was the matter with you, Tom?"

"Oh, Judge, Injun Joe's in the cave!"

The Fate of Injun Joe

Within a few minutes the news had spread, and a dozen skiff-loads of men were on their way to McDougal's cave, and the ferry boat, well filled with passengers, soon followed. Tom Sawyer was in the skiff that bore Judge Thatcher.

When the cave door was unlocked, a sorrowful sight presented itself in the dim twilight of the place. Injun Joe lay stretched upon the ground, dead, with his face close to the crack of the door, as if his longing eyes had been fixed, to the last moment, upon the light and the cheer of the free world outside. Tom was touched, for he knew by his own experience how this wretch had suffered. His pity was moved, but nevertheless he felt an abounding sense of relief and security, now, which revealed to him in a degree which he had not fully appreciated before how vast a weight of dread had been lying upon him since the day he lifted his voice against this bloody-minded outcast.

Injun Joe was buried near the mouth of the cave. The morning after the funeral Tom took Huck to a private place to have an important talk. Huck had learned all about Tom's adventure from the Welshman and the Widow Douglas, by this time, but Tom said he reckoned there was one thing they had not told him; that thing was what he wanted to talk about now.

Huck searched his comrade's face keenly. "Tom, have you got on the track of that money again?"

"Huck, it's in the cave!"

Huck's eyes blazed.

"Tom—honest Injun, now—is it fun or earnest?"

"Earnest, Huck—just as earnest as ever I was in my life. Will you go in there with me and help get it out?"

"I bet I will! I will if it's where we can blaze our way to it and not get lost."

"Huck, we can do that without the least little bit of trouble in the world."

"Good as wheat! What makes you think the money's—"

"Huck, you just wait till we get in there. If we don't find it I'll agree to give you my drum and everything I've got in the world. I will, by jings."

The boys entered the cave, Tom in the lead. They toiled their way to the farther end of the tunnel, then made their spliced kite-strings fast and moved on. A few steps brought them to the spring, and Tom felt a shudder quiver all through him. He showed Huck the fragment of candle-wick perched on a lump of clay against the wall, and described how he and Becky had watched the flame struggle and expire.

"Now I'll show you something else, Huck."

He held his candle aloft and said:

"Look as far around the corner as you can. Do you see that? There—on the big rock over yonder—done with candle-smoke."

"Tom, it's a *cross*!"

When they reached the spot, Huck began to dig. Some boards were uncovered and removed, and sure enough there was the treasure box occupying a snug little cavern.

"Got it at last!" said Huck, plowing among the tarnished coins with his hands. "My, but we're rich, Tom!"

"Now, Huck," said Tom, "we'll hide the money in the loft of the widow's woodshed, and in the morning we'll count and divide it."

When the boys reached the Welshman's house they stopped to rest. Tom then disappeared and returned with an old wagon. They loaded their treasure on this, covered it with rags and were just about to move on when the Welshman stepped out and said:

"Hello, who's that?"

"Huck and Tom Sawyer."

"Good! Come along with me, boys; you are keeping everybody waiting. Here—hurry up, trot ahead—I'll haul the wagon for you. Why, it's not as light as it might be. Got bricks in it?—or old metal?"

"Old metal," said Tom.

The boys wanted to know what the hurry was about.

"Never mind; you'll see when we get to the Widow Douglas's." said the Welshman.

"We ain't been doin' nothin'," said Huck apprehensively.

The Welshman laughed.

"Well, I don't know, Huck, my boy. I don't know about that. Ain't you and the widow good friends?"

"Yes. Well, she's been good friends to me, anyways."

"All right, then. What do you want to be afraid for?"

This question was not entirely answered in Huck's slow mind before he found himself pushed, along with Tom, into Mrs. Douglas's drawing-room. The Welshman left the wagon near the door and followed.

The place was grandly lighted, and everybody that was of any consequence in the village was there. The Thatchers were there, the Harpers, the Rogerses, Aunt Polly, Sid, Mary, the minister, the editor, and a great many more, and all dressed in their best. The widow received the boys as heartily as any one could well receive two such looking beings. They were covered with clay and candle-grease. Aunt Polly blushed crimson with humiliation, and frowned and shook her head at Tom. Nobody suffered half as much as the two boys did, however. The Welshman said:

"Tom wasn't at home, yet, so I gave him up; but I stumbled on him and Huck right at my door, and so I just brought them along in a hurry."

"And you did just right," said the widow. "Come with me, boys."

She took them to a bedchamber and said:

"Now wash and dress yourselves. Here are two new suits of clothes—shirts, socks, everything complete. They're Huck's—no, no thanks, Huck—the Welshman bought one and I the other. But they'll fit both of you. Get into them. We'll wait—come down when you are slicked up enough." Then she left.

Huck said: "Tom, we can slope, if we can find a rope. The window ain't high from the ground."

"What do you want to slope for."

"Well, I ain't used to that kind of a crowd. I can't stand it. I ain't going down there, Tom."

"Oh, bother! It ain't anything. I don't mind it a bit. I'll take care of you."

Some minutes later the widow's guests were at the supper-table, and a dozen children were propped up at little side-tables in the same room, after the fashion of that country and that day. At the proper time the Welshman made his little speech, in which he thanked the widow for the honor she was doing himself and his sons, but said that there was another person whose modesty—

And so forth and so on. He sprung the secret about Huck's share in the

adventure in the finest dramatic manner he was master of, but the surprise it occasioned was largely counterfeit and not as clamorous and effusive as it might have been under happier circumstances. However, the widow made a pretty fair show of astonishment, and heaped so many compliments and so much gratitude upon Huck that he almost forgot the nearly intolerable discomfort of being set up as a target for everybody's gaze and everybody's laudations.

The widow said she meant to give Huck a home under her roof and have him educated; and that when she could spare the money she would start him in business in a modest way. Tom's chance was come. He said:

"Huck don't need it. Huck's rich."

Nothing but a heavy strain upon the good manners of the company kept back the due and proper complimentary laugh at this pleasant joke. But the silence was a little awkward. Tom broke it:

"Huck's got money. Maybe you don't believe it, but he's got lots of it. Oh, you needn't smile—I reckon I can show you. You just wait a minute."

Tom ran out of doors. The company looked at each other with a perplexed interest—and inquiringly at Huck, who was tongue-tied.

Tom entered, struggling with the weight of his sacks, and poured the mass of yellow coin upon the table and said:

"There—what did I tell you? Half of it's Huck's and half of it's mine!"

The spectacle took the general breath away. All gazed, nobody spoke for a moment. Then there was a unanimous call for an explanation. Tom said he could furnish it, and he did. The tale was long, but brimful of interest. There was scarcely an interruption from any one to break the charm of its flow. When he had finished, Mr. Jones said:

"I thought I had fixed up a little surprise for this occasion, but it don't amount to anything now. This one makes it sing mighty small, I'm willing to allow."

The money was counted. The sum amounted to a little over twelve thousand dollars!

Reading Check

1. What is the meaning of the title "Found and Lost Again"?
2. What is the "Fate of Injun Joe"?
3. Why are Tom and Huck taken to the Widow Douglas's house?
4. How do the two boys react to the Widow's kindness?
5. How is the buried treasure used?

The low groaning of the heavy ore-cables and the husky voices of working men had been silenced. The Yellow Dream Mine was now like a peaceful hideaway cradled among the great pines high on a cliff overlooking the Sacramento River. The cable cars hung motionless above the river and the only voices to be heard were those in quiet conversation. It is little wonder that young Jerry never suspected the perilous adventure that was soon to break in upon the serenity of the morning.

The Banks of the Sacramento

Jack London

*"And it's blow, ye winds, heigh-ho,
For Cal-i-for-ni-o;
For there's plenty of gold so I've
    been told,
On the banks of the Sacramento!"*

It was only a boy singing in a shrill treble the sea chantey [sailor's song], which seamen sing the wide world over when they man the capstan bars* and break the anchors out for "Frisco" port. It was only a boy who had never seen the sea, but two hundred feet beneath him rolled the Sacramento. Young Jerry he was called, after Old Jerry, his father, from whom he had learned the song, as well as received his shock of bright-red hair, his blue, dancing eyes, and his fair and inevitably freckled skin.

For Old Jerry had been a sailor, and had followed the sea till middle life,

---

*capstan bars: lever used for hoisting a ship's anchor.

haunted always by the words of the ringing chantey. Then one day he had sung the song in earnest in an Asiatic port, swinging and thrilling round the capstan-circle with twenty others. And at San Francisco he turned his back upon his ship and upon the sea, and went to behold with his own eyes the banks of the Sacramento.

He beheld the gold, too, for he found employment at the Yellow Dream mine, and proved of utmost usefulness in rigging the great ore-cables across the river and two hundred feet above its surface.

After that he took charge of the cables and kept them in repair, and ran them and loved them, and became himself an indispensable fixture of the Yellow Dream mine. Then he loved pretty Margaret Kelly; but she had left him and Young Jerry, the latter barely toddling, to take up her last long sleep in the little graveyard among the great sober pines.

Old Jerry never went back to the sea. He remained by his cables, and lavished upon them and Young Jerry all the love of his nature. When evil days came to the Yellow Dream, he still remained in the employ of the company as watchman over the all but abandoned property.

But this morning he was not visible. Young Jerry only was to be seen, sitting on the cabin step and singing the ancient chantey. He had cooked and eaten his breakfast all by himself, and had just come out to take a look at the world. Twenty feet before him stood the steel drum round which the endless cable worked. By the drum, snug and fast, was the ore-car. Following with his eyes the dizzy flight of the cables to the farther bank, he could see the other drum and the other car.

The contrivance [mechanical device] was worked by gravity, the loaded car crossing the river by virtue of its own weight, and at the same time dragging the empty car back. The loaded car being emptied, and the empty car being loaded with more ore, the performance could be repeated—a performance which had been repeated tens of thousands of times since the day Old Jerry became the keeper of the cables.

Young Jerry broke off his song at the sound of approaching footsteps. A tall, blue-shirted man, a rifle across the hollow of his arm, came out from the gloom of the pine trees. It was Hall, watchman of the Yellow Dragon mine, the cables of which spanned the Sacramento a mile farther up.

"Hello, younker [youngster]," was his greeting. "What you doin' here by your lonesome?"

"Oh, bachin," Jerry tried to answer unconcernedly, as if it were a very ordinary sort of thing. "Dad's away, you see."

"Where's he gone?" the man asked.

"San Francisco. Went last night. His brother's dead in the old country, and he's gone down to see the lawyers. Won't be back till tomorrow night."

So spoke Jerry, and with pride, because of the responsibility which had fallen to him of keeping an eye on the property of the Yellow Dream, and the glorious adventure of living alone on the cliff above the river and of cooking his own meals.

"Well, take care of yourself," Hall said, "and don't monkey with the cables. I'm goin' to see if I can't pick up a deer in the Cripple Cow Canyon."

"It's goin' to rain, I think," Jerry said, with mature deliberation.

"And it's little I mind a wettin'," Hall laughed, as he strode away among the trees.

Jerry's prediction concerning rain was more than fulfilled. By ten o'clock the pines were swaying and moaning, the cabin windows rattling, and the rain driving by in fierce squalls. At half past eleven he kindled a fire, and promptly at the stroke of twelve sat down to his dinner.

No out-of-doors for him that day, he decided, when he had washed the few dishes and put them neatly away; and he wondered how wet Hall was and whether he had succeeded in picking up a deer.

At one o'clock there came a knock at the door, and when he opened it, a man and a woman staggered in on the breast of a great gust of wind. They were Mr. and Mrs. Spillane, ranchers, who lived in a lonely valley a dozen miles back from the river.

"Where's Hall?" was Spillane's opening speech, and he spoke sharply and quickly.

Jerry noted that he was nervous and abrupt in his movements, and that Mrs. Spillane seemed laboring under some strong anxiety. She was a thin, washed-out, worked-out woman, whose life of dreary and unending toil had stamped itself harshly upon her face. It was the same life that had bowed her husband's shoulders and gnarled his hands and turned his hair to a dry and dusty gray.

"He's gone hunting up Cripple Cow." Jerry answered. "Did you want to cross?"

The woman began to weep quietly, while Spillane dropped a troubled exclamation and strode to the window. Jerry joined him in gazing out to where the cables lost themselves in the thick downpour.

It was the custom of the backwoods people in that section of country to cross the Sacramento on the Yellow Dragon cable. For this service a small toll was charged, which tolls the Yellow Dragon Company applied to the payment of Hall's wages.

"We've got to get across, Jerry," Spillane said, at the same time jerking his thumb over his shoulder in the direction of his wife. "Her father's hurt at the Clover Leaf. Powder explosion. Not expected to live. We just got word."

√Jerry felt himself fluttering inwardly. He knew that Spillane wanted to cross on the Yellow Dream cable, and in the absence of his father he felt that he dared not assume such a responsibility, for the cable had never been used for passengers; in fact, had not been used at all for a long time.

"Maybe Hall will be back soon," he said.

Spillane shook his head, and demanded, "Where's your father?"

"San Francisco," Jerry answered briefly.

Spillane groaned, and fiercely drove his clenched fist into the palm of the other hand. His wife was crying more audibly and Jerry could hear her murmuring, "And Daddy's dyin',dyin'!"

The tears welled up in his own eyes, and he stood irresolute [indecisive] not knowing what he should do. But the man decided for him.

"Look here, kid," he said, with determination, "the wife and me are goin' over on this here cable of yours! Will you run it for us?"

Jerry backed slightly away. He did it unconsciously, as if recoiling instinctively from something unwelcome.

"Better see if Hall's back," he suggested.

"And if he ain't?"

Again Jerry hesitated.

"I'll stand for the risk," Spillane added. "Don't you see, kid, we've simply got to cross!"

Jerry nodded his head reluctantly.

"And there ain't no use waitin' for Hall," Spillane went on. "You know as well as me he ain't back from Cripple Cow this time of day! So come along and let's get started."

No wonder that Mrs. Spillane seemed terrified as they helped her into the ore-car—so Jerry thought, as he gazed into the apparently fathomless [too deep to measure] gulf beneath her.

For it was so filled with rain and cloud, hurtling and curling in the fierce blast, that the other shore, seven hundred feet away, was invisible, while the cliff at their feet dropped sheer down and lost itself in the swirling vapor. By all appearances it might be a mile to bottom instead of two hundred feet.

"All ready?" he asked.

"Let her go!" Spillane shouted to make himself heard above the roar of the wind.

He had clambered in beside his wife, and was holding one of her hands in his.

Jerry looked upon this with disapproval. "You'll need all your hands for holdin' on, the way the wind's yowlin'."

The man and the woman shifted their hands accordingly, tightly gripping the sides of the car, and Jerry slowly and carefully released the brake. The drum began to revolve as the endless cable passed around it, and the car slid slowly out into the chasm, its trolley wheels rolling on the stationary cable overhead, to which it was suspended.

It was not the first time Jerry had worked the cable, but it was the first time he had done so away from the supervising eye of his father. By means of the brake he regulated the speed of the car. It needed regulating, for at times, caught by the stronger gusts of wind, it swayed violently back and forth; and once, just before it was swallowed up in a rain squall, it seemed about to spill out its human contents.

After that Jerry had no way of knowing where the car was except by means of the cable. This he watched keenly as it glided around the drum. "Three hundred feet," he breathed to

himself, as the cable markings went by, "three hundred and fifty, four hundred, four hundred and—"

The cable had stopped. Jerry threw off the brake, but it did not move. He caught the cable with his hands and tried to start it by tugging smartly. Something had gone wrong. What? He could not guess; he could not see. Looking up, he could vaguely make out the empty car, which had been crossing from the opposite cliff at a speed equal to that of the loaded car. It was about two hundred and fifty feet away. That meant, he knew, that somewhere in the gray obscurity, two hundred feet above the river and two hundred and fifty feet from the other bank, Spillane and his wife were suspended and stationary.

Three times Jerry shouted with all the shrill force of his lungs, but no answering cry came out of the storm. It was impossible for him to hear them or to make himself heard. As he stood for a moment, thinking rapidly, the flying clouds seemed to thin and lift. He caught a brief glimpse of the swollen Sacramento beneath, and a briefer glimpse of the car and the man and woman. Then the clouds descended thicker than ever.

The boy examined the drum closely, and found nothing the matter with it. Evidently it was the drum on the other side that had gone wrong. He was appalled at thought of the man and woman out there in the midst of the storm, hanging over the abyss [deep gulf], rocking back and forth in the frail car and ignorant of what was taking place on the shore. And he did not like to think of their hanging there while he went round by the Yellow Dragon cable to the other drum.

But he remembered a block and tackle in the toolhouse, and ran and brought it. They were double blocks, and he murmured aloud, "A purchase of four," as he made the tackle fast to the endless cable. Then he heaved upon it, heaved until it seemed that his arms were being drawn out from their sockets and that his shoulder muscles would be ripped asunder. Yet the cable did not

budge. Nothing remained but to cross over to the other side.

He was already soaking wet, so he did not mind the rain as he ran over the trail to the Yellow Dragon. The storm was with him, and it was easy going, although there was no Hall at the other end of it to man the brake for him and regulate the speed of the car. This he did for himself, however, by means of a stout rope, which he passed, with a turn, round the stationary cable.

As the full force of the wind struck him in mid-air, swaying the cable and whistling and roaring past it, and rocking and careening the car, he appreciated more fully what must be the condition of mind of Spillane and his wife. And this appreciation gave strength to him, as, safely across, he fought his way up the other bank, in the teeth of the gale, to the Yellow Dream cable.

To his consternation [bewilderment], he found the drum in thorough working order. Everything was running

smoothly at both ends. Where was the hitch? In the middle, without a doubt.

From this side, the car containing Spillane was only two hundred and fifty feet away. He could make out the man and woman through the whirling vapor, crouching in the bottom of the car and exposed to the pelting rain and the full fury of the wind. In a lull between the squalls he shouted to Spillane to examine the trolley [basket] of the car.

Spillane heard, for he saw him rise up cautiously on his knees, and with his hands go over both trolley wheels. Then he turned his face toward the bank.

"She's all right, kid!"

Jerry heard the words, faint and far, as from a remote distance. Then what was the matter? Nothing remained but the other and empty car, which he could not see, but which he knew to be there, somewhere in that terrible gulf two hundred feet beyond Spillane's car.

His mind was made up on the instant. He was only fourteen years old, slightly and wirily [leanly and strongly] built; but his life had been lived among the mountains, his father had taught him no small measure of "sailoring," and he was not particularly afraid of heights.

In the toolbox by the drum he found an old monkey wrench and a short bar of iron, also a coil of fairly new Manila rope. He looked in vain for a piece of board with which to rig a boatswain's chair. There was nothing at hand but large planks, so he was compelled to do without the more comfortable form of saddle.

The saddle he rigged was very simple. With the rope he made merely a large loop round the stationary cable, to which hung the empty car. When he sat in the loop his hands could just reach the cable conveniently, and where the rope was likely to fray against the cable he lashed his coat, in lieu of the old sack he would have used had he been able to find one.

These preparations swiftly completed, he swung out over the chasm, sitting in the rope saddle and pulling himself along the cable by his hands. With him he carried the monkey wrench and short iron bar and a few spare feet of rope. It was a slightly uphill pull, but this he did not so much mind as the wind. When the furious gusts hurled him back and forth, sometimes half twisting him about, and he gazed down into the gray depths, he was aware that he was afraid. It was an old cable. What if it should break under his weight and the pressure of the wind?

It was fear he was experiencing, honest fear, and he knew that there was a "gone" feeling in the pit of his stomach, and a trembling of the knees which he could not quell.

But he held himself bravely to the task. The cable was old and worn, sharp pieces of wire projected from it, and his hands were cut and bleeding by the time he took his first rest, and held a shouted conversation with Spillane. The car was directly beneath him and only a few feet away, so he was able to explain the condition of affairs and his errand.

"Wish I could help you," Spillane shouted at him as he started on, "but the wife's gone all to pieces! Anyway, kid, take care of yourself! I got myself in this fix, but it's up to you to get me out!"

"Oh, I'll do it!" Jerry shouted back. "Tell Mrs. Spillane that she'll be ashore now in a jiffy!"

In the midst of pelting rain, which half-blinded him, swinging from side to side like a rapid and erratic [irregular] pendulum, his torn hands paining him severely and his lungs panting from his exertions and panting from the very air which the wind sometimes blew into his mouth with strangling force, he finally arrived at the empty car.

A single glance showed him that he had not made the dangerous journey in vain. The front trolley wheel, loose from long wear, had jumped the cable, and the cable was now jammed tightly between the wheel and the sheave block.

One thing was clear—the wheel must be removed from the block. A second thing was equally clear—while the wheel was being removed, the car would have to be fastened to the cable by the rope he had brought.

At the end of a quarter of an hour, beyond making the car secure, he had accomplished nothing. The key [bolt or pin] which bound the wheel on its axle was rusted and jammed. He hammered at it with one hand and held on the best he could with the other, swinging and twisting his body, and made his blows miss more often than not. Nine-tenths of the strength he expended was in trying to hold himself steady. For fear that he might drop the monkey wrench, he made it fast to his wrist with his handkerchief.

At the end of half an hour Jerry had hammered the key clear, but he could not draw it out. A dozen times it seemed that he must give up in despair, that all the danger and toil he had gone through were for nothing. Then an idea came to him, and he went through his pockets with feverish haste, and found what he sought for—a tenpenny nail.

But for that nail, put in his pocket he knew not when or why, he would have had to make another trip over the cable and back. Thrusting the nail through the looped head of the key, he at last had a grip, and in no time the key was out.

Then came punching and prying with the iron bar to get the wheel itself free from where it was jammed by the cable against the side of the block. After that Jerry replaced the wheel, and by means of a rope, heaved up on the car till the trolley once more rested properly on the cable.

All this took time. More than an hour and a half had elapsed since his arrival at the empty car. He removed the detaining ropes, and the trolley wheels began slowly to revolve. The car was moving, and he knew that somewhere beyond, although he could not see, the car of Spillane was likewise moving, and in the opposite direction.

There was no need for a brake, for his weight sufficiently counterbalanced the weight in the other car; and soon he saw the cliff rising out of the cloud depths and the old familiar drum going round and round.

Jerry climbed out and made the car securely fast. He did it deliberately and carefully, and then, quite unheroiclike, he sank down by the drum, regardless of the pelting storm, and burst out sobbing.

There were many reasons why he sobbed—partly from the pain in his hands, which was excruciating; partly from exhaustion; partly from relief and release from the nerve-tension he had been under for so long; and in a large measure from thankfulness that the man and woman were saved.

They were not there to thank him; but somewhere beyond that howling, storm-driven gulf he knew they were hurrying over the trail toward the Clover Leaf.

Jerry staggered to the cabin, and his hand left the white knob red with blood as he opened the door, but he took no notice of it.

He was too proudly contented with himself, for he was certain that he had done well, and he was honest enough to admit to himself that he had done well. But a small regret arose and persisted in his thoughts—if his father had only been there to see!

Reading Check

1. Why is Jerry alone?
2. Following Spillane's demand for Jerry to let them cross, we are told that "Jerry backed slightly away. He did it unconciously, as if recoiling instinctively from something unwelcome." How does this description of Jerry's reaction foreshadow the events to come?
3. What unexpected event turns the Spillane's river crossing into a life-threatening dilemma?
4. How does Jerry react in the face of this danger?
5. In what ways does Jerry's thought— "If only his father had been there to see!"—express sentiments we all have?

The fury of an unexpected storm and the desertion of the ship's crew leave the Swiss Family Robinson alone to face the wild waters. But as you read the following journal entries, you will find that these events were only the first of many adventures this missionary family encountered.

The Swiss Family Robinson

David Wyss

Shipwrecked

The storm lasted for six long and terrible days, and on the seventh it appeared only to redouble its fury. We were driven out of our course and all trace of our position was lost. The water leaking into the hold made us expect every moment to be swallowed up by the waves. I was taking my family to Otaheite [former name for Tahiti], where I had recently been appointed a missionary, yet the storm made it appear as if we were to perish in the wild waters.

To cap off our troubles, the crew made off in the life boats, leaving me with my wife and children to face our fate alone. Fortunately, the ship wedged itself between some great rocks giving us an opportunity to escape to the land we could distinguish nearby.

When the tempest subsided, our little family made a tour of the wreck and found plenty of fresh water and food, as well as a cow, a donkey, a ram, an old pig, two goats, two large dogs, and several sheep, hens, and roosters. Stores of all sorts were available. Our only question now was how we should get these provisions on shore. Several empty casks found in the hold soon answered that question. Fritz, my oldest son, and I found some tools and with the casks contrived a crude tub-boat. The casks were sawed asunder, and after nailing eight half-tubs on a plank, we had a fair boat. With jack-screw and rollers, we raised and launched our craft, and imploring God's blessing we embarked. In the first tub was my wife. Close behind her in the second tub was my youngest son, Franz, who was then just seven years old. The next two tubs contained ammunition, sailcloth, a tent, and tools. Also in this tub were ten hens and two roosters secured under a lattice.

Fritz, who was fifteen, occupied the fifth tub. Then Ernest, thirteen, occupied the sixth and Jack, who was ten, the seventh. I had taken the last for myself, that I might guide the vessel by the stern oar, which served as a rudder. Despite having the tide with us, it was a long and tedious journey before we reached dry land. The two dogs, who had jumped into the sea to follow us, managed to reach the shore first. Steering after them we found ourselves in a small bay or inlet where the water was perfectly smooth. The shore sloped gently upward from the low banks to the cliffs. Everyone sprang gladly out of the boat except for little Franz, who, lying packed in his tub like a potted shrimp, had to be lifted out.

As soon as we could gather our children around us, we knelt to offer thanks and praise for our merciful escape, and with hearts full we commended ourselves to God's good keeping for some time to come.

I was anxious to land the two casks that had been floating alongside our boat, but on attempting to do so I found that I could not get them up the bank on which we had landed. I was therefore obliged to look for a more convenient spot. As I did so I was startled by hearing Jack shouting for help as though in great danger. He was at some distance, and I hurried toward him with a hatchet in my hand. The little fellow stood screaming in a deep pool, and as I approached, I saw that a huge lobster had caught his leg in its powerful claw. Poor Jack was in a terrible fright. Kick as he would, his enemy clung on. I waded into the water, and seizing the lobster firmly by the back, managed to make it loosen

its hold. We brought it safely to land, and Jack, having speedily recovered his spirits, sought to catch the lobster in both hands. When he did so, however, he received such a severe blow from the creature's tail that he flung it down and passionately hit it with a large stone. This display of temper vexed me. "You are acting in a very childish manner," said I. "Never strike an enemy in a revengeful spirit." Once more he lifted the lobster but with greater care. He then ran triumphantly toward the place where my wife, Fritz, Ernest, and Franz were endeavoring to put up the tent.

"Mother, mother! A lobster, Ernest! Look here, Franz, mind, he'll bite you!" All crowded around Jack and his prize, wondering at the lobster's unusual size.

By nightfall we had realized how fortunate we were to have the shelter of our tent, for the night proved to be as cold as the day was hot. We did, however, sleep comfortably, for we were all exhausted by the labors of our first day on shore.

Exploring the Island

At daybreak I awoke my wife that we might take council together while the children slept. It was plain to both of us that we should first discern if possible the fate of our late companions. While searching for other survivors, we might also examine the nature and resources of the country on which we were stranded. We, therefore, came to the resolution that, as soon as we had breakfasted, Fritz and I should start on an expedition with these objects in view, while my wife remained near our landing place with the three younger boys.

Fritz and I and our dog Turk took leave of my wife and the other children, bidding them not to wander far from the boat and tent. We parted not without some anxiety on either side, for we knew not what might assail us in this unknown region.

We reached a rocky summit from which we could obtain a comprehensive view of the surrounding country. The beautiful landscape failed to show us the slightest sign or trace of human beings.

Seeing no evidence of our companions, we descended the hill. As we did so, Turk suddenly darted away from us and sprang furiously among a troop of monkeys, which were gamboling playfully on the turf a little space from the trees. They were taken by surprise completely, and the dog, now really ravenous from hunger, had seized and was fiercely tearing one to pieces before we could approach the spot.

His luckless victim was the mother of a tiny monkey, which, being on her back when the dog flew at her, hindered its flight. The little creature attempted to hide in the grass, and trembling with fear watched its mother. On perceiving Turk's bloodthirsty design, Fritz had eagerly rushed to the rescue, flinging away all he was carrying and losing his hat in his haste. All to no purpose as far as the poor mother was concerned. However, when Fritz reached the sight, the young monkey caught sight of him and with one bound was on his shoulders and holding him fast by his thick curly hair. In spite of all Fritz's efforts the monkey kept firmly seated. Fritz screamed and plunged about desperately trying to shake the creature off, but all in vain. The monkey openly clung closer to his neck, making the most absurd grimaces.

I laughed so much at this ridiculous scene that I could scarcely assist my terrified boy out of his awkward predicament. At last, by coaxing the monkey, offering it a bit of biscuit, and gradually disentangling its small sinewy paws from the curls it grasped so tightly, I managed to relieve poor Fritz, who then looked with interest at the baby ape, no bigger than a kitten, as it lay in his arms. "What a jolly little fellow it is!" exclaimed he. "Do let me try to rear it, father. I dare say coconut milk would do until we can bring the cow and goats from the wreck. If he lives, he might be useful to us. I believe monkeys instinctively know what fruits are wholesome and what are poisonous."

"Well," said I, "let the little orphan be yours. You bravely and kindly exerted yourself to save the mother's life. Now you must train her child carefully, for unless you do, its natural instinct will prove mischievous instead of useful to us."

A Summer House

Next morning while we breakfasted, I made a little speech to my sons. "Remember," said I, "that although you all feel very much at your ease here, we are yet complete strangers to a variety of dangers which may surprise us unawares. I charge you therefore that as we begin our second journey of exploration today that you maintain good order and keep together on the march."

We filled our tent with the things we were leaving behind, for we did not know how long we should be absent. Then, closing it carefully, and ranging chests and casks around it, we were ready to be off. Each of us was well equipped with supplies and in the highest spirits.

We marched on with little interruption until we came upon a most wonderful spot. We stopped spellbound, for surrounding us were several magnificently enormous trees. Presently my wife suggested that if an abode could be contrived among the branches of the trees, it would be the safest and most charming home in the world. We all thought her suggestion a capital idea and immediately set about to prepare a new abode.

By nightfall we were nearly finished. We decided to stay the night and return to our tent the following day to bring more of the provisions to our new home. We lit watch fires and, leaving the dogs on guard below, ascended the handmade ladder to our leafy castle. Fritz, Ernest, and Jack were up in a moment. Their mother followed very cautiously, for though she had originated the idea of building a nest, she yet hesitated to entrust herself at such a terrific height from the ground. When she was safely landed in the house, taking little Franz on my back, I let go the fastenings that secured the lower end of the ladder to the ground, and swinging to and fro, slowly ascended.

Next morning when all were awake I interested the boys by proposing to decide on suitable names for the different spots we had visited on this coast. Names were quickly chosen. Our first place of abode we called Tentholm; the islet in the bay, Shark Island; the reedy swamp, Flamingo Marsh. It was some time before the serious question of our leafy castle could be decided, but finally it was settled that it should be called Falconhurst.

Reading Check

1. List several reasons why the Swiss Family Robinson could have despaired during their first unexpected adventure.
2. How do they maintain their courage in the face of all obstacles?
3. List as many incidents as you can that exemplify God's providential care over this family.
4. What does Fritz's reaction to Turk's attacking the monkey reveal about him?
5. After reading the description of the summer house, what name would you give to this "leafy castle"?

A Winter House

By the end of the first rainy season I realized our need for another, more secure, home during the winter months. Fritz proposed that we should hollow out a cave in the rock, and though the difficulties of such an undertaking appeared almost insurmountable, I yet determined to make the attempt.

Some days afterward the boys and I left Falconhurst with the cart laden with a cargo of spades, hammers, chisels, pickaxes, and crowbars to begin our undertaking. On the smooth face of the rock, I drew out in chalk the size of a proposed entrance, and then, with minds bent on success, we battered away. Six days of hard and incessant toil made but little impression. I do not think that the hole would have been satisfactory for even Master Knips, our pet monkey. But we still did not despair, and were presently rewarded by coming to softer and more yielding substance. Our work progressed, and our minds were relieved.

On the tenth day, as our persevering blows were falling heavily, Jack, who was working diligently with a hammer and crowbar, shouted: "Gone, father! Fritz, my bar has gone through the mountain!"

"Run around and get it," laughed Fritz. "Perhaps it has dropped into Europe—you must not lose a good crowbar."

"But really, it is through; it went right through the rock; I heard it crash down inside. Come and see!"

We sprang to his side, and I thrust the handle of my hammer into the hole he spoke of. It met with no opposition; I could turn it in any direction I chose. Fritz handed me a long pole; I tried the depth with that. I could feel nothing. A thin wall, then, was all that intervened between us and a great cavern.

With a shout of joy, the boys battered vigorously at the rock; piece by piece fell, and soon the hole was large enough for us to enter. I stepped near the aperture, and was about to make a further examination when a sudden rush of poisonous air made me giddy, and shouting to my sons to stand off, I leaned against the rock.

When I came to myself, I explained to them the danger of approaching any cavern or other place where the air has for a long time been stagnant. "Unless air is incessantly renewed it becomes vitiated [corrupted]," I said, "and fatal to those who breathe it. The safest way of restoring it to its original state is to subject it to the action of fire. A few handfuls of blazing hay thrown into this hole may, if the place is small, sufficiently purify the air within and allow us to enter without danger." We tried the experiment. The flame was extinguished the instant it entered. Though bundles of blazing grass were thrown in, no difference was made.

I saw that we must apply some more efficacious [effective] remedy and sent the boys for a chest of signal rockets we had brought from the wreck. We let fly some dozens of these fiery serpents, which went whizzing in, and disappeared at apparently a vast distance from us. Some flew round like radiant meteors, lighted up the mighty circumference, and displayed, as by a magician's wand, a sparkling, glittering roof. They looked like avenging dragons driving a malignant fiend out of a beauteous palace.

We waited for a little while after these experiments, and I then again threw in lighted hay. It burned clearly; the air was purified.

Fritz and I enlarged the opening, while Jack thundered away to Falconhurst to give the astonishing news to his mother.

Great must have been the effect of Jack's eloquence on my wife, for she was quickly at our side. All were in the highest state of excitement. Jack had stowed in the cart all the candles he could find, and now lighting these, we entered. I led the way, sounding the ground as I advanced with a large pole, that we might not fall unexpectedly into any hole or chasm. Silently we marched—my wife, the boys, and even the dogs seeming overawed with the grandeur and beauty of the scene. We were in a grotto of diamonds—a vast cave of glittering crystal.

We returned to Falconhurst with minds full of wonder at our new discovery and plans for turning it to the best possible advantage.

For two months we worked steadily at our salt cave to complete partition walls for rooms and stalls for animals. We desired that our labor be finished before the next long rainy season.

Several days were spent in arranging various rooms. Ernest and Franz undertook the library, fixing shelves and setting in order the books we had salvaged from the wreck.

Jack and his mother took in hand the sitting room and the kitchen, while Fritz and I arranged the workshops. The carpenter's bench, the turning lathe, and a large chest of tools were set in convenient places, and many tools and instruments hung on the walls.

Our rocky home was greatly improved by a wide porch that I made along the whole front of our rooms and entrances by leveling the ground to form a terrace, and sheltering it with a veranda of bamboo, supported by pillars of the same.

The children begged me to settle on a name for our salt cave dwelling, and that of Rockburg was chosen unanimously.

When the rainy season came, we were glad for our new dwelling, for the storms seemed fiercer and wilder than ever. Thunder roared and lightning blazed incessantly. Thankfully, however, we found that the season seemed to pass quickly and soon we were again able to enjoy the outdoors.

The Monster

One evening while seated with my wife and Fritz on the veranda, our conversation was interrupted when Fritz suddenly got up, advanced a step or two, gazed fixedly along the avenue that led from Jackal River, then exclaimed: "I see something so strange in the distance. What in the world can it be, Father? First, it seems to be drawn in coils on the ground like a cable, then uprises as if it were a mast, then it sinks, coils, and moves along again. It's coming toward the bridge."

My wife took alarm at this description, and calling the other boys, retreated into the cave, where I desired them to close up the entrances and keep watch with firearms at the upper

directly, but I must further observe the monster's movements."

Fritz left me unwillingly while I continued to watch the serpent. It was of gigantic size and already much too near the bridge to admit the possibility of removing that means of access to our dwelling. I recollected, too, how easily it would pass through the walls. The reptile advanced with writhing and undulatory [wave-like motion] movements, from time to time rearing its head to the height of fifteen or twenty feet and slowly turning it about, as though on the lookout for prey.

As it crossed the bridge with a slow, suspicious motion, I withdrew and hastily rejoined my little party, which was preparing to garrison our fortress in warlike array.

We placed ourselves at the upper openings, after strongly barricading everything below, and awaited with beating hearts the further advance of the foe.

Its movements appeared to become uncertain, as though puzzled by the trace of human habitation. It turned in different directions, coiling and uncoiling and frequently rearing its head, but keeping about the middle of the space in front of the cave. Suddenly, as though unable to resist doing so, one after another the boys fired, and even their mother discharged her gun. Fritz and I also fired with steadier aim, but with the same want of success, for the monster, passing on with a gliding motion, entered the reedy marsh to the left and entirely disappeared.

A wonderful weight seemed lifted from our hearts, while all eagerly discussed the vast length and awful

windows. These openings we had made in the rock at some elevation and could be reached within by steps.

Fritz remained with me while I examined the object through my spyglass.

"It is, as I feared," I cried, "an enormous serpent. And it is advancing directly this way. We shall be placed in the greatest possible danger, for it will certainly cross the bridge."

"May we not attack it, father?" exclaimed Fritz.

"Only with the greatest caution," returned I. "It is far too formidable [dreadful] and too tenacious of life for us rashly to attempt its destruction. Thank God, we are at Rockburg, where we can keep in safe retreat, while we watch for an opportunity to destroy it. Go up to your mother now and assist in loading the firearms. I will join you though magnificent appearance of the serpent. I had recognized it as the boa constrictor. It was a vast specimen, upward of thirty feet in length.

The near neighborhood of this terrific reptile occasioned me the utmost anxiety. I desired that no one should leave the house on any pretense without my express permission.

During three whole days we were kept in suspense and fear, not daring to stir above a few hundred steps from the door, although during all that time the enemy showed no sign of his presence. In fact, we might have been induced to think that it had passed across the swamp had not the restless behavior of our geese and ducks given proof that it still lurked in the thicket of reeds that the fowl were accustomed to make their nightly resting place. The birds swam anxiously about, and much clapping of wings and disturbed cackling showed their uneasiness. Finally, taking wing, they crossed the harbor and took up their quarters on Shark Island.

My concern increased as time went on. I could not venture to attack with insufficient force a monstrous serpent concealed in dense thickets amidst dangerous swamps. Yet, it was dreadful to live in a state of blockade, cut off from all the important duties in which we were engaged and shut up with our animals in the unnatural light of the cave.

Out of this painful state we were at last delivered by none other than our good old simple-hearted donkey, Grizzle. Not by the exercise of any praiseworthy quality in him, but rather by his sheer stupidity.

Our situation was rendered the more critical from having no stock of provisions or fodder for the animals. The hay failing on the evening of the third day, I determined to set the animals at liberty by sending them, under guidance of Fritz, across the river at the ford.

Fritz was to ride Lightfoot, the onager, and the livestock were to be fastened together that he might guide them easily. Next morning we began to prepare for this by tying them in a line, and while so engaged, my wife opened the door. Suddenly old Grizzle, who was fresh and frolicsome after the long rest and regular feeding, broke away from the halter, cut some awkward capers, then bolting out, careened at full gallop straight for the marsh.

In vain we called him back. Fritz would even have rushed after him had not I held him. In another moment the ass was close to the thicket, and with the cold shudder of horror, we beheld the snake rear itself from its lair, the fiery eyes glanced around, the dark, deadly jaws opened, the forked tongue darted forth, and poor old Grizzle's fate was sealed.

Becoming aware of his danger, the donkey stopped short, spread out all four legs, and set up the most piteous bray that ever wrung echo from the rocks.

Swift and straight as a fencer's thrust, the destroyer was upon him wound round him, entangled, enfolded, compressed him, all the while cunningly avoiding the convulsive kicks of the animal.

A cry of horror arose from the spectators of this miserable tragedy.

"Shoot him, father! Shoot him— save poor Grizzle!"

"It's impossible!" I cried. "Our old friend is lost, but I have hopes that when the snake is gorged with this prey we may be able to attack him with some chance of success."

"But that horrible wretch can't swallow him!" cried Jack.

"It seems utterly impossible," exclaimed Fritz, "that the broad ribs, strong legs, hoofs, and all should go down that throat."

"Only see," I replied, "how the monster deals with his victim. Closer and more tightly he curls his crushing folds, the bones give way, he is kneading him into a shapeless mass. Slowly but surely the donkey will disappear down that disentangled maw!"

My wife and Franz found the scene all too horrible, and hastened into the cave. To the rest of us there seemed a fearful fascination in the dreadful sight, and we could not move from the spot.

This tragic performance lasted from seven in the morning until noon. When the awkward morsel was entirely swallowed, the serpent lay stiff, distorted, and apparently insensible along the edge of the marsh.

I felt now or never was the moment for attack. Calling on my sons to maintain their courage and presence of mind, I left our retreat with a feeling of joyous emotion quite new to me and approached with rapid steps and leveled gun the outstretched form of the serpent. Fritz followed me closely.

Jack, somewhat timidly, came several paces behind; while Ernest, after a little hesitation, remained where he was.

The monster's body was stiff and motionless, which made its rolling and fiery eyes more fearful by contrast.

We fired together, and both shots entered the skull. The light of the eye was extinguished, and the only movement was in the further extremity of the body, which rolled, writhed, coiled, and lashed from side to side.

Advancing closer, we fired our pistols directly into its head, a convulsive quiver ran through the mighty frame, and the boa constrictor lay dead.

Reading Check

1. Having read the description of the winter house, what would you have named this dwelling?
2. What does the father mean when he states: "Out of this painful state [fear of the boa constrictor] we were at last delivered by none other than our good old simple-hearted donkey, Grizzle. Not, however, by the exercise of any praiseworthy quality in him but rather by his sheer stupidity?"
3. Compile a description of the "formidable" boa constrictor.
4. How does each character react to the tragic scene of Grizzle's struggle? Are their reactions consistent with their reactions in the rest of the story?

Ten Years Later

"We spend our years as a tale that is told," said King David. These words recurred to me again and again as I reviewed the past ten years that lay chronicled in the pages of my journal.

The shade of sadness cast on my mind by retrospect of this kind was dispelled by thoughts full of gratitude to God, for the welfare and happiness of my beloved family during so long a period. I had cause especially to rejoice in seeing our sons advance to manhood, strengthened by early training for lives of usefulness and activity wherever their lot might fall.

They were all fine, handsome fellows: Fritz, now twenty-five, was of moderate height, uncommonly strong, active, muscular, and high-spirited.

Ernest, two years younger, was tall and slight; in disposition, mild, calm, and studious. His early faults of indolence and selfishness were almost entirely overcome. He possessed refined tastes and great intellectual power.

Jack, at twenty, strongly resembled Fritz, being about his height, though more lightly built.

Franz, a lively youth of seventeen, had some of the qualities of each of his brothers. He possessed wit and shrewdness, but not the arch drollery [clowning] of Jack.

All were honorable, God-fearing young men, dutiful and affectionate to their mother and myself and warmly attached to each other.

Although so many years had elapsed in total seclusion, it continued to be my strong impression that we should one day be restored to the society of our fellow men.

But time, which was bringing our sons to manhood, was also carrying their parents onward to old age. Anxious, gloomy thoughts relating to their future, should they be left indeed alone, sometimes oppressed my heart.

My elder sons often made expeditions of which we knew nothing until their return several hours later. Any uneasiness I had felt during their absence was then displaced by the joy of their reappearance and reproof died on my lips.

Fritz had been absent on one of these expeditions one whole day, and not until evening did we realize that his kayak was yet gone.

Anxious to see him return before nightfall, I went off to Shark Island with Ernest and Jack, in order to look out for him from the watchtower there.

Long we gazed across the expanse of ocean glittering in the level beams of the setting sun, and finally we discerned a small black speck in the distance which, by telescope, proved to be the returning wanderer.

I remarked that his skiff sailed toward shore at a slower rate than usual. The cannon was fired to let him know that his approach was observed, and then we joyfully hurried back to receive him at the harbor.

It was easy to see as he drew near what had delayed his progress. The kayak towed a large sack heavily laden.

"Welcome, Fritz!" I cried. "Welcome back, wherever you come from, and whatever you bring. You seem to have quite a cargo there!"

"Yes, and my trip has led me to interesting discoveries which will tempt us again in the same direction. Come, boys, let's carry up the things, and while I rest I will relate my adventures."

As soon as possible we all assembled around him. "I think my absence without leave deserves a reproach instead of a warm reception, father, and I must apologize for it," he began. "But ever since I possessed the kayak it has been my ambition to make a voyage of discovery along the coast which we have never explored. Thus I did so, but I must confess that as I progressed I felt anything but comfortable while going through the places held in possession by unfamiliar monsters of the deep. I used every effort to pass through this unknown region quickly and unnoticed. Yet it was more than an hour and a half before I could get clear around the strange rocks, shoals, and cliffs. While journeying I found in the side of one of the rocky walls a lofty entrance to an immense vaulted cave. I entered and found it was tenanted by a number of small species of swallow, scarcely larger than wrens. The walls were covered with thousands of their nests. I pursued my way through the cave which presently opened up into a very lonely bay. The water beneath me was clear as crystal.

"I resumed my survey of the coast, my progress somewhat impeded by a bag of shellfish I had caught and now drew after me. But I proceeded without accident past the mouth of the cave to the further side of the bay.

"The tide was setting strongly inshore, so that I could not attempt a passage through it, but I was still able to examine the crags. I saw nothing remarkable except thousands of sea fowl of every sort and kind, from the gull to the mighty albatross. My approach was regarded as an invasion and trespass by these birds, and they beset me, screaming and wheeling over my head, till, out of patience, I stood up, and hit furiously about me with a boat hook. To my surprise, one blow struck an albatross with such force that he fell stunned. I now once more attempted to cross the reef by the narrow channel and, happily succeeding, found myself in the open sea, and speeding toward home."

Here ended the narrative, but next morning Fritz drew me aside, and confided to me a most remarkable sequel to his story.

The Mysterious Message

"There was something very extraordinary about the albatross," Fritz confided to me. "I allowed you to suppose that I left it as it fell, but in reality I raised it to the deck of the kayak, and then perceived a piece of rag wound round one of its legs. This I removed and, to my utter astonishment, saw English words written on it, which I plainly made out to be: 'Save an unfortunate Englishwoman from the smoking rock!' This little sentence sent a thrill through every nerve. My brain seemed to whirl. I doubted the evidence of my senses. 'Is this reality or delusion?' thought I. 'Can it be true, that a fellow creature breathes with us the air of this lonely region?' I felt stupified for some minutes, but the bird began to show signs of life, which recalled me to myself.

"Quickly deciding what must be done, I tore a strip from my handkerchief, on which I traced the words—'Do not despair! Help is near!' This I carefully bound round one leg, replacing the rag on the other, and then applied myself to the complete restoration of the bird. It gradually revived; and after drinking a little, surprised me by suddenly rising on the wing, faltering a moment in its flight, and then rapidly disappearing from my view in a westerly direction.

"Now, father, one thought occupies me continually: Will my note ever reach this Englishwoman? Shall I be able to find and save her?"

I listened to the account with feelings of the liveliest interest and astonishment. "My dear son," said I, "you have done wisely in confiding to me alone your most exciting discovery. Unless we know more, we must not unsettle the others by speaking of it; for it appears to me quite possible that these words were penned long ago in some distant shore, where, by this time, the unhappy stranger may have perished miserably. By the 'smoking rock' must be meant a volcano. There are none here."

Fritz was not disposed to look at the case from this gloomy point of view. He believed smoke might rise from a rock which was not volcanic; and evidently cherished the hope that he might be able to respond effectually to this touching appeal.

I was in reality as anxious as himself on the subject, but judged it prudent to abate rather than excite hopes of success which might be doomed to bitter disappointment.

After earnest consultation on the subject, we decided that Fritz should go in search of the writer of the message, but not until he had so altered the kayak to fit it for carrying two persons, as well as provisions.

The Search

Fritz had been absent five days. When I could not longer conceal my anxiety, I suggested that we follow him. All were delighted at the proposal, and even my wife, when she heard that we were to sail in the yacht, agreed to accompany us.

On a bright morning, with a favorable breeze, we five, with the dogs, stepped aboard and ran for the cape.

Our beautiful little yacht bounded over the water gaily, and the bright sunshine and delicious sea breeze put us all in the highest spirits. The entrance of the archway was in sight, and thither I was directing the boat's course. Suddenly ahead, I saw a canoe paddled by a tall and muscular savage, who stood up in his skiff and appeared to be examining us attentively.

Seeing that we were staring toward him, the swarthy native seized his paddle and again darted behind a rock. An awful thought now took possession of me. There must be a tribe lurking on these shores, and Fritz must have fallen into their hands. I determined, however, that we should not be easily taken and our guns were reloaded.

Presently a dusky face appeared, peeping at us from a lofty rock. It vanished, and we saw another peeping at us from lower down. Then, again, the skiff put out as though to make further reconnoiter. All, even Jack, looked anxious and glanced at me for orders.

"Hoist a white flag," said I, "and hand me the speaking trumpet."

I seized the trumpet and uttered such peaceable words in the Malay language as I could recall. Neither the flag nor my words seemed to produce any effect, and the savage was about to return to shore.

Jack thereupon lost his patience and took up the trumpet.

"Come here, you!" he exclaimed. "Come on board and make friends, or we'll blow you and your—"

"Stop! Stop! You foolish boy," said I, "you will but alarm the man with your wild words and gestures."

"No! But see," he cried, "he is paddling toward us!"

And sure enough the canoe was rapidly approaching.

Presently a cry from Franz alarmed me. "Look! Look!" he shrieked. "The villain is in Fritz's kayak. I can see the walrus head."

Ernest alone remained unmoved. He took the speaking trumpet. "Fritz, ahoy!" he shouted. "Welcome, old fellow!"

The words were scarcely out of his mouth when I too, recognized the well-known face beneath its dusky disguise.

In another minute Fritz was on board, and in spite of his blackened face was kissed and welcomed heartily. He was now assailed with a storm of questions from all sides: "Where had he been?" "What had kept him?" "Why had he disguised himself?"

"I shall explain all when I give a full account of my adventures," he replied. After removing the stains from his skin, he again sprang into his kayak and piloted us to a picturesque little island in the bay.

When we arrived on shore, we followed Fritz in perfect silence. Presently we emerged from the thicket through which we were passing, and saw before us a hut of sheltering boughs, at the entrance of which burned a cheerful fire. Into this leafy bower Fritz disappeared, leaving his brothers outside in mute astonishment. In another moment he emerged again bringing Jenny Montrose with him.

The Mysterious Guns

Jenny soon became part of the family and greatly aided in helping the long winter evenings at Rockburg to pass quickly. She readily told us many wonderful tales and adventure stories, and proved a particularly comforting companion for my wife.

One evening, our day's work being finished, we decided to stroll up and down the beach. But scarcely had we begun our walk, when there came the sound of three guns booming across the water.

We stopped, speechless. Was it fancy? Had we really heard guns from a strange ship? A tumult of feelings rushed over us—anxiety, joy, hope, doubt, each in turn took possession of our minds. We decided that the sound was definitely from some unfamiliar ship, but was it friend or foe?

"At present," I said, "We can do nothing to discover who fired the shots, for night is drawing on. We must make what preparations we can for inquiry in the morning and pray for guidance."

In the morning we assembled in our little breakfast room. The meal was eaten hurriedly and almost in silence, for our hearts were too full and our minds too busily occupied to allow any outward display of excitement. Fritz and Jack slipped quietly out, and presently returned from the garden with baskets of the choicest fruits in fresh and fragrant profusion. With these as presents for the strangers, Fritz and I boarded the yacht.

As we rounded the cape we spotted the ship, and were greatly relieved to discover that it was a European vessel. As we approached the ship, every eye on board was fixed on us. For all the strange sights which the gallant crew may have looked for, such an anomaly [abnormality] as a pleasure yacht, manned by a party such as ours, was the furthest from their thoughts.

In another minute we were upon her deck. The captain, with the simple frankness of a British seaman, welcomed us cordially.

I gave him an outline of the history of the wreck and our sojourn upon the shores, and spoke to him, too, of Jenny and of the providential way in which Fritz had been the means of rescuing her from her lonely position.

"Then," said the gallant officer, rising and grasping Fritz by the hand, "let me heartily thank you in my own name and in that of Colonel Montrose. For it was the hope of finding some trace of his daughter that led me to these shores. The disappearance of the *Dorcas,* the ship she was on, has been a terrible blow to that great man. Though for three years we have heard no word of survivors, the colonel never entirely abandoned all hope of again hearing of his daughter.

I knew this, and a few weeks ago, when I was about to leave Sydney for the cape, I found three men who declared that they had been on board the *Dorcas.* They said that of the four boats that left the wreck theirs was the only one they knew of that reached the shore safely. From them I learned all the particulars, and applying for permission to cruise in these latitudes, I sailed in hopes of finding further traces of the unfortunate crew. My efforts have been rewarded with unlooked for success."

Fritz replied modestly to the prasies which he received, and then the captain begged to be introduced to my wife, other sons, and Jenny. One of the officers was accordingly dispatched to the yacht with a polite message, and the remainder of our family was soon on board.

That night I had a serious consultation with my wife, as to whether or not we really had any well-grounded reason for wishing to return to Europe. It would be childish to undertake a voyage simply because an opportunity offered for doing so.

Neither of us knew to what decision the other was inclined, and each was afraid of expressing what might run contrary to the feelings of the other. But gradually it became apparent that neither of us entertained any strong wish to leave the peaceful island. Finally we discovered that the real wish which lay at the bottom of both our hearts was to adopt New Switzerland as our home.

My dear wife assured me that she desired nothing more earnestly than to spend the rest of her days in a place to which she had become so much attached, provided I, and at least two of her sons, also wished to remain. From the other two she would willingly part if they chose to return to Europe, with the understanding that they must endeavor to send out emigrants of a good class to join us, and form a prosperous colony.

Then came the question as to which of our sons were best suited to remain with us, and which to go away. This point we left for the boys to decide for themselves.

Fritz, who had grown fond of Jenny, decided to return with her and marry her. Franz also decided to return in order to pursue his education. Both Ernest and Jack willingly decided to remain on the island. Even Captain Littlestone heartily approved of our idea and agreed to consult with English officials on the subject of placing our island under the protection of Great Britain. Thus, every circumstance was wonderfully ordered and linked together by Divine Providence.

I close this journal; it is my great wish that young people who read this record of our lives and adventures should learn from it how admirably suited is the peaceful, industrious life of a cheerful family to the formation of strong, pure, and manly character.

Reading Check

1. Why do you think King David's words "We spend our lives as a tale that is told" come to the father's mind as he reviews the past ten years' adventures?
2. How does each family member change?
3. What discovery does Fritz make on his excursion?
4. Why is the English ship sailing along the coast?
5. What are the most appealing and unappealing aspects of the Robinsons' living in their New Switzerland?

Wartime is often the time when adventurous spirits answer the call to heroic actions. In the following two poems, you will read about two such adventurers and the heroic deeds they performed.

Incident of the French Camp

Robert Browning

You know we French stormed Ratisbon:
    A mile or so away,
On a little mount, Napoleon
    Stood on our storming-day;
With neck out-thrust, you fancy how,
    Legs wide, arms locked behind,
As if to balance the prone brow,
    Oppressive with its mind.

Just as perhaps he mused, "My plans
    That soar, to earth may fall,
Let once my army-leader Lannes
    Waver at yonder wall,"—
Out 'twixt the battery-smokes there flew
    A rider, bound on bound
Full galloping; nor bridle drew
    Until he reached the mound.

Then off there flung in smiling joy,
    And held himself erect
By just his horse's mane, a boy;
    You hardly could suspect
(So tight he kept his lips compressed,
    Scarce any blood came through),
You looked twice ere you saw his breast
    Was all but shot in two.

"Well," cried he, "Emperor, by God's grace
    We've got you Ratisbon!
The marshal's in the market-place,
    And you'll be there anon
To see your flag-bird flap his vans
    Where I, to heart's desire,
Perched him!" The chief's eye flashed; his plans
    Soared up again like fire.

The chief's eye flashed, but presently
    Softened itself, as sheathes
A film the mother eagle's eye
    When her bruised eaglet breathes:
"You're wounded!" "Nay;" his soldier's pride
    Touched to the quick, he said,
"I'm killed, sire!" And, his chief beside,
    Smiling, the boy fell dead.

Emily Geiger

unknown

'Twas in the days of the Revolution,—
    Dark days were they and drear,—
And by Carolina firesides
    The women sat in fear;
For the men were away at the fighting,
    And sad was the news that came,
That the battle was lost; and the death-list
    Held many a loved one's name.

When as heart-sore they sat round the camp-fires,
    "What, ho! Who'll volunteer
To carry a message to Sumter?"
    A voice rang loud and clear.
There was a sudden silence,
    But not a man replied;
They knew too well of the peril
    Of one who dared that ride.

Outspoke then Emily Geiger
    With a rich flush on her cheek,—
"Give me the message to be sent;
    I am the one you seek.
For I am a Southern woman;
    And I'd rather do and dare
Than sit by a lonely fireside,
    My heart gnawed through with care."

They gave her the precious missive;
    And on her own good steed
She rode away, 'mid the cheers of the men,
    Upon her daring deed.
And away through the lonely forests,
    Steadily galloping on,
She saw the sun sink low in the sky,
    And in the west go down.

"Halt!—or I fire!" On a sudden
    A rifle clicked close by.
"Let you pass? Not we, till we know you are
    No messenger or spy."
"She's a Whig,—from her face,—and I will wager,"
    Swore the officer of the day.
"To the guard-house, and send for a woman
    To search her without delay."

No time did she lose in bewailing;
    As the bolt creaked in the lock,
She quickly drew the precious note
    That was hidden in her frock.
And she read it through with hurried care,
    Then ate it piece by piece,
And calmly sat her down to wait
    Till time should bring release.

They brought her out in a little,
    And set her on her steed,
With many a rude apology,
    For his discourteous deed.
On, on, once more through the forest black,
    The good horse panting strains,
Till the sentry's challenge: "Who comes there?"
    Tells that the end she gains.

Ere an hour, in the camp of Sumter
    There was hurrying to and fro.
"Saddle and mount, saddle and mount,"
    The bugles shrilly blow.
"Forward trot!" and the long ranks wheel,
    And into the darkness glides:
Long shall the British rue that march
    And Emily Geiger's ride.

Curdie, a poor young miner, is given the task of saving the king and the kingdom from the selfishness of its subjects. To aid him in his task, Curdie receives a special gift from the grand old princess that enables him to discern the true nature of men. Thus equipped, he and his hideous but faithful beast set out on their perilous adventure.

The Princess and Curdie

George MacDonald

Part I   *The Mountain*

Curdie was the son of Peter the miner. He lived with his father and mother in a cottage built on a mountain, and he worked with his father inside the mountain. The mines belonged to the king of the country, and the miners were his servants, working under his overseers and officers. He was a real king—that is, one who ruled for the good of his people and not to please himself.

About a year before our story begins, a series of very remarkable events had just ended. I will narrate as many of them as will serve to help us understand our present story.

On the mountain, on one of its many claws, stood a grand old house, half farmhouse, half castle, belonging to the king. There his only child, the Princess Irene, had been brought up till she was nearly nine years old, and would doubtless have continued much longer, but for the strange events to which I have referred.

At that time the hollow places of the mountain were inhabited by creatures called goblins, who for various reasons and in various ways made themselves troublesome to all, but to the little princess, dangerous. Mainly by the watchful devotion and energy of Curdie, however, their designs had been utterly defeated, and made to recoil upon themselves to their own destruction, so that now there were very few of them left alive, and many of the miners believed that there was not a single goblin remaining in the whole inside of the mountain.

The king had been so pleased with the boy—then approaching thirteen years of age—that when he carried away his daughter he asked him to accompany them; but he was still better pleased with him when he found that Curdie preferred staying with his father and mother. For the good king knew that the love of a boy who would not leave his father and mother to be made a great man was worth ten thousand offers to die for his sake and would prove so when the right time came. So the king took a kind farewell of them all and rode away with his daughter to the capital city of Gwyntystorm.

A gloom fell upon the mountain and the miners when the princess had gone, and Curdie did not whistle for a whole week. But whoever is diligent will soon be cheerful, and though all the miners missed the household of the castle, they soon managed to get on without them.

The White Pigeon

At the time our story begins, Curdie was growing faster in body than in mind—with the usual consequence, that he was getting rather stupid—one of the chief signs of this was that he believed less and less in things he had never seen. He doubted the princess more and more and he especially doubted the marvelous stories she had told him of her great-great-grandmother, the grand old princess. For he had heard it said that children could not always distinguish betwixt dreams and actual events. He was gradually changing into a commonplace man. Thus, Curdie was not in a very good way. His father and mother had, it is true, no fault to find with him—and yet—neither of them was ready to sing when the thought of him came up.

Now Curdie had made himself a bow and some arrows and was teaching

himself to shoot with them. One evening in the early summer, as he was walking home from the mine with them in his hand, a light flashed across his eyes. He looked, and there was a snow-white pigeon settling on a rock in front of him, in the red light of the level sun. It was a lovely bird. Another moment and it would have been aloft in the waves of rosy light, but just as it was bending its legs to spring, Curdie shot an arrow. The bird fell to the ground, broken-winged and bleeding.

With a gush of pride at his skill, and pleasure at his success, Curdie ran to pick up his prey. I must say for him he picked it up gently. When he held it in his victorious hands, the winged beauty looked up in his face—and with such eyes! As the eyes closed and opened, their look was fixed on his. It did not once flutter or try to get away; it only throbbed and bled and looked at him. Curdie's heart began to grow very large. What could it mean? It was nothing but a pigeon, and why should he not kill a pigeon? Once more it opened its eyes—then closed them again, and its throbbing ceased. Curdie gave a sob. Its last look reminded him of the princess—he did not know why. He remembered how hard he had labored to set her beyond danger, and yet what dangers she had had to encounter for his sake. Now what had he done? He had stopped saving, and had begun killing!

With his tears came the remembrance that a white pigeon, just before the princess and her father went away, came from somewhere and flew round the king and Princess Irene, and then flew away. It was said that the pigeon came from the grand old princess's lamp. This must be that very pigeon! Horrible to think!

Suddenly everything round him seemed against him. The red sunset stung him; the rocks frowned at him; the sweet wind that he had felt against his face as he walked up the hill dropped. It grew darker and darker. An evil something began to move in his heart. "What a fool I am!" he said to himself. Then he grew angry, and was just going to throw the bird from him and whistle, when a brightness shone all round him. He lifted his eyes, and saw a great globe of light. It shone from somewhere above the roofs of the castle. Could she really be there in the tower as Irene had said? It couldn't be! And yet there was the white globe shining, and here was the dead white bird in his hand. That moment the pigeon gave a flutter. "It is not dead!" cried Curdie almost with a shriek. The same instant he was running full speed toward the castle, never letting his heels down, lest he should shake the poor, wounded bird.

The Grand Old Princess

When Curdie reached the castle, and ran into the little garden in front of it, there stood the door wide open. This was as he had hoped, for what could he have said if he had had to knock at it? Those whose business it is to open doors, so often mistake and shut them!

So in he walked. But where to go next he could not tell. It was not quite dark: a dull shineless twilight filled the place. All he knew was that he must go up to the tower, and that proved enough for the present.

There was a great staircase rising before him. At the top of these stairs was yet another. At the top of this second staircase he could go no further, so he left the stairs and went down a passage. This passage was rather dark, but he kept on his way and eventually came to another passage. This passage brought him to a door. He was afraid to open it without first knocking. He knocked, but heard no answer. He was answered nevertheless; for the door gently opened.

As he hesitated, he heard the noise of a spinning wheel. He stood listening, so entranced that he forgot to enter, and the wheel went on and on, spinning in his brain songs and tales and rhymes, till he was almost asleep as well as dreaming, for sleep does not always come first. But suddenly came the thought of the poor bird, which had been lying motionless in his hand all this time, and that woke him up. Just then he heard a voice.

"Come in, Curdie," it said.

Curdie shook. It was getting rather awful. The heart that had never heeded any army of goblins trembled at the soft word of invitation. But then there was the red-spotted white thing in his hand! He dared not hesitate. Quietly he entered, but he could see nothing. Nothing at first—except a sloping shaft of moonlight that came in at a high window, and rested on the floor. He stood and stared at it, forgetting to shut the door.

"Why don't you come in, Curdie?" said the voice.

The gentleness of the voice made Curdie remember his manners. He shut

the door, and drew a step or two nearer to the moonlight.

All the time the sound of the spinning had been going on and on, and Curdie now caught sight of the wheel. Oh, it was such a thin, delicate thing—reminding him of a spider's web in a hedge. It stood in the middle of the room, and it seemed as if the moonlight nearly melted it away. A step nearer, he saw, with a start, two little hands at work with it. And then at last, in the shadow he saw the form of a small withered old woman.

When Curdie saw her, he stood still again. Her grey hair mixed with the moonlight so that he could not tell where one began and the other ended. Her crooked back bent forward over her chest, her shoulders nearly swallowed up her head between them, and her two little hands were just like the grey claws of a hen, scratching at the thread. Indeed Curdie laughed within himself, just a little, at the sight; and when he thought of how the princess used to talk about her huge, great, old grandmother, he laughed more. But that moment the little lady leaned forward into the moonlight, and Curdie caught a glimpse of her eyes, and all the laugh went out of him.

"What do you come here for, Curdie?" she said, as gently as before.

Then Curdie remembered that he stood there as a culprit, and worst of all, as one who had his confession yet to make. There was no time to hesitate over it.

"Oh, ma'am! See here," he said, and advanced a step or two, holding out the pigeon. The moment the rays fell upon it the pigeon fluttered. The old woman put out her hands and took it.

When Curdie saw how distressed she was he grew sorrier still, and said:

"I didn't mean to do any harm, ma'am, I didn't think of its being yours."

"Ah, Curdie! If it weren't mine, what would become of it now?" she returned. "You say you didn't mean any harm. Did you mean any good, Curdie?"

"No," answered Curdie.

"Remember, then, that whoever does not mean good is always in danger of harm."

"But, please ma'am—I don't mean to be rude or to contradict you," said Curdie, "but if a body was never to do anything but what he knew to be good, he would have to live half his time doing nothing."

"There you are much mistaken," said the old quavering voice. "How little you must have thought! Why, you don't seem even to know the good of the things you are constantly doing. Now don't

mistake me. I don't mean you are good for doing them. It is a good thing to eat your breakfast, but you don't fancy it's very good of you to do it. The thing is good—not you."

Curdie laughed.

"There are a great many more good things than bad things to do. Now tell me what bad thing you have done today besides this sore hurt to my little white friend."

"I really don't think I did anything else that was very bad all day," he said to himself. But at the same time he could not honestly feel that he was worth standing up for. All at once a light seemed to break in upon his mind. "I understand now," he said. "I see I have been doing wrong the whole day."

"What wrong were you doing all day, Curdie? It is better to come to the point, you know," said the old lady, and her voice was gentler even than before.

"I was doing the wrong of never wanting or trying to be better. And now I see that I have been letting things go as they would for a long time. Whatever came into my head I did, and whatever didn't come into my head I didn't do. I never sent anything away, and never looked out for anything to come."

"You have got it, Curdie," said the old lady, in a voice that sounded almost as if she had been crying. "When people don't care to be better they must be doing everything wrong. Now that you are sorry my bird will grow better."

The pigeon gave a flutter, and spread out one of its red-spotted wings.

"Oh, thank you! Thank you!" cried Curdie. "I don't know how to thank you."

"Then I will tell you. Do better, and grow better, and be better. And never kill anything without a good reason for it."

"Ma'am, I will go and fetch my bow and arrows, and you shall burn them yourself."

"I have no fire that would burn your bow and arrows, Curdie."

"Then I promise you to burn them all under my mother's porridge pot tomorrow morning."

"No, no, Curdie. Keep them, and practice with them every day, and grow a good shot. There are plenty of bad things that want killing, and a day will come when they will prove useful. But I must see first whether you will do as I tell you."

"That I will!" said Curdie. "What is it, ma'am?"

"But you do not know what I am going to ask."

"You know, ma'am. That is enough."

"You could not have given me a better answer, Curdie," she returned with a radiant smile. "Come to me again tomorrow night—here in the dove tower, and I will tell you more."

"Indeed I will, ma'am," said Curdie. So they parted.

Curdie's Mission

The next night Curdie went home from the mine a little earlier than usual, to make himself tidy before going to the dove tower. The princess had not appointed an exact time for him to be there; he would go as near the time he had gone first as he could.

When he came to the gate of the king's house, he met an unexpected obstruction. In the open door stood the housekeeper, and she seemed to broaden herself out until she almost filled the doorway.

"So!" she said, "it is you, is it, young man? You are the person that comes in and goes out when he pleases, and keeps running up and down my stairs without ever saying by your leave, or even wiping his shoes, and always leaves the door open! Don't you know this is my house?"

"No, I do not," returned Curdie respectfully. "You forget, ma'am, that it is the king's house."

"That is all the same. The king left it to me to take care of and that you shall know!"

"Is the king dead, ma'am, that he has left it to you?" asked Curdie, half in doubt from the self-assertion of the woman.

"Insolent fellow!" exclaimed the housekeeper, "Don't you see by my dress that I am in the king's service?"

"And am I not one of his miners?"

"Ah, that goes for nothing. I am one of his household. You are an out-of-doors laborer. You are a nobody. You carry a pickaxe. I carry the keys. See!"

"But you must not call one a nobody to whom the king has spoken," said Curdie.

"Go along with you!" cried the housekeeper, and would have shut the door in his face, had she not been afraid that when she stepped back he would step in ere she could get the door in motion, for it was very heavy and always seemed unwilling to shut. Curdie came a pace nearer. She lifted the great house

key from her side, and threatened to strike him down with it, calling aloud on Mar and Whelk and Plout, the menservants under her, to come and help her. Ere one of them could answer, however, she gave a great shriek and turned and fled, leaving the door wide open.

Curdie looked behind him, and saw an animal whose gruesome oddity even he, who knew so many of the strange creatures, had never seen equaled. Its eyes were flaming with anger, but it seemed to be at the housekeeper, for it came cowering and creeping up and laid its head on the ground at Curdie's feet. Curdie hardly waited to look at it, however, but ran into the house, eager to get up the stairs before any of the men should come to annoy—he had no fear of their preventing him. Without halt or hindrance, though the passages were nearly dark, he reached the door of the princess's room and knocked.

"Come in," said the voice of the princess.

Curdie opened the door—but, to his astonishment, saw no room there. Could he have opened a wrong door? There was the great sky, and the stars, and beneath he could see nothing—only darkness! But what was that in the sky, straight in front of him? A great wheel of fire, turning and turning, and flashing out blue lights!

"Come in, Curdie," said the voice again.

"I would at once, ma'am," said Curdie, "if I were sure I was standing at your door."

"Why should you doubt it, Curdie?"

"Because I see neither walls nor floor, only darkness and the great sky."

"That is all right, Curdie. Come in."

Curdie stepped forward at once. He was indeed, for the very crumb of a moment, tempted to feel before him with his foot; but he saw that would be to distrust the princess, and a greater rudeness he could not offer her. So he stepped straight in—I will not say without a little tremble at the thought of finding no floor beneath his foot. But that which had need of the floor found it, and his foot was satisfied.

No sooner was he in than he saw that the great revolving wheel in the sky was the princess's spinning wheel, near the other end of the room, turning very fast. He could see no sky or stars any more, but the wheel was flashing out blue—oh, such lovely sky-blue light!

The princess stopped, her wheel stopped, and she laughed. And her laugh was sweeter than running brook and silver bell; sweeter than joy itself, for the heart of the laugh was love.

"Come now, Curdie, to this side of my wheel, and you will find me," she said; and her laugh seemed sounding on still in the words, as if they were made of breath that had laughed.

Curdie obeyed, and passed the wheel, and there she stood to receive him—but she was not the withered creature of the night before. She looked about twenty-five years old and wonderfully fair. Her dress was pale blue and she wore a coronet of silver set with pearls and her slippers were covered with pearls that gleamed every color of the rainbow! Curdie knew, though he could not have told how, that this beautiful woman and the grand old princess of the night before were one in the same. It was some time before he could take his eyes from the marvel of her loveliness. But fearing at last that he was being rude, he turned them away; and, behold, he was in a room that was for beauty marvelous!

The room was so large that looking back, he could scarcely see the end at which he entered; but the other was only a few yards from him—and there he saw another wonder. On a huge hearth a great fire was burning, and the fire was a huge heap of roses, and yet it was fire. The smell of the roses filled the air, and the heat of the flames of them glowed upon his face. He turned an inquiring look upon the lady, and saw that she was now seated in an ancient chair, the legs of which were crusted with gems, but the upper part like a nest of daisies and moss and green grass.

"Curdie," she said in answer to his eyes, "I am going to put you to a hard test. Do you think you are prepared for it?"

"How can I tell," he returned, "seeing I do not know what it is, or what preparation it needs? Judge me yourself, ma'am."

"It needs only trust and obedience," answered the lady.

"I dare not say anything, ma'am. If you think me fit, command me."

"It will hurt you terribly, Curdie, but that will be all; no real hurt but much good will come to you from it."

Curdie made no answer.

"Go and thrust both your hands into that fire," she said quickly, almost hurriedly.

Curdie dared not stop to think. It was much too terrible to think about. He rushed to the fire, and thrust both his hands into the heap of flaming roses. And it *did* hurt! But he did not draw them back. He held the pain as if it were a thing that would kill him if he let it go—as indeed it would have done. He was in terrible fear lest it should conquer him.

But when it had risen to the pitch that he thought he *could* bear it no longer, it began to fall again, and went on growing less and less until by contrast with its former severity it had become rather pleasant. At last it ceased altogether, and Curdie thought his hands must be burned to cinders if not ashes, for he did not feel them at all. The princess told him to take them out and look at them. He did so, and found that all that was gone of them was the rough, hard skin; they were white and smooth like the princess's.

"Come to me," she said.

He obeyed and saw, to his surprise, that her face looked as if she had been weeping.

"Oh, Princess! What is the matter?" he cried. "Did I make a noise and vex you?"

"No, Curdie," she answered; "but it was very bad."

"Did you feel it too then?"

"Of course I did. But now it is over, and all is well. Would you like to know why I made you put your hands in the fire?"

Curdie looked at them again—then said:

"To take the marks of the work off them, I suppose."

"No, Curdie," answered the princess, shaking her head, for she was not

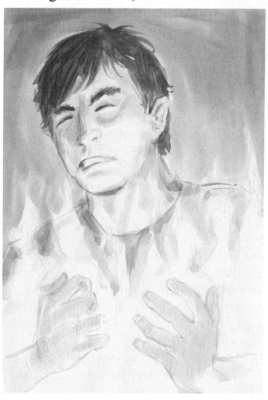

pleased with the answer. "It would be a poor way of making your hands fit for the king's court to take off them signs of service. There is a far greater difference on them than that. Do you feel none?"

"No, ma'am."

"You will, though, by and by, when the time comes. But perhaps even then you might not know what had been given you, therefore I will tell you. All men if they do not take care go down hill. In our country if they continue on their destructive course they eventually go down to the animal's country. What I mean is they grow to be like beasts."

"I am not surprised to hear it, ma'am, when I think of some of our miners."

"Ah! But you must beware, Curdie, how you say of this man or that man that he is traveling beastward. There are not nearly so many going that way as at first sight you might think. When you met your father on the hill tonight, you stood and spoke together on the same spot; and although one of you was going up and the other coming down, at a little distance no one could have told which was bound in the one direction and which in the other. Just so two people may be at the same spot in manners and behavior, and yet one may be getting better and the other worse, which is just the greatest of all differences that could possibly exist between them."

"But ma'am," said Curdie, "where is the good of knowing that there is such a difference, if you can never know where it is?"

"Now, Curdie, you must mind exactly what words I use, because although the right words cannot do exactly what I want them to do, the wrong words will certainly do what I do not want them to do. I did not say *you can never know.* When there is a necessity for your knowing, when you have to do important business with this or that man, there is always a way of knowing enough to keep you from any great blunder. And as you will have important business to do by and by, and that with people of whom you yet know nothing, it will be necessary that you should have some better means than usual of learning the nature of them.

"Listen. Since it is always what they do that makes men go down to be less than men, that is, beasts, the change always comes first in their hands—and first of all in the inside hands, to which the outside ones are but as gloves. They do not know it of course; for a beast does not know that he is a beast, and the nearer a man gets to being a beast the less he knows it. Neither can their best friends, or their worst enemies indeed, see any difference in their hands, for they see only the living gloves of them. But there are not a few who feel a vague something repulsive in the hand of a man who is growing a beast.

"Now here is what the rosefire has done for you; it has made your hands so knowing and wise, it has brought your real hands so near the outside of your flesh gloves that you will henceforth be able to know at once the hand of a man who is growing into a beast; nay, more—you will at once feel the foot of the beast he is growing, just as if there were no glove made like a man's hand between you and it.

"Only there is one beautiful and awful thing about it, that if any one gifted with this perception once uses it for his own ends, it is taken from him, and then, not knowing that it is gone, he is in a far worse condition than before, for he trusts to what he has not got."

"How dreadful!" said Curdie. "I must mind what I am about."

"Yes, indeed, Curdie."

It was a long time before the princess spoke again. But at length she turned and called to someone. "Come here, Lina," she said.

From somewhere behind Curdie, crept forward the same hideous animal which had fawned at his feet at the door, and which, without his knowing it, had followed him every step up the dove tower. She ran to the princess, and lay down at her feet, looking up at her with a most pitiful expression. She had a very short body, and very long legs made like an elephant's, so that in lying down she kneeled with both pairs. Her tail, which dragged on the floor behind her, was twice as long and quite as thick as her body. Her head was something between that of a polar bear and a snake. Her eyes were dark green, with a yellow light

in them. Her under teeth came up like a fringe of icicles, only very white, outside of her upper lip. Her throat looked as if the hair had been plucked off. It showed a skin white and smooth.

"Give Curdie a paw, Lina," said the princess.

The creature rose, and, lifting a long foreleg, held up a great doglike paw to Curdie. He took it gently. But what a shudder, as of terrible delight, ran through him, when, instead of the paw of a dog, such as it seemed to his eyes, he clasped in his great mining fist the soft, neat little hand of a child! He took it in both of his, and held it as if he could not let it go. The green eyes stared at him with their yellow light, and the mouth was turned up towards him with its constant half grin; but here was the child's hand! If he could but pull the child out of the beast! His eyes sought the princess. She was watching him with evident satisfaction.

"Ma'am, here is a child's hand!" said Curdie.

"Your gift does more for you than it promised. It is yet better to perceive a hidden good than a hidden evil."

"But," began Curdie.

"I am not going to answer any more questions this evening," interrupted the princess. "You have not half got to the bottom of the answers I have already given you."

"I will think," said Curdie. "But oh! please! one word more. May I tell my father and mother all about it?"

"Certainly—though perhaps now it may be their turn to find it a little difficult to believe that things went just as you must tell them."

"They shall see that I believe it all the same," said Curdie.

"Tell them that tomorrow morning you must set out for the court—not like a great man, but just as poor as you are. They had better not speak about it. Tell them also that it will be a long time before they hear of you again, but they must not lose heart."

"Yes, ma'am," said Curdie. "Please, am I to go now?"

"Yes," answered the princess, and held out her hand to him.

Curdie took it, trembling with joy. It was a very beautiful hand—not small, very smooth, but not very soft—and just the same to his fire-taught touch that it was to his eyes. He would have stood there all night holding it if she had not gently withdrawn it.

"I will provide you a servant," she said, "for your journey, and to wait upon you afterward."

"But where am I to go, ma'am, and what I am to do? You have given me no message to carry, neither have you said what I am wanted for. I go without a notion whether I am to walk this way or that, or what I am to do when I get I don't know where."

"Curdie!" said the princess, and there was a tone of reminder in his own name as she spoke it, "did I not tell you to tell your father and mother that you were to set out for the court? And you know that lies to the north. You must learn to use far less direction than that. You must not be like a dull servant that needs to be told again and again before he will understand. You have orders enough to start with, and you will find, as you go on, and as you need to know, what you have to do. But I warn you that perhaps it will not look the least like what you may have been fancying I should require of you. I have one idea of you and your work, and you have another. I do not blame you for that— you cannot help it yet; but you must be ready to let my idea, which sets you working, set your idea right. Be true and honest and fearless, and all shall go well with you and your work, and all with whom your work lies, and so with your parents—and me too, Curdie," she added after a little pause.

The young miner bowed his head low, patted the strange head that lay at the princess's feet, and turned away.

Curdie went home, pondering much, and told everything to his father and mother. As the old princess had said, it was now their turn to find what they heard hard to believe. If they had not been able to trust Curdie himself, they would have refused to believe more than half of what he reported.

It was not as if Curdie were leaving them to go to prison, or to make a fortune, and although they were sorry enough to lose him, they were not in the least heartbroken or even troubled at his going.

He came down in the morning dressed in his working clothes. When he had eaten his breakfast, his mother took a pouch made of goatskin, filled it with bread and cheese, and hung it over his shoulder. Then his father gave him a stick he had cut for him in the wood, and Curdie bade them good-bye rather hurriedly, for he was afraid of breaking down. As he went out he caught up his mattock and took it with him. It had on the one side a pointed curve of strong steel for loosening the earth and the ore, and on the other a steel hammer for breaking the stones and rocks. Just as he crossed the threshold the sun showed the first bright ray above the horizon.

Reading Check

1. Which of Curdie's actions show us that he is becoming a "commonplace man"?
2. What decision does Curdie make that changes his direction?
3. Who is the grand old princess, and where does Curdie find her?
4. What hard test does the princess ask Curdie to endure?
5. How does this test prepare him for his adventure at court?

Part II   The Heath

He had to go to the bottom of the hill to get into a country he could cross, for the mountains to the north were full of precipices, and it would have been losing time to go that way.

On and on he fared, and came in a few hours to a country where there were no mountains more—only hills, with great stretches of desolate heath. Here and there was a village, but that brought him little pleasure, for the people were rougher and worse mannered than those in the mountains, and as he passed through, the children came behind and mocked him.

The day went on, and the evening came, and in the middle of a great desolate heath he began to feel tired, and sat down under an ancient hawthorn. It was very old and distorted. There was not another tree for miles around. It seemed to have lived so long, and to have been so torn and tossed by the tempests on that moor, that it had at last gathered a wind of its own, which got up now and then, tumbled itself about, and lay down again.

Curdie had been so eager to get on that he had eaten nothing since his breakfast. He now opened the pouch his mother had given him, and began to eat his supper. The sun was setting.

Now Curdie did not know that this was a part of the country very hard to get through. Nobody lived there, though many had tried to build in it. Some died very soon. Some rushed out of it. Those who stayed longest went raving mad, and died a terrible death. Such as walked straight on, and did not spend a night there, got through well and were nothing the worse. But those who slept even a single night in it were sure to meet something they could never forget, and

which often left a mark everybody could read. The old hawthorn might have been enough for a warning—it looked so like a human being dried up and distorted with age and suffering, with cares instead of loves, and things instead of thoughts. Both it and the heath around it, which stretched on all sides as far as he could see, were so withered that it was impossible to say whether they were alive or not.

While Curdie ate there came a change. Clouds had gathered over his head, and seemed drifting about in every direction, as if not shepherded by the slow, unwilling wind, but hunted in all directions by wolfish claws across the plains of the sky. The sun was going down in a storm of lurid crimson, and out of the west came a wind that felt red and hot the one moment, and cold and pale the other.

As he gazed at the sun, Curdie saw something strange appear against it, moving about like a fly over its burning face. This looked as if it were coming out of the sun's furnace heart, and was

a living creature of some kind surely; but its shape was very uncertain, because the dazzle of the light all around melted the outlines. It was growing larger; it must be approaching! It grew so rapidly that by the time the sun was half down its head reached the top of the arch, and presently nothing but its legs were to be seen, crossing and recrossing the face of the vanishing disc.

When the sun was down he could see nothing of it more, but in a moment he heard its feet galloping over the dry crackling heather, and seeming to come straight for him. He stood up, lifted his pickaxe, and threw the hammer end over his shoulder. He was going to have a fight for his life! And now it appeared again, vague, yet very awful, in the dim twilight the sun had left behind. But just before it reached him, down from its four legs it dropped flat on the ground, and came crawling towards him, wagging a huge tail as it came.

It was Lina. All at once Curdie recognized her—the frightful creature he had seen at the princess's. He dropped his pickaxe, and held out his hand. She crept nearer and nearer, and laid her chin in his palm, and he patted her ugly head. Then she crept away behind the tree, and lay down, panting hard. Curdie did not much like the idea of her being behind him. Horrible as she was to look at, she seemed to his mind more horrible when he was not looking at her. But he remembered the child's hand, and never thought of driving her away. Now and then he gave a glance behind him, and there she lay flat, with her eyes closed and her terrible teeth gleaming between her two huge forepaws.

After his supper and his long day's journey it was no wonder Curdie should now be sleepy. Since the sun set the air had been warm and pleasant. He lay down under the tree, closed his eyes, and thought to sleep. He found himself mistaken, however. But although he could not sleep, he was yet aware of resting delightfully.

Presently he heard a sweet sound of singing somewhere, such as he had never heard before—a singing as of curious birds far off, which drew nearer and nearer. At length he heard their wings, and, opening his eyes, saw a number of very large birds, as it seemed, alighting around him, still singing. It was strange to hear song from the throats of such big birds.

And still singing, with large and round but not less birdlike voices, they began to weave and dance about him, moving their wings in time with their legs. But the dance seemed somehow to be troubled and broken, and to return upon itself in an eddy, in place of sweeping smoothly on. And he soon learned, in the low short growls behind

him, the cause of the imperfection. They wanted to dance all round the tree, but Lina would not permit them to come on her side.

Now Curdie liked the birds, and did not altogether *like* Lina. But neither, nor both together, made a reason for driving away the princess's creature. Doubtless she had been the goblins' creature, but the last time he saw her was in the dove tower and at the old princess's feet. So he left her to do as she would, and the dance of the birds continued only a semicircle, troubled at the edges, and returning upon itself.

But their song and their motions, nevertheless, and the waving of their wings, began at length to make him very sleepy. All the time he had kept doubting whether they could really be birds, and the sleepier he got, the more he imagined them something else, but he suspected no harm.

Suddenly, just as he was sinking beneath the waves of slumber, he awoke in fierce pain. The birds were upon

him—all over him—and had begun to tear him with beaks and claws. He had but time, however, to feel that he could not move under their weight, when they set up a hideous screaming, and scattered like a cloud. Lina was among them, snapping and striking with her paws, while her tail knocked them over and over. But they flew up, gathered, and descended on her in a swarm, perching upon every part of her body, so that he could only see a huge misshapen mass, which seemed to go rolling away into the darkness. He got up and tried to follow, but could see nothing, and after wandering about hither and thither for some time, he found himself again beside the hawthorn.

He feared greatly that the birds had been too much for Lina, and had torn her to pieces. In a little while, however, she came limping back, and lay down in her old place. Curdie also lay down, but, from the pain of his wounds, there was no sleep for him. When the light came he found his clothes a good deal torn and his skin as well, but gladly wondered why the wicked birds had not at once attacked his eyes. Then he turned looking for Lina. She rose and crept to him. But she was in a far worse plight than he—plucked and gashed and torn with the beaks and claws of birds, especially about the bare part of her neck, so that she was pitiful to see. And the worse wounds she could not reach to lick.

"Poor Lina!" said Curdie, "you got all those helping me." She wagged her tail, and made it clear she understood him. Then it flashed upon Curdie's mind that perhaps this was the companion the

princess had promised him. For the princess did so many things differently from what anybody looked for! Lina was no beauty certainly, but already, the first night, she had saved his life.

The Baker and the Barber

Curdie and Lina now passed through a lovely country of hill and dale and rushing stream, and came, at last, to a broad, beautiful river. There was a great rock in the river and on the top of this rock was the city of Gwyntystorm where the king had his court. Surrounding the city were lofty walls, towers, and battlements and above the city could be seen the palace, built like a strong castle. But it had been long neglected.

Curdie crossed the river, and he and Lina began to ascend the long winding road that led to the city. They met a good many idlers along the way, and there was an unfriendliness in their looks which Curdie did not like. At length they reached the principal gate of the city. As they entered this gate, a baker, whose shop was just inside the gate, came out and ran to the shop of his friend, the barber, on the opposite side of the way. But as he ran he stumbled and fell heavily. Curdie hastened to help him up, and found he had bruised his forehead badly. The baker swore grievously at the stone for tripping him up, declaring it was the third time he had fallen over it within the last month; and saying what was the king about that he allowed such a stone to stick up forever on the main street of his royal residence of Gwyntystorm! What was a king for if he would not take care of his people's heads! And he stroked his forehead tenderly.

"Was it your head or your feet that ought to bear the blame for your fall?" asked Curdie.

"Why, you booby of a miner! My feet, of course," answered the baker.

"Nay, then," said Curdie, "the king can't be to blame."

"Oh, I see!" said the baker. "You're laying a trap for me. Of course, if you come to that, it was my head that ought to have looked after my feet. But it is the king's part to look after us all, and have his streets smooth."

"Well, I don't see," said Curdie, "why the king should take care of the baker, when the baker's head won't take care of the baker's feet."

"Who are you to make game of the king's baker?" cried the man in a rage.

But, instead of answering, Curdie went up to the bump on the street, and turning the hammer end of his mattock, struck it such a blow that it flew wide in pieces. Blow after blow he struck until he had leveled it with the street.

Out flew the barber upon him in a rage.

"What do you break my window for, you rascal?"

"I am very sorry," said Curdie. "It must have been a bit of stone that flew from my mattock. I couldn't help it, you know."

"Couldn't help it! A fine story! What do you go breaking the rock for—the very rock upon which the city stands?"

"Look at your friend's forehead," said Curdie. "See what a lump he has got on it with falling over the same stone."

"What's that to my window?" cried the barber. "His forehead can mend itself; my poor window can't."

"But he's the king's baker," said Curdie, more and more surprised at the man's anger.

"What's that to me? This is a free city. Every man here takes care of himself, and the king takes care of us all. I'll have the price of my window out of you!"

Something caught Curdie's eye. He stooped, picked up a piece of the stone he had just broken, and put it in his pocket.

"I suppose you are going to break another of my windows with that stone!" said the barber.

"Oh, no," said Curdie. "I didn't mean to break your window in the first place, and I certainly won't break another."

"Give me that stone," said the barber.

Curdie gave it him, and the barber threw it over the city wall.

"I thought you wanted the stone," said Curdie, as he picked up another rock to put in his pocket.

"No, you fool!" answered the barber. "What should I want with a stone?"

The barber took Curdie by the collar.

"Come now! You pay me for that window."

"How much?" asked Curdie.

The barber said, "A crown." But the baker, annoyed at the heartlessness of the barber, in thinking more of his broken window than the bump on his friend's head, interfered.

"No, no," he said to Curdie. "Don't you pay any such sum. A little pane like that cost only a quarter."

"Well, to be certain," said Curdie, "I'll give a half." For he doubted the baker as well as the barber. "Perhaps one day, if he finds he has asked too much, he will bring me the difference."

"Ha! ha!" laughed the barber. "A fool and his money are soon parted."

As he took the coin from Curdie's hand, Curdie felt that the barber's hand was not like a hand at all but rather like the cold smooth leathery palm of a monkey.

The Dogs of Gwyntystorm

Curdie and Lina continued on their way, and the steep street led them straight up to a large market place with butchers' shops. There were many dogs about the shops and the moment these beasts caught sight of Lina, they came rushing down upon her. When Curdie saw the dogs coming he heaved up his mattock over his shoulder, and was ready. Seeing him thus prepared to defend his follower, a great ugly bulldog flew at him. With the first blow Curdie struck him through the brain and the brute fell dead at his feet. But he could not at once recover his weapon, and a huge mastiff [an ancient breed of dog], seeing him thus hampered, flew at him next.

Now Lina, who had shown herself so brave upon the road thither, had grown shy upon entering the city, and kept always at Curdie's heel. But it was her turn now. The moment she saw her master in danger she seemed to go mad with rage. As the mastiff jumped at Curdie's throat, Lina flew at him, seized him with her tremendous jaws, gave one roaring grind, and he lay beside the bulldog with his neck broken. They were the best dogs in the market, after the judgment of the butchers of Gwyntystorm. Down came their masters, knives in hand.

Curdie drew himself up fearlessly, and awaited their coming, while at his heel Lina sat, her green eyes flashing as yellow gold.

The butchers, not liking the look of either of them, drew back and began to remonstrate in the manner of outraged men.

"Stranger," said the first, "that bulldog belongs to me."

"Take him, then," said Curdie, indignant.

"You've killed him!"

"Yes—else he would have killed me."

"That's no business of mine."

"No?"

"No."

"That makes it the more mine, then."

"This sort of thing won't do, you know," said the other butcher.

"That's true," said Curdie.

"That's my mastiff," said the other butcher.

"And as he ought to be," said Curdie.

"Your brute should be burned alive for it."

"Not yet," answered Curdie. "We have done no wrong. We were walking quietly up your street when your dogs flew at us. If you don't teach your dogs how to treat strangers, you must take the consequences."

"They treat them quite properly," said the butcher. "What right has any one to bring an abomination like that into our city? The horror is enough to make an idiot of every child in the place."

"We are both subjects of the king, and my poor animal can't help her looks. How would you like to be served like that because you were ugly? She's not a bit fonder of her looks than you are— only what can she do to change them?"

"I'll do to change them," said the fellow.

Thereupon the butchers brandished their long knives and advanced, keeping their eyes upon Lina.

"Don't be afraid, Lina," cried Curdie. "I'll kill one—you kill the other."

Lina gave a howl that might have terrified an army, and crouched ready to spring. The butchers turned and ran.

So Curdie and Lina were left standing in the market place. But the terror of them spread throughout the city, and everybody began to shut and lock his door so that by the time the setting sun shone down the street, there was not a shop left open.

"Lina," said Curdie, "the people of this city keep the gates open, but shut up tightly their houses and their hearts."

There was, however, one little thatched house in which lived a poor old woman with her grandchild. And because she never gossiped or quarreled the people called her a witch, and would have done her many an ill if they had not been afraid of her.

Now while Curdie was looking in another direction, the door of this house opened, and out came a little child. She toddled across the market place toward the outcasts. The moment they saw her coming, Lina lay down flat on the road, and with her two huge forepaws, covered her face. Curdie went to meet the child. She took him by the hand, and drew him toward the house.

Lina rose to follow, and when she did the child shrank back frightened. Curdie took the little girl up, then turned to pat Lina. Once safe in Curdie's arms the child wanted to pat Lina too. She did so, and once having patted her decided she would like to ride upon her back. So Curdie set her on Lina's back and she rode home in merry triumph.

At the door the grandmother stood ready to receive them. She warmly welcomed Curdie and showed no dread of Lina. But the moment this door was shut the other doors began to open, and soon there appeared little groups of people here and there.

The baker and the barber joined these groups and quickly began to wag their tongues against Curdie and his horrible beast, and it was not long before the inhabitants of the city were planning evil schemes against the strangers.

The Attack

The wanderers were hospitably entertained by the old woman and her grandchild. Curdie told them stories of the mines and his adventures in them and at length they were all quite tired and went off to bed comfortable and happy.

But Curdie was soon awakened by Lina pulling at him. As soon as he spoke to her she ceased. Curdie listened, and thought he heard someone trying to get in. He rose, and took his mattock, and went about the house, listening and watching. He heard noises, one place then another. The tumult increased every moment until he eventually heard the city marshal shouting outside. Then the people began to shout and rush at the door to cut its fastening.

The moment it was opened, out leaped Lina, with a roar so unnaturally horrible that the people stood paralyzed with terror. They fled in every direction, shrieking and yelling with mortal dismay. Lina vanished—no one knew where, for not one of the crowd had had courage to look upon her.

The moment she was gone, Curdie advanced and gave himself up. The people, so filled with fear and shame were ready to kill him on the spot. But he stood quietly facing them, with his mattock on his shoulder.

They laid his mattock against his back, and tied his arms to it. They then led him up the street to a great dull, heavy-looking building and there imprisoned him.

Once alone, Curdie discovered, to his great relief, that the ropes tied round his mattock had loosened. He got one hand free, and then the other. He then sat down to decide what he must do, but it was not long before he heard the noise of voices outside his cell.

He then heard the sound of the great rusty key in the lock. The door was thrown back, the light rushed in, and with it came the voice of the city marshal, calling upon Curdie to come forth and be tried for his life. The marshal proceeded to read a long list of charges and he was still reading when a scream of agonized terror arose from the farthest skirt of the crowd. In a moment the air was filled with hideous howling. The next moment, in at the door bounded Lina, her two green eyes flaming yellow as sunflowers. With one spring she threw herself at Curdie's feet. Two or three soldiers rushed to the door and pulled it closed. Curdie heard it lock once more, and he and Lina were prisoners together.

Once they were alone, Lina got up, made her way to the back wall and began scratching furiously with all the eighteen great strong claws of her feet. Curdie

rose and went to assist her with his mattock. Once they had broken through the floor, Curdie realized that they were over what seemed a natural cave. But where did the cave lead? In a short time he and Lina had made their way down through the hole and into the darkened passage to explore.

Reading Check

1. Who is the servant the princess sends to aid Curdie?
2. How does Lina's outward appearance differ from her inner nature?
3. List several hazards Curdie faces at the outset of his adventure.
4. How does he escape from these dangers?
5. What does Curdie mean when he says, "The people of this city keep the gates open but shut up tightly their houses and their hearts"?

Part III   The Wine Cellar

They soon came to an old rusted door, and though the door was locked, Curdie found that the lock easily gave way to the prying of his pocket-knife.

When they entered, they could see nothing, but the echo alerted Curdie to the fact that they were in a very large space. He felt about the walls until his hands fell upon a wine cask, and he was about to explore the place thoroughly, when he heard steps coming toward the door. Curdie shrank back just as a man entered carrying a candle and a silver cup.

The man's light revealed row upon row of wine casks stretching away into the darkness of the other end of a long vault. He stopped at the third cask and poured into this cask something from the silver cup. He then turned to the next cask, drew some wine, and rinsed the cup. Throwing this wine onto the floor, he repeated the procedure again. At last, satisfied that the cup was clean he drew some wine and drank it. When he finished, he returned to the third cask, filled the cup, and turned to leave, carefully bearing the full cup of wine.

"There is something wrong here," thought Curdie. "Why would he not drink from the third cask, and to whom is he taking that cup of wine?"

As soon as the man had disappeared, Curdie sat down to think. He must investigate, but it was not yet safe. He and Lina would have to wait until the house was quiet. Then he could move about more freely. For he was certain there was something to do, and if it did not come to him in this cellar, he must go to meet it in other places.

At length he thought it safe to venture out. He made his way to a servant's hall. Lina moved with him. When they reached the hall, they found it quiet. Thus, they left the hall and entered a short passage, which led them to a huge kitchen, vaulted and black with smoke. The fire was still burning so that he was able to see a little of the state of things. The place was dirty and disorderly. Nonetheless, Curdie had, by this time, realized that he was in the palace, and his heart ached to think of the lovely princess Irene and the king living over such a sty.

Leaving the kitchen, he got into the region of sculleries [room for kitchen chores], where he found the horrible smells wandering about like evil spirits. Turning from it in miserable disgust, he re-entered the hall, and crossed to another door. This door opened to a wider passage at the end of which was a large beautiful hall. At one side of the hall was a grand staircase.

At the top of the stairs they entered a large room, dimly lighted by a silver lamp that hung from the ceiling. The splendor of the room told Curdie that he was in the king's chamber. At the far end was a great bed, surrounded with dark heavy curtains. He went softly toward it, his heart beating fast. It was a dreadful thing to be alone in the king's chamber in the dead of night. To gain courage he had to remind himself of the beautiful princess who had sent him.

When he was about halfway to the bed, a figure appeared from the farther side of it, and came towards him with a hand raised warningly. He stood still. The light was dim and he could distinguish little more than the outline of a young girl. But though the form he saw was much taller than the little Princess Irene he remembered, he never doubted it was she.

"You are Curdie," she said.

"And you are the Princess Irene," he returned.

"Then we know each other still. You will help me?"

"That I will," answered Curdie.

From the bed a thin, feeble, hollow voice arose. "I will not, I will not. I am king, and I will be king!" The voice was not at all like the king's voice that Curdie remembered.

The princess rushed to his side. "Never mind them, Father. I am here, and they shan't touch you. They dare not, you know, so long as you defy them."

Curdie drew near the bed on the other side. There lay the grand old

king—he looked grand still, but twenty years older. By degrees his voice sank away and the murmuring ceased.

The princess gave a sigh of relief, and came round to Curdie.

"We can talk a little now," she said, leading him toward the middle of the room. "My father will sleep till the doctor wakes him to give him his medicine. It is not really medicine, though, but wine. Nothing but that, the doctor says, could have kept him alive so long."

"What sort of man is your doctor?" asked Curdie.

"Oh, such a dear, good, kind gentleman!" replied the princess.

"Has your father been long ill?"

"A whole year now," she replied. "Did you not know? The lord chancellor told me that not only Gwyntystorm but the whole land was mourning over the illness of my father."

Now Curdie had not heard a word of his majesty's illness, and had no ground for believing that a single soul in any place he had visited on his journey had heard of it. But just for the time he thought it better not to say anything.

"Does the king cry out like this every night?" he asked.

"Every night," answered Irene. "That is why I never go to bed at night. He is better during the day—a little, and then I sleep."

"I wish he would like me," said Curdie "for then I might watch by him at night, and let you go to bed, Princess."

"Don't you know then?" returned Irene in wonder. "How was it you came? I thought you knew he wanted you."

"Not I," said Curdie, also bewildered, but very glad.

"He used to be constantly saying—he was not so ill then as he is now—that he wished he had you about him."

"The master of the house told papa's own secretary that he had written to the miner-general to find you and send you up. But the miner-general wrote back that they had searched every mine in the kingdom and could hear nothing of you. My father gave a great sigh, and said he feared the goblins had got you, after all, and your father and mother were dead of grief. I cried very much. But one of my grandmother's pigeons with its white wing flashed a message to me through the window one day, and then I knew that my Curdie wasn't eaten by the goblins, for my grandmother wouldn't have taken care of him one time to let him be eaten the next. Where were you, Curdie, that they couldn't find you?"

"We will talk about that another time, when we are not expecting the doctor," said Curdie. "When will he be here?"

The question was answered—not by the princess, but by something which that instant tumbled heavily into the room. On the floor lay a little round man, puffing and blowing and uttering incoherent language. Curdie turned to look for Lina, but she had wisely hidden herself. He then quickly laid his mattock aside lest it should also betray him as the miner prisoner.

"Oh, dear Dr. Kelman!" cried the princess, running up and taking hold of his arm. "I am so sorry. I hope you have not hurt yourself."

"Not at all, not at all," said the doctor, trying to smile and to rise both at once. "Your royal highness has a rather thick mat at the door," said the doctor patting his palms together. "I hope my awkwardness may not have startled His Majesty."

While he talked Curdie went to the door. Lina was no where to be seen.

The doctor approached the bed.

"And how has my beloved king slept tonight?" he asked.

"No better," answered Irene.

"Ah, that is very well!" returned the doctor; his fall seemed to have muddled either his words or their meaning. "When we give him his wine, he will be better still."

Curdie darted at the silver cup which the doctor had dropped in his fall. "I will get more wine," he said and rushed toward the door.

"Come here with that cup, you page!" cried the doctor.

Curdie came a few steps toward him.

"Are you aware, young man," said the doctor, "that it is not just any wine that will do his majesty benefit?"

"Quite, sir," answered Curdie. "The wine for His Majesty's use is in the third cask from the door."

"Fly then," said the doctor looking satisfied.

Curdie stepped outside the room and blew an audible breath. At that moment, up came Lina noiseless as a shadow. He showed her the cup...

"The cellar, Lina. Go," he said, for he knew she would remember the way better than he.

She galloped away on her soft feet, and Curdie had indeed to fly to keep up with her. Not once did she make a dubious turn. When they reached the cellar, Curdie rinsed the cup as he had seen the butler do, then filled it from a good cask and returned to the king's chamber.

Counterplotting

Curdie was already sufficiently enlightened as to how things were going. It was clear that among those about the king there was a plot against him. It was plain also that the doctor was working out a design against the health and reason of His majesty.

The people outside the palace were ignorant of the king's condition. Doubtless this was because His Majesty's councillors desired to alienate the hearts of the king's subjects from their sovereign. Curdie's idea was that they intended to kill the king, marry the princess to one of themselves, and found a new dynasty. But whatever their purpose, he could not doubt that the old princess had sent him expressly to frustrate their plans.

While he stood thinking thus with himself, the young princess was earnestly watching the king, with looks of childish love and womanly tenderness that went to Curdie's heart. He came near and softly called to her.

She came to where he stood under the lamp. "Well, Curdie, what is it?"

"Princess," he replied, "I want to tell you that I have found why your grandmother sent me." He sat down beside her and told her all the story—how her grandmother had sent her good pigeon for him, and how she had instructed him, and sent him there without telling him what he had to do. Then he told her what he had discovered of the state of things generally in Gwyntystorm, and especially what he had heard and seen in the palace that night.

"Things are in a bad state enough," he said in conclusion—"lying, and selfishness and inhospitality and dishonesty everywhere; and to crown all, they speak with disrespect of the good king, and not a man knows he's ill."

"You frighten me dreadfully," said Irene.

"You must be brave for the king's sake," said Curdie.

"Indeed I will," she replied. "But what is to be done? And how *am* I to believe such horrible things about Dr. Kelman?"

"My dear princess," replied Curdie, "you know nothing of him but his face and his tongue, and they are both false. Either you must beware of him, or you must doubt your grandmother and me. For I tell you, by the gift she gave me of testing hands, that this man is a snake. The round body he shows is but the case of a serpent. Perhaps the creature lies there, as in its nest, coiled round and round inside."

"Horrible!" said Irene.

"Horrible indeed; but we must not try to get rid of horrible things by refusing to look at them, and saying they are not there. Is not your father sleeping better since he had the wine I drew for him?"

"Yes."

"Does he sleep better after having the wine the doctor gives him from the butler?"

"No; always worse." she answered.

"Remember that then. Now nothing that passes through any hand in the house except yours or mine must henceforth, till he is well, reach His Majesty's lips."

"But how are we to manage that?"

"That we must contrive," answered Curdie. "I know already how to take care of the wine; but for his food—"

"Alas!" the princess interrupted. "He scarcely ever takes more than a mouthful. I can't think how he lives! And the very thing he would like, and often asks for—a bit of bread—I can hardly ever get for him. Dr. Kelman has forbidden it."

"Bread at least he *shall* have," said Curdie. He promised that as soon as it was light, he would go into the city for some. He asked for her handkerchief to tie it in and said that if he could not bring the bread to her himself, he would send it by Lina, who could keep out of sight better than he.

His hope lay in the fact that bakers everywhere went to work early. But it was yet much too early. So he persuaded the princess to lie down, promising to call her if the king should stir.

His majesty slept very quietly. The dawn had grown almost day, and still Curdie lingered, unwilling to disturb the princess. At last, however, he called her, and she was in the room in a moment.

Curdie got his mattock from where he had hidden it behind a great mirror, and went to find some bread. They took some breakfast with them as they passed through the hall, and as soon as they had eaten it Curdie went out the back door, telling Lina to wait till he came back.

Down the town he went, walking in the middle of the street, that, if any one saw him, he might see he was not afraid, and hesitate to rouse an attack on him. As to the dogs, ever since the death of their two companions, a shadow that looked like a mattock was enough to make them scamper. As soon as he reached the archway of the city gate he turned to the baker's shop, and perceiving no sign of movement, waited there watching for the first.

After about an hour, the door opened, and the baker's man appeared with a pail in his hand. He went to the pump that stood in the street, and filling his pail returned with it into the shop. Curdie stole after him, found the door ajar, opened it very gently and peeped in. Seeing nobody, he entered. He seized a loaf of bread and, after laying the price of it on the counter, sped softly out and up the street.

Now he had to convey the loaf to the princess. Perceiving that there would be a risk in attempting to pass through the palace, and reflecting that the porters in the great hall would probably be awake also, Curdie went to the wine cellar. He took Irene's handkerchief, put the loaf in it, and tied it round Lina's neck telling her to take it to the princess. Using every shadow and every shelter, Lina slid through the servants like a shapeless terror through a guilty mind, and eventually reached the staircase leading to the king's quarters.

Irene trembled a little when she saw Lina glide into the chamber, but she recovered herself at once when she saw the bundle about her neck, for it both assured her of Curdie's safety, and gave her hope of her father's. She untied it with joy, and Lina stole away, silent as she had come.

In the meantime, down below in the cellar, Curdie was lying in the hollow between the upper sides of two great casks, the warmest place he could find. Lina returned and lay at his feet, across the two casks, and did her best to arrange her huge tail that it should be a warm coverlid for her master.

By and by Dr. Kelman called to see his patient; and now that Irene's eyes were opened, she saw clearly enough that he was both annoyed and puzzled at finding His Majesty rather better. He pretended however to congratulate him, saying he believed he was quite fit to see the lord chamberlain. He wanted his signature on something important; only the king must not strain his mind to understand it, whatever it might be. If His Majesty did, he would not be answerable for the consequences. The king said he would see the lord chamberlain, and the doctor went out.

Then Irene gave him more bread and wine, and the king ate and drank, and smiled a feeble smile, the first real one she had seen for many a day. He said he felt much better, and would soon be able to take matters into his own hands again. He had a strange miserable feeling, he said, that things were going terribly wrong, although he could not tell how. Then the princess told him that Curdie had come, and that at night, when all was quiet for nobody in the palace must know, he would pay His Majesty a visit. Her great-great-grandmother had sent him, she said. The king looked strangely upon her, but the strange look passed into a smile clearer than the first, and Irene's heart throbbed with delight.

The Lord Chamberlain

At noon the lord chamberlain appeared. With a long low bow, and paper in hand, he stepped softly into the room. Greeting His Majesty with every appearance of profoundest respect, and congratulating him on the evident progress, he declared himself sorry to trouble him, but there were certain papers, he said, which required his signature. He was a lean, long, yellow man, with a small head, bald over the top, and tufted at the back and about the ears. He had a very thin, prominent, hooked nose, and a quantity of loose skin under his chin and about the throat, which came craning up out of his neckcloth. His eyes were very small, sharp, glittering, and looked black as jet. He had hardly enough of a mouth to make a smile with. His left hand held the paper, and the long, skinny fingers of his right a pen just dipped in ink.

But the king, the moment he saw the paper, resolved that he would not sign without understanding and approv-

ing of it. He requested the lord chamberlain therefore to read it.

His lordship commenced at once but the difficulties he seemed to encounter, and the fits of stammering that seized him, roused the king's suspicion tenfold. He called the princess.

"I trouble His Lordship too much," he said to her. "Take that paper from His Lordship's hand, and read it to me from beginning to end."

"Consider, Your Majesty. The thing would be altogether without precedent. It would be to make sport of statecraft," said the lord chamberlain.

"Perhaps you are right, my lord," answered the king, with more meaning than he intended to manifest. "So this morning we shall read no further. I am indeed ill able for business of such weight."

The lord chamberlain was compelled to retire without having gained his object. And well might his annoyance be keen! For that paper was the king's will, drawn up by the attorney-general. Until they had the king's signature to it there was no venturing further in their schemes. The lord chamberlain began to doubt the doctor's fidelity to the conspiracy, and as soon as he left the chamber he sent in a rage for Dr. Kelman. He came and while professing himself unable to understand the symptoms described by the chamberlain, yet pledged himself again that on the morrow the king should do whatever was required of him.

Meantime, Curdie and Lina had plenty of sleep in the cellar. In the afternoon, having slept all they could, Curdie took his mattock and began to examine the rock walls. This was not merely to pass time; he had reason for it. When he broke the stone in the street, over which the baker fell, its appearance led him to pocket a fragment for further examination. Since then he had satisfied himself that the yellow particles in it were gold. If such stone existed here in plenty, he could soon make the king rich and independent of his ill-conditioned subjects. It was not long before he was persuaded that there were large quantities of gold in the cellar as well.

It was a great delight to him to use his mattock once more. The time went quickly, and when he left the passage to go to the king's chamber, he had already a good heap of fragments behind the broken door.

Dr. Kelman

As soon as he had reason to hope the way was clear, Curdie ventured softly into the hall, with Lina behind him.

When he reached the royal chamber, he found His Majesty awake, and very anxiously expecting him. Curdie informed him that he had already discovered certain of His Majesty's enemies, and one of the worst of them was the doctor.

"Is it possible Kelman can be such a wretch?" he said. "Who then am I to trust?"

"Not one in the house, except the princess and myself," said Curdie.

"I will not go to sleep," said the king.

"That would be as bad as taking the poison," said Curdie. "No, no, sire; you must show your confidence by leaving all the watching to me, and doing all the sleeping you can."

The king smiled a contented smile, turned on his side, and was presently fast asleep. Curdie seated himself behind a curtain at the head of the bed, on the side farthest from the king. He told Lina to get under the bed, and make no noise.

About one o'clock the doctor came stealing in. He looked round for the princess, and seeing no one, smiled with satisfaction as he approached the wine where it stood under the lamp. Having partly filled a glass, he took from his pocket a small phial, and filled up the glass from it. The light fell upon his face from above, and Curdie saw the snake in it plainly visible. He had never beheld such an evil countenance. The man hated the king, and delighted in doing him wrong.

With the glass in his hand, he drew near the bed. Curdie stooped and whispered to Lina. "Take him by the leg, Lina." She darted noiselessly upon him. With a face of horrible consternation, he gave his leg one tug to free it; the next instant Curdie heard a scrunch.

Lina had crushed the bone like a stick of celery. He tumbled on the floor with a yell.

"Drag him out, Lina," said Curdie.

Lina took him by the collar, and dragged him out.

Curdie sat and watched every motion of the sleeping king. All that night the palace lay as quiet as a nursery of healthful children. At sunrise he called the princess.

"How has His Majesty slept?" were her first words as she entered the room.

"Quite quietly," answered Curdie; "that is, since we got rid of the doctor."

"How did you manage that?" inquired Irene; and Curdie had to tell all about it.

"How terrible!" she said.

"Now, Princess," said Curdie, "I must leave you for a few minutes. You must bolt the door, please, and not open it to any one."

Away to the cellar he went with Lina, taking care, as they passed through the servants' hall, to get her a good breakfast. In about one minute she had eaten what he gave her, and looked up in his face. It was not more food she wanted, but work. So out of the cellar they went through the passage. Opening the back door, Curdie let her out. By the time he had returned to the king's chamber, Lina was flying out the gate of Gwyntystorm toward the wood as fast as her mighty legs could carry her.

The Uglies

There was nothing now to be dreaded from Dr. Kelman, but it made Curdie anxious, as the evening drew near, to think that not a soul belonging

to the court had been to visit the king, or ask how he did, that day. He feared, in some shape or other, a more determined assault. He had provided himself a place in the room, to which he might retreat upon approach, and whence he could watch; but not once had he had to take himself to it.

Towards night the king fell asleep. Curdie thought more and more uneasily of the moment when he must again leave them for a little while. Deeper and deeper fell the shadows. No one came to light the lamp. The princess drew her chair close to Curdie. She would rather it were not so dark, she said. She was afraid of something—she could not tell what; nor could she give any reason for her fear but that all was so dreadfully still.

When it had been dark about an hour, Curdie thought Lina might have returned; and reflected that the sooner he went the less danger was there of any assault while he was away. There was more risk of his own presence being discovered, no doubt, but things were

now drawing to a crisis, and it must be run. So, telling the princess to lock all the doors of the bedchamber, and let no one in, he took his mattock, and with here a run there a halt under cover, made his way to the cellar.

He swiftly entered. Lina had done her part. The place was swarming with ugly creatures from the wood—animal forms wilder and more grotesque than ever romped in nightmare dream. Now they all came crowding about Curdie. He counted them. There were forty-nine including Lina.

Reading Check

1. What does Curdie discover in the wine cellar?
2. What is the purpose of Curdie's adventure?
3. How does Curdie discern Dr. Kelman's wickedness?
4. Describe the lord chamberlain.
5. Who are the uglies?

Part IV The Vengeance

It was now close upon suppertime, when Curdie stopped at the door of the king's chamber. The king was still asleep. Curdie talked to the princess for a few minutes, told her not to be frightened whatever noises she heard, only to keep her door locked till he came again. It was time to make himself known.

Curdie now entered the hall and stood before the servants. "I proclaim you all to be villains and traitors to the king."

For a moment all stood astonished into silence by this bold stranger. Then they saw by his mattock over his shoulder that he was nothing but a miner boy. A great roaring laugh burst from the biggest of the footmen as he came shouldering his way through the crowd toward Curdie.

"This is nothing but a gallows bird," he cried, "a fellow the city marshal was going to hang, but unfortunately put it off. He broke prison, and here he is!"

As he spoke, he stretched out his great hand to lay hold of him. Curdie caught it in his left hand, and heaved his mattock with the other. Finding, however, nothing worse than an ox hoof, he restrained himself, stepped back a pace or two, shifted his mattock to this left hand, and struck him a little smart blow on the shoulder. His arm dropped by his side, he gave a roar, and drew back.

"Whoever confesses to having done anything wrong in this house, however small, however great, and means to do better, let him come to this corner of the room, and he shall be pardoned," cried Curdie.

None moved but a page, who went toward him skirting the wall. When they caught sight of him, the crowd broke into a hiss of derision.

Curdie had just put the page between himself and the wall, when in rushed the butler with the huge kitchen poker, the point of which he had blown red-hot in the fire, followed by the cook with the longest spit. Through the crowd, which scattered right and left before them, they came down upon Curdie. Uttering a shrill whistle, he caught the poker a blow with his mattock, knocking the point to the ground, while the page behind him started forward, and seizing the point of the spit, held on to it with both hands, the cook kicking him furiously.

Ere the butler could raise the poker again, or the cook recover the spit, with a roar to terrify the dead, Lina dashed into the room, her eyes flaming like candles. She went straight at the butler. He was down in a moment, and she on the top of him, wagging her tail over him like a lioness.

"Don't kill him, Lina," said Curdie.

"Oh, Mr. Miner!" cried the butler.

"Put your foot on his mouth, Lina," said Curdie. "The truth Fear tells is not much better than her lies."

The rest of the creatures now came stalking, rolling, leaping, gliding, hobbling into the room, and each as he came took the next place along the wall, until, solemn and grotesque, all stood ranged, awaiting orders. He turned to the uglies.

"Go at them," he said.

The whole forty-nine obeyed at once, each for himself, and after his own fashion. A scene of confusion and terror followed. The crowd scattered like a dance of flies. The creatures had been instructed not to hurt much, but to hunt incessantly, until everyone had rushed from the house. The women shrieked, and ran hither and thither through the hall, pursued each by her own horror, and snapped at by every other in passing.

Though they were quite as frightened at first, the men did not run so fast; and by and by some of them finding they were only glared at, and followed, and pushed, began to summon up courage once more, and with courage came impudence. The uglies grew more severe, and the terrors of the imagination were fast yielding to those of experience.

They were flung about in all directions. Their clothes were torn from them. They were pinched and scratched any—and every—where. Ballbody kept rolling up them and over them, confining his attentions to no one in particular. The scorpion kept grabbing at their legs with his huge pincers. A three-foot centipede kept crawling up their bodies, nipping as he went; varied and numerous were their woes.

They were spattered with the dirt of their own neglect; they were soused in the stinking water that had boiled greens; they were smeared with rancid dripping; their faces were rubbed in maggots. I dare not tell all that was done to them. At last they got the door into a back yard open, and rushed out. The door was flung to behind them, and they heard it locked and bolted and barred against them.

More Vengeance

As soon as they were gone, Curdie brought the creatures back to the servants' hall, and told them to eat up everything on the table. It was a sight to see them all standing round it—except such as had to get upon it—eating and drinking, each after its fashion, without a smile, or a word, or a glance of fellowship in the act. A very few moments served to make everything eatable vanish, and then Curdie requested them to clean house, and the page who stood by to assist them.

Curdie meantime was with the king, telling him all they had done. They had heard a little noise, but not much, for he had told the uglies to repress outcry as much as possible; and they had seen to it that the more anyone cried out the more he had to cry out upon, while the patient ones they scarcely hurt at all.

Having promised His Majesty and Her Royal Highness a good breakfast, Curdie now went to finish his business. The leaders must yet be dealt with.

He found the chiefs of the conspiracy holding a final consultation in the smaller room off the hall. These were the lord chamberlain, the attorney-general, the master of the horse, and the king's private secretary; the lord chancellor and the rest, as foolish as faithless, were but the tools of these.

Curdie heard enough to understand that they had determined, in the dead of that night, to bring in a company of soldiers, make away with the king, secure the princess, announce the

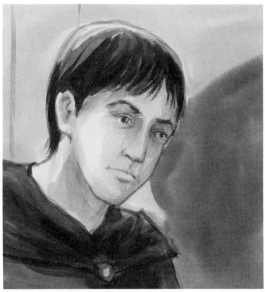

sudden death of His Majesty, read the will they had drawn up, and proceed to govern the country. Everything settled, they agreed to retire, and have a few hours' quiet sleep first—all but the secretary, who was to sit up and call them at the proper moment. Curdie allowed them half an hour to get to bed, and then set about completing his purging of the palace.

First he called Lina, and opened the door of the room where the secretary sat. She crept in, and laid herself down against it. When the secretary, rising to stretch his legs, caught sight of her eyes, he stood frozen with terror. She made neither motion nor sound. Gathering courage, and taking the thing for a spectral illusion, he made a step forward. She showed her other teeth, with a growl neither more than audible nor less than horrible. The secretary sank fainting into a chair.

To the lord chamberlain's door next, Curdie conducted the legserpent, and let him in.

Now His Lordship had had a bedstead made for himself, sweetly fashioned of rods of silver gilt. Upon it the legserpent found him asleep, and under it he crept. But out he came on the other side, and crept over it next, and again under it, and so over it, under it, over it, five or six times, every time leaving a coil of himself behind him, until he had softly folded all his length about the lord chamberlain and his bed. This done, he set up his head, looking down with curved neck right over His Lordship's, and began to hiss in his face.

He woke in terror unspeakable, and would have started up; but the moment he moved, the legserpent drew his coils closer, and closer still, and drew until the quaking traitor heard the joints of his bedstead grinding. Presently he persuaded himself that it was only a horrible nightmare, and began to struggle with all his strength to throw it off. Thereupon the legserpent gave his hooked nose such a bite that his teeth met through it. Then the vulture knew that he was in the grasp of his enemy the snake, and yielded.

The master of the horse Curdie gave in charge to the tapir. When the soldier saw him enter—for he was not yet asleep—he sprang from his bed, and flew at him with his sword. But the creature's hide was invulnerable to his blows, and he pecked at his legs until he jumped into the bed again, groaning, and covered himself up; after which the tapir contented himself with now and then paying a visit to this toes.

As for the attorney-general, Curdie led to his door a huge spider, about two feet long in the body, which, having made an excellent supper, was full of webbing. The attorney-general had not gone to bed, but sat in a chair asleep before a great mirror. He had been trying the effect of a diamond star which he had that morning taken from the jewel room. When he woke he fancied himself paralyzed; every limb, every finger even, was motionless. Coils and coils of broad spider ribbon bandaged his members to his body, and all to the chair. In the glass he saw himself wound about and on a footstool a yard off sat the spider glaring at him.

And now Curdie proceeded to the expulsion of the rest. Great men or underlings, he treated them all alike. From room to room over the house he went, and sleeping or waking took the man by the hand. Such was the state to which a year of wicked rule had reduced the moral condition of the court, that in all he found but three with human hands: the colonel of the guard, the page, and the housemaid. The possessors of these he allowed to dress themselves and move about in peace.

The uglies persecuted the miscreants, and at last sent them shivering outside the palace gates, with hardly sense enough to know where to run.

In the morning Curdie appeared in town. The outcasts were in terror, thinking he had come for them again. But he took no notice of them. He went straight to the old woman and told her that the king required her services. She need take no trouble with her cottage, he said; the palace was henceforward her home. And this very morning she must cook His Majesty a nice breakfast.

With the old woman to minister to the king's wants, with Curdie to protect him, and Irene to nurse him, the king was getting rapidly stronger. Everywhere since the cleaning of the lower regions, the air was clean and sweet, and under the honest hands of one housemaid the king's chambers became a pleasure to his eyes.

But though things in the palace were pure, the king's enemies were still corrupting the city. They went about telling lies among the people until every subject's heart was in rebellion to the king. Furthermore, the moment the lord chancellor reached his house in the country, he dressed and set out for the neighboring kingdom of Borsagrass to invite invasion, and offer a compact with its monarch.

No one from the city dared approach the gates, and seldom did any of the occupants of the palace venture out.

Every night, however, Lina went out hunting, and every morning the legserpent went out fishing. Thus the household was well fed. As to news, the page, in plain clothes, would now and then go into the market place, and gather some. One night he returned with the report that the army of the king of Borsagrass had crossed the border, and two days after, he brought the news that the enemy was now but twenty miles from Gwyntystorm.

Curdie resolved that if no other instructions came from the grand old princess, and the king remained unable to give orders, he would call Lina and the creatures, and march to meet the enemy. If he died, he died for the right, and there was a right end of it. He had no preparations, therefore, to make, except a good sleep.

He asked the king to let the housemaid take his place by His Majesty that night, and went and lay down on the floor of the corridor, no farther off than a whisper would reach from the door of the chamber. There, with an old mantle of the king's thrown over him, he was soon fast asleep.

Somewhere about the middle of the night, he woke suddenly, started to his feet, and rubbed his eyes. He could not tell what had woke him. But could he be awake, or was he dreaming? The curtain of the king's door, which before was a dull red, was now glowing a gorgeous, radiant purple. The crown wrought upon in silks and gems was flashing as if it burned! What could it mean? Was the king's chamber on fire? He darted to the door and lifted the curtain. Glorious terrible sight!

A long and broad marble table, that stood at one end of the room, had been drawn into the middle of it, and thereon burned a great fire, of a sort that Curdie knew—a fire of glowing, flaming roses, red and white. In the midst of the roses lay the king, someone, whom Curdie could not plainly see for the brightness, stood nearby.

At length the glow of the red fire died away, and the glow of the white fire grew gray, and the light was gone. On the table all was black—except for the face of the king, which shone from under the burnt roses like a diamond in the ashes of a furnace.

Then Curdie, no longer dazzled, saw and knew the old princess. The room was lighted with the splendor of her face, of her blue eyes, of her sapphire crown. He turned silently away, and laid himself down again in the corridor. An absolute joy filled his heart. All was safe; all was well.

The King's Army

He woke refreshed.

When he went into the king's chamber, the housemaid sat there and everything in the room was as it had been the night before, save that a heavenly odor of roses filled the air of it. He went up to the bed. The king opened his eyes, and the soul of perfect health shone out of them. Nor was Curdie amazed in his delight.

"Is it not time to rise, Curdie?" said the king.

"It is, Your Majesty. Today we must be doing," answered Curdie.

"What must we be doing today, Curdie?"

"Fighting, sire."

"Then fetch me my armor—that of plated steel, in the chest there."

As he spoke, he reached out his hand for his sword, which hung on the bed before him, drew it, and examined the blade.

"A little rusty!" he said, "but the edge is there. Curdie, my son, I wake from a troubled dream. I know how things are. Call the colonel of the guard."

In complete steel the old man stepped into the chamber. He knew it not, but the old princess had passed through his room in the night.

"Why, Sir Bronzebeard!" said the king, "you are dressed before me! Can you find me a horse think you, Bronzebeard? Alas, they told me my white charger was dead."

"I will go and fright the rabble with my presence, and secure, I trust, a horse for Your Majesty, and one for myself."

"And look you, brother!" said the king, "bring one for my miner boy too, and a sober old charger for the princess, for she too must go to the battle, and conquer with us."

"Pardon me, sire," said Curdie, "a miner can fight best on foot. I might smite my horse dead under me with a missed blow. And besides that, I must be near to my beasts."

"As you will," said the king. "Three horses then, Sir Bronzebeard."

The colonel departed, doubting sorely in his heart how to acquire and lead from the barrack stables three horses, in the teeth of his revolted regiment.

In the hall he met the housemaid.

"Can you lead a horse?" he asked.

"Yes, sir."

"Are you willing to die for the king?"

"Yes, sir."

"Come then. Were I not a man I would be a woman such as you."

When they entered the barrack yard, the soldiers scattered like autumn leaves before a blast of winter. They went into the stable unchallenged—and lo, in a

stall, before the colonel's eyes, stood the king's white charger, with the royal saddle and bridle hung beside him!

"Traitorous thieves!" muttered the old man in his beard, and went along the stalls, looking for his own black charger. Having found him, he returned. He then chose for the princess a great red horse.

The king and Curdie stood in the court, the king in full armor of silvered steel, with a circlet of rubies and diamonds round his helmet. He almost leaped for joy when he saw his great white charger come in gentle as a child to the hand of the handmaid. But when the horse saw his master in his armor, he reared and bounded in jubilation, yet did not break from the hand that held him. Then out came the princess attired and ready, with a hunting knife her father had given her by her side. They brought her mother's saddle, resplendent with gems and gold, set it on the great red horse, and lifted her to it. But the saddle was so big, and the horse so tall, that the child found no comfort in them.

"Please, King Papa," she said, "can I not have my white pony?"

"I did not think of him," said the king. "Where is he?"

"In the stable," answered the colonel. "I found him half starved, the only horse within the gates, the day after the servants were driven out. He has been well fed since."

"Go and fetch him," said the king.

As the colonel appeared with the pony, from a side door came Lina and the forty-nine, following Curdie.

"I will go with Curdie and the Uglies," cried the princess; and as soon

as she was mounted she got into the middle of the pack.

So out they set, the strangest force that ever went against an enemy.

Curdie, happening to look behind him, saw the maid, whom he had supposed stayed at the castle, still following on the great red horse.

About a mile down the river, the king caught sight of the enemy's tents, pitched a few paces in front of him where the bank of the river widened to a little plain.

The Battle

He commanded the page to blow his trumpet; and, in the strength of the moment, the youth uttered a right warlike defiance.

The butchers and the guard, who had gone over armed to the enemy, thought that the king had come to make his peace and were afraid that it might thereafter go hard with them; so they rushed at once to make short work of the good king hoping that their actions would secure and commend them to the king's ememies. The butchers came on first brandishing their knives, and talking to their dogs. Curdie and the page, with Lina and her pack, bounded to meet them. Curdie struck down the foremost with his mattock. The page, finding his sword too much for him, threw it away and seized the butcher's knife, which as he rose he plunged into the foremost dog. Lina rushed raging and gnashing among them. She would not look at a dog so long as there was a butcher on his legs, and she never stopped to kill a butcher, only with one grind of her jaws crushed a leg of him. When they were all down, then indeed she flashed among the dogs.

Meantime the king and the colonel had spurred toward the advancing guard. The king clove the major through skull and collar bone, and the colonel stabbed the captain in the throat. Then a fierce combat commenced—two against many. When the butchers and their dogs were disposed of, up came Curdie and his beasts. The horses of the guard, struck with terror, turned in spite of the spur, and fled in confusion.

Thereupon the forces of Borsagrass, which could see little of the affair, but correctly imagined a small determined body in front of them, hastened to the attack. No sooner did their advancing wave appear than the king, the colonel, the page, Curdie and the beasts, went charging upon them. Their attack, especially the rush of the Uglies, threw the first line into great confusion, but the second came up quickly. The beasts could not be everywhere, there were

thousands to one against them, and the king and his companions were in the greatest possible danger.

A dense cloud came over the sun, and sank rapidly toward the earth. The cloud moved all together, and yet the thousands of white flakes of which it was made up moved each for itself in ceaseless and rapid motion. Those flakes were the wings of pigeons. Down swooped the birds upon each invader; right in the face of man and horse they flew with swift-beating wings, blinding eyes and confounding brain. Horses reared and plunged and wheeled. All was at once in confusion. The men made frantic efforts to seize their tormenters, but not one could they touch; and they outdoubled them in numbers.

The moment the battle began, the princess's pony took fright, and turned and fled. But the maid wheeled her horse across the road and stopped him. Together, then, the princess and the maid awaited the result of the battle.

And as the princess waited, it seemed to her right strange that the pigeons, every one as it came to the rear, and fetched a compass to gather force for the reattack, should make the head of her attendant on the red horse the goal around which it turned; so that about them was an unintermittent flapping and flashing of wings, and a curving, sweeping torrent of the wheeling bodies of birds. Strange also it seemed that the maid should be constantly waving her arm toward the battle. And the time of the motion of her arm so fitted with the rushes of birds, that it looked as if the birds obeyed her gesture, and she was casting javelins by the thousands against the enemy. The moment a pigeon had rounded her head, it went straight as bolt from bow. The enemy stormed back upon their own camp.

"Call off your hounds, Curdie, and let the pigeons do the rest," shouted the king, as he turned to see what had become of the princess.

Before night the bird cloud came back, flying high over Gwyntystorm. Sinking swiftly, it disappeared among the ancient roofs of the palace.

Judgment

The king and his army returned, bringing with them only one prisoner, the lord chancellor. Curdie had dragged him from under a fallen tent, not by the hand of a man, but by the foot of a mule.

When they entered the city, it was still as the grave. The citizens had fled home. "We must submit," they cried, "or the king and his demons will destroy us." The king rode through the streets in silence, ill-pleased with his people. But he stopped his horse in the market place, and called, in a voice loud and clear as the cry of a

silver trumpet. "Go and find your own. Bury your dead, and bring home your wounded." Then he turned him gloomily to the palace.

They found the old woman returned before them, and already busy preparing them food. The king put up his charger with his own hands, rubbed him down, and fed him.

When they had washed, and eaten and drunk, he called the colonel, and told Curdie and the page to bring out the traitors and the beasts, and attend him to the market place.

By this time the people were crowding back into the city, bearing their dead and wounded. And there was lamentation in Gwyntystorm, for no one could comfort himself, and no one had any to comfort him. The nation was victorious, but the people were conquered.

The king stood in the center of the market place. He laid aside his helmet and put on his crown. Then he called the people to him. They dared not disobey. Those, even, who were carrying their wounded laid them down, and drew near trembling.

Then the king said to Curdie and the page:

"Set the evil men before me."

He looked upon them for a moment in mingled anger and pity, then turned to the people and said:

"Behold your trust! Ye slaves, behold your leaders! I would have freed you, but ye would not be free. Now shall ye be ruled with a rod of iron, that ye may learn what freedom is, and love it and seek it. These wretches I will send where they shall mislead you no longer."

He made a sign to Curdie, who immediately brought up the legserpent.

To the body of the animal they bound the lord chamberlain, speechless with horror. The butler began to shriek and pray, but they bound him to the back of Clubhead. One after another, upon the largest of the creatures they bound the whole seven, each through the unveiling terror looking the villain he was. Then said the king:

"I thank you, my good beasts; and I hope to visit you ere long. Take these evil men with you, and go to your place."

Like a whirlwind they were in the crowd, scattering it like dust. Like hounds they rushed from the city, their burdens howling and raving.

What became of them I never heard.

Then the king turned once more to the people and said, "Go to your houses."

They crept home like scolded hounds.

The king returned to the palace. He made the colonel a duke, and the page a knight. But to Curdie he said:

"You are my own boy, Curdie. My child cannot choose but love you, and when you are grown up—if you both will—you shall marry each other, and be king and queen when I am gone. Till then be the king's Curdie."

Irene held out her arms to Curdie. He raised her in his, and she kissed him.

They sat down to supper, and the old woman and the knight and the housemaid waited. The housemaid poured out the wine; and as she poured for Curdie she looked him in the eyes. And Curdie started, and sprang from his seat, and dropped on his knees, and burst into tears. And the maid said with a smile, such as none but one could smile:

"Did I not tell you Curdie, that it might be you would not know me when next you saw me?"

Then she went from the room, and in a moment returned in royal purple, with a crown of diamonds and rubies, from under which her hair went flowing to the floor, all about her ruby-slippered feet. Her face was radiant with joy, the joy overshadowed by a faint mist as of unfulfillment. The king rose and kneeled on one knee before her. All kneeled in like homage. Then the king would have yielded her his royal chair. But she made them all sit down, and with her own hands placed at the table seats for the old woman and the page. Then in ruby crown and royal purple she served them all.

The End

The king sent Curdie out into his dominions to search for men and women that had human hands. And many such he found, honest and true, and brought them to his master. So a new and upright court was formed, and strength returned to the nation.

Queen Irene—that was the right name of the old princess—was thereafter seldom long absent from the palace. Once or twice when she was missing she was with the dear old Uglies in the wood. Curdie thought that perhaps her business might be with others there as well. All the uppermost rooms in the palace were left to her use, and when she was there, he did not always succeed in finding her. She, however, always knew that such a one had been looking for her.

Curdie went to find her one day. As he ascended the last stair, the well-known scent of her roses came to meet him; and when he opened the door, there was the same gorgeous room in which his touch had been glorified by her fire! And there burned the fire—a huge heap of red and white roses. Before the hearth stood the princess, an old grey-haired woman, with Lina a little behind her, slowly wagging her tail, and looking like a beast of prey that can hardly so long restrain itself from springing as to be sure of its victim. The queen was casting roses, more and more roses, upon the fire. At last she turned and said, "Now Lina!"—and Lina dashed burrowing into the fire. There went up a black smoke and a dust, and Lina was never more seen in the palace.

Irene and Curdie were married. The old king died, and they were queen and king. As long as they lived Gwyntystorm was a better city, and good people grew in it. But they had no children, and when they died the people chose a new king. And this king went mining and mining in the rock under the city, and grew more and more eager after the gold, and paid less and less heed to his people. Rapidly they sank toward their old wickednesses.

So greedy was this king after gold, that when at last the ore began to fail, he caused the miners to reduce the pillars which upheld the city. Thus, one day at noon, when life was at its highest, the whole city fell with a roaring crash. The cries of men and the shrieks of women went up with its dust—then there was a great silence. Now all round spreads a wilderness of wild deer, and the very name of Gwyntystorm has ceased from the lips of men.

Reading Check

1. How do the king's enemies corrupt the city?
2. How is the king restored to health?
3. What event turns the battle in favor of the king's forces?
4. Who is the housemaid?
5. How do Curdie's experiences at court qualify him as true adventurer?

Rise Up, O Men of God

William P. Merrill

Rise up, O men of God!
Have done with lesser things;
Give heart and soul and mind and strength
To serve the King of kings.

Rise up, O men of God!
His kingdom tarries long:
Bring in the day of Christ our Lord
And end the night of wrong.

Lift high the cross of Christ!
Tread where His feet have trod:
As brothers of the Son of Man
Rise up, O men of God!

The Triumph of David by Jacupo Vignali from The Bob Jones University Collection of Sacred Art

ELIJAH ON MOUNT CARMEL

And it came to pass, when Ahab saw Elijah, that Ahab said unto him, Art thou he that troubleth Israel?

And he answered, I have not troubled Israel; but thou, and thy father's house, in that ye have forsaken the commandments of the Lord, and thou hast followed Baalim.

Now therefore send, and gather to me all Israel unto mount Carmel, and the prophets of Baal four hundred and fifty, and the prophets of the groves four hundred, which eat at Jezebel's table.

So Ahab sent unto all the children of Israel, and gathered the prophets together unto mount Carmel.

And Elijah came unto all the people, and said, How long halt ye between two opinions? if the Lord be God, follow him: but if Baal, then follow him. And the people answered him not a word.

Then said Elijah unto the people, I, even I only, remain a prophet of the Lord; but Baal's prophets are four hundred and fifty men.

Let them therefore give us two bullocks; and let them choose one bullock for themselves, and cut it in pieces, and lay it on wood, and put no fire under: and I will dress the other bullock, and lay it on wood, and put no fire under:

And call ye on the name of your gods, and I will call on the name of the Lord and the God that answereth by fire, let him be God. And all the people answered and said, It is well spoken.

And Elijah said unto the prophets of Baal, Choose you one bullock for yourselves, and dress it first; for ye are many; and call on the name of your gods, but put no fire under.

And they took the bullock which was given them, and they dressed it, and called on the name of Baal from morning even until noon, saying, O Baal, hear us. But there was no voice, nor any that answered. And they leaped upon the altar which was made.

And it came to pass at noon, that Elijah mocked them, and said, Cry aloud: for he is a god; either he is talking, or he is pursuing, or he is in a journey, or peradventure he sleepeth, and must be awaked.

And they cried aloud, and cut themselves after their manner with knives and lancets, till the blood gushed out upon them.

And it came to pass, when midday was past, and they prophesied until the time of the offering of the evening sacrifice, that there was neither voice, nor any to answer, nor any that regarded.

And Elijah said unto all the people, Come near unto me. And all the people came near unto him. And he repaired the altar of the Lord that was broken down.

And Elijah took twelve stones, according to the number of the tribes of the sons of Jacob, unto whom the word of the Lord came, saying, Israel shall be thy name.

And with the stones he built an altar in the name of the Lord: and he made a trench about the altar, as great as would contain two measures of seed.

And he put the wood in order, and cut the bullock in pieces, and laid him on the wood, and said, Fill four barrels with water, and pour it on the burnt sacrifice, and on the wood.

And he said, Do it the second time. And they did it the second time. And he said, Do it the third time. And they did it the third time.

And the water ran round about the altar; and he filled the trench also with water.

And it came to pass at the time of the offering of the evening sacrifice, that Elijah the prophet came near, and said, Lord God of Abraham, Isaac, and of Israel, let it be known this day that thou art God in Israel, and that I am thy servant, and that I have done all these things at thy word.

Hear me, O Lord, hear me, that this people may know that thou art the Lord God, and that thou hast turned their heart back again.

Then the fire of the Lord fell, and consumed the burnt sacrifice, and the wood, and the stones, and the dust, and licked up the water that was in the trench.

And when all the people saw it, they fell on their faces: and they said, The Lord, he is the God; the Lord, he is the God.

(I Kings 18:17-39)

DISCOVERIES

Discoveries

As the king's adviser pointed with trembling hand toward the other end of the great hall, even the bravest royal guard felt his hand slide involuntarily to the hilt of his sword. There in the doorway stood the lunatic king Nebuchadnezzar. His hair covered his body like the mangy fur of a mad dog, and his fingernails, long and curled like an eagle's talons, clicked against the marble floor as he struggled to draw himself to his full height. Then to everyone's amazement the lunatic spoke. "I Nebuchadnezzar praise and extol and honour the King of heaven, all whose works are truth, and his ways judgment: and those that walk in pride he is able to abase. I have returned—my reason restored. I am the king." The guards released their swords and the royal company breathed easily, for they recognized in Nebuchadnezzar's voice the power and authority that had once caused mighty men to tremble.

We do not actually know how Nebuchadnezzar regained his throne. We do know, however, that God pronounced judgment on this proud king by depriving him of his reason and by forcing him to wander in the fields as a wild beast for seven years. Through this experience Nebuchadnezzar discovered the power of God, a discovery all of us can learn from. To better understand Nebuchadnezzar's specific experience as well as the general process of discovery, let's examine the following chart.

THE PROCESS OF DISCOVERY

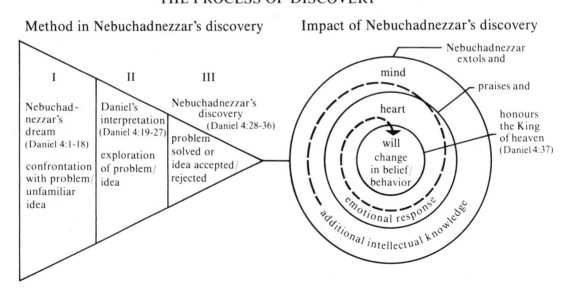

We can see that Nebuchadnezzar's discovery was both powerful and valuable, for this discovery affected not only his mind and heart but also his will. Consequently, the experience did more than increase his knowledge and evoke an emotional response; it totally altered his beliefs and behavior.

All of the characters in this unit's selections make discoveries. Not all of their discoveries, however, have the same impact evidenced in Nebuchadnezzar's experience. Some of the discoveries affect only the mind. For example, the persona in the poem "Opportunity" discovers and records an interesting incident for us, but there is no indication within the poem that his discovery evoked any emotional response or changed his personal beliefs. Likewise, John Burroughs records several specific discoveries for us in his essay, but these discoveries do little more than add to his vast store of knowledge. Though such discoveries may have value, you will find that without the involvement of the heart and will, they have no great impact on the life.

The characters in the stories of "Shago" and "The Necklace" go one step further. Besides adding to their knowledge, their discoveries also evoke a strong emotional response. This may at first appear to change the character, but if we look closely, we can see that there is no real evidence of altered belief. This is particularly true in the case of Mathilde in "The Necklace." Though by the end of the play she regrets her early behavior, she still views herself as a victim of circumstances. Thus, even at the end of the drama there is no essential change in her beliefs.

The selections in which the characters do make essential, lasting changes are "Pivot Play," "You've Got to Learn," and "Symbols." These characters confront a new idea or problem, analyze that idea or problem, respond emotionally, and ultimately modify their behavior in accordance with the discoveries they have made.

You, through your reading, have also confronted many ideas. Through studying the characters in the various unit selections, you have been able to discover the importance of making right choices, building good friendships, maintaining a proper focus, and striving to become a noble adventurer. But what will you do with these discoveries? Will you simply add them to your store of knowledge? Or will you allow what you have learned to also touch your heart and change your attitude and behavior? Before you answer these questions, let's consider this unit's final selection, "Daniel and Belshazzar," for here is the record of a man who refused to benefit from the discovery of another.

You recall in the opening of this essay that we spoke of the lunatic king Nebuchadnezzar. Belshazzar was Nebuchadnezzar's grandson, and Scripture tells us that he knew all that had befallen the proud king.

But instead of allowing the knowledge of his grandfather's experience to touch his heart and alter his behavior, Belshazzar continued in his arrogance until God's patience ran out. And at the height of Belshazzar's prosperity and acclaim the finger of God wrote this condemnation: "God hath numbered thy kingdom, and finished it. Thou art weighed in the balances, and art found wanting. Thy kingdom is divided, and given to the Medes and Persians." Scripture goes on to confirm "In that night was Belshazzar the king of the Chaldeans slain. And Darius the Median took the kingdom."

Belshazzar's negative example reminds us of the value of learning not only from our personal experiences and discoveries but also from those of others. This truth captures for us one of the most significant reasons for studying good literature. In literature we are given the opportunity to gain insight through the characters' experiences, and we can do so without having to stumble over any obstacles or experience unnecessary pain. Let us then allow the discoveries presented to us in our reading to influence us for good that when our Savior returns as conquering king, we shall not "be found wanting."

Now just as the gates were opened to let in Christian,
I looked in after him; and behold, the city shone like the sun,
the streets also were paved with gold, and in them walked
many men with crowns on their heads, palms in their hands,
and golden harps to sing praises withal. There were also of them
that had wings, and they answered one another
without intermission, saying,
"Holy, Holy, Holy, is the Lord."
And after that they shut up the gates: which
when I had seen, I wished myself among them.

A coward's broken sword discovered by a king's son reveals that the greatest weapon in battle is a courageous heart.

Opportunity

Edward Roland Sill

This I beheld or dreamed it in a dream:—
There spread a cloud of dust along a plain;
And underneath the cloud, or in it, raged
A furious battle, and men yelled, and swords
Shocked upon swords and shields. A prince's banner
Wavered, then staggered backward, hemmed by foes.
A craven hung along the battle's edge,
And thought, "Had I a sword of keener steel—
That blue blade that the king's son bears,—but this
Blunt thing!—" he snapt and flung it from his hand,
And lowering crept away and left the field.
Then came the king's son, wounded, sore bestead,
And weaponless, and saw the broken sword,
Hilt-buried in the dry and trodden sand,
And ran and snatched it, and with battle-shout
Lifted afresh he hewed his enemy down,
And saved a great cause that heroic day.

What's under a leaf? Where does the wolf-spider live? Why is the female spider considered a fierce opponent? The following essay was written by a man who took the time to study our world and to discover answers to these and other questions.

The Art of Seeing Things

John Burroughs

The book of nature is like a page written over or printed upon with different-sized characters and in many different languages, interlined and crosslined, and with a great variety of marginal notes and references. There is coarse print and fine print; there are obscure signs and hieroglyphics. We all read the large type more or less appreciatively, but only the students and lovers of nature read the fine lines and the footnotes. It is a book which he reads best who goes most slowly or even tarries long by the way. He who runs may read some things. We may take in the general features of sky, plain and river from the express train, but only the pedestrian, the saunterer [one who walks leisurely], with eyes in his head and love in his heart, turns every leaf

and peruses every line. One man sees only the migrating water-fowls and the larger birds of the air; another sees the passing kinglets and hurrying warblers as well. For my part, my delight is to linger longer over each page of this marvelous record and to dwell fondly upon its most obscure text.

I take pleasure in noting the minute [very small] things about me. I am interested even in the ways of the wild bees, and in all the little dramas and tragedies that occur in field and wood. One June day, in my walk, as I crossed a rather dry, high-lying field, my attention was attracted by small mounds of fresh earth all over the ground, scarcely more than a handful in each. On looking closely, I saw that in the middle of each mound there was a hole not quite so large as a lead pencil. Now, I had never observed these mounds before, and my curiosity was aroused. "Here is some fine print," I said, "that I have overlooked." So I set to work to try to read it; I waited for a sign of life. Presently I saw here and there a bee hovering about over the mounds. It looked like the honeybee, only less pronounced in color and manner. One of them alighted on one of the mounds near me and was about to disappear in the hole in the center when I caught it in my hand. Though it stung me, I retained it and looked it over, and in the process was stung several times; but the pain was slight. I saw it was one of our native wild bees, cousin to the leaf-rollers, that build their nests under stones and in decayed fence rails. Then I inserted a small weed stalk into one of the holes and, with a little trowel [tool for digging holes in the soil] I carried,

proceeded to dig out the nest. The hole was about a foot deep; at the bottom of it I found a little, semitransparent membranous sac or cell, a little larger than that of the honeybee; in this sac was a little yellow pollen—a loaf of bread for the young grub when the egg should have hatched. I explored other nests and found them all the same. This discovery was not a great addition to my sum of natural knowledge, but it was something. Now when I see the signs in a field, I know what they mean: they indicate the tiny earthen cradles of the wild bees.

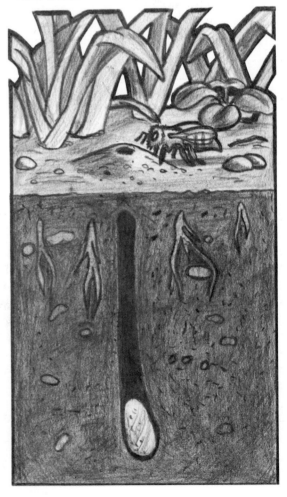

Nearby I chanced to spy a large hole in the turf, with no mound of soil about it. I could put the end of my little finger into it. I peered down and saw the gleam of two small, beadlike eyes. I knew it to be the den of the wolf-spider. Was she waiting for some blundering insect to tumble in? I say she, because the real ogre among the spiders is the female. The male is small and of little consequence. A few days later I paused by this den again and saw the members [legs] of the ogress scattered about her own door. Had some insect Jack the Giant-Killer been there, or had a still more formidable [dreadful] ogress, the sandhornet, dragged her forth and carried away her limbless body to her den in the bank?

What the wolf-spider does with the earth it excavates in making its den is a mystery. There is no sign of it anywhere about. Does it force its way down by pushing the soil to one side and packing it there firmly? The entrance to the hole usually has a slight rim or hem to keep the edge from crumbling in.

As it happened, I chanced upon another interesting footnote that very day. I was on my way to a muck swamp in the woods to see if the showy lady's slipper was in bloom. Just on the margin of the swamp, in the deep shade of the hemlocks, my eye took note of some small, unshapely creature crawling hurriedly over the ground. I stooped down and saw it was some large species of moth just out of its case and in a great hurry to find a suitable place in which to hang itself up and give its wings a chance to unfold before the air dried them. I thrust a small twig in its way,

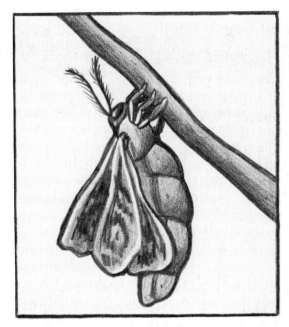

which it instantly seized upon. I lifted it gently, carried it to drier ground, and fixed the stick in the fork of a tree, so that the moth hung free a few feet from the ground. Its body was distended [swelled] nearly to the size of one's little finger, and surmounted by wings that were so crumpled and stubby that they seemed quite rudimentary [simple]. The creature evidently knew what it wanted, and knew the importance of haste. Instantly these rude, stubby wings began to grow. It was a slow process, but one could see the change from minute to minute. As the wings expanded, the body contracted. By some kind of pumping arrangement, air was being forced from a reservoir in the one into the tubes of the other. The wings were not really growing, as they at first seemed to be, but they were unfolding and expanding under this pneumatic [air-filled] pressure from the body. In the course of about half an hour the process was completed, and the winged

creature hung there in all its full-fledged beauty. Its color was checked black and white like a loon's [fish-eating bird in subarctic regions] back, but its name I know not. My chief interest in it, aside from the interest we feel in any new form of life, arose from the creature's extreme anxiety to reach a perch where it could unfold its wings. A little delay would doubtless have been fatal to it. I wonder how many human geniuses are hatched whose wings are blighted by some accident or untoward [unfortunate] circumstance. Or do the wings of genius always unfold, no matter what the environment may be?

One seldom takes a walk without encountering some of this fine print on nature's page. Now it is a little yellow-white moth that spreads itself upon the middle of a leaf as if to imitate the droppings of birds; or it is the young cicadas working up out of the ground, and in the damp, cool places building little chimneys or tubes above the surface to get more warmth and hasten their development; or it is a woodnewt gorging a tree-cricket, or a small snake gorging the newt, or a bird song with some striking peculiarity—a strange defect, or a rare excellence. Now it is a shrike impaling his victim, or blue jays mocking and teasing a hawk and dropping quickly into the branches to avoid his angry blows, or a robin hustling a cuckoo out of the tree where her nest is, or a vireo driving away a cowbird, or the partridge blustering about your feet till her young are hidden. One October morning I was walking along the road on the edge of the woods, when I came into a gentle shower of butternuts; one of them struck my hat brim. I paused and looked about me; here one fell, there another, yonder a third. There was no wind blowing, and I wondered what was loosening the butternuts. Turning my attention to the top of the tree, I soon saw the explanation. A red squirrel was at work gathering his harvest. He would seize a nut, give it a twist, when down it would come; then he would dart to another and another. Farther along I found where he had covered the ground with chestnut burs; he could not wait for the frost and the winds; did he know that the burs would dry and open upon the ground, and that the bitter covering of the butternuts would soon fall away from the nut?

There are three things that perhaps happen near me each season that I have never yet seen—the toad casting its skin, the snake swallowing its young, and the larvae of the moth and butterfly constructing their shrouds [protective coverings]. It is a moot [debatable] question whether or not the snake does swallow its young, but if there is no other good reason for it, may they not retreat into their mother's stomach to feed? How else are they to be nourished. That the moth larva can weave its own cocoon and attach it to a twig seems more incredible. Yesterday, in my walk, I found a firm, silver-gray cocoon, about two inches long and shaped like an Egyptian mummy, suspended from a branch of a bush by a narrow, stout ribbon twice as long as itself. The fastening was woven around the limb, upon which it turned as if it grew there. I would have given something to have seen the creature perform this feat and then incase itself so snugly in the silken shroud at the end of this tether. By swinging free, its firm, compact case was in no danger from woodpeckers, as it might have been if resting directly upon a branch or tree trunk. Nearby was the cocoon of another species that was fastened directly to the limb; but this was vague, loose, and much more involved and netlike. I have seen the downy woodpecker assaulting one of these cocoons, but its yielding surface and webby interior seemed to puzzle and baffle him.

I am interested even in the way each climbing plant or vine goes up the pole, whether from right to left, or from left to right—that is, with the hands of a clock or against them—whether it is under the law of the great cyclonic storms of the northern hemisphere, which all move against the hands of a clock, or in the contrary direction, like the cyclones in the southern hemisphere. I take pleasure in noting every little dancing whirlwind of a summer day that catches up the dust or the leaves before me, and every little funnel-shaped whirlpool in the swollen stream or river, whether or not they spin from right to left or the reverse. If I were in the southern hemisphere, I am sure I should note whether these things were under the law of its cyclones in this respect or under the law of ours. As a rule, our twining plants and toy whirlwinds copy our revolving storms and go against the hands of the clock. But there are exceptions. While the bean, the bittersweet, the morning glory, and others go up from left to right, the hop, the wild buckwheat, and some others go up from right to left. Most of our forest trees show a tendency to wind one way or the other, the hard woods going in one direction, and the hemlocks and pines and cedars and butternuts and chestnuts in another. In different localities, or on different geological formations, I find these directions reversed. I recall one instance in the case of a hemlock six or seven inches in diameter, where this tendency to twist had come out of the grain, as it were, and shaped the outward form of the tree, causing it to make, in an ascent of about thirty feet, one complete revolution about a larger tree close to which it grew. On a smaller scale I have seen the same thing in a pine.

Persons lost in the woods or on the plains, or traveling at night, tend, I believe, toward the left. The movements of men and women, it is said, differ in this respect, one sex turning to the right and the other to the left.

I had lived in the world more than fifty years before I noticed a peculiarity

about the rays of light one often sees diverging from an opening, or a series of openings, in the clouds namely, that they are like spokes in a wheel, the hub, or center, of which appears to be just there in the vapory masses, instead of being, as is really the case, nearly ninety-three millions of miles beyond. The beams of light that come through cracks or chinks in a wall do not converge in this way, but to the eye run parallel to one another. There is another fact: this fan-shaped display of converging rays is always immediately in front of the observer; that is, exactly between him and the sun, so that the central spoke or shaft is always perpendicular. You cannot see this fan to the right or left of the sun, but only between you and it. Hence, as in the case of the rainbow, no two persons see exactly the same rays.

The eye sees what it has the means of seeing, and its means of seeing are in proportion to the love and desire behind it. The eye is informed and sharpened by the thought. My boy sees ducks on the river where and when I cannot, because at certain seasons he thinks ducks and dreams ducks. One season my neighbor asked me if the bees had injured my grapes. I said, "No; the bees never injure my grapes."

"They do mine," he replied; "they puncture the skin for the juice, and at times the clusters are covered with them."

"No," I said, "it is not the bees that puncture the skin; it is the birds."

"What birds?"

"The orioles."

"But I haven't seen any orioles," he rejoined.

"We have," I continued, "because this season we think orioles; we have learned by experience how destructive these birds are in the vineyard, and we are on the lookout for them."

If we think birds, we shall see birds wherever we go; if we think arrowheads, as Thoreau did, we shall pick up arrowheads in every field. Some people have an eye for four-leaved clovers; they see them as they walk hastily over the turf, for they already have them in their eyes. I once took a walk with late Professor Eaton of Yale. He was just then specially interested in the mosses, and he found them, all kinds, everywhere. I can see him yet, every few minutes upon his knees, adjusting his eyeglasses before some rare specimen. The beauty he found in them, and pointed out to me, kindled an enthusiasm also. I once spent a summer day at the mountain home of a well-known literary woman and editor. She lamented the absence of birds about her house. I named a half-dozen or more I had heard or seen in her trees within an hour—the indigo-bird, the purple finch, the yellowbird, the veery thrush, the red-eyed vireo, the song sparrow.

"Do you mean to say you have seen or heard all these birds while sitting here on my porch?" she inquired.

"I really have," I said.

"I do not see them or hear them," she replied, "and yet I want to very much."

"No," said I, "you only want to want to see and hear them."

You must have the bird in your heart before you can find it in the bush.

I was sitting in front of a farmhouse one day in company with the local Nimrod*. In a maple tree in front of us I saw the great crested flycatcher. I called the hunter's attention to it and asked him if he had ever seen that bird before. No, he had not; it was a new bird to him. But he probably had seen it scores of times—seen it without regarding it. It was not the game he was in quest of, and his eye heeded it not.

Human and artificial sounds and objects thrust themselves upon us; they are within our sphere, so to speak. But the life of nature we must meet halfway; it is shy, withdrawn, and blends itself with a vast neutral background. We must be initiated; it is an order the secrets of which are well guarded.

Reading Check

1. To what does the author compare nature?
2. What does the author discover about the small mounds of earth in the field?
3. What does he teach you about the wolf-spider?
4. What three things does the author mention that he has not yet seen in his observation of nature?
5. What does he mean when he says, "The eye sees what it has the means of seeing, and its means of seeing are in proportion to the love and desire behind it"?

*Nimrod: A mighty hunter spoken of in Genesis 10:8-9.

And having food and raiment let us be therewith content. But they that will be rich fall into temptation and a snare, and into many foolish and hurtful lusts, which drown men in destruction and perdition (I Timothy 6:8-9).

The Necklace

Guy de Maupassant

play adaptation by **William Hackett**

MUSIC: *A theme sombre in nature. Forte and fade under.*

NARRATOR: Mathilde was one of those pretty and charming girls who are sometimes, as if by a mistake of destiny, born in a family of clerks. She had no dowry, no expectations, no means of being known, understood, loved or wedded by any rich and distinguished man. As a consequence she let herself be married to a little clerk at the Ministry of Public Information, a man named Claude Loisel. She dressed plainly because she could not dress well. She suffered unceasingly, feeling herself born for all the delicacies and luxuries of life. She hated the poverty of her dwelling. All these things tortured her and made her angry. She thought of long, gracious salons [large rooms in which guests are entertained]; she imagined herself being sought after by famous people, who crowded her charming home just to get a glimpse of her. And Mathilde would like to have been sought after. Instead, she had nothing!

MUSIC: *Out.*

NARRATOR: All she had was a simple little husband, who every night sat at the dinner table covered with a cloth three days old.

CLAUDE (*Expectantly*): Ah, what have we to eat this evening?

SOUND: *Cover lifted from soup tureen.*

CLAUDE: Stew! Wonderful, wonderful stew! What more could a man ask for!

SOUND: *Ladle against plate, as stew is dished out.*

CLAUDE: Mathilde, you are a superb chef. Your stew is nectar of the gods. Just enough herbs. Here you are, my dear.

MATHILDE: I don't want it.

CLAUDE (*Puzzled*): You don't care for any stew?

MATHILDE (*Listlessly*): I do not care for any stew. That is correct.

CLAUDE: B-but it . . . it's—

MATHILDE: Stew!

CLAUDE: But you made it.

MATHILDE: That is just the trouble. I always make the stew. I always cook everything. I'm beginning to smell like a greasy kitchen.

CLAUDE: Mathilde, I don't understand you.

MATHILDE: I know that.

CLAUDE: But what have I done?

MATHILDE: Nothing, and that is just your trouble.

CLAUDE: What do you want of me?

MATHILDE (*Wearily*): Eat your stew, Claude, and don't ask any questions.

MUSIC: *An unhappy theme. Forte and out into:*

SOUND: *Canary chirping in background.*

JEANNE: Won't you have another cake, Mathilde?

MATHILDE: No, thank you.

JEANNE: Some more chocolate?

MATHILDE: Not a thing, dear Jeanne. Every time I come here, I eat much more than I should.

JEANNE (*Laughing*): I always try to please my guests.

MATHILDE (*A trace of envy*): You are a lucky girl, Jeanne. This lovely home, a rich and handsome husband, servants, lovely clothes and jewels—you have everything any wife could ask for.

JEANNE (*Quietly*): Yes, I am fortunate.

MATHILDE: It is strange how life turns out. Here we are, close friends for many years, schoolmates at the convent [Catholic school for girls], both the same, equally pretty—

JEANNE: You're prettier than I, Mathilde.

MATHILDE: You marry a rich husband, while I marry a poor clerk.

JEANNE: Claude is a good man.

MATHILDE: He thinks and looks and acts just like what he is—a little man with no imagination or particular ambition. He is happy to come home and eat his stew and then spend the evening smoking his smelly pipe and reading his newspaper. We never go anywhere. We never attend balls or receptions or dinners.

JEANNE: I've never heard you speak quite like this.

MATHILDE: I need excitement and attention and everything that goes with such a life. Instead, I'm nothing but a drudge [servant]. (*Suddenly*) Good-bye, Jeanne. Thank you for your kindness.

THE NECKLACE   319

JEANNE: Do stay a while longer.

MATHILDE: No, for if I do, I shall become more and more envious of your good fortune. Besides, I have to cook dinner for Claude—stew, again, of course.

JEANNE: You'll call again soon?

MATHILDE: Perhaps. Maybe the next time I won't be in such a foul mood—although I do not guarantee it.

MUSIC: *A short bridge. Forte and out into:*

SOUND: *Door open. In background: A small clock strikes six times.*

CLAUDE: Mathilde, Mathilde! Where are you? It is Claude.

MATHILDE *(Fading in)*: Good evening, Claude.

CLAUDE: You have a small kiss for your husband?

MATHILDE: I suppose so.

CLAUDE *(A pause, then)*: Ah, so! *(Triumphantly)* I have a surprise.

MATHILDE *(Unenthusiastically)*: Oh!

CLAUDE: A great surprise. Here! This is for you.

MATHILDE: A letter.

CLAUDE: But what a letter! Well, open it. Read it.

MATHILDE: Probably a bill.

CLAUDE: And whoever heard of a bill being enclosed in such a fine envelope. Go ahead—open it, Mathilde.

SOUND: *Envelope ripped open. Rustle of paper.*

MATHILDE *(Reading)*: "The Minister of Public Information and Mme. Georges Ramponneau request the honor of M. and Mme. Loisel's company at the palace of the Minister on Monday evening, January 18th." *(Disdainfully)* Well, what do you want me to do with that?

CLAUDE: But, my dear, I thought you would be glad. You never go out, and this is such a fine opportunity. I had trouble to get it.

MATHILDE: Really!

CLAUDE: Don't you understand every one wants to go. It is very select, and they are not giving many invitations to clerks. The whole official world will be there.

MATHILDE: And what do you want me to put on my back?

CLAUDE *(Stammering)*: W-why the . . . the dress you go to the theatre in. It looks very well to me.

MATHILDE *(Practically in tears)*: Oh, oh, Claude!

CLAUDE *(Stuttering)*: What's the matter? Tell me.

MATHILDE *(Controlling herself)*: Nothing, only I have no dress, and therefore I can't go to this ball.

CLAUDE: But of course you can.

MATHILDE: I cannot go. Give your card to some colleague whose wife is better equipped than I.

CLAUDE: Come, let us see, Mathilde. How much would it cost for a suitable dress, something you could use on other occasions, something very simple?

MATHILDE: Well, it would—let me think. *(Pause)* I'd say—I don't know exactly, but I think I could manage it with . . . four hundred francs.

CLAUDE: Four hundred francs.

MATHILDE: See, I told you. It's a great deal of money, too much for us to consider.

CLAUDE: I have four hundred francs laid aside.

MATHILDE: But you've saved that to buy a gun so you can go shooting at Nanterre with your friends.

CLAUDE: That is quite all right.

MATHILDE: I won't hear of it.

CLAUDE: The four hundred francs are for you. And try to have a pretty dress, a very pretty dress.

MATHILDE *(Joyfully)*: Oh, Claude, you are so good to me.

MUSIC: *A cheerful theme. Forte and out.*

CLAUDE: Now turn around, more toward the light. *(Admiringly)* Indeed, it is a very pretty dress, Mathilde. You will be the prettiest woman at the ball. People will ask: "Who is that beautiful woman?" And others will answer: "Don't you know that is Mme. Claude Loisel? Is she not lovely, and that exquisite gown she is wearing, it must have been designed exclusively for her." *(Pause)* Mathilde.

MATHILDE: Yes?

CLAUDE: What is the matter?

MATHILDE: Nothing.

CLAUDE: Come, tell me. You've been so queer these past few days. Are you unhappy?

MATHILDE: It annoys me not to have a single jewel, not a single stone, nothing to put on. I shall look like distress. I should almost rather not go at all.

CLAUDE: You might wear flowers.

MATHILDE *(Not convinced)*: Flowers! Hmph!

CLAUDE: It's very stylish at this time of the year. For ten francs you can get two or three magnificent roses.

MATHILDE: No! There's nothing more humiliating than to look poor among other women who are rich.

CLAUDE: But how stupid you are!

MATHILDE: It is not stupidity. It is a case of not looking well-groomed.

CLAUDE: But you are stupid! Go to your friend, Jeanne Forestier, and ask her to lend you some jewels. You are friendly enough with her to do that.

MATHILDE *(Joyfully)*: It's true. I never thought of it. Oh, but suppose she refuses.

CLAUDE: She won't. You are such close friends, and after all it is merely a loan for the evening.

MATHILDE: I shall go tomorrow. *(Longingly)* She has so many beautiful jewels.

MUSIC: *A short bridge. Forte and out.*

JEANNE: But of course I don't resent your request. You must look well, you know, and I have any number of nice things, and you're welcome to use any of them. Here, let us see what this box holds. *(Pause)* There!

MATHILDE: Bracelets.

JEANNE: I wouldn't wear bracelets, if I were you. Try on this pearl necklace. There! Now look at yourself in the mirror. *(Pause)* Lovely!

MATHILDE *(Reflectively)*: Mmm! Perhaps! *(Eagerly)* What is this?

JEANNE: A Venetian cross—heavy gold.

MATHILDE: I don't think it suits me.

JEANNE: Here are rings—diamonds, black pearl, a ruby, two emerald ones. Do you like them?

MATHILDE: Y-yes, they're very beautiful. Haven't you any more?

JEANNE: Why, yes. Look here, in this box. I don't know what you like. Examine them.

MATHILDE *(After a pause)*: This- . . . this diamond necklace. *(Pause)* How well it looks on me.

JEANNE: It does suit you.

MATHILDE: Can you lend me that, only that?

JEANNE: Why, yes, certainly.

MATHILDE *(Overjoyed)*: You're so kind, Jeanne. Such a wonderful friend. Now I shall indeed look my best. Such a gorgeous necklace!

MUSIC: *A light theme. Forte and out into:*

SOUND: *Background of many voices: the people attending the ball. Hold under.*

FOOTMAN *(Calling out in a loud voice)*: Monsieur and Madame Claude Loisel.

MATHILDE *(Low voice)*: Claude, I'm so excited. Such a beautiful palace and all these beautifully gowned women. And such handsome, distinguished men.

CLAUDE (Nervously): Shh! Look, we are to meet the Minister and his wife. He is my superior.

MATHILDE: Have you ever met him?

CLAUDE: No. I have only seen him from a distance. Quiet, now.

MINISTER: Good evening, er—

CLAUDE: Loisel . . . Claude Loisel. And my wife, Your Excellency.

MINISTER: Good evening, Madame Loisel. May I introduce you to my wife, Madame Ramponneau.

MATHILDE: Good evening, Madame Ramponneau.

MADAME: Good evening, my child.

MINISTER: She is very beautiful, is she not, my dear?

MADAME: Very.

MATHILDE: Thank you.

MINISTER: Young and lovely.

MADAME: And such a beautiful diamond necklace. Did you get it in Paris?

MATHILDE: No! Er, that is—yes, in a way. It's er—new, you see.

MADAME: It sets off your beautiful skin to advantage.

MATHILDE: Thank you, Madame.

MINISTER: Monsieur, er—

CLAUDE: Loisel.

MINISTER: Your face is so familiar. Where have we met? Perhaps at Auteuil or Longchamps?

CLAUDE: I never go to the races, Your Excellency.

MINISTER: I wish I could place you.

CLAUDE: I work for you, sir.

MINISTER (Surprised): Oh!

CLAUDE: I am an under-clerk in the Ministry.

MINISTER: In any event you (Stressing this) and your very lovely wife are welcome. Perhaps Madame Loisel will honor me with a dance later in the evening.

MATHILDE: I shall look forward to it, Your Excellency.

MUSIC: An orchestra playing a bright waltz of the period. Up full and hold under.

SOUND: Background of guests. Weave in and out of scene.

GUEST 1 (A man): That woman dancing—the one with the diamond necklace, who is she?

GUEST 2 (Man): I don't know. Such grace. See how well she dances. I should like to meet her.

GUEST 1: As would I. I want to dance with her.

GUEST 2: His Excellency has danced twice with her. It would seem that she is the belle of the evening.

GUEST 1: Notice how the other women glare at her.

GUEST 2: Small wonder. She puts them to shame with her youth and beauty.

MUSIC: Up full and fade out.

SOUND: The background of guests' voices continues.

ATTACHÉ: And mamselle will save this next dance for me?

GUEST 1: No, she's promised it to me.

GUEST 2: You're both quite mistaken. It is I she has promised it to, messieurs.

MATHILDE (Gay): Now, now, please do not argue over me, gentlemen.

GUEST 2: And why not? After all, you are by far the most beautiful woman present.

ATTACHÉ: The most beautiful woman in Paris.

GUEST 1: In France, you mean.

MATHILDE: You will turn my head, make me vain.

ATTACHÉ: It is only right that a beautiful woman should be complimented, not once, but over and over.

GUEST 1: Your husband, he will be jealous. *(Anxiously)* Are you married?

MATHILDE: Yes.

GUEST 1 *(Disappointed)*: Oh, I was hoping otherwise.

MUSIC: *A waltz. Hold under.*

GUEST 2: Ah, we shall dance.

GUEST 1: This is my dance.

ATTACHÉ: You are both mistaken, for this dance is mine.

MATHILDE: And I am afraid that all three of you are mistaken, for I have already promised this dance to that gentleman who is approaching. See— the tall one.

GUEST 2: Are you dancing with him?

MATHILDE: Yes, who is he? I did not catch his name when we were introduced.

ATTACHÉ: He is the British Ambassador.

MUSIC: *Waltz up full and fade under to background.*

SOUND: *Clock strikes twice.*

CLAUDE *(Yawns deeply)*: Sorry, monsieur. I hope I did not wake you.

HUSBAND *(Wearily)*: Not at all. I really was not asleep—just dozing.

CLAUDE: How much longer does this affair last?

HUSBAND: You still have two hours to go.

CLAUDE: But some of the guests have already left.

HUSBAND: That is your wife dancing—the one with the necklace?

CLAUDE: That is she.

HUSBAND: Then you have two hours to go, my friend. The penalty you have to pay for having such a beautiful and popular wife. See how the men cluster about her.

CLAUDE: I gave up at midnight. I tried to make my way to her, but there was such a crush, I could not pierce even the outer ring. *(Pause)* But you must be in the same position. You are not with your partner.

HUSBAND: My partner is my wife.

CLAUDE: She also must be popular.

HUSBAND: Quite the contrary, she is most unpopular. A remarkably plain woman who receives only barely polite attention from men. You see, in my position, we have to attend many such functions. We dare not leave early, and so, according to our custom, my wife retires to the ladies' cloak room on the pretence of a headache, while I retire to the gentlemen's cloak room, but on no pretence whatsoever. And after dozing several hours, we rise, thank our host, and take our leave. In the morning both of us are well rested. Clever, don't you think?

CLAUDE: If boring.

HUSBAND: Not at all. In these cloak rooms, one meets such interesting people. One night I met the Dey [governor] of Algiers. *(Sighs)* I'm glad I have a plain, uninteresting wife. If I had a beautiful wife like you, I would feel as though I would have to go through some semblance of trying to keep pace with her. But with my dull wife, that is not necessary. Wake me in an hour, please.

MUSIC: *Up full and segue to: Another waltz. Hold under in background.*

SOUND: *Clock strikes four times.*

MATHILDE: Claude, Claude, wake up. Wake up.

CLAUDE *(Sleepily)*: Oh, are we leaving?

MATHILDE: Yes, this is the last dance, and I want to sneak out unnoticed. I don't want the other women to see what a miserable wrap I'm wearing. We'll leave by the side entrance.

CLAUDE: Have you had a fine time?

MATHILDE: Wonderful! And now I return to ugliness, just like Cinderella.

CLAUDE *(Reproachfully)*: Cinderella left the ball at midnight.

MATHILDE: Don't spoil my pleasant memory. Hurry, now, Claude, and hail a cab.

MUSIC: *Up full and fade out.*

CLAUDE *(Yawns)*: Oh, and to think I have to be at work in another four hours. I could fall into bed fully clothed.

MATHILDE: And I'm going to sleep until early afternoon.

CLAUDE: You're lucky.

MATHILDE: It was such a wonderful ball.

CLAUDE: I wouldn't know.

MATHILDE: I could dance every night of my life. *(She hums a bit of a waltz. Suddenly she stops and gives a sharp cry.)*

CLAUDE: What is the matter?

MATHILDE: I have—I have—I've lost Jeanne's necklace.

CLAUDE: What?

MATHILDE: I have lost Jeanne's necklace.

CLAUDE: How? Impossible!

MATHILDE: Look in my cloak . . . my pockets. *(Pause)* Oh, no.

CLAUDE: See if it's caught in the folds of your dress. *(Pause)* Not there. You're sure you had it when you left the ball?

MATHILDE: Yes, I felt it in the vestibule of the palace. Perhaps I dropped it in the street.

CLAUDE: But if you had we should have heard it fall. It must be in the cab.

MATHILDE: Yes, probably. Did you notice his number?

CLAUDE: No. And you, didn't you notice it?

MATHILDE: No. *(Pause)* Whatever will we do?

CLAUDE: I shall go back on foot over the whole route which we have taken. Perhaps I can find it.

MATHILDE: You must find it.

CLAUDE: I will. Now suppose you go to bed.

MATHILDE: Bed! I couldn't sleep. I'll sit up until you return.

MUSIC: *A doleful theme. Forte and out into:*

SOUND: *Small clock strikes seven times. Door open—close.*

MATHILDE *(Anxiously)*: Claude, you found it. Tell me you have found it.

CLAUDE *(Wearily)*: I went over our route, all the way back to the palace. I didn't find it.

MATHILDE: Perhaps a cleaner will discover it. Whoever does may be honest, and will hold it waiting for us to claim it.

CLAUDE: Perhaps. At least, let us hope so, Mathilde.

MATHILDE: I'm going to bed and see if I can't forget the matter, at least for several hours.

CLAUDE: I'll stay up.

MATHILDE: What good will that do?

CLAUDE: I've got to keep searching.

MUSIC: *Grim. Up and under.*

CLAUDE: Monsieur Sous-Prefect, I've come to report the loss of a valuable diamond necklace.

MUSIC: *Up briefly and under.*

CLAUDE: I wish to place in your newspaper the following advertisement. "Lost . . . a valuable diamond necklace—"

MUSIC: *Up and under.*

CLAUDE: If you are the manager, I wish you to ask each of your cab drivers if they have found a diamond necklace.

MUSIC: *Up full and out.*

MATHILDE: I know you are weary, but there must be something you can do. Claude, I've got to return that necklace to Jeanne.

CLAUDE: Perhaps someone will answer the advertisement, or maybe some cab driver will turn it in to us.

MATHILDE: That is what you said yesterday.

CLAUDE: Then the only thing we can do is for you to write to Jeanne that you have broken the clasp of the necklace and that you are having it mended. That will give us time to turn around. Here, I will dictate it to you. "My dear Jeanne: Please forgive the delay in returning your lovely diamond necklace. . . ."

MUSIC: *A short bridge, cuts in over dialogue. Forte and out.*

MATHILDE: We came to you, Monsieur Lavell, because your name is on the box. Right here, it is.

LAVELL: Yes, Madame, that is my box. And it is a diamond necklace you say?

MATHILDE: A very expensive one, too, I fear.

CLAUDE: The name of the purchaser is Forestier, Paul Forestier.

LAVELL: I do not recall having sold a diamond necklace to such a party.

CLAUDE: But you must have, for this is the box it came in. See—your name.

LAVELL: I will consult my books *(Fading)* and see if I cannot find the name Forestier.

MATHILDE *(Low voice)*: Oh, Claude, I hope he finds the record of the sale, for then he will be able to get another just like it.

CLAUDE: We must replace it, and without further delay. Try to look a bit more pleasant. It may not be as expensive as we believe.

MATHILDE: Look pleasant! I'm so weary I could sleep standing up.

CLAUDE: Don't worry. This will straighten out.

MATHILDE: Here he comes.

CLAUDE: What success, Monsieur Lavell?

LAVELL: I have never had a customer named Forestier.

CLAUDE: But your name is on the box.

LAVELL: It was not I who sold the necklace. I must simply have furnished the box. I am sorry I cannot help you.

MATHILDE: Perhaps you can replace the necklace. We can give you an accurate description.

LAVELL: Unfortunately at present, I have no stock of diamond necklaces. I suggest you go to De Remy, the jeweler on the Palais Royal. Undoubtedly there you will find just what you seek. He has a large stock of diamonds of all kinds, including necklaces. *(Fading)* Here, I will give you a card to him. He is a friend of mine for many years.

DE REMY *(Fading in)*: Would it, perhaps, be one like this?

MATHILDE: N-no, not quite. You agree, Claude?

CLAUDE: It isn't like this.

DE REMY: I have shown you almost everything I have in diamond necklaces. Wait! *(Fading a bit)* I have several others. Perhaps one of them may be that for which you are searching. *(Fading in)* Now, here is one. This one here.

MATHILDE: That's it. Look, Claude.

CLAUDE: Yes, it was like the one you're holding Monsieur De Remy.

DE REMY: Success at last, eh!

MATHILDE: Thank heavens!

CLAUDE: How much?

DE REMY: Let me see the tag. *(Pause)* Mmmm! The price is forty thousand francs.

MATHILDE: Forty—

CLAUDE: Forty thousand!

DE REMY: Expensive, I agree, but remember this is a magnificent necklace. The best matched diamonds, each one protected by a full guarantee.

MATHILDE: But forty thousand francs, is a great deal. We are quite poor. My husband is only a clerk.

DE REMY: I wish I could help you, for I appreciate your plight.

CLAUDE: Couldn't you take less, Monsieur De Remy?

MATHILDE: It would help, if you could. Please, Monsieur De Remy. A little less, perhaps.

DE REMY: It would have to be cash, of course. In that case, I could sell you this for thirty-eight thousand francs.

MATHILDE: Thirty-six. Please!

DE REMY: Thirty-six, it is, then.

CLAUDE: I will have to raise the money.

DE REMY: I am not able to hold it, at least not without a deposit. If some other customer wishes it, I must sell it.

CLAUDE: Hold it for three days, just three days. I will be back with the money, I promise.

DE REMY: You look honest. Very well, I shall hold it for three days. And I will do this, in addition: If you find the original before the end of February, I shall buy this one back for thirty-four thousand francs.

CLAUDE: That is fair, Monsieur De Remy. I shall be back inside of three days with the money.

MUSIC: *A bridge. Forte and out.*

MATHILDE: But where are we going to raise such a sum of money in so short a time? It can't be done.

CLAUDE: The money my father left me in bonds, I'll sell them. They are worth, at present, eighteen thousand francs.

MATHILDE: But that is only half.

CLAUDE: My stamp collection, on a quick sale I can get fifteen hundred francs.

MATHILDE: You've spent years collecting it.

CLAUDE: It goes.

MATHILDE: But even with that, we are still far short of the amount we need.

CLAUDE: I'll borrow the rest.

MATHILDE: From whom? All our friends are poor.

CLAUDE (*Wearily*): From anyone who will lend me even a few francs. I can always go to the moneylenders.

MATHILDE: But they're usurers. They'll charge exorbitant interest.

CLAUDE (*Briefly*): It can't be helped. I have to raise the money. We've got to buy that necklace, and you've got to take it to Jeanne before she gets suspicious.

MUSIC: *Up and out.*

JEANNE (*Rather coldly*) Well, my dear Mathilde, I had started wondering what had become of you. I thought perhaps you were ill, or away on vacation.

MATHILDE: No, I have not been away. I'm too poor for that. You did get my note, I hope.

JEANNE: About the necklace. Yes, I received it some days ago.

MATHILDE: I'm sorry about the clasp, but the jeweler replaced it, and it looks as well as ever.

JEANNE: You've brought it with you?

MATHILDE (*As though fumbling*): Yes, I have it right here. This is it.

JEANNE: It is all right?

MATHILDE: Oh, yes. It is in just as good condition as when I borrowed it.

JEANNE: You seem very ill at ease, Mathilde.

MATHILDE (*Uneasily*): I've been working hard. I'm overtired. Rest will help me. Thank you very much for the loan of the necklace. I—I appreciate the great favor you did me.

JEANNE: You should have returned it sooner. I might have needed it.

MATHILDE: Perhaps I never should have borrowed it.

JEANNE (*Stiffly*): No need to feel that way. You asked a favor and I obliged. That's the difficulty in loaning things to friends; they take offense if you show any apprehension about their return.

MUSIC: *Up and out.*

CLAUDE: Good morning, Monsieur Cote. I have brought the manuscripts, copied neatly, just as you wished.

COTE: Ah, good! (*Reflectively*) Hm, hm! So!

CLAUDE (*Anxiously*): The copying, it is all right?

COTE: Yes, fine, as usual. Your copying is excellent, Loisel. (*Pause*) Why are you waiting. Oh, to be sure! Your pay. Five sous a page. Let me see, I owe you—

CLAUDE: Seven francs even, Monsieur Cote.

SOUND: *Clink of coins separately dropped on table.*

CLAUDE: Thank you, Monsieur Cote.

SOUND: *Clink of coins as Claude scoops them up.*

CLAUDE *(Anxiously)*: Perhaps you have more work for me?

COTE: Not immediately. Perhaps the week after next. I will let you know.

CLAUDE: I have a new address.

COTE: You moved again?

CLAUDE: Yes, Monsieur Cote, the rent on the other place was too high for us to pay.

COTE: How long have you been copying for me, Loisel?

CLAUDE: Going on three—no, four years it is.

COTE: And during the day you work at your regular position?

CLAUDE: Yes, sir, at the Ministry of Public Information.

COTE: You must need money badly, to sit up half the night copying manuscripts for five sous.

CLAUDE: Indeed I do, sir.

COTE: Well, leave your new address and I will have some work for you.

CLAUDE *(Eagerly)*: Thank you again, and if you know of anyone else who requires a similar service, perhaps you might recommend me.

MUSIC: *A dreary theme. Forte and out into:*

SOUND: *Street noises. People calling out. (Note: this is Paris during the late nineteenth century, so do not use any modern transcribed traffic sounds.)*

MONGER [TRADER] *(Calling out)*: Fish! Fresh fish! Nice fresh fish!

MATHILDE *(Her voice is older, harder now)*: How much is carp?

MONGER: Carp! Ah, of course! Here is a nice piece.

MATHILDE: Too large. Give me a smaller piece.

MONGER: Here is a fine piece, just right for you and your children.

MATHILDE: I have no children.

MONGER: Ah, they are now grown up and married.

MATHILDE: Stop wagging your tongue long enough to tell me the price of this carp.

MONGER: This piece will cost three francs.

MATHILDE: Three francs! You are mad! Three francs for this miserable segment of carp. I will give you two francs.

MONGER: But no! It is priced at three francs.

MATHILDE: Here is the money—two francs, you thief. Now wrap it up. Hurry!

MONGER *(Grumbling)*: You drive a hard bargain. I am poor—

MATHILDE *(Cutting in)*: And so am I, and I have no time to waste arguing with you. I have work to do.

MONGER: If I had many customers like you, I would have to close my fish stall and enter bankruptcy.

MUSIC *(Cuts in over street noises): Forte and out into:*

SOUND: *Stiff brush scrubbing floor. It continues at brisk pace.*

MATHILDE *(Over sound and matching the pace of the scrubbing)*: I must get this done before Claude comes home . . . must . . . must . . . must.

SOUND: *Scrubbing continues for a few seconds, and then stops.*

MATHILDE: My arms, they are going to drop off. So tired . . . always tired. Look at me—frowsy hair, red, rough hands just like a scrubwoman . . . lines on my face. Oh, I feel so old, so terribly old and tired. *(Philosophically)* Well, no time to worry about my appearance.

SOUND: *Scrubbing continues faster than ever. Door open slowly and close. (Away.)*

CLAUDE: Good evening, Mathilde.

SOUND: *Scrubbing continues.*

CLAUDE: Mathilde!

SOUND: *Scrubbing out.*

MATHILDE *(Listlessly)*: Good evening, Claude. Sit down and I will get your dinner.

CLAUDE: No hurry. I'm not very hungry.

MATHILDE: I have a surprise. Tonight we have stew.

CLAUDE: Do you recall when even the mention of the word stew used to anger you? Now stew is a luxury.

(Tenderly) Oh, Mathilde, it bothers me so to see you looking so tired, so worn out. And why?

MATHILDE: Because of my vanity and heedlessness. Because for one evening eight years ago I had to pretend I was something I was not. What would have happened to us if I had not lost that necklace?

CLAUDE *(Gently)*: Who knows.

MATHILDE: Life is so strange. How little a thing is needed for us to be lost or to be saved.

CLAUDE: Only this morning I figured that it will be another two years before I have completely repaid the money I borrowed.

MATHILDE: Ten years of slavery for both of us. Suffering, no new clothes or holiday journeys; ten long years of doing without even the simple

comforts. *(Softly)* And sometimes when I am alone working here, I think. I think of that wonderful, gay evening of long ago when I was so beautiful, and when I danced and danced to that music. *(Crying)* And then I immediately put those thoughts from my mind.

CLAUDE: You're crying, Mathilde.

MATHILDE: Yes, I cry for myself, for having been such a lightheaded and foolish woman. But it was such a beautiful evening.

MUSIC: *Up and out into:*

SOUND: *A Sunday in park pattern: children laughing and chattering.*

CLAUDE *(Breathing in)*: This air is so clean and the sun so strong. Sunday in Champs Élysées. A bit of Heaven!

MATHILDE: We should come here more often, Claude. It is good for us to see other people enjoying themselves. See those little boys sailing their boat. How happy they are.

CLAUDE: I hope they never grow up. You know, I feel just like an old man.

MATHILDE: But you are not.

CLAUDE: My hair is thinning and what I have left is gray.

MATHILDE: Time changes all of us outwardly and inwardly. Ten years ago if you had told me that I would take a Sunday stroll clad in such a gown, I would have hooted at you. Now I wear it and don't care what anyone says about my appearance. I have learned much these past ten years, very much. *(Pause)* Claude, what is the matter?

CLAUDE: That lady approaching.

MATHILDE: It's Jeanne Forestier.

CLAUDE *(Hurriedly)*: Come let us leave.

MATHILDE: Why should we?

CLAUDE: I cannot bear her face.

MATHILDE: Well, I can. Now I feel perfectly free to speak what is on my mind.

CLAUDE *(Fading a bit)*: Mathilde, come back. Mathilde.

MATHILDE: Good day, Jeanne.

JEANNE: But madame, I do not know you. You mistake me for someone else.

MATHILDE: No, I have made no mistake. I am Mathilde Loisel.

JEANNE: Oh, my poor Mathilde! How you've changed!

MATHILDE: Yes, I have had days hard enough, since I've seen you, days wretched enough—and all because of you!

JEANNE: Because of me! How so?

MATHILDE: Do you remember the diamond necklace which you lent me to wear at the ministerial ball?

JEANNE: Yes. Well?

MATHILDE: Well, I lost it.

JEANNE: What do you mean? You brought it back.

MATHILDE: I brought you back another just like it. And for this we have been ten years paying. You can understand that it was not easy for us, us who had nothing. At last it is ended, and I am very glad.

JEANNE: You say that you brought back a necklace of diamonds to replace mine?

MATHILDE: Yes. You never noticed it, then! They were very like, almost identical.

JEANNE: Oh, my poor Mathilde! Why, my necklace was paste. It was worth at most five hundred francs!

MUSIC: *Curtain theme. Forte and out.*

Reading Check

1. How does the narrator describe Mathilde?
2. List several quotations that show us that Claude's outlook differs from Mathilde's.
3. How is Mathilde's outlook evidenced in her actions?
4. What discovery does Mathilde make at the end of the story?
5. How do the opening Scripture verses apply to Mathilde's discovery?

Shago had a keen, sharp eye, an eye that allowed him not only to pitch a baseball with deadly accuracy but also enabled him to discern the subtle changes of a summer sun. Unfortunately, Shago's friends were not as quick to discern subtle changes.

Shago

James Pooler

When the summer sun moves its heat a little low in the sky and there's a stir out of doors in the late afternoon's hush, I wonder if the Indian boys still gather under the bluff.

The bluff must be much the same. A gash of naked sand and stone upright for fifty feet and then the slope of green junipers and pines going to cover the top of the hill. And at the foot of the bluff the flat field where the marsh and quack grass grow, fed by the waves that in storms reach up to the very foot of the bluff. And, toward the lake, all those huge rocks, too big for man to move, and reasonless, stand in strange, silent rows for the waves to break on their outer sentinels.

That field was a fine one with the high wind singing in the pines of the bluff overhead and the colder wind outdistancing the waves to come across the rocks and freshen us at our play. Always around us the steady roar of the waves breaking and their hiss as they ran up the slope of sand to die.

The Indian lads must be there, and I know the island boys are. There, with

the ebbing of the day and before cows must be sought in their roaming, the lads must join in their game.

We used a ball hard-woven of fisher twine with a rock of rubber for its heart. It was a grand hard ball and our bats were good—they came polished off the Michigan shore, but some of us fancied the island ones cut and honed of our own woods. Shawn Laferty owned the gloves which the catcher and first baseman wore. And the bases were white driftwood.

Once we had a quarter ball, which one of the resort men bought us, but we played only a few innings before it got lopsided and sorry bits of wood and string flew from it, and we went back to our own wound ball.

It was Shago White, who had a curve that would break your back, who wound the balls. Shago lived in Indian Town, though his mother once was of the Irish. Shago would take twine from the fishing shanties and, with the old bits of hard rubber we carefully saved, wind a ball that was as round as any of the store kind.

When first I played I remember Shago's pitching well. He was not much older than I, but had been playing longer, and already he was a pitcher for at least a few innings of every game. He had feathers for feet, a strong arm, a sure eye. It always was Shago who was picked first if you won the choosing up.

The first time I came to bat, Shago was pitching. It was sick of heart, I was, and shaking and in great fear that I would make a fool of myself and the others would laugh. I still see Shago grinning there and whirling his arm like a windmill and the ball shooting at me and I making a helpless swing, a full ninny! And how I stood, decided to wait the next one out, and Shago blazing another one past me and the umpire calling it a strike.

And I spit on my hands as the older boys did and glared out at Shago. I'll never know if it was my luck or skill, or the kindness of Shago, that I hit the next ball and got on base. For I remember Shago rolled on the sand and laughed and laughed and so did I— except I stood still on the base. I felt a man.

It would have done you who love boys good to see Shago. He was lean and sharp like a knife blade, and there seemed to be the glint of steel in his eyes. But his mouth was merry and was quicker to laugh or shout than any other. There was a strange Indian madness on him, too.

I remember well the day that we had two men on the bases and Shago stopped his windup, pegged the ball to the catcher, and was away running fast to the foot of the bluff. He went up it like smoke up a chimney, only more quietly, and we saw him reach the summit, go swiftly along its edge, pounce, and hold up for us to see a young puppy, one of Pegh Mahone's brood, that might have tumbled down the bluff.

And again a day that the sun in strange complexion was dyeing all the sky and the hill and the rocks beside us, even our faces, with a grand blush, and Shago stopped the game. He would do it often when his side was way ahead by drawing back his arm and throwing the ball far over the catcher's head. It was what he did this evening and ran to a big rock right at the water's edge. We followed Shago up on the rock and sat beside him, perched like gulls. First he pointed out into the deep water where, just below the calm surface, you could see rocks big enough to farm, and then he pointed to the sun.

"A blood sun," he said.

"A red sunset, a fine day tomorrow," John Gallagher answered.

"You lie there," said Shago. "A blood sun." And our eyes followed his over the bluff and the world that had grown a strange hue and still.

"A bad sun," said Shago. "Any tug not in by midnight will end on rocks like those. The sun says so."

We all grew still and looked out at the mountain rocks in the lake. Many of us had fathers who were fishermen, and we had some dread of the lake. And we listened to the little waves patting the big rocks. Color was over everything. It was Shago who spoke first.

"We'll have to hurry for the cows," he said. "They'll be restless, and it will be no night to be out late looking for them."

We went together up over the bluff, and toward the cows in the fields and the woods to hurry them home with clods and sticks. There was little shouting that night, for a mood was on us, and when we'd eaten we went to the docks and in the early night counted the tugs. They all were home.

That night the winds quarreled and slammed water on the island from all sides. You could hear the boom of water and the scream of wind when you first awoke the next morning. There were no ball games, for the waves poured

through the rocks, up to the foot of the bluff. Beyond, out in deep water where Shago had pointed, you could see between the rolling waves the heads of rocks four times the size of a tug. Big rocks which should not have been lifting their heads up into our world.

It was in my third year of playing there afternoons below the bluff that I saw something strange in Shago. He would squint long from the box before he threw the ball. It always came fast and with a sweep, but we were learning that if we waited, often we got a walk. As the summer went, they came oftener. Shago, too, was losing his skill at the plate and not hitting as well.

With the next spring we knew. Shago's eyes were red, and his pitching was hard, fast, and with great curves that did not seem to find the plate. Once in a while Shago would steady and pitch and his side never would lose, but by September he was a bad pitcher, a poor hitter, and had taken to playing with the fielders.

That winter, I remember, his mother bought him glasses from a man in Charlevoix, but because we laughed at him with the glint of glass on his dark face he only wore them going home.

The summer that came after found Shago early at the bench, but he no longer pitched. He pretended that he had no liking for that, and a custom grew up that whatever side took Shago always asked him if he would pitch. He would say "No," and would turn to go out into left field close to the bluff where the ball, if hit, never went far. His sight was such that he could not field well, and even when they would pitch easy to him he could not hit.

As fall came on, Shago, who had a pride to him, would come out late after the game had started, pretending he had been busy for his mother. He would sit with the little boys, who hoped to get into the game if we ran short.

School came to an end for him, too. The nuns, soon learning that sight was going from Shago, told his mother that she need not make him study any more, but to send him to school to listen. Shago went for a while, but after they asked him questions a couple of times to see if he were following the work, and he knew none of the answers, he would come no more. We saw him less and less. We found he had gone to work for one of the fishermen, cleaning hooks, which took nimble fingers and which one might do with only a sense of touch.

It was early spring, and a few plucky [spirited] crickets already had started their fiddling when Shago came slowly down the single street of St. James to stop in front of us. We stood in the light of the store where candy was sold and where we often met.

In Shago's hands there were five baseballs. They were wondrously tight in their winding and each as round as ever a baseball was. There never had been the like of such balls on the island.

"You'll be starting the game soon," said Shago. "So I got these ready."

We took them in our hands. We all told Shago how fine they were and thanked him. He stood curling his fingers around one wound so tightly you could feel where strand lay next to strand.

"But aren't you going to bat one?" Shago asked. "I think they have a fine fly to them."

We stood helpless and looked from one to the other. Why were we so thick of head we could not have said we would go for a bat and so changed his thoughts to other things? But we stood there as helpless as once we were at bat when Shago was in fine form. It was Laferty who blurted it out:

"We can't, Shago," he said.

It was night.

Reading Check

1. How does the author describe Shago?
2. List several of Shago's actions that reveal to us his ability to keenly observe his surroundings.
3. Why does Shago stop pitching and become a fielder?
4. What reason does he give for this change?
5. What discovery do his friends make at the end of the story?

All the Cliffside players were quick to say that Joe Woods was the most valuable shooter on the basketball team. But the coach's definition of "valuable" differed greatly from the teams', and this difference was bound to cause trouble.

Pivot Play

Joseph Olgin

Joe Woods, six-foot-one captain of Cliffside's basketball team; looked at his pal Fred Casper, and winked. He nodded toward the blackboard, where the new coach was drawing diagrams of plays.

Coach Dever's voice was earnest. "And so, Joe, your height should make you a good pivot man. It will be your job to get the ball; whirl to shake off your opponent, and then feed it to one of your teammates. You are not to do the shooting for baskets yourself."

The other players looked at Joe, their center and a perfect shot.

"It sounds good, Joe," whispered Bill Daly, a short boy who played guard. "With your long arms you're a cinch to get the ball. And you're so tall they can't reach it as you turn to make the pass.

But wait till our new coach sees how you make baskets! Then he'll forget all about that 'feeding stuff.' "

Joe was busy with his thoughts.

Humph! Feeding! He hadn't been in the Conference last year because of an ability to pass the ball on to someone else. Not at all! Everyone knew that he was a dead shot. And from either side of the basket, too!

Coach Dever suddenly shot a question at him. "Now do you understand how I want you to play, Joe?"

"Sure, sure," said Joe lightly. "It's better to have five fellows scoring than to depend on just one."

The coach seemed to relax a little. If Joe cooperated with him, he'd have little trouble in installing his new system of play.

"That's all for today, boys," he said. "But we've lots to do. First game's in two weeks."

The first game of the season was only five minutes old when the Cliffside spectators were on their feet cheering. Joe Woods, their star performer was showing that during the summer's vacation he had forgotten nothing about how to make baskets. The score was already ten to two, and all five of Cliffside's baskets were of Joe's making. Rockdale, the opposing team, had called time out.

Joe felt great as he approached Coach Dever on the side line. He certainly had shown the coach that pivot playing, though all right for practice, wasn't needed in a real game. But the coach didn't seem convinced. His face was set in stern lines.

"Look, Joe," he snapped, "you should have passed to Skip on that last play—and to Frank Thomas twice before that."

Joe's temper rose. "I made the baskets, didn't I? and they're what count!"

The coach turned abruptly and beckoned to a player on the bench. "Stan, go in and take Joe's place."

Sitting on the bench, Joe glumly watched Stan, who was only five-feet-six, try to handle the difficult job of being pivot man. Cliffside's playing suffered. When the gun sounded for the half, the score stood at 25-23. Rockdale was only one basket behind.

During the intermission the coach took Joe aside. "Look, Joe," he said, "I'm giving it to you straight. With the fellows we have on the team this year, we can win the championship if we play

right. You're the one who can bring it in—if you'll work with me."

But Joe was still angry. "What's the use of my feeding the ball to the others when I can score with it myself?" he argued. "Rockdale's center is five inches shorter than I am. He can't stop me."

"That's true—*tonight*," agreed Coach Dever. "But it won't always be that way. Sooner or later, we'll run into someone who'll be able to hold you. And then we'll be licked if you are the only one who can make baskets. Understand?"

Joe started in the second half, and the Cliffside crowd cheered. But their cheers turned to groans as Joe, unaccustomed to his new role, played poorly. Rockdale took the lead in the third quarter; but in the fourth, Cliffside came storming back to ring up four baskets. The game ended at 50-46, with Cliffside ahead.

But there was no rejoicing in the Cliffside dressing room. Joe was the most disgruntled of all. "We'll be lucky

if we win half our games this year," he muttered.

"Let's rebel," growled Fred Casper. "Coach says we can play his way or turn in our suits. But after a few games with the second-string fellows, he'd be glad to have us back—on our own terms, too."

Joe thought about Fred's proposal for a long moment, then shook his head. "No, Fred," he said, "We can't let the school down. We'll play coach's way till he sees for himself that he's all wrong."

Joe did his best to adapt himself to the new style; but as the season progressed, he became more and more resentful. When Cliffside barely nosed out its two weakest competitors in the Conference, he exploded.

"We should have beaten them by thirty points!" he raged.

"We beat them by twenty-five last year," muttered Fred. Then he perked up. "Well, we beat them anyway—so what's the difference?"

All the difference in the world, thought Joe. His own dreams of breaking the individual player's scoring record, for instance.

Joe's feelings reached a new low when Fred, and later Skip, passed him in making scores. He was now third man from the top—and if this kept up he'd probably be the last.

Gradually the other members on the team stopped grumbling about the new style of playing.

"It's not bad at all," cried Bill after Cliffside trounced Bay City, a strong rival. "Cheers! We're going places this year!"

"Humph," thought Joe. "Not bad for you fellows! You've scored more points this fall than you did in the last two years combined."

In the next game, against York, Joe yielded to an overpowering temptation to get back into the scoring race. He passed up several chances to feed the ball to his companions and made baskets himself, using his favorite left-hand shots.

Coach Dever promptly yanked him out of he game. And this time, to Joe's surprise, there was no howl of dismay from his teammates or from the watching crowd.

People certainly forget you in a hurry, thought Joe. Bitterly, he realized that he could not disobey orders any more. It was Coach's way—or nothing.

One thing in particular increased Joe's heartache—the newspaper articles about Bob Marvin, Fairview's new center. Fairview, a neighboring town, was Cliffside's strongest opponent in the Conference. Young Marvin's scoring average of an amazing 28 points a game was far ahead of Joe's old record of 22 points.

Joe agonized as he read each new account of Bob's skill. All Joe had to show this year was a miserable six-points average.

Finally, the day of the Conference championship game arrived. And Cliffside, having defeated all the others, was face to face with Fairview. When the visiting team came trotting out on the floor, Joe stared in amazement. Their center, red-headed Bob Marvin, was at least six-feet-four. For the first time in his life, Joe felt dwarfed.

The game started with fast action. Bob took a pass on the right, about five feet out from the basket. Joe, playing

behind him, leaped up desperately as Bob whirled and aimed for the basket. But Joe's leap was useless, for Bob's longer arms held the ball out of reach—and it zoomed into the basket.

When Cliffside did get the ball, Joe fed it to Fred for the shot; but Bob reached over and grabbed it easily from the shorter boy. The tall youth seemed to be everywhere! In spite of Cliffside's best effort, Bob sank four more baskets in the next three minutes. The score was now 10-0.

Cliffside called for a time out. Joe was mad. He felt he was being made a fool of. Talk about a one-man show! The Fairview star player *proved* that Coach Dever was wrong. Five men

against one was "the bunk" if the one always got the ball. Grimly, Joe determined to get back into the scoring picture. The coach wouldn't dare take him out. He was Cliffside's only chance!

When play resumed, Fred Casper got the ball, and being strongly guarded, passed it on to Joe. Joe whirled and aimed for the basket; but before he could complete the shot, Bob Marvin had leaped up and batted the ball down. Three more times Joe attempted to shoot, but each time Bob calmly smothered the shot.

Joe's heart sank. Bob could block all his shots, and he couldn't stop the big Fairview center at all! Suddenly Joe was glad that Coach Dever *had* installed the new system. He knew Bob couldn't stop him from feeding the ball to the other Cliffside players. And if they ganged up on Bob, they could make him run around a lot to get the ball. The killing pace would soon tell on the tall star-player.

As the game progressed, Fairview's scoring began to fall off. The ball sped from one Cliffside player to another, and some of them found the opportunity to make a few lucky shots. The first half ended 36-26, with Fairview in the lead.

Between halves, Coach Dever came up to Joe and patted him on the back. Then he ordered a new strategy.

"We'll have two of our men cover Bob," he said. "Joe, you play right behind him. And, Frank, you stay right in front. Keep a careful watch, and don't let Bob's teammates get the ball to him."

The coach's plan worked fairly well as the second half got under way. From force of habit, the Fairview players kept trying to pass the ball to Bob so that he would make the shots. And with him so heavily guarded, they found it difficult to do this. Time after time the ball was seized from them by Cliffside, who then began passing it back and forth from one Cliffside player to another.

Gradually Cliffside's score went up, and at the end of the third quarter the score was 45-44!

As the fourth quarter progressed, Bob Marvin became nearly frantic as his inability to escape from the two Cliffside men who were guarding him. The swift pace was wearing him down, too. Yet, when he did get the ball, his shots were true. And three minutes before closing time the score was tied— 60-60. Cliffside took time out.

Coach Dever's voice was quiet as he gave his final instructions. "This time, Joe, don't feed off. I think I can read Bob's mind. He's giving up his idea of shooting. He intends to keep an eye on you and prevent you from making passes. This time just pretend to pass; then instead of completing the pass, shoot for the basket. You might succeed in fooling him."

It was Cliffside's ball, and the clock was ticking off the last seconds of play. Fred fired the ball to Joe. Joe faked a pass as Fred cut around him to the left. Bob, fooled by the motion, leaped over to prevent completion of the pass. Then, Joe, whirling quickly, aimed and shot for the basket. The shot was good! A roar rose from the crowd as the ball dropped, giving Cliffside a two-point lead.

Fairview threw themselves into the play as if their very lives depended on it. But Bob, nervous and weary, missed the basket. Joe pounced on the falling ball, and started a brisk series of passes that continued until the closing gun sounded. The game was over!

The Cliffside fans went wild, and Joe had difficulty in reaching the locker room. There, the congratulations continued until Jim Arnold, sports writer for the *Post*, hurried into the room.

"Got some inside stuff for you," he cried spotting Joe. "You've been voted the Conference's most valuable player. You've broken the record for 'assisting plays.' I never saw anything like the work you did for the good of your team!"

Joe stared, then blinked to clear a sudden mist from his eyes.

"Come on," cried the reporter, "say something for the press."

"That's easy," smiled Joe. "Five men can beat one man any time. Right, team?"

"Right!" roared the new Conference champions in chorus.

Reading Check

1. What is Joe's attitude at the opening of the story?
2. How does he display this attitude in the opening game?
3. What is the new coach's response to Joe's actions in the first game?
4. How do you think Joe's attitude hinders him and his teammates?
5. As a result of the Fairview game, what discoveries do Joe and his teammates make?

Though the following short story and poem differ in form, you will find that both deal with the theme of revenge and that both reveal a very personal discovery.

You've Got to Learn

Robert Murphy

It was a little after dawn when the big dog otter's broad, whiskered muzzle broke the calm and flawless mirror of the lake. A widening circle of ripples slid away from him, and he reared half length from the water to look about. The near shore was dim and quiet; on the far shore, the spruce and hemlock made a dark band against the paling sky. The otter whistled, cocked his head to the rolling echoes, and dropped back into the water again. He was an animal of great and happy vitality [energy]; he began diving and rolling, with movements as effortless and fluid as a dance, hardly disturbing the calmness of the water.

Presently, he vanished as silently as he had appeared. A swift line of bubbles followed him toward the banks; he dived deeper for the submerged entrance of the burrow, followed it above water line, and in the dark den bounded by roots found his mate with the one pup beside her, and waked them both. There was a short, good-natured scuffle among the three, and then they pushed the pup before them down the tunnel. When they all appeared on the lake's surface, the pup tried to climb upon his mother's back and ride. She shook him off and ducked him when he whimpered, and they began to hunt the bank. They hunted with great thoroughness, from surface to bottom, exploring every hole and cranny, every root hollow and crack among the stones, finding a few crawfish and an occasional frog. These were some easy kills and they let the pup make most of them. His little belly began to bulge, and his mother, growing hungry, left them to catch a pickerel in deeper water and bring it in. They climbed out on the bank and shared it; then, gleaming and sleek from the water, they rolled and galloped about, hissing at one another with mock ferocity.

Day stole in upon them. Out on the lake, the trailing mists of night thinned and vanished; the serrated [uneven] line of spruces on the distant shore took on depth and shape in the strengthening light. As the long rays of the sun fell on the otters, they gave over their play, cleaned their fur, and went into the water again. They continued up the lake toward one of the streams which fed it. When they reached the stream mouth, the mother and the pup swung away along the shore line. The otter remembered the great brown trout which lived above the bend of the stream, and left them. The trout was old and wise, and

the otter had missed it so many times that the contest between them had become a fascinating game.

It was characteristic of the otter that he didn't go directly, his mind fixed on the trout. He zigzagged to and fro across the stream, playing as he went. When he came out of the water to cross the rocks at the first shallows, he heard the distant barking of a dog, up the lake in the direction his mate and the pup had gone. He hesitated for a moment and went on.

He rounded the bend carefully, and began his stalk of the trout. He knew it would be lying like a shadow a little above the sandy bottom in the rushing green gloom of the pocket under a great gray rock. It would be facing upstream, and he would gain an advantage by coming up from the rear. He stretched out full length and, paddling gently and slowly with his forepaws, slid through the water like a stealthy shadow, close to the bank and halfway to the bottom. He came to the corner of the rock and paused, sank until his belly softly scraped the sand, and became one with the bottom's shadows; then sinuous [winding] as a snake, he began to flow around the rock. He saw the trout several yards away, hanging motionless, and tensed for the spring.

The trout caught a slight movement of the otter's shadowy form in the tail of its eye. It drifted a little farther out and swung quartering to him; the otter arched his back swiftly, thrust against the water and darted in. An explosive burst of power sent the trout to the surface; the otter's teeth scored a thin bloody line on its side and the power of its tail stroke rolled him over and over. The trout reached the surface and shattered it by a leap, and the otter righted himself and breached [broke the surface] for air. Although a wild chase upstream and through the rapids was

as much a part of the game as the stalk, this time the otter didn't follow. He lay for a moment resting, his sleek head dappled by the sunlight falling through the leaves, and then remembered the barking of the dog.

His game with the trout was over. He started swiftly downstream and came to its mouth. Good fishing water was there, but he didn't hesitate; he turned up the lake. As he rounded the bend, he saw, fifty yards away, the head of his mate break water a good distance from the shore. The pup was just sliding down the bank; and, as the otter watched, the brown-and-white shape of the dog ran out of the hemlocks toward the pup and snapped at it. The pup was startled and confused; it scrambled between the dog's legs, turned again, and leaped from the bank. The dog leaped after it with a great splash; and, because the pup had lost time and couldn't get out of the shallows, the dog's long jaw closed on it and it was tossed into the air.

The otter was moving before the dog left the bank, swimming with desperate speed. As the pup curved into the air, a boy ran out on the bank, yelling, and although the otter avoided man above any other creature, he paid no attention to the boy now. He reached the dog a little before his mate, as it leaped for the falling pup, and, rising beneath it, fastened upon its throat. The female swirled away from them, getting behind the pup and driving it before her out into the lake.

The dog reared to free its throat, but the otter overbalanced it, fighting with deadly coolness to get it into deeper water. He was all about it, attacking and slipping away with disconcerting swiftness always maneuvering it a little farther out. The boy on the bank realized this; he grabbed a branch to use as a club, and, jumping from the bank, began to splash toward them. The otter saw the boy coming and pulled the dog into deeper water. The dog tried wildly to free itself, but the otter fastened implacably [relentlessly] on its haunches, pulled it down and entangled it in a pile of brush on the bottom. The dog struggled desperately in a world alien to it, but in which the otter was at home. But it was trapped; the air in its lungs fled in silver bubbles to the surface, and the otter struck again.

Standing up to his chest in the water, Andy Gates stared in helpless anguish

at the spot where the dog had gone down. He saw the bubbles burst to the surface, and, a short time later, a swirl far out where the otter breached for air as it followed its mate and the pup. At first he couldn't believe that the dog wouldn't come up again. But time drew out and realization finally came upon him; he dropped the branch he was holding, his fists clenched at his sides and his blue eyes filled with tears. The world about him was suddenly a new and terrible place. He forgot that the dog had been brash and foolishly quarrelsome, that no one had ever been able to teach it anything, and that it had usually been a nuisance. All that he remembered was his brother, standing by the gate before he left for the South Pacific, saying, "Take care of the pup, Andy. We'll make a bird dog of him when I get back."

He didn't realize that Joe, who knew the dog would never amount to anything, had said that to make them feel closer to each other for a moment and hold off the threatening tears, to make the parting easier for them both. The dog was a trust Joe had placed upon him, his most immediate link with his brother, and he had let it be killed. He turned and stumbled out of the water, tears blurring his sight. When his feet found the hard-packed surface of the path, he started along it toward home, stumbling a little now and then. There was an aching emptiness within him, an emptiness which seemed to have swallowed up all his strength; halfway up the long hill, he had to stop, and stood panting, unconscious of the dry fragrance of sun-warmed hemlock on the morning air.

He stopped crying after a while, and the world slowly came back to him. He grew aware of the birds that moved about him, the leaf shadows on the path, and the slow movement of clouds across the sky. But he didn't go on. He sat down beside the path, dry-eyed now, but the emptiness hadn't gone, and he saw his surroundings as though from a great distance. Time stopped as his mind tried to rationalize the dog's death and soften the shock of it. The afternoon was growing late when he crossed the top of the hill and saw the farm in the little valley below, the big barn and the sprawling house among the willows, the file of ducks moving up from the stream shining white in the lowering sun, the cows coming in, and his father walking slowly between the house and the barn.

His father saw him and waited with his hands tucked into the top of his Levis. Gates was a kindly and unhurried man; he looked at the boy's face and didn't mention the chores that he'd done himself.

"Trouble, Andy?" he asked.

The boy's chin trembled. "Nicky," he said. "There was an otter—" He couldn't go on. He began to cry again, and suddenly went to his father as he hadn't done for years, and leaned against him, crying. "He went after the little one," he said, shaking with sobs, "and the big one drowned him. And Joe—" He couldn't talk about Joe.

"Joe would understand it, boy," his father said, sliding an arm around him. "Joe would know you couldn't help it."

"I was keeping him for Joe," Andy said. "Joe left him with me. He was Joe's and mine." He began to cry violently again.

"Joe's and mine," he repeated, remembering Joe at the gate, going away. "I'll kill him!" he burst out, thumping his father's broad chest.

"I'll find him and kill him!"

The man started to speak and checked himself, realizing the futility of words. The boy was extraordinarily moved; it was useless to talk against an emotion so deep that he could only guess at it. Time would have to smooth it out—time and what patient understanding he could give. The man was silent for a long time, holding the boy in the crook of his arm.

"Supper, Andy," he said finally. "Get ready for supper, boy."

"I don't want any supper, dad," Andy said. "I-I couldn't eat any supper."

"All right," Gates said. "Go along up to your room, then. Go up the front stairs. I'll tell mother you won't be down."

The boy went into the house; after waiting for a few minutes. Gates went around to the back door and into the warm kitchen. Mrs. Gates was taking a pie from the oven. She looked around, smiled, and straightened up to put the pie on top of the stove. She was small and very neat; her movements were deft and quick, and her eyes were blue like the boy's.

"Andy won't be down, Helen," Gates said. "We'd better eat without him."

"Why?" she asked. "What's the matter?"

"Well," Gates said. He took off his hat, hung it behind the door and thought a moment. "That fool dog," he said finally, "got himself killed by an otter. There was a young one, I think, and he went for it. Andy is—I've never seen

him so worked up. Joe must have said something about taking care of the dog, and Andy thinks he's let Joe down. He's going to kill the otter, he says."

"But it's not like him," she said. "He doesn't just kill things, Harry."

"No," Gates said. "He's not a cruel boy."

"You'll have to talk to him" she said. "I don't want him to be that way. Vengeful like, I mean."

"It's not revenge," Gates said. "It's— he's—" He shook his head, irritated by his inarticulateness [inability to speak]. "This is a deep thing, Helen. He'll have to work it out himself. Maybe he'll kill that otter, but I hope not. If he kills it, then I'll have to talk to him."

She looked at him, puzzled. "What do you mean, Harry?"

"That's the trouble," he said, exasperated. "I don't know what I mean. I can't say, I just feel it. Let's eat, shall we?"

"All right," she said, and began to fill their plates. Upstairs, the boy lay on his bed. The picture of Joe in his uniform smiled at him from the bureau, but he had stopped looking at it. He felt that he couldn't look at it again until he'd found the otter. As his father had said, he wasn't a cruel boy, but all his emotions confirmed the decision, made so suddenly, that the otter must pay with its life for the life of the dog. The justice of the matter, the fact that the otter had been defending the pup, never occurred to him. Many plans went through his mind, but there was no pleasure, no anticipation of exciting sport, connected with any of them.

He went about his hunting with a singleness of purpose unusual in a boy, with a definite and unvarying schedule. First he'd do the chores, carefully and thoroughly, then get his old single-shot 22 rifle and go out. At first, he spent a lot of time at the lake, hiding near the place where the dog had been drowned. He knew, from remembered bits of Gate's talk, that otters didn't stay in one place, but made a wide, periodic circle about the ponds and streams of the countryside. Sooner or later, he thought, they'd come past him again. He spent days hidden among the hemlocks, and, although he learned a great deal about other animals and birds, he never saw the otters.

The thought came to him finally that they might have passed near dawn, before he got there, or after dusk, when he couldn't see them or had left for home. For several days, disappointment took all the energy out of him; he stayed at home, and his mother thought, with relief, that he'd given up.

"I'm glad it's over, Harry," he said to Gates. "It wasn't like a boy to act like that, going wherever he went, so regular all the time. It was more like a funny little old man."

But Gates had been quietly watching the boy, and he shook his head. "No," he said. "He's not through yet. He's just trying to get away from the place."

Gates was right; the boy was deciding that he would have to move about, to find the otters' route and intercept them somewhere. The place where the dog had died had held him through a wistful, boyish hope that somehow it might come back again. But the bond weakened; reality came closer to him than it had ever come before, and, as hope died, some of his boyishness died with it. He finally broke away from the place and made his first circuit of the lake.

He went too fast at first and found nothing. The otters left very little indication of their passing along the shore line—a few fish scales and bones in widely separated places, a single rare pad mark in damp ground not covered by leaves or vines. On his first trip up the shore he found nothing. Slowing down and going very carefully, he found faint sign at last, and knew how painstakingly he would have to search from then on. He found the place where they left the lake, the stream they used, and how far they followed before leaving it.

In time he knew, between the actual points where they touched and guesses at the routes which connected these points, the otters' entire twenty-five-mile circuit of the country. It was an achievement in woodcraft which few men could have accomplished, because few men would have had the patience or the time. He had covered a tremendous amount of country; he was well scratched by briers, but he was brown and strong, and had filled out surprisingly.

He changed, little by little, during those weeks. The boyish heedlessness with which he had formerly moved through the woods was gone. He grew somewhat like an Indian, a part of the woods rather than an alien presence, drifting quietly about with a mind empty of thought, but blank and clean for the impressions which flowed into it. Time ceased to exist for him. He took no more account of hours than a squirrel, and learned the causes of sounds and the little chains of circumstance which stem from them—the techniques of the hunters and the defenses of the hunted. He saw young grouse freeze and blend with the leaves when the shadow of a hawk swung over them; he watched the steps by which a litter of young foxes learned to catch mice. The play of life about him increased with his skill in seeing it, but his understanding of it and his growing sympathy with it were both completely subconscious until his adventure with the lynx [a type of wildcat].

He had found its tracks several times. They seemed to be near the places where he had walked or hidden, and he grew curious. He gave over the otters for a time and hunted it, and found that it was stalking him. He spent a good deal of time in the thick hemlock it liked best; finally, he went through this woods noisily, backtracked with great care, and hid in a very thick place.

A long time went by before he saw a movement, an indistinct blur as the pale fawn-colored fur slipped across a patch of sunlight. It came closer, silently, never distinct in the thicket; and then it was standing in a little opening not thirty feet away, the yellow eyes staring at him, the big, soft paws tense, and the tufted ears cocked. There was a good deal of wild power in it, but he never thought of being afraid. It stood regarding him, poised, unblinking and feral [untamed], framed against the wild tangle of the thicket, but without menace. He smiled, and there suddenly seemed to come upon it a look, an expression, of shame that it had been outmaneuvered and taken in. It made a little sound, turned, and, with great care for its dignity, moved off and vanished.

For the first time, he realized how much a part of his life the otters had become and how much he liked them. He realized, too, how clear and simple their reasons for action were, even when they killed.

His thought naturally came to the otters, and swung quickly away, but the fact that he had almost looked upon them sympathetically confused him. He got up, puzzled and a little ashamed, and went home. The disturbing questions which came to him refused to be dismissed. His father was alone in the kitchen; he looked up and saw that the boy was troubled.

"Yes, son?" he asked.

"Dad," he began, knowing that his father would help him, "the otters—"

Just then, his mother came in. "There's a letter from Joe for you, Andrew," she said. "I put it in your room."

His father watched the swift change of his expression, the closing of his mind against the question, with regret. "I wish you hadn't mentioned that letter, mother," he said after the boy left. "I

wish you'd hidden it. I think he's seen something he liked about those otters, and it was about to change his mind."

"Oh, I'm so sorry," she said. "I'm so sorry, Harry. Do you think—"

"I think it's too late," Gates said. "He's right back now where he was before."

✓The uneasiness which at first had been like a formless shadow in the old dog otter's brain was sharper now, for he encountered the man-smell which evoked [to draw out] it more frequently. To be followed was a new experience to him, and he didn't know what to make of it. It had not been difficult to avoid the infrequent and casual encounters all animals have with man sooner or later; his senses were superior to theirs, and vigilance and care were all that was necessary. He saw or heard or scented them and got out of the way; they passed and were gone, and places which held evidence of their presence were better left alone. But this was different; the smell waited in many places for him, clinging to the underbrush or the banks. His temper grew short with constant watchfulness, and he began to avoid the daylight hours.

The female didn't take well to the curtailed activity either. She was of a more casual temperament than her mate; she had never, as he had long ago, been caught in a trap and nearly drowned. She had not felt the blind terror of it nor lost two toes; her brain wasn't marked by an experience impossible to forget. She chafed [became annoyed] at being quiet in the dank [damp] blackness of a bankside den when she knew that the world was filled

with sunshine and freedom and sport a few feet away. She remembered so many happy places—gloomy thickets they went through between streams where a complexity of fine scents lingered and birds flashed in and out of shadow; deep pools below falls where trout hid among the sunken rocks; long, easy stretches of lazily sparkling water, and precipitous [steep] banks where the three of them made slides and plunged down them until they were too weary for anything but lying happily in the sun.

She grew morose [gloomy] as they all did. Their rollicking vitality, with its urge toward ceaseless activity and play, was frustrated and turned against them. They bickered and snarled at one another.

But this retreat, which would eventually have discouraged the ordinary hunter, was doomed to failure with the boy. All his determination and effort were concentrated solely upon them, and because they could not exist by moving about altogether in the dark, it was inevitable that he find them. The impulse to change his range came to the old otter many times, but he resisted it. The old range was home, familiar and somehow comforting; the memories of his life along its banks and streams were deeply etched into his brain, and they held him there.

Clouds were beginning to cover the late-afternoon sun when the boy found the pad mark on the little sandy margin of the stream. It was very fresh; water was still oozing slowly into it, and he

began to tremble. The facts that he had always got home before dark, to avoid worrying his mother, and that he wouldn't be able to do it this time if he didn't start at once were forgotten. A strange sort of surety came upon him, and, after a moment, the trembling stopped and he grew calm. He knew that the stream didn't go much farther; that within a quarter of a mile the otters would leave it and go across country, through a hemlock swamp and over a low ridge, to reach the stream on the other side which flowed finally into the lake.

He knew the thicket so well that he could predict where they would pass through it—a marshy little path which had once been a lumber road, cut through a high and tangled bank. He knew he could intercept them there by going through the woods; he knew he had them.

He had so often imagined the feeling of triumph that would be his when he found them that he was confused by the lack of it, by a sort of unwillingness that had suddenly come into his heart. This emotion was inexplicable [not able to be understood] to him, and seemed like a betrayal of his brother. He thought of his father, who did not approve of the thing he was doing, but who had been patient and kind and had said nothing against it, and suddenly he felt lost and alone. He stood indecisively for a moment in the darkening woods; the thoughts of his father changed to thoughts of Joe, and his back stiffened.

He started to walk. A deeper gloom fell upon him as he went into the hemlock, and a deeper silence; he moved like a ghost, for his feet made no sound in the fallen needles. When he came to the place, the bank above the lumber road, the setting sun came out more brightly, and the thicket was filled with a banded, coppery light. The low branches were so thick that he had to crawl to the top on his hands and knees. He reached the top and lay down, stretching out with the rifle cocked in his hands. It was very quiet. The swampy little path lay before him for a few yards, meandering and crooked, masked here and there by low hemlock branches and brown old stumps rotting and green with moss.

The coppery light faded again, and after a long time the brooding silence was suddenly broken by a spitting snarl. The boy raised himself on his elbows quickly; there was a rapid, slurred pattering of feet, and the three otters were bunched below him. The old male's back was claw-raked and bleeding; he snarled at his mate and moved toward her as though to drive her along the path, then turned and galloped the other way. A lynx materialized in front of him, crouched and spitting, its ears laid flat and its teeth gleaming. He went at it hissing, and it gave ground; another bounded off the bank toward the pup, but he whirled and drove it off. Short-legged and awkward on land, he was at a great disadvantage before the pair of lynxes, but somehow he managed to be everywhere at once.

The snarling lynxes, trying to draw both otters away from the pup, were very quick, but the old otter moved like a dark flame. He closed with one of them, took his raking and punished it, and broke away in time to fasten on

the throat of the other, which was batting with a hooked claw at his mate. He shook its big body, threw it aside and whirled again toward the first. Quiet suddenly fell; the lynxes drew off a little, and they all stood panting, glaring at one another.

The path had been so quiet and empty one moment and so full of violent action the next that the boy was held immobile and staring. The sudden quiet freed him. He got up on his knees, his eyes on the otter; he was so filled with a sudden overwhelming admiration for its courage that he nearly shouted encouragement as it stood, black and bloody, and so obviously ready to carry the fight on. One of the lynxes moved; it drew off a little farther, as though deciding to abandon the fight. The boy didn't think; he raised the rifle and fired a quick shot at it. The shot missed, but the lynx turned tail with a snarl and bounded off through the hemlocks. The other went after it, and the old otter turned its head and looked at him for a moment with curiosity, but no fear. Then it shook itself and drove the female and the pup before it down the path and out of sight.

It was well dark when the boy heard his father shouting in the distance and answered him; presently, he saw the lantern moving far off among the dark trees, and hurried toward it.

"Are you all right, Andy?" Gates called. "Are you all right, boy?"

"Yes, dad," he said. He came to the circle of yellow light and stopped.

"Your ma was a little worried," Gates said gently.

"I'm sorry," he said; and then, "I found them, dad."

Gates didn't say anything. He just stood there holding the lantern, and the boy could see a star or two among the scattering clouds and branches high above his head. "I found them," he said again. "There were two lynxes after them, and he—the old one, the otter—fought them off. He was wonderful, dad; he licked them both."

"Rabbits must be scarce," Gates said, "to make them tackle him."

"It was the little one," Andy said. "They were after him. But the old one—I-I shot at the lynxes, dad."

There was silence for a long moment, then Gates said, "You're not sorry?"

"No," the boy said. "No. He's not mean, dad. It was the little one all the time. He was watching out for it—even the day he took Nicky; but I didn't know it then. Do you think Joe will understand that, dad?"

"Sure," Gates said. "He'll understand it. He'll be glad you understand it too." His long arm went around the boy's shoulders. "Come on," he said. "Let's get on home."

Reading Check

1. What does the author tell us about otters in the opening of the story?
2. Why is Andy so determined to kill the otter?
3. What discoveries does Andy make about nature while stalking his prey?
4. How do these discoveries contribute toward changing his attitude?
5. What key event completes this change in attitude?
6. What personal discovery does Andy make through this experience?

Symbols

Christina Rossetti

I watched a rosebud very long
  Brought on by dew and sun and
    shower,
  Waiting to see the perfect flower:
Then, when I thought it should be
    strong,
  It opened at the matin hour
And fell at evensong.

I watched a nest from day to day,
  A green nest full of pleasant shade,
  Wherein three speckled eggs were
    laid:
But when they should have hatched
    in May,
  The two old birds had grown
    afraid
Or tired, and flew away.

Then in my wrath I broke the bough
  That I had tended so with care,
  Hoping its scent should fill the air:
I crushed the eggs, not heeding how
  Their ancient promise had been
    fair:
I would have vengeance now.

But the dead branch spoke from the
    sod,
  And the eggs answered me again:
  Because we failed dost thou com-
    plain?
Is thy wrath just? And what if God,
  Who waiteth for thy fruits in vain,
Should also take the rod?

Christ Returneth

H. L. Turner

It may be at morn, when the day is awaking,
When sunlight thro' darkness and shadow is breaking,
That Jesus will come in the fullness of glory,
To receive from the world "His own."

    Chorus:
O Lord Jesus, how long, how long
Ere we shout the glad song,
Christ returneth!
Hallelujah! hallelujah! Amen.

The Ascension by Gustave Doré from The Bob Jones
University Collection of Sacred Art

It may be at midday, it may be at twilight,
It may be, perchance, that the blackness of midnight
Will burst into light in the blaze of His glory,
When Jesus receives "His own."

While its hosts cry Hosanna, from heaven descending,
With glorified saints and the angels attending,
With grace on His brow, like a halo of glory,
Will Jesus receive "His own."

Oh, joy! oh, delight! should we go without dying,
No sickness, no sadness, no dread and no crying,
Caught up thro' the clouds with our Lord into glory,
When Jesus receives "His own."

DANIEL AND BELSHAZZAR

Belshazzar the king made a great feast to a thousand of his lords, and drank wine before the thousand.

Belshazzar, whiles he tasted the wine, commanded to bring the golden and silver vessels which his father Nebuchadnezzar had taken out of the temple which was in Jerusalem; that the king, and his princes, his wives, and his concubines, might drink therein.

Then they brought the golden vessels that were taken out of the temple of the house of God which was at Jerusalem; and the king, and his princes, his wives, and his concubines, drank in them.

They drank wine, and praised the gods of gold, and of silver, of brass, of iron, of wood, and of stone.

In the same hour came forth fingers of a man's hand, and wrote over against the candlestick upon the plaister of the wall of the king's palace: and the king saw the part of the hand that wrote.

Then the king's countenance was changed, and his thoughts troubled him, so that the joints of his loins were loosed, and his knees smote one against another.

The king cried aloud to bring in the astrologers, the Chaldeans, and the soothsayers. And the king spake, and said to the wise men of Babylon, Whosoever shall read this writing, and shew me the interpretation thereof, shall be clothed with scarlet, and have a chain of gold about his neck, and shall be the third ruler in the kingdom.

Then came in all the king's wise men: but they could not read the writing, nor make known to the king the interpretation thereof.

Then was king Belshazzar greatly troubled, and his countenance was changed in him, and his lords were astonied.

Now the queen by reason of the words of the king and his lords came into the banquet house: and the queen spake and said, O king, live for ever: let not thy thoughts trouble thee, nor let thy countenance be changed:

There is a man in thy kingdom, in whom is the spirit of the holy gods; and in the days of thy father light and understanding and wisdom, like the wisdom of the gods, was found in him; whom the king Nebuchadnezzar thy father, the king, I say, thy father, made master of the magicians, astrologers, Chaldeans, and soothsayers;

Forasmuch as an excellent spirit, and knowledge, and understanding, interpreting of dreams, and shewing of hard sentences, and dissolving of doubts, were found in the same Daniel, whom the king named Belteshazzar: now let Daniel be called, and he will shew the interpretation.

Then was Daniel brought in before the king. And the king spake and said unto Daniel, Art thou Daniel, which art of the children of the captivity of Judah, whom the king my father brought out of Jewry?

I have even heard of thee, that the spirit of the gods is in thee, and that light and understanding and excellent wisdom is found in thee.

And now the wise men, the astrologers, have been brought in before me, that they should read this writing, and make known unto me the interpretation thereof: but they could not shew the interpretation of the thing.

And I have heard of thee, that thou canst make interpretations, and dissolve doubts: now if thou canst read the writing, and make known to me the interpretation thereof, thou shalt be clothed with scarlet, and have a chain of gold about thy neck, and shalt be the third ruler in the kingdom.

Then Daniel answered and said before the king, Let thy gifts be to thyself, and give thy rewards to another; yet I will read the writing unto the king, and make known to him the interpretation.

O thou king, the most high God gave Nebuchadnezzar thy father a kingdom, and majesty, and glory, and honour:

And for the majesty that he gave him, all people, nations, and languages, trembled and feared before him: whom he would he slew; and whom he would he kept alive; and whom he would set up he set up; and whom he would he put down.

But when his heart was lifted up, and his mind hardened in pride, he was deposed from his kingly throne, and they took his glory from him:

And he was driven from the sons of men; and his heart was made like the beasts, and his dwelling was with the wild asses: they fed him with grass like oxen, and his body was wet with the dew of heaven; till he knew that the most high God ruled in the kingdom of men, and that he appointeth over it whomsoever he will.

And thou his son, O Belshazzar, hast not humbled thine heart, though thou knewest all this;

But hast lifted up thyself against the Lord of heaven; and they have brought the vessels of his house before thee, and thou, and thy lords, thy wives, and thy concubines, have drunk wine in them; and thou hast praised the gods of silver, and gold, of brass, iron, wood, and stone, which see not, nor hear, nor know: and the God in whose hand thy breath is, and whose are all thy ways, hast thou not glorified:

Then was the part of the hand sent from him; and this writing was written.

And this is the writing that was written, MENE, MENE, TEKEL, UPHARSIN.

This is the interpretation of the thing: MENE; God hath numbered thy kingdom, and finished it.

TEKEL; Thou art weighed in the balances, and art found wanting.

PERES; Thy kingdom is divided, and given to the Medes and Persians.

Then commanded Belshazzar, and they clothed Daniel with scarlet, and put a chain of gold about his neck, and made a proclamation concerning him, that he should be the third ruler in the kingdom.

In that night was Belshazzar the king of the Chaldeans slain.

And Darius the Median took the kingdom, being about threescore and two years old.   Daniel 5

"And the light shineth in darkness; and the darkness comprehended it not."

As you read the following novel, Wine of Morning, *you will have opportunity to use the insights you have gained through your study of the unit introductions. You will be able to do so by evaluating the character of Joel. Like Ben-Hur, Joel experiences many adventures, and these adventures ultimately bring him to the same discovery. But unlike Ben-Hur, Joel's behavior throughout most of the story is villainous, rather than heroic. By examining Joel's choices, the friends that he had, and the focus of his life, you will better understand the suffering that results from wrong choices.*

Wine of Morning

Bob Jones

PROLOGUE

He had never imagined such absolute blackness. He had known the gloom of mountain caves, of starless nights spent among the crumbling stones and fallen columns of an old and nameless temple of some half-forgotten god. He had known the darkness of the desert when the winds howl through the night and the sky is hidden by the blowing sand. He remembered the secret darkness of cellars, the stuffy darkness of windowless rooms, the dusty darkness of old tombs. Theirs had been the darkness of safety and in them he had hidden secure from pursuit. Darkness, he knew, could be as friendly as a fireside, as comfortable as an old cloak. But now he felt smothered by this blackness—crushed down, hemmed in. So, he thought, must guilt press down upon a tender conscience.

How long he had been imprisoned here, he had no way of knowing. At intervals the heavy door was opened on its squeaky hinges, and the hard bread and gourd of water were left upon the stone floor by the taciturn jailer, who only grunted in answer to his questions. Whether once a day or twice, his smoky torch dispelled for a moment the gloom; whether he came at regular or irregular intervals the prisoner had no way of knowing, for once the heavy door was shut again no sound could pierce its thickness or relieve the stillness of the cell.

He would lie quietly upon the bare floor, seeking in sleep to pass away the hours. He would walk until exhausted—six paces this way, three paces that—back and forth, up and down. He would sit in the corner directly under the small fissure[1] through which came his only ventilation, his arms clasped about his knees, his head resting against the stone walls until his nerves could no longer endure the screaming silence. Then, to keep from going mad, he would burst into speech. Sometimes he sang the Psalms of David. Sometimes he cursed long and bitterly until exhausted and relaxed by the vehemence of his profanity. More and more he found his thoughts turning backward to familiar scenes of by-gone days. Sometimes he forgot the darkness as the lamp of memory was lighted in his mind. Sometimes the silence gave way to the remembered voices of old friends. So for a while his thoughts walked free under the sky.

Chapter 1

He and Stephen lay at full length on the summit of the hill. Propped upon their elbows, straws between their teeth, they could see his house near the synagogue as the whole little town of Nazareth lay spread out before them. Some half dozen houses huddled around the common well, where the road wound down the valley. Several score more clung to the lower slope directly beneath them, and a few staggered crazily up the steep hillside toward the crest.

It was the time of day when young hearts feel a strange and inexplicable melancholy. They watched as from chimney after chimney the gray smoke began to rise as fires were lighted for the cooking of the evening meal. One by one the women and girls came with their water pots to the town well, stopping to exchange a bit of gossip or discuss the weather with the neighbors before they turned homeward, filled pitchers borne gracefully upon heads or shoulders.

On the horizon the sun, brilliant as pagan priest in golden vestment, seemed to be shedding the blood of day in crimson sacrifice upon the altar of the West. All at once he was conscious of the suddenly awakened breeze upon his cheek and watched half idly how it ruffled with gentle fingers the thick and tousled hair of his friend. It was Stephen who broke the silence.

"I wonder what Irene looks like, Joel?"

"Oh, I imagine she is short and fat and has stringy hair and pimples on her nose."

This was an old joke between them. Twenty times in the last few weeks Stephen had said, "What do you think she's like?" and twenty times had Joel turned over in his mind all the unattractive features and disagreeable qualities he could think of, selecting each time some horrible new combination of possibilities. These he delighted to offer his long-suffering friend. Sometimes she was "angular and bony as Simon's old mule." Again Stephen was assured she would prove "knock-kneed and cross-eyed with a temper like Jonathan's granny," the latter being known for twenty miles around as the meanest woman in Galilee. She had now "teeth like a spavined[2] horse," again "no teeth at all." The possibility of pimples had just occurred to Joel and it gave him special pleasure to suggest them to Stephen.

"That's just the trouble," said Stephen. "She may have pimples or worse. Any other fellow around here is able to see the girl his family has arranged for him to marry and he knows what he is getting, but it is just my luck to be betrothed to a girl from Cyprus whom I won't see until she comes for the wedding."

"Well, anyway," said Joel, "it's too late now to do anything about it. How soon is she coming?"

"Within a month," sighed his friend. Then, after a moment of silence, he added fervently, "Oh, Joel, I hope she won't be too bad! Well, if I'm to be home before dark, I'd better get started."

He got up, brushing off his tunic, and stood looking down at Joel, his handsome features gloomy. Then his accustomed smile returned.

"All mother can talk about is her plans for the wedding. It's a good thing I haven't any brothers. She'd never live through more than one. I never saw her so excited about anything. Come over to Cana when you can." With this customary invitation he was gone.

Joel watched the lithe[3] figure leaping gracefully from ledge to ledge down the steep northern shoulder of the hill. Going this way, Stephen saved at least a mile. He half ran, half slid down the final hundred feet or so, arriving midst a cloud of dust and a small avalanche of loose shale and stones in the ravine below. Soon he had left the narrow defile[4] and stood in the broad valley upon the road that wound north and west by way of Cana to Gennesaret. Here he paused to wave to Joel, who

returned the farewell and then went slowly down the footpath on the gentle southern slope toward Nazareth while his friend turned homeward to Cana.

Stephen's mother had grown up in Jerusalem and, until her marriage to the richest man in Cana, had been like a sister to Joel's mother, Miriam. Their boys, born within a few days of each other, were as different in temperament and appearance as summer and winter— Joel, dark haired, brown-eyed, impetuous, hot-tempered, and rebellious against the strict Pharisaism of his father, the rabbi; Stephen, fair and blonde, quiet, poetical, and deeply religious. Yet these two, different as they were, shared a passionate love for their nation and an intense and burning hatred for the Roman oppressor. They had been equally well taught, for Stephen had been sent by his parents to study under Ephraim, Joel's father. This studious and quiet man was no ordinary small-town rabbi, but a man of exceptional wisdom, profoundly respected far and wide and having considerable influence even among the priests and rabbis of Jerusalem, where he had lived before his marriage. A cousin of the high priest himself, he might, had he so desired, have been prominent in the temple circles of the Holy City; but he preferred the quiet of Nazareth to the political wrangling and theological arguments of his colleagues in Jerusalem. Rabbi Ephraim felt his time well spent in study and in the teaching of a few promising young men.

The next afternoon, passing along the street of Nazareth, Joel stopped as he frequently did in front of the

carpenter shop of old Joseph. Removable shutters were down and the whole front of the building opened to the street. Joseph, a dignified and kindly graybeard, stood by his workbench painstakingly planing a cedar plank while James, one of several sons, a young man only a few years older than Joel, was putting the finishing touches on a simple table. The work of Joseph's shop was famous far and near and he was respected as both artist and artisan. Though most of the objects he made were as plain as the simple homes into which they went, they were carefully and beautifully constructed, and Joel never tired of watching the skillful hands at work or wearied of the smell of freshly planed lumber and of glue which pervaded the shop. There was an older son called Jesus, whom Joel, in common with most of the villagers, had always considered somehow different from the others. His patience was unfailing and His goodness taken for granted in the district. He was never too busy to help a neighbor and the quality of His carpentry excelled even that of Joseph. More than this, He was a scholar, possessing an extraordinary knowledge of the Scriptures, frequently surprising rabbi Ephraim by the keenness of his questions.

Some weeks before, Jesus had left Nazareth quietly one day, and the gossip was that He had gone down into Judea.

Now exchanging the time of the day with James and Joseph, Joel inquired, "Do you expect Jesus home soon?"

Joseph laid down his plane before he replied. "His mother and I hope He will come back to see us soon, but of course, now that He is about His Father's business we can't expect to see much of Him in Nazareth."

There was about the answer such infinite resignation and such a mixture of pride and sadness that Joel was puzzled. He wanted to ask Joseph what he meant by "His Father's business." As a child playing near the well, Joel had occasionally heard from the lips of chattering women fragments of half understood gossip about Joseph, about Jesus and Mary, His mother. Now these came to his mind as James, who had been humming as he worked, broke off suddenly, glancing quickly at his father.

Never one to keep silent when his curiosity was touched, Joel was turning over in his mind the best way to frame his question. His attention, however, was diverted by a party coming along the road from Jerusalem and drawing rein beside the well, a short distance from where he stood just inside the open shop. There were three travelers—a man mounted on a beautiful little Arabian steed and two women riding mules. The man, probably forty years old, was slight of stature, wiry, and well built. The older of the two women seemed to be a servant. The other, whom the man was helping to alight, was so turned that Joel could not see her face. Now as she approached the well, Joel beheld her fully for the first time. For a moment he forgot to breathe! Never had Joel glimpsed such beauty as this girl's who, having handed her traveling cloak of blue wool to the serving woman, stood clothed in a Grecian gown of the most delicate rose color, her hair hidden after the Jewish fashion under a flowing veil.

Without realizing he had begun to move, he found himself drawn as if by a magnet toward the well, never taking his eyes from the lovely creature who was accepting a cup of water from the man. As she started to drink, she noticed Joel for the first time, and over the lifted cup her eyes met his for a brief instant. Joel was practically overpowered by their brilliance. Large, dark, and expressive, they were ringed by long curved lashes so black as to be almost blue. Above them were finely arched brows, and as she returned the cup with a smile of thanks to the man, Joel caught the gleam of fine white teeth behind rosy lips and saw a dimple come and go. Long-limbed and full-bosomed, she was almost as tall as Joel. Such beauty of face and form would have attracted attention at the court of Caesar. Overwhelming was the effect of all this loveliness upon a village lad like Joel.

Noting now the intense and unwavering glance of the smitten youth, she blushed a delicate rose from her throat to her cheek, and lowering her eyes, turned to speak to the servant woman. Joel, oblivious to all but this exquisite creature, was startled by the sound of the man's voice.

"Peace be with you friend. What's the name of this place?"

If he had been asked his own name at that moment, Joel could not have replied directly, and it was not until the question was repeated that he managed to stammer, "Naz—Nazareth."

"And how far is it to Cana?"

"About five miles," said Joel. "Are you going there?"

"Yes; is it hard to find the way?"

"Uh—very," replied Joel.

The truth was that the road led directly to Cana with no crossroads or byways that could possibly lead a traveler astray.

"As a matter of fact, I was just going over there to see a friend. I'll be glad to show you the way, if you'd like."

Joel was surprised to hear himself saying these words. Until that moment he had not entertained any idea of going to see Stephen that day, but the thought of this lovely creature's passing out of his life so quickly was more than he could endure. He had to remain in her company a little while longer if only to steal a glance at her now and then. The journey to Cana seemed a God-given opportunity.

The stranger welcomed the suggestion. "You are very kind. We are ready whenever you are."

"Just a moment until I give a message to a friend," replied Joel.

And, hurrying to the door of Joseph's shop, he said in a low voice to James, "Tell mother when she comes by on her way to the well that I'll spend the night in Cana with Stephen and be home tomorrow, won't you?"

"Sure, I'll tell her."

Then with a twinkle in his eye and a glance toward the group by the well, James added, "Don't get lost and go all the way around by Damascus in getting there."

The women had remounted their mules, but the man out of courtesy had remained afoot to walk with Joel. The only disadvantage from Joel's standpoint was that by walking at the head of the little caravan, he could not keep his eyes fixed upon the girl. Not so much because courtesy required that he make conversation as because curiosity demanded that he find out all that he could about the beauty riding quietly behind him, he said, "Have you come a long way? Where are you from?"

"We have come from Jerusalem, now, but our home is in Cyprus," replied the stranger. "My daughter is betrothed to a young man of Cana and I am bringing her now to be married."

Joel stopped so suddenly that he was almost run over by the horse his companion was leading. He turned and looked toward the girl. "Then you're Irene!"

Her eyes opened wide in surprise. "How did you know my name?"

As though he had not heard the question, Joel continued, "Every time I talked to Stephen, he said, 'What do you think she'll look like?' And—."

"And," said Irene smiling now, "how did you reply?"

Thinking of all the answers he had given, he turned crimson, "I certainly had no idea his bride would be the most beautiful woman in the world."

At this fervently spoken compliment, the serving woman, who had been listening for all she was worth, gave a sort of snort. At least, Joel presumed it was she—from the sound it might equally as well have been her mule— and Irene's father cleared his throat loudly and suggested, "Perhaps we had better be getting along."

Joel remembered very little of the further details of the journey. He scarcely heard and afterwards could recall very little of the Cypriote's conversation, although he kept up a constant monologue and disclosed his entire life's history.

A prosperous merchant who had been converted to Judaism and had married a Jewish girl, he was making his first journey into the land of the Chosen People. He and his daughter and her maid had come by ship to Joppa and had spent a few days in Jerusalem seeing the sights and worshiping in the temple. Irene's aunt, her mother's sister, lived in Cana and it was through her influence that the betrothal had been arranged with Stephen's parents. Shortly after his wife's death, Irene's father had a letter from this sister-in-law informing him that pious and wealthy neighbors of hers had a handsome son just two years older than Irene and suggesting a betrothal contract. Overjoyed at the prospect of finding such a husband for his daughter, he had commissioned her to negotiate the engagement. All this information and much more went in one of Joel's ears and out the other.

There were, however, a few moments of that journey Joel never forgot. They were those spent in conversation with her. She had called to him saying, "Come, tell me all about Stephen. What is he like?"

Joel dropped back to walk beside her, confused as he had never been before by conflicting emotions. The sound of her voice speaking to him as she eagerly and gaily questioned him about Stephen, about Stephen's family, about Cana, was like music in his ears, but music in a minor key, for the theme of that musical voice was always Stephen. A feeling of frustration and unreasonable fury swelled in his heart as he tried to do justice to Stephen in his description of his friend when he wanted so badly to say, "Forget about Stephen."

Impetuous, he knew himself incurably in love with this girl whom he had first seen only an hour ago. Impressionable son of a hot-blooded race, he had been attracted by other girls, had fancied himself briefly in love with this one or that. But this was an altogether different thing. He wanted to be loyal to his friend, but he knew in his heart it was not loyalty that kept him from saying, "Can't you see, I love you?" Neither was it the presence of her father and serving woman, but only the certainty that such a declaration would shut off from him altogether her smile and conversation.

All too soon they reached Cana. Joel's legs lagged as he approached the house of his friend. Esther, Irene's aunt, lived on the edge of the village nearest Nazareth. Here he had taken reluctant leave of Irene and had bidden her father a courteous, absent-minded farewell.

He dreaded the thought of meeting Stephen and having to talk to him about Irene. He wished he had not left the message for his mother, for he knew if he returned home now she would besiege him with questions as to why he had changed his mind. "Had he quarreled with Stephen? Was there any trouble in Cana? Was he sick?" He could not face her insistent curiosity and demanding motherhood—not now. Besides, his conscience demanded that he see Stephen. Logic told him that sooner or later he must face his friend; better then to get it over.

The family was at supper when Joel came in. Stephen's mother called a servant to set a place for Joel while another came with water and a basin to wash his hands and feet. They welcomed him as they always had—as another son, a member of the family. Casually he said, as he sat down at the table, "Oh, by the way, Irene has come. I walked from Nazareth with her and her father."

For a moment, utter silence greeted this announcement. Stephen's mother sat, her hands in her lap. Stephen's mouth dropped open. His father paused, hand halfway to mouth, the bread it held forgotten.

It was the woman who spoke first, "Do you mean they are here? In Cana? This soon? But nothing is ready for the wedding!"

"Tell me, what is she like?" cried Stephen, jumping up from his place and running around the table to lay his hands upon the shoulders of his friend. Turning to face him, Joel managed to force his lips to smile. Though it was a smile edged with bitterness, Stephen did not seem to notice.

"No pimples," said Joel.

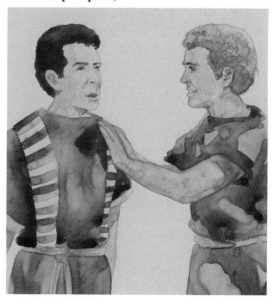

Chapter 2

Rebekah, Stephen's mother, was a kindly inefficient and helpless soul. With much more heart than head, she felt weighted down by her responsibilities as the wife of the wealthiest man in Cana and one of the wealthiest in all of Galilee. The more effort she made to discharge her social responsibilities, the more confusion resulted.

The wedding was to be a grand affair. "After all," she said to her husband, "he is our only child. And, besides, the neighbors expect it. Anything less than a seven-day feast would be unbecoming. There is so much to do," she wailed. "I wonder, Joel, if you couldn't arrange to stay on here for a few days and keep Stephen company and help us with the preparations. You are like one of the family, you know, and it would be such a help to have someone to keep Stephen out from underfoot."

Having no good excuse for refusing and secretly hoping that he might have an opportunity of catching a glimpse of Irene if he remained in Cana, Joel consented.

Rebekah, who had taken his acceptance for granted, had not even stopped for breath. "Let's see, day after tomorrow is the Sabbath. We'll make what preparation we can before sundown tomorrow. It will take two days at least to get ready—that's if we hurry. Perhaps we can complete the preparations the day after the Sabbath and have the wedding the next day. But, of course, I suppose I should talk to Esther and to Irene and her father and see if that's convenient for them."

Apparently it was, because early the next morning preparation got under way. Extra servants were hired. Nothing but the best would do for Rebekah— she must send over to Gennesaret for a woman known as the best baker in the district. No one else could make such delicious cakes and pastries and only the best would do for this feast! The house was filled from morning to night with the smell of roasting meats and the odor of almond tarts and honey cookies. Figs and dates and raisins were bought. Wine was ordered.

Amid all the preparation Rebekah fluttered helplessly, giving orders and countermanding them, and getting in everyone's way. Her mind always on something else besides the detail under discussion, she would ask endless questions and never hear the answers. Fortunately, she had good servants and somehow they got things done in spite of her. It was worse than spring-cleaning time. Rugs and tapestries were taken out to be dusted and aired. Additional beds and coverings were borrowed from the neighbors to take care of the guests from out of town. Neighbors came with offers of a spare room or dishes and utensils.

Messengers were sent through all the countryside with invitations to relatives and friends. Much of those two busy days, Stephen and Joel spent on horseback—sometimes together, sometimes apart—delivering such invitations. Twice passing Esther's house—once because he had to go that way, once because he made a detour for that purpose—Joel saw Irene. Each time he exchanged a few words with her. He was glad for the excitement that kept him occupied; but, riding alone over the hills, he had much time for thought. This he knew: he could never stay in Nazareth after the marriage. It was too close to Cana, and there would be visits back and forth. He felt he could not bear the sight of Stephen's happiness, and he knew he could not see Irene often and avoid saying to her things which must be left unsaid.

Stephen was much too excited to note anything unusual about his friend's manner, but the demons of jealousy and bitterness were at work in the soul of Joel. Once as they were riding along a narrow road at the top of a steep cliff some little distance from Cana, Joel thought, "If his horse should stumble or slip, perhaps Irene—." His brow broke out in a cold sweat. By force of will he turned his thoughts from the contemplation of the strong young body of his friend lying broken on the rocks

below, and spurred his horse into a gallop, widening the distance between himself and Stephen. For he had been riding on the inside and he dared not trust himself in a position where by a sudden turn of his horse in an act of treachery he could force his friend over the edge.

He hated himself for the blackness of his thought, and that night long after Stephen had fallen asleep, he lay staring into the darkness, praying for an end to his anguish. He wanted Stephen to be happy, but a thousand times more intensely he wanted Irene for himself.

Finally, the day of the wedding arrived and with it the friends and invited guests. Promptly at midnight, dressed in a new linen robe embroidered with silk, his hair perfumed with ointment, Stephen set out in company of all the guests to the house where his betrothed was staying. With singing and musical instruments the gay procession moved through the darkness. Hearing the sound of the music, a group of the young girls of the village who had gathered earlier at Esther's house came out with lighted lamps in their hands to meet the bridegroom and his companions. Greeted by Irene's father at the door of the house, they were led to an upper room decorated with garlands and flowers, and perfumed with incense.

Here Irene waited. There was about her nothing to suggest that she was not entirely of Hebrew blood. The robes of Grecian design she customarily wore with such unconscious grace had been laid aside. Dressed like every Jewish bride in embroidered garments, with bracelets upon wrists and ankles and strands of coins upon her forehead, she stood in the center of the room, face hidden by a green veil.

Stephen, on entering, first presented the gifts which he had brought—golden earrings set with lapis from Damascus, a multi-colored scarf of softest cashmere, bracelets of silver and beads of carnelian, crystal bottles and alabaster boxes of perfume and ointment.

Then the actual marriage ceremony began. The Elder of the village handed the bridegroom a silver cup of wine with which to pledge his bride. When Stephen had done so, the cup was handed to Irene as two of the bridesmaids lifted her veil. Her dark eyes, shaded and accented by cosmetics, looked even larger and more lustrous than usual as she smiled at Stephen. Now she, in turn lifting the cup, pledged her faith to the tall blond youth standing so proudly beside her.

Esther gave a signal and her servants passed wine among the visitors that all might drink the toast. Next, the marriage contract was signed; the Elder pronounced a sevenfold blessing; and Stephen and Irene were bonded together for life.

During all this time, Joel, utterly miserable, had stood alone in a corner, hoping that his face did not betray his heart.

Now the procession returned to Stephen's house, the bride riding upon a white mare in the midst, torches blazing and songs echoing in the night, and there, without interruption they feasted and sang until morning. Such a wedding had never been seen in Cana. Day after day for seven days, the sound of music was heard in the village; and no stranger passed along the road through town but was invited to stop for food and wine. Some coming from distant places were especially welcomed and urged to linger until the end of the feast that all might have opportunity to hear their news and gossip of great cities and far lands. Friends who had not seen each other for months talked endlessly of old times. New babies were admired and, much to their disgust, comments about how they had grown rang in the ears of older children.

Joel gave himself with reckless abandon to an outward show of enjoyment. But about his soul there was a kind of numbness. One incident only stood out in his mind long afterward and this was something so strange that it would have been impossible to forget.

Mary, the wife of Joseph the carpenter, had come to the feast with James, and on the third day Jesus also appeared, accompanied by four or five men who were strangers to Joel. There was about Jesus an air of power of which Joel had never before been aware. His face seemed thinner than when He had left Nazareth, and His eyes disconcerted the unhappy youth, who had a feeling that all his inner thoughts and hidden conflicts were quite obvious to Mary's Son. All at the feast seemed to be drawn to this Man and listened eagerly to His words, which had somehow the ring of conscious authority, though He spoke in gentle tones and conducted Himself with a quiet humility.

Toward sundown on this third day of the feast, Joel, who had felt unable longer to endure the laughter of the celebrating crowd, had gone into the yard. Through the open door he noticed that there was quite a space of time when

no servants came with pitchers of wine to replenish the cups of the guests. He saw Rebekah fluttering about more helpless and confused than usual, whispering to the servants and wringing her hands.

Mary, always kind and helpful, sensing an unfortunate situation, arose from her place and, slipping her arm around Rebekah, took her to one side apparently to inquire the cause of her obvious distress. Watching Rebekah's vague but anguished gestures as she talked to her sympathetic friend, Joel felt a twinge of pity for Mary, who he knew from experience was in for a long and repetitious recital. She listened patiently, however, until finally able to get in a reassuring word. Then going to her Son, she stooped to whisper in His ear. Excusing Himself, He arose from His place and walked out with His mother into the yard, pausing near where Joel was seated under a fig tree.

"Son," she said, "the wine has given out. Poor Rebekah is so helpless about housekeeping affairs we must do something."

Jesus paused for a moment, looking tenderly at His mother before speaking. "Woman, what have I to do with you? My time has not come yet."

Mary merely smiled at Him and, reaching up, patted His arms in mock disapproval. Then she turned to some servants who were roasting a kid over an open fire not far away.

"Do whatever He tells you," she called, pointing to Jesus, and with another smile for her Son walked away.

Jesus sighed. Then indicating six waterpots which stood on a rack against the wall near the door of the house, He said, "Fill them with water."

Looking at each other as if to say, "What's this all about?" the two men shrugged their shoulders but set out to obey. They took the jars to the well a short distance from the house and one by one filled them to the brim with the cool water drawn from deep underground.

"Now," said Jesus, taking an empty pitcher from a serving girl who had stopped to watch the proceedings, "fill this from one of the pots."

His curiosity stirred, Joel watched one of the men lift the heavy pot to pour the water into the pitcher which the other servant was holding. To his amazement the liquid that poured from the jar was a deep amethyst color. The hand of the man holding the pot jerked involuntarily with surprise, and the liquid poured forth so rapidly that it overran the small mouth of the pitcher and stained the hand and the sleeve of the servant who was holding it. Before he could control himself, several cupfuls had been spilled on the ground and the smell of wine was in their nostrils. When the pitcher was filled the Carpenter said, "Take it in to the toastmaster." With many a backward glance at Jesus, both servants, followed by the gaping serving maid, entered the house with the pitcher of miraculous liquid.

Joel, following them as far as the doorway, heard the toastmaster say, "Fill up the cups all around." Then after a moment, "This is a strange feast, Stephen. It's customary to bring out the best wine at the beginning and the poor wine after everyone has drunk well. But you have saved the best for the last."

Joel turned to face Jesus, who all the while had remained standing under the shade of the fig tree near the cooking pit. He could not believe what his eyes had seen. He wanted to ask questions, but somehow for the first time in his life he dared not. Mary brushed past him as she came from the house. Going to Jesus, she put her arm around Him and said, "Thank you, my Son."

Reading Check

1. Where is the man in the prologue, and what is he thinking?
2. Why has Stephen not seen his bride?
3. What phrase of Joseph's puzzles Joel?
4. Why does Joel plan to leave Nazareth after the wedding?
5. In what way does Jesus now seem different to Joel?

Chapter 3

Summer was everywhere in the land, but winter was in the heart of Joel.

He had not seen Stephen and Irene since the wedding feast several months before. In fact, he had spent most of the time in Capernaum. Desperate with unhappiness and determined to leave Nazareth, he had come here to this big and bustling town, resolved to find some means of support. And, fortunately, almost at once through the good offices of a friend, he was engaged as a bookkeeper and clerk by a merchant named Jonathan. This good man, the owner of a small business, had been afflicted for several years with palsy and lately his condition had grown so bad that he could not leave his bed. His son, who had taken over more and more the management of his father's affairs, had passed away suddenly a few weeks before Joel had come. Jonathan, desperate for an educated and reliable man who could look after the business and keep the accounts in order, welcomed Joel as an answer to his prayers. After his son's death and until Joel's arrival, the shop had been in the hands of Dysmas, a young lad of sixteen, who was honest and earnest enough but who had neither the maturity nor judgment necessary to maintain a business. Jonathan's wife tried to look in on things, but, being a weak and sickly woman, had found her hands full with managing the household affairs and caring for her invalid husband.

Though Joel had never desired to be a merchant and chafed at life indoors, he was thankful for the opportunities of Capernaum. The salary, though not large, was enough for his needs and the young man from Nazareth was practically his own boss. He shared a nice room behind the shop with young Dysmas; and Jonathan and his wife who lived upstairs, though kind and friendly enough, left him pretty much to his own devices. This arrangement suited Joel perfectly.

The shop, dealing in fishing supplies, salt and tar, rope and canvas, was directly on the lake shore; and when business was slack he would sit in the doorway and look out over the water, only half listening to Dysmas' cheerful and ceaseless chatter. Joel never tired of watching the fishermen mending their nets on the beach or patching their sails and repairing the rigging after a night spent in wresting a living from the treacherous waters. Many of these fishermen were customers of Jonathan's shop; and Joel, attracted to these free and independent men, some as young as himself, quickly made friends among them and was sometimes invited to go out for a night of fishing.

One day Simon, a neighbor from Nazareth—he of the bony mule— arrived in Capernaum with news that Joel's father was ill, and the sympathetic Jonathan, hearing of it, insisted that his clerk take a few days to go home for a visit. Thus Joel happened one midsummer Sabbath to be in the old familiar home town synagogue. Jesus, who had arrived in Nazareth a few days

before, stood up to read the Scriptures. The passage selected was one familiar to the congregation.

"The Spirit of the Lord God is upon me because the Lord hath anointed me to preach good tidings unto the meek. He hath sent me to bind up the broken hearted, to proclaim liberty to the captives and the opening of the prison to them that are bound. To proclaim the acceptable year of the Lord."

Here, Jesus, rolling up the scroll, returned it to the elder and sat down in the seat facing the people—a sign that He intended to teach for the first time in the synagogue where He had worshiped on so many other Sabbaths.

A stir of interest ruffled through the congregation. They had heard amazing rumors about the wonderful acts performed by this Man whom they had known as a neighbor, and the miracle at the wedding feast in nearby Cana had been spread abroad by the servants who had witnessed it.

"Today is this Scripture fulfilled in your hearing." The effect of this simple, direct sentence spoken in the clear, rich, resonant voice was profound, and in the pause that followed, the crowded congregation seemed to hold its breath. The Scripture He had read they all recognized as Isaiah's prophecy of the signs that would accompany the coming of Messiah. No wonder then that the declaration of Jesus took their breath away. He could scarcely have said more plainly, "Messiah is here."

As He began again to speak, all in the synagogue, although compelled to admit the grace and power of His words, were nevertheless, shocked at His implied claim. Of course, they knew He was not Messiah. He was the carpenter, their neighbor, a rabbi even, but not Messiah. Then some began to grow angry. Some glanced at their neighbors and shook their heads as if to say, "Such outrageous things should not be spoken in the synagogue."

There was particular agitation among the eight or nine men occupying the chief seats. Most of them middle aged or elderly, this group had assumed special leadership in the affairs of the synagogue and considered themselves preeminent in piety and righteousness. Delighting in arguments, no two of them would have agreed exactly on any point of doctrine, nor would any one have conceded preeminence to the others in the matter of observing strictly all outward religious ceremonies and traditional practices.

In his heart Joel disliked and despised several of this group and had little respect for the others. He knew them to be in varying degrees, selfish and greedy, ruthless and cruel. Rabid nationalist that he was, Joel was convinced that the only force that could unify the Jewish nation was the religion of Abraham. But that religion he realized must be a burning vital faith, not merely hypocritical appearances and pious cant. And he thought, "It is such frauds as these that have betrayed our nation." He watched them—glancing from one to the other—observing their reactions as Jesus spoke.

There were three for whom he felt a special contempt. One of these, Saul by name, was as stingy as he was wealthy. His stubby-fingered hands, covered with coarse reddish hair, were clasped around a stomach so large and flabby as to be almost obscene. His little pig's eyes were closed and his puffy face was twisted into what was intended for an expression of outraged righteousness.

Reuben, another of the three, was hunched forward, skinny neck drawn in, hawk-like head half hidden by hunched shoulders. The thin lips under the hooked nose were curled in scorn, and his hands were clasped like the talon of some unclean bird upon the gnarled head of his staff. He, rich old miser, had recently allowed the only son of the poorest widow in the village to be sold into slavery in payment of a small debt she owed him.

The other, Zacharias, his cap pushed to the back of his bald head with its bulging forehead, was leaning forward in his seat as though about to rise in protest. His sensuous face, thick-lipped and heavy-lidded, was red with fury as he turned to those near him and said in a loud and sarcastic whisper, "This *is* Joseph's son, isn't it?"

Just then Joses, a poor widower with several sickly children—one far gone with consumption—leaned over and whispered to Joel, "They say Jesus healed a nobleman's sick son in Capernaum. Did you see Him do it?"

Before Joel could reply, the village cynic just in front of them, having overheard the remark, turned around and muttered wisely out of the corner of his mouth, "I heard all about that. It was just a coincidence that the boy got well about that time."

Now the words of a familiar proverb were on the lips of Jesus, " 'Physician, heal thyself.' This proverb you will without doubt quote to me and say, 'We have heard what you have done in Capernaum; do it here at home also.' " He paused and glanced deliberately around the crowded synagogue as if to read on their scornful, angry faces the doubts of their disbelieving hearts. Sadly then, He shook His head.

"I tell you truly, no prophet is accepted in his own country. Let me remind you of the fact that in the time of Elijah, when the heavens were shut for three and a half years and great famine was throughout the land, there were many widows in Israel. But Elijah was sent into Sidon to the city of Sarepta to a woman who was a widow there, but not unto any of the others. And in the time of Elisha many lepers were in Israel. None of them were cleansed but Naaman, a Syrian."

The reference was quite plain to their biased minds. Jesus was saying that the foreigner, whom they despised, was more worthy of blessing than they were. The synagogue was humid with the stench of sweating and excited bodies and the atmosphere was tense with emotional strain.

Old Reuben's lips curled still more as he began to hiss at Jesus. Saul, porcine[5] eyes now open, raised clenched fists to heaven and cried, "Blasphemer!"

Even among the ordinary folks there was muttering, and cries of "Cast Him out" were heard. Others echoed Saul, crying, "Blasphemer!"

But it was Zacharias who leaped to his feet and, rushing upon Jesus, pulled Him from the Seat of the Rabbi.

"Let's see if He is a miracle-worker. When we throw Him over the cliff He can show us whether He is Messiah."

Joel also was stirred with anger. He resented with all the inborn prejudice of his Jewish soul the implication of Jesus' words. But he alone of the entire congregation had seen the water become wine. So he stood irresolute in the midst of all the confusion. All about him now were the cries of "To the cliffs! Throw Him over!"

The hands of half a dozen were laid upon Jesus, His clothes almost torn

from Him by their roughness, and He was hustled unceremoniously from the synagogue by the erstwhile worshippers.

Joel, swept outside by the crowd, stood blinking in the bright sunlight of the midsummer day. He was thankful that Mary and Joseph were not witnessing this scene, for the good old carpenter, shortly after Joel moved to Capernaum, had died suddenly and James had taken Mary to Bethsaida to visit relatives. He was glad also that his own father had not been present in the synagogue, for Joel was not sure just what attitude he might have taken. Kindly and gentle, he was nonetheless a strict Pharisee and Joel, though undecided and irresolute in his own attitude, was somehow thankful that his father had no part in the proceedings.

Meanwhile, the Sabbath calm of little Nazareth was disturbed by such commotion as the old town had never looked upon before. Jesus was being half dragged, half carried down the steps of the synagogue and the street echoed with the shouts. "To the hill of precipitation!" "Cast Him down!"

Joel's father, attracted by the noise, appeared in the doorway of his house next to the synagogue, a robe hastily wrapped around him, his face wan and pale, his eyes feverish. He leaned with one hand upon the facing of the door and cried out, "What's the matter?"

At first his voice was inaudible amid the general confusion, but presently those nearest the house, hearing him, called to the others, "The rabbi wants to know the trouble."

Because they respected Ephraim and because they felt sure of the approval

of so learned and pious a man, the mob halted, and a dozen voices began at once to exclaim.

"One at a time, please," said the rabbi, "one at a time!"

Old Reuben, as the eldest, felt it his prerogative to speak and, hobbling toward Ephraim, began in high-pitched and trembling voice to bewail the horrible blasphemies they had heard and the insults they had endured from the lips of Jesus.

But Zacharias, quivering with passion and still clutching Jesus by the wrist, interrupted Reuben to give his version of the sermon. "So," he concluded with the anger of outraged bigotry, "we are going to take Him to the place of precipitation[6] and cast Him down."

Joel's father, who had listened intently all the while, looked from one to the other of the rulers of the synagogue. "Is this then the way you keep the Sabbath?" he inquired. "Is this deed worthy of good Jews? Does this bitterness please God who said, 'Thou

shalt not kill'? Which one of you has He ever injured? For years He lived among us and no one was able to find sin or unkindness in Him. If, as you say, He has blasphemed, cannot God avenge Himself?"

His quiet voice full of scorn was plainly heard by all in the street and it was apparent that the words of the venerable and respected rabbi made a strong impression upon many, but their leaders were not to be deprived of their revenge for what they considered the insults of Jesus.

"Blasphemy is deserving of death," intoned Saul in pious tones.

"Shall His blasphemies go unpunished?" shrilled Reuben.

"Shall we permit this fellow, whom we have tolerated in our midst so many years, to look down upon respectable people and good Jews?" screamed Zacharias.

Thus they stirred the crowd to a new pitch of frenzy, undoing the effect of the rabbi's reasonable and arresting words.

"Cast Him down! This blasphemer, who calls Himself Messiah, defiles the town."

With these cries and others they again moved forward, pulling and shoving Jesus, Who all this time had said not a word. The old rabbi, sick as he was, sought to stop them by thrusting himself in their way, his arms outspread, but he was thrust so roughly aside that he fell in the street as the mob surged by.

Joel ran to his father, lifted him like a child in his arms to carry him into the house. Tears of rage and shame were running down Joel's face. He appreciated his father as he never had before and a furious and bitter hatred against the whole town flamed in his soul.

"I could kill them all," he cried between clenched teeth. "Did they hurt you, Father?"

"No, no," said the old man. "It's because I'm so weak from the sickness. Put me down quickly and go and stop them somehow. They must not do this thing!"

Assuring himself that his father was not injured, he laid him upon his couch and, leaving him in the care of his mother, ran from the house. The mob was already above the town, passing the outlying houses, taking the path toward the brow of the hill where he and Stephen had so often gone together. He overtook them just as they reached the summit. Short of breath from excitement, anger, and the running climb, he was scarcely able to call, "Stop, stop! Don't! Wait a moment!"

They did not seem to hear and, in any event, would not have obeyed. They stood now only twenty or thirty feet from the edge of the cliff at the spot where the drop was most abrupt. Joel shoved and elbowed his way through the crowd, attempting to reach the side of Jesus, too angry to care if he were thrown over with Him, provided that he could take just one of the mob along in the plunge.

At this moment Zacharias said, "Over you go, blasphemer." And he and several others took hold of Jesus to thrust Him headlong to His death. Then before Joel could interfere a strange thing happened. Their surprised hands grasped only thin air. Jesus was gone! He had disappeared from the midst of the mob. One moment he had stood there disheveled[7] from their rough handling, but enveloped in silent dignity. The next, He had vanished.

"Did you throw Him over?" came a cry from the outskirts of the mob, from someone who had been unable to see the one miracle granted that day to the eyes of Nazareth.

"What happened?" asked another.

"Where did He go?" said Zacharias.

A strange feeling of exaltation filled the heart of Joel. He had seen a man, standing in the center of almost the entire population of the town, disappear in broad daylight from the very grasp of half a dozen men. This thing he could not understand but he could gloat over the discomfort of these bitter men. How he reveled in their thwarted fury! Noting the stupid and blank expression of Zacharias, Joel planted himself squarely in front of the disconcerted Pharisee, looked him full in the face, and broke into a scornful laugh.

Then for the first time in his life he swore, bitterly cursed them and the town of his birth. Then, pushing his way through the surprised citizens, he started down the hill to take leave of his parents, determined never after that day to set foot again in Nazareth.

Chapter 4

Joel arrived in Capernaum in the midst of a torrential downpour of rain. The sullen clouds, which had been moving in from the west to black out all sign of moon and stars, were suddenly shot through with terrific flashes of lightning, and deafening claps of thunder echoed back and forth from the hills surrounding the lake. Then when Joel was scarcely a mile from town the bottom seemed to drop out of the sky. Instead of seeking shelter as he might very well have done, Joel trudged on with the blinding rain in his face, his own mood as dark as the sky between lightning flashes, and his thoughts as stormy as the weather.

Never prone to soul-searching and self-analysis, Joel would have said that his anger was due to the rough treatment his father had received from the Nazarenes when he tried to interfere with their plans to destroy Jesus and to his own contempt for the leaders of the mob. Though he did not realize it, a good deal of disgust with himself underlay his gloomy mood. He had not yet conquered the passion for Irene and the jealousy of Stephen which had made him move away from Nazareth. Added to this was confusion and uncertainty in regard to his own attitude toward Jesus. The incidents of the morning were a jumbled and muddled series of pictures in his thoughts. He tried to recall the exact words of Jesus. Had He actually claimed to be Messiah or had they misinterpreted and misunderstood Him? One thing was certain: He had

disappeared. And, Joel reminded himself, he had seen the water changed to wine.

On returning from the hilltop, he had gone into the house determined to give his parents an account of what had happened and then leave for Capernaum without delay. In his anger the fact that such a journey was unlawful on the Sabbath had not occurred to him, and, as far as he was concerned, he would have been perfectly willing to disregard the law anyway. His father had seemed so grieved at the idea that he had permitted himself to be persuaded to remain by his bedside until sundown, but had refused absolutely to spend another night in Nazareth. Thus it was that he arrived in Capernaum close to midnight, soaked to the skin and exhausted from the twenty-mile walk and the strain and excitement of the day.

At Jonathan's house it was not until he had banged the third time on the shutter that he succeeded in waking Dysmas, who was sleeping soundly through all the noise of the storm. The lad finally came, doped with slumber, to unbolt the door. Without even lighting a lamp, Joel tore off his sodden garments and, falling into bed, dropped off instantly into a sound sleep.

The next thing he knew, bright sunshine was in his face and Dysmas was shaking him roughly by the shoulder, saying, "Hey, wake up, wake up! Jonathan wants to see you."

As soon as he was dressed, Joel went through the shop, left the house, and turning into the alley, climbed the outside stair, which led to the second story. Jonathan, too shaken by disease to feed himself, propped up in bed, was being fed by the faithful Sarah. Though ordinarily Joel did not take his meals with his employer, nothing would do the kindly woman but that he sit down and eat breakfast before he and Jonathan talked business.

He made a good meal of broiled fish, hard-boiled eggs, and little rolls freshly baked that morning. Between mouthfuls, he answered the questions of the old couple: "Was his father better?" "Had he enjoyed his visit home?" "Wasn't that storm last night an unheard of thing for this time of year?"

The youth was careful to make no mention of the riot the previous day, though he could not explain to himself his reticence[8] to discuss an occurrence which he knew the old people would have found exciting and thrilling. At length, both the meal and questions being finished, Sarah went about her housekeeping duties, leaving her husband and his clerk to talk business.

Joel received from Jonathan full instructions about laying in new stock and asked his advice about a number of matters. Finally, as Joel arose to leave, the invalid said, "While you were gone we had a message from Levi, the tax collector, that our taxes are delinquent.[9] You had better go and see him this morning."

A few hundred yards from Jonathan's shop, several large buildings set in a grove of trees were surrounded by a high wall. This was the official seat of the government in Capernaum. One of the houses was a barracks for the Roman soldiers. Another was the residence of the centurion and his family. The third, two stories high and surrounded by a kind of open colonnade or covered walk, was the headquarters of various petty officials and contained the courts of law. The tax office was located on the ground floor. Levi, the chief collector, sat just inside the office behind a table placed across the open doorway so that those doing business with him were required to remain outside in the colonnade. Behind Levi several clerks were busy with their records.

Joel, in common with all patriotic Jews, felt a particular contempt for any Hebrew who became a petty official under the Roman conquerors and looked upon him as a traitor to his own people. This attitude was not without foundation. It was almost impossible for a Jew to remain long in a governmental position unless he was completely subservient[10] to the Roman authorities or had some strong influence at the court of Herod. In the last analysis this was practically the same, for Herod owed his tetrarchy[11] to Rome and was cordially hated as a sycophant[12] of Caesar's.

Joel was determined for Jonathan's sake to veil his contempt for the tax collector, since to antagonize one of these men could mean an increase in assessment. As long as these officials delivered promptly what their superiors considered sufficient taxes for their districts, they could be fairly sure of remaining in office, and anything additional which they might collect they could pocket with no one the wiser. Theirs was a business which permitted large-scale graft and theft.

For the greater part of an hour, the youth conferred with Levi, who demanded an increase in payment because Jonathan's taxes were delinquent. Joel explained that the old man's son had died just at the time the taxes were due and that Jonathan was bedridden and unable to look after business. He apologized for his employer and assured the official that there would be no delay in any future payments. Had he desired, Levi could have waived the fine, which Joel suspected would go into his own pocket anyway, but in a technical, letter-of-the-law interpretation he refused to do so.

It was plain that Joel was accomplishing nothing. Levi's manner indicated growing impatience and several men and a woman were waiting their turn to speak to the tax collector. Finally, with bad grace, the youth counted out the coins demanded while Levi watched with a bored air as if to say, "The life of a public official is a monotonous one—nothing to do but take in money all day long."

As Joel turned on his heels and started down the covered walk, all unnoticed by him, a cadaverous-looking individual who had been idling against a column just opposite the desk of Levi, yawned and stretched, and, moving as one who had all the time in the world and no particular purpose in view, followed the youth down the colonnade, across the courtyard, and through the gates to the street. The cool, shaded portico was a favorite loitering place for the idlers of the town. A number of benches were set between the columns and these were occupied by people waiting to transact business or by lawyers whose affairs required their presence at the courts that day or who, having no business, sat around hoping

for a client. No one, therefore, paid any particular attention to the stroller.

Once past the sentries at the gate, his attitude underwent a decided change. His aimless manner dropped away and he set out with purposeful steps in the direction taken by Joel, being careful, however, not to decrease the distance between them. When Joel turned into the alley beside Jonathan's house, the tracker quickened his pace, but when he had arrived at the intersection, Joel was nowhere in sight, having gone up the stairs to Jonathan's apartment.

The stranger, presuming the young man had passed through the alley to the street beyond, now went this way himself—of course, without finding Joel.

Meanwhile the indignant young man was expressing himself freely to his employer on the subject of tax collectors and of the government in general. Joel with the radicalism of youth and his natural hatred of oppression of any sort was much more upset than Jonathan, who had learned through experience and suffering to bear injustice patiently. Taxes were so high that only a small margin of profit was left to the old man after they had been paid and the expense of the business cared for. As the old couple had no other income except that from the little shop, the heavy fine which Levi had exacted worked a real hardship.

Knowing this, Joel expected Jonathan to echo his tirade but the old man lifted a trembling hand to silence the angry youth. Instead of uttering complaints, the quiet voice said, "God permits our nation to be punished for our sins. He gave our fathers into the hands of the Egyptians and the Assyrians and they were oppressed. But when repentance and revival came, God gave relief from the chastening of the pagan. God uses Rome to chasten us because of the corruption and selfishness of our leaders and because our religion has become only a dead thing."

"But are we just to put up with all the rottenness and bend our necks and grovel in the dirt? At least we can fight! The Macabees did!" interrupted Joel.

"The hope of the Jew is not in the resistance and rebellion which you advocate, my son; our hope is in a spiritual revival." The lids dropped over the bright eyes of the old man. Softly he quoted:
"If my people who are called by my name, shall humble themselves and pray, and seek my face, and turn from their wicked ways, then I will hear from heaven, and will forgive their sin, and will heal their land."
Then he opened his eyes and fixed them upon Joel. "My boy, these are God's words."

He paused for a moment, plucking at the coverlet with his poor palsied hands, "God hasn't forsaken us; we have forsaken Him. His promise stands. Someday His King will rule in justice and in equity. The glories will be restored when Messiah comes, my son."

Messiah! The thoughts of Joel were upon Jesus as the old man spoke. He had strange powers certainly, but were they the powers of a king? Could they be great enough to drive out the Roman and destroy the corrupt Herod? Could the hand that knew the hammer and saw wield a sword? God's Messiah surely would come in a burst of glory with blasting trumpets and flaunting banners, with rolling drums and all the panoply of royal power. Jesus' claim that He was Messiah might be only a delusion on His part, Joel decided, but at least He had the gift of miracles, and His enemies could have no power over a man who could vanish from their grasp. Perhaps He might even be a prophet. In the olden days prophets had been simple men—farmers and shepherds, and they had worked miracles. Why should God not call a carpenter?

Joel's thought went racing on. Perchance this Man then might be the leader they needed—one around whom the nation could rally. No, not Messiah, certainly, but a man who could perhaps lead an army and wear a crown. Already He had attracted wide attention and captured the popular imagination. The rumors that had preceded Him from Judea were evidence of that.

Joel pondered upon these possibilities long after he had taken leave of Jonathan, and, during the days that followed, they were never far from his thoughts. Meanwhile, Jesus had appeared in Capernaum and crowds followed Him everywhere. Early one morning as Joel opened the shop, he stopped to watch as usual the fishermen coming in from their night's work. Already several of the boats had been drawn up in shallow water. It was apparent that they had had no luck during the night because no shining fish were being placed in baskets for market.

Joel by now was able to recognize the boats of the different men and he knew more or less intimately their owners and crews. That dark craft with the green sails belonged to Zebedee, a man whose temper was as uncertain as winter weather on Galilee. He sat now in unaccustomed silence mending the nets which had been badly torn by some submerged object, and James and John, his sons, were helping with what was always a tedious and unpleasant task. A little distance out, Joel could see a red head bending over the side of another boat as a man pulled in the nets for the last time before making for shore. This he knew to be Simon, a rugged giant of a man about forty years old and a loud and incessant talker. He was as impulsive and impetuous as Joel, and between the fisherman and the youth from Nazareth a warm friendship had developed. Andrew, his brother, gave him a hand in getting the last of the nets aboard and two hired hands at the oars began to pull for the landing.

At the same time Jesus approached from the town, pressed upon by a surprisingly large crowd for such an early hour. He reached the shore just as the keel of the ship of Simon and Andrew grated upon the pebbles. That the brothers were acquainted with the Nazarene, Joel knew, for when he had first met them in Capernaum, he had recognized them, as well as James and John, as the companions of Jesus at the wedding in Cana. As they leaped out now to greet Him, Joel presumed that Jesus asked them a question, for he saw them nod assent and help Him into the boat. Then Andrew and Peter shoved the craft backward from the beach, wading in up to their waists to free the

vessel before climbing aboard. With the crew settling to the oars, they maneuvered the boat broadside to the shore.

Now Jesus, sitting down, his back against the mast, began to teach the people while the fishermen, maintaining their distance from the beach, held the boat steady against the drift and the slight breeze. Meanwhile, Joel had come down to stand in the edge of the intently listening crowd. After He had spoken briefly to them, Jesus turned to Simon and said, "Now, go out into deep water and let down your nets."

Simon's bass voice rumbled across the water, as he replied, "Master, we've been at it all night and haven't caught anything, but if You say so, over they go."

The crowd watched with keen interest. The boat was rowed out a few hundred yards and Simon and Andrew let the net out over the stern while their two crewmen rowed the ship around in a great circle. Now came the business of pulling in.

To the amazement of the observers, although Simon and Andrew exerted all their great strength, they were unable to get the net aboard. The two oarsmen left their places to lend a hand, but still the nets resisted their efforts. Now they beckoned to Zebedee and his sons, who cast off from the shore and rowed out to help them. Muscular backs straining, they bent to the task. Slowly the nets came up tearing with the weight of a catch great enough to fill both boats to the gunwales with glistening fish until they were in such danger of capsizing that some had to be thrown back into the water. When the over-laden crafts reached the shore, there were many eager hands to draw the prows up on the small round pebbles which edged the lake.

As the boat grounded, Simon, kneeling, half upon the plank seat and half upon the heaped-up fish at the feet of Jesus, exclaimed, almost choked with tears, "Leave me, Lord, for I am a sinful man."

Jesus laid His hand upon the red head and promised, "After this, you shall catch men."

Then leaping from the boat, He turned and said to the brothers, "Follow Me, and I will make you fishers of men."

Andrew and Simon, with no further thought for the nets, the ship, or the load of fish, fell into step behind Jesus as He moved down the beach to Zebedee's ship. Here He stopped only a moment.

"James, John," He called; and the two lads—John, just younger, and James, just older than Joel—straightened up from their nets and, without a word to their father, joined Simon and Andrew as they followed Jesus into Capernaum.

Reading Check

1. What claim of Jesus stirs up the crowd in Nazareth?
2. What is Joel's opinion of the religious leaders?
3. To Joel's surprise, who tries to stop the attempt to kill Jesus?
4. How do the religious leaders treat Joel's father?
5. What reason does Jonathan give for Israel's bondage to Rome?

Chapter 5

"So then he screamed, fell down and rolled on the floor for a minute, and then after a while, when he sat up, he was all right." Dysmas' voice broke with excitement and he was quite out of breath as he finished his story.

"Wait a minute," Joel said, confused by the excited narrative. "Calm down, calm down. Start over and tell it all from the beginning."

"But I've just told you," protested the lad, though nothing could have stopped him from repeating it.

"Here," said Joel, pushing the youth down on to the side of the bed. "Relax. Now, come again."

Dysmas took a deep breath. "Well, we were all in the synagogue, listening to Jesus. All at once Darsis lifts both hands up and starts yelling, 'Let us alone!'"

"Right in the middle of the sermon?"

"Uh, huh, right in the middle. Then he came down and stood in front of Jesus."

"Didn't anybody try to stop him?"

"Well, of course, most people in town are afraid of him, anyway; so they just sort of drew back to give him plenty of room."

"What did Jesus do all this time?"

"Oh, He just looked at the man. Say, Joel, have you ever seen Darsis when the spell is on him?"

Joel shook his head.

"Then you can't imagine what it's like. His voice is different. It's as though somebody else was inside of him, speaking with another voice through his mouth. It was this strange voice that said, 'What have we to do with you, Jesus of Nazareth? Are You come to destroy us?' He stood there looking at Jesus, shivering as if he had a chill, and then in the terrible hollow whisper that was loud enough for us all to hear, he said, 'I know You—Who You are—the Holy One of God!' "

"Then?" pressed Joel.

"Then Jesus, Who all the time had been sitting in the Rabbi's Seat, just as He had been when Darsis interrupted the sermon, got up suddenly and looked at Darsis almost as if He were angry, and cried, 'Hold your peace!' "

"Did he?"

"Yes, that's the strange thing—He did! Usually when the demon is upon him, nothing can make him be quiet. He began to tremble harder than ever, but he didn't say anything else. Then Jesus spoke like a centurion commanding a soldier, 'Come out of him!' and that's when he screamed and fell down. After a moment he sat up and looked around and the strange expression was gone from his eyes, and he acted just like anybody else."

"What happened to him?" asked Joel.

"Well, you could tell by looking at him that the demon was gone; so people weren't afraid of him any more. Two or three helped him up and he actually thanked them. Then he knelt down and took the hem of Jesus' robe and began to kiss it."

It was an amazing story. This Darsis was a town character and though Joel had never witnessed one of the strange demoniacal attacks which came upon him at intervals, he had often seen him on the street and in the marketplace, a wild-eyed and frenzied figure, mumbling outlandish gibberish or croaking terrible prophecies. He slept here and there in nooks and crannies or on the beach or the steps of the synagogue. He never wanted for food because it was an unheard-of thing to refuse any demoniac who came begging. Superstition and fear assured creatures like Darsis of being well fed. Though demon possession was not uncommon, no one had ever heard of an unclean spirit leaving its victim at the command of any man.

"I'll bet you're sorry you stayed home today," said Dysmas, with a wide grin. "The first time, too, and something exciting like this happens."

Remembering that experience of the previous Sabbath in the synagogue at Nazareth, Joel had suggested that he stay with Jonathan so that Sarah could go with Dysmas to worship. The lad was right; he was sorry he had stayed home. He would like to have seen the demon cast out; but, having seen it, he knew he would have been no better able to explain it. When Dysmas asked, "What sort of man is Jesus that even evil spirits obey Him?" Joel had no answer for the lad or for his own questioning mind.

Dysmas, too excited by the events of the morning to stay quietly at home, went out looking for young friends in the town with whom he might discuss, over and over, the strange, dramatic incident of the morning. He came back about dark with word that Jesus had spent the afternoon at the house of Simon, where He had healed his mother-in-law of fever. The news having got around, people had come as soon as the Sabbath was over, immediately after sundown, from all over Capernaum, bringing their sick and blind and crippled relatives until they had filled the whole street around Simon's house. Jesus had come out and put His hands upon them and healed them all.

Meantime, Joel had spent the afternoon on the housetop, lying under a piece of sailcloth that had been rigged as an awning, watching the changing colors of the lake and busy with his own thoughts.

As they were preparing for bed, Dysmas stopped, one sandal on, one off, "Maybe He could heal Jonathan." And it was agreed between them that right after breakfast the next day they would somehow get their employer to Jesus.

Their disappointment, therefore, was keen when the first customer of the morning brought the information that Jesus had set out with His followers at sunrise for the hills. Though news drifted back of His visit to other cities in Galilee, together with rumors of great miracles, it was many weeks before Capernaum saw Him again.

Meantime, Joel was growing day by day more bitter and cynical about the conditions of the land and its hopes for the future. He saw a delegation of scribes, accompanied by several elders, wait fawningly[13] upon Herod's steward when he came by boat one day from Tiberias. This fat and treacherous individual, the son of a Galilean father and an Idumean slave, was known through all the province for his ruthless cruelty and greed. By pandering[14] to Herod's vices, he had made himself indispensable to his dissipated master.

Not to enjoy the favor of the steward was sooner or later to lose the favor of the tetrarch, for his influence over Herod was uncanny.

As he watched the leading citizens of the town with flattery and gifts feed the vanity and avarice[15] of this low-born man, Joel felt actual physical nausea.

Another day the kind Sarah, having seen from her upper window the gathering of a crowd and signs of commotion up the shore, had come down to the shop saying, "Jonathan is sleeping for a little while and I'll look out for things if you boys would like to go and see what the excitement is all about."

It was a group of manacled slaves passing through Capernaum on their way down the lake to Tiberias, where Herod was engaged in architectural and engineering projects involving the construction of a new wing of his palace, the enlarging of his orchard and gardens, and the erection of a great stone pier to accommodate the large pleasure craft he intended to have built for himself. This unhappy group was comprised largely of young men in their late teens and twenties, strong bodied and able to do heavy work. Pointing this out to Dysmas, whom he unconsciously was infusing with something of his own bitter resentment, Joel cried, "These are not criminals or prisoners of war; they are good Jews. Do you know how they became slaves?"

"I suppose because they were sold for debts they couldn't pay," answered the lad.

"Because they were unlucky enough not to be able to pay the taxes piled on their backs. It's a case of pay for Herod's palace or help build it. Their wives and children can starve while they work for the pleasure of a man who's a parasite and the most useless creature in Galilee."

Of course, such talk was treason and dangerous in a crowd like this gathered to watch the unfortunate conscripts being loaded into the boat. The only one who gave any indication that he might have overheard was the tall, thin individual just behind the youths, and sudden gleam in his dark-circled eyes and the tightening of his thin lips might have been entirely unrelated to Joel and his conversation with Dysmas. But this time when Joel, still talking intently to his companion, turned homeward, this man was careful not to lose sight of the two until he had tracked them all the way to Jonathan's and seen them go into the shop.

Now as the stranger walked past the open door, Joel was describing to Sarah in even more bitter language the unhappy scene they had just witnessed. Had anyone been observing the mysterious individual at that moment he would have detected on the lean face the expression of satisfaction a woman wears when she has succeeded in getting her way, and a man when he has found out something he needs to know in order to put over a successful business deal.

About mid-morning several days later as Joel was seated in the door of the shop, half dozing in the sunshine, a shadow fell across his face. Lifting his head, he found himself looking up at a tall, sallow and unhealthy appearing man. Supposing him a customer, Joel

rose to his feet, greeting him politely with the usual "Peace be with you."

"And with you," replied the stranger, his thin-lipped mouth drawing to one side in a smile that disclosed yellow and broken teeth. "I'm not exactly a customer; I was just—" he broke off vaguely, then added, "If I might sit down?"

Joel, puzzled, indicated the doorstep.

The stranger promptly folded his long legs and sat down, his shoulder

against the doorpost. Joel resumed his own seat beside him. After the custom of the Jews, the stranger made polite conversation for a while upon a wide variety of general topics before he came to the point of his business.

"I am a newcomer to town and thought I'd settle in Capernaum. Someone told me that this business was for sale—that is, I mean to say, that the owner of the business was an invalid and might be interested in selling."

Joel had a strange feeling that this was not the real purpose of the stranger's visit, but he could think of no other reason why he might have come, so dismissed his suspicions as silly and unreasonable.

"I don't think Jonathan would be interested in selling," Joel answered slowly. "I've never heard him mention it."

"But he might consider it?"

"I doubt it. His father owned the place before him. He's never lived anywhere else, and I think he'd be miserable in a strange house, particularly now that he's bedridden."

"Well, you might mention it to him if it's convenient, and I can stop by again and find out what he says."

As he got to his feet, he looked out over the lake, lying like shiny green silk in the sunlight. "It reminds me of a bay in the Aegean," he said.

Joel was interested as the visitor had intended he should be. "But you are not a Greek!" he exclaimed.

"No, no, I was born in Joppa, but I lived for a while in Greece."

"Some day I shall travel," declared Joel with conviction. "Tell me, where else have you been?"

"I have been to Egypt and as far as Crete and Rhodes. As a boy living in a seaport and watching the ships come in, I got a yen to know what was beyond the horizon. One day I ran away to sea."

"I'll bet you had some interesting times."

"Yes, strange sights I've seen and a bit of adventure now and then. Well, I must be going. I'll stop back by in a day or two and find out what Jonathan has to say."

Joel could scarcely wait for the return of the tall man whose name he was ashamed he had forgotten to inquire. Brought up in a small town like Nazareth, he had, like every imaginative youth, dreamed of adventures in strange lands, of looking on foreign towns and observing the strange customs of other peoples. Though he had been brought up to believe the Jews, as God's chosen race, were superior to other nations, and though he agreed with his father, who for hours on end decried the influence of paganism upon their nation, he was fascinated by what he had heard of the wonders of pagan civilizations. Though he was sure that Jerusalem, which he had visited, must be the most wonderful city in the world because in it was the temple of Jehovah, he nonetheless wanted to see Athens and Rome. Having had little contact with widely traveled men, Joel made up his mind to become well acquainted with the ex-sailor, and he was determined to hear the stories of his adventures.

He mentioned this interesting visitor to Jonathan and inquired, as he had promised, whether there was any possibility that the property could be purchased.

"I was born here, and here, if God wills, I shall die," the old man exclaimed, almost indignant that anyone should think that he would part with his home.

Joel, forgetting his initial suspicions of the man from Joppa, felt compelled to defend him to Jonathan. "I am sure he meant no harm in inquiring. He struck me as a very nice man."

"Well, nice or not, tell him I'm not interested," he snapped. And then, as if ashamed of his outburst, he added, "Of course, I suppose we should thank him for inquiring."

Chapter 6

To Joel, waiting impatiently, it seemed that the stranger would never return. Whenever he was on the street, he found himself watching for a tall figure with dark-circled eyes and a thin-lipped mouth and a twisted smile. So wise had been this stranger's approach and so strong the force of his personality that he had made upon Joel a profound impression. It had been his object to arouse the curiosity of the young man in order to insinuate himself into his confidences, but he little realized how decidedly he had awakened the interest of the youth.

Several days following the visit from the stranger, Joel and Dysmas were returning to Capernaum just after sundown. They had gone out late in the afternoon for a swim in the lake at a spot about a mile south of town. Now as they were headed homeward, cool and refreshed, Joel saw the man from Joppa, walking with long strides toward them, who after an exchange of greetings, suggested, "If you don't mind, I'll walk along with you."

"But, weren't you going the other way?" asked Dysmas, who felt something of the same instinctive distrust which Joel had experienced when he first met this man.

"I am just taking a stroll," said the stranger. "I like to walk along the beach at this time of day. I think it's the spell and charm of the lake more than anything else that makes me want to settle down in Capernaum."

"Well," said Joel. "I'm afraid you'll have to settle in some other house than Jonathan's."

"He won't sell?"

"Not at any price. He almost had apoplexy[16] at the very thought of it."

If the stranger was disappointed he did not show it. In fact, Dysmas, to whom Joel had, of course, mentioned this stranger's visit to the shop and his object in coming, thought the man even seemed relieved at Joel's answer.

"Well, I shall just have to look around a bit further. I appreciate your kindness in inquiring about it for me." Then dismissing the matter entirely, he turned to other topics. Now as they arrived at Jonathan's, instead of bidding them good-bye, the man from Joppa insisted that they have supper with him. Though both young men were reluctant to put themselves under obligation to one who was practically a stranger, he was so insistent that they could not refuse without being rude; besides, the walk and the swim had whetted youthful appetites. Dysmas and Joel kept bachelor's quarters and the thought of something besides their own erratically prepared meals was a temptation they could scarcely resist.

Presently, therefore, they found themselves seated at a well-laden table in a little courtyard. This was a popular spot with travelers who passed through Capernaum. Business was good in the courtyard and other diners were being served in an inner room. The round and jolly woman who ran this little eating place seemed to be well acquainted with their host and she, herself, waddled back and forth from table to kitchen hurrying the servant and seeing that they were properly looked after and that everything was to their tastes.

Finally, rather more than pleasantly filled, and quite at ease with the world, the two youths sat over cups of wine listening to the fascinating tales of their host, whose name they had discovered was Omah. There was no doubt about it: he was a talented teller of tales with a flair for description and an unfailing sense of humor and a gift for dramatic language.

As he talked his hearers forgot his strange appearance, and any feeling of mistrust quite vanished as he spun his yarns. Older men than these boys, sixteen and nineteen, had fallen under the spell of Omah's personality.

Frequently thereafter Joel could be found in the evenings in Omah's company. Sometimes Dysmas was along, but more often Joel would go alone to meet his new-found friend.

From his vantage point of nineteen Joel was rather inclined to look down upon the younger lad and consider him immature and something of a nuisance. For his part, Dysmas looked up to Joel with an admiration which amounted almost to worship and was quite unwarranted. He would do anything for Joel and followed him about like a faithful dog, and it was only because Joel gave him no encouragement that Dysmas so seldom accompanied him when he spent the evenings with Omah.

These two, the tall man and the broad-shouldered youth, could be seen night after night walking along the beach in the moonlight or sitting together in a wine shop somewhere. Omah had introduced Joel to several of his friends and sometimes these joined them under the smoke-stained beams of a low-ceilinged inn or in the upper room which Omah had rented in the house of a widow. The two who appeared most frequently were an ill-matched pair: Hosea, one-eyed and pock-marked and practically bald; Zelon, dark-haired and handsome. Though Joel was frequently with them, it occurred to him that he knew very little about these men, though he gathered from their conversation that they were from Judea. Hosea, at least, spoke frequently of Jerusalem as one speaks of his native town.

The rabbi, Ephraim, would have been considerably distressed had he seen his son night after night in such company. But actually, aside from the fact that they drank rather too much Syrian beer, the conduct of Joel and his companions was harmless enough. When not listening to stories of Omah's adventures, they spent their evenings discussing for hours on end the state of the world and of their homeland in particular. Though at first more careful than Joel in the expression of their opinion about the government of Galilee, Omah and his friends were certainly in accord with him; and their sympathetic attitude and expressions of agreement, dropped from time to time, did nothing to modify Joel's radicalism or discourage the increasing treason of his thoughts.

One evening the feelings of the three older men were less conservatively expressed than heretofore. The town had buzzed all day with news of the crucifixion by the Romans of a rebel leader. This man, Jeshua, had rallied to himself in the wilderness beyond Jordan a band of disgruntled followers and runaway slaves. He had even dared to attack with success one or two small Roman outpost garrisons. It had been his hope that his countrymen would rally around the banner of rebellion he had raised, but the Jewish leaders themselves had, of course, given no encouragement, and the Romans had only to send from Jerusalem a small well-equipped troop under the command of a centurion to put down the abortive mutiny. The little band was scattered, some having been slain in the skirmish, during which Jeshua was captured along with a number of his followers, who were sent to the galleys. Pilate, the Roman procurator of Judea, had ordered the execution of their leader.

Discussing the collapse of Jeshua's dreams of Jewish freedom, Joel said bitterly, "The whole trouble lies primarily in the selfishness of our leaders. There are too many traitors in the Sanhedrin and among the priests and scribes."

"Well, you can't very well expect them to encourage uprisings against the Romans," said Hosea. "As long as things are peaceful the procurator keeps his hands off religious affairs and they can enjoy their revenues and profits in peace."

"And," added Joel, "strut their piety."

The quiet Zelon, who made now what was the longest speech Joel had yet heard from him, revealed an unsuspected turn of mind. "The priests keep saying to the people that the Romans respect religious freedom and urge them, therefore, to give their conquerors no trouble. The difficulty is that the whole philosophy of our history is against this attitude. With the Jew, religion and nationalism are all one. By their compromise with the conquerors, they've taken all the force out of religion and reduced it to outward sacrifices and ceremonies."

"Well," interrupted Omah, "they are certainly dogmatic enough about these."

"Sure, they're dogmatic," Joel agreed. "Sacrifices bring income to the temple. They are the livelihood of the priests and their hangers-on; and by observing all the ceremonies and traditions, these hypocritical priests persuade the common people that they are the defenders and sustainers of the religion of our fathers."

"My own personal opinion," said Omah at this point, "is that the only kind of rebellion that will ever flame into a real success is rebellion against religion as well as against Rome; but then," he added, "of course, I'm a complete atheist."

Joel was shocked. He had never suspected his friend of being anything but a believing, if somewhat religiously negligent, Jew. The strict upbringing of the Pharisee's son showed in his somewhat stilted reply. "Our nation has been most prosperous when most true to God. Genuine religion and prosperity have always been found together, and all the prophets teach that when Messiah sets up His government, spiritual life will flourish along with our national glories."

Omah laid a friendly hand upon Joel's arm. "I'm sorry if my atheism offends you, Joel. But I think we're going to waste our time if we wait for a God I don't believe in to send a Messiah—a leader. We're going to have to find one for ourselves, a man of courage and imagination, with popular appeal and plenty of contempt for the Pharisees and the Sadducees, and the scribes, and all the rest."

"Maybe," Zelon suggested, "this man Jesus is what we need. They say He has plenty of courage and the way He skins the scribes and Pharisees is something to hear."

"I'm afraid He's too religious," objected Omah. "I don't mean too pious like the professional religionists in Jerusalem. I mean sincerely religious. I'm afraid He's one of those deluded souls that actually believe all the law and prophets through and through. He's too sincere for His own good. Religion of that sort always betrays a man by making him soft when he needs to be tough."

"But," Joel insisted, "He does denounce hypocrisy and He certainly has power to work wonders."

Hosea's one bright eye looked around the table. "They tell me He thinks He is the Messiah. He's either crazy or, more likely, possessed of evil spirits that give Him power to work miracles."

"But He casts the evil spirits out of others!" protested Joel.

"Well," laughed Hosea, "maybe He Himself has the king of all evil spirits whom the others have to obey."

Somehow the conversation turned to a comparison of relative conditions in Judea and Galilee. In many respects they were parallel. The Romans maintained garrisons in each and demanded revenues and tribute from both. Upon the death of Herod the Great about thirty years before, the Romans had divided into three parts his kingdom, which had included not only Judea and Galilee, but Perea to the northeast also. As far as the Jews were concerned, their situation was little changed by the division. The Romans still ruled them. The only difference was that in Judea Herod's son, Archelaus, had been deposed and banished about twenty years before, and the Romans had sent a procurator or governor to take his place. In Galilee Herod Antipas, another son of Herod the Great, still was the nominal representative of Caesar with the title of tetrarch.

"When all's said and done," offered Hosea, "I'd rather live under a Roman governor like Pilate than a tricky Romanized Jew like Herod. With all their faults, the Romans are usually fair and they're great sticklers for law. But Herod, as far as he dares, when he thinks Caesar won't hear of it, does as he pleases."

"But," said Omah, "he's careful not to anger or upset the Romans. He goes out of his way to flatter every mere centurion in his effort not to miss any string he can pull in his ambition to have Caesar change his title from tetrarch to king!"

Hosea chuckled. "That prophet called John has given Herod plenty of headaches. I heard him preach a whole sermon against adultery, using Herod as an example. He called on him to repent and demanded that he get rid of Herodias. I'm sure if any man in the congregation had an idea of stealing his brother's wife, he changed his mind after that sermon!"

Zelon took up the subject, "He's still a headache for Herod. Now that the tetrarch has him clapped into jail he

doesn't know what to do with him. He's too superstitious to put a prophet to death and he'd lose face if he released him without a retraction of his statements about Herodias."

"And he's sure it's bad luck to keep him in prison," finished Omah. "Well, if John gets out he might be just the man to head a rebellion against the powers that be. He should have sufficient grudge after being in jail and he can certainly sway the crowds."

"Sure," agreed Hosea, "if he would quit preaching repentance long enough to get interested in something as practical as a rebellion."

"Well, we could promise John that after he has got rid of Herod and the Romans he can go back to preaching again. That might be a good thing, too, if he could get the priests converted."

In this note the gathering broke up and Joel went home, head heavy with wine and with the unsatisfactory feeling that he was talking entirely too much about the corruption destroying his nation and the oppression which was weighing it down. The need, he told himself, was not talk, but action—not words, but deeds. Though it was late when he went to bed, he lay for a long time listening to the regular breathing of Dysmas across the room. He felt he had to *do* something, but the question he kept asking himself as he tossed from side to side was "what?"

Reading Check

1. What story of Christ's power does Dysmas relate to Joel?
2. What aspect of the stranger's background interests Joel?
3. Who are Omah's two friends?
4. Which of Joel's new group of "friends" claims to be an atheist?
5. Which two men are discussed as potential leaders of the Israelite rebellion against Rome?

Chapter 7

The next day Jesus reappeared in Capernaum as suddenly as He had left. And the town was filled within a few hours by throngs of people who had flocked to listen to His words and see His miracles.

He had gone again to Simon's house, but, according to Dysmas, who, much too excited to be of any use in the shop, had been given the day off, Jesus had been invited to the residence of Jonas, the most prominent Pharisee in Capernaum and the leading force in the administration of the synagogue. Apparently to get away for a while from the insistent multitude, Jesus had accepted the invitation and had gone out by a back way from Simon's house.

But he was not to escape the crowd. When He arrived at Jonas's Jesus found a number of important men already there. A delegation of scribes and Pharisees from Jerusalem was present,

as well as representatives of other cities in Judea and Galilee. They had come quite obviously to form an opinion of this strange Teacher Who had flashed into such sudden prominence and whose influence was becoming rapidly nationwide.

Meantime, word had got around that Jesus was no longer at Simon's house, but had gone to Jonas's, and the milling throng that followed Him there had pushed through the gates and into the courtyard in front of the large home of the prominent and wealthy citizen. By noon men and women were packed into an impatient and sweating mass that could not get into the house and would not disperse.

It was this scene of confusion that greeted the arrival of Jonathan before the house. Squinting in the bright sunlight, pale from his weeks of confinement, he lay shaking with his affliction upon a litter borne at one end by Joel and Dysmas and at the other by Zebedee, the fisherman, and Enos, one of the two nephews who had taken the places of his sons on the fishing boat.

"Looks as if we're going to have a hard time getting through the crowd," said Dysmas.

"Pardon us, please," cried Joel, attempting to shoulder his way into the mass of closely packed bodies.

"Stop shoving. You can't get through here!"cried voices. And a large woman with several chins and two or three enormous warts on her face walled her popped eyes indignantly and croaked in a hoarse voice, "I wonder who they think *they* are."

"Old frog," mumbled Zebedee, and the description was so apt that Dysmas burst out laughing.

By now they had managed to get through the edge of the crowd until they stood just outside the gate, but it was plain to them all that there was no possibility of getting into the yard. One thin man with the instincts of a cat or a serpent might have been able to insinuate himself bit by bit through the crowd; but for four men weighted down by a sick man on a stretcher, it was an absolute impossibility. With great difficulty Dysmas choked back tears of vexation. Joel's face showed his disappointment. Zebedee was living up to his nickname of "Thunder" by rumbling fiercely in his throat what sounded suspiciously like oaths. Enos's sweaty face was creased in a frown. Only the sick man seemed patient and undisturbed.

"There must be some other way in," mused Joel.

This gave Enos an idea. "Let's get out of this mob," he said, giving a push to the stretcher that surely would have caused Dysmas, just in front of him, to lose his footing had he not been wedged in by the crowd. Instead, therefore, of Dysmas moving, only his hand holding the stretcher pole moved, and the end of the pole was rammed vigorously against the ample back of the frog-like woman.

"Why, you!" she exclaimed furiously, slapping Dysmas resoundingly. Then turning to the interested onlookers, she announced in a loud croak, "Poked me with that pole, he did, right in the small of the back!"

A serious situation might have developed if it hadn't been for Zebedee. "Nothing about your back is small," he rumbled. "Besides, I saw him; he poked you in the widest part."

The crowd roared with laughter; and, taking advantage of the moment of good humor, the stretcher bearers worked themselves and their burden down the street and beyond the house. At the corner of the wall Enos said, "Let's turn down here."

Out of sight of the crowd they set Jonathan down and stood flexing their arms and rubbing their muscles.

"I know how we might get in," suggested Enos. "Farther down there," he pointed, "is a little door in the wall. It's the way I've gone in when I've come delivering the fish. It leads into the kitchen yard."

"Won't that be full of people, too?" inquired Joel.

"I don't think so; it's separated from the front court by a wing of the house and a cross wall. This back yard is used only by the servants."

"Suppose the door is locked," said Joel.

"Then break it down!" suggested Zebedee fiercely.

For the first time Jonathan joined the discussions, "I'm afraid that would be a little noisy, old fellow, and I'd hate to think of my four friends going to jail for trying to help me."

I'll tell you what," suggested Dysmas. "I can climb over the wall and unbolt the door from the inside."

This as it turned out was the solution of the problem, but it was accomplished not without difficulty. The small side door was almost exactly opposite the back entrance to the governmental quadrangle and two soldiers were always on guard there.

"Let me carry the front end by myself," directed Joel. "You go on down

the street, up the alley, and climb over the wall from the back of the house. If any of the servants see you and start to howl, tell them Zebedee sent you to find out how many fish they want delivered tomorrow. Tell them the door was bolted and you climbed the wall to ask because you were scared to come back to Zebedee without finding out."

Enos laughed, "Nobody knowing Zebedee will doubt that."

The lad hurried off and presently the watchers, seeing the little door open, picked up the stretcher, walked down the street, and, under the eyes of the disinterested soldiers not thirty feet away, passed nonchalantly into Jonas's back yard. Bolting the door behind them, Dysmas was grinning with excitement.

"I didn't see anybody. All the servants must be in the house trying to overhear what's going on."

Crossing the yard, Jonathan's faithful bearers now encountered another difficulty. Walking boldly up to the back door, they found the inside of the house as packed as the courtyard in front. Just inside the back door were the servants, but the rest of the room as far as they could see from outside was filled with well-dressed and important-looking people, all of whom were trying to see through the archway into the main reception room beyond.

The stretcher bearers backed away for further consultation.

"May I have my keel ripped out if I'm going to be stopped now!" roared Zebedee.

Through an open window he saw Simon, a head taller than any of the rest standing near the center of the large room, which seemed to occupy the whole one-story wing between the paved courtyard and the back yard.

"That's where Jesus is," pointed out the fisherman, "because Simon won't be very far from Him."

"Look," said Joel, pointing to the stairs leading from the yard to the roof. "Let's go up there."

"Why?" inquired Dysmas and Enos in one breath.

"Come on and I'll show you."

With great difficulty and much juggling to keep the stretcher level, they made the rooftop. Surrounded with a parapet bearing boxes of shrubs and flowers and fitted with a number of stone benches, this was obviously used as a sort of outdoor room during the warm weather. The roof was floored with large terra-cotta tile laid edge to edge, the joints sealed up with pitch to turn the rain.

The bearers having set down the stretcher, Joel moved to a point near the center of the roof. "This should be about the spot," he said. "Zebedee, lend me your knife." The fisherman took from his belt the sharp-bladed tool for cleaning his catch and handed it to the youth, who knelt and began using it to work one of the tiles loose from the soft pitch. In a few moments he lifted the tile from its place. With one removed it was a simple matter to lift out the next. Now the others quickly joined in, Dysmas practically trembling with excitement and Enos grinning and Zebedee chuckling with mischievous pleasure as his big hands joined the attack upon the roof.

Looking down through the opening, Joel beheld a sea of upturned faces.

Jonas, the owner, was squinting and trying to move his head out of a blinding ray of direct sunlight. Only Jesus was not looking up, but calmly was continuing to speak as if there were no interruption.

"They look like a boatload of fish," chuckled Zebedee, winking down at his surprised sons, who were standing with Simon and Andrew just behind their Master.

Now the priests and the scribes, with whom the room was filled, began turning to one another with inquiring looks; and voices began to be heard asking, "What's going on?" "What are they doing?" "What's the meaning of this?"

Jonas, embarrassed at the thought of disturbing Jesus while He was speaking, and bewildered with surprise, was making all kinds of queer faces and gesturing excitedly to the men on the roof. He plainly meant, "Here I have all these distinguished people under my roof, and you go tearing that roof away from over their heads. Stop it this instant!" Self-important little man—Joel felt a twinge of pity for him, though he could not help smiling at his antics. As the volume of voices rose in the room, Jesus ceased speaking and sat quietly, watching the faces about Him.

By now an opening some eight feet long had been made between two of the beams, the space being just wide enough to permit the lowering of the stretcher. Quickly unwinding the long sash wrapped several times about his waist, Joel tied it securely to one of the stretcher handles. Seeing what he intended to do, the other three followed his example. Now, using their sashes as

cords, they very carefully lowered Jonathan, bed and all, into the room. The ceiling was not very high and, by lying on their stomachs and stretching their arms full length through the opening, they were able to lower the litter to within about three feet of the floor.

Meantime, several lawyers and one priest who had been standing just under the opening, when they saw the bed coming down, scrambled frantically out of the way, pushing themselves in among the other guests in an undignified fashion that they would have been most embarrassed to assume under any circumstances. Now their only thought was to get out from under.

One of Zebedee's sons who was standing close by took hold of one end of the stretcher with both hands and Simon, to get where he could take hold of the other, thrust two or three prominent men vigorously aside, indifferent to their grunts of protest. Seeing the stretcher supported from below, the men on the roof, their task of friendship completed, turned loose the ends of the scarves and James and Simon laid Jonathan at the very feet of Jesus.

Jesus turned upon Jonathan, now so dazed by the excitement of his journey and the unconventional means of his entrance as to scarcely know where he was, a smile of reassurance and understanding. Then bending over, He said in a clear voice, "Son, your sins are forgiven you."

Aside from the sound of a sharp intake of breath here and there, the room was deathly still. It was a silence pregnant with shock and indignation. Straightening up, Jesus stood for a moment looking down at Jonathan.

Then raising His eyes, He turned a piercing glance upon the room. To the watchers on the roof it seemed as if every man upon whom that glance fell winced and withered into smallness. Though they could not see His eyes from their position above, they had the strange feeling that He was reading hearts. The impression was confirmed when Jesus spoke in a voice in which contempt was mingled with pity, "Why do you reason this way in your hearts? Which is easier to say, 'Your sins are forgiven,' or 'Get up and walk'?" Then looking down at Jonathan, He said, "Arise, and take up your bed, and go home."

Jesus, bending above the invalid, reached down and took the trembling hand. Instantly the quivering muscles of the emaciated body became still. Jonathan seemed for a moment as tense as a runner at the starting line, waiting for the signal. Then he relaxed, breathing a long-drawn sigh of complete contentment. The face, a moment before so pallid,[17] was suffused[18] with the warm color of glowing health. The body so wasted from years of disease had become before their gaze well rounded and strong.

As Jesus raised him to his feet, it seemed as if the hand clasping Jonathan's rather gave a signal of command than offered a means of assistance.

Oblivious to all in the room, Jonathan, his face radiant, turned to Jesus and poured out his thanks. Meanwhile, Simon and James rolled up the stretcher, tying the ends of the poles together with the scarves. Jonathan took it from them; and, carrying it in front of him against his chest as a spear is borne by a soldier on parade, he left the house by the back door, all crowding aside to make way for him. Overhead, Joel and his companions were replacing as best they could the disarranged tile.

Jesus with His disciples had followed Jonathan from the house and left the yard by the small side door in the wall. Their task on the roof completed, the four friends descended and while his companions gathered around Jonathan, Joel slipped out through the little gate and followed Jesus. The Nazarene and His disciples were just appearing through the gate into the governmental compound, apparently intending to cross through the grounds on their way to Simon's house on the other side of the town. Joel trailed them between the barracks and the centurion's house and was only a short distance behind as they turned down the covered colonnade along the law court building.

Just as they came abreast of the tax collector's office, Jesus stopped and looked at Levi. Joel pressed closer, hoping to hear some scathing denunciation from the lips that had often rebuked scribe and Pharisee. Now, thought Joel, this crook will get what's coming to him.

"Follow me," said Jesus.

Joel could scarcely believe his ears. Surely he had not heard correctly. But apparently there was no mistake, for Levi arose and, pulling to one side the table that blocked the doorway, came out and joined the disciples as Jesus and His companions moved on down the colonnade. The exaltation which had come with the healing of Jonathan left the breast of Joel, to be replaced by a feeling of disappointment which during the next few hours changed to a dull anger. The vague hopes which he had cherished that somehow Jesus might be the leader Israel needed were shattered by the calling of Levi to be His disciple. Though he had never admitted to himself that Jesus might be Messiah, subconsciously he must have accepted the possibility, so keen was his disap-pointment at an act which appeared to be irrefutable evidence that Jesus could not be the Promised One. Messiah was to bring freedom from oppression. Surely, Joel told himself, there would be no room in His government for traitors who had profited by oppression.

Chapter 8

Joel thought he had sounded the depths of disappointment as he knocked that night upon the door of Omah's room in the widow's house, but he was to find still deeper valleys. He had not come here to talk about the shattering of his half-formed dreams. Though he could not have told why, he had no desire to discuss Jesus with Omah. That experienced individual quickly observed his young friend's preoccupation and ill-disguised melancholy, but was far too wise to inquire directly as to its cause. Instead he acted as if there was nothing unusual in Joel's manner, and kept up a running monologue so infrequently and briefly punctuated by remarks from his visitor that it could hardly be called a conversation.

The sound of music and occasional burst of laughter through the open window formed a background to Omah's voice. For the first time since he had met this man, the youth paid little attention to what he was saying and he had not heard the music and laughter at all, preoccupied as he was with all his own dark thoughts. Suddenly the youth noted that his companion had stopped speaking, as if waiting for an answer. He pulled himself together with an effort.

"I beg your pardon. What did you say?"

"I said it's quite a party our neighbor's having," replied the older man, nodding toward the open window.

Joel crossed the room and looked down. Just below was a large garden belonging to the next house, only partially visible through the trees that grew thickly around it. Torches fastened by brackets to their trunks illuminated a scene of festivity. About a large table was gathered a gay company laughing and feasting to the accompaniment of a small orchestra playing on a balcony. Beautifully dressed and well-trained servants came and went. Looking down upon the scene through the leaves, he could not distinguish, by the flickering torch light, the faces of the diners.

Behind him Joel heard Omah saying, "Our neighbor lives on quite a lavish scale. Profitable business, tax collecting!"

Joel turned, "Is that where Levi lives?"

Omah nodded, his mouth twisted into the familiar crooked grin. Joel turned back to the window and, laying both hands upon the sill, leaned out to peer intently down. Then straightening up but without looking around, he spoke over his shoulder.

"Who are his guests?" Each word was uttered separately as if by a great effort. Carelessly the answer was tossed back, "Oh, Jesus and His disciples. It appears Levi joined their number today and this is a sort of farewell to the comforts of home and the enjoyment of ill-gotten gains."

Joel gave no sign of having heard, but to Omah's ear during a lull in the music came a sound which might have been that of the evening breeze rustling the leaves of the garden. It might also have been a deep sigh. A moment later Joel started as Omah's hand was laid upon his shoulder. He had not heard him come across the room to stand behind him.

"Well, fellow," said the warm musical voice with its underlying tone of irony, "I suppose Israel will have to look elsewhere for a champion in the time of her distress. A fine Messiah He makes, feasting with tax gatherers and sinners."

Joel kept his face turned away from his friend. He was ashamed of the tears which overflowed his eyes and ran unchecked down his cheeks. The hand on Joel's shoulder tightened in a grip almost painful. The voice in Joel's ear rang with a new note—vibrant, incisive as a sword thrust.

"Since your gifted fellow-townsman makes friends with those who collaborate[19] with our conquerors, perhaps it's up to us to do something for the cause of freedom."

Now as he finally turned to look at Omah, astonishment was written on Joel's face. Not only the careless bantering[20] tone was gone from Omah's voice, but the expression of amused cynicism to which Joel had become so accustomed no longer lay on his mocking features and danced in his narrowed eyes. This was not the man from Joppa that Joel had come to know—a cynic sitting idly, watching life go by, satisfied to comment amusingly upon its tragedies and sins.

"Come," said this new voice, "sit down. It's time you and I had a real talk."

Joel crossed the room to his chair. Omah closed the blind and they could no longer hear the laughter and music. Omah resumed his seat, facing Joel

across the table, on which a lamp was burning.

"How much are you willing to give to see our nation great and strong and free?"

"I haven't anything to give," answered Joel slowly, "except myself."

"Are you ready to give that?"

"Certainly, if it will do any good."

"Do you know what it means to be a fugitive—an outlaw hiding in caves, hungry and cold? Can you endure filthy prisons, torture, death?"

Now it was Joel whose smile was twisted and bitter. "A man endures what he has to, I suppose. After all, I haven't much to lose. The woman I love is married to somebody else. My parents are comfortably fixed. Nobody is dependent upon me. Even old Jonathan can take over his business again."

The room was silent for a moment. "But what's this all about?" inquired the perplexed youth.

"Before I answer let me tell you a story. No, wait," he continued, holding up his hand in a gesture of command, silencing Joel, who had been about to interrupt. "Not just another adventure story. When you have heard it, you'll understand why I tell it. It won't take long."

"Some years ago," he began, "there was in my home town a particularly affectionate and godly little family of Jews. The man was a craftsman—a goldsmith, to be exact—honest and hard-working. His wife was a woman of great beauty and sweetness. There were only two children—a boy about eight and a girl half that age.

"Now a seaport town is always filled with rough men—dock workers, sailors,

the general riffraff that haunts the wharves. Because of this the father tried whenever possible to avoid being away from home after dark, but one night he was kept at his shop putting the finishing touches on a carved bowl which had been ordered by a wealthy merchant from Athens, who intended it as a gift for his wife. The merchant was sailing the next morning and the jeweler, who had promised to have it ready, worked late on the finishing touches, the final polishing. When he arrived home he was appalled to find the door, which was always kept locked, banging in the wind.

"With sinking heart he entered the house and lighted a lamp. His little daughter was dead, her head smashed in, the boy was unconscious and bleeding, and his wife, who had been cruelly assaulted, sat staring into space, unmoving and unspeaking. Her mind was gone, and until the day of her death nearly twenty years later, she lived in a dark, secret world of her own, never seeming to recognize anyone she had known and never speaking a word.

"The frantic father finally succeeded in reviving his son, who told a horrible story. The house had been broken into by a drunken man, one who had, even when sober, made advances to the beautiful young Jewess which she had indignantly rebuffed. This night, crazed with lust and drink, he had attacked the woman, tearing her robe from her shoulders. The boy leaped to his mother's defense but was easily knocked down, of course, and kicked into unconsciousness.

"Before the night was over the heartbroken jeweler, fired by his wrongs to vengeful fury, had sought out his wife's attacker and his daughter's murderer and killed him. But because this man was a Roman citizen, the Jew was sent without a trial, without consideration for the wrongs which he had suffered, to the galleys and his son never heard of his father again. The fact that he, a Jew, had killed a Roman was enough for the authorities. It did not matter that this particular Roman had been banished from Rome for robbery and murder. He was the son of one of Caesar's courtiers. The murder of a four-year-old girl, the rape of a godly Jewish mother were small offenses compared to the vengeance of the father and the husband."

Omah's voice died away and there was a long silence in the room, the flickering lamp casting a shadow large and distorted upon the wall behind him. After a moment he continued, "That man was my father, that woman my mother. It was my sister who was murdered and I was the boy left unconscious on the floor."

Joel did not speak. There was nothing he could say. Omah shuddered slightly and when he resumed speaking it was as if the gesture had rid him of his mood. His voice was no less earnest but now cold and businesslike.

"I grew up swearing vengeance upon the Romans. Hardly more than a boy, I went to sea and visited other lands. Always with a loathing for the Romans in my heart, I observed the effects of their tyranny in other countries. Five years later I returned to Judea old in experience of cruelty and mature in a hatred full grown. As time went by I found there were other men whose hearts were as crammed with bitterness as my own and I became active in a secret organization that throughout all Judea and Galilee is planning for the day of rebellion and vengeance."

Joel could not take his eyes from the speaker. He had never heard of such an organization and he had never suspected that this man was dedicated to any cause.

Now Omah's words concerned Joel. "I was sent here for the purpose of contacting our leaders in this district. The day you paid your taxes I happened to be standing nearby. I was impressed with the way you handled that affair. I could feel your waves of anger but you dealt like a diplomat with that serpent Levi. I followed you to find out where you lived and who you were, but stupidly I lost you when you turned into the alley by Jonathan's house. I saw you again the day Herod's conscripts came through town and I managed to get near you in the crowd. I overheard your conversation and knew then that my impression of you had been right."

"Then," interrupted Joel, "you weren't interested in buying Jonathan's business."

For a moment the sidewise smile appeared. "I had to have some excuse to get acquainted and I had learned from my inquiries that Jonathan was an invalid; so the idea of trying to buy the business was as practical as any."

"But suppose he had taken you up?"

"Then," Omah chuckled, "I would have quarreled with him over the price. We never would have worked out a deal."

Now he was serious again. "Zelon and Hosea feel about you as I do. Oh, you see how I trust you. I don't hesitate to tell you they are members of our organization, too. No man can be admitted unless three of our people vouch for him. They left it to me to approach you in any way I thought best. I chose frankness. Will you join us, Joel?"

Then as the youth opened his mouth to reply, Omah interrupted, "No, you don't have to answer now. Think it over for a day or two and count the cost. It may mean death. It will certainly mean sacrifice. I know I can trust you, whether you come with us or not, never to mention this conversation or speak of our plans."

Joel's heart beat fast. Here was the opportunity to do something worthwhile. His impulsive temperament, his love for adventure, his passionate patriotism—all these answered "Yes" to Omah's invitation. He got up, tall for his years, vigorous muscular body fired with youthful enthusiasm. He extended his hand to Omah.

"You can count me in," he said. "When do I start?"

Reading Check

1. What "shocking" statement does Jesus make in healing Jonathan?
2. What action undermines Joel's confidence in Jesus?
3. What question does Omah ask Joel?
4. Why does Omah hate the Romans?
5. What is Joel's response to Omah's invitation?

Chapter 9

Earth lay blushing in the embrace of autumn and his breath on her cheeks sent ripples through the field of ripened grain, as Joel stepped from the boat at the little town of Tarichaeae on the southmost tip of Galilee to begin the long walk to Jerusalem. He had left Capernaum before daybreak and the sun was rising over the hills of Gadara as he bade good-bye to Enos and his brother, who had brought him thus far on his journey, and to Omah, who had come with them to see him well on his way.

In his breast the sadness of departure was allayed[21] by the excitement of the journey. He had spent the evening before in Omah's room, where he had received his final instructions and learned for the first time that Zelon was the son of a prince of Judah, and Hosea the brother of Malchus, the captain of the temple guards. Finally, Omah, lifting his wine cup had proposed, "A toast to Joel, our brother and comrade in the cause of freedom."

Hosea and Zelon had cried, "To Joel." The toast was drunk, and one by one the three older men had embraced the young recruit. By the time he got home to bed, it lacked only six hours until he must meet Enos and his brother on the beach. But Joel, too excited to sleep, lay staring at the ceiling for a longer time than it took the crescent of the waning moon to sail that portion of the sea of sky visible through his open window. For half a year this familiar room had been his home and he realized now with surprise how accustomed he had become to it all—to the business of the shop, the sight of bright-colored sails burning in the fires of dawn, to Dysmas's endless talking and dog-like devotion, to Sarah's thoughtfulness and Jonathan's fatherly kindness.

Presently these waking thoughts, domesticated flocks shepherded by his will, gave way to dreams—those untamed imaginings of the mind, misbegotten, eerie visions that wander, wild creatures, through the silent lands of sleep. His gentle father with torch in hand ran screaming through the temple courts to fire the veil before the Most Holy Place. The busy flames ran up the drape and where they burned away the inlaid ceiling, he saw his own face staring down to watch as Jesus and His followers feasted with Herod to the wailing strains of savage music. Now Irene on her white mule rode between the columns and Stephen, suddenly beside him on the roof, began to grapple with him as they had wrestled many times, till suddenly both plunged down as Irene's laughter soared with the music to a crashing climax.

Joel sat up suddenly, wide awake. He shivered, whether from his dream, or the chill air of early morning he could not tell. As he crossed the room to the window, Dysmas spoke.

"It's about time to get up, isn't it, Joel?"

Judging from the sky that it was close to dawn, Joel answered, "It's about time, Dysmas."

Both the youths were unusually quiet as they dressed. A knock sounded on the door. It was Jonathan, who had waked to find fresh wonder in his own strength and who from sheer exuberance could hardly wait to shift about the heavy bales of canvas and the jars of tar and oil that stocked his shop.

"Sarah has breakfast ready. If you're going to get away before sun-up we had better eat," he said.

Joel was touched by this final manifestation of kindness from the couple who had been like understanding parents. Joel's eyes were moist and the old woman was unashamedly crying when she kissed him good-bye and put into his hand the lunch she had wrapped in a napkin.

"You might not be near a place where you can buy food when you get hungry at noon," she said.

They all went down to see him off; and looking back from where he sat in the stern of the boat, he saw what was to be his last memory of Capernaum— Sarah's white scarf waving in the slowly thinning darkness.

Now walking briskly southward in the cool morning air, he gazed at Mount Tabor on his right, between him and the village of his birth. He had wanted to see his parents before leaving the district and regretted his vow not to return to Nazareth. He had written them a long letter in which he said that Jonathan had been healed and had no further need of him, and therefore, he had decided to go to Jerusalem to look for a job there. It was, of course, impossible to tell them of his real purpose. He had written a similar note to Stephen and had added, half ashamed, "It's a pity we haven't seen each other since you were married. I know you and Irene have been too happy for you to miss your old friend." He concluded by sending Irene his greetings and best wishes to them both.

The sun was high when he descended into the plain of Esdraelon, passing through Endor, where ill-fated Saul had come to consult the witch. That night he slept in the province of Judea at a little roadside inn near the city of Sychar in the country of the Samaritans, and the next afternoon he stood looking across a valley upon the battlemented walls circling Jerusalem.

Entering the city, Joel followed the instructions Omah had given and inquired for the mansion of Prince Manaen. "He is well enough known in Jerusalem that anybody you meet can tell you where he lives," Omah had said. And Joel found this was no exaggeration. Manaen had been brought up in the household of Herod the Great, who treated him like an adopted son. Speculation had it that he was actually an illegitimate child of that lustful monarch, who had seemed to hold for Manaen an affection to which his three acknowledged sons were strangers.

The charm and virtue of Prince Manaen lent little support to such conjecture,[22] for he was as different from Herod Antipas as it was possible for a man to be. As cordially as the tetrarch was hated, the prince was loved. As profoundly as Herod was despised, Manaen was admired. "How," people inquired, "could these two opposites possibly be half brothers?"

The prince lived quietly as a private citizen, but naturally he could not altogether escape public attention and was as well known for his charity as his charm. Faces brightened at the mention of his name and Joel found himself cheerfully directed to his house.

Outside the palace, for such it proved to be, Joel sat down upon the marble steps to wait for a reply to Omah's letter which he had sent in by the porter. He had scarcely settled himself when the doorkeeper returned, accompanied by a strongly built young man whom he presented as Toron, steward of the prince's household. It occurred to Joel that he looked more like a soldier than a household official. His broad chest and large limbs would have been more appropriately clothed with armor than with the striped silk robe and the multi-colored shawl.

Toron greeted Joel as courteously as a visiting prince. And when the servant who followed him with a basin, a jug of water, and a towel, had removed Joel's sandals, he himself knelt to pour the water over his feet, dusty from the journey. Joel was surprised by so unusual a token of respect and wondered what Omah had said about him in his letter.

The prince awaited him in a large hall decorated in classic Greek style, the walls of cream-colored marble. Toron had drawn aside the heavy violet silk hanging between the Doric columns, but had himself remained without when the drapes fell into place behind the young Nazarene. Prince Manaen, a handsome man twice Joel's age, walked toward him as the youth descended three broad steps to the inlaid floor. The few strands of gray that blended at the temples into the dark brown of his wavy hair contributed but one final touch to the distinguished appearance of this man, everything about whom spoke of lofty birth and noble breeding. His features were well-formed and not particularly Jewish in cast. Even his beard was more closely trimmed than was usual among the men of his race. If he had been clean shaven he might have passed for a Greek with his soft light olive complexion, long lashes, and delicate brows.

Joel found it was difficult to believe that this man in these Hellenistic[23] surroundings was the head of a secret band of zealots dedicated to the cause of Jewish freedom. He was dressed in a robe of soft black wool embroidered at the neck and the cuffs with threads of gold. Instead of the usual sash he wore a belt of black leather embossed with circles of gold and fastened with a topaz clasp.

The prince embraced Joel warmly and welcomed him to Jerusalem. Taking him by the arm, he led him the length of the magnificent apartment to a double doorway just opposite the columned entrance, down a short corridor, and into a smaller room in astonishing contrast to the reception hall. This chamber, apparently the private study of the prince, could not have been more Hebraic in mood and decoration. Manaen, who had been inquiring affectionately about Omah, courteously indicated that Joel should be seated. Noting Joel's glances examining the room, Manaen said with a charming smile, "You're amazed at the contrast?"

"I find it interesting, sir," replied Joel truthfully.

"You might say the difference in the style of these rooms represents the disparity[24] between my public and my

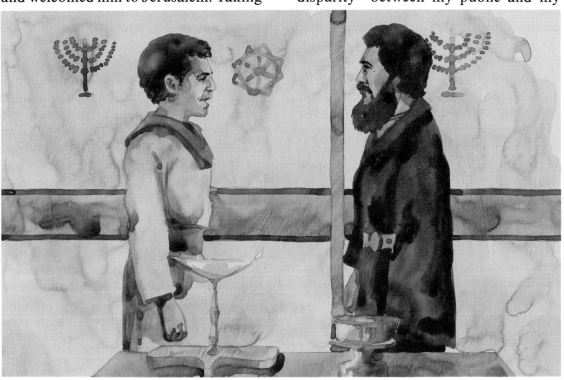

private life," Manaen explained. "I find it expedient to present a —how shall I say?—cosmopolitan[25] face to the world, but my heart is completely Jewish. That my secret activities may go unsuspected, I find it advisable to give no outward indication of undue nationalism, though sometimes even that is a good disguise.

Joel's raised eyebrows indicated that he did not quite follow this line of reasoning.

"It's simple enough," continued the prince. "No one ever expects a loud and constant talker of being anything more than a windbag. A man can talk so endlessly upon one subject as to make himself ridiculous. No one considers a ridiculous man dangerous; so a seeming monomania on the subject of freedom can become a most effective cloak to cover the armor and sword of freedom hidden beneath it."

"I see what you mean," confessed Joel, adding, "I suppose I have a great deal to learn, Your Excellency."

The hearty, merry laugh, which had been known to disarm many a suspicious enemy and which the prince's friends found so infectious that it was impossible not to join, rang out like deep-toned bells. "You'll be amazed at the disguises we wear and the strange places in which you find our comrades. There are, thank God, lovers of liberty everywhere eager for any chance to strike a blow for freedom."

"And the Romans suspect nothing?" inquired Joel.

"They suspect everything except the right people," said Manaen. "It's their nature to be suspicious. That's why they've been so successful in establishing an empire. No nation can last long occupying a conquered territory unless she's suspicious. They have their spies everywhere and occasionally one of our people is picked up. Sometimes they are tortured for information but they don't talk and few of them know enough to do much harm if they did."

"Omah said that the identity of the leader is not known to many in the organization. I can't understand how it happens that I should be sent here and receive your—I hope you will pardon me—seeming confidence."

"I have need of a new man without any contacts among our people to do a special job. I instructed Omah, who is one of our most valuable men, to be on the lookout for a young Jew, well educated in the Scriptures and the traditions of our race, radical in his views, full of patriotism, and attractive in appearance and personality. Omah, whose judgment and intuition I have found always reliable, sent you. You please me."

Tactfully noting Joel's embarrassment, he cleared his throat and changed the subject. "Now let's get down to business. Toron has given orders for a room to be prepared for you. You shall live here in my house. Wait, does anyone in Jerusalem know you?"

"I doubt it, sir," answered Joel. "My father is a cousin of the present high priest and rather widely acquainted in Jerusalem, but I have not been here for seven years."

"And you have grown up considerably in that time," said Manaen lightly; "so we won't worry about your being recognized. You shall be introduced as the son of an old friend of mine. The princess is giving a dinner tonight. You will be there. I should like you to get acquainted with as many of the guests as possible and afterwards give me your impression of each. That will be a good test of your ability to size people up, something very essential in your new job."

Chapter 10

Thus Joel found himself installed in the palace of Prince Manaen, where he was to reside off and on for over two years. His quarters were more luxurious than any others he had ever known and life moved smoothly in that well-ordered household.

The princess, Loda, a strong-willed but pleasant woman, treated Joel with unfailing courtesy. This was at first a trifle impersonal, perhaps, but as the passing weeks convinced her of Joel's loyalty and devotion to her husband her manner became less and less formal. Ostensibly Joel was simply a guest in the home and the friends and acquaintances of the prince began to take it for granted that this, as they thought, son of a boyhood friend had been adopted by Manaen.

Actually his duties were largely those of a private secretary and confidential messenger. At first Joel was puzzled by the fact that he had been accepted seemingly untried and unproven into a position of such confidence. This seemed to indicate an almost childlike trust on the part of a man who was anything but inexperienced and gullible and who was in a position where his very life depended upon his sagacity[26] and cleverness.

As time passed, the reason for the prince's action became apparent to Joel; and once understood, it was another evidence of the care and caution which had enabled Manaen to carry on his dangerous work so long undetected.

Sometimes it was necessary to assign a man to a task that carried with it considerable danger; it was occasionally necessary to order him into a position where he was almost sure to be caught, in which case imprisonment and death were inevitable. Joel, having no contacts among the secret workers aside from the three acquaintances he had made in Capernaum, would not be emotionally involved by a possible friendship when he delivered to a man an order which he knew might mean almost certain death for him.

Shortly before Omah had been commissioned to look for a new man for the position of secretary, the Romans had seized a load of arms being smuggled into the country; and so fortuitous[27] had been the arrival of the Roman squadron on the scene that the prince was convinced that somewhere along the line there had been a leak in information. His investigations convinced him that his secretary had been responsible. Whether the plans had been deliberately betrayed or whether the man had been merely indiscreet, the prince was never able to determine. Fortunately, the authorities had not seemed to connect Manaen in any way with the smuggling operations, but it was a setback for the patriots and cost the lives of a number of valuable men.

When Joel inquired what had become of the former secretary, the prince adroitly avoided the question. Apparently he had simply disappeared. Thinking about his probable fate, Joel could not help shuddering but was too much of a realist not to regard his removal as anything but a necessity. Besides, Joel, with a feeling of contempt for his predecessor, told himself that he deserved whatever happened to him.

By nature Joel was open and blunt to a fault, but under the prince's tutelage[28] he was becoming skilled in the arts of subterfuge and intrigue. These were necessary tools in their dangerous task, but Joel could not help feeling a contempt for himself for resorting to them. He knew that pretense and deceit were their only defense and felt the ultimate liberty of his people justified the means necessary to attain it, but in spite of this, Joel could not help losing respect for himself. It was an occupational hazard which would not have fazed a man of a different temperament. The prince, for instance, was completely unaffected. Absolutely honest in his business, personally generous and tenderhearted in the extreme, where the cause was concerned he could be completely ruthless in his dealings and gag at nothing that could advance his purposes. Joel was convinced that he would have sacrificed his own son without hesitation had it been necessary or even expedient; and so perverse is the human mind that Joel admired in his master those very qualities which, acquired with so much difficulty, he despised in himself.

After six months under the influence and pedagogy[29] of Prince Manaen, Joel began to notice that everywhere he went he was followed and spied upon. Thinking that perhaps the authorities were suspicious and fearing for the safety of his master, Joel mentioned this to Manaen, who answered calmly, "Yes, I know. I'm disappointed in you that you have only just discovered it. They have been on your trail every time you have left this house since the day you arrived in Jerusalem."

"You mean you knew it all along?" asked the amazed Joel.

"Certainly, I knew it. I had them follow you."

Joel looked so astonished that the prince broke into laughter and the study echoed with his merriment.

"Surely, Joel, you know me well enough to realize that I take no chances. By now I'm as convinced of your honesty and judgment as I could be of any man's. I think your devotion to the cause for which we are fighting is unassailable[30] and I flatter myself that you bear me some degree of affection, but I run no more risks than necessary and I thought it a good idea to keep an eye on you."

Meantime the handsome Joel had been accepted in the upper circles of the society of the Holy City. The friendship of Prince Manaen opened all doors to the youth, and his charm and good looks made him a welcomed guest in the mansions and palaces of Jerusalem. Having trained himself to disguise his contempt for them, he was entertained by self-important scribes and, careful always to represent himself as a strict Pharisee, he rubbed shoulders with religious leaders at receptions and dinners. Into most of these households no Romans were ever invited socially, however willing his hosts might be to do business with a Roman when a profit could be made. He even went with Prince Manaen to dine in the palace of the high priest and could scarcely repress a smile to think how that pompous ecclesiastic was entertaining a cousin all unawares.

Always his ears were open for information that might be useful, and he went out of his way to cultivate those who were in position to lend, however inadvertently or unconsciously, aid to the conspirators. Among the wearers of the wide phylacteries he found few men who were not in some way despicable, if not for their vices, for their pride and self-righteousness. He discovered few signs of greatness in the upper brackets of the priesthood. Joel could not make up his mind which was worse—the acrimonious and bitter Pharisees, who contended for every jot and tittle of the law and the observance of every useless outward practice of what with them was obviously a dead religion, or the scoffing Sadducees, who with scornful superiority laughed at divine revelation and sought to make of Judaism no religion at all but merely a philosophy. He did now and then come across examples of genuine goodness, unstained life and sincere faith. There was, for example, Gamaliel, a member of the Sanhedrin. Joel found him a reasonable, logical man, unbiased and untainted with the prejudice of his class. There was Nicodemus, a rich young nobleman and friend of Prince Manaen. Most of all, Joel was drawn to Joseph of Arimathea, one of those souls so rarely found, a man of such immaculate conscience and perfect integrity he can neither suspect the possibility of evil in others nor know the meaning of compromise or fear himself.

Joel's life in Jerusalem was by no means a mere round of social calls and visitation. He put in long hours in the study with the prince, pen in hand, taking dictation. Frequently Manaen would not begin to attend to his more important affairs until after the household was asleep and there was no likelihood of his being disturbed by the arrival of some visitor too eminent or influential to be turned away with a message that the Prince was engaged. Often the sky was rosy with dawn before the lamps were extinguished in the little room.

Occasionally Joel would be away from the city for several days at a time, attending to important matters elsewhere. He arranged for the transfer of funds to pay for arms purchased abroad and smuggled in by various and devious means to be hidden away until the day of the uprising. He bribed border patrols. He paid off ship captains. Twice he was able to arrange for the escape of prisoners. On one occasion he bribed a guard. On the other he arranged an attack upon a squad of soldiers leading the prisoner to execution. All but two of the soldiers were killed and their prisoner disappeared into Moab. Manaen particularly commended Joel upon the latter coup, which caused terrible repercussions and drove the Roman governor into such a fury that he ordered the execution of the guards that had escaped the weapons of those who rescued the prisoner. Manaen laughed heartily when he heard of the governor's action.

"If we can get Pilate mad enough, often enough, he'll kill off all his army and save us the trouble. When the Roman slays his own legions he fights with the Jews against Rome."

When he had been in Jerusalem just a year, something occurred that was to have a profound effect upon the life of Joel. Returning home late one evening through the dark and narrow streets, he was passing an archway when he heard the sound of a struggle and the sharp cry of a woman. Without stopping to think, he turned and, running through the arch, found himself in a small courtyard. Dimly seen by the faint moonlight, two figures were struggling. Joel grasped the larger of the two by the shoulder, swung him around and with all the power of his muscular arm and the weight of his body struck him on the point of the jaw with his clenched fist. Though the man was heavier than Joel, he was taken by surprise and so accurate was Joel's blow that the man went down in a heap, striking the back of his head upon the cobblestones, where he lay faintly groaning.

"Thank you," said a low breathless voice, as the woman moved around the prostrate[31] figure of her assailant to take Joel's hand.

She was trembling violently and, afraid she might faint, Joel slipped an arm around her. As the quivering form

leaned against him, Joel was conscious of the scent of a heavy Arabian perfume.

"You'd better get out of here," warned the woman, "quickly before he comes to. He will . . . come . . . to, won't he?" The voice was still breathless.

Joel released the woman and knelt beside the prostrate form. Placing his hand upon the chest, he found the heartbeat steady. Then, bending over to peer into the face of the man, he received a distinct shock. It was Toron, the steward of Prince Manaen.

Joel, still kneeling, looked up at the woman. "What were you doing here with him?" he asked.

"He offered to see me home," she said, "and when I would not let him come in he attempted to—" her voice broke off.

This was a strange situation. No respectable Jewish woman was ever found on the streets at night unless in the company of her husband or of some man of her family or of armed servants with torches; yet this woman, virtuous or not, had certainly been resisting the advances of Toron.

Joel got to his feet as he turned this over in his mind.

"Where do you live?" he asked.

"Just there." She indicated a door to the right.

"Have a key?"

She handed it to him. He found the lock. The key turned easily and the door opened.

"You are very kind. Thank you again," said the woman. "Peace be with you."

"I'm going in," he spoke in no uncertain terms.

The woman hesitated a moment. Joel was standing just inside the entrance, his back against the open door. There was nothing else she could do but let him come with her. She moved past Joel, who closed and locked the door. They were in a bare hallway with a stone floor, unfurnished except for a stand on which a lamp was burning. The woman opened a door at the end of the hall.

"In here," she said.

The woman removed her hooded cloak and flung it carelessly upon a divan built around three walls of the room. Joel recognized her now as Myra, the most popular dancer in Jerusalem. He had often seen her perform as a hired entertainer at banquets and it was evident from her dress that she was just returning from such an affair. Her young and graceful figure was only slightly concealed by an Egyptian costume of transparent green silk with a wide beaded collar. Around her waist was a girdle of soft yellow linen fitting tightly over her hips and tied in front with the two fringed ends falling to her knees. Bracelets in the form of serpents adorned her rounded arms above the elbows. Completing the costume was a wig of black silk thread cut in straight bangs across the forehead and falling to her shoulders. By the light of the lamp she made an exotic and pulse-quickening picture, in spite of the worried frown that drew together the brows so carefully stressed and elongated[32] by the make-up brush.

"Do you suppose we ought to do something about him?" she asked, nodding in the direction of the street.

"I mean, pour some water on him or something?"

Joel had no desire to revive the man. "Let him alone," he grinned. "He'll come around eventually."

Since Joel had not recognized Toron by the dim light of the courtyard, in the excitement of the brief instant before he knocked him unconscious, he thought it quite likely that the steward had no idea who his assailant was. Joel was deterred from making any effort to restore him to consciousness by the wish to save Toron the acute discomfort of realizing that he had been laid low by a man smaller and lighter in weight than himself, for although Joel was tall and muscular, Toron was built like a gladiator. Although Joel had plenty of physical courage and was not afraid of any reprisals the steward might attempt, he dreaded the thought of the embarrassing situation in the household, if Toron should know his identity.

"Except for a headache tomorrow he'll be all right," said Joel.

Myra's gray-green eyes narrowed slightly as she regarded him appraisingly.

"You are not a man who's afraid. You proved that just now," she said musingly. "Is it because you prefer Myra's company all to yourself that you do not revive the man?"

"Perhaps!"

"Then perhaps you would enjoy her conversation more across a table with food and wine. So if you'll pardon me for a moment—." She left the room.

Joel sank upon the divan and, finding it soft and comfortable, stretched out at full length, feet on the cushions, hands clasped behind his head. A little fountain tinkled musically in the center of the large room, which smelled of sandalwood as if incense had been recently burning. Joel sighed comfortably. In a few moments Myra returned with a copper tray, which she placed upon the low inlaid table.

"A moment more," she said, and went out again to return immediately with a pitcher of wine. "Now, if you think you can manage to pull yourself up, you can bring those cushions and put them here on the floor. Now some more."

When they were seated on the cushions, the table between them, Joel, who had not realized he was hungry, found the impromptu midnight meal delicious. There were dried dates and fresh figs, barley wafers and cheese and luscious round cakes filled with ground nuts. The Persian wine was sweet and heavy. When Joel had finished, from a bottle of Phoenician glass Myra poured into two tiny cups a liquid clear and sparkling as the purest water. This was a very potent liquor made by distilling strong fermented wine. Flavored with anise,[33] it burned like fire as they sipped it slowly.

Joel found his companion constantly more fascinating. All during the meal she had kept up a running conversation. Her wit was keen, and she was a consummate[34] actress. She had Joel roaring with laughter by her impersonations of some of the more eminent figures of Jewish society. So accurate was her delineation of character, so subtly did she underline the peculiarities of her subjects, so delicately indicate their weaknesses, so exactly duplicate their mannerisms that Joel had no difficulty in recognizing them.

Finally Joel said, "And Toron? He's a friend of yours, isn't he?"

"Ah, he's a pig, that Toron. Strutting like a Roman legionnaire who makes himself important before the eyes of children. He thinks that because he's big and handsome no woman can resist him. Always he leers at me. Tonight I had been entertaining in the house of Dostes. He is waiting for me when I come out. He takes me by the arm and says, 'Tonight I'll take you home.' "

She slipped into a caricature of Toron as she talked, squaring her shoulders, jutting out her jaw, lowering her voice and speaking in the soft, insinuating manner of the man she was describing. "But enough of him. Tell me, who are you?"

"One who has watched you dance and found you charming," answered Joel lightly.

"Yes? I have observed you watching now and then."

"If I could believe that I'd be flattered," said Joel, "but when you dance you are so withdrawn, I don't believe you ever notice anybody."

For a moment her laughter tinkled; then she said, "If you just knew. Sometimes the expressions on the faces of the men are so absurd I can hardly keep from laughing while I dance."

"So that's how you noticed me then—with an absurd expression on my face?"

She lifted a supple long-fingered hand as if to brush aside this last remark and spoke quite seriously, "No, I remember now. You were with Prince Manaen. So, you are the young man who has come to live with him. Joel. See, I even know your name, but then the hearts of half the young ladies of Jerusalem beat faster at the mention of your name. No, you needn't blush. You are quite the idol of the town. Now I shall dance for you."

As the girl got gracefully to her feet, Joel finished the last of his drink, then went to sit on the divan. Myra stood for a moment poised like a bird for flight. Then she began softly to hum a strange rhythmic melody. Slowly she raised her hands, arms moving gracefully, wrists curved, each pointed finger hinting of caresses. Her slender body stirred sinuously, every movement singing of passion and desire.

Joel had never before seen her dance like this. Watching, he felt the blood pound in his temples. Closer and closer came the dancer. More and more rapid became the movements of her whirling body. Then suddenly Myra dropped to her knees, the dance ended.

Joel sprang from the divan and, going to Myra, put his hands under her elbows and lifted her to her feet. For a moment he stood looking down into her face; then his arms were around her.

*   *   *   *   *

It was broad daylight when Joel strode through the portals of Manaen's palace. As he crossed the mosaic floor turning toward the marble stair, the voice of the prince said, "Good morning, Joel."

Looking up, he saw his master descending the steps. The prince stopped, right hand resting lightly on the carved balustrade, and looked down at Joel with a quizzical smile.

"Perhaps I called my watchdogs off too soon," he jested lightly. "Such an hour to be coming home!"

Still continuing to smile, he resumed his descent. Meantime Joel was standing at the foot of the stairs, conscious of embarrassment he was unable to hide. The prince stopped again two steps above him. Placing both hands on the shoulders of the young man, he declared, "I believe you actually look guilty." He broke off serious now, "A woman, I suppose?"

Joel said nothing.

The prince shrugged slightly. "Come to breakfast," he invited, taking Joel by the arm; "I don't know what my household's coming to. My steward looks this morning like a man who got the worst of a fight and my secretary gets home barely in time for breakfast."

Reading Check

1. How does Prince Manaen appear to the public?
2. How does Manaen introduce Joel?
3. What are Joel's new duties?
4. How does Joel feel about these new duties?

Chapter II

Joel's involvement with Myra had begun on what was exactly the first anniversary of his arrival in Jerusalem. A year before, his conscience would have made him miserable, but during that year the son of the small town rabbi had grown into a sophisticated and ruthless man. Engaged in a dangerous game with men's lives for the pawns and freedom as the stakes, Joel felt need for relief from the strain and this he found in the company of the charming and entertaining Myra. Joel did not pretend to himself that he was in love with the dancer, but her attraction for him was tremendous and she became a habit with him as insidious[35] and necessary as a narcotic.

The prince, considering emotional involvements as dangerous for a revolutionist, had drawn upon the means at his disposal to discover the object of Joel's attachment. At first determined that the young man must break off relations with the dancer, upon mature reflection Manaen decided the contact might be useful. He managed to suggest in subtle fashion to Joel that a popular dancer was in position to overhear a good deal that might be important to the conspirators and implied that Joel could make use of this in the service of the cause.

In spite of all the young man's discretion, gossip was inevitable. Joel, familiar with Toron's nature and habits by now, knew that no breath of scandal escaped his ears and fancied that he detected lurking hatred in the eyes of the steward and wondered whether Toron had guessed that it was he who had rescued Myra from his clutches and left him unconscious on the cobblestones.

Three months had gone since Joel's encounter when closeted with him one night in the study, Manaen said, "I hope in a little over a year we'll be ready to strike."

Joel looked up from the parchment in his hand. "Can we be ready as soon as that, my lord?"

"I think we can. The Passover is the logical time for an uprising. It's now three months until the feast. I think we'll stage a little token demonstration then. It will give us an opportunity to observe the reaction of the people. Then during the following year we will have it whispered everywhere that on the next Passover the Romans will feel a real blow."

"But," objected Joel, "the Romans will be sure to hear the rumor and be warned—if the demonstration this year isn't warning enough."

"That's quite true," agreed Manaen. "But they feel secure. Next year they will not anticipate anything much bigger than this year's incident. Even if they double the present garrison of Judea, which they won't, they'll still have only a relatively small force. No, I think there is more to gain than lose by this plan.

We must have the farmers, the shepherds and merchants—all the plain men who love freedom—ready for the struggle, eager to use the arms we will have ready."

"But will we have enough arms ready?" Joel asked.

"It will keep us busy, but I think it can be done. Besides, we'll have to risk it; it's dangerous to wait longer. Our group has grown as large as is safe. The greater the number, the greater the risk of discovery. Now here is what I have in mind."

Briefly the prince unfolded his plans. The conspirators were to be instructed to begin a campaign of agitation throughout both Judea and Galilee to stir the common people to a new pitch of hatred of their conquerors by playing upon religious bigotry and the nationalism born in every Jewish breast. Meantime the gathering of arms was to be pushed, and they were to contact the outlaw chieftains, who from the wilderness of Moab made occasional forays[36] into Judea, robbing caravans and preying upon the villagers. Some of these men were patriots, who, with a price on their heads, had resorted to this type of life through necessity. Occasionally troops were sent against them, but the robber bands would scatter and hide out among the hills until the troops gave up and withdrew; then they would reassemble and resume their depredations.[37]

"You, Joel," said the prince, "shall personally enlist the aid of these men. Omah and his companions have been busy in Galilee. Perhaps I'll need to send you there with some final instructions for organizing and arming the slaves

that Herod has gathered in Tiberius. How many are there by your last report?"

"Almost five hundred, sir," the young man replied.

"Enough to overthrow the palace guard and the Roman garrison in Capernaum as well. Besides, by next year there will be twice as many. Of course, Herod with his personal bodyguard will come to Jerusalem for the Passover. My foster brother has to throw his annual sop of piety to his people," said Manaen disgustedly.

"And what are we going to do for money for all this?" asked Joel.

The prince sat silent, his chin resting on his hand. Almost his entire personal fortune, Joel knew, had been expended. There were very few rich men in the organization and these, too, had impoverished themselves in the interest of freedom.

"May I suggest something, Your Excellency?" inquired the young man.

The prince, who had come to rely upon Joel's advice, waited for him to speak.

"Not a day goes by but somebody arrives in Jerusalem with gifts for the temple and with money for sacrifices. If we could discover through our spies when a wealthy man from, say, Caesarea or Joppa plans to make a pilgrimage to Jerusalem, some of our people could meet him on the way and quietly relieve him of his burden."

The prince shook his head, "I don't like it"; after a moment he added, "but it could be done."

"And why shouldn't it?" said Joel. "After all, those rich men are being heavily taxed by Rome and when we rid them of their conquerors we'll be doing them a favor. Why shouldn't they contribute in their own interest?"

The prince smiled at this logic, then grew serious. "When I think of all the money poured into the laps of those parasites on the hill," he nodded in the direction of the temple, "I froth at the mouth. What they pocket in one month would be all we need for the next fifteen."

"Then why not accept my plans?" insisted Joel.

"We'll think it over," answered Manaen slowly.

"And meantime," continued the young man, "would it not also be a good idea to consider having a few of our people lift a little from 'those parasites on the hill' direct?"

"You mean we should stoop to robbery and house-breaking?" Manaen inquired aghast.

"I mean a little jewelry, a handful of gold pieces; every little bit helps, and some of them have plenty."

All this was the beginning of an entirely new phase of activity in the program of the conspirators and was to bring Joel into a fame that he did not anticipate and would not have desired.

Chapter 12

The next weeks were busy ones for Joel, who was finding it difficult to lead two lives at once. In Jerusalem he was, when in the public eye, the young dilettante.[38] Privately and on the occasions of his frequent disappearance from the Holy City, he was the scheming revolutionary. That he might eliminate every possibility of any connection between the two, the young man had from the beginning never even used his own name in his conspiratorial contacts. The rank and file of the underground workers knew him only as "The Son of the Rabbi"—Barabbas, a suitable *nom de guerre* implying as it did a heritage of Jewish tradition and training. Becoming progressively more daring in his exploits, appearing with dramatic suddenness in the most unexpected and widely separated places, he indulged in ever more and more spectacular deeds, none of which had any military value but all of which were calculated to have decided psychological effects. The authorities were constantly nettled and irritated and quite frequently made to appear incompetent and ridiculous. The common people were impressed with the fact that someone was busy in their behalf and gradually everywhere the hopeless acceptance of a bad situation began to give way to expectancy and a faint anticipation of eventual relief.

With ever-increasing frequence, the name of Barabbas was whispered in shocked awe or spoken in respectful terms. In one of the popular taverns Joel listened with concealed amusement to an outraged centurion offering to his drinking companions a much exaggerated version of the burning of the barracks at Azotus. Another time, he heard how "that clever rascal, Barabbas" had arranged the kidnapping of a tax collector in Hebron who, relieved of several weeks' revenues and frightened within an inch of his life, had been released upon his promise to resign his public office. In his hearing, scandalized priests bewailed the loss of temple offerings which had been stolen from pilgrims on the way to Jerusalem "by that unspeakable creature, Barabbas, or his band of ruffians." Joel smiled deprecatingly[39] or nodded seriously as the mood of the speaker warranted, never failing to agree fervently that something certainly should be done.

With the gusty winds of early spring, the young man arrived in Capernaum, too well known here to be anything but Joel. He was welcomed as a long absent son by Jonathan and Sarah. Nothing would do the delighted Dysmas but that Joel occupy his old bed in the room behind the shop, and the suggestion that he had intended to go to an inn was met with protestations of injured feelings and a grieved countenance.

Joel regretted missing Zelon and Hosea, but the handsome young man of noble birth was in Phoenicia and the Cyclops with the hearty laugh had been sent briefly to Caesarea Philippi. Omah, however, welcomed him with the warmth of genuine pleasure, and, looking into his angular face, Joel felt again the power of the personality that had captivated the young clerk so many months ago.

"You make me very proud of my abilities to judge men," said the man of Joppa when they were closeted in the rented room he still occupied. "There's certainly very little about you to suggest the lad who left here for Jerusalem."

Joel smiled but his voice was serious. "I hardly remember him myself. Sometimes I wish I could recapture his innocence."

"He was a tempestuous young radical," declared Omah with the crooked smile Joel so well remembered.

"And should I finish the description, I should add, full of angry words as a cloud is full of wind," stated Joel.

When Joel had delivered Manaen's message in regard to the program of agitation during the next twelve months, Omah replied, "I shall pass that on to Hosea and if the prince does not object, leave him to head up the work here. I was arrested by Herod's police ten days ago and questioned about my activities."

"They proved nothing, of course?"

"Much to my surprise they released me, but they are at least suspicious and I know I'm being watched."

"Since it wasn't the Romans but Herod's men, the chances are you'll be safe enough in Judea," predicted Joel, who continued after a moment's consideration. "Perhaps it would be wise for you to go to Caesarea and meet Hosea there. If he comes back here and you are seen together, their suspicion of you will extend to him."

"Meantime," Omah said, "I hope no one noticed your coming in."

Joel looked cautiously around as he left the house. As far as he could tell, the dark streets were empty but he returned by a devious route to the home of Jonathan, confident that he had thrown any possible watcher off the trail.

Next morning across the breakfast table Joel inquired, "Is Jesus in town?"

"I think He is at Simon's house. Since the news of John the Baptist's death was made public yesterday, He has not been seen on the street," replied Jonathan, whose eyes always brightened at the mention of the Nazarene.

"I hear," interposed Dysmas, "that the men He sent out to preach and cast out demons have been coming back two by two for the last several days."

"Rachel was telling me while we were washing clothes in the lake together that Herod is terribly upset by the reports of their miracles." Sarah spoke with the satisfaction of a woman passing along private information

"How did Rachel hear all this?" her husband inquired.

"Oh, her daughter is one of the court dressmakers and she told her mother that Herod has been like a crazy man ever since Herodias tricked him into having the Baptist beheaded. He has the blackest circles under his eyes and he has lost weight just in the last week!"

"Which he could very well stand to lose," interpolated[40] her husband.

"Well, anyway," the good woman declared with an air of finality, "he goes around mumbling, 'This John I beheaded, is he coming back to haunt me by these miracles?' "

The meal was scarcely over when Zebedee walked into the shop to greet Joel with loud and heartily spoken expressions of pleasure, pounding the young man so enthusiastically upon the back that he coughed and caught his breath.

"Well, you arrived right on the tail of the excitement, didn't you, young fellow?" said the brown and weather-beaten old sailor, seating himself on a coil of rope. "That spineless old beer-belly certainly got himself outfoxed by a pair of women, didn't he! And one John the Baptist is worth twenty Herods any day."

The old man whistled disgustedly through the space left by a missing front tooth.

Joel agreed heartily but briefly with the old man's sentiments, then, changing the subject, inquired, "How are James and John?"

He noted that Dysmas sitting on the steps whittling a piece of soft cedar looked at him strangely. Idly he wondered why.

"Fine, fine, took them across the lake this morning, I did. Jesus and four or five others in my boat. The rest of them went over in Simon's old craft."

"Who owns it now?" Joel inquired.

"Oh, I do. We were partners, you know. I've got enough nephews and cousins to man every boat on the lake; so I bought it. Paid his mother-in-law for it. Simon wouldn't take any money."

"Where were they going?" asked the young man.

"Oh, up into the hills. Want to get away from the crowd. Needs rest, He does, but half the town has gone around the lake looking for Him. Unless they hide in a cave He'll never get any peace."

Dysmas threw away the stick now whittled to a sharp point, slipped his knife into his girdle and got up. "Wouldn't you like to go, Joel? Always when there's a big crowd around He teaches them and heals the sick people."

"If you'd like to go I'll give you a ride across the lake and save you the walk around," offered the friendly Zebedee.

Joel thought it over for a moment. Yes, he decided, he would like to see Jesus again and, with the background of his recent experiences, he was curious as to what opinions he would now form of this strange Man whose reputation was so great everywhere.

He patted Dysmas affectionately on the shoulder. "That's a good suggestion, fellow." "Thanks, Zebedee, I should like to go."

It was Jonathan who spoke now. "If you boys go before noon, Sarah will never forgive you. She's roasting a leg of spring lamb and cooking a great pot of herbs and she expects you here to eat it. I'll tell you what, Zebedee, you have lunch with us and they can leave in the early afternoon. If today is like every other day, the Master still will be healing and teaching even at sundown."

It was, therefore, in the middle of the afternoon that Dysmas and Joel, with a word of thanks to Zebedee for the pleasant trip, stepped over the side into the shallow water and waded to the eastern shore of the lake. An hour later, climbing up into the rocky, barren hills covered with short grass, they came upon the multitude, grouped as in a natural amphitheater around the side of a hill. Jesus, on a slight hummock[41] a little apart, sat preaching, a group of disciples ringed about Him as if to form a barrier between Him and the thousands of listeners. Dysmas and Joel had scarcely settled themselves near the summit of the hill at the back of the crowd when each felt a heavy hand upon his shoulder and, turning to look up, saw Simon, the great redhead, grinning down.

"Well, well, well, it's good to see you, Joel. My, you've broadened out. Hello, Dysmas." He spoke in a whisper so as not to disturb the audience intent upon the words of Jesus.

The big disciple squatted down between them. "I like to circulate around the crowd. Interesting to listen to their comments. They say He is Isaiah, Jeremiah, or one of the prophets."

"Who do you say He is?" Joel questioned.

Simon's low tones rang with conviction as he replied, "I say He's the Christ, the Son of the Living God."

Presently, Jesus stopped speaking and one by one the sick and afflicted were brought before Him, passed through the ring of circling disciples. Jesus touched them or spoke to them and they were healed. Watching the miracles, Joel remembered the broken roof. A blind man was led by his son, a boy about twelve, to Jesus, Who touched his eyes, speaking a few words which Joel could not hear. But he could not miss the man's cry, which rang out through the little valley, "I can see, oh, I can see!"

Falling on his knees, he kissed the hand of Jesus and then as one of the disciples stepped forward to lift him gently to his feet, he turned, with a heart-hunger long denied, to look at his boy.

A plain woman, poorly dressed, ran forward to throw herself into his arms. The man took her face between his hands and stood gazing for a long time at the wife he had never seen. Even Joel's armor of sophistication was pierced by the sight and it was through misty eyes that he saw Jesus give the signal that He was too exhausted to do more. Several of the disciples turned and moved among the people, explaining that Jesus was weary and asking them not to demand anything else of the Master.

Joel turned to Dysmas. "What's the name of that disciple Jesus is talking to now?"

"That's Philip."

Joel's attention was diverted by a young lad near him who had grasped the skirt of Andrew's robe as he passed through the crowd.

"Look," the boy was saying, "here's a lunch that Mother packed for me this morning and I didn't eat. I guess I was so interested in Jesus I forgot to be hungry. Would you give it to Him? Maybe if He ate something He'd be rested."

Andrew patted the lad on the shoulder. "I'll tell you, son, you get up and come with me and give it to Him yourself."

"You mean I could really speak to Him?" asked the boy, eyes wide.

"Certainly, certainly, now you just come along. By the way, what's in the basket?"

The boy's voice grew less audible as he followed Andrew toward Jesus. "Some barley rolls and a couple of fish."

Philip and the Lord were still talking as Andrew came up with the boy. Andrew spoke to the Master, Jesus turned and smiled at the lad, who held out the little basket; and Andrew, obviously referring to the contents, lifted the napkin that covered the lunch.

Jesus took the basket in His right hand, laying His left upon the head of the boy as He spoke His thanks. Now above the hubbub of the crowd they heard Jesus' voice as He called His disciples.

"Have them all sit down again on the grass in groups of fifty or a hundred."

The disciples, plainly wondering at the instructions, nevertheless, hastened to obey and, moving among the people, soon had them arranged in groups as their Master had instructed. Waiting for further orders, the disciples gathered around Jesus, Who was standing now upon the rise where He had sat to preach, the basket in His hand. The crowd sat silent, watching. Lifting His face toward Heaven, Jesus began to pray. It was a simple grace, a prayer of thanksgiving for a meal. When it was

ended Jesus, giving Andrew the basket to hold, took out one of the rolls and broke it. Returning the pieces to the basket, He removed another which He also broke and replaced. After five loaves had been broken, He divided the fish in the same fashion.

"Now," said Jesus to the disciples, "take and feed the people."

Joel felt a tingle run up his spine as Andrew passed the basket to the disciples one by one and each reached in and drew out pieces of roll and fish by the handfuls.

At Simon's suggestion they took off their cloaks and laid them on the ground and piled them up with the food. Then, folding the cloaks together to make a bundle, the disciples went from group to group, passing out the simple meal. It was Simon who approached the company in which Dysmas and Joel had been placed.

As the two young men helped themselves from the bountiful supply in

the fisherman's cloak, Simon asked them, "How can I help but believe He's the Christ of God?"

Great peace seemed to settle with the twilight shadows on the assembled thousands. Joel, eating of the miraculous supper, kept thinking, "What a leader He would make! What a king who can feed his subjects by the thousands from a boy's lunch basket!" His thoughts were warring in him. "He feasted with a tax collector and called him to be a disciple," said one part of his mind. "Yes," said the other, "but He seems to have as little respect for hypocrisy as any man. He shows that by His dealing with the scribes and Pharisees." "But nobody has ever heard Him speak out against the Roman oppression." "True," his thoughts answered themselves, "but He is merciful to the oppressed and His heart is tender toward the poor."

Chapter 13

Joel and Dysmas had been among the first to start homeward. Both young and strong and used to long walks, they had already left the crowd strung out some distance behind them. When they reached the shore and turned north and west, the wind sprang up, roaring in angry gusts between the hills that girded the lake and churning the waters into choppy foam-capped waves. Low-hanging, heavy clouds marched like a defeated army in ragged formation across the sky, trailing ragged scraps of mist like dragging banners.

"It's going to be a rough night," Dysmas said.

Joel agreed, his mind elsewhere. He was wishing that he might have an opportunity to talk with Jesus privately. If He could be persuaded to claim the throne, then they could rally the people easily against the Romans. Both Joel and Prince Manaen were aware that the weakness of their plans was the lack of a leader. They needed a monarch with a crown, a symbol of Jewish sovereignty, but he must be a man in whom the people had confidence and whom they would follow. If Jesus would just declare Himself king, Joel decided he could even overlook His attitude toward Levi, the tax collector.

While his mind was busy with these thoughts, Joel's body was struggling against the wind. So terrific were the intermittent gusts that it was practically impossible to make any progress against them. Then with alarming abruptness the wind ceased. There was no gradual abatement of the fury of the blasts. One moment the storm was at its height; the next all nature was at peace. As if by magic the clouds dissolved and the smiling moon was mirrored in the placid water of the lake. From a nearby thicket the sad voice of a nightbird rang in benediction on the calm sweet air of spring.

The next day they learned that this strange phenomenon had accompanied a miraculous appearance of Jesus to His disciples. Their informant was Zebedee, who had heard the story from his sons. After the supernatural feeding of the hungry multitudes, Jesus had gone farther up into the hills to pray, and His disciples had embarked for Capernaum in Zebedee's other boat, the one that had been Simon's.

"The wind suddenly blew up a gale from the northwest. They were having a hard time keeping the ship from foundering. Part of 'em were bailing for all they were worth and the rest of 'em were at the oars trying to hold her nose into the wind. They were just about exhausted when they see a figure walking right across the top of the waves. First they think it's a ghost but when He comes closer they recognize Jesus. You know how Simon is—always pushing himself forward. Well, Simon hollers out, 'If that's really you, Lord, tell me to come to you.' "

Dysmas interrupted, "You mean Simon wanted to get out of the boat and swim to Jesus?"

"Nope," answered Zebedee, "he wanted to get out of the boat and *walk*. And that's just what he did, too! Jesus said, 'Come on.' Then Simon stood up on the seat and jumped over the side. But he didn't sink—not then! He started walking to Jesus, stepping over the little waves and climbing up the big ones."

The fisherman interrupted his narrative to spit with gusto through the open door.

"Go on," said Joel, "finish the story."

"Well, Simon can't keep from strutting. He's just got to show off whenever there's anybody around to see him. When he first left the boat, he kept his eyes right on Jesus and was walking straight toward Him, but he gets more and more confident as he goes along. He is almost to the Master when he wants to be sure the fellows in the boat aren't missing his performance; so he turns around and looks over his shoulder. He opens his mouth to say something. Knowing Simon, I'd be willing to wager it was something like 'I'm doing all right! Why don't you fellows try this?'

"Just then he sees a great big wave, the daddy of 'em all coming toward him. It looks like it's going to break clear over him and he gets panicky and right then he starts to sink."

Zebedee chuckled at the thought of his erstwhile partner's ducking.

"Go on," cried Joel.

"Then what?" inquired Dysmas at the same instant.

"Simon yells, 'Save me, Lord, I'm drowning!' Jesus just reaches out His hand and pulls him up and puts an arm around him and they walk to the boat together. All the pride's gone out of Simon. The boys say he didn't open his mouth for the rest of the night, and that's some kind of a record for Simon."

Zebedee's boisterous chuckle became a trio as the others joined in. Presently the old fisherman recollected, "This is what I meant to tell you. When Simon got into the boat the wind stopped! And suddenly the boat was just off Capernaum, though a moment before it had been in the middle of the lake."

Joel and Dysmas exchanged glances. Zebedee, changing the subject without a pause for breath, went on talking. "I understand since yesterday the people are saying Jesus is the One Whom God promised to send. They are talking everywhere about making Him king. Well, He'd be a good one."

It was at this moment that Sarah returned from market all out of breath. "Did you know Jesus is back in Capernaum?" she panted.

"Yes, Zebedee just told us."

"Well, nobody seems to know how He got here. There was only one boat on the other side and the disciples left in that without Jesus, and He never passed the crowd walking around the lake. But He slept at Simon's house last night."

The windy fisherman, nothing loath to hear his own voice, opened his mouth to repeat the story he had just told the young men. But great talker that he was, he was no match for the woman. Before he could get a word out, Sarah was saying, "The crowd was so thick around Him on the street that, to find a little relief, He went into the synagogue. He's there now preaching."

"I think I'll go over," said Joel.

"You'll never get in," objected Sarah.

Dysmas and Zebedee started to the door, showing their intention of going also.

But Joel was not destined that day to stand face to face with Jesus. When they reached the ornate marble synagogue for which Capernaum was famous, the crowd was dispersing, discussing the sermon just heard. Seeing a friend in the crowd, Zebedee called to him; and as he pushed his way in their direction, the fisherman informed the young man that this was one of Jesus' most enthusiastic followers.

"There's nothing about him that suggests enthusiasm," said Joel doubtfully.

"What did Jesus say?" called out the irrepressible[42] Zebedee while his friend was still fifty feet away.

"I don't know. I couldn't understand. He spoke of eating His flesh and drinking His blood. It was the strangest sermon I ever heard Him preach. It is very obvious He doesn't intend to let us make Him king. I'm convinced there's little use in going along with Him any further," said Zebedee's friend dejectedly.

Before the day was over Joel heard from at least a dozen sources the same report, and by nightfall it was said in Capernaum that of the scores who had been disciples of Jesus there remained only the twelve intimate friends.

This was the last day Joel was ever to spend in the Galilean town. The next morning, taking leave of Jonathan and his wife, he said, "I wonder what's become of Dysmas. I don't want to leave without telling him good-by."

Just at that moment the young man appeared, a bundle of clothes in his hand.

"I've decided to go with you, Joel," Dysmas announced in a tone which said, "It's all settled; there's no use to argue about it."

The old couple protested vigorously, saying all in a breath they couldn't spare him and he was too young to go and "wouldn't he be in Joel's way?"

Dysmas only smiled and said, "I'm going."

A year and a half ago if Dysmas had insisted upon coming with him, Joel angrily would have refused to permit it. But now, somewhat to his own surprise, Joel discovered he was glad of the boy's company. Dysmas, the talkative lad of sixteen, had matured and grown until he was almost as tall as Joel. Quieter now and less exuberant,[43] he had restrained his happy spirits and cheerful outlook. During the last few days Joel had found him a most pleasant companion, who knew how to adapt himself to the moods of his older friend. Even now, trudging along beside him, Dysmas seemed to sense that Joel was in no mood for conversation.

That young man meantime was wondering what he was going to do with the boy when they reached Jerusalem. He certainly could not admit him to the secrets of his conspiratorial[44] life and he was forced to face the truth that he was ashamed to have Dysmas discover about Myra, as he would be sure to in Jerusalem.

"Barabbas?" said Dysmas.

Joel was surprised into a quick glance at the lad. This was the first word he had spoken since they had left Capernaum. Attempting to cover his confusion, Joel said in a nonchalant voice, "What about Barabbas?"

"I wasn't going to say anything about him. I was just getting ready to say something to him," said Dysmas, mischief in his eyes.

"Are you crazy?"

"Uh, uh, just a light sleeper."

Joel stopped in his tracks and turned to face the youth, waiting for him to continue.

"The night you arrived, you talked in your sleep."

"And said what?"

"Oh, a few words about a riot on the Passover. You said only two things that were clear. One was 'They don't suspect that I'm Barabbas.' "

"Well," probed Joel. "And the other?"

Dysmas' gaze shifted and his cheeks grew red. "Uh-h, I don't exactly remember," he stammered.

"Come on, come on, let's have it."

"It was 'I'll always come back to you, Myra,' " the boy spoke reluctantly, obviously embarrassed.

In the early days of their acquaintance Dysmas would have asked bluntly, "Who is Myra?" but now he tactfully changed the subject, disgusted with himself for having inadvertently admitted that there had been more than one clear sentence muttered by Joel as he slept.

"The next day when Zebedee blustered about Herod's having beheaded John, you had very little to say," Dysmas continued. "Why, when you lived in Capernaum you would have talked all day about a thing like that, but this time you were glad to change the subject."

"So what?"

"So I remembered what you had said in your sleep and decided you might be Barabbas after all because he is fighting our oppressors, and when a man *does* things he doesn't have such an urge to *talk*."

"A clever deduction," Joel admitted with admiration, determined to be more careful about his reactions from now on.

"I made up my mind then I'd come with you. You used to say so much about oppression and tyranny that you got me to thinking and I decided I had to *do* something too."

"Well!" said Joel. The word was not a question; it was an exclamation. Plainly it meant, "So that's what I've done—betrayed myself by talking in my sleep, been so transparent in my manner that this stripling saw through me, had such an unconscious influence upon this youngster that I now have him on my hands for good."

Joel's pride slipped considerably. He had thought himself a master of subterfuge and he had boasted to himself that he was too clever to reveal his secret. His ego was saved from a complete collapse only by the unstinted admiration in Dysmas' eyes and his admission that Joel's influence had been so potent upon him.

"I won't get in your way, Joel. You know I can keep a secret and I'll try to be a help."

Joel smiled and flung his arm affectionately about the boy's shoulders. "All right, pal, we'll see what we can

do. But for heaven's sake forget this Barabbas business. Remember for the time being, at least, that my name is Joel. I take orders myself but I'll get you in if I can, though for your sake I would a thousand times rather you had stayed in Capernaum. This life you are so eager to live is plenty rotten in lots of ways. You'll keep telling yourself you're a hero, but your heart will call you a liar every time."

Reading Check

1. What is Prince Manaen's opinion of Joel's involvement with Myra?
2. Why is Joel called "Barabbas"?
3. What proves to Joel that Jesus is "merciful to the oppressed" and "tender toward the poor"?
4. How does Joel's rebellion influence Dysmas?
5. What statement does Joel make to Dysmas that indicates that Joel has not found satisfaction in his rebellion?

Chapter 14

The seething mass of bright-robed pilgrims made of the temple court a caldron[45] boiling with color. Standing upon the stone terrace, the lofty walls of the sacred enclosure rising behind him, Dysmas looked down upon the scene, wide-eyed, overcome.

"There's more to see," said Joel, plucking him by the sleeve, turning to pass through one of the nine gates covered with gold and silver.

Joel had made it habit to come frequently to the temple when he was in Jerusalem, realizing that appearances here were an essential part of his masquerade. He knew that even the talk about Myra would not hurt his standing with the corrupt religious leaders as long as he kept up an outward pretense of piety. Joel was glad now of his familiarity with the sacred place, for he was finding great pleasure in leading his

young friend through its majestic expanse. That small-town lad, tongue-tied with wonder, followed him now across the Court of Women.

To their left a flight of fifteen semicircular steps led to an upper gate. They mounted the stairs, passed through the portal to the inner court where a score of priests were busy slaying the sacrificial victims and offering them upon the great stone altar, forty feet square. Just beyond the altar was the temple itself, a glittering mass of white marble and gleaming gold.

Joel could imagine something of what Dysmas was feeling as he saw all these glories for the first time. As often as Joel had been here he always felt a thrill of pride and religious fervor. No matter that the monstrous and bloody Herod had erected this temple, no matter that its architecture was a mixture of classical Greek and decadent Egyptian, this was the throbbing heart of Jewry, this blazing altar, the hearthstone of an enslaved nation.

Retracing their steps and passing out through the Court of the Gentiles, Dysmas remarked, "This looks like a market place."

"That's all it is," answered Joel, "the biggest, busiest, crookedest market in the world. Here they buy and sell God's favor, overcharging for a beast that some poor sinner wants to offer for a reconciliation with Jehovah. The racket and the wrangling and the rattling of the coins must make a pleasant sound in the ears of the Most High."

At this moment the noise was increased by shouts of "Down with the robbers!" "Kill the priests!" Oaths and curses echoed resoundingly. Plainly a riot had broken out.

"Quick! Let's get out of here!" said Joel, as the temple guards on duty attempted to break up the melee.[46] "They'll bring up additional guards and lock the gates. We'd better get out," urged Joel, fairly pulling Dysmas along.

All this was a part of Manaen's well-laid scheme. Dysmas was totally unaware that it was Joel who had covertly given the signal that started the trouble. At almost the same instant an attempt was being made to set fire to Herod's palace and several Roman soldiers on their solitary patrols were attacked in different sections of the city and a mob gathered with well-timed vehemence outside the barred gates of the Castle of Antonia, screaming, "Down with the Romans! Destroy the oppressors!"

Pilate, the governor, hating the noise and confusion of Jerusalem during the Passover season, had imprudently decided to spend the period of the feast at the castle in Herodium, some ten miles southwest of the city. The captain left in command, finding matters getting entirely out of hand, sent posthaste for reinforcements, and it was not until Pilate arrived with additional troops some hours later that the mob was dispersed and a semblance of quiet restored to the Holy City.

Manaen's delight in the success of his plans was mitigated[47] somewhat by regret at the loss of several good men whom it had been necessary to sacrifice in order to accomplish his purpose. Four had been killed in street fighting, six others were imprisoned at the Fortress of Antonia by the Romans, and several others lay chained in the temple dungeons. The city was seething with excitement under its enforced calm, the Romans were nervous, and the Sanhedrin in furious agitation sat late into the night.

Joel and his master sat in the study, congratulating themselves upon the success of their plan. "Now that's over, we'll have time to talk about this young friend of yours," said Manaen finally. "What's his name?"

"Dysmas."

"You know how I feel about personal relationships entangling with the business at hand?"

"I know, Sir," said Joel smoothly, "but I will not be working alone nearly so much during the crucial twelve months ahead and I'd prefer to have in my company men whom I know and can trust."

"And how do you know you can depend upon this youngster? He's completely untried."

"I grant you that, my lord, but so was I when you accepted me here," replied Joel.

Manaen, having no answer to this, attempted none.

"The boy is intelligent," continued Joel truthfully; "he's young, vigorous, full of fire, and I'm convinced he's absolutely devoted to me." Joel was pushing Manaen now for a decision, hoping to avoid any questions from the prince as to how much the boy knew about his activities. Joel would have been chagrined[48] to admit to his master that by talking in his sleep he had betrayed himself.

Finally Manaen, leaning back in his chair, square-fingered, well-kept hands thrust under his belt, said, "All right, Joel. I've got in the habit of taking your recommendations and trusting your advice. Do whatever you think best about this boy; but remember, he's *your* responsibility. Tell him no more about our affairs than necessary."

"Would you like to see him, sir?"

"Not here," answered Manaen, "and not when he knows it. I'll manage to see him, but he'll not meet me or know he's being looked over."

After a moment's pause the prince leaned across the desk, elbows resting on the polished surface. "Since we're going to break our custom in regard to friends working together, I'd suggest that you attach Omah also to your little—what shall we call it?—bodyguard?"

"I should prefer another name," answered Joel stiffly.

The prince smiled deprecatingly. "I meant no offense. Perhaps the word was ill chosen. Shall we say 'shock troops'?"

"Call it what you will," said Joel smiling. "I shall be delighted to have Omah, though it will seem strange my giving him orders."

"But not strange to Omah. I am confident he'll feel honored to serve under you."

Joel had spoken truthfully. He would be glad to have Omah, but he knew Prince Manaen well enough by now to realize that worthy gentleman had suggested him because he felt his maturity and experience valuable in compensating for Dysmas' lack of both.

"Will you need more men?" inquired the prince.

"No, Your Excellency," answered Joel, "I think three will be plenty, at least for most of the jobs; a large company attracts attention, and the more men, the more difficult it is to hide out when necessary."

Joel spent very little time in Jerusalem from then on. Robbery, sabotage, and negotiations of various sorts kept the three friends busy the length and breadth of the land. For months, though they were hunted unceasingly, no Roman patrol caught sight of Barabbas and his companions. So well organized were the conspirators that they had workers everywhere and it was possible for the three confederates to disappear into a perfect hiding place whenever and wherever it was necessary. Now it was the cellar of a respectable inn similar to that run by Omah's fat friend in Capernaum; again it was the straw in a farmer's stable that concealed the three. Sometimes it was a rock-hewn tomb, sometimes a cave; but there was scarcely a square mile in Judea and Galilee but afforded them some sort of cover.

Again and again the feared Barabbas would strike and disappear. The Romans offered a reward for his capture and the Sanhedrin doubled it, but from Dan to Beersheba the common people talked of his exploits and wished him Godspeed.

Briefly Joel would appear in the city to make a report to the prince or to discuss with him the point of delivery for the booty they had cached, but much of the brief time he spent within the walls of Jerusalem was passed with Myra.

Joel was less and less in evidence and Barabbas more and more apparent in the personality of this young man, and the robber had no scruples against holding back from the service of his country an occasional valuable bauble[49] taken from some pilgrim or stolen from the country house of some rich ruler or priestly official. Careful always to select something not easily identified or some jewel pried from its setting, he gave it to the dancer.

Chapter 15

Winter was dragging its slow, cold way toward spring. Roads were icy or bogged with mud; travel was difficult. But about two months before the Passover, Joel made his arduous[50] way from Ashkelon to Jerusalem, leaving Dysmas and Omah, who would meet him four days later in En-gedi on the shore of the great Salt Sea, prepared to accompany him into the land of Moab.

He warmed himself on his cold journey with thoughts of Myra. All through his conference with Manaen she was never out of his mind, and when, toward evening, he could get away from the prince's study, he hurried to her house. Letting himself in with the key which she had given him, he called from the hall, "Myra! Myra!" but it was not the lovely dancer who appeared, but the little black serving maid, who informed him that her mistress was performing that night and would not be home until late.

Asking her to bring food, Joel sat down by a brazier[51] of charcoal in the room with the fountain to wait with as much patience as possible for Myra's return. He would have liked to go to meet her, but did not want to add fuel to gossip by doing so. Upon Joel's insistence, since her experience with Toron, she consented to perform only when her employer provided an escort to see her home.

When it lacked one hour of midnight, a loud pounding was heard at the front door. The little ebony-colored serving maid, who lived some distance away, had long since left the house. Joel, ever on his guard of late, knew this could not be Myra, who had a key. Fearing treachery, he extinguished the lamp before he opened the door to the hall. Taking off his sandals he slipped softly across the cold stone flooring. He put his ear against the crack of the door. Muffled, but quite clear, came the sound of voices.

"Are you sure Barabbas is in there?" From the accent Joel judged that this was a Roman.

Smooth and venemous as poisoned honey were the answering tones. "He is in there, all right." The voice became suggestive now. "I'm afraid our visit is a bit—inopportune."

Joel cursed silently, red mists of fury before his eyes in the darkness. He had recognized that voice, and for the first time in his life the lust to kill was hot upon him. Hate coursed like fire in his veins. Heretofore, hatred had been largely an abstract thing with Joel—hatred of tyranny, hatred of oppression, hatred of Rome; the hatred of the mob on the hill of precipitation at Nazareth—

that hatred had been the most intense, and it was to this as death to life, as dull ashes to this crimson fury flaming in his heart. The pounding of the blood in his temples made it difficult to hear. He took a deep breath, forcing himself to calmness, and listened intently.

". . . wake the neighborhood if we break down the door, and by all the gods there'll be Hades to pay if you've led us a wildgoose chase and we break in and he's not there."

"Listen, soldier, when Jerusalem wakes up tomorrow and finds out *who* Barabbas is—well there'll be a sensation, I can tell you that! And for the soldiers who captured him, there's bound to be promotion. Besides, don't forget the reward!"

It was not until this loathsome voice had died away that Joel was conscious that his nails were biting into his palms, so tightly clenched were his fists.

"What do you think?" It was the voice with the accent.

Apparently, the Roman soldier was conferring with his companions; Joel strained to discover how many voices would answer. He could detect only one.

"It would be better if we could find another way in. The door looks strong and we haven't anything to break it down."

Apparently, then, there were only two soldiers. Joel's mind was working fast. Quietly he dropped to his knees, peering intently at the floor. There was a faint flicker of light under the door. They had torches. Unfortunate, but it couldn't be helped.

The smooth voice flowed again, "I don't think we need to worry about noise. Only blank walls face this little court. The door is thick I grant you.

But the wood of the jamb is old and dry. Surely, it's no match for a pair of Roman legionnaires."

"Especially with a Jewish Hercules to help," snarled a Roman voice sarcastically. "Well, we'll try it, and if Barabbas isn't here, you'll sleep tonight in the cell that would have been his, my massive friend."

Joel retreated hurriedly down the hall as the door shuddered with the first attack upon its solid panels. Quickly he replaced his sandals on feet cold from the stone floor. Working swiftly, his only light the dim red glow of the charcoal brazier, he snatched up cushions, arranging them in rough suggestion of a sleeping form on the divan farthest from the door. Quickly he stripped off his cloak, threw it like a blanket over the pillows, giving them a final prod or two here and there.

Next he crossed to the low table. Picking up pitcher and goblet, he returned with rapid strides to the divan. The goblet he laid on its side on the floor beside the trailing corner of the cloak. From the pitcher he poured wine generously, staining the garment and making a fragrant rivulet[52] on the stone.

As he worked he had been listening intently to the sounds of the blows on the door. Now came a splitting of wood. In an instant Joel had set the pitcher beside the overturned goblet and crossed the room. The door to the hall he had left open purposely that he might follow the progress of his hunters. Now he closed it silently, just as the front door gave way and flew open, striking with a crash against the wall.

In the dark room Joel, thankful for the dull brown of his tunic, pressed his back against the plaster beside the door. Every sense alert, he heard the sound of approaching feet. Cautiously his door began to open, a wedge of light growing along the floor. Now the door swung open, shoved by a cautious hand, and Joel was completely hidden behind it. The torch was thrust into the room.

"Looks empty."

"Sh-h look! There! Asleep! Strange he didn't hear the noise."

"No, he's drunk! Smell the wine? See, he dropped the goblet when he passed out."

Only a faint creak of leather and a slight rattle of arms told Joel they were moving across the room. He waited tense, counting silently, "One, two, three, four." Joel stepped from behind the door, catching only a brief glimpse of two startled Roman faces turned toward him in surprise. Then he was in the hall, the door slammed shut behind him, bolt drawn. There was no time now to be concerned with the banging upon the panel—with the cries of the trapped legionnaires.

Where in this darkness was Toron? Joel suspected that the Romans, always on guard against treachery, had insisted the Jew remain outside when they entered the house. He was sure of it now as a dark shadow blacked out the faint gray outline of the door to the courtyard. Stealthily Joel slipped across the hall. His groping fingers touched the lamp stand, feeling for the unlighted lamp it bore. Now his hand closed over the smooth round copper vessel. Drawing back his arm he hurled it through the darkness in the direction of his unseen enemy. He heard it strike. There was an oath and simultaneously the

crash of the lamp hitting the floor, where it rolled, clattering across the stone.

Now Joel's eyes, accustomed to the darkness, saw the dim outline of the giant figure lunging toward him. With a shove of his hand he threw the lamp stand to the floor directly in the path of Toron, who tripped and plunged headlong. Joel, dagger in hand, sprang just as the giant struggled to his knees and the two bodies went down together. Rolling upon the stone floor, Joel felt huge hands at his throat. Joel's arm, strong with fury, rose and fell in short fierce blows.

"There, there, there. Again. Once more!"

The choking hands relaxed. In the darkness anguished gasps, then gurgling sighs.

Silence!

Breathing hard, Joel pushed himself to his knees. He was calm, satisfied, clear in mind as he wiped his sticky hands on the garment of the dead man. The legionnaires, reduced to silence by the noise of the struggle outside their prison, now resumed their blows upon the door. Their cries, growing ever fainter, followed Joel as he stepped out into the night.

Chapter 16

Two things must be done quickly: intercept Myra and get her hidden away somewhere before the Romans could arrest her for questioning, then warn Manaen. As far as Joel knew, Myra had no reason to suspect that her lover was the most notorious criminal at large in Judea. Her relationship with Joel might be common talk in the city; but if she disappeared, the authorities, ever ready to suspect the worst, would come to the conclusion she had been deceiving Joel with Barabbas and would never associate the two.

Aside from the dead steward, only Manaen and the little Negress had known that Joel was in Jerusalem. Should the authorities locate the black girl, Joel felt he could rely upon her loyalty and intelligence not to betray him. He had good cause now to be glad for the generosity and kindness with which he had always treated the maid, and he remembered thankfully many little evidences of her devotion to him. Joel, waiting in the shadow of a buttress for Myra to pass, hoped her escorts would be men to whom he was unknown.

There was the glimmer of an approaching torch. Joel, shivering without his cloak in the wintry night, drew farther back into the shadows. Now they were in range of his view— a woman and two armed servants, one with a torch. Wrapped in a heavy cloak though she was, Joel easily recognized Myra's walk. Nonchalantly, he stepped from his hiding place directly into the path of the three.

"Peace be with you, Myra."

The servants had come to a halt, prepared for trouble from the cloakless stranger. Myra, recognizing Joel, flashed him a smile; but before she could call his name, Joel interrupted, "I've only a moment and something important to say; so if you'll do me the honor of letting me see you the rest of the way home, it will give me the opportunity of talking to you."

Myra had not become the most popular dancer in Jerusalem only because of her beauty and talent. She was clever as well. Having lived by her wits so long, she was quick to sense something out of the ordinary and with perfect ease took up her cue.

"Certainly," she responded. "It is very kind of you to come. I suppose it's Mother! You want to spare me the shock?"

Clever actress that she was, there were tears in her eyes as she turned to the servants. "My mother was not feeling well when I left home tonight. Her heart, you know. I never expected this. If I'd known, I would not have left her! If you'll let us have the torch, we can make out very nicely."

With a word of thanks and "Peace be with you," she dismissed the sympathetic servants.

When they were scarcely out of earshot around the corner, Myra whispered, her arms around his neck and lips close to his ear, "What's the matter, Joel? Tell me quickly."

"Let me get rid of this," replied the young man, thrusting the hissing torch

flame through the thin crust of ice that covered a puddle of water. He slipped his arm around Myra's waist. "No, not that way. This!" he said, turning her in the direction from which she had come.

"What's the matter, Joel? Where are we going?"

"To Prince Manaen's"

"But why? Joel, what are you laughing about?"

"So many questions at once," said Joel between his chuckles. "I suppose it's the reaction after the tension I've been through, but the way you played up to my little act was the funniest thing I ever saw. Your poor, poor mother!"

He was off again into another gale of laughter. "You practically had those poor servants weeping. It's a good thing they don't know that your mother's with a Roman captain in Alexandria."

"He's not a captain. He's a centurion, I'll have you know," answered Myra in mock indignation. "Now stop being a fool and tell me what this is all about or I won't go another step with you."

"Toron is dead in your front hallway and two Roman legionnaires are locked in your house. No, don't ask any questions," he added, to the astonished girl. "Here we are at the palace. I'll explain it all when we get inside."

Joel did not mount the marble stairs nor pull the bell cord to summon the porter. Instead, he led the girl to a small unobtrusive door lower by three steps than the uneven cobbles of the street. Signalling Myra to precede him, they entered, Joel bolting the door behind them. Taking Myra's hand, he led her up a narrow stone stair. At the top he drew aside a hanging and they stepped into the little corridor connecting the reception hall with Manaen's study, but it was not toward either of these that Joel turned. Instead, he took up a lighted lamp and escorted Myra into a little sitting room just opposite the room with the Hebraic decorations.

"Wait here. I'll be back in a moment," he said, indicating a chair of ivory and cedar wood.

Leaving the lamp beside her, he went out.

Entering the study, Joel crossed the room, stepping around a chair in the darkness. Lifting the tapestry on the wall behind the desk, he found a rope, which he gave three short, quick pulls. Unheard in the study, a soft-toned bell chimed thrice in the bedroom of the prince upstairs.

Soon after his arrival his master had disclosed this mechanism to Joel with the instructions that should any emergency arise late at night, Joel might, in this confidential fashion, summon the prince. Until tonight he had never had cause to resort to it.

Awaiting his master's arrival, Joel struck a flint and lighted the lamp, first making sure that the heavy draperies were fully drawn across the window. Almost at once Manaen entered, dressed as usual in black, immaculately groomed, every hair in place. From his appearance, it might have been mid-afternoon rather than an early hour of the morning. Seated behind his carved desk, he manifested no sign of shock or surprise as Joel hurriedly related the night's adventure. Manaen heard him through without interruption, then asked, "Had you any reason to suspect Toron of being your enemy?"

Frankly Joel answered, giving the prince for the first time a full account of the incident that had taken place in the little courtyard more than a year before. The prince sighed, "I trusted Toron, of course, or he wouldn't have been my steward, but he knew nothing of the details of my affairs. The only way he could have known that you are Barabbas is to have eavesdropped."

"I can understand, Sir, how his enmity and jealousy might have led him to betray me to the Romans, but surely the thought that he was inevitably involving you should have kept him from it."

The prince shook his head sadly. "I suppose you see now why I fear emotional involvements more than anything else in this business of ours."

Rising, he paced up and down the little room, hands clasped behind him. "We'll have to move quickly. The Roman legionnaires should have been able to break out of their prison by now. If they know Toron's identity, which from what you have told me I doubt, the authorities will be here at any moment."

"And if he wasn't known and the body is not identified?" asked Joel.

"I shall certainly have to report my steward missing in a day or two, in any case," was the reply. "If I know our pagan conquerors, and I've had enough experience with them that I ought to know, the city gates will be guarded to prevent this dancer's leaving the city and in an effort to capture Barabbas, of whom they have only a vague and general description."

"So vague and general that nobody has applied it to me. I could ride openly through the gate," said Joel.

"You could if you wanted them to know you had been in Jerusalem, which you don't. In a situation like this you can be very sure they would ask plenty of questions about where you were going and on what business. That's also something we must avoid."

"And Myra?" asked Joel. "What are we to do with her, my lord? How much must she be told?"

"Nothing, gentlemen," said a musical voice. "She has heard everything."

Both men turned quickly to the beautiful woman who had opened the door and walked in so unexpectedly. Nothing disconcerted, the courteous prince said with all his usual suavity[53] and charm, "Won't you sit down? This unexpected entrance takes us rather by surprise, but you are as always ointment for the eyes."

"Thank you, my lord."

She had retained her cloak against the chill of the house. Now as she seated herself, she threw it back from her shoulders. She did not address her lover, but turned her smile entirely upon Prince Manaen.

"Your Excellency is a man of wisdom and experience. I think it might be wise for you to tell your young friend that no woman's curiosity can stand the sort of treatment he's given me tonight."

Manaen smiled and turned to Joel, saying, "You hear, Joel?"

Myra continued, "I hope you'll pardon my eavesdropping. The sound carries so easily through the door I simply could not resist the temptation."

"Apparently neither could Toron," said Joel angrily.

"You shouldn't be upset with Myra," the prince rebuked him. "She has solved a very difficult problem for us—how and how much we were to tell of the real situation."

Myra smiled at the prince and continued, "Well, I need no great wisdom to see that I'm involved in a serious situation because of my foolish love for Joel—I'm afraid I could never get used to calling him Barabbas. Oh, I know, Prince Manaen, that he feels no real love for me, but, in spite of all, my foolish heart that I thought so well controlled—"

She broke off, turning now to the young man. "You needn't worry, Joel, I love you far too much to care whether you are Barabbas or who you are, and you need have no fear that I shall betray you."

She turned back to Manaen, who was standing, head to one side, regarding her with a hint of admiration on his usually well-masked features. "I take it the problem now is to get us—Joel and me—out of the city. I think that's a simple matter."

"Simple!" exclaimed Joel.

The prince with a glance and an upraised hand silenced him. "Yes, Myra?"

"The body of your treacherous steward will have to be buried, though, personally, I think it would be more fitting to fling it into a ditch."

"Yes?" said Manaen again, interest evident in the word.

"Well, the Romans are very careful not to interfere in Jewish religious observances, and a funeral even for a Jew like Toron is a religious ceremony."

"Yes?" said Prince Manaen for the third time.

"Who will count the mourners that accompany his corpse to its grave or know whether two more leave the city than return from the ceremony?"

Joel's admiration was written on his face. Manaen smiled and bowed from the waist.

"Though I have often had the pleasure of seeing you dance, I regret, Myra, that I have not before had the benefit of your advice!"

As had been predicted, the next morning when the city gates were opened, they were heavily guarded. And no traveler passed from the Holy City who was not carefully scrutinized and questioned—that is, nobody except the mourners that followed the body of Prince Manaen's steward to its burial place on the Mount of Olives, outside the wall.

In that company, perfectly disguised by the ashes heaped on their heads and smeared on their faces, tearing their garments and wailing lustily, Joel, feeling like an awkward fool, and Myra, thoroughly enjoying one of the most dramatic performances of her entire career, left Jerusalem.

Prince Manaen's sigh of relief at their safe departure changed to a hearty peal of laughter at the thought of the Romans busy looking everywhere for the killer of Toron except among those mourning at his funeral.

Chapter 17

Myra's three loves—for Joel, for adventure, and for acting—made her a valuable addition to the little company of conspirators. It was her charm, more than Joel's impassioned words or the bribes and promises of great rewards, which won over the bandit chief they met by appointment at midnight in the ruins of an ancient Moabitish temple. With her mobile face and vari-timbered voice,[54] she could be as the occasion warranted—the innocent young maiden, doting wife, railing shrew, refined young lady, or cheap woman. Her gift for sizing up a situation, her intuition, and her understanding of men served them well on more than one occasion; and the very presence of a woman made their little group less liable to suspicion of banditry and outlawry. But not even her wit or devotion were charm enough to prevent the blow that shattered all their well-made plans and dashed their brave dream of Jewish freedom.

As Joel had predicted, rumors of an outbreak on the Passover had reached the ear of Pilate. He had indicated his intention of leaving the palace of Herod, his usual residence in Jerusalem, and occupying for the duration of the Passover the Castle of Antonia. This cold, uncomfortable fortress commanded the temple courts and afforded a strategic position from which a strong hand might reach forth to crush rebellion lifting its head either in the sacred enclosures or elsewhere in the city.

From Galilee came the rumor that Herod was eagerly preparing for his trip southward to the Holy City. Outwardly he was only making his annual religious pilgrimage, but it was whispered everywhere that Herod was eager to be under the shadow of the protection of Pilate's doubled garrison; and it was said that he was trying by gifts and overtures of friendship to be reconciled to the Roman Governor, with whom his relations had been strained.

So throughout the land, preparations were being made and alliances strengthened among those of common interests. The religious leaders of Jerusalem—the priests, the scribes, and elders of the city—fearing anything that might upset the status quo, were frequently in council. Telling themselves that any change would be for the worse, they dreaded the thought of a rebellion, which might give Rome an excuse to enact new measures curtailing their prestige and incomes. Added to all this was an even graver concern about the influence of Jesus. Their pride had been cut by their failures to trap Him into an unfortunate utterance, though they had sent their most skillful lawyers in the attempts. Their hatred had been aroused by His stinging denunciation of their hyprocrisy and pretense. Their leadership was being undermined by the sincerity of His kindness and the wonders He had wrought. Their monopoly on religion was being threatened by the simplicity of the faith He taught, their pretenses of piety made ridiculous by His modest manner and unassuming humility. Everywhere men were listening to His words, attracted by an authority lacking in the language of their religious leaders.

Fear and hope, dread and expectancy, like the blossoms of the springtime, seemed to clothe the very hills and valleys of the land. It lacked only two weeks of the Feast and Joel and his friends were congratulating themselves on a job thus far well done and almost finished. Supplies of arms were hidden in strategic points readily available everywhere. Orders had been carefully transmitted for the insurrection that now awaited only the final signal to blaze forth and consume the structure of tyranny throughout Jewry.

Riding along a deserted stretch of road through a narrow valley near Lydda, Joel and his companions saw coming toward them two men on horseback, each leading a well-laden pack beast.

"Well, well, this is too good an opportunity to miss," asserted Joel.

"But Joel, we don't need to rob any more," objected Myra. "We've raised all the funds we need. All that sort of thing is done with."

Dysmas, still so young in crime as to feel constantly the pricking of his conscience, added his words to hers. "No, Joel, let's don't. I feel we shouldn't."

As Joel was about to give way to their pleadings, he glanced toward Omah, on whose face he observed the cynical smile and an expression that Joel fancied seemed to say, "Wrapped around the fingers of a woman and a boy!"

So instead of the words he was about to speak, Joel cried, "If you're soft, stay here. Omah and I can handle this."

Though armed, the well-dressed middle-aged pilgrims made no resistance as the two men rode down upon them, but only poured forth a torrent of words, prayers that their lives should be spared, interspersed with wails over the loss of their property.

As Joel and Omah were reaching for the bridles of the pack animals, intending to lead them to a place of seclusion away from the road before examining their burdens, Dysmas called, "Look, Joel! Soldiers."

It was evident they had fallen into a trap. From the hills on both sides armed men were riding rapidly down upon them, spreading out to cut off their escape.

Calling, "This way," Joel spurred his Arabian straight down the road in the direction of Joppa, the others right

behind, hoping to escape in this direction before the spreading soldiers could completely block the way. They had almost made it when a Roman legionnaire pulled his galloping horse to a stand directly ahead of them. Joel's sword flashed once, twice and the soldier's headless body dropped from the saddle. The delay was fatal, however, and now they were pressed in on every side by the legionnaires. All fought valiantly, even Myra striking right and left in an effort to force a way through the mass of encircling men and horses. The conspirators knew that orders were to take them alive. They also knew that capture meant an eventual death, as cruel as possible. Better then to fight for their lives here; for should they die now, such a death would be better than that which awaited them in the form of an official execution.

So fierce and courageous was their defense that four legionnaires had fallen before them. Finally, the captain, realizing it was going to be an almost impossible task to take Barabbas alive, raised his sword, aiming a terrific blow at the young man. Joel, drawing his own weapon from the body of a slain soldier, failed to see the descending sword. Myra, struggling with the reins and pressing her spurs viciously into the flank of her horse, managed to interpose herself between her lover and his attacker, receiving the full force of the descending weapon. Striking her shoulder, the blade, backed by a powerful Roman arm, cut through flesh and bone and muscle, halfway to her

waist. Dysmas, striving also to save Joel, simultaneously plunged his weapon into the heart of the captain. Joel, struck with horror by Myra's sacrifice, was disarmed and bound before he could rally himself. Dysmas, seeing Joel captured, offered no further resistance; and Omah, fighting alone, was soon overpowered.

The Romans, angered by the loss of their comrades, their pride stung by the death of their captain at the hands of a stripling, rode rapidly toward Jerusalem, eager to see their three prisoners safely stowed in a dungeon and to collect the reward for the capture of Barabbas.

Entering the city, they rode past Manaen's mansion, where the porter stared, wide-eyed, opened-mouthed, at the spectacle of Joel's being led bound toward the Castle of Antonia. Joel was thinking, "Thank God, he saw me. He'll tell the prince and perhaps he can escape before Barabbas is identified as Joel, his friend."

Now clattering across the drawbridge and through one of the arched tunnels piercing the great entrance tower, its barred gates standing open for their passage, they rode into the stone-paved sunlit courtyard of the Castle of Antonia. Unceremoniously the captives were dragged from their horses, through a stone archway, down steep rough stairs. They halted in a dusty underground corridor. One of a row of heavy planked doors creaked open. Dysmas and Omah were dragged inside and Joel heard the rattle of chains as they were secured to the wall. Then rough hands shoved Joel forward as the door was locked on his friends. Through a barred door at the end of the corridor, down a winding flight of stone steps in Stygian darkness, they led him. He heard the protesting cry of a knife blade cutting the ropes that bound his wrists. A heavy hand was placed in the small of his back; and with a Latin curse and a shove, he was thrust forward into the inky darkness, behind him like a groan of despair the noise of the hinges, like a death rattle the sound of bolts.

Reading Check

1. Who betrays Barabbas to the Romans?
2. How does Joel deceive the soldiers?
3. Where does Joel take Myra, and what does she overhear?
4. How does Myra help Joel escape from Jerusalem?
5. What part does Joel's pride play in his capture and Myra's death?

"He came unto his own, and his own received him not. But as many as received Him, to them gave He power to become the sons of God."

Part 2, Chapter 1

Pontius Pilate, procurator of Judea, stood at his window watching the dawn fire the temple of Jehovah, God of the Jews. Gazing on the magnificent spectacle and listening to the prayer horns of the priests proclaim the morning sacrifice, he was wishing the magnificence a mass of ruins and all these tricky, scheming priests dead in the rubble.

The governor had spent a bad night. In twenty years of campaigning he had slept in many places and on all kinds of beds, including the hard ground, but in no place did he sleep so poorly as in this Castle of Antonia. He loathed the place, stinking with the burning flesh of the sacrifices in the courtyard of the temple adjoining, and with the smoke of the altar sooting its rooms and stinging the eyes of its occupants whenever the winds blew from the south. Any part of Jerusalem was bad enough, but the Castle of Antonia was the worst of all; and the Jews were difficult people at any time, but on the days of their feasts, impossible.

Four years before when he had received this appointment he had thought himself greatly honored to be made at the age of thirty-six procurator of even so relatively unimportant a province as Judea. Many times since, he had wondered if that appointment had not been a scheme of his enemies. Instead of a promotion it amounted, he thought, to banishment. He picked up for the twentieth time the parchment on the table and his eye fell upon a paragraph halfway down the page:

"From the coldness that Caesar showed me when I last had the honor of being invited to the palace I surmise that Marcus is up to his old tricks—more successfully than last time, I'm afraid. Porcina tells me that every time Marcus had been alone with the emperor, Caesar mumbles for hours afterwards about the 'inefficiency of certain officials in the east' and frequently refers to the Jews. I hope, my son, that you can contrive that good reports shall reach his ear from Jerusalem; for, as we both know, there are those here in Rome who would like to see you recalled in disgrace from your position of responsibility and honor."

"Responsibility! Certainly," Pilate sighed; "but honor!" he wondered as he tossed the letter angrily onto the table. His mother, Jupiter be praised, could be depended upon to keep track of the gossip of the imperial court and pass on to him anything which might affect her son.

Well had he tried to be fair to these quibbling Jews and as tactful as his nature permitted and pride allowed. The trouble was that when he pleased the rulers and religious leaders he offended the common folk. The former could gain the ear of Caesar but the latter could break out in rebellion, the imminent threat of which was responsible for his being here in this stinking castle.

Even when Julia Procula came to call him to breakfast he could not leave his problems behind. Usually just the presence of his wife and the sweetness of her gentle smile had a soothing effect upon Pilate, but this morning talking things over with her did little good, and after a night haunted by troubled dreams her smile was wan and forced.

"It's either please the priests by flattering and giving in to them so they will send good reports to Caesar—in which case we risk a rebellion—or it's to somehow placate[55] the riffraff and avoid a rebellion and let the priests and leaders write what they will to Caesar," he summarized petulantly.[56]

"Well, when one must choose between two evils it's always wise to choose the lesser," philosophized the Roman lady.

"Agreed," said her husband. "But who understands the mind of these Jews enough to know what will placate them?"

"But," continued Julia with a wife's gift of ignoring her husband's interruptions, "if it were possible to please the common folks, avoid rebellion, and at the same time manage to get a few good reports to Caesar you would completely outplay these big-nosed priests at their own game of political intrigue."

"That sounds extremely wise, my dear, but how can it be done? Tell me that!"

"Well, in the first place you must release a prisoner today. It's an old custom. Remember? One which I have always considered extremely stupid. It's as if Rome were bribing those whom she rules, but today it may prove a means to an end for you—release the prisoner most popular with the rabble. You're not eating your melon, dear," she added irrelevantly.

But Pilate's mind was busy; he saw a glimmer of light and the melon was forgotten.

"This fellow Barabbas is a crook and a scoundrel but something of a fabulous figure in the imagination of the average Jew."

"Then he's the one to release."

"Of course, he may give us trouble later on but I'll think of some way to get around that. Did you know that he's the adopted son of Prince Manaen?"

"The one who's Herod's foster brother?" asked his wife.

"He! And apparently the Sanhedrin and the temple crowd are furious to think that the prince knowingly or not took a thief under his patronage, particularly since that thief specialized in robbing pilgrims on their way to the temple with gifts."

Julia spoke now with that "see how simple it all is" air which wives use to their husbands. "Well, send for Prince Manaen and tell him you will release his adopted son if he will guarantee that Herod, his foster brother, will advise Caesar that you are the most efficient and capable governor with whom he has ever dealt."

"The prince has disappeared. Wait a minute. Herod has held it against me because I put nine of his Galileans to death a year or so ago—that and the fact that I put military standards dedicated to Augustus on the walls of his palace—but in the last few weeks he's been trying to make up. I have been cold to his advances as a matter of Roman pride."

"But now if you should release his adopted brother's adopted son—dear me, what a distant relationship!—you will be making a gesture of friendship toward Herod and you'll be pleasing the masses at the same time."

"That certainly should more than counteract the animosity of the Sanhedrin and the bigoted priests." Pilate, actually smiling, began to eat his melon with a show of relish. "Nothing would please me more than to insult and irritate those bigots and make friends with Herod and win the good will of this unpredictable Jewish rabble all at the same time."

Thus spoke Pilate, little realizing that, with Barabbas in jail and Prince Manaen fled to points unknown, there was no danger of rebellion on this Passover. And thus Barabbas, who had risked his life in the cause of revolution, was to become unwittingly the chief weapon of the Roman governor in avoiding revolution.

Part 2, Chapter 2

Joel awakened to the urging of a Roman boot. He sat up blinking in the glare of torches.

"Come on! Get up, murderer! The governor is doing you the honor of entertaining you for breakfast," drawled a Roman voice, and the harsh laughter of his companions applauded this sarcasm.

Joel got to his feet and preceded the soldier from the cell, the silent jailer stepping aside to let them pass and following them torch in hand. In the antechamber at the foot of the stairs were his fellow men-at-arms, one of them with a torch. Up the winding stairs they went—two soldiers, Joel, the other soldier, and the jailer—and in this same order passed through the barred doorway into the long corridor. Joel expected them to stop for Omah and Dysmas; but seeing they had no intention of doing so, he cried out, "Dysmas! Omah!"

"Shut up there and move along," commanded a soldier harshly.

But Joel had the satisfaction of hearing above the faint rattling of chains the sound of his name being called by his friends, their voices muffled by the thick planks of their door.

As they neared the top of the second flight of stairs, Joel caught a glimpse of daylight. The soldier with the torch stepped to the side of the corridor until Joel, following his companion, had passed him. Handing his torch to the jailer who went no farther, he hurried to resume his former position at the head

of the little procession. In a moment they had passed through an arched entrance and were in the great paved fore-court of the Fortress of Antonia.

Joel, long accustomed to musty underground air and darkness, blinked and half closed his eyes in the light of early morning, taking long deep breaths of the fresh air. Crossing the pavement, his eyes becoming momentarily more accustomed to the daylight, Joel saw that even at this early hour the courtyard was bustling with activity. Several horsemen were riding through the gateway. Soldiers were coming and going; others were lounging on the steps or kneeling on the paving stones intent upon their gambling games. Joel's escort took him diagonally across the great paved quadrilateral, up the flight of wide stone stairs on the south side, and down a long covered porch, its archways overlooking the courtyard and the entrance of the fortress opposite.

Presently Joel stood in a large room, stone walled and austerely[57] furnished. Pilate, the procurator, was writing at a table as Joel was led in by his guards.

Pilate looked up. Before him stood a stalwart[58] young Jew with unkempt hair and ragged beard, the grime of confinement upon his body and garments. Pilate's slender, high-bridged nose wrinkled delicately. Here, at least, was a change from the smell of burning beasts.

The governor stared for a long moment into the dark, burning eyes before him. Just as he was opening his mouth to address his prisoner, a soldier entered the room hurriedly, saluted the governor, and burst out with "Your Excellency, there's quite a large group of Jews, at least forty or fifty, coming from the Bezetha Hill toward the castle."

"Are they armed?"

"I think not, sir, except for the temple guards. There are a number of them and quite a lot of priests. I should say it's a delegation from the Sanhedrin."

Without a further word for Joel or his guards, whom he seemed to have forgotten, Pilate left the room. Standing on the portico,[59] the governor looked across the court to the great double arches of the entrance. The heavy gates were being closed; but through the bars the approaching group was plainly visible, its leaders stepping now upon the drawbridge. Recognizing the high priest and other prominent ecclesiastics and various members of the Sanhedrin, Pilate, cursing the poor judgment of his subordinate in ordering the gates closed, called instructions that they were to be opened promptly. To his surprise, however, the Jews made no effort to enter the courtyard but stopped on the drawbridge just beyond the gates.

"Invite them to enter," said Pilate to the soldier who had brought the news of their approach. Saluting, the young legionnaire crossed the courtyard and spoke to the high priest. In a moment he had returned.

"They say, Your Excellency, they cannot defile themselves on their feast day by entering the dwelling of Gentiles."

"Any apologies?"

"None, Sir," answered the young soldier. "They say they have brought a prisoner named Jesus for you to examine and sentence to death."

Pilate's high forehead wrinkled, his chin was raised. "So they have come to bring me a prisoner and to tell me in advance what judgment I shall pass upon him. Well, we shall see."

His hands resting upon the stone balustrade,[60] Pilate leaned over to call an order to several soldiers standing in the courtyard just below. Crossing the pavement, they received the Prisoner from the hands of the temple guard. Pilate beheld a man of slightly more than medium height with a slender muscular build returning between them across the court.

Pilate met the Prisoner at the top of the stairs. He certainly did not look like a criminal. For a moment the governor gazed into His face, then dropped his eyes, uncomfortable before the glance of the Prisoner, unflinching yet kind, sad yet pitying. Descending the

in his dealings with this dangerous and powerful figure.

Instead of answering the question specifically, the priest said defiantly, "If He were not a malefactor,[61] we would not have delivered Him up to you."

Pilate shrugged and prepared to turn away, saying, "Very well, if you do not care to make your charges known, I'll have nothing to do with it. Take Him yourself and judge Him according to your law." Profound contempt was in the way he spoke the last two words. It was plain that to the Roman there was no real law except that of Rome.

The Jewish lawyer standing next to the high priest spoke now, resentment of Roman domination in his surly tone, "It is not lawful for us to put any man to death."

Another voice from somewhere in the forefront of the crowd cried, "We found this Fellow perverting the nation."

A short young Sadducee, attempting to give himself height by an aggressive, self-confident manner, cried officiously, "He has been forbidding to pay tribute to Caesar." And the bigoted features of the high priest fairly writhed with malevolence as he spat out, "He has been saying that He Himself is Christ the King."

In their intense animosity for the Prisoner they had raised points which they knew Pilate could not lightly push aside, but he was determined he would not give these scowling zealots the satisfaction of listening to his examination. He would question the Prisoner on the gallery and bait their curiosity by letting them see what they could not hear.

steps, Pilate strode toward the delegation, silently cursing the stupid custom that forbade their coming in to him. He addressed the high priest, Caiaphas by name, a man with a great beak of a nose and full red lips showing through his beard.

"What accusation do you bring against this Man?" he inquired coldly but resolved to be as judicial as possible

Returning to Jesus, whom he had left standing at the top of the stairs between the soldiers, Pilate was convinced that he had to deal with the delusions of a madman. Yet when he came to look again into the face of the Prisoner, he could not bring to his tones the imperious mockery that he had intended. Instead he found himself inquiring almost as if he expected a reasonable answer, "Are you the King of the Jews?"

There was about the reply the quiet dignity of an innate authority that gave Pilate the uncomfortable sensation that not the Prisoner but the governor was on trial.

"Do you ask this for yourself or did others say it to you about Me?"

"Am I a Jew?" flashed Pilate in quick petulancy. "Your own nation and the chief priests have delivered You unto me." He waited a moment, uncomfortable and perplexed, then almost appealing cried, "What have You done?"

"My kingdom is not of this world. If My kingdom were of this world, then would My servants fight that I should not be delivered to the Jews; but now is My kingdom not from here."

Pilate took a deep breath before asking, "Then You are a King?"

Stronger than ever was the procurator's feeling that he was being weighed in the balances as Jesus responded, "You say whether I am a King. For this purpose I was born and for this cause I came into the world that I should bear witness to the truth. Everyone that is of the truth hears My voice."

Pilate had never in his life been concerned with truth but always with expediency, yet for this moment at least truth seemed more important than personal advancement or the honor of the empire. Partly in sadness, partly in irony, and partly from a real desire to discern the connection of such an abstract matter with this question of life and death, Pilate, searching the face of his Prisoner, asked, "What is truth?"

He did not know whether he expected an answer but he received none unless it was from the eyes of Jesus, which seemed to search his heart and bring to light all the lies and deceit and pretense which were the fabric of his life. Turning swiftly, greatly perturbed, and feeling that he must at all costs save this Man, Pilate descended the steps part way and called across the fifty yards of pavement to the accusers in the gateway, "I find no fault in this Man."

He was reminded of the cries of jackals slinking by night across a deserted battlefield, busy among the bodies of the rotting dead, as he heard their yappings in reply, "He stirs up the people! He teaches throughout Judea." It was impossible for him to distinguish further details of their accusations, so numerous were the voices calling at once; but amid the babble he caught the word "Galilee!"

Here, thought Pilate, is a way out from under unpleasant responsibility. He held up his hands imperiously. Voices died away into rebellious silence.

"Is He from Galilee?"

Beards wagged affirmatively.

"Then, He's Herod's responsibility. Take Him to the Tetrarch." Pilate signaled the soldiers to return the Prisoner to His priestly accusers and ordered an officer to accompany them to Herod.

Part 2, Chapter 3

The procurator, returning to his private quarters, found Barabbas standing at the end of the porch, the three soldiers still guarding him. Always short tempered, Pilate spoke with more than his usual asperity to the unfortunate legionnaire in charge of the guard detail, "What are you doing here? I left you inside."

The legionnaire, standing rigidly at attention, apology in voice and manner answered, "I beg your pardon, Your Excellency, but we thought perhaps you wouldn't want us to remain in your private quarters; so we brought the prisoner outside."

"In order to see what was going on! When you're on duty it is not your business to think but to obey commands," the governor answered gruffly though secretly thankful that the odoriferous[62] prisoner had not been all this time in his office.

Now as they were preparing to follow him inside, Pilate said, "I don't want him now. Later."

"Shall we return him to the lower dungeon?"

"No, chain him there where he'll be convenient when I'm ready." He indicated a heavy iron loop imbedded in the mortar of the gallery wall for the purpose of holding a torch. "That's solid. He'll be safe enough there." And the governor, without waiting to see his orders carried out, passed into the castle.

He was congratulating himself on his cleverness in sending Jesus to Herod. He had heard somewhere that the Tetrarch was eager to meet this famous Miracle-Worker face to face; so he hoped that the Galilean ruler would consider Pilate had done him a favor in bringing him into contact with Jesus and that he had paid him a subtle compliment by stepping aside and relinquishing to him the authority of dealing with this case. Yes, concluded Pilate, he had indulged in a brilliant bit of diplomacy. Still he was angry with himself, knowing that he had been a coward in not facing the issue squarely and releasing, as he might very well have done, this Man of whose innocence he was convinced.

But Pontius Pilate had not escaped the responsibility of deciding the case of Jesus of Nazareth. A soldier entered to inform him that the Jews had returned with their Prisoner. The governor appeared on the gallery, determined this time to make a short work of releasing the persecuted Jesus, but he lacked the moral fiber to risk his own interests in doing so. He was settled, therefore, on a compromise which he felt would satisfy the Jews and save Jesus from their antagonism. He looked down across the courtyard, crowded now with all the soldiers not on duty, drawn here by the noise and the excitement. In the great double arches of the gateways stood the Jewish leaders and ecclesiastics, but this time they were backed by a great mob of vicious-looking Jews who had apparently come together from the back alleys of the worst quarters of Jerusalem.

In the center of the paved quadrilateral, midway between Pilate and the priests, stood Jesus, wearing now a magnificent white cloak which Herod had ordered thrown in mockery around Him. This Pilate learned from the captain whom he had ordered to follow the Jews with their Prisoner to Herod's palace and bring him information of the results of that expedition. His report was brief: "Herod asked the Prisoner a great many questions but He would make no reply. He seemed disappointed that the Man would not perform a miracle for him and was apparently bored by the noise of His accusers. He and his palace guard mocked Him, put this cloak upon Him, and ordered Him returned to you with the Tetrarch's compliments."

Pilate, hands on the balustrade, called to the priests, "You brought this Man to me as one who perverts the people and, as you have seen, I examined Him. I found Him not guilty of the things of which you accuse Him. Neither did Herod—I sent you to him and he found nothing deserving death. I intend, therefore, to scourge Him and release Him."

The murmur of anger that rose from the assembled Jews was mingled with the cries of a smaller band which was trying to approach the castle gate, making an effort to push through the mob already gathered. Barabbas's eyes brightened. These were Prince Manaen's men—his fellow conspirators. Their cries could be plainly heard in the courtyard and on the gallery, above the voices of the chief priests and their followers. "We've come to claim a prisoner! Observe the Passover custom, Pilate! Release Barabbas. We want Barabbas!"

Until that moment Pilate had forgotten the insurrectionist.[63] Now he thought he saw an easy way out of his dilemma. He knew how extreme was the hatred of these priests and scribes for this robber and was confident if they had to choose between Barabbas and Jesus, they would be glad to take Jesus.

He spoke a word of brisk command, "Unchain the murderer and lead him to the head of the stairs." He motioned to another legionnaire to bring Jesus up the steps. A moment later they stood side by side—Jesus and Barabbas—in full view of priests and leaders, rabble and assembled Roman soldiers.

Pilate, standing on a lower step, cried in a voice accustomed to calling commands above the noise of the battlefield. "Whom shall I release, Barabbas or Jesus which is called Christ the King of the Jews?"

So sure was he that the majority would call for Jesus that he descended to the courtyard and prepared to seat himself upon the curial chair. This seat of Roman authority was set up in whatever place the procurator was in residence. Since the Castle of Antonia afforded no room appropriate for a judgment hall, a dais had been placed in the open courtyard, and upon it under an awning stood the chair. Pilate, about to seat himself and give the official order of release for Jesus, felt a tugging at his toga. It was the little Greek waiting maid of Julia Procula.

"Excellency, my mistress sent me to ask you not to have anything to do with this Just Man." She pointed to Jesus.

"She said that I should say to you in her own words, 'I have suffered many things in a dream because of Him.' "

Pilate, always superstitious and already perplexed by the mystery which he felt surrounded Jesus, could scarcely repress a shudder. Well, his problem would be solved in a moment. He seated himself, only to start up again in agitation and astonishment at the cries, "Barabbas, release Barabbas!"

It was not only the voice of the late arrivals he heard. The cry was being taken up by the followers of the priests, whose leaders were moving among them, instigating and commanding. The governor could not believe his ears. These unpredictable Jewish officials, loving money as they did, had added their reward to his for the capture of Barabbas; yet now, faced with the choice of his release or Jesus', they were asking for Barabbas to go free. He held up his hand for silence. "What shall I do with Jesus Who is called Christ, Whom you name King of the Jews?"

A single voice like a geyser of hate rose from the gateway, "Let Him be crucified!"

Another and another took up the cry until the stones of the entrance tower echoed and shook with its malevolence. "Let Him be crucified! Let Him be crucified!"

The pagan governor, to whom the life of one of the lesser races was of small importance, used to cruelty as he was, could not understand such black and venomous hatred. Snatching a spear from the hand of the soldier standing at attention beside the curial chair, Pilate smote it furiously against the great bronze eagle, the emblem of

Roman authority, hanging above and behind the judgment seat. Like the sound of a great dissonant bell, the blows vibrated across the courtyard. It was a brazen voice demanding silence, and the howling mob obeyed its command.

"Why, what evil has He done?" demanded Pilate.

But the cries rose again, fiercer than ever, "Let Him be crucified!"

Pilate, thwarted and browbeaten, knowing himself a coward, fancied contempt was in the eyes of the soldiers whom he ordered to strike the bands from the robber and murderous insurrectionist.

Barabbas was free but he made no move toward the castle entrance. He felt impelled to remain for the end of the scene now being enacted. He had no wish to brush against the chief priests and their hired mob and he wanted to learn, if possible, the fate in store for Dysmas and Omah. He stepped back to the side of the great stone stair, making himself as inconspicuous as possible in the entrance of the low room under the gallery, used by the common soldiers as a place of relaxation, where they gathered to drink or gamble and to boast profanely of their deeds of valor or lust.

Pilate meantime had turned with a word of command to the Greek maid who, impelled by curiosity, had remained near his dais. The governor's order sent her up the stairs and across the gallery to his quarters. The chief priests and the rest watched in silence, interest having quieted their angry voices. She returned now with a large bronze basin of water which she held

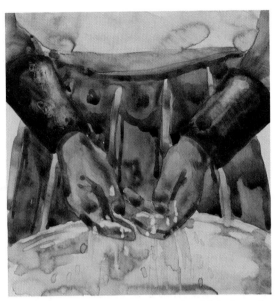

for the governor as he washed his hands in dramatic gesture, saying, "I'm innocent of the blood of this just Man. You answer for it."

The response of the multitude sent a shudder down the back of the murderer standing inconspicuously in the background. "His blood be upon us and upon our children!"

Pilate, his schemes all gone awry,[64] had still the faint hope that he might yet release Jesus without the necessity of asserting the authority he was too great a coward to exercise. Perhaps if these Jews saw Jesus bleeding and suffering, their blood-lust would be satisfied; so he turned Him over to the soldiers with the command, "Scourge Him."

No task was more enjoyable to the sadistic[65] legionnaires, whose livelihood was warfare and whose pleasure cruelty. The whole troop, about a tenth of a legion or some five hundred men, swarmed after Jesus and His guards into the hall beneath the gallery with its walls scrawled with obscenities. Here, while the son of the Rabbi watched from the doorway, they stripped the Nazarene and chained Him to a column. Then one after another, some forty of the brutal Romans laid blows upon His back with a leathern whip tied with scraps of sharp metal and bits of bone. They made a game of this cruelty, betting on who could strike the hardest blow and vying for the opportunity to prove their strength and brutality.

Among the various gambling games chiseled in the large flagstones with which the open court was paved was one just beside the entrance hall. The knuckle bones with which four soldiers had been playing when they were interrupted by the prospect of a more cruel diversion had been left practically at Barabbas's feet. Its complex design covered several flagstones with its intricacies, among which frequently recurred a capital B. At the top of the design was carved a rough, prickly crown.

Barabbas recognized this as Basilicus, one of the most popular games played by the Romans in which the loser permitted each of the other players to smite him with their belts upon his bare back. The game had its origin in the custom on the Saturnalia of choosing a burlesque king by lot, of loading him with ludicrous[66] honors and giving him liberty to satisfy any caprice, and then when the Saturnalia was ended, of putting him to death. One of the last to lay the whip across the torn shoulders of Jesus was the slow ape-like soldier who had been on the point of losing this game when it was interrupted. Relieved at escaping the forfeit he would have had to pay, he laid down the whip and, wiping the sweat from his forehead, said with a vicious grin, "This is better than Basilicus."

"Hey," cried another, his keener imagination fired by the comparison, "it could be better yet! This Fellow says He's a King; let's make Him one."

Quickly his companions entered into the spirit of the vicious jest. One hardhanded Latin went into the courtyard to return dragging a branch of thorn tree he had pulled from a heap of firewood piled against the wall. With oaths when the thorns pricked his fingers, he wove the barbed twigs into the rude semblance of a victor's coronet. Two or three others, using the handles of their daggers to protect their hands from the pricks, pressed the crown upon the brow of the patient suffering Man Who hung half fainting upon the chains that bound Him to the column. Then roughly they released Him and flung Him down upon a crude stool.

"A robe for His Majesty," cried one of the tormentors. "No, not the white one. Here, take Captain Marcus's. He's on duty and won't miss it."

Across the mangled back and shoulders the rough scarlet-purple wool was flung.

"That's all but the scepter."

How will this do?" cried the ape-like brute, picking up one of the rushes with which the stone hall was carpeted. He smote Jesus viciously across the cheek with the filthy reed and then thrust it into His hand.

"Hail, King of the Jews."

With laughter and mockery they cried, "Hail! King of the Jews!" One squint-eyed fellow dropped on his knees in mock reverence and from that position spat full in the face of the pathetic Figure. Others followed his example, smiting Him with the backs of their hands or with clenched fists. Some pulled at His beard with violent tugs that took out strands of hair.

It was at this moment that Pilate swept past Joel into the door of the common room, calling, "That's enough! Bring Him out now!" His voice broke off as he caught a full view of the pitiful thorn-crowned, scarlet-robed Figure, dripping with spittle and blood.

The anger of the procurator blazed forth. Stinging with the consciousness of his own weakness and with self-contempt for the way he had dealt with Jesus, Pilate cursed and berated the soldiers for presuming to have exceeded his commands in these additional mockeries and torments beyond the scourging which he had ordered. Finally, out of breath, he cried hoarsely, "Bring Him forth now! Quickly!"

Still furious with the soldiers, with the Jews, and, above all, with himself, Pilate crossed the pavement to the entrance tower where the chief priests and their mob were still crowded into the shadows of the embrasures[67] or packed on the drawbridge beyond. Pilate, who felt sure that the blood-stained mockery of royal robe and thorny coronet, that the spittle of humiliation and the anguish of lacerated back would purchase pity even from these stony hearts, said to the high priest, "See, I bring Him forth to you that you may know that I find no fault in Him."

At this moment Jesus, thrust from the shadowy doorway of the common room, stood revealed in the full glare of a shaft of direct sunlight streaming through the opening between two lofty eastern towers. Pilate, to whom the harsh Aramaic language was both difficult to speak and unpleasant to hear, was not aware that under the tension of that dramatic moment he relapsed into the language of his birth, as pointing to the still Figure he cried, "Ecce Hommo!" "Behold the Man!" But instead of the pity which Pilate had expected, the crown of thorns, the broken reed of a scepter reminded these chief priests and ambitious Jewish rulers of the authority which the Prisoner had been acquiring over the minds and hearts of men. Pilate was standing close enough to feel the warmth of their breath and the spraying drops of their saliva as, their hatred bursting forth in fresh torrents, they shrieked, "Crucify Him! Crucify Him! Crucify Him!"

Losing all semblance of self-control as he had lost all vestige of self-respect, Pilate matched their screaming, angry tones as he cried, "You take Him and crucify Him, for I find no fault in Him!"

Gone was the majesty of Roman law, the dignity of Roman justice. It was the lawyer who had writhed not an hour before under the procurator's contempt for Jewish law who now with triumph in his tone mocked Pilate with the words "WE have a law, and by that law He ought to die because He made Himself the Son of God."

The phrase, "the Son of God," his wife's dreams, the sad, deep voice saying, "My kingdom is not of this world"—all these and the silent witness of his own heart inspired the procurator with a fear—half reverential, half superstitious. He retired again to the gallery and had Jesus brought hither. He commanded the soldiers to withdraw out of earshot. They stood alone on the shadowy gallery, plainly visible to the Jews and to the soldiers the purple-bordered toga of the Roman Governor and the faded, blood-stained, scarlet robe draped in mock royalty about the Man of Nazareth. Fear was in the low voice of the Roman. "Whence are you?" But though he waited for a long moment there was no answer.

More urgent now that questioning voice, "You do not speak to me? Don't you know that I have power to crucify you and power to release you?"

Now the bruised lips moved and the rich minor melody of the anguished voice flowed over the coward Roman, "You could have no power at all against Me except it were given you from above. Therefore he that delivered Me unto you has the greater sin."

Pilate, eyes cast down in thought, again crossed the pavement. This time, almost a suppliant,[68] he appealed to the Jews. Their answer was "If you let this Man go, you are not Caesar's friend. Whoever makes himself a king speaks against Caesar."

The chief priests, experienced in their judgments of men, even in their blind hatred of Jesus, were wise enough to realize that the weak point in the armor of Pilate was his fear of being thought lacking in loyalty to Caesar. As well Pilate knew as they that Tiberias, half-crazed by disease and the constant fear of assassination or overthrow, could not brook[69] in any subordinate the slightest indication of disloyalty or compromise with treason.

Slowly Pontius Pilate ascended the dais; reluctantly he assumed the Judgment Seat. Lacking the courage of a man to release the Prisoner and defy the Jews, he resorted to the weapon of a woman and made mockery serve him. With a scornful gesture he indicated the Figure standing in pathetic majesty at the top of the stairs. With contemptuous tongue he cried, "Behold! Your King!" Their echoing chorus of hatred beat against the walls of the castle. "Away with Him! Crucify Him! Crucify Him!"

With a supercilious[70] smile, an attitude of mock surprise, Pilate leaned forward to ask, "Shall I crucify your KING?" But he was no match for these Jews. Sarcasm for sarcasm they gave him. "We have no king but Caesar!"

Eager now to be rid of them and to forget as quickly as possible this whole affair, with its embarrassment, fear and defeat, Pilate gave the necessary orders. A band of soldiers under the command of a centurion was assigned to convey the Prisoner to the place of execution and to stand by until the deed should be accomplished.

As they were dragging timbers from the storeroom to make a cross, Pilate thought of yet another insult with which he might avenge himself upon these scheming priests and cruel Jewish leaders. "Bring out the companions of Barabbas," he commanded. "They'll make nice courtiers for a Jewish King."

Forgotten in the background, Barabbas saw his friends dragged before the Judgment Seat—so settled their fate that even before sentence was passed the sounds of the hammers nailing together their crosses reverberated across the court. Then the instruments of their

deaths upon their backs, three figures moved slowly from the castle to the accompaniment of muted trumpets and the martial tread of flanking soldiers.

Reading Check

1. What news from Rome disturbs Pilate?
2. How does Pilate plan to appease the Jews and Herod simultaneously and to insult the Sanhedrin?
3. What effect does Pilate's conversation with Jesus have on the procurator?
4. How does Pilate try to escape responsibility for Jesus?
5. How is the destiny of Omah and Dysmas linked to Jesus?

Part 2, Chapter 4

Dazed by his narrow escape from death, Joel was sickened by the treatment Jesus had endured. Joel, who had long since overcome any squeamishness at the shedding of blood when necessary, had been physically sickened by the display of such wanton cruelty nor could he understand natures so perverted as to find enjoyment through inflicting suffering. Remembering that Sabbath in Nazareth long ago, he could not help wondering why Jesus permitted Himself to be thus dealt with. Surely He had not lost His strange gifts and supernatural powers. If He could heal, then certainly He could destroy. Why then had He not used His powers against the fiendish soldiers? Perhaps He was waiting, biding His time, to perform some spectacular act of vengeance and destruction.

He knew unspeakable torments were in store for his friends. His conscience smote him about Dysmas, and he blamed himself for the horrible fate of the youth. He regretted the fiery words he had spoken so freely and cursed the unconscious influence he had exerted upon the susceptible heart and mind of an impressionable boy. He rebuked himself for ever having permitted Dysmas to join him in his career of insurrection and robbery. For Omah he felt pity; for Dysmas, remorse as well.

Impelled by an irresistible impulse to see the tragedy through to its end, he followed the procession from the castle. Once across the drawbridge, he turned into the first side street, feeling that he could not at the moment endure the sight of his former co-workers, the conspirators who had clamored for his freedom. Through the narrow, winding ways of the old city the column would, he knew, move slowly. Jesus, weakened by His suffering and loss of blood, had been staggering painfully under the weight of the heavy wood and His progress was bound to be slow.

Joel, thoroughly familiar with all the short-cuts and byways, reached the western gate well in advance of the cortege of the condemned. Here the guards on duty were holding back all traffic into the city until the procession should pass the walls. Now around a bend in the narrow street came the first of the crowd, followed closely by the centurion glittering in his armor; immediately behind him, the ranks of the soldiers escorting the three unfortunates to the hill of death.

As they neared the portal, just beyond which he was waiting, Joel heard the sound of a heavy plank striking the cobblestone and the cry, "He's fallen again!"

The centurion stopped. "He can't make it," he said in disgust to the guard at the gate. "It's a wonder He got this far with that cross on His back. We'll have to conscript somebody to carry it."

"How about him?" suggested the guard, pointing to a dark-skinned giant who, coming in from the country, had been among those held back at the gate.

"Here, you!" called the centurion. "Where are you from?"

"Cyrene in Africa," answered the black man with dignity.

"What's your name?"

"Simon."

"Well, Simon, we have a special honor for you today. You're going to carry a King's throne," and without waiting for a word of agreement or objection, he ordered the cross placed upon the back of the African.

Jesus was half kicked, half lifted to His feet and the slow march resumed. Joel moved ahead of the crawling serpent of humanity with its heart of suffering as it wound its way under a cloud of choking dust along the twisting road to Golgotha. Ahead loomed the Hill of the Skull, the bare rock rising like the bald pate of ancient death, long-abandoned burial caves like staring, empty sockets in the stony cranium. Precipitate on the side facing Jerusalem, the summit of the hill could be reached only by a narrow lane branching off from the main road and curving around to ascend the less sheer incline on the west.

Among the first to turn in to this rough tract, Joel climbed the slope.

About this bare and melancholy spot was the hideous atmosphere of death and from the very stones of this unwholesome hill seemed to rise the sickening smell of mortality. Their broken beams rotting beside them, stumps of crosses, monuments to the sufferings of long-dead malefactors, afforded roosting places to the vultures that, disturbed by this new invasion of their horrible aerie, now wheeled and circled against the clear sky, their hoarse screechings answering the jeering voices of the mob. Standing on the brow of this grisly hill, Joel looked down upon the road. All the way back to Jerusalem stretched the procession, swollen by the blood thirsty and the idly curious, its numbers increased by pilgrims and strangers eager for any excitement and by proselyte Jews from the ends of the earth who had come to celebrate the feast of the Passover in the Holy City. From the eminence Joel marked the costumes of a dozen nations, but directly behind the condemned men and their Roman guard were the priestly robes and rich garments that distinguished the rulers of the Jews.

Part 2, Chapter 5

Three crosses loomed against the morning sky, their long shadows dulling the gleam of Roman helmets where the soldiers quarreled over the garments of the anguished trio hanging naked above them.

Efficiency resulting from past experience had made quick work of impaling their victims. The crosses had been laid flat upon the rocky crest, the condemned stripped and flung roughly upon them, arms and legs held in place by brawny hands, spikes driven into palms and feet. Omah had screamed curses as the nails tore through his flesh and Dysmas had cried out in fear and anguish, but Jesus had prayed, "Father, forgive them for they know not what they do." The weathered remnants of old crosses had been pried from their sockets and these three had been raised in their places.

Now all the clothes had been divided among the executioners, except for the seamless robe of soft blue wool woven by Mary for her Son. It was the most valuable of all and a fight seemed imminent as four angry soldiers laid claim to it.

"Here, you," ordered the centurion, "none of that now. If you can't settle it any other way, use these." From the leather pouch at his side he took a pair of dice and flung them on the ground.

Gamblers by instinct, their animosities vanished at the prospect of the play. While their companions gathered to watch, they knelt quickly, each certain that luck would be his. "You, Sextus, roll first and remember high man wins."

"A six and a three. See if you can beat that!"

The second soldier shook the ivory cubes vigorously, then blew upon his fist before tossing. "A deuce! Hades!"

"It should have been low man the winner, eh Vestus?" cried out a stocky legionnaire and the disgusted Vestus retorted, "With you looking over my shoulder with your evil eye, I should have expected bad luck."

Now all were intent upon the rolling dice which had been tossed by the third soldier. "Five and four," called several voices at once, and the centurion added, "That makes it a tie between you and Sextus unless Vinicius can raise it."

His face red with excitement, the youthful Vinicius called upon the god of luck, as he picked up the dice. Briefly he rattled them in his fist, then with his eyes closed made the cast. A low whistle sounded from one of his opponents before Vinicius raised his lids. The dice had fallen six and six. The centurion spoke. "Don't begrudge him his luck, boys. After all, its his first crucifixion."

"Yeah," jeered Vestus, "He needed something to brace him up. Did you see how green he turned when we nailed 'em?"

Barabbas with a shudder lifted his eyes from the soldiers to their victims. Above the head of Jesus was a parchment inscribed in Greek and Latin and Hebrew, "This is Jesus of Nazareth, the King of the Jews." No sooner had it been read than the chief priests in anger had demanded that the centurion remove it. "The governor wrote it and there it stays," he retorted.

"We'll see about that" was their angry rejoinder,[71] and a delegation set off to Pilate.

Now they returned hot and crestfallen.[72] "Well, what did the old man say?" asked the grinning officer. Ignoring him, they whispered to their fellow priests who gathered around them with eager questions and Barabbas heard their reply, "He says, 'What I have written I have written.' "

Their bitterness and chagrin at this new insult from the pagan governor was vented in fresh fury upon Jesus. Pressing upon the cross, they screamed, "You, You that destroyed the temple and built it in three days, let's see You save Yourself now!" Their mockery was like a torch touched to dried grass and through the entire mob there seemed to race a flame of unreasoning anger. Bestial faces distorted with hatred, the lowest types of humanity from the gutters of the city sought to outdo the scribes and elders in the vileness of their insults. Thugs and harlots, priests and religious leaders made themselves allies in that moment and Barabbas, sick with disgust, cursed the God who had made him a Jew.

"If He is the King of Israel, let Him come down from the cross and we'll believe Him," they shrieked. "He trusted in God, let Him deliver Him now," cried one. "Yeah, if God will save Him," answered another. "Sure," mocked a third, "He said, 'I'm the Son of God.' "

The centurion, smarting under the treatment he had received from the Jewish leaders, sought to goad them by fresh pricks at their nationalistic pride. "If You really are the King of the Jews, save Yourself," he challenged Jesus, implying that only a base people could have so helpless a King and the cry which on their own lips had mocked Jesus became on those of the Roman a mockery of all Jews.

Even the fellow sufferers joined their words to the others. "Yes, save Yourself and us!" There was in Dysmas' voice the remembrance of miracles in Galilee and a hope somehow even now for another. But there was only contempt mingled with the pain in Omah's demand, "If You are Christ, show it. Save Yourself and us!" Again and again he spat out the stinging phrases from dry and tortured lips, his face turned toward the central Figure. Jesus met his scornful gaze for a moment and then turned His head toward Dysmas. The young lad, suffering as he was, nevertheless managed a smile as if to say, "Don't mind him." And to Omah, he called, "Haven't you any fear of God? Here we are under the same sentence, only we deserve ours. We are getting the punishment our crimes demand, but this Man hasn't done anything wrong!"

Perhaps, thought Barabbas, he recollects that afternoon in the hills when Jesus fed the people and gave sight to the blind man. Then as the lad spoke again Barabbas wondered if Dysmas was recalling Simon's words of faith that day, for there was an echo of the same deep confidence in the anguished voice of the crucified youth as he prayed, "Lord, remember me when You come into Your kingdom." The crowd had grown silent, listening to the speeches of the suffering malefactors and in that silence the answer of Jesus was plainly heard by them all, "You shall be with

Me in Paradise today." Jesus' bruised lips parted in a smile of infinite tenderness and into the eyes of Dysmas came a look of peace that pain could not conquer.

The eyes of Jesus turned toward the little group standing a short distance from the cross. Barabbas, turning to follow the glance, saw Mary and two or three other women. Trying to comfort them was John, the youngest of Zebedee's sons.

"Woman." The word had about it such a tone of love and compassion, as Jesus had always used in speaking to Mary, but now a thousand times more evident. "See thy Son!"

And He addressed young John, saying, "Look to thy mother." Barabbas watching saw the glance of the crucified Nazarene go from His friend to Mary. How, marvelled Barabbas, can He think of others when He is suffering so?

The sun was now at the zenith and for three hours the crosses had been erected. No breath of air stirred to cool the fevered bodies of the dying men. Suddenly the heaven darkened. One moment, the skies were clear and cloudless; the next, blackness lay upon the land. At noon it had become as midnight.

There were cries of fright and wonder heard in the crowd. The centurion ordered a fire built against the sudden darkness, using bits of the old crosses for the purpose. Torches were sent for from Jerusalem. Barabbas stood his ground against the jostling and the shuffling bodies stumbling blindly against him in the darkness.

For almost three hours, Jesus hung silent on the central cross, His distorted limbs outlined grotesquely by the flickering torches.

About what must have been mid-afternoon, though with the sun veiled, Barabbas had no way of knowing the hour, Jesus cried in extreme anguish, "Eli, Eli, lama sabachthani."[73] The words were like a scream of torment, chilling Barabbas's blood. For a moment there was dead silence on the hill of death. Then cruelty rang out in the laughing voice of a priest.

"He is calling for Elias." It rose like an antiphonal chorus all about Barab-bas in the darkness. When at length it died away, Jesus' voice was heard again, saying, "I thirst."

Before they had nailed Him to the cross, they had offered Jesus sour wine in which gall and myrrh had been dissolved. A group of pious women in Jerusalem had demanded of the Roman conquerors the right to extend this one act of pity to condemned malefactors that their pain might be somewhat dulled by the narcotic effect of the drug, but Jesus after one taste had refused the drink.

Barabbas had wondered at this and had been thinking how much more intense His pain must have been than that of His companions who had taken the cup. Now, the centurion, contrary to custom, his hard heart moved by an impulse of pity Barabbas had not imagined he possessed, took a sponge and poured it full of the dark red wine, sour as vinegar, with which the soldiers refreshed themselves. Placing the sponge on the point of a spear, he lifted the shaft, bringing the wine in this fashion to the lips of the Sufferer, disregarding the new cries of "Let Him alone. We are waiting to see whether Elias will come and save Him."

Having drunk the two or three mouthfuls of wine He could get from the sponge, Jesus prayed, "Father, into Thy hands I commend My spirit."

A moment He was silent: then there arose from His lips like a shout of victory the words "It is finished!" His deep breathing was plainly audible; then it stopped, and the thorn-crowned head dropped forward.

At this instant a roaring as of thunder filled the air. The earth groaned as a great quake shook the hillside. Rocks ground together, great boulders cracked open, and across the summit of Golgotha fissures appeared. Some in the crowd flung themselves upon their knees in terror; others were hurled down, as the earth heaved like the ocean under them. Only the centurion, clinging to the central cross, remained standing, when with a final sigh the earth settled itself.

Barabbas rose to his feet. At that moment, the darkness lifted as suddenly as it had fallen. The afternoon sunlight revealed pale and frightened faces. The crosses of the conspirators were tilted at grotesque angles, but the central cross stood straight and upright.

The priests and elders were clawing their way through the mob in their eagerness to be gone from the place. Chastened and panic-stricken, the multitude was hurrying headlong down the rocky path, some beating their breasts and others crying out in fear and lamentation. Barabbas felt he, too, could no longer bear to remain on this accursed hill; no longer endure Jerusalem; no longer tolerate the sight of priestly robes or Jewish faces. Staggering like a drunken man, he felt a compelling need to be gone—he knew not where, but away from this hill, this city, this land. As one possessed, he turned to flee, pausing only for one last look at his crucified friends and the still figure of Jesus of Nazareth. The last sight he remembered of that terrible day was the blood trickling down the rough wood of the cross. The last words that registered in his consciousness were those of the awed centurion, saying, "Surely this Man was the Son of God."

Reading Check

1. What puzzles Joel about Jesus?
2. Why does Joel blame himself for Dysmas's capture and death?
3. Who comes to a saving knowledge of Christ on Golgotha?
4. What are the last words Joel remembers hearing on the day of the crucifixion?

Part 2, Chapter 6

A whirling speck in the ocean of infinity, the earth moved on along its planetary path. Nightly the points of fire that men call stars reflected the glory of Omnipotence. Daily the sun, a burning preacher, proclaimed Omniscient Wisdom creating and sustaining an ordered universe. Light succeeded darkness, and darkness light. The ever-circling seasons marched in order by, and the seeds of the spring planting fathered the harvest of the autumn, but few there were who stopped to consider all these wonders; few who regarded such accustomed nightly miracles and daily marvels. Man, taking all for granted, went about his little ways, and if the morning stars sang together, few were the mortal ears that caught their melody. Man was too busy with birth and death, with love and war, with food for the belly, and clothes for the back to lift his eyes often heavenward.

So the years came and passed and with them, little men and Caesars. Tiberius, at whose name the world trembled, unhappy amid the splendid isolation and magnificence of his island in the Sapphire Bay, exchanged at last the ample villa and sunlit gardens of Capri for the confining darkness of a tomb. Caligula, worse than he, feasted for a few brief years at the table of imperial power until, drunk with flattery and sated[74] with blood, he became himself a dish for worms, the menial scavengers of a mightier monarch, Death. Now the honors of empire were paid to Claudius, whose name and profile adorned the coins pouring from

every corner of the world a steady stream into his coffers.

Pontius Pilate had been recalled from his position of doubtful honor and banished to Vienne in Gaul. A whim of Caligula's had deposed Herod Antipas; and now his nephew, Herod Agrippa I, wielded in Jerusalem a vassal scepter over all the country of the Jews, both Judea and Galilee.

For Joel these had been thirteen lagging years. A restless wanderer, unable anywhere to lay down the burden of remorse, he had sought to escape from the past in strange lands and far places. But guilt journeyed where he journeyed, and memory lodged with him. Daily she sat down with him to eat; her voice interrupted his reading, distracted his attention from every task he undertook, broke the thread of his conversation. When at night he lay down, memory was his bedfellow, beside him in the darkness; and when at last he fell asleep, she shared his dreams.

A natural leader of men, he sought no followers and encouraged no friendships. He made no permanent alliances. He was employed for a while by a merchant of Corinth. He journeyed with traders into Persia. He spent six months in Rome, where he worked as a public letter-writer. Finally, he crossed to North Africa, working his way eastward until he came to Alexandria. Here his wide reading and good education stood him in hand, and he secured a position on the staff of the great library. Here he had remained for more than a year.

During all these thirteen years, he had never set foot on the soil of Jewry. Less than a year after he left Jerusalem, his parents had been stricken with a contagion and died within a few days of each other. This he learned from a distant cousin, a rabbi, in Corinth and it was the chance meeting with this relative that led to his moving on from the Greek city.

Now he had no ties to bind him to Galilee. Indeed, in his heart he was glad. He told himself he was no longer by instinct or desire a Jew; yet such was his Jewish training that he found paganism repulsive. Jewish bigotry and cruelty had alienated him from his own people, but he could feel no kinship with the idolatrous Gentiles among whom he moved.

For a time he gave himself freely to drink and dissipation.[75] Women found him attractive, but he would not let himself grow fond of any. He thought of Myra's death, for which he blamed himself; he saw again Dysmas, suffering on a cross, and cursed the power in himself that had attracted the friendship and admiration of the lad.

But strangely enough, more than these, he felt the guilt of Jesus' death. Had he not been a prisoner then, he told himself, Pilate would have released his Fellow Townsman. He had been guilty, and Jesus innocent; but Barabbas had gone free, and Jesus been nailed to his cross. He had brought only grief and death to those closest to him, and he felt somehow to blame that an Innocent Man had died instead of him.

Part 2, Chapter 7

From the afterdeck of the slow-moving vessel, Joel gazed out over the gray-green expanse of the Mediterranean. Four days ago, he had embarked from Alexandria and now off to the starboard, below the horizon, lay the shores of Judea. Beneath him the heavy-laden vessel rose and fell on the long, low swells. Upon the afterdeck Arteses, her Greek master, was studying the horizon with a worried scrutiny. The dark eyes of this large man were changeable as the sea, sparking one moment with bright humor, and the next, dark and lowering as a thundercloud. Under the short-cropped gray hair his wrinkled face was tanned as old parchment and weather-beaten as granite cliffs.

Until this morning, they had made good time with a favorable wind. Now the canvas flapped idly on the mast, and the strong arms of the galley slaves, manning the single bank of oars, drove the vessel, laden as she was to the gunwale with a cargo of Egyptian grain, but slowly ahead. One of a busy fleet employed in supplying hungry Rome with bread, she flaunted[76] on her bows, in sharp contrast to her utilitarian[77] purpose, the romantic name *Luna Aegyptia,* Egyptian Moon.

The head and shoulders of a Roman officer appeared at the top of the ladder leading up from the mid-ship deck, where the slaves sat upon their benches, massive backs bent, muscled arms moving mightily as they pulled at the oars. An instant later, Metellus stood beside the captain. A landsman to the core, he hated the ocean and despised these long sea voyages. They had been scarcely out of the wide delta of the Nile before he had acquainted Joel with this fact.

"What a life," he had grumbled. "Here I am an inland man, born on a farm with a stomach never happy on the sea. Yet I spend my time sailing back and forth across these blasted waves."

"But, why?" inquired Joel.

"Because when you're in the army, you obey orders. I never could get along with the captain of the garrison where I was, there in Ostia, and out of spite, the old boy had me assigned to this tub."

"Why must they have a Roman officer on board a grain ship?" asked Joel.

"Oh, Caesar must have a representative everywhere. It's my job to see that the hatches aren't tampered with en route and that the grain arrives safely in Ostia."

"Well," laughed Joel, "it doesn't sound like a very strenuous job."

"Not strenuous, no; but with hard biscuit and salt meat, I never get fat at it, and you should see this floating rattrap roll in rough weather. Cramped quarters, no women, and rarely an intelligent passenger to talk to; in fact rarely a passenger at all. It's worse than a desert garrison."

Now with a nod at Joel, the Roman spoke to the captain. "How long will we be becalmed, would you say?"

The muscular shoulders of the master were lifted in a shrug, his deep voice rumbling in reply, "By Neptune, who can tell? But I don't like the feel of the air or the look of the sea."

"Oh, gods," sighed the officer. "I suppose we'll have a blow then. I turn green at the thought."

They had a blow indeed. At nightfall, the storm struck in violent fury. Fortunately the captain had anticipated it, and the sails were furled. The winds, which seemed to blow from every quarter at once, buffeted the vessel, howling like demons in the rigging and whipping and bending the mast.

Her laboring planks lashed by the furious billows, the *Luna* groaned like a woman in childbirth. So sudden was the storm that a number of the oars were broken before they could be shipped and the steering sweep was snatched from the hand of the helmsman, who was knocked to the deck as it swung free. The captain sprang to lay hold of the wildly flailing handle, and it took all his strength and that of three sailors to hold it steady. Meanwhile he bawled out profane orders for sea anchors to be set out from the bow. It was impossible to maintain a course, and all that could be done was to keep the vessel head-on to the wind; and thus they ran before the storm, a plaything of the ferocious elements.

The unfortunate slaves, chained to the benches, were soaked to the bone as they were doused again and again by the furious waves that broke over the ship.

Throughout the night the storm raged, its fury unabated. The gray light of a gloomy dawn revealed only mountainous crests and rushing clouds. Below deck, in his bunk, Joel, sick and weak, expected every moment to capsize or founder. At length, unable longer to endure the stifling dampness and stench of the tight-closed cabin, he staggered to the deck, gripping the lifeline stretched by the seamen. Now he half lay, half sat in the shelter of a bulkhead, a rope around his chest lashing him to a stanchion lest he be washed overboard.

It had not occurred to him that nature had any powers held in reserve, but as the day wore on, it was apparent that there had been furies yet unleashed. A sudden blast snapped the mast like a twig, and it went overboard, leaving shattered benches and crushed and broken bodies among the galley slaves.

The captain boomed frantic orders. His voice was snatched away by the wind but the seamen did not need his commands. Recognizing the danger, they sprang with axes to cut the tackle that bound the floating mast to the ship. Like a battering ram in the hands of the waves, it was pounding against the sides of the vessel, splintering the planks and threatening to stove in the hull. Sliding and falling on the slippery deck, the seamen clung to the lifelines with one hand, hacking away at the tangled rigging with the other. A towering wave hung for a moment motionless above

the vessel wallowing in the trough of the sea, then dashed in tons of cold brine upon the slanting deck.

For a long moment, Joel's straining eyes were blinded and he gasped for breath. Slowly the ship lifted like an old fat mongrel shaking herself free of an unwelcome bath. The mast was gone and so were the sailors who had cut it free.

For three long days and interminable[78] nights more, the storm flailed the hapless vessel. Toward dawn on the fourth day, faint points of light were visible through the howling darkness and when day broke, they saw a rocky coast ahead. Though the gale still blew, it was evident that the storm was abating, but there was little hope for them. The planks of the deck were already gaping where the swollen grain in the water-logged holds was pushing the ship apart. Plainly above the sound of the wind, they could hear the roar of the breakers. The captain ordered the slaves unchained that they might have some little chance of life.

Steadily the vessel was being carried toward the reef. Joel thought to himself, "Thus, at last, I find death," and wondered if it would bring him peace.

Now the reef was only three ship lengths away. Beyond the high wall of the breakers the waters were relatively calm, and he could see the sandy beach at the foot of the cliff. Suddenly, the ship struck broadside! There was a sound of wrenching timbers. Joel was flung overboard by the impact and the waters closed over him.

Part 2, Chapter 8

From the top of the cliff, the woman and the boy watched the doomed vessel being driven toward the reef as toward gaping jaws. The boy beat his fists excitedly upon the stone wall atop the precipice, saying, "Look, Mother. Look!"

She stood with her hand at her temple, striving to hold the long hair out of her eyes, against the busy wind; her cloak, fluttering and billowing like a banner behind her; her linen dress molded to her breast.

Above them the agitated branches of the orchard trees whispered and bowed excitedly, and the wind snatched greedily at the smoke from the chimney of the house behind them.

"If we could just do something. Will they all be drowned, Mummy?" asked the boy.

"God knows," she replied. "Pray, Son; pray for them. She's almost on the reef. Oh—. She has struck!"

"Maybe we could do something, Mother," said the boy, his eager young face looking up at her. "If Grandpa were only here, maybe he'd know what to do."

"Come, Son, let's go down to the beach. Perhaps some of them will get

to shore. At least we can be there to help. Wait, first oil and light for a fire. They'll need it if any reach the sand."

They hurried down the rough steps carved in the stone face of the cliff, she carrying live coals in a long-handled pot, and the boy the bottle of oil in his strong little hand.

The beach was littered with shells and seaweed and with driftwood cast up by the storm. This was too wet to burn; but from under the overhanging ledges and from behind the boulders, they dragged out enough wood, fairly dry, to make a large pile on top of the coals they had placed on the sand. Over it, they poured the oil, and before long a blaze flaunted its defiant pennants of flame in the face of the dying storm. Already flotsam[79] from the wreck was bobbing in the bay and grating against the sand of the beach. The ship itself had disappeared.

It must have been at least an hour later that the boy cried, "Mother, isn't that a man?" She had seen him, at the same moment, clinging to a cask, still a long way out, but being washed slowly toward the shore.

"Oh, I hope he can hold on," cried the boy.

It seemed an eternity before the man reached the shallow water. Once he lost his hold and disappeared, but he came up again, weakly trying to grasp the slippery keg. Finally, he managed to secure a hold. Saying to the boy, "Stay here," she waded in the rough surf up to her shoulders to meet the man. She grasped him just as exhaustion overcame him.

His arm was a dead weight around her shoulders, as she slipped hers around his waist, saying, "Steady, you're almost ashore. You're safe now."

He nodded faintly, no energy left for speech.

The boy met them at the water's edge, putting his arm about the man from the other side, saying, "Here, lean on me." Together they half dragged, half carried him across the sands to the fire, where he dropped limply upon the ground. The woman turned to the boy, "Go to the house, Son. Bring the heavy covers from my bed and my cloak, and one of Grandfather's, too." Then when the boy was some distance away, she cried, "And Joel,"—

As she spoke the boy's name, the man's eyes opened, bewilderment in their depths. "Be sure to bring some wine, too," she called after the lad.

Then the man understood she had not been calling him. But his bloodshot eyes, seeing her features clearly, were more bewildered than ever. He tried to lift himself upon his arm, but the effort was too great for him.

As she came around the fire to his side, saying, "It's all right, you'll be warm in a moment; my son will bring clothes and wine for you," she heard in a husky whisper from the lips of this bedraggled and exhausted stranger cast up by the sea her own name called. Then his eyes closed again. His labored breathing grew regular.

Striving to keep warm, she puzzled over the problem. How had this man known her name and who was he? She studied his features. Surely he was no one she knew.

When the boy returned, she shrugged aside the question. They removed the man's soaked tunic and wrapped him in a cloak. Then the woolen covers were thrown over him, tucked around and under. Once the stranger stirred and opened his eyes, and she held the pitcher of wine to his lips, while the lad lifted his head. He drank deeply and went to sleep again.

For several hours she and the boy scanned the waters for the sight of other survivors, but none appeared. It was almost noon when her father and her cousin Aeneas joined them on the beach. They had returned home from their business in the city to find the house empty. Noting from the garden the fire on the beach, they descended the cliff.

The shipwrecked man, still unconscious, was racked now with chills and hot fever. The two men, with frequent stops for rest, managed to carry him up the rough stairs. Finally they got him to bed.

For twelve days the fever gripped him. Sometimes he raved and muttered incoherently. They forced him to take the herbs and medicine prescribed by the physician they sent for, and to swallow warm broth. They nursed him tenderly, sitting for hours by his bedside, keeping the wet cloths upon his forehead. Almost never was he left alone, day or night—even the boy taking his turn at the vigil.

Eventually the fever left him, weak and helpless, but rational again, with eyes that looked at the ceiling or stared listlessly at the faces bending over him.

One morning as the woman laid him back upon the pillow after she had lifted him to give him a drink, he said softly, "Thank you, Irene."

She set the cup down and turned to him with the question that had never been far from her mind since the day she had taken him from the sea, "Tell me, how do you know me? How do you know my name?"

He smiled weakly. "That is the second time that you have asked me that. Do you remember one day long ago you journeyed to Cana and passed through Nazareth?"

"Yes, I remember that day."

"But not the boy who met you at the well of Nazareth and showed you the road to Cana."

"But you—you are not Joel," she cried incredulously.[80]

He nodded. "Yes, I'm Joel."

Embarrassed now by her failure to recognize him, she said, "But, of course, I should have known you, but that was long ago. I saw you for such a little time."

"I have changed, but you are much the same. And Stephen, where is he?"

Her eyes looked past him for a moment as if seeing again some distant scene; then she replied simply, "He is with the Lord."

Joel did not understand. Stephen, the Galilean, had no lord, except Herod, and he would never enter his service. Of that Joel was sure. Before he could speak Irene continued, "And now we live here in Cyprus in the old home place, and God has brought you here."

Joel had never thought of it that way. He had explained his rescue to himself on the basis that he was too vile a morsel, even for the hungry sea.

During the days of his convalescence,[81] he learned many things. Stephen was dead, had died five years ago in Jerusalem. In this home, they talked of Jesus, as if He were God, and called Him Christ, the Anointed One. Confused by all this, Joel hesitated for a long time to ask the question stirring in his brain. But one day, in the garden he spoke. They had brought a couch from the house and set it in a sunny spot beside the stone bench. He lay there under a woolen coverlet. Irene, her sewing in her hand, sat beside him and young Joel in a red tunic was romping with his puppies nearby. "It's very peaceful here."

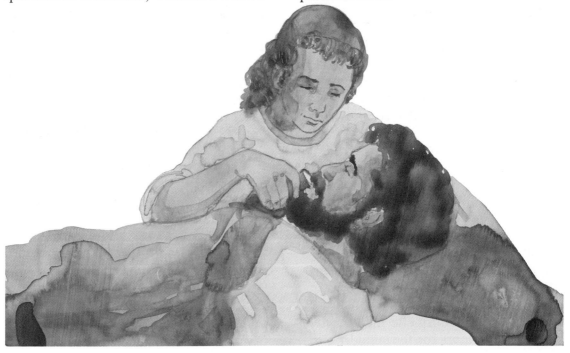

"Yes," answered the woman, "but lonesome sometimes. If it weren't for the boy—!" Her voice trailed away, her glance following the bright-clothed figure lovingly.

"That day on the beach, I thought you were calling my name when you spoke to him."

"Stephen named him for you," she said simply.

"Tell me, what happened—how Stephen died—how you happened to come back here?"

"It's a long story," she answered. She leaned back against the trunk of the tree under which the bench was set. "Four years after we were married we moved to Jerusalem, and my father and Aeneas came to live with us. There, a year later, the boy was born. We often saw the old friends from Galilee. James and John, the sons of Zebedee were there, and Mary, the mother of Jesus, and Peter."

"Peter?" interrupted Joel.

"Yes, the big red-headed fisherman. Simon was his name in Galilee, but Jesus had changed it to Peter, the Rock."

"With Jesus dead, what were they doing?" he asked, and then half to himself he mused, "They must have been lost without Him."

For the first time in twelve years, Joel had spoken aloud the name of the crucified Nazarene, and he was surprised to find how, talking to Irene, that name which he had long avoided came so easily to his lips. Irene looked at him steadily. "But He is not dead."

"Jesus not dead? But I saw Him—dead."

"They crucified Him, yes," she answered, "but He's alive again—alive forevermore."

This was too much for Joel. He shook his head, "I can't understand."

"It's quite simple. They took Him down from the cross and buried Him. But three days later, He came out of the tomb."

"Who saw Him?"

"Oh, a great many people; the disciples saw Him several times in Jerusalem and Galilee."

"A vision or a spirit, perhaps."

"One does not handle a spirit, and they touched Him," she answered. "A vision does not prepare a meal of fish and He fed them one morning on the beach." Joel pondered this for a moment, a strange exultation stirring in him. Then he asked, "But are they with Him now? And where is He?"

"He has gone back to Heaven to the Father. Forty days after He came from the grave, He took them to the Mount of Olives and left them. He blessed them there and rose up into Heaven."

"Surely, Irene, you don't believe this."

"How can I not!" she answered firmly. "I talked with those who saw Him go. You remember, Joel, how He turned water into wine at our wedding. Surely you must know that He had divine power."

"Yes, He had power to do miracles." Joel's eyes were upon the bright blossoms of the garden, but his thoughts were upon other things—a miraculous draught of fish, a palsied man healed, a multitude fed. "Yes," he said again, "He had power." His face darkened with his thoughts, "But not enough power to stay off the cross."

"Too much love to stay off a cross," she corrected, speaking now in the tone

one uses to a slow, dull child. "He came into the world to die on that cross, Joel."

"What do you mean by that?"

"I mean He came to pay the price of sin that sinners might go free. You're a rabbi's son, Joel." He shuddered at the words. That was something he had tried for years to forget. "Surely," she was saying, "you remember the words of Isaiah. He was speaking of Jesus when he said, 'For our transgressions He was wounded, for our evils He was bruised, the punishment of our sin was upon Him and with His lashings we are healed.' "

Unnoticed by either of them, the young laughter of the boy rang out under the trees. Joel was silent on his couch under the glance of the soft, earnest eyes of the woman. After a moment he changed the subject. "And you and Stephen?" He could not comprehend all this she had told him about Jesus. He must have time alone to digest this strange story of resurrection. It was not a thing to be easily comprehended. He must read again the words of the prophet, unseen and neglected by him all these years.

"Stephen and I became followers of the Lord. We were baptized and witnessed among the Jews that He was the Messiah, the Chosen One of God, the Saviour of men."

"And did the Jews believe?" Joel questioned.

"Some believed, but the leaders grew angry. They feared the message, and they hated those who were followers of Christ." She sighed and said quite simply, "They stoned Stephen to death because of it."

Joel stirred in anger, "The same old bigots. How I hate those Jewish leaders!"

"But you must not hate them," she cried.

"Don't you?" he asked surprised.

"No."

Joel looked at her in wonder. The clear simple statement left no doubt of her sincerity. She was continuing her story, "After Stephen's death, they sought to persecute those who followed Christ. We had to leave Jerusalem and came back home to Cyprus. There are others here on the island who also fled from Jerusalem with us."

"Are they Jews?" he asked.

"Some Jews; some, like my father, Jewish proselytes."

"And all accept Jesus as the Messiah?"

"Yes," was the answer, "they, too, believe in Him."

The next day Joel met some of them. They came to the house to worship together in a simple ceremony. They sang one of the old familiar Psalms, and Joel, sitting to one side, joined in the phrases he thought he had long forgotten. Then Irene's father prayed the strangest prayer that the rabbi's son had ever heard. He thanked God for the salvation Jesus had brought. He prayed for forgiveness for their enemies and he ended it, "in the name of Jesus Christ, Thy Son, our Lord." Then they broke bread together and passed a cup of wine among them. They did not include Joel, but later they prayed for him, one after another, thanking God for his rescue and asking that he might come to know the joy of following Jesus. Again they sang and the service was over.

They tarried for a while, talking of

simple, commonplace matters; but underlying the whole conversation was their love for Jesus. His name was often spoken, and Joel envied them their simple faith and coveted the peace which seemed to abide upon all in the house. Even the ten-year-old boy, who sat beside Joel, his little hand clasping that of the man for whom he had been named, even he, talked about Jesus as about a friend whom he loved. And when the bright eyes looked up into the man's and he asked the question, "You love Jesus, don't you, big Joel?" he could only look away, silent.

As his strength returned, Joel worked in the garden and helped with the tasks of the farm. In the long conversations with Irene and her father and her cousin Aeneas, he learned the details of Stephen's death and of the rapid increase of the number who in those days in Jerusalem had believed on Jesus.

He never discussed his own life of conspiracy and outlawry, never revealed that he had been Barabbas, the robber. He told them of his wanderings, but not of his bitterness and anguish of heart, or of the weight of his burden of guilt. He tried to believe as they believed and his mind knew that what they told him of the resurrection of Jesus was true. He even shared with them the certainty that He was the Son of God, but in his heart he could not believe that freedom for a guilty past was possible for Barabbas. It seemed too simple and ingenuous that by merely trusting in the death of Jesus as an atonement for his sins, they would be forgiven of God.

Nightly, Joel sat with them as they read from the prophets and he knelt beside them for the evening prayer. Irene's father was always kind and considerate of him, and he and Aeneas became good friends. Joel and his young namesake spent hours together walking on the beach or playing in the garden, and he came to love him as he would a son; and as the ties of friendship grew tight between them, he became more and more uncomfortable and alarmed. All the old love for Irene had blazed up afresh, but he did not dare to speak of it, both because he did not share her faith and because he thought himself an unlucky man who brought misfortune upon those who loved him. He would have liked to spend his life here, a member of this family, but regarding himself as a Jonah, he felt he must leave. So when Aeneas spoke of plans to go to Antioch, Joel expressed the wish to go with him and the friends who were to make up the party. Fortunately, he had funds for the journey in the pouch at his belt saved with him from the wreck.

On the evening before his departure, sitting on the stone bench with Irene, the leaves of autumn underfoot and falling around them, he tried to express his thanks for his rescue and her kindness.

"We thank God for bringing you here, Joel," she responded. "And we hate to see you go."

"I have been happier here than any time since Stephen and I were boys together."

"Stephen often talked of those days," she said, "and he was grieved that you never came to see us. Why was that, Joel?"

The colors of the sunset had grown

faint in the sky, and the night was gathering about them. Through the gloom, his voice came to her, "Don't you know why, Irene? It was because I loved you from the moment I saw you by the well at Nazareth, and I knew I must not come."

"The few times I saw you, you hid it very well, Joel. For Stephen's sake I used to wish you would come. Now for his sake, I thank you that you did not come."

"Irene, I am as one who carries the plague of misfortune. I bring only suffering to those who befriend me. No, do not interrupt," he went on, as she started to speak. "If I feel that I am ever freed from this curse, I will return."

"And I will welcome you, Joel."

"Stephen was fine and good. He died nobly. I am none of these things, and I have lived basely. I am not worthy to ask it now, but some day, perhaps, I may dare to ask for your love."

"And I shall pray for you, Joel, every day, that you may come to know the peace that Christ can bring—freedom from the past." She hurried on, "I know, though you have never spoken of it, in your life there are dark secrets and much suffering. I do not ask to share these, but remember, Joel, He bore your griefs and He wants to carry your sorrows."

She rose from her place beside him. "We must go in now. Remember this evening, as I shall. And when you find the Light of the World for your own darkness, Joel, come back to Cyprus."

Side by side, they entered the house. Overhead blazed the evening star and at the foot of the cliff the calm sea whispered to the sands.

Reading Check

1. What characterizes the thirteen years of Joel's life following the crucifixion?
2. Who rescues Joel after the shipwreck?
3. What startling news about Jesus and Stephen does Irene tell Joel?
4. Who does Irene say Jesus is?
5. What does Joel reveal to Irene?

Part 2, Chapter 9

Of the score of cities named Antioch, by far the largest and most important was that in Asia Minor. Like an old bejeweled queen with painted face above dirty robes and unwashed body, she sprawled on the banks of the Orontes. Her palaces gleamed like amethysts and emeralds on her breast. The Triumphal Way built by the Emperor Tiberius across the city was her stomacher of pearl and ivory, and the great Temple of Jupiter her diadem. Her forums, her shrines, her public edifices—these were her glories, but throughout three of the four great divisions which made up Antioch, the mass of the buildings were like those of every other Eastern city—huddled together like whispering women. In the fourth and oldest section, the houses, as if overcome by the stench of the alleys, seemed to be fainting against each other, too closely packed to fall. The chief capital of all the Roman provinces of the East, Antioch's strategic location was of the utmost military importance, Situated at the crossroads of travel—north and south, east and west—she was one of the great trade centers of the world. A cosmopolitan city of two hundred thousand free men and at least that number of slaves, she was a Babel echoing with all the languages of the world. In her temples a thousand gods were worshiped, for within her walls more than perhaps in any other city there was a breadth of religious freedom—a freedom not so much of tolerance as of indifference. Such was Antioch when Joel and his companions entered her gates and took up their residence in the Jewish quarter.

The Cypriotes had a number of friends and kinsmen in the city who had preceded them from Cyprus more than a year before. They made the new arrivals welcome, and Joel was hospitably received among them. He found here the same amazing spirit of peace which had been manifest in the home of Irene and her father. These, too, were followers of Jesus, and the rabbi's son had never seen such zeal as theirs—not even among the most ardent contenders for Jewish freedom in the old days at Jerusalem.

Lucius of Cyrene, the silk merchant by whom Joel was employed, spent a great deal more time talking about salvation than he did about business,

and no customer entered his shop without hearing a discourse on the power of Jesus Christ to change lives and bring joy to men. Joel was amazed and touched at the confidence placed in him, a stranger, by Lucius, who often trusted him alone with the shop while he went out through the city talking about Jesus everywhere.

One evening as Joel was about to close for the day, the owner came in, followed by a stranger, obviously a servant.

"An old customer of mine has asked me to send him over some of the new silks which came in yesterday," said Lucius. "He wants to make a selection."

"How about this?" Joel laid his hand upon a bolt of crimson cloth.

"No, not that; only black or black with gold and silver threads."

Together they selected a number of pieces. As the laden servant turned to leave, Lucius suggested, "Suppose you go along with him, Joel. I'd like you to meet the prince."

Thus it happened that Joel found himself a few moments later in the house of Prince Manaen in Antioch. The shock and surprise of seeing his old friend and patron again was almost overpowering. He had followed the servant into a simple room, beautifully but unostentatiously[82] furnished, where three men were seated together at the evening meal. The two who were facing the door were strangers to Joel; of the third, Joel saw the back of a head crowned with white hair above black-robed shoulders. Then at the sound of their footsteps, the head was turned toward the door. As the man rose and came toward them, Joel caught his breath sharply. It seemed impossible that the passing of a decade could have left Manaen so unchanged. He was exactly as Joel remembered him except that the hair, once dark with the distinguishing gray at the temples, was now snow-white and the beard scarcely less so. Joel knelt, partly because his knees had grown so weak he felt he could not stand, partly in honor of this man whom he so greatly admired. Scarcely

above a whisper he cried, "My Lord Manaen!"

The familiar voice spoke, "Get up my son. There is no Lord here but Christ." Manaen extended his hand and Joel grasped it with both his own, covered it with kisses, then laid it against his forehead. Embarrassed, Manaen tried to withdraw his hand. Then recognition came. He stood for a moment, gazing transfixed at Joel's upturned face. "It can't be—Joel! Joel, my son! Thank God!" Then they were in each other's arms.

It was some moments later that Prince Manaen, wiping the tears from his cheeks, turned to the servant, indicating a chair. "Put the goods there and leave us." Then with his arm around Joel, he led him across the room toward the two men standing near the table. "This, my friends, is the boy of whom you've heard me speak so often and for whom you've seen me weep. This is— Joel. Joel, I want you to meet Barnabas and Saul of Tarsus, known as Paul."

As he acknowledged the introduction, Joel, according to long habit, made a quick mental estimate of the two men. Barnabas, still under thirty, was well set up, with a handsome clean-shaven face. Obviously a man of education and good background; the sternness of character suggested by the firm chin was modified by the sweetness of his smile.

His homely companion seemed to have tried to compensate for the baldness of his high and bulging forehead by the luxuriance of his fierce beard, dark and forked. His nose was large and hooked like an eagle's beak, but when Joel looked into the dark and luminous[83] eyes, he forgot the ugliness

of the face. There was something of hypnotic beauty about those eyes. The voice which issued from behind the terrifying beard, though not deeply pitched, was resonant and powerful— a voice to sway multitudes and bend men to the will of the speaker. Refinement and culture were in its accents; self-assurance in its tone. "Manaen has spoken of you almost every day since we became acquainted," Paul said.

Barnabas added, "I'm sure no father ever grieved so over a lost son."

As Joel turned, smiling affectionately at the prince, Manaen said, "You cannot imagine, Joel, how burdened I've been, wondering what had become of you—whether you were alive or dead."

Here Paul's vibrant[84] voice dominated the room again. "And Manaen had us pray together with him every day that God somehow would bring you here that he might tell you of the new life he has found in Jesus Christ."

Thinking how, without any effort on his own part, he had been so strangely reunited, first with Irene and now with Manaen, the two people living whom he most deeply loved, Joel knew this could be no mere accident or whim of chance and was conscious that these happenings must be ordained of Heaven for its own purpose.

Manaen called a servant, had a place set for Joel at the table, and insisted that he sit and eat, but with a heart so full Joel found little appetite for the delicious meal. On both his part and Manaen's there were many questions to be asked and answered. Manaen had told Paul and Barnabas all the details of the unhappy conspiracy, but Joel learned this evening for the first time how his master, warned by the porter of Joel's arrest, had left Jerusalem hurriedly and fled northward.

"About all that was left of my estate aside from the palace at Jerusalem was this house and garden," Manaen explained, "and so, naturally, it was the place to which I came."

"And you've stayed here, then, ever since?"

"Bitter and despondent," Manaen replied, "for over a decade because of our failure and the death of my wife."

Joel interrupted him, ashamed that in his surprise at meeting Manaen he had failed to inquire about her. "I'm sorry to hear that the Princess—" he broke off. How long ago?"

"Shortly after she joined me here. She was killed in the earthquake eleven years ago."

"And you have lived here alone since then?"

"Yes, and my life was empty until I met this young man." He indicated Barnabas. "He brought me into the light of the truth of God's love for me."

Here Barnabas took up the story. "The church at Jerusalem had sent me to Asia Minor to check on reports that the gospel was being preached to the Greeks and the foreigners and that many of them were believing. My father had been a friend of Prince Manaen's; so I looked him up when I got to Antioch."

"And changed his life," finished Manaen.

There could be no doubt that something had changed it. Though outwardly, except for the white hair, his old friend looked the same, Joel could sense some new quality—a settled peace, a quiet radiance—that he had not possessed in the old days. "It is," Joel analyzed silently, "more perhaps a gentle humility than anything else."

Now it was Joel's turn to speak of himself, and to his own surprise he was soon discussing freely the past years filled with despondence and hopelessness. It may have been the joy of meeting his old friend again that broke down the barriers of restraint. It may have been the powerful eyes of Paul and the man's genius for understanding the workings of his mind, the hungerings of his heart. Paul seemed to know instinctively so much about his soul-struggle that Joel found himself supplying the details. When he described the scene at Calvary, they wept—all of them. Finally he came to the shipwreck, to his meeting with Irene.

"You mean this woman who took you from the sea was a girl whom you had loved years ago?" asked Paul.

"Loved from a distance, yes," replied Joel. "I saw her only a few times and for a few days. She had married my friend."

"And the friend, where is he?" asked Manaen.

"Dead! Stephen was stoned by the Jews."

Manaen and Barnabas looked at Paul. "Stephen?" His face was pale. "I was there," he said to Joel. I saw him die."

"You saw it—his death?"

"I was a party to his death, and those who threw the stones asked me to watch their cloaks when they bared their arms to slay him." Seeing the mounting horror and repulsion in the face of the rabbi's son, Paul spoke more quickly. "I have seen others suffer, too, for

Christ's sake—have *made* them suffer. But God in His mercy has forgiven, and I pray that when I suffer for Christ, as I shall, I may bear it as nobly as Stephen. His face was like the face of an angel when he died."

Joel did not speak for a moment. Then in a low voice he asked incredulously, "And you say God has forgiven you *that?*"

"That, and much more."

"Then—perhaps there is hope for me."

"He has power to save to the very limit all who come to God by Him."

And that night Joel came. He laid down the burden of all the sinful years and for the first time had peace of soul. As the dawn was in the sky he was baptized where the Orontes flowed past the marble terrace of the house of his friend, Prince Manaen, and then Paul laid his hands upon Joel and prayed that he should receive the gift of the Holy Ghost. When Joel arose from his knees the sun was visible above the horizon, flooding the terrace with light. So the grace of God was flooding his soul, long darkened by sin and doubt. The ecstasy within seemed more than he could bear! He was as one intoxicated, one who had sipped of the Day Spring, drunk with the Wine of Morning.

Part 2, Chapter 10

Nothing would do Prince Manaen but that Joel come and live with him. Frequently the church assembled in his house, more numerous every day, for God was working in Antioch and a strange, new life was stirring in the old city.

In all Antioch there was no happier man than Joel. The radiance within shone out like a bright lamp for all to see, and from that flame other lives were kindled. Everywhere he went, he preached Christ. Jews, Greeks, barbarians—all with whom he came in contact—heard of the miracle wrought in his life.

Once as Joel was preaching in the market place a magistrate, passing by, stopped to listen, a cynical smile upon his dissipated face. He interrupted with a sneer. "What a polyglot religion this is! We all have our gods, each nation its own, but this is an absurd religion you preach."

"I preach the truth of the eternal God, revealed in Jesus Christ His Son, for all men, for every nation," Joel replied.

"You are not a very good Jew then. They're a snooty lot that have no use for any man uncircumcised. And look what this new faith does to the Romans

"Yes, we are Christians," cried the little band of believers gathered around Joel. "Christians!" echoed the crowd.

"Christians?" asked the cynical magistrate.

The new name took hold, and from that day the disciples were called Christians in Antioch, and wherever they went to the ends of the earth, preaching the gospel, the name went with them.

Joel had planned to return in the spring to Cyprus and to Irene. He had written her of his conversion, but did not know whether across the stormy winter seas his letter had ever reached her. Now in the first month of spring he felt compelled to change his plans and to delay his voyage.

The Christians at Antioch had raised money for the relief of the persecuted church at Jerusalem. Paul and Barnabas had been selected as the envoys to deliver the gift, and they urged Joel to accompany them. The thought of spending the Passover season in the Holy City appealed to him. He longed, as a free man, to walk the streets of Jerusalem, to stand again on the Hill of Death and thank God there for His love and sacrifice for him. He wanted to break bread with the little band who had known the Lord and join with them in their Easter hymn of praise. He determined, therefore, to journey southward with his new friends and then from Joppa take ship for Cyprus.

It lacked but seven days of the Feast when they reached Jerusalem. Prince Manaen had suggested that Joel lodge with his old porter who, crippled by rheumatism, had retired to a little house near the Joppa gate. Here he lived on

who embrace it! They refuse to sacrifice at the shrine of the Emperor. You're overthrowing the whole social structure, too, saying free men and their slaves are brothers! What are you, after all?"

"We are Christians," answered Joel impulsively.

the pension which Manaen sent to him. "You were always a favorite of his," the Prince had said, "and it would make his old heart happy to have you as his guest. Besides, I am concerned for his soul, and I believe you can bring him to faith in Christ."

The prince had been right. The old man had welcomed Joel with such enthusiastic and effusive[85] joy as was almost embarrassing, and Joel had not been three days with him before he too became a believer.

But they found the church of Jerusalem in travail and sorrow. James, the eldest of Zebedee's sons, had been beheaded at the order of Herod Agrippa, a tyrannical act which caused much enthusiasm among the Jewish leaders. When the politic king observed this, he determined to continue his attack upon the Christians and had seized Simon, now called Peter, the name the Lord had given him. This disciple's martyrdom seemed inevitable also because the king had announced his intentions of putting Peter to death following the Passover.

Those who loved Christ remained quietly in their homes, for the most part behind locked doors, venturing out only after dark when they would hurry through the streets to gather somewhere, praying all night for Peter's release. Such a group, Joel among them, were in the house of a woman named Mary on the night following Easter. She and her son, John Mark, were among the most faithful and devoted believers; and their home had become a regular meeting place for the Christians.

Toward morning they were startled by a loud knocking at the gate of the walled garden. Fearing that this might mean the arrival of Herod's soldiers, Mark said to their little maid, Rhoda, "Find out who it is before you let him in."

She hurried out and returned in a moment, her face beaming. "It's Peter! Peter's at the gate."

"Nonsense, child," said Mary, "you know Peter's in prison. That's why we have been praying here."

"But it is Peter," Rhoda insisted. "I know his voice."

"Perhaps, Mother," said Mark, "the Lord has heard our prayer." And he went himself to the gate, leaving his mother ashamed of her lack of faith.

When the tall fisherman followed young Mark into the room, they gathered around him joyfully.

"Thank God," cried one, "Herod decided to set you free."

"How did this miracle happen?" asked Mary. "We were praying for your release."

"Before I answer your questions, let me thank you for your prayers." He looked around the room, his eyes resting questioningly upon Joel. Mary, noting it, said, "This is a new believer; he comes from Antioch. His name is Joel."

"Joel," rumbled Peter's deep voice, "don't tell me you're the lad that worked for Jonathan of Capernaum. You've changed, but I recognize you, lad." And Joel clasped the hand of still another old friend.

"But tell us," Mark insisted, "how Herod happened to change his mind about you."

Simon Peter shook his head, chuckling, "His Majesty hasn't changed his mind; God has changed his plans for him."

"You mean—?"

"I mean Herod thinks he has me still chained in my cell."

"Then how is it you're free?" asked Joel. "Surely the jailer didn't release you without an order."

"God gave the order that set me free, but not to the jailer. I was asleep. I was awakened by a blow on my side. The prison was full of light and an angel stood beside me. 'Get up quickly,' he said, 'dress yourself, put on your sandals.' The chains fell off my arms and I got up, put on my clothes. Then the angel said, 'Follow me.' The cell door opened. We went out and the heavy door of the corridor also opened. Then we came to the iron gate; without a sound or a creak of the hinges, it opened, too. All the time I thought I was dreaming. When we were in the street, the angel vanished, and I knew then that it wasn't a dream—that God had set me free; and here I am."

"We are glad that you came to us," said Mark, "but you can't stay here. This is one of the first places they'll search."

"I had thought of that," said Peter, "but the names of all the Christians in Jerusalem are known to the authorities. Where can I go?"

A sudden idea struck Joel. To think quickly had been necessary to him when he was a conspirator, and the experience gained then proved useful now. "I have a suggestion," he said. "I am staying with an old man who lives near the Joppa gate. His house is right against the city wall. I can hide you there."

Peter shook his head dubiously. "I don't know. It's a terrific risk for him to take. Would he be willing to chance it?"

"Delighted," Joel assured him. "He has known Christ only a few days. Just yesterday, he said to me, 'Here I am, old and crippled with rheumatism. I am not much good for anything, but I want you to pray that the Lord will give me one chance to really serve Him before I die.'" Joel smiled. "It looks as if you're the answer to that prayer, Peter."

Peter appealed to the entire group, "What do you think?"

An old man spoke, "It seems to me it's the only chance." Heads nodded in agreement.

Rhoda, the maid, said now, "You had better hurry. It's almost dawn."

Bundled in dark cloaks, their faces concealed as far as possible by the folds, Peter and Joel hurried through the streets, racing against daylight across the city. There was only a faint gray in the east when they reached the little house built against the city wall.

They had encountered only two people on the way—a pair of soldiers on the night watch. Realizing that their safety lay in apparent indifference to the patrol, Joel and Peter had passed them nonchalantly by. Unfortunately the light of the soldier's torch struck them full in the face. The guards had looked after them curiously.

"If I didn't know he was in jail, I would swear that tall fellow was that fanatic, Simon Peter," said one.

"And I have seen the other man, too, somewhere. I never forget a face, and he looks familiar to me," replied his companion.

"Who is he, then?"

"I can't quite place him. I'm sure he's a jailbird," he pondered, "and sometime or other I have guarded him. Well," he yawned, "they acted honest enough; besides, it's time for us to check in."

About an hour later, Herod Agrippa, roused from slumber, heard a white and trembling jailer confess that his prisoner had vanished and the furious king ordered the death of the soldiers assigned to guard Peter.

Naturally, the news of the disciple's disappearance seeped quickly into every part of Jerusalem. Herod commanded the garrison to search the house of every known Christian. The members of the watch who had been on duty the night before were awakened and turned out of the barracks for questioning. Had they seen any signs of the prisoners? Only two reluctantly reported that they had seen a man who might have been he. Brought before the king himself, they described their encounter with the two men in the streets a few hours before. "Well, have you made up your mind who the other was?" snarled Herod Agrippa when they had finished.

"The more I think about it, Your Majesty," mumbled the frightened soldier, "the more I believe he was a fellow named Barabbas. It's been fourteen or fifteen years since I saw him, but I never forget a face."

"Barabbas? Who's he?"

"He was taken for conspiracy in the time of the procurator Pilate and was released at the Passover time."

The king paced the mosaic floor angrily. "Can you describe him?"

"Yes, sire, I think I can."

"All right, give the captain his description and have the city searched for him, too."

Jerusalem was turned inside out— all to no avail. The next morning the monarch, seething with rage, departed for the great games at Caesarea, leaving furious orders to continue the search and commanding that when Peter and Barabbas were found they should be sent to him immediately under double guard.

Reading Check

1. With whom is Joel reunited, and to whom is he introduced in Antioch?
2. What convinces Joel that God is willing to forgive any sin?
3. What city does Joel go to visit?
4. Why is the church in this city beset with confusion and sorrow?
5. How does Joel help his old friend Peter?

Part 2, Chapter 11

In the packed stadium of Caesarea, tension was high. The games and athletic contests held here were among the most famous and popular in the East and Herod the Great, who had built this city, would have rejoiced in the spectacle of the massed thousands, feverish with excitement. The entire city was gay with silken banners and tapestries. Wreaths and garlands decorated private homes and public buildings. Visitors from many nations had thronged the streets, pushing their way toward the great arena. For these three days, ordinary business and commonplace matters were neglected or forgotten, and the ships in the artificial harbor behind the great breakwater were unmanned, their crews having joined the pleasure-seeking crowd.

The day was perfect. The sun shone down in warm brilliance, and the soft spring breeze played with the gold fringe of the purple awning above the royal podium. Herod had almost forgotten his anger and irritation in his delight that the Jewish champions had taken the lead in almost every contest of the morning— in the foot races, in the discus throw, in the javelin toss. Only his archers had been defeated by those of Egypt, who were the world champions and who were expected to win, anyway. Toward noon, however, something occurred which completely spoiled for him the triumphs of the previous hours.

A huge owl, blinded by the glaring sunshine, had flopped and fluttered awkwardly above the crowd, finally alighting on one of the gold cords of the canopy above the king's head. To the frightened and superstitious monarch, this was an omen of the utmost evil, and the unseeing eyes of the night bird appeared to glare balefully down upon him.

Most of the crowd, intent upon the contestants in the arena, had failed to notice the arrival of the owl, but the courtiers and the attendants in the royal box were as disturbed by its presence as the king, who sat cowering upon his throne, unable to concentrate upon the games before him. It was with a sigh of relief that Herod heard the trumpets proclaim the end of the morning's sport. Abruptly he dismissed his courtiers and, accompanied only by his chamberlain, retired to lunch.

"Have the canopy taken down," he commanded.

"But, Your Majesty," protested the chamberlain, "the sun is hot."

"Never mind, take it down!" repeated the king with a shudder.

In the great towering circle of the seats, the crowd relaxed. Determined not to lose their places, the common folks had come provided with bread and cheese and olives, which they now began to eat. Those who had reserved places repaired to the great hallways circling the building underneath the seats to buy their lunches from the food venders whose counters were set up here. Hawkers moved through the stands selling fruit juices and wine.

The architect who had designed the coliseum for Herod the Great had provided a luxurious retiring room for the sovereign, accessible by a marble stair rising from the corridor behind the royal box. The tall windows of this room opened upon a balcony behind and above the podium. Here workers, in obedience to Herod's orders, were already busy loosening the ropes which held the canopy. As his meal was placed before the king, a breathless messenger

arrived. "Your Majesty, a guard has just come from Jerusalem, bringing Barabbas, whom you ordered sent to you when found."

"And Peter?"

"I'm sorry, but there is no word of him."

"Well, where is this Barabbas?" asked Herod petulantly.

"In the Caesarea prison, Sire."

"Have him brought here at once." He dismissed the messenger with a wave of his hand.

Added to the other irritations which plagued Agrippa was the unexplained absence of Marta, his mistress, who should have been at the palace to greet him when he arrived in Caesarea. For over a year now, she had never failed to appear at his command to help him forget the annoying worries of royalty. He turned to his steward. "Where is Marta? I have sent for her three times and she hasn't come."

The official shrugged his narrow shoulders and spread his thin hands in a gesture which said, "You should know women by now. Who can explain their moods?"

"Find her at once and bring her here. Tell her that I command her presence."

The king had barely finished shellfish and squab and begun on the pastry, when the chamberlain returned with a tall woman of uncommon beauty. "Here is Marta, Your Majesty. We found her, as it happened, here in the stadium."

"All right, now get out and leave us," ordered the king.

When he and Marta were alone, Herod Agrippa, pouting like a spoiled child, questioned, "Why have you treated me like this, Marta? You know

I need you." He patted the silken cushions beside him, "Come, sit down."

The lovely Marta shook her golden head and remained standing. "No, Your Majesty, it's all over."

"Over?" gasped the king.

"Yes."

"But why? Is it something I have done to anger you?"

"No, Sire."

"Then I suppose it's a trick to get some present from me. What is it you want? A pink sapphire, perhaps, or a necklace of rubies?"

"Nothing. I have everything I need. You see, my wants are changed now; my desires are different. I have become a follower of the Christ."

"You—a long-faced follower of that dead Carpenter!" Herod laughed. "Come you vixen, you do have a sense of humor, don't you? That's always been half your charm for me."

"But I am serious, Your Majesty; I am not playing a part now to entertain you. Christ is my Saviour."

Herod, realizing now that this was no jest and stirred by his passion for her, said, "Surely you cannot be led astray by these fanatics. You must be crazy, girl."

They were interrupted by the chamberlain, whose head appeared at the top of the stairs, as he said apologetically, "Excuse me, Your Majesty, but the soldiers are here with Barabbas."

"His arrival is opportune," cried Herod. "Have him brought up. No, Marta, don't go, not yet. I want you to see something. I will show you what these Christians are like."

Herod frowned at the man who stood, respectful but uncowered, before him. "You were seen on the street with Simon Peter after he escaped from prison." The man said nothing. "It was Simon Peter, wasn't it?"

"Yes, King Herod, it was," Joel responded.

"Where is he?"

"I don't know."

"Where did you take him? You were with him. Where did he go?"

"I cannot tell you that."

"So? My torturers are expert. We'll see whether you can tell me that." Agrippa looked from Joel to Marta, then back at his prisoner. "You are one of those who follow that Jesus, are you not?"

"I am a Christian, yes."

"Now, Marta, listen and see how merciful Herod Agrippa can be." The king smiled wickedly at Joel. "If you will renounce your faith, you shall go free this instant with the guarantee of my pardon; if not, you shall be tortured to death. Take your choice."

The man stood, head erect, looking the monarch full in the face, as he said, "Bring on your tortures, King."

The lovely woman standing near Herod turned toward the sovereign a look of mingled triumph and sadness. "You see, Your Majesty." She started to the stair. As she passed Joel, she stopped and laid her hand on his arm, "Thank you, my brother. I shall pray for you." Then she was gone.

Strong through the open window came the notes of silver trumpets. Herod, his sullen face livid with anger, said, "Take him to jail; he'll die tomorrow." Then to his chamberlain, he added, "Remind me to sign the order tonight."

As the king swept down the stairs, one of the guards said to the other, "We shall have to miss the chariot race, and I have three pieces of silver on the Sidonian driver."

"Why, you traitor!" cried his companion. "Why don't you bet on your own man? I've put my money on the Jew."

"I bet where I think I can win," retorted the first soldier.

"Then I should like to stand by you at the race and see your face when you lose."

The maid who had come in to clear the table said with a flirtatious smile, "Well, there's the window and the balcony. Why don't you see the race and then take this poor man to jail."

The soldiers exchanged glances. "Shall we risk it?"

"Why not?"

With Joel between them they stepped upon the balcony. The sun was covered by a passing cloud. To their right the chariots were lined up at the starting point, the eager horses rearing, manes tossing, their grooms hard put to hold them. King Herod Agrippa had just seated himself upon his throne, and the crowd which had cheered the king's appearance was settling now into silence, since it was evident that Herod intended to speak.

"It looks like the old windbag could wait until after the race," muttered a soldier beside Joel.

Preoccupied as he was with his problems, Herod's speech was brief, and it certainly did not merit the terrific applause with which it was received.

"It's those Sidonians," said the soldier, leaning across Joel to speak to his companion. "They are trying to make up to Herod by flattering him."

"I know. It's because of the new trade agreement they want him to sign."

At this moment the cloud passed, and the sun shone down in brilliance. With the canopy removed, it fell full upon the figure of the king, dazzling in a golden robe, striking colored fire from the jeweled circlet on his head.

"It's a god. He's a god," cried a voice from the section where the Sidonians were seated.

Others took up the cry. Flattered by this blasphemy, Herod rose in acknowledgment. Then a strange thing happened. One moment he stood erect in his pride. The next he was doubled over in agony, retching horribly. Then he was prostrate upon the Damascene carpet, writhing and screaming.

A moment, spellbound and panic-stricken, the multitude was silent. Then pandemonium broke out in the stadium.

"Quick, let's get out of here," cried the soldier at Joel's right to his companion.

"Yes, they may bring him here. If they find us, we're done for!"

Headlong they rushed Joel down the stairs and out of the corridor toward the street just as King Herod was carried in from the podium.

Part 2 Chapter 12

The fat and tipsy jailer who brought Joel his supper was in a talkative mood. He slapped the wooden trencher down on the stone ledge, splashing the wall with grease. "You're the new prisoner, aren't you? I hear Herod intended to have you executed tomorrow but the order isn't signed. I don't think they know what to do with you—whether to go ahead with the execution or turn you loose. Well," he exhaled fumes of sour wine in a long sigh, "that's life. Anyway, old Herod's gone. He died horribly, they tell me—vomiting blood. It had fat white worms crawling in it, too." He nodded sagely, his bloated fingers wiggling in graphic demonstration. "I hope you have a good appetite. We've got meat tonight. That's only for special occasions in this jail. Of course, it's because of the celebration of the games, but it looks almost like it's in honor of Herod's death, doesn't it? Don't tell anybody I said it, but it seems to me that's a good enough reason to celebrate." His fat stomach shook with laughter. "That's what I've been doing

ever since I heard the news—celebrating! Here, I can't stop and talk all night. Where did I put that spoon?"

Joel had hardly been able to take his eyes off the spoon since this windy fellow had entered the cell. The handle was thrust into the open front of his tunic and the wooden bowl protruded bottom up, resting against the tangled yellow hair of his chest. It looked like a brown egg in a nest of straw.

"Here it is," said the jailer, drawing it forth and slapping it into the stew.

When he had gone, Joel sat for a long time in the darkness, the unappetizing meal untouched. For all his drunken wordiness the jailer had given him something to think about. The order for Joel's death had not been signed and perhaps he would be released. A general amnesty for prisoners was a common enough custom whenever there was a change of rulers and a new sovereign took the throne. Well, if he died tomorrow, he would be with his Lord and see again the One Whom his soul had come to love. If he lived, there was Irene, waiting in the quiet garden above the ever-changing sea; and there was a world beyond, waiting, too, waiting for the message of God's love.

After a long while he knelt on the rough stone. "Whether I shall live to preach Thy gospel to distant lands, or whether I shall die tomorrow, Thou knowest. If it be by life or by death that I can best glorify Thee, Thy will be done."

Then perfectly content, he lay down and went to sleep.

Reading Check

1. Why does Herod want the canopy down?
2. How does Herod try to convince Marta to give up her faith in Christ?
3. What happens to Herod and why?
4. Why does Joel have hope for being released?
5. What is Joel's sole desire for his future?

1. fissure: narrow crack in a rock.
2. spavined: diseased.
3. lithe: flexible.
4. defile: pass or gorge.
5. porcine: pig-like.
6. precipitation: headlong fall.
7. disheveled: in disarray.
8. reticence: reserve.
9. delinquent: late.
10. subservient: submissive.
11. tetrarchy: rule as governor.
12. sycophant: flatterer.
13. fawningly: grovelingly.
14. pandering: catering to.
15. avarice: greed.
16. apoplexy: a stroke.
17. pallid: pale.
18. suffused: overspread.
19. collaborate: cooperate.
20. bantering: jesting.
21. allayed: lessened.
22. conjecture: speculation.
23. Hellenistic: like the classical Greek.
24. disparity: difference.
25. cosmopolitan: universal.
26. sagacity: shrewdness.
27. fortuitous: fortunate.
28. tutelage: teaching.
29. pedagogy: education.
30. unassailable: unquestionable.
31. prostrate: lying flat.
32. elongated: lengthened.
33. anise: small licorice-flavored plant.
34. consummate: accomplished.
35. insidious: harmful.
36. forays: raids.
37. depredations: plunderings.
38. dilettante: connoisseur.
39. deprecatingly: disapprovingly.
40. interpolated: inserted.
41. hummock: ridge or hill.
42. irrepressible: unable to be restrained.
43. exuberant: enthusiastic.
44. conspiratorial: involved in conspiracy.
45. caldron: large kettle.
46. melee: hand-to-hand battle.
47. mitigated: moderated.
48. chagrined: embarrassed.
49. bauble: trinket.
50. arduous: difficult.
51. brazier: metal pan.
52. rivulet: small brook.
53. suavity: graciousness.
54. vari-timbered: varying in pitch.
55. placate: appease.
56. petulantly: ill-temperedly.
57. austerely: severely.
58. stalwart: resolute.
59. portico: porch
60. balustrade: staircase railing.
61. malefactor: criminal.
62. odoriferous: giving off an odor.
63. insurrectionist: revolutionary.
64. awry: amiss.
65. sadistic: extremely cruel.
66. ludicrous: ridiculous.
67. embrasures: openings or doorways.
68. suppliant: petitioner.
69. brook: tolerate.
70. supercilious: scornful.
71. rejoinder: reply.
72. crestfallen: depressd.
73. "Eli, Eli, lama sabachthani": "My God, my God, why hast Thou forsaken me."
74. sated: glutted.
75. dissipation: intemperate living.
76. flaunted: displayed.
77. utilitarian: useful.
78. interminable: extremely tiresome.
79. flotsam: debris.
80. incredulously: unbelieving.
81. convalescence: recuperation.
82. unostentatiously: without show.
83. luminous: shining.
84. vibrant: energetic.
85. effusive: expressive.

Crown Him with Many Crowns

Crown Him with many crowns,
The Lamb upon His throne;
Hark! how the heavenly anthem drowns
All music but its own!
Awake, my soul and sing
Of Him who died for thee;
And hail Him as thy matchless King
Thro' all eternity.

Crown Him the Lord of love!
Behold His hands and side,—
Rich wounds, yet visible above,
In beauty glorified:
No angel in the sky
Can fully bear that sight,
But downward bends his wondering eye
At mysteries so bright.

Crown Him the Lord of life!
Who triumphed o'er the grave;
Who rose victorious to the strife
For those He came to save:
His glories now we sing,
Who died and rose on high;
Who died eternal life to bring,
And lives that death may die.

Crown Him the Lord of heaven!
One with the Father known,
One with the Spirit through Him given
From yonder glorious throne!
To Thee be endless praise,
For Thou for us hast died;
Be Thou, O Lord, through endless days
Adored and magnified.

The Ascension by Benjamin West from
The Bob Jones University Collection of Sacred Art

THE STONING OF STEPHEN

And in those days, when the number of the disciples was multiplied, there arose a murmuring of the Grecians against the Hebrews, because their widows were neglected in the daily ministration.

Then the twelve called the multitude of the disciples unto them, and said, It is not reason that we should leave the word of God, and serve tables.

Wherefore, brethren, look ye out among you seven men of honest report, full of the Holy Ghost and wisdom, whom we may appoint over this business.

But we will give ourselves continually to prayer, and to the ministry of the word.

And the saying pleased the whole multitude: and they chose Stephen, a man full of faith and of the Holy Ghost, and Philip, and Prochorus, and Nicanor, and Timon, and Parmenas, and Nicolas a proselyte of Antioch:

Whom they set before the apostles: and when they had prayed, they laid their hands on them.

And the word of God increased; and the number of the disciples multiplied in Jerusalem greatly; and a great company of the priests were obedient to the faith.

And Stephen, full of faith and power, did great wonders and miracles among the people.

Then there arose certain of the synagogue, which is called the synagogue of the Libertines, and Cyrenians, and Alexandrians, and of them of Cilicia and of Asia, disputing with Stephen.

And they were not able to resist the wisdom and the spirit by which he spake.

Then they suborned men, which said, We have heard him speak blasphemous words against Moses, and against God.

And they stirred up the people, and the elders, and the scribes, and came upon him, and caught him, and brought him to the council,

And set up false witnesses, which said, This man ceaseth not to speak blasphemous words against this holy place, and the law:

For we have heard him say, that this Jesus of Nazareth shall destroy this place, and shall change the customs which Moses delivered us.

And all that sat in the council, looking stedfastly on him, saw his face as it had been the face of an angel.   (Acts 6)

Then said the high priest, Are these things so?

And he (Stephen) said . . . Ye stiffnecked and uncircumcised in heart and ears, ye do always resist the Holy Ghost: as your fathers did, so do ye.

Which of the prophets have not your fathers persecuted? and they have slain them which shewed before of the coming of the Just One; of whom ye have been now the betrayers and murderers:

Who have received the law by the disposition of angels, and have not kept it.

When they heard these things, they were cut to the heart, and they gnashed on him with their teeth.

But he, being full of the Holy Ghost, looked up stedfastly into heaven, and saw the glory of God, and Jesus standing on the right hand of God,

And said, Behold, I see the heavens opened, and the Son of man standing on the right hand of God.

Then they cried out with a loud voice, and stopped their ears, and ran upon him with one accord,

And cast him out of the city, and stoned him: and the witnesses laid down their clothes at a young man's feet, whose name was Saul.

And they stoned Stephen, calling upon God, and saying, Lord Jesus, receive my spirit.

And he kneeled down, and cried with a loud voice, Lord, lay not this sin to their charge. And when he had said this, he fell asleep. (Acts 7:1-2a, 51-60)

INDEX

OF AUTHORS, TITLES, AND FIRST LINES OF POETRY

GENRE INDEX

Scripture

Photo Credits

The Bob Jones University Collection of Sacred Art: 1-2, 78, 131, 204, 301, 356, 498
George Collins: Cover, 80-81, 136-137, 208-209, 304-305
Unusual Films: 360-361